CIMA

MANAGEMENT

PAPER P2

PERFORMANCE MANAGEMENT

STUDY TEXT

Our text is designed to help you study **effectively** and **efficiently**.

In this edition we:

- **Highlight** the **most important elements** in the syllabus and the **key skills** you will need

- **Signpost** how each chapter links to the syllabus and the learning outcomes

- **Provide** lots of **exam alerts** explaining how what you're learning may be tested

- **Include examples** and **questions** to help you apply what you've learnt

- **Emphasise key points** in **section summaries**

- **Test your knowledge** of what you've studied in **quick quizzes**

- **Examine your understanding** in our **exam question bank**

- **Reference all the important topics** in the **full index**

SUITABLE FOR EXAMS UP TO SEPTEMBER 2014

BPP LEARNING MEDIA

First edition 2009
Fifth edition June 2013

ISBN 9781 4453 7133 7
(Previous ISBN 9781 4453 9609 5)

eBook ISBN 9781 4453 7178 8

British Library Cataloguing-in-Publication Data
A catalogue record for this book
is available from the British Library

Published by

BPP Learning Media Ltd
BPP House, Aldine Place
London W12 8AA

www.bpp.com/learningmedia

Printed in the United Kingdom by Polestar Wheatons

Hennock Road
Marsh Barton
Exeter
EX2 8RP

Your learning materials, published by BPP Learning Media Ltd, are printed on paper sourced from sustainable, managed forests.

We are grateful to the Chartered Institute of Management Accountants for permission to reproduce past examination questions. The suggested solutions in the exam answer bank have been prepared by BPP Learning Media Ltd.

BPP
LEARNING MEDIA

Contents

How our Study Text can help you pass

Streamlined studying	• We show you the best ways to study efficiently
	• Our Text has been designed to ensure you can easily and quickly navigate through it
	• The different features in our Text emphasise important knowledge and techniques
Exam expertise	• **Studying P2** on page xiii introduces the key themes of the syllabus and summarises how to pass
	• We highlight throughout our Text how topics may be tested and what you'll have to do in the exam
	• We help you see the complete picture of the syllabus, so that you can answer questions that range across the whole syllabus
	• Our Text covers the syllabus content – no more, no less
Regular review	• We frequently summarise the key knowledge you need
	• We test what you've learnt by providing questions and quizzes throughout our Text

Our other products

BPP Learning Media also offers these products for the P2 exam:

Practice and Revision Kit	Providing lots more question practice and helpful guidance on how to pass the exam
Passcards	Summarising what you should know in visual, easy to remember, form
Success CDs	Covering the vital elements of the P2 syllabus in less than 90 minutes and also containing exam hints to help you fine tune your strategy
i-Pass	Providing computer-based testing in a variety of formats, ideal for self-assessment
Interactive Passcards	Allowing you to learn actively with a clear visual format summarising what you must know

You can purchase these products by visiting www.bpp.com/cimamaterials

CIMA Distance Learning

BPP's distance learning packages provide flexibility and convenience, allowing you to study effectively, at a pace that suits you, where and when you choose. There are four great distance learning packages available.

Online classroom live	Through Live interactive online sessions it provides you with the traditional structure and support of classroom learning, but with the convenience of attending classes wherever you are
Online classroom	Through pre-recorded online lectures it provides you with the classroom experience via the web with the tutor guidance & support you'd expect from a face to face classroom
Basics Plus	A guided self study package containing a wealth of rich e-learning & physical content
Basics Online	A guided self study package containing a wealth of rich e-learning content

You can find out more about these packages by visiting www.bpp.com/cimadistancelearning

Features in our Study Text

 Section Introductions explain how the section fits into the chapter

 Key Terms are the core vocabulary you need to learn

KEY TERM

 Key Points are points that you have to know, ideas or calculations that will be the foundations of your answers

KEY POINT

 Exam Alerts show you how subjects are likely to be tested

 Exam Skills are the key skills you will need to demonstrate in the exam, linked to question requirements

 Formulae To Learn are formulae you must remember in the exam

LEARN

 Exam Formulae are formulae you will be given in the exam

EXAM

 Examples show how theory is put into practice

 Questions give you the practice you need to test your understanding of what you've learnt

 Case Studies link what you've learnt with the real-world business environment

CASE STUDY

 Links show how the syllabus overlaps with other parts of the qualification, including Knowledge Brought Forward that you need to remember from previous exams

 Website References link to material that will enhance your understanding of what you're studying

 Further Reading will give you a wider perspective on the subjects you're covering

 Section Summaries allow you to review each section

Streamlined studying

What you should do	In order to
Read the Chapter and Section Introductions	See why topics need to be studied and map your way through the chapter
Go quickly through the explanations	Gain the depth of knowledge and understanding that you'll need
Highlight the Key Points, Key Terms and Formulae To Learn	Make sure you know the basics that you can't do without in the exam
Focus on the Exam Skills and Exam Alerts	Know how you'll be tested and what you'll have to do
Work through the Examples and Case Studies	See how what you've learnt applies in practice
Prepare Answers to the Questions	See if you can apply what you've learnt in practice
Revisit the Section Summaries in the Chapter Roundup	Remind you of, and reinforce, what you've learnt
Answer the Quick Quiz	Find out if there are any gaps in your knowledge
Answer the Question(s) in the Exam Question Bank	Practise what you've learnt in depth

Should I take notes?

Brief notes may help you remember what you're learning. You should use the notes format that's most helpful to you (lists, diagrams, mindmaps).

Further help

BPP Learning Media's *Learning to Learn Accountancy* provides lots more helpful guidance on studying. It is designed to be used both at the outset of your CIMA studies and throughout the process of learning accountancy. It can help you **focus your studies on the subject and exam**, enabling you to **acquire knowledge, practise and revise efficiently and effectively**.

Syllabus and learning outcomes

Paper P2 Performance Management

The syllabus comprises:

Topic and Study Weighting

		%
A	Pricing and product decisions	30
B	Cost planning and analysis for competitive advantage	30
C	Budgeting and management control	20
D	Control and performance measurement of responsibility centres	20

Learning Outcomes		
Lead	**Component**	**Syllabus content**
A Pricing and product decisions		
1 Discuss concepts of cost and revenue relevant to pricing and product decisions.	(a) Discuss the principles of decision-making including the identification of relevant cash flows and their use alongside non-quantifiable factors in making rounded judgements. (b) Discuss the possible conflicts between cost accounting for profit reporting and stock valuation and information required for decision-making. (c) Discuss the particular issues that arise in pricing decisions and the conflict between 'marginal cost' principles and the need for full recovery of all costs incurred.	• Relevant cash flows and their use in short-term decisions, typically concerning acceptance/rejection of contracts, pricing and cost/benefit comparisons. • The importance of strategic, intangible and non-financial judgements in decision-making. • Relevant costs and revenues in decision-making and their relation to accounting concepts. • Marginal and full cost recovery as bases for pricing decisions in the short and long-term.

Learning Outcomes		
Lead	**Component**	**Syllabus content**
2 Analyse short-term pricing and product decisions.	(a) Explain the usefulness of dividing costs into variable and fixed components in the context of short-term decision-making. (b) Interpret variable/fixed cost analysis in multiple product contexts to breakeven analysis and product mix decision-making, including circumstances where there are multiple constraints and linear programming methods are needed to identify 'optimal' solutions. (c) Discuss the meaning of 'optimal' solutions and how linear programming methods can be employed for profit maximising, revenue maximising and satisfying objectives. (d) Analyse the impact of uncertainty and risk on decision models based on CVP analysis.	• Simple product mix analysis in situations where there are limitations on product/service demand and one other production constraint. • Multi-product breakeven analysis, including breakeven and profit/volume charts, contribution/sales ratio, margin of safety etc. • Linear programming for more complex situations involving multiple constraints. Solution by graphical methods of two variable problems, together with understanding of the mechanics of simplex solution, shadow prices etc. (Note: questions requiring the full application of the simplex algorithm will not be set although candidates should be able to formulate an initial tableau, interpret a final simplex tableau and apply the information it contained in a final tableau). • Sensitivity analysis of CVP-based decision models.
3 Discuss pricing strategies and their consequences.	(a) Apply an approach to pricing based on profit maximisation in imperfect markets. (b) Discuss the financial consequences of alternative pricing strategies. (c) Explain why joint costs must be allocated to final products for financial reporting purposes, but why this is unhelpful when decisions concerning process and product viability have to be taken.	• Pricing decisions for profit maximising in imperfect markets. (Note: tabular methods of solution are acceptable). • Pricing strategies and the financial consequences of market skimming, premium pricing, penetration pricing, loss leaders, product bundling/optional extras and product differentiation to appeal to different market segments. • The allocation of joint costs and decisions concerning process and product viability based on relevant costs and revenues.

Learning Outcomes		
Lead	**Component**	**Syllabus content**
B **Cost planning and analysis for competitive advantage**		
1 Evaluate techniques for analysing and managing costs for competitive advantage.	(a) Compare and contrast value analysis and functional cost analysis.	• Value analysis and quality function deployment.
	(b) Evaluate the impacts of just-in-time production, the theory of constraints and total quality management on efficiency, inventory and cost.	• The benefits of just-in-time production, total quality management and theory of constraints and the implications of these methods for decision-making in the 'new manufacturing environment'.
	(c) Explain the concepts of continuous improvement and Kaizen costing that are central to total quality management.	• Kaizen costing, continuous improvement and cost of quality reporting.
	(d) Prepare cost of quality reports.	• Learning curves and their use in predicting product/service costs, including derivation of the learning rate and the learning index.
	(e) Apply learning curves to estimate time and cost for new products and services.	• Activity-based management in the analysis of overhead and its use in improving the efficiency of repetitive overhead activities.
	(f) Apply the techniques of activity-based management in identifying cost drivers/activities.	• Target costing.
	(g) Explain how process re-engineering can be used to eliminate non-value adding activities and reduce activity costs.	• Life cycle costing and implications for marketing strategies. • The value chain and supply chain management, including the trend to outsource manufacturing operations to transition and developing economies.
	(h) Explain how target costs can be derived from target prices and the relationship between target costs and standard costs.	• Gain sharing arrangements in situations where, because of the size of the project, a limited number of contractors or security issues (eg in defence work), normal competitive pressures do not apply.
	(i) Discuss the concept of life cycle costing and how life cycle costs interact with marketing strategies at each stage of the life cycle.	• The use of direct and activity-based cost methods in tracing costs to 'cost objects', such as customers or distribution channels, and the comparison of such costs with appropriate revenues to establish 'tiered' contribution levels, as in the activity-based cost hierarchy.
	(j) Discuss the concept of the value chain and the management of contribution/profit generated throughout the chain.	• Pareto analysis.
	(k) Discuss gain sharing arrangements whereby contractors and customers benefit if contract targets for cost, delivery etc are beaten.	

Learning Outcomes		
Lead	**Component**	**Syllabus content**
	(l) Analyse direct customer profitability and extend this analysis to distribution channel profitability through the application of activity-based costing ideas.	
	(m) Apply Pareto analysis as a convenient technique for identifying key elements of data and in presenting the results of other analyses, such as activity-based profitability calculations.	

C	**Budgeting and management control**	
1 Explain the principles that underlie the use of budgets in control.	(a) Explain the concepts of feedback and feed-forward control and their application in the use of budgets for planning and control.	• Control system concepts.
	(b) Explain the concept of responsibility accounting and its importance in the construction of functional budgets that support the overall master budget.	• The use of budgets in planning: 'rolling budgets' for adaptive planning.
	(c) Identify controllable and uncontrollable costs in the context of responsibility accounting and why uncontrollable costs may or may not be allocated to responsibility centres.	• Responsibility accounting and the use of budgets for control: controllable costs and treatment of uncontrollable costs; the conceptual link between standard costing and budget flexing.
2 Evaluate performance using budgets, recognising alternative approaches and sensitivity to variable factors.	(a) Evaluate projected performance using ratio analysis.	• Assessing the financial consequences of projected performance through key metrics including profitability, liquidity and asset turnover ratios.
	(b) Evaluate the consequences of 'what if' scenarios and their impact on the master budget.	• What-if analysis based on alternate projections of volumes, prices and cost structures and the use of spreadsheets in facilitating these analyses.
	(c) Evaluate performance using fixed and flexible budget reports.	• The evaluation of out-turn performance using variances based on 'fixed' and 'flexed' budgets.

BPP LEARNING MEDIA

Learning Outcomes		
Lead	**Component**	**Syllabus content**
3 Discuss the broader managerial issues arising from the use of budgets in control.	(a) Discuss the impact of budgetary control systems and setting of standard costs on human behaviour. (b) Discuss the role of non-financial performance indicators. (c) Compare and contrast traditional approaches to budgeting with recommendations based on the 'balanced scorecard'. (d) Discuss the criticisms of budgeting, particularly from the advocates of 'beyond budgeting' techniques.	• Behavioural issues in budgeting: participation in budgeting and its possible beneficial consequences for ownership and motivation; participation in budgeting and its possible adverse consequences for 'budget padding' and manipulation; setting budget targets for motivation; implications of setting standard costs etc. • Non-financial performance indicators. • Criticisms of budgeting and the recommendations of the advocates of the balanced scorecard and 'beyond budgeting'.
D Control and performance measurement of responsibility centres		
1 Discuss the use of responsibility centres in devising organisation structure and in management control.	(a) Discuss the use of cost, revenue, profit and investment centres in devising organisation structure and in management control.	• Organisation structure and its implications for responsibility accounting.
2 Discuss information suitable for management decision-making in responsibility centres.	(a) Discuss cost information in appropriate formats for cost centre managers, taking due account of controllable and uncontrollable costs and the importance of budget flexing. (b) Discuss revenue and cost information in appropriate formats for profit and investment centre managers, taking due account of cost variability, attributable costs, controllable costs and identification of appropriate measures of profit centre 'contribution'. (c) Discuss alternative measures of performance for responsibility centres.	• Presentation of financial information representing performance and recognising issues of controllable/uncontrollable costs, variable/fixed costs and tracing revenues and costs to particular cost objects. • Return on investment and its deficiencies; the emergence of residual income and economic value added to address these.

Learning Outcomes

Lead	Component	Syllabus content
3 Discuss the broader managerial issues arising from the division of the organisation into responsibility centres.	(a) Discuss the likely behavioural consequences of the use of performance metrics in managing cost, profit and investment centres.	• The behavioural consequences of performance management and control.
	(b) Discuss the typical consequences of a divisional structure for performance measurement as divisions compete or trade with each other.	• The theory of transfer pricing, including perfect, imperfect and no market for the intermediate good. • Use of negotiated, market, cost-plus and variable cost based transfer prices. 'Dual' transfer prices and lump sum payments as means of addressing some of the issues that arise.
	(c) Discuss the likely consequences of different approaches to transfer pricing for divisional decision-making, divisional and group profitability, the motivation of divisional management and the autonomy of individual divisions.	• The interaction of transfer pricing and tax liabilities in international operations and implications for currency management and possible distortion of internal company operations in order to comply with Tax Authority directives.
	(d) Discuss in principle the potential tax and currency management consequences of internal transfer pricing policy.	

Studying P2

1 What's P2 about

1.1 Pricing and product decisions

This section focuses on **short-term decision-making** and the issues that must be considered in this process. Some of the areas covered will be revision but it is important to be familiar with the impact that **costs, pricing strategies and constraints on production and sales** have on decisions.

Chapters 1A, 1B and 2 cover **relevant costs, short-term decisions and limiting factor analysis**. The focus is on both the calculations and also **discussion** of issues such as why certain costs are included in the decision-making process. Decision-making when there is more than one constraint is the covered in Chapters 3 and 4, with **linear programming**. There is strong emphasis on **interpretation and analysis**.

Finally, we consider **pricing** and how different pricing strategies can affect short-term decision-making.

1.2 Cost planning and analysis for competitive advantage

We look at the various techniques that can be used for **cost planning and analysis** in this section. We start off with cost planning in Chapter 7, looking at such techniques as learning curves, life cycle costing and target costing. Cost analysis – covered in Chapter 8 – focuses on such techniques as ABC, direct product profitability and customer profitability analysis. **Application** of Pareto analysis is also covered.

Cost management techniques such as JIT, total quality management (TQM) and outsourcing are covered in Chapters 9A and 9B.

1.3 Budgeting and management control

This section is primarily concerned with **performance evaluation** using budgets rather than the mechanics (which were covered in Paper P1). It begins with looking at the use of flexible budgets for evaluation and control purposes and then looks at the behavioural aspects of budgeting. There is also considerable focus on financial and non-financial performance indicators as well as the Balanced Scorecard.

In this section the main focus is on **interpretation and analysis** rather than on mechanical calculations (although you may need to perform numerical calculations before moving onto the discussion elements).

1.4 Control and performance measurement of responsibility centres

Finally, we look at measuring performance in divisionalised organisations. After understanding different types of **responsibility centres**, we focus on measures of performance such as residual income and return on investment. The effects of **transfer pricing strategies** on divisional performance are also considered.

2 What's required

You will be expected to demonstrate knowledge and understanding of various techniques as well as the ability to apply these techniques to different scenarios. Key higher skills include evaluation, interpretation and analysis.

The examiners are looking for

- Clear layout and labelling of workings
- Ability to apply knowledge to given scenarios rather than the production of generic answers
- Understanding of key techniques
- Ability to analyse and discuss data and information rather than just production of the numbers

What the examiner means

The table below has been prepared by CIMA to help you interpret the syllabus and learning outcomes and the meaning of exam questions.

You will see that there are 5 levels of Learning objective, ranging from Knowledge to Evaluation, reflecting the level of skill you will be expected to demonstrate. CIMA Certificate subjects were constrained to levels 1 to 3, but in CIMA's Professional qualification the entire hierarchy will be used.

At the start of each chapter in your study text is a topic list relating the coverage in the chapter to the level of skill you may be called on to demonstrate in the exam.

Learning objectives	Verbs used	Definition
1 Knowledge		
What you are expected to know	• List	• Make a list of
	• State	• Express, fully or clearly, the details of/facts of
	• Define	• Give the exact meaning of
2 Comprehension		
What you are expected to understand	• Describe	• Communicate the key features of
	• Distinguish	• Highlight the differences between
	• Explain	• Make clear or intelligible/state the meaning of
	• Identify	• Recognise, establish or select after consideration
	• Illustrate	• Use an example to describe or explain something
3 Application		
How you are expected to apply your knowledge	• Apply	• Put to practical use
	• Calculate/ compute	• Ascertain or reckon mathematically
	• Demonstrate	• Prove with certainty or to exhibit by practical means
	• Prepare	• Make or get ready for use
	• Reconcile	• Make or prove consistent/compatible
	• Solve	• Find an answer to
	• Tabulate	• Arrange in a table
4 Analysis		
How you are expected to analyse the detail of what you have learned	• Analyse	• Examine in detail the structure of
	• Categorise	• Place into a defined class or division
	• Compare and contrast	• Show the similarities and/or differences between
	• Construct	• Build up or compile
	• Discuss	• Examine in detail by argument
	• Interpret	• Translate into intelligible or familiar terms
	• Prioritise	• Place in order of priority or sequence for action
	• Produce	• Create or bring into existence

Learning objectives	Verbs used	Definition
5 Evaluation		
How you are expected to use your learning to evaluate, make decisions or recommendations	• Advise	• Counsel, inform or notify
	• Evaluate	• Appraise or assess the value of
	• Recommend	• Propose a course of action

3 How to pass

3.1 Study the whole syllabus

You need to be comfortable with **all areas of the syllabus**, as questions will often span a number of syllabus areas. A little wider reading will help you keep up to date with the global environment and new technologies.

3.2 Lots of question practice

You can **develop analysis and application skills** by attempting questions in the Exam Question Bank and later on questions in the BPP Practice and Revision Kit.

3.3 Analysing questions

For P2 it's particularly important to **consider the question requirements carefully** so that you understand exactly what the question is asking.

If you are given a scenario, make sure you relate your answer to it where possible as the examiner will be expecting you to demonstrate ability to apply techniques in particular contexts.

Always read the question carefully and answer the question set, not the question you hoped would be set!

3.4 Answering questions

Well-judged, clear recommendations grounded in the scenario will always score well as markers for this paper look to reward good answers. Lists of points memorised from texts and reproduced without any thought won't score well – you must always relate your knowledge to the specific question that you are facing. Additionally, only include scenario information or detailed theory in your answer if it supports the points you're making.

3.5 Exam technique

The following points of exam technique are particularly relevant to this paper.

- If you are asked to produce your answer in a **particular format** (for example, a report) make sure you do so as there will be marks for **presentation and coherence**.

- **Read the questions carefully** to ensure you are clear about what is being asked. **Answer the question set** and relate it to the scenario if there is one.

- Don't spend all your time on the longer Section B questions – make sure **you allocate the correct amount of time** to answering each question.

- You should consider in advance how you are going to use the **20 minute reading time.** You might decided to concentrate on reading through the longer Section B questions or you might prefer to skim read all the questions to ensure you know what is required in each.

- Leave time to **check your answers** at the end to identify and correct any silly mistakes.

- Practise **the presentation and layout** of answers, and pay attention to the legibility of your handwriting!

4 Brought forward knowledge

The examiner may test knowledge or techniques you've learnt at lower levels. As P2 is part of the Performance pillar, the content of Paper P1 will definitely be significant.

Remember that brought forward knowledge will only be useful if it is linked to the learning outcomes of Paper P2. For example, you might not be asked to produce a detailed budget but you might be required to comment on how budgets can affect individuals' behaviour in the workplace.

5 Links with other exams

You will make use of the knowledge gained from studying the Paper P2 syllabus in later papers so make sure you keep your study materials. For example, knowledge of relevant costs will be useful in Paper F3 *Financial Strategy* when evaluating investment proposals and strategies.

The exam paper

Format of the paper

		Number of marks
Section A:	Five compulsory medium answer questions of 10 marks each. Short scenarios may be given, to which some or all questions relate	50
Section B:	One or two compulsory questions. Short scenarios may be given, to which questions relate	50
		100

Time allowed: 3 hours, plus 20 minutes reading time

Numerical content

The paper is likely to have a mixture of numerical and written elements. The percentage of numerical versus written parts is likely to vary from sitting to sitting.

Breadth of question coverage

Questions in *both* sections of the paper may cover more than one syllabus area.

Knowledge from other syllabuses

Candidates should also use their knowledge from papers, particularly Paper P1.

May 2013 exam paper

Section A

1   Customer profitability statements
2   Learning curve
3   Zero based budgeting
4   Risk and uncertainty in decision making: decision rules
5   Beyond budgeting

Section B

6   (a) Limiting factor analysis
     (b) Linear programming
     (c) Value analysis
7   Transfer pricing

March 2013 exam paper – resit exam

Section A

1   Learning curve
2   Costs of quality, value chain
3   Activity based costing
4   Variance analysis
5   Balanced scorecard

Section B

6   Graphical linear programming
7   (a) Divisional performance measures
     (b) Investment appraisal and divisional performance

November 2012 exam paper

Section A

1 Learning curve
2 Flexible budgets
3 Participation in budget setting
4 Costs of quality
5 Production plans and JIT

Section B

6 (a) Limiting factor analysis
  (b) Shadow prices
  (c) Multi-product CVP analysis
  (d) Sensitivity analysis
7 (a) Demand function
  (b), (c) Transfer pricing

September 2012 exam paper – resit exam

Section A

1 Learning curve
2 Balanced Scorecard
3 Flexible budgets: variance analysis
4 Costs of quality
5 Product life cycle

Section B

6 (a), (b) Contract pricing: relevant costs
7 (a) Perfromance ratios
  (b) Multi-product CVP analysis
  (c) Investment appraisal, multi-product CVP analysis

May 2012 exam paper

Section A

1 The learning curve
2 Balanced scorecard
3 Flexing a budget and participation in budget setting
4 JIT
5 Cost plus and target costing

Section B

6 (a) & (b) Limiting factor analysis and restricted freedom of action
  (c) Linear programming
7 (a) Profit maximising price
  (b) Transfer prices

March 2012 exam paper – resit exam

Section A

1   The learning curve
2   Kaizen costing and performance reporting
3   Business process re-engineering
4   Budget control – feedforward and feedback control
5   Balanced scorecard

Section B

6   Graphical linear programming
7   (a) Measuring performance in divisionalised businesses
     (b) Investment appraisal

November 2011 exam paper

Section A

1   Learning curve
2   Kaizen costing
3   Value analysis and functional cost analysis
4   Budget control – feedforward and feedback control
5   Balanced Scorecard

Section B

6   (a) Relevant costs
     (b) & (c) Transfer pricing
7   (a) Measuring performance in divisionalised businesses
     (b) Costs of quality

September 2011 exam paper – resit exam

Section A

1   Pricing decisions and the demand curve equation
2   Customer life cycle
3   Kaizen costing
4   Variance analysis - operational variances
5   Balanced Scorecard

Section B

6   (a), (b) & (c) Break-even analysis
     (d) Value analysis
7   (a) Contribution
     (b) NPV
     (c) Transfer Pricing

May 2011 exam paper

Section A

1 Pricing decisions and the demand curve equation
2 The product life cycle
3 Target costing and Kaizen costing
4 Variance analysis - planning and operational variances
5 Non-financial performance measures and performance reports

Section B

6 (a) & (b) Relevant cost analysis
7 (a) & (b) Transfer pricing
 (c) Investment appraisal
 (d) Divisional performance measures

March 2011 exam paper – resit exam

Section A

1 The learning curve
2 Just-in-time production
3 Budget participation
4 Performance statements and variance analysis
5 Total quality management

Section B

6 (a) - (c) Short-term decisions and limiting factor analysis
 (d) Linear programming: the simplex method
7 (a) & (b) Measuring performance in divisionalised businesses
 (c) Transfer pricing

November 2010 exam paper

Section A

1 The learning curve and planning & operational variances
2 Costs of quality
3 Total quality management and JIT
4 Budgeting systems – rolling budgets
5 Activity-based costing

Section B

6 (a) Limiting factor analysis
 (b) & (c) Linear programming: the simplex method
7 (a) Performance measurement
 (b) Investment appraisal
 (c) Residual income

September 2010 exam paper – resit exam

Section A

1   Multi-product breakeven analysis
2   Kaizen and costs of quality
3   Customer profitability analysis
4   Participative budgeting and motivation
5   The learning curve, target costing and variance analysis

Section B

6   (a) Limiting factor analysis
     (d) Pricing strategies
     (c) The product life cycle
7   (a) Measuring performance in divisionalised businesses
     (b) & (c) Transfer pricing

May 2010 exam paper

Section A

1   Flexed budgets and the learning curve
2   The product life cycle
3   Just-in-time production
4   Budgeting systems and non-financial performance indicators
5   Reporting performance in divisionalised businesses and activity based costing

Section B

6   (a) & (b) Limiting factors
     (c) & (d) Linear programming: the graphical method

7   (a) Return on investment
     (b) NPV and ROI
     (c) Transfer pricing

Specimen exam paper

Section A

1   The value chain and gain sharing arrangements
2   The learning curve and planning & operating variances
3   Budgeting
4   Activity based costing and Pareto analysis
5   Cost planning and pricing decisions

Section B

6   (a) – (c) Relevant costs and short-term decisions

7   (a)   Measuring performance in divisionalised businesses
     (b)   Negotiated transfer pricing
     (c)   Measuring performance in divisionalised businesses
     (d)   Dual transfer prices

INTRODUCTION

INTRODUCTION – A REVISION OF BASIC COST ACCOUNTING CONCEPTS AND TECHNIQUES

Before you start your P2 studies, read through this chapter to remind yourself of basic cost accounting concepts and techniques. These areas were introduced at Certificate level but are fundamental to your understanding of many topics covered in the P2 syllabus.

If you are confident you understand the contents of this chapter, have a go at the questions and then feel free to move onto Chapter 1A. If you are a bit rusty, read the chapter in full and attempt the questions as you go along. You can also continue to refer to this introduction as you move through the P2 syllabus.

topic list	learning outcomes	syllabus references	ability required
1 Some basic cost accounting concepts	Revision	n/a	knowledge
2 The problem of overheads	Revision	n/a	application
3 Revision of absorption costing	Revision	n/a	application
4 Overhead absorption	Revision	n/a	analysis
5 Revision of marginal costing	Revision	n/a	analysis
6 Revision of variance analysis	Revision	n/a	analysis
7 Reconciling profit figures	Revision	n/a	analysis

1 Some basic cost accounting concepts

Introduction

This section reviews a number of key terms that you must be familiar with.

KEY POINTS

- **Costs** can be **classified** according to their **nature** or according to their **purpose** (inventory valuation/profit measurement, decision making, control).

- **Costs** can **behave** in **variable, fixed, semi-variable/semi-fixed/mixed** or **stepped** fashion in relation to changes in activity level.

- **Semi-variable costs** can be **analysed** using the **high-low** or **scattergraph methods**.

Knowledge brought forward from earlier studies

Cost units and cost centres

Cost unit

- Anything that is measurable and useful for cost control purposes

- Can be tangible (such as a tonne of coal) or intangible (such as an hour of accountant's time)

- Composite cost units are made up of two parts (such as the passenger/kilometre (the cost of transporting one passenger for one kilometre) for a bus company)

Cost centre

- Act as collecting places for costs before they are analysed further

- Examples: A production department, a service location such as the canteen, a function such as a sales representative, an activity such as quality control or an item of equipment such as a key production machine

Cost classification

According to their nature

- Into materials, labour, expenses and then further subdivided (such as raw materials, components, consumables)

According to their purpose

- For **inventory valuation and profit measurement**, costs might be classified as **product costs and period costs, direct costs and indirect costs/overheads**, or they might be **classified by function** (production/manufacturing, administration, marketing/selling and distribution)

- For **decision making**, costs are **classified by behaviour** (see below) or as **relevant and non-relevant** (a concept covered in Chapter 2)

- **Classification for control** involves dividing costs into those that are **controllable** and those that are **uncontrollable**, or into **normal and abnormal costs**

Cost behaviour

Variable costs

- Tend to **vary directly with the level of output** (so that there is a **linear relationship** between **variable cost per unit and output**)

- Variable cost per unit is the **same amount for each unit produced** but **total variable cost increases as volume of output increases** (for example, materials)

Fixed costs

- Tend to be **unaffected by increases or decreases in the level of output**

- Relate to a span of time and so are a **period charge** (as the **time span increases so too will the cost**)

- Only **constant** at all levels of output **within the relevant range** of output (the range of output at which the organisation has had experience of operating in the past and for which cost information is available)

- Examples: local government taxes for commercial properties (rates) and UK road fund licence

Semi-variable (or semi-fixed or mixed) costs

- Made up of a **fixed cost element** and a **variable cost element** and so **partly affected by changes in the level of activity**

- Can be **analysed** using the **high-low method** or the **scattergraph method**

Stepped costs

- **Behave like fixed costs within certain ranges of activity**

- Example: rent (of an organisation's one factory) may be a fixed cost if production remains below 1,000 units a month, but if production exceeds 1,000 units a second factory may be required and the cost of rent (on two factories) would go up a step

- Do not behave like variable costs and so, continuing the example above, if monthly output is 1,500 units, two factories are required – not 1.5 factories

---

Section summary

Costs can be **classified** according to their **nature** or according to their **purpose** (inventory valuation/profit measurement, decision-making, control).

Costs can **behave** in **variable, fixed, semi-variable/semi-fixed/mixed** or **stepped** fashion in relation to changes in activity level.

Semi-variable costs can be **analysed** using the **high-low** or **scattergraph** methods.

---

2   The problem of overheads

Introduction

Traditionally, the view has been that a fair share of overheads should be added to the cost of units produced. This fair share will **include a portion of all production overhead expenditure** and possibly administration and marketing overheads too. This is the view embodied in the principles of **absorption costing**.

2.1 Using absorption costing to deal with the problem of overheads

The **theoretical justification** for using absorption costing is that all production overheads are incurred in the production of the organisation's output and so each unit of the product receives some benefit from these costs. Each unit of output should therefore be charged with some of the overhead costs.

2.1.1 Practical reasons for using absorption costing

(a)   **Inventory valuations**

Inventory in hand must be valued for two reasons.

(i)   For the **closing inventory** figure in the balance sheet (statement of financial position)
(ii)   For the **cost of sales** figure in the income statement (statement of comprehensive income)

(b)   **Pricing decisions**

Many companies attempt to set selling prices **by calculating the full cost of production or sales** of each product, and then adding a margin for profit. 'Full cost plus pricing' can be particularly useful for companies which do jobbing or contract work, where each job or contract is different, so that a standard unit sales price cannot be fixed. Without using absorption costing, a full cost is difficult to ascertain.

(c)   **Establishing the profitability of different products**

This argument in favour of absorption costing states that if a company sells more than one product, it will be difficult to judge **how profitable each individual product is**, unless overhead costs are shared on a fair basis and charged to the cost of sales of each product.

2.2 Using marginal costing to deal with the problem of overheads

Advocates of **marginal costing** take the view that only the variable costs of making and selling a product or service should be identified. **Fixed costs should be dealt with separately** and treated as a cost of the accounting period rather than shared out somehow between units produced. Some overhead costs are, however, variable costs which increase as the total level of activity rises and so the marginal cost of production and sales should include an amount for variable overheads.

Section summary

The traditional approach to dealing with overheads is **absorption costing**. It is recommended in financial accounting, but in some situations the information it provides can be **misleading**.

3   Revision of absorption costing   3/13

Introduction

This section acts as a reminder of how to calculate cost per unit using absorption costing and the terminology used in this costing technique.

KEY TERM

ABSORPTION COSTING is 'A method of costing that, in addition to direct costs, assigns all, or a proportion of, production overhead costs to cost units by means of one or a number of overhead absorption rates'.

(CIMA *Official Terminology*)

Knowledge brought forward from earlier studies

Absorption costing

- Product costs are built up using absorption costing by a process of **allocation,** apportionment and **overhead absorption**.

- **Allocation** is the process by which whole cost items are charged directly to a cost unit or cost centre. **Direct costs are allocated directly to cost units. Overheads clearly identifiable with cost**

centres are allocated to those cost centres but costs which **cannot be identified with one particular cost centre** are **allocated to general overhead cost centres**. The cost of a warehouse security guard would therefore be charged to the warehouse cost centre but heating and lighting costs would be charged to a general overhead cost centre.

- The **first stage of overhead apportionment** involves sharing out (or apportioning) the overheads within **general overhead cost centres** between the other cost centres using a fair basis of apportionment (such as floor area occupied by each cost centre for heating and lighting costs).

- The **second stage of overhead apportionment** is to apportion the costs of **service cost centres** (both directly allocated and apportioned costs) to production cost centres.

- The **final stage** in absorption costing is the **absorption into product costs** (using overhead absorption rates) of the overheads which have been allocated and apportioned to the production cost centres.

3.1 Calculating the cost per unit

The diagram below illustrates the procedures you should follow when trying to calculate the cost per unit using absorption costing. Note the process of **allocating, apportioning** and **reapportioning** indirect costs to cost centres and ultimately production centres.

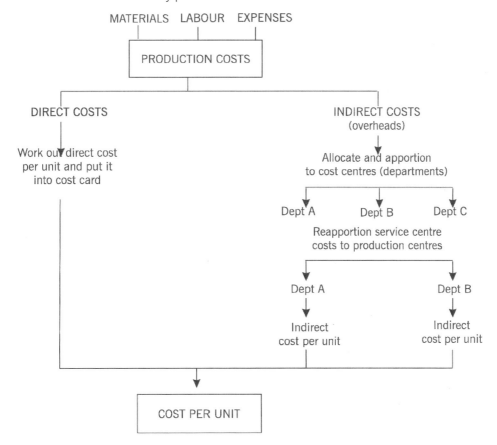

Question 1   Apportionment

A company is preparing its production overhead budgets and determining the apportionment of those overheads to products. Cost centre expenses and related information have been budgeted as follows.

	Total $	Machine shop A $	Machine shop B $	Assembly $	Canteen $	Maintenance $
Indirect wages	78,560	8,586	9,190	15,674	29,650	15,460
Consumable materials	16,900	6,400	8,700	1,200	600	–
Rent and rates	16,700					
Buildings insurance	2,400					
Power	8,600					
Heat and light	3,400					
Depreciation (machinery)	40,200					
Value of machinery	402,000	201,000	179,000	22,000	–	–
Power usage (%)	100	55	40	3	–	2
Direct labour (hours)	35,000	8,000	6,200	20,800	–	–
Machine usage (hours)	25,200	7,200	18,000	–	–	–
Area (sq ft)	45,000	10,000	12,000	15,000	6,000	2,000

Required

Using the direct apportionment to production departments method and bases of apportionment which you consider most appropriate from the information provided, calculate overhead totals for the three production departments.

Section summary

The three stages of absorption costing are **allocation**, **apportionment** and **absorption**.

---

4 Overhead absorption

Introduction

Having allocated and/or apportioned all overheads, the next stage in absorption costing is to add them to, or absorb them into, the cost of production or sales.

KEY TERM

ABSORBED OVERHEAD is 'Overhead attached to products or services by means of absorption rates'.
(CIMA *Official Terminology*)

4.1 Use of a predetermined absorption rate

KEY TERM

OVERHEAD ABSORPTION RATE is 'A means of attributing overhead to a product or service, based for example on direct labour hours, direct labour cost or machine hours'.   (CIMA *Official Terminology*)

Knowledge brought forward from earlier studies

 The overhead likely to be incurred during the coming year is estimated.

 The total hours, units or direct costs on which the overhead absorption rates are based (activity levels) are estimated.

 Absorption rate = estimated overhead ÷ budgeted activity level

4.2 Choosing the appropriate absorption base

The choice of an absorption basis is a **matter of judgement and common sense**. There are no strict rules or formulae involved. The ease of collecting the data required for the chosen rate is a major factor. But the basis should realistically reflect the characteristics of a given cost centre, avoid undue anomalies and be 'fair'. It is generally accepted **time-based bases** should be used if possible as many overheads, such as rent and rates, increase with time. The **choice will be significant in determining the cost of individual products, but the total cost of production overheads is the budgeted overhead expenditure, no matter what basis of absorption is selected.** It is the relative share of overhead costs borne by individual products and jobs which is affected.

Question 2	Bases of absorption

List as many possible bases of absorption (or 'overhead recovery rates') that you can think of, and give their advantages and disadvantages.

Question 3	Absorption rates

Using the information in and the results of **Question 1: apportionment** (in Section 3), determine budgeted overhead absorption rates for each of the production departments using appropriate bases of absorption.

4.3 Under- and over-absorption of overheads

KEY POINT

Under-/over-absorbed overhead occurs when overheads incurred do not equal overheads absorbed.

The rate of overhead absorption is based on **estimates** (of both numerator and denominator) and it is quite likely that either one or both of the estimates will not agree with what actually occurs.

- **Over absorption** means that the **overheads charged to the cost of sales are greater than the overheads actually incurred**.

- **Under absorption** means that **insufficient overheads have been included in the cost of sales**.

KEY TERM

UNDER- OR OVER-ABSORBED OVERHEAD (or UNDER- OR OVER-RECOVERED OVERHEAD) is 'The difference between overhead incurred and overhead absorbed, using an estimated rate, in a given period'.

(CIMA *Official Terminology*)

Suppose that the budgeted overhead in a production department is $80,000 and the budgeted activity is 40,000 direct labour hours, the overhead recovery rate (using a direct labour hour basis) would be $2 per direct labour hour. Actual overheads in the period are, say $84,000 and 45,000 direct labour hours are worked.

	$
Overhead incurred (actual)	84,000
Overhead absorbed (45,000 × $2)	90,000
Over-absorption of overhead	6,000

In this example, the cost of production has been charged with $6,000 more than was actually spent and so the cost that is recorded will be too high. The over-absorbed overhead will be an adjustment to the income statement at the end of the accounting period to reconcile the overheads charged to the actual overhead.

Question 4   Under- and over-absorption

The total production overhead expenditure of the company in **Question: apportionment and Question: absorption rates** (in Sections 3 and 4) was $176,533 and its actual activity was as follows.

	Machine shop A	Machine shop B	Assembly
Direct labour hours	8,200	6,500	21,900
Machine usage hours	7,300	18,700	–

Required

Using the information in and results of the two questions mentioned above, what is the under or over absorption of overheads?

4.3.1 The reasons for under-/over-absorbed overhead

The overhead absorption rate is predetermined from budget estimates of overhead cost and activity level. Under or over recovery of overhead will occur in the following circumstances.

- Actual overhead costs are different from budgeted overheads.
- The actual activity level is different from the budgeted activity level.
- Actual overhead costs **and** actual activity level differ from those budgeted.

Question 5   Reasons for under/over absorption

Elsewhere Ltd has a budgeted production overhead of $180,000 and a budgeted activity of 45,000 machine hours.

Required

Fill in the blanks and choose the correct terms from those highlighted in the following statements.

(a)   If actual overheads cost $170,000 and 45,000 machine hours were worked, **under-absorbed/over-absorbed** overhead will be $ .... because ....

(b)   If actual overheads cost $180,000 and 40,000 machine hours were worked, **under-absorbed/over-absorbed** overhead will be $ .... because ....

(c)   If actual overheads cost $170,000 and 40,000 machine hours were worked, **under-absorbed/over-absorbed** overhead will be $ .... because ....

4.3.2 Accounting for under-/over absorbed overheads

If overheads are **under-absorbed**, the cost of units sold will have been understated and therefore the under-absorption is charged to the income statement for the period. It is not usually considered necessary to adjust individual unit costs and therefore inventory values are not altered.

Any **over-absorption** is credited to the income statement for the period.

4.3.3 The problems caused by under-/over-absorption of overheads

If **under-absorption** occurs, product prices may have been set too low as managers have been working with unit rates for overheads that are too low. This could have a significant impact on profit levels.

If overhead rates have been unnecessarily high (**over-absorption**), it is likely that prices have been set too high which could significantly reduce sales of the product.

Section summary

After apportionment, overheads are absorbed into products using an **appropriate absorption rate based on budgeted costs and budgeted activity levels.**

Under-/over-absorbed overhead occurs when overheads incurred do not equal overheads absorbed.

5   Revision of marginal costing

Introduction

This section acts as a reminder of the marginal costing technique that was covered in your previous studies. Make sure you read the 'knowledge brought forward' to ensure you are familiar with the terminology and the differences between a marginal costing income statement and one used for absorption costing.

KEY TERMS

MARGINAL COST is 'The part of the cost of one unit of a product or service which would be avoided if that unit were not produced, or which would increase if one extra unit were produced'.

CONTRIBUTION is 'Sales value less variable cost of sales'.

MARGINAL COSTING is 'The accounting system in which variable costs are charged to cost units and fixed costs of the period are written off in full against the aggregate contribution. Its special value is in recognising cost behaviour, and hence assisting in decision-making.'   (CIMA *Official Terminology*)

Knowledge brought forward from earlier studies

Marginal costing

- In **marginal costing**, closing **inventories are valued at marginal (variable) production cost** whereas, in **absorption costing**, inventories are **valued at their full production cost** which includes absorbed fixed production overhead.

- If the opening and closing inventory levels differ, the **profit reported** for the accounting period **under the two costing systems will therefore be different**.

- But **in the long run, total profit for a company will be the same** whichever is used because, in the long run, total costs will be the same by either method of accounting. Different accounting conventions merely affect the profit of individual periods.

Income statements

- **Absorption costing**

	$	$
Sales		X
Opening inventory (at full cost)	X	
Full production cost	X	
Less closing inventory (at full cost)	X	
Cost of sales	X	
Under-/over-absorbed overhead	X	
Total cost		X
Gross profit		X
Less non-manufacturing costs		X
Net profit		X

- **Marginal costing**

	$	$
Sales		X
Opening inventory (at variable cost)	X	
Production cost (variable costs)	X	
Less closing inventory (at variable cost)	X	
Cost of sales		X
Contribution		X
Less fixed production costs		X
Gross profit		X
Less non-manufacturing fixed costs		X
Net profit		X

Question 6	Marginal costing and absorption costing

RH makes and sells one product, which has the following standard production cost.

		$
Direct labour	3 hours at $6 per hour	18
Direct materials	4 kilograms at $7 per kg	28
Production overhead	Variable	3
	Fixed	20
Standard production cost per unit		69

Normal output is 16,000 units per annum. Variable selling, distribution and administration costs are 20 per cent of sales value. Fixed costs are $180,000 per annum. There are no units in finished goods inventory at 1 October 20X2. The fixed overhead expenditure is spread evenly throughout the year. The selling price per unit is $140. Production and sales budgets are as follows.

	Six months ending 31 March 20X3	Six months ending 30 September 20X3
Production	8,500	7,000
Sales	7,000	8,000

Required

Prepare profit statements for each of the six-monthly periods, using the following methods of costing.

(a)   Marginal costing   (b)   Absorption costing

Section summary

In **marginal costing**, inventories are valued at **variable (marginal) production cost** whereas in **absorption costing** they are valued at their **full production cost**.

If **opening and closing inventory levels differ, profit** reported under the two methods will be **different**.

In the **long run, total profit** will be the **same** whatever method is used.

6 Revision of variance analysis   3/11, 5/11, 9/11, 3/13

Introduction

Variance analysis reconciles actual to budgeted costs, revenue or profit. It is a way of explaining the difference between actual and budgeted results. They can either be favourable (F), better than expected or adverse (A), worse than expected.

You should remember the variances summarised below from your previous studies.

Variance	Favourable	Adverse	Calculation	
Material price	– Unforeseen discounts received – Greater care in purchasing – Change in material standard	– Price increase – Careless purchasing – Change in material standard	Price Based on actual purchases What should it have cost? What did it cost?	$ X (X) X
Material usage	– Material used of higher quality than standard – More efficient use of material – Errors in allocating material to jobs	– Defective material – Excessive waste or theft – Stricter quality control	Usage Based on actual production What should have been used? What was used? Difference valued at standard cost per kg	Kgs X (X) X $X
Labour rate	– Use of workers at a rate of pay lower than standard	– Wage rate increase	Rate Based on actual hours paid What should it have cost? What did it cost?	$ X (X) X

Variance	Favourable	Adverse	Calculation	
Idle time	– The idle time variance is always adverse	– Machine breakdown – Illness or injury to worker	Idle time Hours worked Hours paid Difference valued at standard rate per hour	Hrs X (X) $X
Labour efficiency	– Output produced more quickly than expected because of worker motivation, better quality materials etc – Errors in allocating time to jobs	– Lost time in excess of standard – Output lower than standard set because of lack of training, sub-standard materials etc – Errors in allocating time to jobs	Efficiency Based on actual production How long should it have taken? How long did it take? Difference valued at standard rate per hour	Hrs X (X) X $X
Variable overhead expenditure	– See fixed overhead expenditure (below)	– See fixed overhead expenditure (below)	Based on actual hours worked What should it have cost? What did it cost?	$ X (X) X
Variable overhead efficiency	– See labour efficiency (above)	– See labour efficiency (above)	Based on actual production How long should it have taken? How long did it take? Difference valued at std rate per hour	Hrs X (X) X $X

Note: This assumes variable overheads are incurred per labour hour

Variance	Favourable	Adverse	Calculation	
Fixed overhead expenditure	– Savings in costs incurred – More economical use of services	– Increase in cost of services used – Excessive use of services – Change in type of service used	Budgeted expenditure Actual expenditure	$ X (X) X

Overhead expenditure variances ought to be traced to the individual cost centres where the variances occurred.

Variance	Favourable	Adverse	Calculation	
Fixed overhead volume	Production or level of activity greater than budgeted	Production or level of activity less than budgeted	Budgeted units Actual units Difference valued at OAR per unit	Units X (X) X $X

Remember that where inputs can be substituted for one another, the efficiency/usage variance can be subdivided. Material and labour variances can both be split into mix and yield (or output) components.

Variance	Description	Calculation	
Yield	Measures the effect on costs of inputs yielding more or less than expected.	Calculated as the difference between the expected output and the actual output, valued at the standard cost per unit.	
Mix	Measures whether the actual mix is cheaper or more expensive than the standard	Calculated as the difference between the actual total quantity used in the standard mix and the actual quantity used in the actual mix, valued at the standard input price of each material.	

Planning and operational variances are summarised below.

Variance	Description	Calculation	
Planning variance	A planning variance arises because of inaccurate planning or faulty standards.	Original standard Revised standard Difference valued at standard rate	Hrs X (X) $X
Operational variance	An operational variance compares actual results with the revised (or ex-post) standard.	How long should it have taken? How long did it take? Difference valued at standard rate	Hrs X (X) $X

Section summary

Whilst you are unlikely to be required to calculate a number of variances in the exam, you should understand how different variances are inter-linked and be able to discuss potential causes of variances.

7   Reconciling profit figures

Introduction

Now that you can calculate profits using absorption costing and marginal costing, the final issue is how to reconcile the profits. You might be required to reconcile profits calculated using the two methods. Alternatively you might be asked to reconcile profits for different periods calculated using the same method.

7.1 Reconciling the profit figures given by the two methods

KEY POINT

The **difference in profits** reported using marginal costing and absorption costing is **due** to the **different inventory valuation methods** used.

(a)   **Inventory levels increase during the period**

Absorption costing will report the higher profit. Some of the fixed production overhead incurred during the period will be carried forward in closing inventory (which reduces cost of sales) to be set against sales revenue in the following period instead of being written off in full against profit in the period concerned.

(b) **Inventory levels decrease during the period**

Absorption costing will report the lower profit. As well as the fixed overhead incurred, fixed production overhead which had been carried forward in opening inventory is released and is also included in cost of sales.

Example: reconciling profits

The profits reported for the six months ending 31 March 20X3 in the previous question would be reconciled as follows.

	$'000
Marginal costing profit	191
Adjust for fixed overhead in inventory (inventory increase of 1,500 units × $20 per unit)	30
Absorption costing profit	221

Question 7
Profit reconciliation

Reconcile the profits reported for the six months ending 30 September 20X3 in **Question 6: marginal costing and absorption costing**.

Question 8
Differences between absorption costing and marginal costing profits

D&M report an absorption costing profit of $112,500 for the year to 31 December 19X0. Opening inventory consisted of 58,000 units, closing inventory 43,000 units. The fixed overhead absorbed per unit is $19.50.

Required

Fill in the blank in the following statement.

The marginal costing profit for the period would be $ ....

7.2 Reconciling the profits for different periods

KEY POINTS

When **marginal costing** is used, differences in profits in different periods are **due to changes in sales volume.**

When **absorption costing** is used differences are **due to changes in sales volumes and adjustments made for over-/under-absorbed overhead.**

Example: reconciling marginal costing profit with absorption costing profit

Look back at the information in **Question 6: marginal costing and absorption costing**.

Reconcile the marginal costing profits for the two periods and also the absorption costing profits for the two periods.

For marginal costing

The difference in profits in the two periods is due entirely to **changes in units sold** (everything else has remained the same). Higher sales volume means higher contribution and thus greater profits.

Contribution per unit

	$
Selling price	140
Less direct labour	((18)
direct materials	(28)
variable production overhead	(3)
variable selling and other costs (20% × $140)	(28)
Contribution	63

The **marginal costing profit figures** can be reconciled as follows.

	$'000
Marginal costing profit for six months to 31 March 20X3	191
Increase in contribution in second six-month period due to increase in sales volume	
((8,000 – 7,000) × $63)	63
Marginal costing profit for six months to 30 September 20X3	254

For absorption costing

Profit per unit

	$
Selling price	140
Less standard production cost	(69)
variable selling and so on costs	(28)
Profit	43

The **absorption costing** profit figures can be reconciled as follows.

	$'000
Absorption costing profit for six months to 31 March 20X3	221
Increase in profit in second six-month period due to increase in sales volume	
((8,000 – 7,000) × $43)	43
Adjustments for under/over absorption	
Six months to 31 March 20X3	(10)
Six months to 30 September 20X3	(20)
Absorption costing profit for six months to 30 September 20X3	234

The **over absorption** in the first six months must be **deducted** in the reconciliation because it made that period's profit higher (and we are reconciling from the first six months' figure to the second six months'). The **under absorption** in the second six months must also be **deducted**, however, as it made that period's profits lower than the first six months'.

This is a bit confusing so go over the paragraph above until you have the reasoning clear in your mind. Then try the following question.

 Question 9   Reconciliation of profits for different periods

In a reconciliation of the absorption costing profits of 20X0 to those of 20X1, there was under absorption of fixed production overhead in both periods. How should the under absorbed overhead figures be dealt with in the reconciliation?

	20X0 figure	20X1 figure
A	Add	Add
B	Deduct	Add
C	Add	Deduct
D	Deduct	Deduct

Section summary

When **marginal costing** is used, differences in profits in different periods are **due to changes in sales volume**.

When **absorption costing** is used differences are **due to changes in sales volumes and adjustments made for over-/under-absorbed overhead**.

Chapter Roundup

✓ Costs can be **classified** according to their **nature** or according to their **purpose** (inventory valuation/profit measurement, decision-making, control).

✓ **Costs** can **behave** in **variable, fixed, semi-variable/semi-fixed/mixed** or **stepped** fashion in relation to changes in activity level.

✓ **Semi-variable costs** can be **analysed** using the **high-low** or **scattergraph methods**.

✓ The traditional approach to dealing with overheads is **absorption costing**. It is recommended in financial accounting, but in some situations the information it provides can be **misleading**.

✓ The three stages of absorption costing are **allocation, apportionment** and **absorption**.

✓ After apportionment, overheads are absorbed into products using **an appropriate absorption rate based on budgeted costs and budgeted activity levels**.

✓ **Under-/over-absorbed overhead** occurs when overheads incurred do not equal overheads absorbed.

✓ In **marginal costing**, inventories are valued at **variable (marginal) production cost** whereas in **absorption costing** they are valued at their **full production cost**.

✓ If **opening and closing inventory levels differ**, **profit** reported under the two methods will be **different**.

✓ In the **long run**, **total profit** will be the **same** whatever method is used.

✓ When **marginal costing** is used, differences in profits in different periods are **due to changes in sales volume**.

✓ When **absorption costing** is used differences are **due to changes in sales volumes and adjustments made for over-/under-absorbed overhead**.

Quick Quiz

1   The behaviour of fixed costs depends on whether marginal costing or absorption costing is used. *True or false?*

2   How is an overhead absorption rate calculated?

   A   Estimated overhead ÷ actual activity level
   B   Estimated overhead ÷ budgeted activity level
   C   Actual overhead ÷ actual activity level
   D   Actual overhead ÷ budgeted activity level

3   Over absorption means that the overheads charged to the cost of sales are greater than the overheads actually incurred. *True or false?*

4   *Fill in the blanks in the statements about marginal costing and absorption costing below.*

   (a)   If inventory levels .... between the beginning and end of a period, absorption costing will report the higher profit.

   (b)   If inventory levels decrease, ... costing will report the lower profit.

5   *Fill in the following blanks with either 'marginal' or 'absorption'.*

   (a)   Using .... costing, profits can be manipulated simply by changing output and inventory levels.

   (b)   Fixed costs are charged in full against the profit of the period in which they are incurred when .... costing is used.

   (c)   .... costing fails to recognise the importance of working to full capacity.

   (d)   .... costing could be argued to be preferable to .... costing in management accounting in order to be consistent with the requirements of SSAP 9.

   (e)   .... costing should not be used when decision-making information is required.

6   What are the three practical reasons cited in the chapter for using absorption costing?

   (a)   ....
   (b)   ....
   (c)   ....

Answers to Quick Quiz

1   False. The behaviour of fixed costs remains the same regardless of the costing system being used.

2   B. Actual figures are *not* used.

3   True

4   (a)   Increase
       (b)   Absorption

5   (a)   absorption
       (b)   marginal
       (c)   marginal
       (d)   absorption, marginal
       (e)   absorption

6   (a)   Inventory valuation
       (b)   Pricing decisions
       (c)   Establishing profitability of different products

Answers to Questions

1 Apportionment

	Total $	A $	B $	Assembly $	Canteen $	Maintenance $	Basis of apportionment
Indirect wages	78,560	8,586	9,190	15,674	29,650	15,460	Actual
Consumable materials	16,900	6,400	8,700	1,200	600	–	Actual
Rent and rates	16,700	3,711	4,453	5,567	2,227	742	Area
Insurance	2,400	533	640	800	320	107	Area
Power	8,600	4,730	3,440	258	–	172	Usage
Heat and light	3,400	756	907	1,133	453	151	Area
Depreciation	40,200	20,100	17,900	2,200	–	–	Val of mach
	166,760	44,816	45,230	26,832	33,250	16,632	
Reallocate	–	7,600	5,890	19,760	(33,250)	–	Direct labour
Reallocate	–	4,752	11,880	–	–	(16,632)	Mach usage
Totals	166,760	57,168	63,000	46,592	–	–	

2 Bases of absorption

(a) **Percentage of direct materials cost**. It is safe to assume that the overhead costs for producing brass screws, say, are similar to those for producing steel screws. The cost of brass is, however, very much greater than that of steel. Consequently, the overhead charge for brass screws would be too high and that for steel screws too low, if a percentage of cost of materials rate were to be used.

(b) Using **prime cost** as the absorption base would lead to anomalies because of the inclusion of the cost of material, as outlined above.

(c) **Percentage of direct labour cost**. If the overhead actually attributable to units was incurred on, say a time basis, but one highly-paid employee was engaged on producing one item, while a lower-paid employee was producing another item, the overhead charged to the first item using a percentage of wages rate might be too high while the amount absorbed by the second item might be too low. This method should therefore only be used if similar wage rates are paid to all direct employees in a production department. A direct labour hour rate might be considered 'fairer'.

(d) A **direct labour** hour basis is most appropriate in a **labour intensive** environment.

(e) A **machine hour** rate would be used in departments where production is controlled or dictated by **machines**. This basis is becoming more appropriate as factories become more heavily automated.

(f) A **rate per unit** would be effective only if all units were identical.

3 Absorption rates

Machine shop A:	$57,168/7,200	= $7.94 per machine hour
Machine shop B:	$63,000/18,000	= $3.50 per machine hour
Assembly:	$46,592/20,800	= $2.24 per direct labour hour

4 Under- and over-absorption

		$	$
Actual expenditure			176,533
Overhead absorbed			
Machine shop A	7,300 hrs × $7.94	57,962	
Machine shop B	18,700 hrs × $3.50	65,450	
Assembly	21,900 hrs × $2.24	49,056	
			172,468
Under-absorbed overhead			4,065

Option B is incorrect because actual expenditure was greater than overhead absorbed. Not enough overhead was therefore absorbed.

Options C and D are based on absorption using direct labour hours for the two machine shops. Their overheads are incurred in line with machine hours.

5 Reasons for under/over absorption

The overhead recovery rate is $180,000/45,000 = $4 per machine hour.

			$
(a)	Actual overhead		170,000
	Absorbed overhead (45,000 × $4)		180,000
	Over-absorbed overhead		10,000

Reason: Actual and budgeted machine hours are the same but actual overheads cost less than expected.

			$
(b)	Actual overhead		180,000
	Absorbed overhead (40,000 × $4)		160,000
	Under-absorbed overhead		20,000

Reason: Budgeted and actual overhead costs were the same but fewer machine hours were worked than expected.

			$
(c)	Actual overhead		170,000
	Absorbed overhead (40,000 × $4)		160,000
	Under-absorbed overhead		10,000

Reason: A combination of the reasons in (a) and (b).

6 Marginal costing and absorption costing

(a)   **Income statements for the year ending 30 September 20X3: Marginal costing basis**

	Six months ending 31 March 20X3		Six months ending 30 September 20X3	
	$'000	$'000	$'000	$'000
Sales at $140 per unit		980		1,120
Opening inventory	–		73.5	
Std. variable prod. cost (at $49 per unit)	416.5		343.0	
	416.5		416.5	
Closing inventory (W1)	73.5		24.5	
Cost of sales		343		392
		637		728
Variable selling and so on costs		196		224
Contribution		441		504
Fixed costs: production (W2)		160		160
Gross profit		281		344
Fixed costs: selling and so on		90		90
Net profit		191		254

(b)   **Income statements for the year ending 30 September 20X3: Absorption costing basis**

	Six months ending 31 March 20X3		Six months ending 30 September 20X3	
	$'000	$'000	$'000	$'000
Sales at $140 per unit		980		1,120
Opening inventory	–		103.5	
Std. cost of prod. (at $69 per unit)	586.5		483.0	
	586.5		586.5	
Closing inventory (W1)	103.5		34.5	
Cost of sales	483.0		552.0	
(Over-)/under-absorbed overhead (W3)	(10.0)		20.0	
Total costs		473		572
Gross profit		507		548
Selling and so on costs				
Variable	196		224	
Fixed	90		90	
		286		314
Net profit		221		234

Workings

1

	Six months ending 31 March 20X3	Six months ending 30 September 20X3
	Units	Units
Opening inventory	–	1,500
Production	8,500	7,000
	8,500	8,500
Sales	7,000	8,000
Closing inventory	1,500	500
Marginal cost valuation (× $49)	$73,500	$24,500
Absorption cost valuation (× $69)	$103,500	$34,500

2   Budgeted fixed production o/hd = 16,000 units × $20 = $320,000 pa = $160,000 per six months

3

	Six months ending 31 March 20X3		Six months ending 30 September 20X3	
Normal output (16,000 ÷ 2)	8,000	units	8,000	Units
Budgeted output	8,500	units	7,000	Units
Difference	500	units	1,000	Units
× std. fixed prod. o/hd per unit	× $20		× $20	
(Over-)/under-absorbed overhead	(($10,000)		$20,000	

7 Profit reconciliation

	$
Marginal costing profit	254
Adjust for fixed overhead in inventory (inventory decrease of 1,000 units × $20 per unit)	(20)
Absorption costing profit	234

8 Differences between absorption costing and marginal costing profits

The correct answer is $405,000.

	$
Absorption costing profit	112,500
Adjust for fixed overhead in inventory	
(inventory decrease of 15,000 × $19.50 per unit)	292,500
Marginal costing profit	405,000

9 Reconciliation of profits for different periods

The correct answer is C.

The under absorption in 20X0 made the 20X0 profit lower and so it should be added. The under absorption in 20X1 made the 20X1 profit lower than the 20X0 profit and so it should be deducted.

Now try the question from the Exam Question Bank			

Number	Level	Marks	Time
Q1	Introductory	10	18 mins

PRICING AND PRODUCT DECISIONS

Part A

RELEVANT COSTS

The chapter begins with an **introduction** to decision-making (**Sections 1 and 2**) and provides some general information about the decision-making process.

In **Sections 3 to 5** of this chapter you will learn how to identify the **relevant costs and revenues** in decisions, so that management time is not wasted in considering irrelevant information. You will also learn about the importance of considering the **non-quantifiable factors** in every decision (in **Section 7**) and about the **assumptions** underlying the relevant costing approach to decision-making (**Section 6**). These are topics that you looked at in your Certificate level studies, so they won't be completely new to you.

This chapter links closely with **Chapter 1B** which deals with the actual decision-making process.

topic list	learning outcomes	syllabus references	ability required
1 Decisions	A1(a)	A1(i)	analysis
2 Information for decision-making	A1(a), (b)	A1(i)	analysis
3 Relevant costs and revenues	A1(a), (b)	A1(i)	analysis
4 Non-relevant costs and revenues	A1(a)	A1(i)	analysis
5 Some rules for identifying relevant costs	A1(a), (b)	A1(i), (ii)	analysis
6 The assumptions in relevant costing	A1(a), (b)	A1(i), (ii)	analysis
7 Relation to accounting concepts	A1(b)	A1(iii)	analysis
8 Non-quantifiable factors in decision-making	A1(a), (b)	A1(ii)	analysis

1 Decisions

Introduction

This section looks briefly at the different types of decisions you will encounter in the P2 syllabus.

1.1 Accept or reject decisions

These decisions are taken on the **merits of a particular opportunity** under consideration, **without the need to compare** that opportunity to other available opportunities (although alternative uses for the resources that will be needed if the opportunity is accepted have to be taken into account).

If a decision is taken to go ahead with a particular course of action (the '**accept**' option), the organisation will **still be free to consider and take on any other opportunities** presented.

1.2 Ranking decisions

These decisions involve a **choice between one or more competing opportunities**, and so the different opportunities have to be **compared**. They tend to arise for one of two reasons.

(a)   Because there are not enough resources to pursue all the available opportunities.

(b)   The opportunities offer different means to the same or similar ends. In a decision whether a new regional office should be located in city A or city B, for example, both opportunities are different means towards the same end of the choice of an office location.

In this chapter and the ones that follow we will be looking at how to make these types of decision.

Section summary

Most decisions can be categorised as one of two types - **accept or reject** decisions or **ranking** decisions.

2 Information for decision-making

Introduction

Information required for decision-making differs considerably from that used for profit reporting and inventory valuation. This section examines the differences between the provision of different types of information.

2.1 Cost accounting versus information for decision-making

Information derived from **cost accounting data** accumulation systems is **totally misleading** for **decision-making purposes.** Absorption costing is used for profit reporting and inventory valuation purposes but as it does not separate fixed and variable costs, it does not provide relevant information for decision-making.

KEY POINT

For one-off decisions or decisions affecting the use of marginal spare capacity, absorption costing information about unit profits is irrelevant and misleading. On the other hand, since total contribution must be sufficient to cover the fixed costs of the business, marginal costing would be unsuitable as a basis for establishing long-term sales prices for all output.

2.2 Marginal costing for decision-making

As mentioned above, absorption costing is not useful for decision-making as it produces misleading information. **Marginal costing** is used for decision-making purposes as it splits costs clearly into fixed and variable elements. This distinction is important as fixed costs are not relevant for short-term decision-making.

Typically, in the short run, fixed costs remain unchanged, which means that the **marginal cost, revenue and contribution** of each decision option are **relevant**.

When marginal costing is used for short-term decision-making, the best option is always the one that **maximises contribution**.

Even if fixed costs do change, the division of costs into their fixed and variable components is still needed to allow you to identify contribution.

2.2.1 Costs that vary with activity levels

A large proportion of **short-term decisions require information** about how **costs and revenues vary with activity** so that the alternative options of each decision can be evaluated. Here are some examples.

(a)   At what level should budgeted output be set?
(b)   Should component X be manufactured internally or purchased from a supplier?
(c)   Should a one-off special order be accepted?

For each of these decisions, **management require estimates of costs at different levels of activity of the alternative courses of action**. An organisation might decide to accept a one-off order without understanding that the extra work will mean taking on new staff. Fulfilling the order at the agreed price might therefore result in an overall loss for the organisation.

For short-term decision-making, **costs** should therefore be **divided** into:

(a)   **Purely variable costs**, such as direct materials, which can be easily attributed to products, services, customers and so on.

(b)   **Variable costs** that are **fixed in the short term** and which **cannot be directly attributed to cost objects**, **but** which are **avoidable** if the product is not produced, the service not provided and so on.

(c)   **Fixed costs**, which become **variable in the longer term, or if activity levels change significantly.** They are **not relevant to short-term decision-making** based on marginal costing principles as they do not change in the short term.

By classifying costs in this way, it is then **possible to predict total costs** at different levels of output.

Section summary

There is a **conflict** between cost accounting for **profit reporting** and **inventory valuation** and the convenient availability of information for **decision-making**.

The division of **costs** into their **variable and fixed components** is **useful** in the context of **short-term decision-making**.

3 Relevant costs and revenues

5/11, 11/11, 9/12

Introduction

Section 2 highlighted the need to use marginal costing for short-term decision-making purposes. This section focuses on how to identify relevant costs and revenues. Make sure you understand how to identify such costs before moving onto the next section as this is a key part of the syllabus.

3.1 Relevant costs

The costs which should be used for **decision-making** are often referred to as **relevant costs**

KEY TERM

In its *Official Terminology,* CIMA defines RELEVANT COSTS as 'Costs appropriate to a specific management decision. These are represented by future cash flows whose magnitude will vary depending upon the outcome of the management decision made'.

(a) **Future costs.**

    (i)   A cost that has been incurred in the past is totally irrelevant to any decision that is being made 'now'. Such costs are **past costs** or **sunk costs.**

    (ii)   **Committed** costs are those that result from legally binding contracts. These are also not relevant (even if they have not yet been paid) as they cannot be avoided.

(b) Relevant costs are **cash flows**. This means that costs or charges such as the following, which do not reflect additional cash spending, should be ignored for the purpose of decision-making.

    (i)   **Depreciation** (does not involve the movement of cash).

    (ii)   **Notional rent or interest** (a fixed overhead that does not change in the short-term).

    (iii)   **All overheads absorbed**.

(c) Relevant costs are **incremental costs**.

KEY TERM

The CIMA *Official Terminology* defines INCREMENTAL or DIFFERENTIAL COSTS as 'The difference in total cost between alternatives; calculated to assist decision-making'.

For example, suppose a company decides to accept a contract from a customer. An existing supervisor currently earning £1,000 per month is given an extra £100 per month for taking on the extra responsibility associated with this contract. The **incremental** cost is the **additional** salary paid to the supervisor (£100) – the original salary of £1,000 was being paid anyway.

3.2 Avoidable costs and opportunity costs

Other potential relevant costs include **avoidable costs** and **opportunity costs**.

Avoidable costs (as the name suggests) are costs that could be **avoided** if an activity or sector of a business is discontinued. These costs are usually associated with shutdown or divestment decisions.

KEY TERM

AVOIDABLE COSTS are defined as 'The specific costs of an activity or sector of a business which would be avoided if that activity or sector did not exist'.

(CIMA *Official Terminology*)

Opportunity cost is the **benefit sacrificed** by choosing one opportunity rather than the next best alternative. You will often encounter opportunity costs when there are several possible uses for a scarce resource.

For example, if a material is in short supply, it may be transferred from the production of one product to that of another product. The opportunity cost is the **contribution lost** from ceasing production of the original product.

KEY TERM

OPPORTUNITY COSTS is 'The value of a benefit sacrificed when one course of action is chosen, in preference to an alternative. The opportunity cost is represented by the forgone potential benefit from the best rejected course of action'.   (CIMA *Official Terminology*).

Question 1A.1	Relevant costs

Learning outcome A1(a)

An information technology consultancy firm has been asked to do an urgent job by a client, for which a price of $2,500 has been offered. The job would require the following.

(a)   30 hours' work from one member of staff, who is paid on an hourly basis, at a rate of $20 per hour, but who would normally be employed on work for clients where the charge-out rate is $45 per hour. No other member of staff is able to do the member of staff in question's work.

(b)   The use of 5 hours of mainframe computer time, which the firm normally charges out to external users at a rate of $50 per hour. Mainframe computer time is currently used 24 hours a day, 7 days a week.

(c)   Supplies and incidental expenses of $200.

Required

Fill in the blank in the sentence below.

The relevant cost or opportunity cost of the job is $......... .

3.3 Relevant revenues

Relevant revenues are also **future, incremental cash flows**.

(a)   (i)   Revenue **received in the past** is totally **irrelevant** to any decision that is being made now.

(ii)   Revenue that has **not yet been received but will be received regardless of the decision made** is **not relevant**.

(b)   Relevant revenues are **cash flows**. The book profit on the sale of a non-current asset is therefore not relevant to a decision on whether or not to sell that asset, whereas the cash received for the asset is.

(c)   Relevant revenues are **incremental revenues**. If project A earns revenue of $1,000 and project B earns revenue of $2,500, the relevant revenue in a decision about whether to choose project B instead of project A is $(2,500 – 1,000) = $1,500.

3.4 Minimum price quotations for special orders

The total relevant cost of an order represents the minimum price that the company should charge for an order if they wish to make neither a profit or a loss.

Section summary

Relevant costs are **future, incremental cash flows**.

4 Non-relevant costs and revenues

Introduction

Just as important as being able to identify relevant costs is the ability to identify non-relevant costs. This section focuses on the types of costs that are irrelevant to short-term decision-making.

4.1 Sunk costs

KEY TERM

A SUNK COST is 'Cost that has been irreversibly incurred or committed and cannot therefore be considered relevant to a decision. Sunk cost costs may also be deemed **irrecoverable** costs.'

(CIMA *Official Terminology*)

An example of a sunk cost could be **development costs already incurred**. Suppose that a company has spent $250,000 in developing a new service for customers, but the marketing department's most recent findings are that the service might not gain customer acceptance and could be a commercial failure. The decision whether or not to abandon the development of the new service would have to be taken, but the $250,000 spent so far should be ignored by the decision makers because it is a sunk cost.

4.2 Committed costs

A committed cost is a **future cash outflow** that will be **incurred anyway, whatever decision is taken now** about alternative opportunities. Committed costs may exist because of contracts already entered into by the organisation, which it cannot now avoid.

4.3 Notional costs

KEY TERM

The CIMA *Official Terminology* definition of a NOTIONAL COST is 'A cost used in product evaluation, decision-making and performance measurement to reflect the use of resources which have no "**actual** (observable) cost".

Examples of notional costs in cost accounting systems

(a) **Notional rent**, such as that charged to a subsidiary, cost centre or profit centre of an organisation for the use of accommodation which the organisation owns.

(b) **Notional interest charges on capital employed**, sometimes made against a profit centre or cost centre.

4.4 Historical costs

Although historical costs are irrelevant for decision making, historical cost data will **often** provide the **best available basis for predicting future costs**.

4.5 Non-relevant variable costs

There might be occasions when a variable cost is in fact a sunk cost. For example, suppose that a company holds some units of raw material. They have been paid for already, and originally cost $2,000. They are now obsolete and are no longer used in regular production, and they have no scrap value. However, they could be used in a special job which the company is trying to decide whether to undertake. The special job is a 'one-off' customer order, and would use up all the materials currently held.

In deciding whether the job should be undertaken, the relevant cost of the materials to the special job is nil. Their **original cost** of $2,000 is a **sunk cost**, and should be ignored in the decision.

However, if the materials did have a **scrap value** of, say, $300, then their relevant cost to the job would be the **opportunity cost** of being unable to sell them for scrap, ie $300.

4.6 Attributable fixed costs

Exam alert

There might be occasions when a fixed cost is a relevant cost, and you must be aware of the distinction between 'specific' or 'directly attributable' fixed costs, and general overheads.

(a) **Directly attributable fixed costs** are those costs which, although fixed within a relevant range of activity level are relevant to a decision for either of the following reasons.

  (i) They would increase if certain extra activities were undertaken. For example, it may be necessary to employ an extra supervisor if a particular order is accepted. The extra salary would be an attributable fixed cost.

  (ii) They would decrease or be eliminated entirely if a decision were taken either to reduce the scale of operations or shut down entirely.

(b) **General fixed overheads** are those fixed overheads which will be **unaffected** by decisions to increase or decrease the scale of operations. An apportioned share of head office charges is an example of general fixed overheads for a local office or department. General fixed overheads are not relevant in decision making.

Exam alert

Fixed costs are assumed to be irrelevant in decision-making (unless given an indication to the contrary). In ABC, however, the crucial assumption is that many so-called 'fixed' costs are actually variable with business complexity given a long enough period of time.

Section summary

Non-relevant costs include **sunk costs**, **committed costs**, **notional costs** and **historical costs**.

Unless you are given an indication to the contrary, you should assume that **variable costs** will be **relevant** costs and that **fixed costs** are **irrelevant** to a decision.

5 Some rules for identifying relevant costs

Introduction

In order to be able to make correct decisions, you must be able to identify the costs that are relevant to that decision. This section covers the general rules that you should follow when trying to identify relevant costs for decision-making.

5.1 The relevant cost of materials

If the materials have no resale value and no other possible use, then the relevant cost of using them for the opportunity under consideration would be nil. The following diagram will be useful to help you identify the relevant cost of materials.

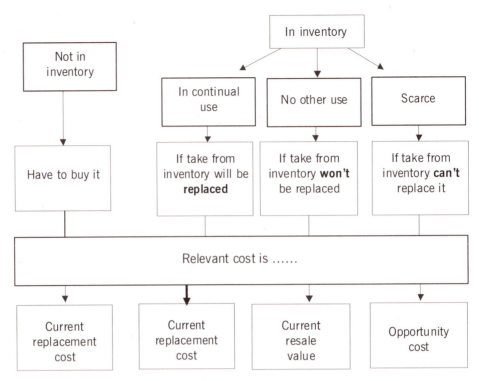

You should test your knowledge of the relevant cost of materials by attempting the following question.

Learning outcome A1(a)

DLN has been approached by a customer who would like a special job to be done for him, and who is willing to pay $22,000 for it. The job would require the following materials.

Material	Total units required	Units already held	Book value of units held $/unit	Realisable value $/unit	Replacement cost $/unit
A	1,000	0	–	–	6.00
B	1,000	600	2.00	2.50	5.00
C	1,000	700	3.00	2.50	4.00
D	200	200	4.00	6.00	9.00

Material B is used regularly by DLN, and if units of B are required for this job, they would need to be replaced to meet other production demand.

Materials C and D are held as the result of previous over buying, and they have a restricted use. No other use could be found for material C, but the units of material D could be used in another job as substitute for 300 units of material E, which currently costs $5 per unit (and of which the company holds no units at the moment).

Required

Fill in the blank in the sentence below.

The relevant cost of material for deciding whether or not to accept the contract is $ ....

5.2 The relevant cost of using machines

The relevant cost of using machines depends on whether the machines can be used for **another purpose** (which will create an opportunity cost) or if they have to be **acquired specifically** for the job in question.

Example: the relevant cost of using machines

An organisation is considering whether to undertake some contract work for a customer. The machinery required for the contract would be as follows.

(a)   A special cutting machine will have to be hired for three months for the work (the length of the contract). Hire charges for this machine are $75 per month, with a minimum hire charge of $300.

(b)   All other machinery required in the production for the contract has already been purchased by the organisation on hire purchase terms. The monthly hire purchase payments for this machinery are $500. This consists of $450 for capital repayment and $50 as an interest charge. The last hire purchase payment is to be made in two months' time. The cash price of this machinery was $9,000 two years ago. It is being depreciated on a straight line basis at the rate of $200 per month. However, it still has a useful life which will enable it to be operated for another 36 months.

The machinery is highly specialised and is unlikely to be required for other, more profitable jobs over the period during which the contract work would be carried out. Although there is no immediate market for selling this machine, it is expected that a customer might be found in the future. It is further estimated that the machine would lose $200 in its eventual sale value if it is used for the contract work.

Required

Calculate the relevant cost of machinery for the contract.

Solution

(a)   The cutting machine will incur an incremental cost of $300, the minimum hire charge.

(b)   The historical cost of the other machinery is irrelevant as a past cost; depreciation is irrelevant as a non-cash cost; and future hire purchase repayments are irrelevant because they are committed costs. The only relevant cost is the loss of resale value of the machinery, estimated at $200 through use. This user cost will not arise until the machinery is eventually resold and the $200 should be discounted to allow for the time value of money. However, discounting is ignored here.

(c)   **Summary of relevant costs**

	$
Incremental hire costs	300
User cost of other machinery	200
	500

 Question 1A.3   Relevant cost of using machines

Learning outcome A1(a)

A machine which originally cost $12,000 has an estimated life of ten years and is depreciated at the rate of $1,200 a year. It has been unused for some time, however, as expected production orders did not materialise.

A special order has now been received which would require the use of the machine for two months.

The current net realisable value of the machine is $8,000. If it is used for the job, its value is expected to fall to $7,500. The net book value of the machine is $8,400.

Routine maintenance of the machine currently costs $40 a month. With use, the cost of maintenance and repairs would increase to $60 a month for the months that the machine is being used.

Ignore the time value of money.

What is the relevant cost of using the machine for the order?

5.3 The relevant cost of labour and variable overheads

The relevant cost of **labour** and **variable overheads** will depend on whether labour is working at **full capacity**.

If labour is working at full capacity, it will have to be taken away from another activity in order to work on the new project. This will create an **opportunity cost** that must be accounted for during the decision-making process.

The diagram below can be used to determine the relevant cost of labour and variable overheads.

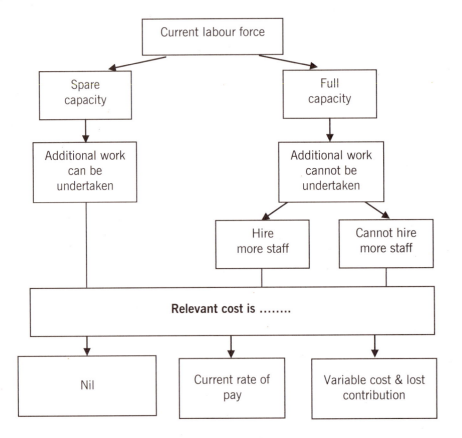

Example: Relevant costs of labour and variable overheads

A company has been offered $21,000 by a prospective customer to make some purpose-built equipment. The extra costs of the machine would be $3,000 for materials. There would also be a requirement for 2,000 labour hours. Labour wages are $4 per hour, variable overhead is $2 per hour and fixed overhead is absorbed at the rate of $4 per hour.

Labour, however, is in limited supply, and if the job is accepted, workers would have to be diverted from other work which is expected to earn a contribution of $5 per hour towards fixed overheads and profit.

Required

Assess whether the contract should be undertaken.

Solution

The relevant costs of the scarce resource, labour, are the sum of the following.

- The variable costs of the labour and associated variable overheads
- The contribution forgone from not being able to put it to its alternative use

Fixed costs are ignored because there is no incremental fixed cost expenditure.

	$
Materials	3,000
Labour (2,000 hours at $4 per hour)	8,000
Variable overhead (2,000 hours at $2 per hour)	4,000
	15,000
Opportunity cost:	
Contribution forgone from other work (2,000 hours × $5 per hour)	10,000
Total costs	25,000
Revenue	21,000
Net loss on contract	(4,000)

The contract should not be undertaken.

It is worth thinking carefully about labour costs. The labour force will be paid $8,000 for 2,000 hours work, and variable overheads of $4,000 will be incurred no matter whether the workers are employed on the new job or on other work. Relevant costs are future cash flows arising as a direct consequence of a decision, and the decision here will not affect the total wages paid. If this money is going to be spent anyway, should it not therefore be ignored as an irrelevant cost?

The answer to this crucial question is 'no'. The labour wages and variable overheads are relevant costs even though they will be incurred whatever happens. The reason for this is that the other work earns a contribution of $5 per hour **after having covered** labour and variable overhead costs. Work on the purpose-built equipment ought therefore to do at least the same.

Question 1A.4

More relevant costing

Learning outcome 1(i)

LAM is involved in a project that requires 100kg of material J. The company holds 50kg of material J. It purchased this material, which has a standard cost of $10 per kg, six months ago for $12 per kg. Material J can currently be purchased for $9 per kg. If the 50kg of material J held is not used, it could be sold for $8 per kg.

The relevant cost of the material J required for the project is $900. *True or false?*

Section summary

The **relevant cost of raw materials** is generally their current replacement cost unless the materials have already been purchased and will not be replaced, in which case the relevant cost of using them is the higher of their current resale value and the value they would obtain if they were put to an alternative use.

Using **machinery** will involve some **incremental costs**.

- Repair costs arising from use
- Hire charges
- Any fall in resale value of owned assets which results from their use

Depreciation is **not** a relevant cost.

The relevant cost of **labour** and **variable overheads** will depend on whether labour is working at **full capacity**.

6 The assumptions in relevant costing

Introduction

Relevant costs are future costs. Whenever anyone tries to predict what will happen in the future, the predictions are often incorrect. Cost accountants have to make the best forecasts of relevant income and costs that they can and at the same time recognise the assumptions on which their estimates are based. This section covers the variety of assumptions that may be made – you must be aware of these.

Exam alert

If you make an assumption in answering an examination question and you are not sure that the examiner or marker will appreciate or recognise the assumption you are making, you should include a narrative explanation in your solution.

(a) **Cost behaviour patterns are known**; if a department closes down, for example, the attributable fixed cost savings would be known.

This is not necessarily so, and it is always important to question assumptions of this nature. For example, if you are told in an examination question that a factory intends to increase production by 50%, and you are invited to assume in your number work that fixed costs and unit variable costs would be unaffected, it is important to challenge this assumption as a footnote to your solution, making the following points.

(i) Is it clear that the factory could handle such a large increase in output?

(ii) If so, fixed costs would probably change dramatically, and there might also be a shift in unit variable costs.

(b) **The amount of fixed costs, unit variable costs, sales price and sales demand are known with certainty**. However, it is possible to apply risk and uncertainty analysis to decisions and so recognise that what will happen in the future is not certain.

(c) **The objective of decision-making in the short run is to maximise 'satisfaction'**, which is often regarded as 'short-term profit'. However, there are many qualitative factors or financial considerations, other than those of profit, which may influence a final decision. You should point these out in your answers.

(d) **The information on which a decision is based is complete and reliable.** This is obviously unrealistic and decision makers must be made aware of any inadequacies of the information that they are using for their decisions.

Section summary

There are a number of **assumptions** typically made in relevant costing.

7 Relation to accounting concepts

Introduction

Relevant revenues and costs are used for decision-making purposes rather than for reporting to external parties. This means that accounting concepts are not necessarily consistent with information for decision making.

Accounting concept	Relevance to relevant costs and decision-making
Accruals	The accruals concept seeks to report transactions in the period to which they relate. However, relevant costs and revenues are calculated on a cash basis rather than an accruals basis and do not include such items as depreciation and allocated fixed costs. Decision-making focuses on future costs - past costs are never relevant.
Reliability	Relevant costs and revenues are in the future, they can never be 100% reliable.
Relevance	By their very nature, relevant costs and revenues should always be relevant to the decision being made. However detailed knowledge of the decision is necessary in order to determine what is relevant and what is not.
Completeness	Relevant costs and revenues should be complete for the decision being made but will not include any items that do not affect that decision.
Comparability	If companies are trying to make a choice between alternatives, the potential outcomes of these alternatives must be comparable – that is, all relevant costs and revenues relating to each alternative must be included. Sunk costs, non-cash costs and costs that are not affected by the decision must always be excluded.
Going concern	While future projects will only be considered if the business is still trading, not all decisions are based on the assumption that the company will continue in profitable business for the foreseeable future – for example, shutdown decisions. In addition, it should be noted that if all projects are undertaken on a relevant cost basis and are priced using the minimum price, the projects will not make enough money to cover the fixed costs of the business

Section summary

Accounting concepts for financial reporting purposes only have **limited relevance** to decision-making. Such concepts include accruals, reliability, relevance, completeness, comparability and going concern.

8 Non-quantifiable factors in decision-making

Introduction

Of equal importance to quantifiable factors in decision-making are the non-quantifiable factors. This section looks at examples of such factors and also offers advice on how you might treat such factors in an exam situation.

Non-quantifiable factors in decision making are factors which might influence the eventual decisions but which have not been quantified in terms of relevant costs or benefits. They may stem from **two sources**.

(a)   Non-financial objectives

(b)   Factors which might be quantifiable in **money terms**, but which have not been quantified, perhaps because there is **insufficient information to make reliable estimates.** Such factors tend to focus on the **long-term implications** of decisions.

Exam alert

Decision-making questions in the exam often ask you to detail 'other factors that should be considered' after you have completed the figurework for the decision. However, even if the question does not invite you to do so, it is a good idea to get into the habit of adding a few notes concerning 'other factors'. This applies especially if you feel that you have made any assumptions that could be challenged.

8.1 Examples of non-quantifiable factors

Non-quantifiable factors in decision making will vary with the circumstances and nature of the opportunity being considered. Here are some examples.

Factors	Details
Availability of cash	An opportunity may be profitable, but there must be sufficient cash to finance any purchases of equipment and build-up of working capital.
Inflation	The effect of inflation on the prices of various items may need to be considered, especially where a fixed price contract is involved in the decision: if the income from an opportunity is fixed by contract, but the costs might increase with inflation, the contract's profitability would be over-stated unless inflation is taken into account.
Employees	Any decision involving the shutdown of a plant, creation of a new work shift, or changes in work procedures or location will require acceptance by employees, and ought to consider employee welfare.
Customers	Decisions about new products or product closures, the quality of output or after-sales service will inevitably affect customer loyalty and customer demand. It is also important to remember that a decision involving one product may have repercussions on customer attitudes towards a range of products.
Competitors	In a competitive market, some decisions may stimulate a response from rival companies. For example, the decision to reduce selling prices in order to raise demand may not be successful if all competitors take similar action.
Timing factors	There might be a choice in deciding when to take up an opportunity. The choice would not be 'accept or reject'; there would be three choices. • Accept an opportunity now • Do not accept the opportunity now, but wait before doing so • Reject the opportunity
Suppliers	Some decisions will affect suppliers, whose long-term goodwill may be damaged by a decision to close a product line temporarily. Decisions to change the specifications for purchased components, or change inventory policies so as to create patchy, uneven demand might also put a strain on suppliers. In some cases, where a company is the supplier's main customer, a decision to reduce demand or delay payments for goods received might drive the supplier out of business.
Feasibility	A proposal may look good in financial terms, but technical experts or departmental managers may have some reservations about their ability to carry it out.

Factors	Details
Flexibility and internal control	Decisions to subcontract work, or to enter into a long-term contract have the disadvantages of inflexibility and lack of controllability. Where requirements may be changeable, it would be preferable to build flexibility into the organisation of operations.
Unquantified opportunity costs	Even where no opportunity costs are specified, it is probable that other opportunities would be available for using the resources to earn profit. It may be useful to qualify a recommendation by stating that a given project would appear to be viable on the assumption that there are no other more profitable opportunities available.
Political pressures	Some large companies may suffer political pressures applied by the government to influence their investment or disinvestment decisions.
Legal constraints	A decision might occasionally be rejected because of doubts about the legality of the proposed action.

Question 1A.5

Using relevant costs

Learning outcome A1(a)

An organisation in the civil engineering industry with headquarters located 22 miles from London undertakes contracts anywhere in the United Kingdom.

The organisation has had its tender for a job in north-east England accepted at $288,000 and work is due to begin in March 20X3. However, the organisation has also been asked to undertake a contract on the south coast of England. The price offered for this contract is $352,000. Both of the contracts cannot be taken simultaneously because of constraints on staff site management personnel and on plant available. An escape clause enables the organisation to withdraw from the contract in the north-east, provided notice is given before the end of November and an agreed penalty of $28,000 is paid.

The following estimates have been submitted by the organisation's quantity surveyor.

COST ESTIMATES

		North-east $	South Coast $
Materials:	Held at original cost, Material X	21,600	
	Held at original cost, Material Y		24,800
	Firm orders placed at original cost, Material X	30,400	
	Not yet ordered – current cost, Material X	60,000	
	Not yet ordered – current cost, Material Z		71,200
Labour – hired locally		86,000	110,000
Site management		34,000	34,000
Staff accommodation and travel for site management		6,800	5,600
Plant on site – depreciation		9,600	12,800
Interest on capital, 8%		5,120	6,400
Total local contract costs		253,520	264,800
Headquarters costs allocated at rate of 5% on total contract costs		12,676	13,240
		266,196	278,040
Contract price		288,000	352,000
Estimated profit		21,804	73,960

Notes

(a)   X, Y and Z are three building materials. Material X is not in common use and would not realise much money if re-sold; however, it could be used on other contracts but only as a substitute for another material currently quoted at 10% less than the original cost of X. The price of Y, a material in common use, has doubled since it was purchased; its net realisable value if re-sold would be its

new price less 15% to cover disposal costs. Alternatively it could be kept for use on other contracts in the following financial year.

(b) With the construction industry not yet recovered from a recent recession, the organisation is confident that manual labour, both skilled and unskilled, could be hired locally on a sub-contracting basis to meet the needs of each of the contracts.

(c) The plant which would be needed for the south coast contract has been owned for some years and $12,800 is the year's depreciation on a straight-line basis. If the north-east contract is undertaken, less plant will be required but the surplus plant will be hired out for the period of the contract at a rental of $6,000.

(d) It is the organisation's policy to charge all contracts with notional interest at 8% on the estimated working capital involved in contracts. Progress payments would be receivable from the contractee.

(e) Salaries and general costs of operating the small headquarters amount to about $108,000 each year. There are usually ten contracts being supervised at the same time.

(f) Each of the two contracts is expected to last from March 20X3 to February 20X4 which, coincidentally, is the company's financial year.

(g) Site management is treated as a fixed cost.

Required

As the management accountant to the organisation, do the following.

(a) Present comparative statements to show the net benefit to the organisation of undertaking the more advantageous of the two contracts.

(b) Explain the reasoning behind the inclusion in (or omission from) your comparative financial statements of each item given in the cost estimates and the notes relating thereto.

Section summary

Non-quantifiable factors should **always be considered** alongside the quantitative data in a decision.

Chapter Roundup

✓   **Most decisions** can be categorised as one of two types, **accept or reject** decisions or **ranking** decisions.

✓   There is a **conflict** between cost accounting for **profit reporting** and **inventory valuation** and the convenient availability of information for **decision making**.

✓   The division of **costs** into their **variable and fixed components** is **useful** in the context of **short-term decision-making**.

✓   Relevant costs are **future, incremental cash flows**.

✓   Non-relevant costs include **sunk costs, committed costs, notional costs** and **historical costs**.

✓   Unless you are given an indication to the contrary, you should assume that **variable costs** will be **relevant** costs and that **fixed costs** will be **irrelevant** to a decision.

✓   The **relevant cost of raw materials** is generally their current replacement cost unless the materials have already been purchased and will not be replaced, in which case the relevant cost of using them is the higher of their current resale value and the value they would obtain if they were put to an alternative use.

✓   Using **machinery** will involve some **incremental costs**.

    –   Repair costs arising from use
    –   Hire charges
    –   Any fall in resale value of owned assets which results from their use

    Depreciation is **not** a relevant cost.

✓   The relevant cost of **labour** and **variable overheads** will depend on whether labour is working at **full capacity**.

✓   There are a number of **assumptions** typically made in relevant costing.

✓   **Accounting concepts** for financial reporting purposes only have **limited relevance** to decision-making. Such concepts include accruals, reliability, relevance, completeness, comparability and going concern.

✓   **Non-quantifiable factors** should **always be considered** alongside the quantitative data in a decision.

Quick Quiz

1   Tick the correct box for each of these types of cost.

	Relevant cost	Non-relevant cost
Incremental cost	☐	☐
Sunk cost	☐	☐
Committed cost	☐	☐

2   An attributable fixed cost is never a relevant cost. *True or false*?

3   The total relevant cost of a scarce resource is equal to the sum of the variable cost of the scarce resource and

A   the price that the resource would sell for in the open market
B   the fixed cost absorbed by a unit of the scarce resource
C   the contribution forgone from the next-best opportunity for using the scarce resource
D   the price that would have to be paid to replace the scarce resource

4   Which of the following is not an assumption typically made in relevant costing?

A   Cost behaviour patterns are known.

B   The amount of fixed costs, unit variable costs, sales prices and sales demand are known with certainty.

C   The objective of decision making in the short run is to maximise satisfaction.

D   There is no scarcity of resources.

5   What are the six steps in the decision-making process?

STEP ① ....

STEP ② ....

STEP ③ ....

STEP ④ ....

STEP ⑤ ....

STEP ⑥ ....

6   We detailed 12 non-quantifiable factors in decision making. List ten of them.

7   *Choose the correct words from those highlighted.*

Opportunity cost is the **value/cost** of a **benefit/cost** which is **sacrificed/purchased** when one course of action is chosen, in preference to an alternative. The opportunity cost is represented by the forgone **potential/expected/net realisable value** benefit from the **best/worst** rejected course of action.

Answers to Quick Quiz

1 Relevant; non-relevant; non-relevant

2 False. It is relevant to a decision because it is a fixed cost that would be affected by the decision being taken.

3 C. It is a common mistake to forget to include the opportunity cost.

4 D. This is *not* an assumption in relevant costing.

5

 Identify objectives

 Search for alternative courses of action

 Collect data about the alternative courses of action

 Select the appropriate course of action

 Implement the decision

 Compare actual and planned outcomes and take any necessary corrective action if the planned results have not been achieved

6 Here are all 12.

- The availability of cash
- Inflation
- Employees
- Customers
- Competitors
- Timing factors
- Suppliers
- Feasibility
- Flexibility and internal control
- Unquantified opportunity costs
- Political pressures
- Legal constraints

7 Opportunity cost is the value of a benefit which is sacrificed when one course of action is chosen, in preference to an alternative. The opportunity cost is represented by the forgone potential benefit from the best rejected course of action.

Answers to Questions

1A.1 Relevant costs

The correct answer is $1,800.

The relevant cost or opportunity cost of the job would be calculated as follows.

	$
Labour (30 hours × $45)	1,350
Computer time opportunity cost (5 hours × $50)	250
Supplies and expenses	200
	1,800

1A.2 Relevant cost of materials

The correct answer is $15,450.

(a) **Material A** is not yet owned. It would have to be bought in full at the replacement cost of $6 per unit. Total = $6,000.

(b) **Material B** is used regularly by the company. There is existing inventory (600 units) but if these are used on the contract under review a further 600 units would be bought to replace them. Relevant costs are therefore 1,000 units at the replacement cost of $5 per unit. Total = $5,000.

(c) 1,000 units of **material C** are needed and 700 are already held. If used for the contract, a further 300 units must be bought at $4 each. The existing inventory of 700 will not be replaced. If they are used for the contract, they could not be sold at $2.50 each. The realisable value of these 700 units is an opportunity cost of sales revenue forgone. Total = (300 × $4) + (700 × $2.50) = $2,950.

(d) The required units of **material D** are already held and will not be replaced. There is an opportunity cost of using D in the contract because there are alternative opportunities either to sell the existing inventory for $6 per unit ($1,200 in total) or avoid other purchases (of material E), which would cost 300 x $5 = $1,500. Since substitution for E is more beneficial, $1,500 is the opportunity cost.

Total relevant cost is therefore $15,450.

1A.3 Relevant cost of using machines

	$
Loss in net realisable value of the machine through using it on the order $(8,000 − 7,500)	500
Costs in excess of existing routine maintenance costs $(120 − 80)	40
Total marginal user cost	540

1A.4 More relevant costing

The correct answer is $850 and so the statement is false.

	$
Material already held, relevant cost = 50kg × $8 =	400
Material to be purchased, relevant cost = 50kg × $9 =	450
	850

$900 is incorrect because the material held should be valued at its realisable value of $8.

1A.5 Using relevant costs

One way of determining which is the more advantageous of the two contracts is to calculate the net cost or benefit of cancelling the north-east contract in favour of the work on the south cost. We are asked to present comparative statements, however, and so our approach will be to prepare statements of the relevant costs of each contract.

Did you read note (c) properly? Rent receivable is *not* an expense. Make sure that the explanations you give in part (b) do not differ from the treatment of items in part (a).

(a)   **Statements of the relevant costs of each contract**

	Note	North-East $	South Coast $
Material X held ($21,600 × 90%)	1	19,440	
Material Y held ($24,800 × 2)	2		49,600
Material X on order ($30,400 × 90%)	1	27,360	
Material X not yet ordered	3	60,000	
Material Z not yet ordered	3		71,200
Labour	4	86,000	110,000
Site management	5	–	–
Staff accommodation and travel	6	6,800	5,600
Plant for north-east contract	7	(6,000)	
Plant for south coast contract	8	–	–
Interest on capital	9	–	–
Headquarters' costs	10	–	–
Penalty payment	11		28,000
Total relevant costs		193,600	264,400
Contract price		288,000	352,000
Net benefit		94,400	87,600

The **north-east** contract is therefore the **more advantageous**, with a net benefit to the organisation of $94,400.

(b)   The **reasoning** behind the treatment of each cost item is given in the following notes.

Notes

1   The relevant cost of the material X held and on order is the **opportunity cost** of the saving which is forgone by not using X as a substitute material.

2   Ignoring the time value of money and the cost of storing the material, it would not be worth selling material Y and then repurchasing it next year. In fact the cost of borrowing is 8%, which is much less than the 15% cost of disposing of the material. The relevant cost of using material Y is the **replacement cost** which would have to be paid to obtain more material for next year's contracts.

3   Since this material has not yet been ordered, the **current cost** is the relevant cost of a decision to proceed with each contract.

4   The labour costs are the **incremental costs** which would have to be incurred if the contract goes ahead. They are therefore relevant costs of both contracts.

5   The statement that site management is treated as a fixed cost is assumed to mean that it is a **committed cost** which will be incurred irrespective of the decision concerning these contracts.

6   It is assumed that these are **incremental costs** which will only be incurred if the contracts go ahead.

7   If the north-east contract is undertaken, the **rental value received** will be $6,000. The **depreciation cost is not relevant** (see note 8).

8   It is assumed that the depreciation cost is an accounting book entry and that the **value of the plant will not be affected** by using it on either contract.

9   Although there would probably be some incremental **working capital financing costs** as a result of the contracts, we have **no way of knowing** how much they would be. They would be somewhat reduced by the effect of the progress payments received from the contractee.

10   It is assumed that the total amount of headquarters' costs **would not be affected** by the decision to undertake either contract. This is therefore not a relevant cost.

11   The penalty payment is a relevant cost of cancelling the north-east contract in order to proceed with the south coast contract.

Now try the question from the Exam Question Bank	Number	Level	Marks	Time
	Q2	Examination	25	45 mins

SHORT-TERM DECISIONS

In this chapter we will be continuing our study of relevant cash flows and short-term decision making.

Section 1 provides some guidelines on **layout and labelling of workings** that you should adhere to when attempting short-term decision-making questions. This is an important section that you should not ignore.

Sections 2 to 8 cover a **range of short-term decision-making scenarios**. Regardless of the scenario you encounter in an exam question, remember that the key to short-term decision-making is identifying and accounting for the **relevant** cash flows (that were covered in Chapter 1A).

Section 9 covers **joint cost allocation**, a topic that was originally covered at Certificate level (Paper C01).

topic list	learning outcomes	syllabus references	ability required
1 Presentation guidelines	A1(a), (c)	A1(i), (iii), (iv)	analysis
2 Acceptance/rejection of contracts	A1(a), (c)	A1(i), (iv)	analysis
3 Minimum pricing	A1(a)	A1(i), (iii)	analysis
4 Extra shift decisions and overtime	A1(a)	A1(i)	analysis
5 Make or buy decisions	A1(a)	A1(i)	analysis
6 Either/or problems	A1(a)	A1(i)	analysis
7 Shutdown problems	A1(a)	A1(i)	analysis
8 Choosing between options	A1(a)	A1(i)	analysis
9 Allocation of joint costs	A3(c)	A3(iii)	comprehension

1 Presentation guidelines

Introduction

One of the most important skills in tackling short-term decision-making questions is the layout of your answer and the correct labelling of workings. This section gives you some guidelines you should follow when you are answering such questions. Get into the habit of following these guidelines when you are practising questions so that you will be able to apply them in an exam situation.

1.1 The importance of showing workings

If the marker can **see** from your workings that you have **read the question**, extracted the **right information**, and had a good go at **using the techniques** that you should know about, having studied for this paper, there is a good chance that you will get through the exam quite comfortably.

(a) **Number your workings** consecutively. You may end up with workings 1 to 50 if you are not quite sure how to proceed at the outset, and experiment with the numbers a bit, or just workings 1 to 3 if you sorted out exactly how to do the question from the start. It does not matter **how many** workings you do. Only **layout, labelling** and **cross-referencing** matter in the exam.

(b) Always **label your workings** and tables with headings and sub-headings, and show units used ($, kg, units, etc). (Note the extent of the labelling in the workings shown above, in spite of the fact that most of the figures are given.)

(c) As you go along, **do a summary** on a separate clean page of whatever you expect to be your **final figures** and **state your conclusion** if it is not immediately clear.

(d) Without fail your summary **must be cross-referenced** to your **workings**, because you will get marks for sensible workings, even if the answer is wrong.

Section summary

Ensure your workings are shown clearly and your answer presented neatly to maximise your chances of gaining marks.

2 Acceptance/rejection of contracts

Introduction

This section focuses on the decision of whether a 'special' one-off contract should be accepted. Make sure you understand how the accept/reject decision is made and note the importance of layout and labelling of workings.

2.1 The accept/reject decision

'Special' one-off contracts are usually considered when a company has **spare capacity** (that is, resources do not have to be taken from existing work).

As with all short-term decisions, a 'special' one-off contract should be accepted if it **increases contribution** (that is, if the variable costs are less than the price to be paid by the customer) once all relevant costs have been taken into consideration.

Relevant costs and revenues will include the **price paid** by the customer, **variable costs** incurred as a result of the contract and any **additional fixed costs** incurred that are **directly related** to the contract.

Where there is **no spare capacity**, the company should only accept the contract if its contribution **exceeds** the contribution that had to be sacrificed from existing business (the **opportunity cost**).

Example: Accepting or rejecting contracts

HP makes a single product which sells for $20, and for which there is great demand. It has a variable cost of $12, made up as follows.

	$
	$
Direct material	4
Direct labour (2 hrs)	6
Variable overhead	2
	12

The labour force is currently working at full capacity producing a product that earns a contribution of $4 per labour hour. A customer has approached the company with a request for the manufacture of a special contract for which he is willing to pay $5,500. The costs of the contract would be $2,000 for direct materials, and 500 labour hours will be required.

Recommend whether the contract should be accepted and state any other factors that may have to be considered before the final decision is made.

Solution

(a)   The labour force is working at full capacity. By accepting the contract, work would have to be diverted away from the standard product, and contribution will be lost, that is, there is an **opportunity cost** of accepting the new contract, which is the contribution forgone by being unable to make the standard product.

(b)   Direct labour pay costs $3 per hour, but it is also usually assumed that variable production overhead varies with hours worked, and must therefore be spent in addition to the wages cost of the 500 hours.

(c)

	$	$
Value of contract		5,500
Cost of contract		
Direct materials	2,000	
Direct labour (500 hrs × $3)	1,500	
Variable overhead (500 hrs × $1)	500	
Opportunity cost (500 hrs × $4) (contribution forgone)	2,000	
Relevant cost of the contract		6,000
Loss incurred by accepting the contract		(500)

Although accepting the contract would earn a contribution of $1,500 ($5,500 – $4,000), the lost production of the standard product would reduce contribution earned elsewhere by $2,000 and so the contract should not be accepted.

Other considerations must also be taken into account, however.

(a)   Will **relationships with existing customers**, or prices that can be commanded in the market, be affected if the contract is accepted?

(b)   As a loss leader, could it create **further business opportunities**?

(c)   Should existing business be turned away in order to fulfil a one-off enquiry or could a **long-term contract** be established?

Exam skills

It is easy to forget to make your recommendation as to whether the contract should be accepted. Make sure you include your recommendation and explanation for your decision. 'Other factors' are often non-financial considerations and should be relevant to the given scenario.

Question 1B.1

Accept or reject

Learning outcome A1(a)

A company has been making a machine to order for a customer, but the customer has since gone into liquidation, and there is no prospect that any money will be obtained from the winding up of the company.

Costs incurred to date in manufacturing the machine are $50,000 and progress payments of $15,000 had been received from the customer prior to the liquidation.

The sales department has found another company willing to buy the machine for $34,000 once it has been completed.

To complete the work, the following costs would be incurred.

(a)   Materials: these have been bought at a cost of $6,000. They have no other use, and if the machine is not finished, they would be sold for scrap for $2,000.

(b)   Further labour costs would be $8,000. Labour is in short supply, and if the machine is not finished, the work force would be switched to another job, which would earn $30,000 in revenue, and incur direct costs of $12,000 and absorbed (fixed) overhead of $8,000.

(c)   Consultancy fees $4,000. If the work is not completed, the consultant's contract would be cancelled at a cost of $1,500.

(d)   General overheads of $8,000 would be added to the cost of the additional work.

Should the contract be accepted?

Section summary

In general terms, a **contract** will probably be **accepted** if it **increases contribution** and profit, and rejected if it reduces profit.

If an organisation **does not have sufficient spare capacity, existing business** should only be **turned away** if the **contribution from the contract is greater than the contribution from the business which must be sacrificed.**

3 Minimum pricing

Introduction

Another important decision that a company must make is the minimum price that should be quoted for a particular one-off product or contract. This section demonstrates how the minimum price is determined.

3.1 Determination of minimum price

The **minimum price** for a one-off product or contract is its **total relevant costs**. At this price the company will make no extra (incremental) profit or loss. It is really the **breakeven price**.

The following example will illustrate the technique.

Example: Minimum price using an opportunity cost approach

Minimax has just completed production of an item of special equipment for a customer, only to be notified that this customer has now gone into liquidation. After much effort, the sales manager has been able to interest a potential buyer who might buy the machine if certain conversion work could first be carried out.

(a)   The sales price of the machine to the original buyer had been fixed at $138,600 and had included an estimated normal profit mark-up of 10% on total costs. The costs incurred in the manufacture of the machine were as follows.

	$
Direct materials	49,000
Direct labour	36,000
Variable overhead	9,000
Fixed production overhead	24,000
Fixed sales and distribution overhead	8,000
	126,000

(b)   If the machine is converted, the production manager estimates that the cost of the extra work required would be as follows.

Direct materials (at cost) $9,600
Direct labour
    Department X: 6 workers for 4 weeks at $210 per worker per week
    Department Y: 2 workers for 4 weeks at $160 per worker per week

(c)   Variable overhead would be 20% of direct labour cost, and fixed production overhead would be absorbed as follows.

Department X: 83.33% of direct labour cost
Department Y: 25% of direct labour cost

(d)   Additional information is available as follows.

(i)   In the original machine, there are three types of material.

(1)   Type A could be sold for scrap for $8,000.

(2)   Type B could be sold for scrap for $2,400 but it would take 120 hours of casual labour paid at $3.50 per hour to put it into a condition in which it would be suitable for sale.

(3)   Type C would need to be scrapped, at a cost to Minimax of $1,100.

(ii)   The direct materials required for the conversion are already in inventory. If not needed for the conversion they would be used in the production of another machine in place of materials that would otherwise need to be purchased, and that would currently cost $8,800.

(iii)   The conversion work would be carried out in two departments, X and Y. Department X is currently extremely busy and working at full capacity; it is estimated that its contribution to fixed overhead and profits is $2.50 per $1 of labour.

Department Y, on the other hand, is short of work but for organisational reasons its labour force, which at the moment has a workload of only 40% of its standard capacity, cannot be reduced below its current level of eight employees, all of whom are paid a wage of $160 per week.

(iv)   The designs and specifications of the original machine could be sold to an overseas customer for $4,500 if the machine is scrapped.

(v)   If conversion work is undertaken, a temporary supervisor would need to be employed for four weeks at a total cost of $1,500. It is normal company practice to charge supervision costs to fixed overhead.

(vi)   The original customer has already paid a non-returnable deposit to Minimax of 12.5% of the selling price.

Required

Calculate the minimum price that Minimax should accept from the new customer for the converted machine. Explain clearly how you have reached this figure.

Solution

The minimum price is the price which reflects the **relevant costs** of the work. These are established as follows.

(a)   **Past costs are not relevant**, and the $126,000 of cost incurred should be excluded from the minimum price calculation. It is necessary, however, to consider the alternative use of the direct materials which would be forgone if the conversion work is carried out.

	$
Type A	
Revenue from sales as scrap (note (i))	8,000
Type B	
Revenue from sales as scrap, minus the additional cash costs necessary to to prepare it for sale ($2,400 – (120 × $3.50)) (note (i))	1,980
Type C	
Cost of disposal if the machine is not converted (a negative opportunity cost) (note (ii))	(1,100)
Total opportunity cost of materials types A, B and C	8,880

By agreeing to the conversion of the machine, Minimax would therefore lose a net revenue of $8,880 from the alternative use of these materials.

Notes

(i)   Scrap sales would be lost if the conversion work goes ahead.
(ii)   These costs would be incurred unless the work goes ahead.

(b)   The cost of additional **direct materials for conversion** is $9,600, but this is an historical cost. The relevant cost of these materials is the **$8,800** which would be spent on new purchases if the conversion is carried out. If the conversion work goes ahead, the materials held would be unavailable for production of the other machine mentioned in item (d)(ii) of the question and so the extra purchases of $8,800 would then be needed.

(c)   **Direct labour** in departments X and Y is a fixed cost and the labour force will be paid regardless of the work they do or do not do. The cost of labour for conversion in **department Y is not a relevant cost** because the work could be done without any extra cost to the company.

In **department X**, however, acceptance of the conversion work would oblige the company to divert production from other profitable jobs. The minimum contribution required from using department X labour must be sufficient to cover the cost of the labour and variable overheads and then make an additional $2.50 in contribution per direct labour hour.

Department X: costs for direct labour hours spent on conversion

6 workers × 4 weeks × $210 = $5,040

Variable overhead cost $5,040 × 20% = $1,008

Contribution forgone by diverting labour from other work

$2.50 per $1 of labour cost = $5,040 × 250% = $12,600

(d)   **Variable overheads** in department Y are **relevant** costs because they will only be incurred if production work is carried out. (It is assumed that if the workforce is idle, no variable overheads would be incurred.)

Department Y   20% of (2 workers × 4 weeks × $160) = $256

(e)   If the machine is converted, the company cannot sell the **designs and specifications** to the overseas company. $4,500 is a **relevant** (opportunity) cost of accepting the conversion order.

(f)   **Fixed overheads**, being mainly unchanged regardless of what the company decides to do, should be ignored because they are **not relevant** (incremental) costs. The additional cost of **supervision** should, however, be included as a **relevant** cost of the order because the $1,500 will not be spent unless the conversion work is done.

(g)   The **non-refundable deposit** received should be **ignored** and should not be deducted in the calculation of the minimum price. Just as costs incurred in the past are not relevant to a current decision about what to do in the future, revenues collected in the past are also irrelevant.

Estimate of minimum price for the converted machine

	$	$
Opportunity cost of using the direct materials types A, B and C		8,880
Opportunity cost of additional materials for conversion		8,800
Opportunity cost of work in department X		
Labour	5,040	
Variable overhead	1,008	
Contribution forgone	12,600	
		18,648
Opportunity cost: sale of designs and specifications		4,500
Incremental costs		
Variable production overheads in department Y		256
Fixed production overheads (additional supervision)		1,500
Minimum price		42,584

Section summary

The **minimum price** for a one-off product or service contract is its total relevant costs. This is the price at which the company would make no incremental profit and no incremental loss from undertaking the work, but would just achieve an incremental cost breakeven point.

4 Extra shift decisions and overtime

Introduction

Extra shift decisions are another type of decision problem and must be considered (where appropriate) when trying to make short-term decisions. They are concerned with whether or not it is worth opening up an extra shift for operations.

4.1 Factors to be considered

Qualitative factors in extra shift decisions include the following.

(a) **Would the work force be willing** to work the shift hours, and if so, what overtime or shift work premium over their basic pay might they expect to receive?

(b) **Do extra hours have to be worked just to remain competitive**? Banks might decide to open on Saturdays just to match what competitors are doing and so keep customers.

(c) Would extra hours result in **more sales revenue, or would there merely be a change in the demand pattern**? For example, if a shop were trying to decide whether to open on Sundays, one consideration would be whether the customers it would get on Sunday would simply be customers who would otherwise have done their shopping on another day of the week instead, or whether they would be additional customers.

When a business expands, the management is often faced with the problems of whether to acquire larger premises and more plant and machinery and whether to persuade existing personnel to work longer hours (on an overtime basis) or to engage extra staff who would use the existing equipment but at a different time (on a shift basis).

If the management decide to **incur additional expenditure on premises** and plant, that expenditure is a **fixed cost**. It will therefore be necessary to determine how much additional contribution will be required from the anticipated increased production to cover the extra fixed cost.

If it is decided to use the existing non-current assets, but for a longer period each day, the choice of shift working or overtime will also involve a marginal costing consideration.

(a) If **overtime** is selected, the **direct wages cost per unit produced will be increased** because the wages paid to workers on overtime are a basic rate plus an overtime bonus.

(b) If the management opt for **shift working** the shift premium may not be as expensive as the overtime premium so the **direct wages cost may be relatively lower**. On the other hand, there may be **an increase in fixed (or semi-fixed) costs** such as lighting, heating and canteen facilities.

Section summary

The decision to work an **extra shift** should be taken on the basis of whether the costs of the shift are exceeded by the benefits to be obtained.

5 Make or buy decisions

Introduction

Make or buy decisions are quite common in companies as they try to decide whether it would be more profitable to outsource production to an external organisation. This section looks at the procedures involved in reaching the correct decision.

5.1 Factors to consider in make or buy decisions

Whilst it is often tempting to outsource responsibility for a product to an external party, there are various factors that must be considered before the best decision for the company can be made.

The most important factor to remember is that the decision **should not be based solely on cost considerations**. Management should weigh up the non-financial benefits of internal production against those of outsourcing.

The **'make' option** should give management **more direct control** over the work, but the **'buy' option** often has the benefit that the external organisation has a **specialist skill and expertise** in the work. Other issues to consider are:

(a) How can **spare capacity** freed up by subcontracting be used **most profitably**?

(b) Could the decision to use an outside supplier cause an **industrial dispute**?

(c) Would the subcontractor be **reliable** with delivery times and product quality?

(d) Does the company wish to be **flexible** and maintain **better control** over operations by making everything itself?

5.2 Reaching the correct decision

Where there are **no scarce resources** and the company has **freedom of choice**, the relevant costs of a make or buy decision are the **differential costs** between the make and buy options.

The variable cost of producing the goods in-house is likely to be less than the cost of buying in. However the company must also consider the **savings in directly attributable fixed costs** that will arise from using an outside supplier.

The following example illustrates the process.

Example: Make or buy

An organisation makes four components, W, X, Y and Z, for which costs in the forthcoming year are expected to be as follows.

	W	X	Y	Z
Production (units)	1,000	2,000	4,000	3,000
Unit marginal costs	$	$	$	$
Direct materials	4	5	2	4
Direct labour	8	9	4	6
Variable production overheads	2	3	1	2
	14	17	7	12

Directly attributable fixed costs per annum and committed fixed costs are as follows.

	$
Incurred as a direct consequence of making W	1,000
Incurred as a direct consequence of making X	5,000
Incurred as a direct consequence of making Y	6,000
Incurred as a direct consequence of making Z	8,000
Other fixed costs (committed)	30,000
	50,000

A subcontractor can supply units of W, X, Y and Z for $12, $21, $10 and $14 respectively.

Required

Decide whether the organisation should make or buy the components and state any other issues that may be considered before the final decision is reached.

Solution

(a) The relevant costs are the differential costs between making and buying, and they consist of differences in unit variable costs plus differences in directly attributable fixed costs. Subcontracting will result in some fixed cost savings.

	W $	X $	Y $	Z $
Unit variable cost of making	14	17	7	12
Unit variable cost of buying	12	21	10	14
	(2)	4	3	2
Annual requirements (units)	1,000	2,000	4,000	3,000
Extra variable cost of buying (per annum)	(2,000)	8,000	12,000	6,000
Fixed costs saved by buying	1,000	5,000	6,000	8,000
Extra total cost of buying	(3,000)	3,000	6,000	(2,000)

(b) The company would save $3,000 pa by subcontracting component W (where the purchase cost would be less than the marginal cost per unit to make internally) and would save $2,000 pa by subcontracting component Z (because of the saving in fixed costs of $8,000).

(c) Important **further considerations** would be as follows.

(i) If components W and Z are subcontracted, the company will have spare capacity. How should that **spare capacity be profitably used**? Are there **hidden benefits** to be obtained from subcontracting? Would the company's workforce resent the loss of work to an outside subcontractor, and might such a decision cause an **industrial dispute**?

(ii) Would the subcontractor be **reliable with delivery times**, and would he supply components of the same **quality** as those manufactured internally?

(iii) Does the company wish to be **flexible** and **maintain better control** over operations by making everything itself?

(iv) Are the **estimates** of fixed cost savings **reliable**? In the case of product W, buying is clearly cheaper than making in-house. In the case of product Z, the decision to buy rather than make would only be financially beneficial if the fixed cost savings of $8,000 could really be 'delivered' by management

Section summary

If an organisation has the freedom of choice about whether to **make internally or buy externally and has no scarce resources** that put a restriction on what it can do itself, the relevant costs for the decision will be the differential costs between the two options.

6 Either/or problems

Introduction

This section contains a detailed example of how to tackle the more complicated type of relevant cost question – the either/or decision. You will notice that proper layout makes the task much easier and it also increases your chances of gaining marks!

Example: Do now or do later?

MM currently carries out Process B the output from which can be sold for $20 per unit and has variable unit costs of $7.50 per unit. Process B has directly attributable fixed operating costs of $40,000 per annum. MM also carries out Process C by using equipment that has running costs of $25,000 per annum. The equipment could be sold *now* for $50,000 (but this would incur dismantling costs of $7,500) or in one year's time for $45,000 with dismantling costs of $8,750.

Process B could be adapted so that it incorporated Process C.

(a) The existing Process B machinery would have to be removed, either now at a dismantling cost of $12,500 and with the sale of the machinery for $100,000, or in one year's time for $75,000 with dismantling costs of $13,750.

(b) Alternative Process B machinery would have to be leased. This would cost $10,000 per annum and have annual fixed running costs of $30,000.

The existing Process B machinery originally cost $250,000 when bought five years ago. It is being depreciated at 10% per annum.

Required

Prepare an analysis on an incremental opportunity cost basis to decide on financial grounds whether to adopt Process B immediately or to delay it for one year. *Ignore the time value of money.*

Solution

	Adapt Now $	Adapt in one year $	Net (savings) /costs $
Savings			
Sale of Process C equipment	(50,000)	(45,000)	(5,000)
Sale of Process B machinery	(100,000)	(75,000)	(25,000)
Costs			
Fixed operating costs	0	40,000	(40,000)
Removal of Process B machinery	12,500	13,750	(1,250)
Process C – running costs	0	25,000	(25,000)
Process C – dismantling costs	7,500	8,750	(1,250)
Leased Process B equipment running costs	30,000	0	30,000
Leasing costs	10,000	0	10,000
Net (savings) less costs			(57,500)

Conclusion. Adapting now will bring savings of $57,500 more than adapting in one year.

There are lessons to be learned here about extracting information from complex Paper 2 questions. Note the following points.

(a)   You should do **savings and costs separately** and put **one type in brackets** (it doesn't matter which way round you do this as long as you are consistent within the question: we have put savings in brackets in keeping with the accounting convention that they are credits). This is important because it is easy to get the signs wrong when you come to work out the differences.

(b)   Subtract column 2 from column 1 taking **care with the minus signs**. For instance:

$-50,000 - (-45,000) = -5,000$

(c)   Adapting now means that the fixed operating costs of $40,000 will not be incurred so a **nought** goes in the Now column. Adapting in one year means that fixed operating costs of $40,000 will have to be paid for another year. The net benefit of adapting now is therefore a saving of $40,000.

(d)   There are some **red herrings** in the information given. Unit selling prices and costs are not relevant, since they do not change, whenever Process B is adapted. Original cost and depreciation are not relevant because they are not future cash flows.

Section summary

The best approach to a complex **either/or problem** is to draw up a three-column table with columns for the first option (say, adapt now) and the second (say, adapt later), and a third column for the differences between the options (Column 1 minus Column 2).

7   Shutdown problems

Introduction

Another decision that a company may have to take is whether to discontinue an operation. This could mean the closure of a production line, factory, division or other activity. This section focuses on the costs and other factors that must be considered before this important decision can be made. As with previous sections, note how the information in the solution is presented.

7.1 Types of shutdown decisions

Decisions to be made in shutdown or discontinuance problems include

*   Whether or not to close down a product line, department or other activity.
*   If the decision is to shut down, whether the closure should be permanent or temporary.
*   If there is a choice about the timing of the closure, when should it take place.

Read our four step guide method in Section 5.2 below when you come to work through these decisions.

7.2 Financial considerations

The basic method is to use short-run relevant costs to calculate contributions and profits or losses.

1   Calculate what is earned by the process at present (perhaps in comparison with others).

2   Calculate what will be the financial consequences of closing down (selling machines, redundancy costs etc).

3   Compare the results and act accordingly.

4   Bear in mind that some fixed costs may no longer be incurred if the decision is to shut down and
        they are therefore relevant to the decision.

Bear these in mind as you read through the example below.

Example: Adding or deleting products

An organisation manufactures three products, Pawns, Rooks and Bishops. The present net annual income
from these is:

	Pawns	Rooks	Bishops	Total
	$	$	$	$
Sales	50,000	40,000	60,000	150,000
Variable costs	30,000	25,000	35,000	90,000
Contribution	20,000	15,000	25,000	60,000
Fixed costs	17,000	18,000	20,000	55,000
Profit/loss	3,000	(3,000)	5,000	5,000

The organisation is concerned about its poor profit performance, and is considering whether or not to
cease selling Rooks. It is felt that selling prices cannot be raised or reduced without adversely affecting
net income. $5,000 of the fixed costs of Rooks are direct fixed costs which would be saved if production
ceased. All other fixed costs, it is considered, would remain the same.

Solution

By stopping production of Rooks, the consequences would be a $10,000 fall in profits:

	$
Loss of contribution	(15,000)
Savings in fixed costs	5,000
Incremental loss	(10,000)

Suppose, however, it were possible to use the resources realised by stopping production of Rooks and
switch to producing a new item, Crowners, which would sell for $50,000 and incur variable costs of
$30,000 and extra direct fixed costs of $6,000. A new decision is now required:

	Rooks	Crowners
	$	$
Sales	40,000	50,000
Less variable costs	25,000	30,000
	15,000	20,000
Less direct fixed costs	5,000	6,000
Contribution to shared fixed costs and profit	10,000	14,000

It would be more profitable to shut down production of Rooks and switch resources to making Crowners,
in order to boost profits by $4,000 to $9,000.

7.3 Non-quantifiable considerations

As usual the decision is not merely a matter of choosing the best financial option.

(a)   A product may be retained if it is providing a contribution, albeit a small one. Retaining a wide
        range of **low volume/low contribution products** would add to the **complexity** and hence costs of
        manufacture, however, but very little to overall profit. Low volume/low contribution products
        should therefore be examined on a regular basis.

(b) The **effect on demand for other products** if a particular product is no longer produced should be taken into account.

(c) The extent to which demand for **other products** (existing or new) can expand to **use** the **capacity** vacated by the product being deleted is an issue.

(d) **Pricing policy**. Is the product a **loss leader?** Is the product in the introductory stage of its **life cycle** and consequently priced low to help it to become accepted and hence maximise its long-term market share **(penetration pricing).** (These are issues you will cover in Chapter 9.)

Question 1B.2

Deleting products

Learning outcome A1(a)

A company's product range includes product F, on which the following data (relating to a year's production) are available.

	$
Revenue	200,000
Materials cost	157,000
Machine power cost	14,000
Overheads: type A	28,000
type B	56,000

Type A overheads would be avoided if production of product F ceased, but type B overheads would not be. Both types of overheads are absorbed in direct proportion to machine power cost, and that cost is a purely variable cost.

Production of product F should be discontinued. *True or false?*

7.4 Relative profitability

The relative profitability of products can be judged by **calculation** of their contribution to sales **(C/S) ratios**. Suppose an organisation produces three products A, B and C, and that production capacity is limited. If product A has a C/S ratio of 22%, product B a C/S ratio of 27% and product C a C/S ratio of 25%, given unlimited demand for the three products the organisation should concentrate on producing product B.

Example: Shutdown decisions

You may consider by now that you understand the basic principles of selecting relevant cash flows for decision making and it may therefore be useful at this stage to test your understanding with a more advanced example. Attempt your own solution before reading on.

Ayeco, with a head office in Ayetown, has three manufacturing units. One is in Beetown, the second in Ceetown and the third in Deetown. The company manufactures and sells an air-conditioner under the brand-name of Ayecool at a price of $200. It is unable to utilise fully its manufacturing capacity.

Summarised income statements for the year are shown below.

	Beetown $'000	Ceetown $'000	Deetown $'000	Total $'000
Costs				
Direct materials	200	800	400	1,400
Direct wages	200	900	350	1,450
Production overhead: variable	50	300	150	500
fixed	200	600	300	1,100
Sub-total	650	2,600	1,200	4,450
Selling overhead: variable	25	200	100	325
fixed	75	250	150	475
Administration overhead	100	450	200	750
Sub-total	850	3,500	1,650	6,000
Head office costs	50	200	100	350
Total	900	3,700	1,750	6,350
Profit	100	300	250	650
Sales	1,000	4,000	2,000	7,000

The management of the company has to decide whether or not to renew the lease of the property at Beetown, which expires next year. The company has been offered an extension to the lease at an additional cost of $50,000 per annum. This situation concerning the lease has been known for some time, so the accountant has collected relevant information to aid the decision. It is estimated that the cost of closing down Beetown would be offset by the surplus obtained by the sale of plant, machinery and inventories.

If Ayeco does not renew the lease of the Beetown property it has two alternatives.

(a)   Accept an offer from Zeeco, a competitor, to take over the manufacture and sales in the Beetown area and pay to Ayeco a commission of $3 for each unit sold.

(b)   Transfer the output at present made in Beetown to either Ceetown or Deetown. Each of these units has sufficient plant capacity to undertake the Beetown output but additional costs in supervision, salaries, storage and maintenance would be incurred. These additional costs are estimated as amounting yearly to $250,000 at Ceetown and to $200,000 at Deetown.

If the Beetown sales are transferred to either Ceetown or Deetown, it is estimated that additional transport costs would be incurred in delivering to customers in the region of Beetown, and that these would amount to $15 per unit and $20 per unit respectively.

Required

Present a statement to the board of directors of Ayeco to show the estimated annual profit which would arise from the following alternative courses of action.

(a)   Continuing production at all three sites
(b)   Closing down production at Beetown and accepting the offer from Zeeco
(c)   Transferring Beetown sales to Ceetown
(d)   Transferring Beetown sales to Deetown

Comment on your statement, indicating any problems which may arise from the various decisions which the board may decide to take.

Solution

The main difficulty in answering this question is to decide what happens to fixed cost expenditure if the Beetown factory is closed, and what would be the variable costs of production and sales at Ceetown or Deetown if work was transferred from Beetown.

Fixed costs

It should be assumed that the direct fixed costs of the Beetown factory will be saved when shutdown occurs. These costs will include rent, depreciation of machinery, salaries of administrative staff and so on and it is therefore probably correct to assume that savings on shutdown will include all fixed costs charged to Beetown with the exception of the apportioned head office costs.

Variable cost of production

The variable cost of production at Ceetown or Deetown is more tricky, because the variable cost/sales ratio and the contribution/sales ratio differs at each factory.

	Beetown	Ceetown	Deetown
	%	%	%
Direct materials/sales	20.0	20.0	20.0
Direct wages/sales	20.0	22.5	17.5
Variable production overhead/sales	5.0	7.5	7.5
Variable selling overhead/sales	2.5	5.0	5.0
Total variable costs/sales	47.5	55.0	50.0
Contribution/sales	52.5	45.0	50.0

Labour appears to be less efficient at Ceetown and more efficient at Deetown, but variable overheads are more costly at both Ceetown and Deetown than at Beetown. It is probably reasonably accurate to assume that the variable cost/sales ratio of work transferred from Beetown will change to the ratio which is current at the factory to which the work is transferred. Transport costs would then be added as an additional cost item.

Statement of estimated annual profit

Option 1 Continuing production at all three sites

	$
Profit before rent increase on lease	650,000
Increase in annual cost of lease	50,000
Revised estimate of annual profit	600,000

Option 2 Accepting the offer from Zeeco

	$	$
Current estimate of total profit		650,000
Less revenue lost from closing Beetown	(1,000,000)	
Direct costs saved at Beetown	850,000	
	(150,000)	
Commission from Zeeco* (5,000 × $3)	15,000	
Net loss from closure		(135,000)
Revised estimate of total profit		515,000

- Number of units = $1,000,000 ÷ $200 per unit = 5,000 units.

Option 3 Transfer work to Ceetown

	$	$	$
Current estimate of total profit			650,000
Direct costs saved by closing Beetown		850,000	
Extra costs at Ceetown			
Variable costs (55% of $1,000,000)	(550,000)		
Extra costs of supervision etc	(250,000)		
Extra costs of transport (5,000 units × $15)	(75,000)		
		(875,000)	
Net extra costs of transfer			(25,000)
Revised estimate of total profit			625,000

Option 4 Transfer work to Deetown

	$	$	$
Current estimate of total profit			650,000
Direct costs saved by closing Beetown		850,000	
Extra costs at Deetown			
Variable costs (50% of $1,000,000)	(500,000)		
Extra costs of supervision etc	(200,000)		
Extra costs of transport (5,000 units × $20)	(100,000)		
		(800,000)	
Net savings from transfer			50,000
Revised estimate of total profit			700,000

Conclusion. The preferred option should be to transfer production from Beetown to Deetown, since profits would rise to $700,000, and would be $75,000 higher than profits obtainable from the next most profitable option (option 3).

Comments on the example

The example above illustrates how accounting information for decision-making can often be presented in a concise form, without the need to reproduce a complete table of revenues, costs and profits for each option. You should study the presentation of the figures above, and note how they show only the relevant costs or benefits arising as a direct consequence of each decision option.

The eventual management decision may not be to transfer to Deetown, because other **non-quantifiable factors** might influence the final decision.

(a) Concern for employees at Beetown and the wish to avoid redundancies.

(b) Problems in recruiting additional staff at Deetown.

(c) The possibility that the extra workload at Deetown might reduce labour efficiency there, making costs of production higher than those estimated in the statement.

(d) Difficulties in assembling and organising a transport fleet might persuade management to reject options 3 and 4.

7.5 When to close

As well as being able to deal with 'whether to close' situations you may also be required to handle 'when to close' situations. This is similar to the 'do now or do later' example above.

Example: When to close

Daisy currently publish, print and distribute a range of catalogues and instruction manuals. The management have now decided to discontinue printing and distribution and concentrate solely on publishing. Stem will print and distribute the range of catalogues and instruction manuals on behalf of Daisy commencing either at 30 June 20X0 or 30 November 20X0. Stem will receive $65,000 per month for a contract which will commence either at 30 June 20X0 or 30 November 20X0.

The results of Daisy for a typical month are as follows.

	Publishing $'000	Printing $'000	Distribution $'000
Salaries and wages	28.0	18.0	4.0
Materials and supplies	5.5	31.0	1.1
Occupancy costs	7.0	8.5	1.2
Depreciation	0.8	4.2	0.7

Other information has been gathered relating to the possible closure proposals.

(a) Two specialist staff from printing will be retained at their present salary of $1,500 each per month in order to fulfil a link function with Stem. One further staff member will be transferred to publishing to fill a staff vacancy through staff turnover, anticipated in July. This staff member will be paid at his present salary of $1,400 per month which is $100 more than that of the staff member who is expected to leave. On closure all other printing and distribution staff will be made redundant and paid an average of two months redundancy pay.

(b) The printing department has a supply of materials (already paid for) which cost $18,000 and which will be sold to Stem for $10,000 if closure takes place on 30 June 20X0. Otherwise the material will be used as part of the July 20X0 printing requirements. The distribution department has a contract to purchase pallets at a cost of $500 per month for July and August 20X0. A cancellation clause allows for non-delivery of the pallets for July and August for a one-off payment of $300. Non-delivery for August only will require a payment of $100. If the pallets are taken from the supplier, Stem has agreed to purchase them at a price of $380 for each month's supply which is available. Pallet costs are included in the distribution materials and supplies cost stated for a typical month.

(c) Company expenditure on apportioned occupancy costs to printing and distribution will be reduced by 15% per month if printing and distribution departments are closed. At present, 30% of printing and 25% of distribution occupancy costs are directly attributable costs which are avoidable on closure, whilst the remainder are apportioned costs.

(d) Closure of the printing and distribution departments will make it possible to sub-let part of the building for a monthly fee of $2,500 when space is available.

(e) Printing plant and machinery has an estimated net book value of $48,000 at 30 June 20X0. It is anticipated that it will be sold at a loss of $21,000 on 30 June 20X0. If sold on 30 November 20X0 the prospective buyer will pay $25,000.

(f) The net book value of distribution vehicles at 30 June 20X0 is estimated as $80,000. They could be sold to the original supplier at $48,000 on 30 June 20X0. The original supplier would purchase the vehicles on 30 November 20X0 for a price of $44,000.

Required

Using the above information, prepare a summary to show whether Daisy should close the printing and distribution departments on financial grounds on 30 June 20X0 or on 30 November 20X0. Explanatory notes and calculations should be shown.

Solution

		Handover 30.6.X0 $	Handover 30.11.X0 $	Net savings/ (costs) of 30.6.X0 handover $
Relevant inflows				
Inventory (W2)		10,000		10,000
Pallet sale (W3)		380		380
Rent	(5 × $2,500)	12,500		12,500
Non-current asset sales				
Printing		27,000	25,000	2,000
Distribution		48,000	44,000	4,000
Total inflows		97,880	69,000	28,880
Relevant outflows				
Salaries and wages (W1)		15,500	110,000	(94,500)
Materials and supplies (W2)			142,500	(142,500)
Pallets (W3)		600		600
Occupancy costs (W4)				
Apportioned		29,112	34,250	(5,138)
Direct			14,250	(14,250)
Stem fee	(5 × $65,000)	325,000		325,000
Total outflows		370,212	301,000	69,212
Net inflow/(outflow)		(272,332)	(232,000)	(40,332)

Conclusion. The operation should be kept open until 30.11.20X0.

Workings

1   *Salaries and wages*

	Printing $	Distribution $	Total $
Costs if 30.6.X0 handover			
2 × $1,500 × 5 months	15,000	–	15,000
$100 × 5 months		500	500
			15,500
Costs if 30.11.X0 handover			
5 months usual costs	90,000	20,000	110,000

2   *Inventory*

The $18,000 cost of production is a sunk cost from previous periods. Therefore only the income is recorded. Also, the $10,000 income could be seen as one of the opportunity costs of continuing production.

			$
Therefore materials costs are	printing:	($31,000 × 5 – $18,000) =	137,000
	distribution:	($1,100 × 5) =	5,500
			142,500

3   *Pallets*

The alternative flows can be estimated as follows.

Take both deliveries

	$
Payment (2 × $500) =	1,000
Resale (2 × $380) =	760
Net flow	240

Take one delivery (ie July)

	$
Payment	500
Cancellation fee (August)	100
	600
Sale to Stem	380
Net flow	220

Take no deliveries

Cancellation fee	$300

Only the July delivery should be taken.

4   *Site costs*

	Printing $	*Distribution* $	*Total* $
Total occupancy costs (5 months)	42,500	6,000	48,500
of which directly attributable (30%/25%)	(12,750)	(1,500)	(14,250)
∴ Apportioned costs	29,750	4,500	34,250
Reduction in apportioned costs (15%)	(4,463)	(675)	(5,138)
Apportioned costs after closure	25,287	3,825	29,112

7.5.1 Temporary closure

The decision whether to shut down temporarily should take into account the following factors.

(a)   The impact on the organisation's other products and the product in question
(b)   Problems of recruitment of skilled labour when production begins again
(c)   Possibility of plant obsolescence
(d)   Problems of closing down and restarting production in some industries
(e)   Expenditure on disconnection of services, start up costs and so on

If contribution is only just covering fixed costs but improved trading conditions in the future seem likely it may be worth continuing the business.

Exam alert

Be very careful when setting out any relevant cost evaluation. **Do not** incorporate in the same analysis both the incremental costs and revenues that would apply if the decision proceeded (such as continuing with a product) *and* the avoidable costs if it did not (deleting the product). This is an easy mistake to make. You should consider first a decision to continue with the product and then compare it with a decision to delete the product.

7.6 Idle production capacity

If an organisation does decide to shut down a factory, department, product line or other activity, it may well be faced with a decision about what to do with the resulting idle production capacity.

(a) **Marketing strategies** could be used to increase demand for existing products.

(b) **Idle plant and machinery could be moved to another department** or factory, thereby reducing expenditure on new plant and machinery and/or interest charges.

(c) **Special orders could be accepted**, providing that the contribution generated is either greater than any reduction in fixed overheads which would occur if the idle capacity was not used or greater than any increase in fixed overheads if the idle capacity were to be used.

(d) **Space could be sub-let** to a third party.

Such considerations are particularly important if the closure is only temporary.

Section summary

Non-quantifiable factors in shutdown problems include the impact on employees, customers, competitors and suppliers.

8 Choosing between options

Introduction

In this section we look at an alternative choice type question, which is basically a matter of comparing relevant costs and revenues.

8.1 Presentation, presentation, presentation

KEY POINT

The **key point** in decision-making questions is that you **let the marker see** what you are doing. This is simply a matter of **layout and labelling**. Every examiner, in every subject, for every professional body, always complains about the layout and labelling of students' answers. Get wise to this!

We have been emphasising the need for good presentation in short-term decision-making questions throughout this chapter. Whilst you might be thinking we are overdoing the emphasis, you should be aware that layout and labelling of students' answers is a frequent concern in examiners' post-exam guidance.

The example we have chosen is one where there is a strong temptation to just tap away on a calculator and write down the final answer. This will not earn you any marks if you happen to tap the wrong figure, because nobody will know what you did wrong. In other words the main issue is the value of **good presentation.**

Example: Options available

AA has three options for Machine A.

Option 1 Dispose of Machine A in one year's time for $8,750

Option 2 Modify Machine A now at a cost of $6,250. This choice is being considered in conjunction another decision, Decision A.

Decision A would mean that production output would increase by 25,000 units per annum except in the first year when 25% of the production enhancement would be lost due to running in. Production units sell for $20 per unit and have variable costs of $7.50 per unit.

The modification will mean that Machine A can only be sold for $5,000 in one year's time. However, it will reduce the production enhancement loss from 25% to 15%.

Option 3 Modify Machine A now at a cost of $2,500, which will mean that the company does not have to hire an alternative machine at a cost of $7,500. This modification would mean that Machine A will have a disposal cost of $625 in one year's time.

Required

Determine what the company should do with Machine A. *Ignore the time value of money.*

Solution

Easy marks if you're a prize winner

Here is how to lay out a **summary** of your answer that would instantly put you in the running for **Best Overall Answer**.

Summary final answer

	(Saving)/Cost	Reference
Option 1	$(8,750)	W1
Option 2	$(30,000)	W2
Option 3	$(4,375)	W3

Conclusion. Option 2 is clearly the best because it gives the highest revenue.

Solution

Easy marks if you're keen to get on

Here, on the other hand, is how good **pass-standard** students should **lay out** the **workings** that markers would scrutinise if the overall answer happened not to be right.

1   **Option 1**

The revenue from **Option 1** is given in the question: $8,750.

2   **Option 2**

	$
Reduction in impact of production losses(25,000 x (25-15)% x $(20 −7.50))	(31,250)
Modification (given)	6,250
Sales value after one year (given)	(5,000)
Saving	(30,000)

3   **Option 3**

	$
Modification (given)	2,500
Hire costs avoided (given)	(7,500)
Disposal cost (given)	625
Saving	(4,375)

Wording

The 'double negative' wording of Option 2 may have confused you. The enhancement is 25,000 units x $12.50 contribution = $312,500. Decision A reduces this enhancement by 25% to $234,375. Use of machine A only reduces it by 15% to $265,625 and therefore *saves* $31,250.

Section summary

Many of the decision scenarios covered in this chapter could be described as cost/benefit comparisons because you need to compare the costs and benefits associated with the decision in order to determine what action to take.

9 Allocation of joint costs

Introduction

In your earlier studies you covered the techniques of process costing, which is the costing method which applies when goods or services are produced in a sequence of continuous processes. Here we look at the methods of accounting for joint products and by-products which arise as a result of a continuous process and the various decision problems that can occur.

9.1 Joint products and by-products

KEY TERM

JOINT PRODUCTS are defined in CIMA *Official Terminology* as 'Two or more products produced by the same process and separated in processing, each having a sufficiently high saleable value to merit recognition as a main product'.

KEY POINT

Features of joint products

(a)   They are produced in the same process.
(b)   They are indistinguishable from each other until the separation point.
(c)   They each have a substantial sales value (after further processing, if necessary).
(d)   They may require further processing after the separation point.

For example in the oil refining industry the following joint products all arise from the same process.

(a)   Diesel fuel
(b)   Petrol
(c)   Paraffin
(d)   Lubricants

KEY TERM

A BY-PRODUCT is defined in CIMA *Official Terminology* as 'Output of some value produced incidentally in manufacturing something else (main product)'.

What exactly distinguishes a joint product from a by-product?

The answer lies in management attitudes to their products, which in turn is reflected in the cost accounting system.

(a)   A **joint product** is regarded as an important saleable item, and so it should be **separately costed**. The profitability of each joint product should be assessed in the cost accounts.

(b)   A **by-product** is not important as a saleable item, and whatever revenue it earns is a 'bonus' for the organisation. It is not worth costing by-products separately, because of their relative insignificance.

It is therefore equally irrelevant to consider a by-product's profitability. The only question is how to account for the 'bonus' net revenue that a by-product earns.

9.2 Problems in accounting for joint products

Costs incurred prior to this point of separation are **common or joint costs**, and these need to be allocated (apportioned) in some manner to each of the joint products. In the following sketched example, there are two different split-off points.

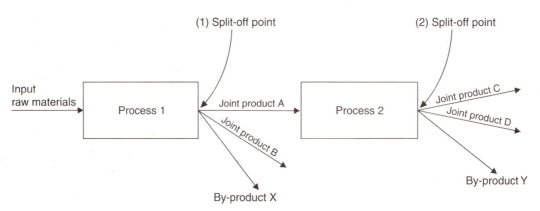

The special problems in accounting for joint products are basically of two different sorts.

(a)   How joint costs should be apportioned between products.

(b)   Whether it is more profitable to sell a joint product at one stage of processing, or to process the product further and sell it at a later stage. In the above diagram, product A has been processed further but product B has been sold at the split-off point.

We will return to the second problem later in this section. Let us for now consider the first problem.

9.3 Apportioning joint costs to joint products

The problem of costing for joint products concerns **joint costs**, that is those common processing costs shared between the units of eventual output up to their 'split-off point'. Some method needs to be devised for sharing the joint costs between the individual joint products for the following reasons.

(a)   **To put a value to inventory held at the period end** of each joint product for **financial reporting purposes** in particular, but also for management reports. For external reporting it is necessary that inventory valuation includes an apportionment of the common costs of production, as well as any directly attributable costs of further processing.

(b)   **To record the costs and therefore the profit from each joint product.** This is of **limited value** however, because the costs and therefore profit from one joint product are influenced by the share of costs assigned to the other joint products. Management decisions would be based on the apparent relative profitability of the products which has arisen due to the arbitrary apportionment of the joint costs.

(c)   Perhaps to assist in **pricing decisions**.

9.4 Some examples of the joint costs problem

(a)   How to spread the joint costs of oil refining between the joint products made (petrol, naphtha, kerosene and so on).

(b)   How to spread the joint costs of running the telephone network between telephone calls in peak rate times and cheap rate times, or between local calls and long-distance calls.

KEY POINT

Methods used to apportion joint costs to joint products

(a)   Physical measurement

(b)   Relative sales value apportionment method 1; sales value at split-off point

(c)   Relative sales value apportionment method 2; sales value of end product less further processing costs after split-off point

(d)   A weighted average method

9.5 Dealing with joint costs: physical measurement

With physical measurement, the joint cost is apportioned to the joint products on the basis of the proportion that the output of each product bears by weight or volume to the total output. An example of this would be the case where two products, product 1 and product 2, incur joint costs to the point of separation of $3,000 and the output of each product is 600 tons and 1,200 tons respectively.

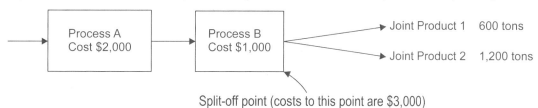

Product 1 sells for $4 per ton and product 2 for $2 per ton.

The division of the joint costs ($3,000) between product 1 and product 2 could be based on the tonnage of output.

	Product 1	Product 2	Total
Output	600 tons	1,200 tons	1,800 tons
Proportion of joint cost	$\frac{600}{1,800}$	$\frac{1,200}{1,800}$	
	$	$	$
Apportioned cost	1,000	2,000	3,000
Sales	2,400	2,400	4,800
Profit	1,400	400	1,800
Profit/sales ratio	58.3%	16.7%	37.5%

This method is unsuitable where the products separate during the processes into **different states**, for example where one product is a gas and another is a liquid. Furthermore, this method does not take into account the **relative income-earning potentials of the individual products**, with the result that one product might appear very profitable and another appear to be incurring losses.

9.6 Dealing with joint costs: sales value at split-off point

With relative sales value apportionment of joint cost, the cost is **apportioned according to the product's ability to produce income**. This method is most widely used because the assumption that some profit margin should be attained for all products under normal marketing conditions is satisfied. The joint cost is apportioned to each product in the proportion that the sales value of that product bears to the sales value of the total output from the particular processes concerned. Using the previous example where the sales price per ton is $4 for product 1 and $2 for product 2.

(a)   Joint costs of processes to split-off point $3,000

(b)   Sales value of product 1 at $4 per ton $2,400

(c)   Sales value of product 2 at $2 per ton $2,400

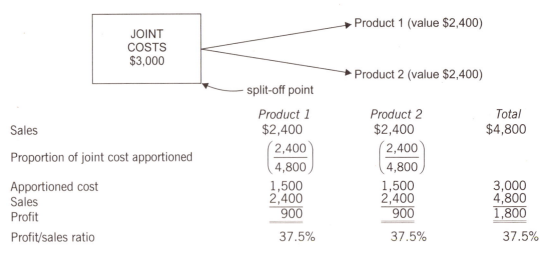

	Product 1	Product 2	Total
Sales	$2,400	$2,400	$4,800
Proportion of joint cost apportioned	$\left(\dfrac{2,400}{4,800}\right)$	$\left(\dfrac{2,400}{4,800}\right)$	
Apportioned cost	1,500	1,500	3,000
Sales	2,400	2,400	4,800
Profit	900	900	1,800
Profit/sales ratio	37.5%	37.5%	37.5%

A comparison of the different gross profit margins resulting from the application of the above methods for allocating joint costs will illustrate the greater acceptability of the relative sales value apportionment method. Physical measurement gives a higher profit margin to product 1, not necessarily because product 1 is highly profitable, but because it has been given a smaller share of joint costs.

9.7 Dealing with joint costs: sales value minus further processing costs

Joint products may have no known market value at the point of separation, because they need further separate processing to make them ready for sale. The allocation of joint costs should be accomplished as follows.

(a)   Ideally, by determining a **relative sales value at the split off point** for each product.

(b)   If a relative sales value cannot be found, a residual sales value at the split-off point can be determined.

(i)   Take the final sales value of each joint product

(ii)   Deduct the further processing costs for each product

This residual sales value is sometimes referred to as the **notional** or **proxy sales value** of a joint product.

Example: Sales value minus further processing costs

JT has a factory where four products are originated in a common process.

During period 4, the costs of the common process were $16,000. Output was as follows.

	Units made	Units sold	Sales value per unit
Product P1	600		
Product Q1	400		
Product R	500	400	$7
Product S	600	450	$10

Products P1 and Q1 are further processed, separately, to make end-products P2 and Q2.

	Units processed	Units sold	Cost of further processing	Sales value per unit
Product P1/P2	600	600	$1,000	$10 (P2)
Product Q1/Q2	400	300	$2,500	$20 (Q2)

Required

Calculate the costs of each joint product and the profit from each of them in period 4. There was no inventory at the beginning of the period.

Solution

(a)   It is helpful to begin a solution to joint product problems with a diagram of the process.

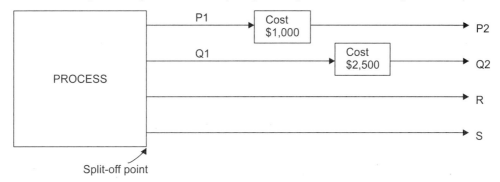

(b)   Next we calculate the notional sales values of P1 and Q1 at the split-off point.

	P2	Q2
	$	$
Sales value of production	6,000	8,000
Less further processing costs	1,000	2,500
Notional sales value, P1, Q1	5,000 (P1)	5,500 (Q1)

(c)   Now we can apply sales values to apportion joint costs.

Joint product	Sales value of production	%	Apportionment of joint costs
	$		$
P1	5,000	25	4,000
Q1	5,500	27.5	4,400
R	3,500	17.5	2,800
S	6,000	30	4,800
	20,000	100	16,000

(d)   We can now draw up the profit statement.

	P1/2	Q1/2	R	S	Total
	$	$	$	$	$
Joint costs	4,000	4,400	2,800	4,800	16,000
Further processing	1,000	2,500	–	–	3,500
Cost of production	5,000	6,900	2,800	4,800	19,500
Less inventory at period end	0	1,725	560	1,200	3,485
Cost of sales	5,000	5,175	2,240	3,600	16,015
Sales	6,000	6,000	2,800	4,500	19,300
Profit	1,000	825	560	900	3,285
Profit/sales ratio	17%	14%	20%	20%	17%

Question 1B.3

Units method of splitting common costs

Learning outcome A3(c)

Refer back to the example above and fill in the blanks in the sentence below.

The profit for the period is $............... and the value of the inventory held at period end is $......... if joint costs are apportioned using the units method.

9.8 Dealing with joint costs: weighted average method

The weighted average method of joint cost apportionment is a development of the units method of apportionment. Since units of joint product may not be comparable in physical resemblance or physical weight (they may be gases, liquids or solids) units of each joint product may be multiplied by a weighting factor, and '**weighted units**' would provide a basis for apportioning the joint costs.

Example: Weighted average method

MG manufactures four products which emerge from a joint processing operation. In April, the costs of production were as follows.

	$
Direct materials	24,000
Direct labour	2,000
	26,000

Production overheads are added using an absorption rate of 400% of direct labour costs. Output from the process during April was as follows.

Joint product	Output
D	600 litres
W	400 litres
F	400 kilograms
G	500 kilograms

Units of output of D, W, F and G are to be given weightings of 3, 5, 8 and 3 respectively for apportioning joint costs.

Required

Apportion the joint costs.

Solution

Total costs are $26,000 for direct costs plus $8,000 overhead. The costs would be $34,000, apportioned as follows.

Joint product	Output units	Weighting	Weighted units
D	600	3	1,800
W	400	5	2,000
F	400	8	3,200
G	500	3	1,500
			8,500

The costs are therefore apportioned at a rate of $34,000/8,500 = $4 per weighted unit.

Joint product	Apportionment of common cost
	$
D	7,200
W	8,000
F	12,800
G	6,000
	34,000

KEY POINT

You should be able to appreciate the **arbitrary nature of joint cost allocation**. The resulting product costs should never be used as a basis for decisions concerning process or product viability because the apparent relative profitability of the products has arisen due to the arbitrary apportionment of the joint costs.

9.9 The further processing decision

A different type of decision making problem with joint products occurs when there is a **choice between selling part-finished output or processing it further**. This decision problem is best explained by a simple example.

Example: Further processing

An organisation manufactures two joint products, A and B. The costs of common processing are $15,000 per batch, and output per batch is 100 units of A and 150 units of B. The sales value of A at split-off point is $90 per unit, and the sales value of B is $60 per unit. An opportunity exists to process product A further, at an extra cost of $2,000 per batch, to produce product C. One unit of joint product A is sufficient to make one unit of C which has a sales value of $120 per unit.

Should the organisation sell product A, or should it process A and sell product C?

Solution

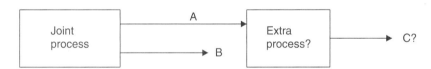

The problem is resolved on the basis that product C should be sold if the sales value of C minus its further processing costs exceeds the sales value of A.

	$
Sales value of C, per batch (100 × $120)	12,000
Sales value of A, per batch (100 × $90)	9,000
Incremental revenue from further processing	3,000
Further processing cost	2,000
Benefit from further processing in order to sell C	1,000 per batch

If the further processing cost had exceeded the incremental revenue from further processing, it would have been unprofitable to make and sell C. It is worth noting that the **apportionment of joint processing costs between A and B is irrelevant to the decision**, because the total extra profit from making C will be $1,000 per batch whichever method of apportionment is used.

KEY POINT

When there is a **choice between processing part-finished output further or selling it**, the further processing is worthwhile if the further processing cost is less than the incremental revenue gained from further processing.

Exam skills

You must be able to apportion joint costs using the four methods illustrated.

| **Question 1B.4** | Joint products decision |

Learning outcome A3(c)

PCC produces two joint products, Pee and Cee, from the same process. Joint processing costs of $150,000 are incurred up to split-off point, when 100,000 units of Pee and 50,000 units of Cee are produced. The selling prices at split-off point are $1.25 per unit for Pee and $2.00 per unit for Cee.

The units of Pee could be processed further to produce 60,000 units of a new chemical, Peeplus, but at an extra fixed cost of $20,000 and variable cost of 30p per unit of input. The selling price of Peeplus would be $3.25 per unit.

Required

Choose the correct words from those highlighted.

The organisation **should convert/should not convert** Pee to Peeplus.

9.10 Costing by-products

A by-product is a supplementary or secondary product (arising as the result of a process) whose **value is small relative to that of the principal product**. Nevertheless the by-product has some commercial value, and has to be accounted for.

| **Question 1B.5** | Accounting for by-products |

Learning outcome A(v)

Randolph manufactures two joint products, J and K, in a common process. A by-product X is also produced. Data for the month of December 20X2 were as follows.

Opening inventory	nil	
Costs of processing	direct materials	$25,500
	direct labour	$10,000

Production overheads are absorbed at the rate of 300% of direct labour costs.

		Production Units	Sales Units
Output and sales consisted of:	product J	8,000	7,000
	product K	8,000	6,000
	by-product X	1,000	1,000

The sales value per unit of J, K and X is $4, $6 and $0.50 respectively. The net realisable value of the by-product is deducted from process costs before apportioning costs to each joint product. Costs of the common processing are apportioned between product J and product K on the basis of sales value of production.

Required

Fill in the blanks in the sentences below.

The profit for December 20X2 is $ .... The profit attributable to product J is $ ...., while that attributable to product K is $ ....

Question 1B.6

Another joint products decision

Learning outcome A3(c)

Ruffage manufactures two products, T42 and 24T. These products are made jointly in process A, and then processed further, separately, with the manufacture of T42 completed in process B and 24T in process C. Costs and revenues for September were as follows.

2,000 tonnes of material (costing $36,000) were input to process A, 500 tonnes (costing $5,000) were added in process B and 1,000 tonnes (costing $8,000) were added in process C. Labour and overhead were $24,000 in process A, $20,000 in process B and $25,000 in process C.

Output from process A was 1,000 tonnes of part-finished T42 and 1,000 tonnes of part-finished 24T. At this stage in processing the sales value of T42 is $26 per tonne and of 24T is $39 per tonne. All completed output of T42 (1,500 tonnes) was sold in the month for $66,000 and all completed output of 24T (2,000 tonnes) was sold for $66,000.

Required

(a)   Calculate the profitability of each product in the month, assuming that joint costs in process A are apportioned using the following methods.

    (i)   On a physical units basis

    (ii)   On the basis of sales value at the point of separation

(b)   Comment on what these figures suggest about the following.

    (i)   Whether either product makes losses and ought not to be manufactured

    (ii)   Whether either product should be sold partially-finished as output from process A, instead of processed further in process B or C

Section summary

- **Features of joint products**

  (a) They are produced in the same process.

  (b) They are indistinguishable from each other until the separation point.

  (c) They each have a substantial sales value (after further processing, if necessary).

  (d) They may require further processing after the separation point.

- A **by-product** is a product which is similarly produced at the same time and from the same common process as the 'main product' or joint products. The distinguishing feature of a by-product is its relatively low sales value in comparison to the main product. In the timber industry, for example, by-products include sawdust, small offcuts and bark.

- Joint products are not separately identifiable until a certain stage is reached in the processing operations. This stage is the **'split-off point'**, sometimes referred to as the **separation point**.

- **Methods used to apportion joint costs to joint products**

  (a) Physical measurement

  (b) Relative sales value apportionment method 1; sales value at split-off point

  (c) Relative sales value apportionment method 2; sales value of end product less further processing costs after split-off point

  (d) A weighted average method

- The usual method of **accounting for a by-product** is to deduct its net realisable value from the cost of production of the main product.

Chapter Roundup

✓   Ensure your workings are shown clearly and your answer presented neatly to maximise your chances of gaining marks.

✓   In general terms, a **contract** will probably be **accepted** if it **increases contribution** and profit, and rejected if it reduces profit.

✓   If an organisation **does not have sufficient spare capacity, existing business** should only be **turned away if the contribution from the contract is greater than the contribution from the business which must be sacrificed.**

✓   The **minimum price** for a one-off product or service contract is its total relevant costs: this is the price at which the company would make no incremental profit and no incremental loss from undertaking the work, but would just achieve an incremental cost breakeven point.

✓   The decision to work an **extra shift** should be taken on the basis of whether the costs of the shift are exceeded by the benefits to be obtained.

✓   If an organisation has the freedom of choice about whether to **make internally or buy externally and has no scarce resources** that put a restriction on what it can do itself, the relevant costs for the decision will be the differential costs between the two options.

✓   The best approach to a complex **either/or problem** is to draw up a three-column table with columns for the first option (say, adapt now) and the second (say, adapt later), and a third column for the differences between the options (Column 1 minus Column 2).

✓   **Non-quantifiable factors** in **shutdown problems** include the impact on employees, customers, competitors and suppliers.

✓   Many of the decision scenarios covered in this chapter could be described as cost/benefit comparisons because you need to compare the costs and benefits associated with the decision in order to determine what action to take.

✓   **Features of joint products**

  –   They are produced in the same process.
  –   They are indistinguishable from each other until the separation point.
  –   They each have a substantial sales value (after further processing, if necessary).
  –   They may require further processing after the separation point.

✓   A **by-product** is a product which is similarly produced at the same time and from the same common process as the 'main product' or joint products. The distinguishing feature of a by-product is its relatively low sales value in comparison to the main product. In the timber industry, for example, by-products include sawdust, small offcuts and bark.

✓   Joint products are not separately identifiable until a certain stage is reached in the processing operations. This stage is the **'split-off point'**, sometimes referred to as the **separation point**.

✓   **Methods used to apportion joint costs to joint products**

  –   Physical measurement
  –   Relative sales value apportionment method 1; sales value at split-off point
  –   Relative sales value apportionment method 2; sales value of end product less further processing costs after split-off point
  –   A weighted average method

✓   The usual method of **accounting for a by-product** is to deduct its net realisable value from the cost of production of the main product.

Quick Quiz

1   Fixed costs should never be taken into account in an accept/reject decision. *True or false?*

2   What are the relevant costs in a make or buy decision?

      A   The sum of the relevant costs of the two options
      B   The opportunity costs associated with the decision
      C   The differential costs between the two options
      D   The incremental costs of the two options

3   *Choose the correct words from those highlighted.*

      In a situation where a company must sub-contract work to make up a shortfall in its own in-house capabilities, its total costs will be minimised if those units bought have the **lowest/highest** extra **variable/fixed** cost of **buying/making** per unit of scarce resource.

4   *Fill in the blank.*

      An organisation produces four products for which there is unlimited demand. Production capacity is limited. The organisation should concentrate on producing the product with the .... C/S ratio.

5   Sunny plc manufactures both work and leisure clothing. The company is considering whether to cease production of leisure clothing. List the **costs, which are relevant** to the decision to cease production.

6   Joint cost allocations are essential for the purposes of determining relative product profitability. *True or false?*

7   When deciding, purely on financial grounds, whether or not to process a joint product further, the information required is:

      (i)   the value of the joint process costs;
      (ii)   the method of apportioning the joint costs between the joint products;
      (iii)   the sales value of the joint product at the separation point;
      (iv)   the final sales value of the joint product;
      (v)   the further processing cost of the joint product.

      Which of the above statements are correct?

      A   (i), (ii) and (iii) only
      B   (iii), (iv) and (v) only
      C   (iv) and (v) only
      D   (i), (ii), (iv) and (v) only

8   *Choose the correct words from those highlighted.*

      A joint product should be processed further if **post-separation/pre-separation** costs are **greater than/ less than** the **increase in revenue/additional fixed costs**.

9   *Fill in the blanks.*

      The accounting treatment of a by-product usually consists of deducting the .... of the by-product from the .... of the main product.

Answers to Quick Quiz

1   False. Additional fixed costs incurred as a result of accepting the order must be taken into account.

2   C. You need to know the difference in cost between the two options.

3   lowest, variable, buying

4   highest

5   Those costs which will be saved if production of leisure clothing ceases (that is, all variable costs plus any fixed costs which are specific to producing and selling leisure clothing (such as advertising))

   •   Any closure costs such as the cost of equipment disposal and staff redundancies

   •   **Opportunity costs** such as the loss of any contribution which would have been earned from the continued manufacture and sale of leisure clothing

   •   The **opportunity costs** of continuing to produce leisure clothing such as the potential contribution which could be earned from using the capacity released to produce work clothing (although these costs will only occur if work clothing production has capacity constraints)

   Any fixed costs, which will continue whether or not leisure clothing ceases are not relevant.

6   False

7   B. Any costs incurred up to the point of separation are irrelevant.

8   post separation, less than, increase in revenue

9   net realisable value, cost of production

Answers to Questions

1B.1 Accept or reject

(a) Costs incurred in the past, or revenue received in the past are not relevant because they cannot affect a decision about what is best for the future. **Costs incurred to date of $50,000** and **revenue received** of $15,000 are 'water under the bridge' and should be **ignored**.

(b) Similarly, the **price paid in the past for the materials** is **irrelevant**. The only relevant cost of materials affecting the decision is the opportunity cost of the revenue from scrap which would be forgone – $2,000.

(c) **Labour costs**

	$
Labour costs required to complete work	8,000
Opportunity costs: contribution forgone by losing other work $(30,000 – 12,000)	18,000
Relevant cost of labour	26,000

(d) The **incremental cost of consultancy from completing the work** is $2,500.

	$
Cost of completing work	4,000
Cost of cancelling contract	1,500
Incremental cost of completing work	2,500

(e) **Absorbed overhead** is a notional accounting cost and should be **ignored**. **Actual overhead incurred** is the only overhead cost to **consider**. **General overhead** costs (and the absorbed overhead of the alternative work for the labour force) should be **ignored**.

(f) **Relevant costs** may be summarised as follows.

	$	$
Revenue from completing work		34,000
Relevant costs		
Materials: opportunity cost	2,000	
Labour: basic pay	8,000	
opportunity cost	18,000	
Incremental cost of consultant	2,500	
		30,500
Extra profit to be earned by accepting the completion order		3,500

The contract should be accepted as it will increase the company's profit.

1B.2 Deleting products

Production of product F should continue and so the statement is false.

	$	$
Revenue		200,000
Less: materials cost	157,000	
machine power cost	14,000	
type A overheads	28,000	
		199,000
Contribution		1,000

Production of product F should be continued, because it makes a contribution of $1,000 a year.

1B.3 Units method of splitting common costs

The correct answers are $3,091 and $3,291.

Joint product	Units produced	%	Apportionment of common costs $
P1	600	28.6	4,576
Q1	400	19.0	3,040
R	500	23.8	3,808
S	600	28.6	4,576
	2,100	100.0	16,000

Profit statement

	P1/2 $	Q1/2 $	R $	S $	Total $
Joint costs of production	4,576	3,040	3,808	4,576	16,000
Further processing	1,000	2,500	–	–	3,500
Cost of production	5,576	5,540	3,808	4,576	19,500
Less closing inventory	0	1,385	762	1,144	3,291
Cost of sales	5,576	4,155	3,046	3,432	16,209
Sales	6,000	6,000	2,800	4,500	19,300
Profit/(loss)	424	1,845	(246)	1,068	3,091
Profit/sales ratio	7%	31%	–	24%	16%

1B.4 Joint products decision

The correct answer is 'should convert'.

The only relevant costs/incomes are those which compare selling Pee against selling Peeplus. Every other cost is irrelevant: they will be incurred regardless of what the decision is.

	Pee			Peeplus
Selling price per unit	$1.25			$3.25
	$		$	$
Total sales	125,000			195,000
Post-separation processing costs	–	Fixed	20,000	
	–	Variable	30,000	50,000
Sales minus post-separation (further processing) costs	125,000			145,000

It is $20,000 more profitable to convert Pee into Peeplus.

1B.5 Accounting for by-products

The correct answers are $12,000, $5,250 and $6,750.

The **sales value of production** was $80,000.

	$
Product J (8,000 × $4)	32,000 (40%)
Product K (8,000 × $6)	48,000 (60%)
	80,000

The costs of production were as follows.

	$
Direct materials	25,500
Direct labour	10,000
Overhead (300% of $10,000)	30,000
	65,500
Less NRV of by-product (1,000 × 50p)	500
Net production costs	65,000

The **profit statement** would appear as follows (nil opening inventory).

		Product J $		Product K $	Total $
Production costs	(40%)	26,000	(60%)	39,000	65,000
Less closing inventory	(1,000 units)	3,250	(2,000 units)	9,750	13,000
Cost of sales		22,750		29,250	52,000
Sales	(7,000 units)	28,000	(6,000 units)	36,000	64,000
Profit		5,250		6,750	12,000

1B.6 Another joint products decision

(a)   (i)   **Units basis of apportionment**

	Product T42 $	Product 24T $	Total $
Process A costs (apportioned 1:1)	30,000	30,000	60,000
Process B costs	25,000	–	25,000
Process C costs	–	33,000	33,000
Total costs	55,000	63,000	118,000
Revenue	66,000	66,000	132,000
Profit	11,000	3,000	14,000

        (ii)   **Sales revenue basis of apportionment**

	Product T42 $	Product 24T $	Total $
Process A costs (apportioned 26:39)	24,000	36,000	60,000
Process B costs	25,000		25,000
Process C costs	–	33,000	33,000
Total costs	49,000	69,000	118,000
Revenue	66,000	66,000	132,000
Profit	17,000	(3,000)	14,000

(b)   (i)   Product 24T makes a loss when the sales revenue basis of apportionment is used, but not when the units basis of apportionment is used. The difference between income statement is due simply to how the common costs in Process A are shared between the two products.

Although product 24T **makes a loss by one method**, it would be **wrong to conclude that it should not be made at all**. If the company continues to make T42, it has got to make 24T as well, at least in process A, since the products are output jointly from a common process. And if product 24T does **make some contribution** towards covering fixed overheads, it is **worth making and selling**, if no better alternative exists.

(ii)   In this situation, there is some **choice**. Product 24T can either be sold as part-finished output from process A, for $39 per tonne, or processed further in process C. The **relevant analysis** of this decision would be:

	$
Revenue from process C output	66,000
Revenue obtainable from sale of process A output (1,000 × 39)	39,000
Extra revenue from further processing	27,000
Costs of process C	33,000
Possible loss in process C	(6,000)

Not all of the $33,000 of process C costs might be **avoidable**. If there are some fixed and unavoidable costs charged to process C, there would be a smaller loss incurred by operating process C instead of selling part-finished product 24T. It might even be profitable to run process C, for example if avoidable costs were only $25,000, say, out of the $33,000 total costs for process C.

Even so, the possibility ought to be drawn to management's attention that it **might be more profitable to close down process C and sell product 24T in its part-complete form**. Neither method of cost apportionment that we used brings out this information for management's attention, and so both methods of costing are **inadequate** in this respect.

Now try the question from the Exam Question Bank	Number	Level	Marks	Time
	Q3	Examination	25	45 mins

LIMITING FACTOR ANALYSIS

You have **already encountered limiting factor analysis** in your earlier studies and so we have included at the beginning of this chapter a reminder of the key concepts and basic techniques involved in this approach to allocating resources. Work through the examples and do the questions in **Section 1** to ensure that you are perfectly happy with the basics.

You need to build on this knowledge, however, and deal with situations in which organisations have 'restricted **freedom of action'**. This type of problem is covered in **Section 2**.

In **Section 3** we will be considering the approach to take if an organisation has to buy in some of its products because it **cannot make sufficient quantities in-house** to meet demand.

Shadow prices are covered in **Section 4**. Some students find it quite difficult to get their head around the concept so go over the material a number of times if necessary until you really understand it.

We end the chapter by looking at the issues to bear in mind when **using limiting factor analysis**.
Limiting factor analysis can only be used if there is **one** limiting factor. If there are **two or more limiting factors**, a technique known as linear programming must be applied. This is covered in **Chapters 3 and 4**.

topic list	learning outcomes	syllabus references	ability required
1 Limiting factors	A1(a), 2(a)	A1(i)	analysis
2 Limiting factor analysis and restricted freedom of action	A1(a), 2(a)	A1(i)	analysis
3 Make or buy decisions and scarce resources	A1(a)	A1(i)	analysis
4 Limiting factors and shadow prices	A1(a)	A1(i)	analysis
5 Using limiting factor analysis	A1(a), 2(b)	A1(i), 1(ii)	analysis

1 Limiting factors

Introduction

All companies are limited in their capacity, either for producing goods or providing services. There is always one resource that is most restrictive (the limiting factor). This section looks at examples of how to deal with limiting factors when making production decisions.

KEY TERM

A LIMITING FACTOR is any factor that is in scarce supply and that stops the organisation from expanding its activities further, that is, it limits the organisations activities'. (CIMA *Official Terminology*)

Knowledge brought forward from earlier studies

Limiting factor analysis

- An organisation might be faced with just one limiting factor (other than maximum sales demand) but there might also be several scarce resources, with two or more of them putting an effective limit on the level of activity that can be achieved.

- Examples of limiting factors include sales demand and production constraints.

  - Labour. The limit may be either in terms of total quantity or of particular skills.

  - Materials. There may be insufficient available materials to produce enough units to satisfy sales demand.

  - Manufacturing capacity. There may not be sufficient machine capacity for the production required to meet sales demand.

- It is assumed in limiting factor analysis that management would make a product mix decision or service mix decision based on the option that would maximise profit and that profit is maximised when contribution is maximised (given no change in fixed cost expenditure incurred). **In other words, marginal costing ideas are applied.**

  - Contribution will be maximised by earning the biggest possible contribution per unit of limiting factor. For example if grade A labour is the limiting factor, contribution will be maximised by earning the biggest contribution per hour of grade A labour worked.

  - The limiting factor decision therefore involves the determination of the contribution earned per unit of limiting factor by each different product.

  - If the sales demand is limited, the profit-maximising decision will be to produce the top-ranked product(s) up to the sales demand limit.

- In limiting factor decisions, we generally assume that fixed costs are the same whatever product or service mix is selected, so that the only relevant costs are variable costs.

- When there is just one limiting factor, the technique for establishing the contribution-maximising product mix or service mix is to rank the products or services in order of contribution-earning ability per unit of limiting factor.

KEY POINTS

If resources are limiting factors, **contribution** will be **maximised** by earning the biggest possible contribution per unit of limiting factor.

Where there is just one limiting factor, the technique for establishing the contribution-maximising product or service mix is to rank the products or services in order of contribution-earning ability per unit of limiting factor.

Example: Limiting factor decision

Sausage makes two products, the Mash and the Sauce. Unit variable costs are as follows.

	Mash	Sauce
	$	$
Direct materials	1	3
Direct labour ($3 per hour)	6	3
Variable overhead	1	1
	8	7

The sales price per unit is $14 per Mash and $11 per Sauce. During July the available direct labour is limited to 8,000 hours. Sales demand in July is expected to be as follows.

Mash	3,000 units
Sauce	5,000 units

Required

Determine the production budget that will maximise profit, assuming that fixed costs per month are $20,000 and that there is no opening inventory of finished goods or work in progress.

Solution

 Confirm that the limiting factor is something other than sales demand.

	Mash	Sauces	Total
Labour hours per unit	2 hrs	1 hr	
Sales demand	3,000 units	5,000 units	
Labour hours needed	6,000 hrs	5,000 hrs	11,000 hrs
Labour hours available			8,000 hrs
Shortfall			3,000 hrs

Labour is the limiting factor on production.

 Identify the contribution earned by each product per unit of scarce resource, that is, per labour hour worked.

	Mash	Sauce
	$	$
Sales price	14	11
Variable cost	8	7
Unit contribution	6	4
Labour hours per unit	2 hrs	1 hr
Contribution per labour hour (= per unit of limiting factor)	$3	$4

Although Mashes have a higher unit contribution than Sauces, two Sauces can be made in the time it takes to make one Mash. Because labour is in short supply it is more profitable to make Sauces than Mashes.

 Determine the budgeted production and sales. Sufficient Sauces will be made to meet the full sales demand, and the remaining labour hours available will then be used to make Mashes.

(a)

Product	Demand	Hours required	Hours available	Priority for manufacture
Sauces	5,000	5,000	5,000	1st
Mashes	3,000	6,000	3,000 (bal)	2nd
		11,000	8,000	

(b)

Product	Units	Hours needed	Contribution per unit $	Total $
Sauces	5,000	5,000	4	20,000
Mashes (balance)	1,500	3,000	6	9,000
		8,000		29,000
Less fixed costs				20,000
Profit				9,000

Conclusion

(a) Unit contribution is *not* the correct way to decide priorities.

(b) Labour hours are the scarce resource, therefore **contribution per labour hour** is the correct way to decide priorities.

(c) The Sauce earns $4 contribution per labour hour, and the Mash earns $3 contribution per labour hour. Sauces therefore make more profitable use of the scarce resource, and should be manufactured first.

1.1 Two potentially limiting factors

You may be asked to deal with situations where two limiting factors are potentially limiting (and there are also product/service demand limitations). The approach in these situations is to find out which factor (if any) prevents the business from fulfilling maximum demand.

KEY POINT

Where there is a **maximum potential sales demand** for an organisation's products or services, they should still be ranked in order of contribution-earning ability per unit of the limiting factor. The contribution-maximising decision, however, will be to produce the top-ranked products (or to provide the top-ranked services) up to the sales demand limit.

Example: Two potentially limiting factors

Lucky manufactures and sells three products, X, Y and Z, for which budgeted sales demand, unit selling prices and unit variable costs are as follows.

		X		Y		Z	
Budgeted sales demand		550 units		500 units		400 units	
		$	$	$	$	$	$
Unit sales price			16		18		14
Variable costs:	materials	8		6		2	
	labour	4		6		9	
			12		12		11
Unit contribution			4		6		3

The organisation has existing inventory of 250 units of X and 200 units of Z, which it is quite willing to use up to meet sales demand. All three products use the same direct materials and the same type of direct labour. In the next year, the available supply of materials will be restricted to $4,800 (at cost) and the available supply of labour to $6,600 (at cost).

Required

Determine what product mix and sales mix would maximise the organisation's profits in the next year.

Solution

There **appear to be two scarce resources**, direct materials and direct labour. This is not certain, however, and because there is a limited sales demand as well, either of the following might apply.

- There is **no limiting factor at all**, except sales demand.
- There is **only one scarce resource** that prevents the full potential sales demand being achieved.

 STEP 1 **Establish which of the resources, if any, is scarce.**

	X Units	Y Units	Z Units
Budgeted sales	550	500	400
Inventory in hand	250	0	200
Minimum production to meet demand	300	500	200

	Minimum production to meet sales demand Units	Required materials at cost $	Required labour at cost $
X	300	2,400	1,200
Y	500	3,000	3,000
Z	200	400	1,800
Total required		5,800	6,000
Total available		4,800	6,600
(Shortfall)/Surplus		(1,000)	600

Materials are a limiting factor, but labour is not.

 STEP 2 **Rank** X, Y and Z in order of contribution earned per $1 of direct materials consumed.

	X $	Y $	Z $
Unit contribution	4	6	3
Cost of materials	8	6	2
Contribution per $1 materials	$0.50	$1.00	$1.50
Ranking	3rd	2nd	1st

 STEP 3 **Determine a production plan.** Z should be manufactured up to the limit where units produced plus units held in inventory will meet sales demand, then Y second and X third, until all the available materials are used up.

Ranking	Product	Sales demand less units held Units	Production quantity Units		Materials cost $
1st	Z	200	200	(× $2)	400
2nd	Y	500	500	(× $6)	3,000
3rd	X	300	175	(× $8)	*1,400
		Total available			4,800

* Balancing amount using up total available.

Draw up a budget. The profit-maximising budget is as follows.

		X Units	Y Units	Z Units
Opening inventory		250	0	200
Add production		175	500	200
Sales		425	500	400

	X $	Y $	Z $	Total $
Revenue	6,800	9,000	5,600	21,400
Variable costs	5,100	6,000	4,400	15,500
Contribution	1,700	3,000	1,200	5,900

Exam alert

A question could ask you to calculate the optimum production plan for a business and the contribution that would result from adopting the plan.

Section summary

A **scarce resource** is a resource of which there is a limited supply. Once a scarce resource affects the ability of an organisation to earn profits, a scarce resource becomes known as a limiting factor.

If resources are limiting factors, **contribution** will be **maximised** by earning the biggest possible contribution per unit of limiting factor.

Where there is just one limiting factor, the technique for establishing the contribution-maximising product or service mix is to rank the products or services in order of contribution-earning ability per unit of limiting factor.

Where there is a **maximum potential sales demand** for an organisation's products or services, they should still be ranked in order of contribution-earning ability per unit of the limiting factor. The contribution-maximising decision, however, will be to produce the top-ranked products (or to provide the top-ranked services) up to the sales demand limit.

2 Limiting factor analysis and restricted freedom of action
5/12

Introduction

Companies are not always able to produce the profit-maximising mix of products or services due to certain restrictions on production or sales. This section focuses on such situations and how to arrive at the optimal solution.

2.1 Restrictions on freedom of action

In certain circumstances an organisation faced with a limiting factor on production and sales **might not be able to produce the profit-maximising product mix** because the mix and/or volume of products that can be produced and sold is also restricted by a factor other than a scarce resource.

(a) A contract to **supply a certain number of products** to a customer

(b) Production/sales of a minimum quantity of one or more products to **provide a complete product range and/or to maintain customer goodwill**

(c) Maintenance of a **certain market share** of one or more products

In each of these cases, the organisation might have to **produce more of a particular product or products than the level established by ranking** according to contribution per unit of limiting factor.

KEY POINT

Where companies are restricted in their freedom of what to produce, the optimum production plan must take minimum production requirements into account first. The remainder of the limiting factor can then be allocated in the normal way according to contribution per unit of that factor.

Example: Restricted freedom of action

Harvey is currently preparing its budget for the year ending 30 September 20X2. The company manufactures and sells three products, Beta, Delta and Gamma.

The unit selling price and cost structure of each product is budgeted as follows.

	Beta	Delta	Gamma
	$	$	$
Selling price	100	124	32
Variable costs:			
Labour	24	48	6
Materials	26	7	8
Overhead	10	5	6
	60	60	20

Direct labour rate is budgeted at $6 per hour, and fixed costs at $1,300,000 per annum. The company has a maximum production capacity of 228,000 direct labour hours.

A meeting of the board of directors has been convened to discuss the budget and to resolve the problem as to the quantity of each product which should be made and sold. The sales director presented the results of a recent market survey which reveals that market demand for the company's products will be as follows.

Product	Units
Beta	24,000
Delta	12,000
Gamma	60,000

The production director proposes that since Gamma only contributes $12 per unit, the product should no longer be produced, and the surplus capacity transferred to produce additional quantities of Beta and Delta. The sales director does not agree with the proposal. Gamma is considered necessary to complement the product range and to maintain customer goodwill. If Gamma is not offered, the sales director believes that sales of Beta and Delta will be seriously affected. After further discussion the board decided that a minimum of 10,000 units of each product should be produced. The remaining production capacity would then be allocated so as to achieve the maximum profit possible.

Required

Prepare a budget statement which clearly shows the maximum profit which could be achieved in the year ending 30 September 20X2.

Solution

 STEP 1   **Ascertain whether labour hours are a scarce resource.**

	Units demanded	Labour hours per unit	Total labour hours
Beta	24,000	4 ($24/$6)	96,000
Delta	12,000	8 ($48/$6)	96,000
Gamma	60,000	1 ($6/$6)	60,000
			252,000

 STEP 2   **Rank the products.**

Since only 228,000 hours are available we need to establish which product earns the greatest contribution per labour hour.

	Beta	Delta	Gamma
Contribution ($)	40	64	12
Labour hours	4	8	1
Contribution per labour hour	$10	$8	$12
Ranking	2nd	3rd	1st

 STEP 3   **Determine a production plan.**

The optimum production plan must take into account the requirement that 10,000 units of each product are produced, and then allocate the remaining hours according to the above ranking.

		Hours
Beta	10,000 units × 4 hours	40,000
Delta	10,000 units × 8 hours	80,000
Gamma	10,000 units × 1 hour	10,000
		130,000
Gamma	50,000 units × 1 hour (full demand)	50,000
Beta	12,000 units × 4 hours (balance)	48,000
		228,000

 STEP 4   **Draw up a budget.**

BUDGET STATEMENT

	$
Contribution	
Beta (22,000 units × $40)	880,000
Delta (10,000 units × $64)	640,000
Gamma (60,000 units × $12)	720,000
	2,240,000
Fixed costs	1,300,000
Profit	940,000

Question 2.1

Learning outcome A2(b)

JJ makes two products, the K and the L. The K sells for $50 per unit, the L for $70 per unit. The variable cost per unit of the K is $35, that of the L $40. Each unit of K uses 2 kgs of raw material. Each unit of L uses 3 kgs of material.

In the forthcoming period the availability of raw material is limited to 2,000 kgs. JJ is contracted to supply 500 units of K. Maximum demand for the L is 250 units. Demand for the K is unlimited.

What is the profit-maximising product mix?

Section summary

Where companies are restricted in their freedom of what to produce, the optimum production plan must take minimum production requirements into account first. The remainder of the limiting factor can then be allocated in the normal way according to contribution per unit of that factor.

3 Make or buy decisions and scarce resources   3/11, 5/13

Introduction

We have already met make or buy decisions in Chapter 1B. This section extends the decision-making process by introducing scarce resources and the issue of restricted freedom of choice.

3.1 Combining internal and external production

An organisation might **want to do more things than it has the resources for**, and so its alternatives would be as follows.

(a)   Make the best use of the available resources and ignore the opportunities to buy help from outside
(b)   Combine internal resources with buying externally so as to do more and increase profitability

Buying help from outside is justifiable if it **adds to profits**. A further decision is then required on how to split the work between **internal** and **external** effort. What parts of the work should be given to suppliers or sub-contractors so as to maximise profitability?

KEY POINT

In a situation where a company must **sub-contract work to make up a shortfall in its own in-house capabilities**, its total costs will be minimised if those units bought have the lowest extra variable cost of buying per unit of scarce resource saved by buying.

Example: Make or buy decision with scarce resources

MM manufactures three components, S, A and T using the same machines for each. The budget for the next year calls for the production and assembly of 4,000 of each component. The variable production cost per unit of the final product is as follows.

	Machine hours	Variable cost
		$
1 unit of S	3	20
1 unit of A	2	36
1 unit of T	4	24
Assembly		20
		100

Only 24,000 hours of machine time will be available during the year, and a sub-contractor has quoted the following unit prices for supplying components: S $29; A $40; T $34.

Required

Advise MM.

Solution

The organisation's budget calls for 36,000 hours of machine time, if all the components are to be produced in-house. Only 24,000 hours are available, and so there is a shortfall of 12,000 hours of machine time, which is therefore a limiting factor. The shortage can be overcome by subcontracting the equivalent of 12,000 machine hours' output to the subcontractor.

The assembly costs are not relevant costs because they are unaffected by the decision.

The decision rule is to **minimise the extra variable costs of sub-contracting per unit of scarce resource saved** (that is, per machine hour saved).

	S	A	T
	$	$	$
Variable cost of making	20	36	24
Variable cost of buying	29	40	34
Extra variable cost of buying	9	4	10
Machine hours saved by buying	3 hrs	2 hrs	4 hrs
Extra variable cost of buying per hour saved	$3	$2	$2.50

This analysis shows that it is **cheaper to buy A than to buy T** and it is **most expensive to buy S**. The **priority for making** the components in-house will be in the **reverse order**: S, then T, then A. There are enough machine hours to make all 4,000 units of S (12,000 hours) and to produce 3,000 units of T (another 12,000 hours). 12,000 hours' production of T and A must be sub-contracted.

The cost-minimising and so profit-maximising make and buy schedule is as follows.

Component	Machine hours used/saved	Number of units	Unit variable cost	Total variable cost
			$	$
Make: S	12,000	4,000	20	80,000
T	12,000	3,000	24	72,000
	24,000			152,000
Buy: T	4,000	1,000	34	34,000
A	8,000	4,000	40	160,000
	12,000			346,000

Total variable cost of components, excluding assembly costs

Question 2.2   Make or buy and limiting factors

Learning outcome A2(b)

TW manufactures two products, the D and the E, using the same material for each. Annual demand for the D is 9,000 units, while demand for the E is 12,000 units. The variable production cost per unit of the D is $10, that of the E $15. The D requires 3.5 kgs of raw material per unit, the E requires 8 kgs of raw material per unit. Supply of raw material will be limited to 87,500 kgs during the year.

A sub contractor has quoted prices of $17 per unit for the D and $25 per unit for the E to supply the product. How many of each product should TW manufacture in order to maximise profits?

Required

Fill in the blanks in the sentence below.

TW should manufacture .... units of D and .... units of E to maximise profits.

Section summary

In a situation where a company must **sub-contract work to make up a shortfall in its own in-house capabilities**, its total costs will be minimised if those units bought have the lowest extra variable cost of buying per unit of scarce resource saved by buying.

4 Limiting factors and shadow prices   11/12

Introduction

You will meet shadow prices when you cover linear programming in Chapters 3 and 4. However they are relevant wherever there are scarce resources. This section deals with the concept of shadow prices and their relevance to short-term decision-making.

4.1 Shadow prices and opportunity costs

KEY TERM

A SHADOW PRICE is 'An increase in value which would be created by having available one additional unit of a limiting resource at the original cost'.   (CIMA *Official Terminology*)

Whenever there are limiting factors, there will be **opportunity costs**. As you know, these are the **benefits forgone by using a limiting factor in one way instead of in the next most profitable way.**

For example, suppose that an organisation provides two services X and Y, which earn a contribution of $24 and $18 per unit respectively. Service X requires 4 labour hours, and service Y 2 hours. Only 5,000 labour hours are available, and potential demand is for 1,000 of each of X and Y.

Labour hours would be a limiting factor, and with X earning $6 per hour and Y earning $9 per hour, the profit-maximising decision would be as follows.

	Services	Hours	Contribution $
Y	1,000	2,000	18,000
X (balance)	750	3,000	18,000
		5,000	36,000

Priority is given to Y because the **opportunity cost** of providing Y instead of more of X is $6 per hour (X's contribution per labour hour), and since Y earns $9 per hour, the incremental benefit of providing Y instead of X would be $3 per hour.

If extra labour hours could be made available, more X (up to 1,000) would be provided, and an extra contribution of $6 per hour could be earned. Similarly, if fewer labour hours were available, the decision would be to provide fewer X and to keep provision of Y at 1,000, and so the loss of labour hours would cost the organisation $6 per hour in lost contribution. This $6 per hour, the **marginal contribution-earning potential of the limiting factor at the profit-maximising output level**, is referred to as the **shadow price** (or **dual price**) of the limiting factor.

Note that the shadow price only applies while the extra unit of resource can be obtained at its normal variable cost. The shadow price also indicates the amount by which contribution could fall if an organisation is deprived of one unit of the resource.

The shadow price of a resource is its **internal opportunity cost.** This is the marginal contribution towards fixed costs and profit that can be earned for each unit of the limiting factor that is available. A knowledge of the shadow price of a resource will help managers to decide how much it is worth paying to acquire another unit of the resource.

Section summary

The **shadow price** or **dual price** of a limiting factor is the increase in value which would be created by having one additional unit of the limiting factor at the original cost.

5 Using limiting factor analysis

Introduction

Limiting factor analysis provides us with a profit-maximising product mix, within the assumptions made. It is important to remember, however, that other considerations, so far not fully considered in our examples, might entirely alter the decision reached. These issues are considered here.

Exam alert

Don't ignore this wordy section – if you were to get a full limiting factor analysis question in the exam there would undoubtedly be marks for discussion of pertinent non-quantifiable issues.

5.1 Non-quantifiable factors

The following table gives examples of non-quantifiable factors that may have an effect on the final decision reached.

Factor	Examples
Demand	Will the decision reached (perhaps to make and sell just one product rather than two) have a harmful effect on customer loyalty and sales demand? For example, a manufacturer of knives and forks could not expect to cease production of knives without affecting sales demand for the forks.
Long-term effects	Is the decision going to affect the long-term as well as the short-term plans of the organisation? If a particular product is not produced, or produced at a level below sales demand, is it likely that competitors will take over vacated markets? Labour skilled in the manufacture of the product may be lost and a decision to reopen or expand production of the product in the future may not be possible.
Labour	If labour is a limiting factor, is it because the skills required are difficult to obtain, perhaps because the organisation is using very old-fashioned production methods, or is the organisation a high-tech newcomer in a low-tech area? Or perhaps the conditions of work are so unappealing that people simply do not want to work for the organisation.
Other limiting factors	The same sort of questions should be asked whatever the limiting factor. If machine hours are in short supply is this because more machines are needed, or newer, more reliable and efficient machines? If materials are in short supply, what are competitors doing? Have they found an equivalent or better substitute? Is it time to redesign the product?

5.2 Assumptions in limiting factor analysis

When you are dealing with short-term decision-making questions, certain assumptions have to be made. If any of the assumptions are not valid, then the profit-maximising decision might be different. These assumptions are as follows.

(a) **Fixed costs will be the same** regardless of the decision that is taken, and so the profit-maximising and contribution-maximising output level will be the same.

   This will not necessarily be true, since some fixed costs might be directly attributable to a product or service. A decision to reduce or cease altogether activity on a product or service might therefore result in some fixed cost savings, which would have to be taken into account.

(b) **The unit variable cost is constant,** regardless of the output quantity of a product or service. This implies the following.

   (i)   The price of resources will be unchanged regardless of quantity; for example, there will be no bulk purchase discount of raw materials.

   (ii) Efficiency and productivity levels will be unchanged; regardless of output quantity the direct labour productivity, the machine time per unit, and the materials consumption per unit will remain the same.

(c) **The estimates of sales demand** for each product, and the **resources required** to make each product, **are known with certainty**.

   In the example in Section 1.2, there were estimates of the budgeted sales demand for each of three products, and these estimates were used to establish the profit-maximising product mix. Suppose the estimates were wrong? The product mix finally chosen would then either mean that some sales demand of the most profitable item would be unsatisfied, or that production would exceed sales demand, leaving some inventory unsold. Clearly, once a profit-maximising output decision is reached, management will have to keep their decision under continual review, and adjust their decision as appropriate in the light of actual results.

(d) **Units of output are divisible**, and a profit-maximising solution might include fractions of units as the optimum output level.

Where fractional answers are not realistic, some rounding of the figures will be necessary.

Exam skills

An examination problem might present you with a situation in which there is a limiting factor, without specifically stating that this is so, and you will have the task of recognising what the situation is. You may be given a hint with the wording of the question.

(a) 'It is possible that the main raw material used in manufacturing the products will be difficult to obtain in the next year.'

(b) 'The company employs a fixed number of employees who work a maximum overtime of eight hours on top of the basic 36 hour week. The company has also agreed that no more staff will be recruited next year.'

In (a) there is a hint that raw materials might be a limiting factor. In (b), perhaps less obviously, a maximum limit is placed on the available labour hours, and so the possibility should occur to you that perhaps labour is a limiting factor.

If you suspect the existence of a limiting factor, some quick computations should confirm your suspicions.

(a) Calculate the amount of the scarce resource (material quantities, labour hours, machine hours and so on) needed to meet the potential sales demand.

(b) Calculate the amount of the scarce resource available (for example number of employees multiplied by maximum working hours per employee).

(c) Compare the two figures. Obviously, if the resources needed exceed the resources available, there is a limiting factor on output and sales.

Exam alert

Always remember to state any assumptions you make when answering limiting factor analysis questions. The marker will find them useful when working through your script as they may justify your approach to certain parts of the question.

Section summary

Non-quantifiable factors, such as effect on customer goodwill, ability to restart production and reasons for a resource being a limiting factor, should also be borne in mind in product mix decisions.

Various **assumptions** are made in limiting factor analysis.

- Fixed costs remain the same regardless of the decision taken.
- Unit variable cost is constant regardless of the decision taken.
- Estimates of sales demand and resources required are known with certainty.
- Units of output are divisible.

Chapter Roundup

- ✓ A **scarce resource** is a resource of which there is a limited supply. Once a scarce resource affects the ability of an organisation to earn profits, a scarce resource becomes known as **a limiting factor**.

- ✓ If resources are limiting factors, **contribution** will be **maximised** by earning the biggest possible contribution per unit of limiting factor.

- ✓ **Where there is just one limiting factor**, the technique for establishing the contribution-maximising product or service mix is to rank the products or services in order of contribution-earning ability per unit of limiting factor.

- ✓ Where there is a **maximum potential sales demand** for an organisation's products or services, they should still be ranked in order of contribution-earning ability per unit of the limiting factor. The contribution-maximising decision, however, will be to produce the top-ranked products (or to provide the top-ranked services) up to the sales demand limit.

- ✓ Where companies are restricted in their freedom of what to produce, the optimum production plan must take minimum production requirements into account first. The remainder of the limiting factor can then be allocated in the normal way according to contribution per unit of that factor.

- ✓ In a situation where an organisation must **subcontract work to make up a shortfall in its own in-house capabilities**, its total costs will be minimised if the units bought have the lowest extra variable cost of buying per unit of scarce resource saved by buying.

- ✓ The **shadow price** or **dual price** of a limiting factor is the increase in value which would be created by having one additional unit of the limiting factor at the original cost.

- ✓ **Non-quantifiable factors**, such as effect on customer goodwill, ability to restart production and reasons for a resource being a limiting factor, should also be borne in mind in product mix decisions.

- ✓ Various **assumptions** are made in limiting factor analysis.
    - – Fixed costs remain the same regardless of the decision taken.
    - – Unit variable cost is constant regardless of the decision taken.
    - – Estimates of sales demand and resources required are known with certainty.
    - – Units of output are divisible.

Quick Quiz

1 *Choose the correct word from those highlighted.*

When there is just one limiting factor, the product with the **biggest/smallest** contribution earning ability per unit of limiting factor should be produced first.

2 Which of the following is not an example of a limiting factor?

   A   Sales demand
   B   Materials
   C   Machine time
   D   Profit

3 Marginal costing ideas are applied in limiting factor analysis. True or false?

4 Put the following in the correct order of approach to adopt when dealing with limiting factor analysis and limited freedom of action.

   (a)   Allocate resource according to ranking
   (b)   Rank the products
   (c)   Take into account minimum production requirements

5 Choose the correct words from those highlighted.

If an organisation has to subcontract work to make up a shortfall in its own in-house capabilities, its total costs will be minimised if those units bought have the **highest/lowest** extra **variable cost/resource requirement** of buying per **unit of scarce resource/$** saved.

6 Fill in the blanks.

The shadow price of a scarce resource indicates the amount by which contribution would .... if an organisation were deprived of one unit of the resource. The shadow price only applies while the extra unit of resource can be obtained at its .... cost.

7 *Use the words listed below to fill in the blanks in the following statements about the assumptions in limiting factor analysis.*

Missing words: units of output; sales demand and resources required per unit; unit variable cost; fixed costs.

   (a)   .... will be the same regardless of the decision taken.

   (b)   The .... is constant, regardless of the output quantity.

   (c)   The estimates of .... are known with certainty.

   (d)   .... are divisible.

8 The following details relate to three services offered by DSF.

	V $ per service	A $ per service	L $ per service
Selling price of service	120	170	176
Direct labour	20	30	20
Variable overhead	40	56	80
Fixed overhead	20	32	40
	80	118	140
Profit	40	52	36

All three services use the same direct labour, but in different quantities.

In a period when the labour used on these services is in short supply, the most and least profitable use of the labour is:

	Most profitable	Least profitable
A	L	V
B	L	A
C	V	A
D	A	L

Answers to Quick Quiz

1   Biggest

2   D. Limiting factors are resources or demand.

3   True

4   (b), (c), (a)

5   Lowest
     Variable cost
     Unit of scarce resource

6   fall
     normal variable

7   (a)   Fixed costs
     (b)   Unit variable cost
     (c)   Sales demand and resources required per unit
     (d)   Units of output

8   B

	V	A	L
	$	$	$
Selling price per service	120	170	176
Variable cost per service	60	86	100
Contribution per service	60	84	76
Labour cost per service	$20	$30	$20
Contribution per $ of labour	$3	$2.80	$3.80
Ranking	2	3	1

Answers to Questions

2.1 Restricted freedom of action

	K	L
Contribution per unit	$15	$30
Contribution per unit of limiting factor	$15/2 = $7.50	$30/3 = $10
Ranking	2	1

Production plan	Raw material used kg
Contracted supply of K (500 x 2 kg)	1,000
Meet demand for L (250 x 3 kg)	750
Remainder of resource for K (125 x 2 kg)	250
	2,000

The profit-maximising mix is 625K and 250L.

2.2 Make or buy and limiting factors

The correct answer is: TW should manufacture 9,000 units of D and 7,000 units of E.

	D $ per unit	E $ per unit
Variable cost of making	10	15
Variable cost of buying	17	25
Extra variable cost of buying	7	10
Raw material saved by buying	3.5 kgs	8 kgs
Extra variable cost of buying per kg saved	$2	$1.25
Priority for internal manufacture	1	2

Production plan	Material used kgs
∴ Make D (9,000 × 3.5 kgs)	31,500
E (7,000 × 8 kgs)	56,000
	87,500

The remaining 5,000 units of E should be purchased from the contractor.

Now try these questions from the Exam Question Bank	Number	Level	Marks	Time
	Q4	Examination	10	18 mins
	Q5	Examination	10	18 mins
	Q6	Examination	10	18 mins

LINEAR PROGRAMMING: THE GRAPHICAL METHOD

 In the previous chapter we saw how to determine the profit-maximising allocation of resources when an organisation is faced with just one resource constraint. When there is **more than one resource constraint**, the technique of **linear programming** can be used. This technique can be applied to problems with the following features.

- There is a single objective, which is to maximise or minimise the value of a certain function. The objective in commercial decision making is usually to maximise contribution and thus maximise profit.

- There are several constraints, typically scarce resources, that limit the value of the objective function.

There are two linear programming techniques. The graphical method is used for problems involving two products. The simplex method is used if the problem involves more than two products.

We will be looking at the graphical method in this chapter. The simplex method is covered in the next chapter.

Section 1 provides a detailed step-by-step approach to graphical linear programming. Make sure that you really understand how to carry out each step before you move on to the next.

topic list	learning outcomes	syllabus references	ability required
1 The graphical method	A2(c)	A2(iii)	analysis
2 The graphical method using simultaneous equations	A2(c)	A2(iii)	analysis
3 Sensitivity analysis	A2(d)	A1(iv)	analysis

1 The graphical method   5/10, 3/12, 5/12, 3/13

Introduction

Linear programming is used when there is more than one scarce resource. This section looks at the steps involved in solving a linear programming problem using the graphical method. There are several steps in the process so make sure you understand each step before moving onto the next one.

1.1 A definition of linear programming

Before we work through the steps involved in solving this constraints problem using the graphical approach to linear programming, it is worth reading the CIMA *Official Terminology* definition of linear programming to get a glimpse of what we will be doing.

KEY TERM

LINEAR PROGRAMMING is 'The use of a series of linear equations to construct a mathematical model. The objective is to obtain an optimal solution to a complex operational problem, which may involve the production of a number of products in an environment in which there are many constraints'.

(CIMA *Official Terminology*)

Exam alert

Linear programming has been flagged by the examiner as an important topic that students have struggled with. Make sure you can construct the graph and interpret the results – question practise is essential.

Example: WX Ltd

The following example will be used throughout the chapter to illustrate the graphical method of linear programming.

WX Ltd manufactures two products, A and B. Both products pass through two production departments, mixing and shaping. The organisation's objective is to maximise contribution to fixed costs.

Product A is sold for $1.50 whereas product B is priced at $2.00. There is unlimited demand for product A but demand for B is limited to 13,000 units per annum. The machine hours available in each department are restricted to 2,400 per annum. Other relevant data are as follows.

Machine hours required	Mixing Hrs	Shaping Hrs
Product A	0.06	0.04
Product B	0.08	0.12

Variable cost per unit	$
Product A	1.30
Product B	1.70

Question 3.1   Constraints

Learning outcome A2(c)

What are the constraints in the situation facing WX Ltd?

1.2 Solving the problem using the graphical method: steps 1 – 3

KEY POINT

The steps in the graphical method are as follows.

1   Define variables.
2   Establish objective function.
3   Establish constraints.
4   Draw a graph of the constraints.
5   Establish the feasible region.
6   Determine the optimal product mix.

Let's start solving WX's problem.

Define variables

What are the **quantities that WX can vary**? Obviously not the number of machine hours or the demand for product B. The only things which it can vary are the **number of units of each type of product produced**. It is those numbers which the company has to determine in such a way as to obtain the maximum possible profit. Our variables (which are usually products being produced) will therefore be as follows.

Let x = number of units of product A produced.
Let y = number of units of product B produced.

Establish objective function

KEY TERM

The OBJECTIVE FUNCTION is a quantified statement of the aim of a resource allocation decision.

We now need to introduce the question of contribution or profit. We know that the **contribution on each type of product** is as follows.

		$ per unit
Product A	$(1.50 − 1.30) =	0.20
Product B	$(2.00 − 1.70) =	0.30

The **objective of the company is to maximise contribution** and so the **objective function to be maximised** is as follows.

Contribution (C) = 0.2x + 0.3y

Establish constraints

KEY TERM

A CONSTRAINT is 'An activity, resource or policy that limits the ability to achieve objectives'.

(CIMA *Official Terminology*)

The **value of the objective function** (the maximum contribution achievable from producing products A and B) is **limited by the constraints** facing WX, however. To incorporate this into the problem we need to **translate the constraints into inequalities involving the variables** defined in Step 1. An inequality is an equation taking the form 'greater than or equal to' or 'less than or equal to'.

(a) Consider the **mixing department machine hours** constraint.

   (i) **Each unit of product A** requires 0.06 hours of machine time. Producing five units therefore requires 5 × 0.06 hours of machine time and, more generally, **producing x units will require 0.06x hours**.

   (ii) Likewise producing **y units of product B will require 0.08y hours**.

   (iii) The total machine hours needed in the mixing department to make x units of product A and y units of product B is 0.06x + 0.08y.

   (iv) We know that this **cannot be greater than 2,400 hours** and so we arrive at the following inequality.

0.06x + 0.08y ≤ 2,400

Question 3.2   Inequalities

Learning outcome A2(c)

How can the constraint facing the shaping department be written as an inequality?

(b) The final inequality is easier to obtain. The **number of units of product B produced and sold is y** but this has to be **less than or equal to 13,000**. Our inequality is therefore as follows.

y ≤ 13,000

(c) We also need to add **non-negativity constraints** (x ≥ 0, y ≥ 0) since negative numbers of products cannot be produced. (Linear programming is simply a mathematical tool and so there is nothing in this method which guarantees that the answer will 'make sense'. An unprofitable product may produce an answer which is negative. This is mathematically correct but nonsense in operational terms. Always remember to include the non-negativity constraints. The examiner will not appreciate 'impossible' solutions.)

The **problem** has now been reduced to the following **four inequalities** and **one equation**.

Maximise contribution (C) = 0.2x + 0.3y, subject to the following constraints:

0.06x + 0.08y ≤ 2,400

0.04x + 0.12y ≤ 2,400

0 ≤ y ≤ 13,000

0 ≤ x

Question 3.3   Formulation of linear programming model

Learning outcome A2(c)

An organisation makes two products, X and Y. Product X has a contribution of $124 per unit and product Y $80 per unit. Both products pass through two departments for processing and the times in minutes per unit are as follows.

	Product X	Product Y
Department 1	150	90
Department 2	100	120

Currently there is a maximum of 225 hours per week available in department 1 and 200 hours in department 2. The organisation can sell all it can produce of X but EU quotas restrict the sale of Y to a maximum of 75 units per week. The organisation, which wishes to maximise contribution, currently makes and sells 30 units of X and 75 units of Y per week.

Required

Assume x and y are the number of units of X and Y produced per week. Formulate a linear programming model of this problem, filling in the blanks in (a) and (b) below.

(a)   The objective function is to maximise weekly contribution, given by C = ...

(b)   The constraints are:

Department 1 .... EU quota ....

Department 2 .... Non-negativity ....

1.3 Steps 4 and 5 – graphing the problem and establishing feasible region

A **graphical solution** is **only possible** when there are **two variables** in the problem. One variable is represented by the **x axis** of the graph and one by the **y axis**. Since non-negative values are not usually allowed, the graph shows **only zero and positive values of x and y**.

1.3.1 Graphing equations and constraints

A **linear equation with one or two variables** is shown as a **straight line on a graph**. Thus $y = 6$ would be shown as follows.

If the problem included a **constraint that y could not exceed 6**, the inequality $y \leq 6$ would be represented by the **shaded area of the graph below**.

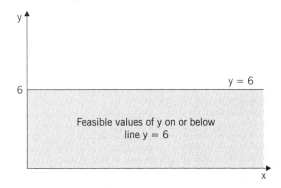

The equation $4x + 3y = 24$ is also a straight line on a graph. To **draw any straight line**, we **need only to plot two points and join them up**. The easiest points to plot are the following.

*   x = 0 (in this example, if $x = 0$, $3y = 24$, $y = 8$)
*   y = 0 (in this example, if $y = 0$, $4x = 24$, $x = 6$)

By plotting the points, (0, 8) and (6, 0) on a graph, and joining them up, we have the line for 4x + 3y = 24.

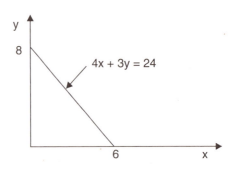

Any combination of values for x and y on the line satisfies the equation. Thus at a point where x = 3 and y = 4, 4x + 3y = 24. Similarly, at a point where x = 4.5 and y = 2, 4x + 3y = 24.

If we had a **constraint 4x + 3y ≤ 24, any combined value of x and y within the shaded area below (on or below the line) would satisfy the constraint.**

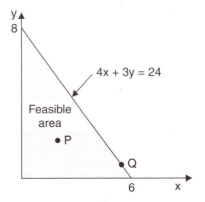

Consider point P which has coordinates of (2, 2). Here 4x + 3y = 14, which is less than 24; and at point Q where x = 5½, y = 2/3, 4x + 3y = 24. **Both P and Q lie within the feasible area** or **feasible region. A feasible area enclosed on all sides may also be called a feasible polygon.**

1.3.2 Establishing the feasible region

KEY TERM

A **FEASIBLE REGION** is 'The area contained within all of the constraint lines shown on a graphical depiction of a linear programming problem. All feasible combinations of output are contained within or located on the boundaries of the feasible region'. (CIMA *Official Terminology*)

When there are **several constraints**, the **feasible area** of combinations of values of x and y must be an area **where all the inequalities are satisfied**. Thus, if **y ≤ 6 and 4x + 3y ≤ 24** the **feasible area** would be the **shaded area** in the following graph.

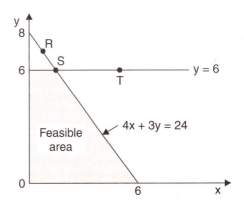

(a)   Point R (x = 0.75, y = 7) is not in the feasible area because although it satisfies the inequality 4x + 3y ≤ 24, it does not satisfy y ≤ 6.

(b)   Point T (x = 5, y = 6) is not in the feasible area, because although it satisfies the inequality y ≤ 6, it does not satisfy 4x + 3y ≤ 24.

(c)   Point S (x = 1.5, y = 6) satisfies both inequalities and lies just on the boundary of the feasible area since y = 6 exactly, and 4x + 3y = 24. Point S is thus at the intersection of the two lines.

Similarly, if y ≥ 6 and 4x + 3y ≥ 24 but x is ≤ 6, the feasible area would be the shaded area in the graph below.

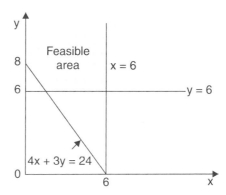

 Question 3.4   Feasible region

Learning outcome A2(c)

Draw the feasible region which arises from the constraints facing WX on the graph below.

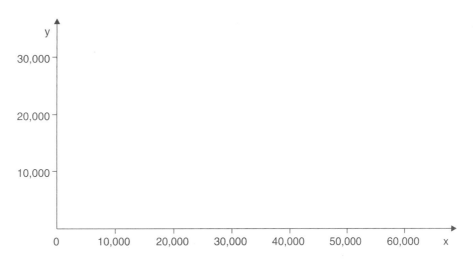

1.4 Step 6 – finding the optimum allocation of resources

KEY POINT

The **optimal solution** can be found by 'sliding the iso-contribution (or profit) line out'.

Having found the feasible region (which includes all the possible solutions to the problem) we need to **find which of these possible solutions is 'best'** or **optimal** in the sense that it yields the maximum possible contribution.

Look at the feasible region of the problem faced by WX (see the solution to the question above). Even in such a simple problem as this, there are a **great many possible solution points within the feasible area.**

Even to write them all down would be a time-consuming process and also an unnecessary one, as we shall see.

Here is the graph of WX's problem.

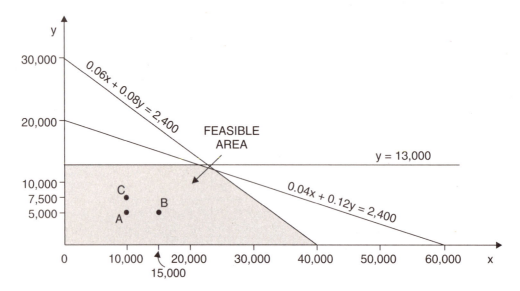

(a) Consider point A at which 10,000 units of product A and 5,000 units of product B are being manufactured. This will yield a contribution of (10,000 × $0.20) + (5,000 × $0.30) = $3,500.

(b) We would clearly get more contribution at point B, where the same number of units of product B are being produced but where the number of units of product A has increased by 5,000.

(c) We would also get more contribution at point C where the number of units of product A is the same but 2,500 more units of product B are being produced.

This argument suggests that the **'best' solution** is going to be at a **point on the edge of the feasible area** rather than in the middle of it.

This still leaves us with quite a few points to look at but there is a way in which we can **narrow down still further the likely points at which the best solution will be found.** Suppose that WX wishes to earn contribution of $3,000. The company could sell the following combinations of the two products.

(a) 15,000 units of A, no B.
(b) No A, 10,000 units of B.
(c) A suitable mix of the two, such as 7,500 A and 5,000 B.

The **possible combinations required to earn contribution of $3,000** could be **shown by the straight line 0.2x + 0.3y = 3,000.**

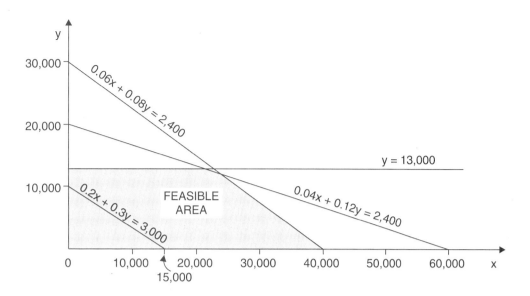

Likewise for profits of $6,000 and $1,500, lines of 0.2x + 0.3y = 6,000 and 0.2x + 0.3y = 1,500 could be drawn **showing the combination of the two products** which would **achieve contribution of $6,000 or $1,500.**

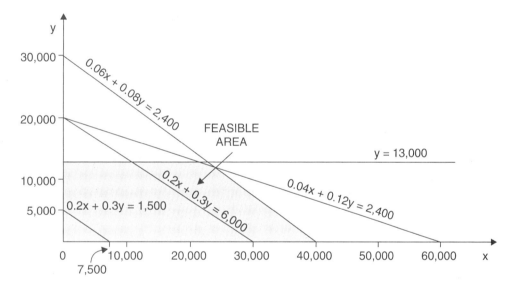

The **contribution lines are all parallel**. (They are called **iso-contribution lines**, 'iso' meaning equal.) A similar line drawn for any other total contribution would also be parallel to the three lines shown here. **Bigger contribution is shown by lines further from the origin** (0.2x + 0.3y = 6,000), smaller contribution by lines closer to the origin (0.2x + 0.3y = 1,500). As WX tries to increase possible contribution, we need to 'slide' any contribution line outwards from the origin, while always keeping it parallel to the other contribution lines.

As we do this there will come a point at which, if we were to **move the contribution line out any further, it would cease to lie in the feasible region**. Greater contribution could not be achieved, because of the constraints. In our example concerning WX this will happen, as you should test for yourself, where the contribution line just passes through the intersection of 0.06x + 0.08y = 2,400 and 0.04x + 0.12y = 2,400 (at coordinates (24,000, 12,000)). The point (24,000, 12,000) will therefore give us the optimal allocation of resources (to produce 24,000 units of A and 12,000 units of B).

Exam alert

You may be asked to prepare a graph to show the optimum production plan for a business and discuss how the graph could be used to help to determine a revised optimum production plan if the actual resources available were to change.

1.5 The graphical solution with a twist

Example

This example shows that it is not always necessarily easy to identify the decision variables in a problem.

DCC operates a small plant for the manufacture of two joint chemical products X and Y. The production of these chemicals requires two raw materials, A and B, which cost $5 and $8 per litre respectively. The maximum available supply per week is 2,700 litres of A and 2,000 litres of B.

The plant can operate using either of two processes, which have differing operating costs and raw materials requirements for the production of X and Y, as follows.

Process	Raw materials consumed Litres per processing hour		Output Litres per hour		Cost $ per hour
	A	B	X	Y	
1	20	10	15	20	500
2	30	20	20	10	230

The plant can run for 120 hours per week in total, but for safety reasons, process 2 cannot be operated for more than 80 hours per week.

X sells for $18 per litre, Y for $24 per litre.

Required

Formulate a linear programming model, and then solve it, to determine how the plant should be operated each week.

Solution

Define variables

You might decide that there are two decision variables in the problem, the quantity of X and the quantity of Y to make each week. If so, begin by letting these be x and y respectively.

You might also readily recognise that the aim should be to maximise the total weekly contribution, and so the objective function should be expressed in terms of maximising the total contribution from X and Y.

The contribution per litre from X and Y cannot be calculated because the operating costs are expressed in terms of processing hours.

	Process 1			Process 2	
	$ per hour	$ per hour		$ per hour	$ per hour
Costs:					
Material A		100			150
Material B		80			160
Operating cost		500			230
		680			540
Revenue:					
X (15 × $18)	270		(20 × $18)	360	
Y (20 × $24)	480		(10 × $24)	240	
		750			600
Contribution		70			60

The **decision variables** should be **processing hours in each process**, rather than litres of X and Y. If we let the processing hours per week for process 1 be P_1 and the processing hours per week for process 2 be P_2 we can now formulate an objective function, and constraints, as follows.

 Establish objective function

Maximise $70P_1 + 60P_2$ (total contribution) subject to the constraints below

 Establish constraints

$$20P_1 + 30P_2 \leq 2,700 \text{ (material A supply)}$$
$$10P_1 + 20P_2 \leq 2,000 \text{ (material B supply)}$$
$$P_2 \leq 80 \text{ (maximum time for } P_2)$$
$$P_1 + P_2 \leq 120 \text{ (total maximum time)}$$
$$P_1, P_2 \geq 0$$

 Graph the problem

The graphical solution looks like this.

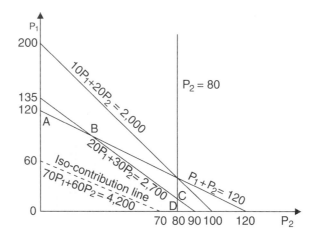

 Define feasible area

The material B constraint is not critical, and the feasible area for a solution is shown as ABCDO on the graph.

 Determine optimal solution

The optimal solution, determined using the iso-contribution line $70P_1 + 60P_2 = 4,200$, is at point A, where $P_1 = 120$ and $P_2 = 0$.

Production would be (120 × 15) 1,800 litres of X and (120 × 20) 2,400 litres of Y.

Total contribution would be (120 × $70) = $8,400 per week.

Question 3.5 | Determining the optimal solution

Learning outcome A2(c)

On 20 days of every month GS makes two products, the Crete and the Corfu. Production is carried out in three departments – tanning, plunging and watering. Relevant information is as follows.

	Crete	Corfu
Contribution per unit	$75	$50
Minutes in tanning department per unit	10	12
Minutes in plunging department per unit	15	10
Minutes in watering department per unit	6	15
Maximum monthly sales (due to government quota restrictions)	3,500	4,000

	Tanning	Plunging	Watering
Number of employees	7	10	5
Hours at work per day per employee	7	6	10
Number of idle hours per day per employee	0.5	1	0.25

Due to union restrictions, employees cannot be at work for longer than the hours detailed above.

Required

Use the graphical method of linear programming to determine the optimum monthly production of Cretes and Corfus and the monthly contribution if GS's objective is to maximise contribution.

Section summary

The **graphical method** of linear programming is used for problems involving two products.

The steps in the graphical method are as follows.

1　Define variables.
2　Establish objective function.
3　Establish constraints.
4　Draw a graph of the constraints.
5　Establish the feasible region.
6　Determine the optimal product mix.

The **optimal solution** can be found by 'sliding the iso-contribution (or profit) line out'.

2 The graphical method using simultaneous equations

Introduction

Instead of a 'sliding the contribution line out' approach, simultaneous equations can be used to determine the optimal allocation of resources. This section also considers the impact of slack and surplus in solving linear programming problems.

Example: Using simultaneous equations

An organisation manufactures plastic-covered steel fencing in two qualities: standard and heavy gauge. Both products pass through the same processes involving steel forming and plastic bonding.

The standard gauge sells at $15 a roll and the heavy gauge at $20 a roll. There is an unlimited market for the standard gauge but outlets for the heavy gauge are limited to 13,000 rolls a year. The factory operations of each process are limited to 2,400 hours a year. Other relevant data is given below.

Variable costs per roll

	Direct material $	Direct wages $	Direct expense $
Standard	5	7	1
Heavy	7	8	2

Processing hours per 100 rolls

	Steel forming Hours	Plastic bonding Hours
Standard	6	4
Heavy	8	12

Required

Calculate the allocation of resources and hence the production mix which will maximise total contribution.

Solution

Define variables

Let the number of rolls of standard gauge to be produced be x and the number of rolls of heavy gauge be y.

Establish objective function

Standard gauge produces a contribution of $2 per roll ($15 – $(5 + 7 + 1)) and heavy gauge a contribution of $3 ($20 – $(7 + 8 + 2)).

Therefore the objective is to maximise contribution (C) = 2x + 3y subject to the constraints below.

Establish constraints

The constraints are as follows.

$$0.06x + 0.08y \leq 2,400 \quad \text{(steel forming hours)}$$
$$0.04x + 0.12y \leq 2,400 \quad \text{(plastic bonding hours)}$$
$$y \leq 13,000 \quad \text{(demand for heavy gauge)}$$
$$x, y \geq 0 \quad \text{(non-negativity)}$$

Graph problem

The graph of the problem can now be drawn.

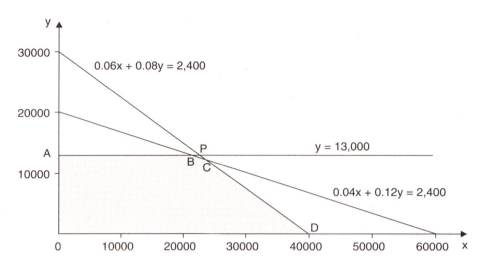

STEP 5

Define feasible area

The combinations of x and y that satisfy all three constraints are represented by the area OABCD.

STEP 6

Determine optimal solution

Which combination will maximise contribution? Obviously, the more units of x and y, the bigger the contribution will be, and the optimal solution will be at point B, C or D. It will not be at A, since at A, y = 13,000 and x = 0, whereas at B, y = 13,000 (the same) and x is greater than zero.

Using simultaneous equations to calculate the value of x and y at each of points B, C and D, and then working out total contribution at each point from this, we can establish the contribution-maximising product mix.

Point B

$$
\begin{array}{rcl}
y & = & 13,000 \ (1) \\
0.04x + 0.12y & = & 2,400 \ (2) \\
0.12y & = & 1,560 \ (3) \ ((1) \times 0.12) \\
0.04x & = & 840 \ (4) \ ((2) - (3)) \\
x & = & 21,000 \ (5)
\end{array}
$$

Total contribution = (21,000 × \$2) + (13,000 × \$3) = \$81,000.

Point C

$$
\begin{array}{rcl}
0.06x + 0.08y & = & 2,400 \ (1) \\
0.04x + 0.12y & = & 2,400 \ (2) \\
0.12x + 0.16y & = & 4,800 \ (3) \ ((1) \times 2) \\
0.12x + 0.36y & = & 7,200 \ (4) \ ((2) \times 3) \\
0.2y & = & 2,400 \ (5) \ ((4) - (3)) \\
y & = & 12,000 \ (6) \\
0.06x + 960 & = & 2,400 \ (7) \ (\text{substitute in } (1)) \\
x & = & 24,000 \ (8)
\end{array}
$$

Total contribution = (24,000 × \$2) + (12,000 × \$3) = \$84,000.

Point D

Total contribution = 40,000 × $2 = $80,000.

Comparing B, C and D, we can see that contribution is maximised at C, by making 24,000 rolls of standard gauge and 12,000 rolls of heavy gauge, to earn a contribution of $84,000.

If you are finding it difficult to follow this approach, go back to your previous notes to revise how to solve simultaneous equations.

2.1 Slack and surplus

KEY POINT

Slack occurs when maximum availability of a resource is not used. **Surplus** occurs when more than a minimum requirement is used.

If, at the optimal solution, the resource used equals the resource available there is **no spare capacity** of a resource and so there is **no slack**.

If a resource which has a **maximum availability** is **not binding** at the optimal solution, there will be **slack**.

In the example above, the optimal solution is x = 24,000, y = 12,000.

If we substitute these values into the inequalities representing the constraints, we can determine whether the constraints are binding or whether there is slack.

Steel forming hours:	(0.06 × 24,000) + (0.08 × 12,000) = 2,400 = availability Constraint is **binding**.
Plastic bonding hours:	(0.04 × 24,000) + (0.12 × 12,000) = 2,400 = availability Constraint is **binding**.
Demand:	Demand of 12,000 ≤ maximum demand of 13,000 There is **slack**.

Note that because we had already determined the optimal solution to be at the intersection of the steel forming hours and plastic bonding hours constraints, we knew that they were binding!

If a minimum quantity of a resource must be used and, at the optimal solution, **more than that quantity is used**, there is a **surplus** on the minimum requirement.

For example, suppose in a particular scenario a minimum of 8,000 grade A labour hours had to be worked in the production of products x and y, such that (say) 3x + 2y ≥ 8,000. If 10,000 hours are used to produce the optimal solution, there is a surplus of 2,000 hours.

We will be looking at this form of constraint in the next section.

Section summary

Simultaneous equations can be used to solve linear programming problems rather than using the iso-contribution (profit) lines.

Slack occurs when maximum availability of a resource is not used. **Surplus** occurs when more than a minimum requirement is used.

3 Sensitivity analysis

Introduction

Sensitivity analysis is used to find out what would happen to the optimal solution if variables were **changed**. This is an essential process as variables such as the availability of material and labour and the contribution for individual products are not certain. This section focuses on how to carry out sensitivity analysis. Make sure you understand the concept of **shadow prices**.

KEY POINT

Sensitivity analysis with linear programming can be carried out in one of two ways.

(a) By **considering the value of each limiting factor or binding resource constraint**

(b) By **considering sale prices (or the contribution per unit)**

3.1 Limiting factor sensitivity analysis

We use the shadow price to carry out sensitivity analysis on the availability of a limiting factor.

3.1.1 Shadow prices

KEY TERM

The SHADOW PRICE or DUAL PRICE of a limiting factor is the increase in value which would be created by having one additional unit of the limiting factor at the original cost.

Question 3.6	Shadow prices 1

Learning outcomes A2(c), A2(d)

Choose the correct words from those highlighted.

A shadow price is the **increase/decrease** in **contribution/revenue** created by the availability of an extra unit of a **resource/limiting resource** at **its original cost/a premium price**.

So in terms of linear programming, the shadow price is the **extra contribution or profit that may be earned by relaxing by one unit a binding resource constraint**.

Suppose the availability of materials is a binding constraint. If one extra kilogram becomes available so that an alternative production mix becomes optimal, with a resulting increase over the original production mix contribution of $2, the shadow price of a kilogram of material is $2.

Note, however, that this increase in contribution of $2 per extra kilogram of material made available is calculated on the **assumption** that the **extra kilogram would cost the normal variable amount**.

Note the following points.

(a) The shadow price therefore represents the maximum **premium** above the basic rate that an organisation should be **willing to pay for one extra unit** of a resource.

(b) Since shadow prices indicate the effect of a one unit change in a constraint, they provide a measure of the **sensitivity** of the result.

(c) The **shadow price** of a constraint that is **not binding** at the optimal solution is **zero**.

(d) Shadow prices are **only valid for a small range** before the constraint becomes non-binding or different resources become critical.

Depending on the resource in question, shadow prices enable management to make **better informed decisions** about the payment of overtime premiums, bonuses, premiums on small orders of raw materials and so on.

3.1.2 Calculating shadow prices

In the earlier example of WX, the availability of time in both departments are limiting factors because both are used up fully in the optimal product mix. Let us therefore calculate the effect if **one extra hour of shaping department machine time** was made available so that 2,401 hours were available.

The **new optimal product mix would be at the intersection of the two constraint lines** $0.06x + 0.08y = 2,400$ and $0.04x + 0.12y = 2,401$.

Solution by simultaneous equations gives $x = 23,980$ and $y = 12,015$.

(You should solve the problem yourself if you are doubtful about the derivation of the solution.)

Product	Units	Contribution per unit $	Total contribution $
A	23,980	0.20	4,796.0
B	12,015	0.30	3,604.5
			8,400.5
Contribution in original problem ((24,000 × $0.20) + (12,000 × $0.30))			8,400.0
Increase in contribution from one extra hour of shaping time			0.5

The **shadow price of an hour of machining time in the shaping department is therefore $0.50**.

The **shadow price** of a limiting factor also shows by **how much contribution would fall if the availability of a limiting resource fell by one unit**. The **shadow price** (also called **dual price**) of an hour of machine time in the shaping department would again be calculated as $0.50. This is the **opportunity cost** of deciding to put an hour of shaping department time to an alternative use.

We can now make the following points.

(a)   The management of WX should be prepared to **pay up to $0.50 extra per hour** (ie $0.50 over and above the normal price) of shaping department machine time to obtain more machine hours.

(b)   This **value** of machine time **only applies as long as shaping machine time is a limiting factor**. If more and more machine hours become available, there will eventually be so much machine time that it is no longer a limiting factor.

Question 3.7	Shadow prices 2

Learning outcomes A2(c), A2(d)

What is the shadow price of one hour of machine time in the mixing department?

3.1.3 Ranges for limiting factors

We can calculate **how many hours will be available before machine time in the shaping department ceases to be a limiting factor.**

Look back at the third graph in Section 1.4. As more hours become available the constraint line moves out away from the origin. It ceases to be a limiting factor when it passes through the intersection of the sales constraint and the mixing department machine time constraint which is at the point (22,667, 13,000).

So, if x = 22,667 and y = 13,000, our new constraint would be 0.04x + 0.12y = H (hours) where H = (0.04 × 22,667) + (0.12 × 13,000) = 2,466.68 hours.

The shadow price of shaping department machine time is therefore $0.50 but only up to a maximum supply of 2,466.68 hours (that is 66.68 hours more than the original 2,400 hours). Extra availability of machine time above 2,466.68 hours would not have any use, and the two limiting factors would become sales demand for product B and machine time in the mixing department.

3.2 Selling price sensitivity analysis

KEY POINT

Selling price sensitivity analysis is carried out by changing the slope of the 'iso-contribution' line.

The optimal solution in our WX example was to make 24,000 units of product A and 12,000 units of product B. Would this solution change if the **unit sales price of A increased by 10c?**

The **contribution would increase** to 0.3x + 0.3y (in place of 0.2x + 0.3y). The **iso-contribution lines would now have a steeper slope** than previously, parallel (for example) to 0.3x + 0.3y = 3,000.

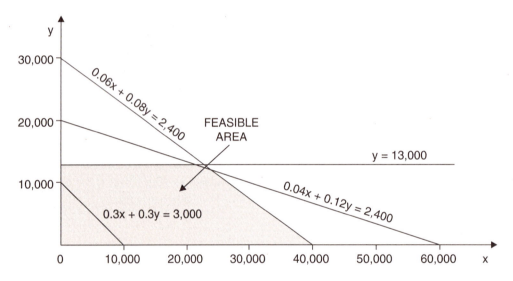

If you were to place a ruler along the iso-contribution line and move it away from the origin as usual, you would find its **last point within the feasible region** was the point (40,000, 0).

Therefore if the sales price of A is raised by 10c, WX's contribution-maximising product mix would be to produce 40,000 units of A and none of B.

Example: Sensitivity analysis

SW makes two products, X and Y, which each earn a contribution of $8 per unit. Each unit of X requires four labour hours and three machine hours. Each unit of Y requires three labour hours and five machine hours.

Total weekly capacity is 1,200 labour hours and 1,725 machine hours. There is a standing weekly order for 100 units of X which must be met. In addition, for technical reasons, it is necessary to produce at least twice as many units of Y as units of X.

Required

(a) Determine the contribution-maximising production plan each week.
(b) Calculate the shadow price of the following.

    (i) Machine hours
    (ii) Labour hours
    (iii) The minimum weekly demand for X of 100 units

Solution

Solution (a): production plan

The linear programming problem may be formulated as follows.

Define variables

Let x = number of units of X produced and y = number of units of Y produced.

Establish objective function

Maximise contribution (c) = 8x + 8y subject to the constraints below.

Establish constraints

4x + 3y	$\leq$	1,200 (labour hours)
3x + 5y	$\leq$	1,725 (machine hours)
X	$\geq$	100 (minimum demand)
Y	$\geq$	2x (technical constraint)
Y	$\geq$	0 (non-negativity)

Graph the problem

The graph of this problem would be drawn as follows, using 8x + 8y = 2,400 as an iso-contribution line.

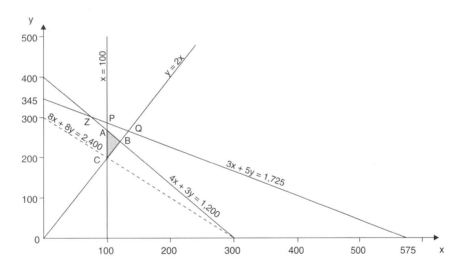

Establish feasible polygon

The feasible polygon is ABC. Using the slope of the iso-contribution line, we can measure that the contribution-maximising point is point A.

Determine optimal solution

At point A, the effective constraints are x = 100 and 4x + 3y = 1,200.

$\therefore$ If x = 100, (4 × 100) + 3y = 1,200

$\therefore$ 3y = 1,200 – 400 and so y = 266$^2/_3$

It is important to be aware that in linear programming, the optimal solution is likely to give values to the decision variables which are in fractions of a unit. In this example, contribution will be maximised by making 266$^2/_3$ units of Y.

	Contribution $
Make 100 units of X	800.00
266$^2/_3$ units of Y	2,133.33
Total weekly contribution	2,933.33

Solution (b): sensitivity analysis

(i) **Machine hours** are not fully utilised in the optimal solution. 100 units of X and 266$^2/_3$ units of Y need (300 + 1,333.33) = 1,633.33 machine hours, leaving 91.67 **machine hours unused**. Machine hours, not being an effective constraint in the optimal solution, have a **shadow price of $0**. Obtaining one extra machine hour would add nothing to the contribution.

(ii) The shadow price of **labour hours** would be obtained by calculating the total weekly contribution if the labour hours constraint were 1,201 hours. It should be possible to see fairly easily that the **new optimal solution** would be where x = 100 and 4x + 3y = 1,201. Therefore x = 100, y = 267 and total weekly contribution would be (100 + 267) × $8 = $2,936.

Since contribution with 1,200 labour hours as the constraint was $2,933.33, the **shadow price** of **labour hours** is $(2,936 – 2,933.33) = $2.67 per hour. This is the amount by which total contribution would rise if one extra labour hour per week were made available.

Note that there is a **limitation** to the number of extra labour hours that could be used to earn extra contribution. As more and more labour hours are added, the constraint line will move further and further away from the origin. For example if we added 800 labour hours capacity each week, the constraint 4x + 3y ≤ (1,200 + 800) (ie 4x + 3y ≤ 2,000) would be so much further away from the origin that it would no longer be an effective constraint. Machine hours would now help to impose limitations on production, and the profit-maximising output would be at point P on the graph.

Labour hours could only be added to earn more contribution up to point P, after which they would cease to be an effective constraint. At point P, x = 100 and 3x + 5y = 1,725. Therefore y = 285.

The labour hours required to make 100 units of X and 285 units of Y are (4 × 100) + (3 × 285) = 1,255 hours, which is 55 hours more than the initial constraint limit.

Total contribution at point P = (100 + 285) × $8 = $3,080. Since total contribution at point A, where labour hours were limited to 1,200 hours, was $2,933.33, the extra contribution from the 55 extra labour hours would be $(3,080 – 2,933.33)/55 = $2.67 per hour (as calculated previously).

Thus, the shadow price of labour hours is $2.67 per hour, for a maximum of 55 extra hours per week, after which additional labour hours would add nothing to the weekly contribution.

(iii) The shadow price of the **minimum weekly demand for X** may be obtained by calculating the weekly contribution if the minimum demand is reduced by one unit to 99, so that x ≥ 99, given no change in the other original constraints in the problem.

The new optimal solution would occur where x = 99 and 4x + 3y = 1,200. Therefore y = 268.

Total contribution per week when x = 99 and y = 268 is (99 + 268) × $8 = $2,936. Since the contribution when x ≥ 100 was $2,933.33, the **shadow price** of the minimum demand for X is $(2,936 – 2,933.33) = **$2.67 per unit**. In other words, by reducing the minimum demand for X, the weekly contribution can be raised by $2.67 for each unit by which the minimum demand is reduced below 100 per week.

As with the constraint on labour hours, this shadow price is **only applicable up to a certain amount.** If you refer back to the graph of the problem, you should be able to see that if the minimum constraint on X is reduced beyond point Z, it will cease to be an effective constraint in the optimal solution, because at point Z the machine hours limitation will begin to apply.

Question 3.8
Ranges for shadow prices

Learning outcomes A2(c), A2(d)

By how many units per week can the minimum demand be reduced before the shadow price of $2.67 per unit referred to above ceases to apply?

Section summary

The **shadow price** or **dual price** of a limiting factor is the increase in value which would be created by having one additional unit of the limiting factor at the original cost.

Selling price sensitivity analysis is carried out by changing the slope of the 'iso-contribution' line.

Chapter Roundup

✓   The **graphical method** of linear programming is used for problems involving two products.

✓   The **steps in the graphical method** are as follows.

- –   Define variables.
- –   Establish objective function.
- –   Establish constraints.
- –   Draw a graph of the constraints.
- –   Establish the feasible region.
- –   Determine the optimal product mix.

✓   The **optimal solution** can be found by 'sliding the iso-contribution (or profit) line out'.

✓   **Simultaneous equations** can be used for solving linear programming problems rather than using the iso-contribution (profit) lines.

✓   **Slack** occurs when maximum availability of a resource is not used. **Surplus** occurs when more than a minimum requirement is used.

✓   The **shadow price** or **dual price** of a limiting factor is the increase in value which would be created by having one additional unit of the limiting factor at the original cost.

✓   **Selling price sensitivity analysis** is carried out by changing the slope of the 'iso-contribution' line.

Quick Quiz

1   *Fill in the blanks in the statements below with one of the following terms.*

Objective function; decision variable; constraint; inequality; non-negativity constraints.

(a)   .... should be included when formulating linear programming solutions to ensure that the answer makes sense in operational terms.

(b)   An .... is an equation taking the form 'greater than or equal to' or 'less than or equal to'.

(c)   An .... is a quantified statement of the aim of a resource allocation decision.

2   *Choose the correct words from those highlighted.*

A feasible **polygon/area** enclosed on all sides is known as a feasible **polygon/area.**

3   *Put the following steps in the graphical approach to linear programming in the correct order.*

Draw a graph of the constraints
Define variables
Establish the feasible region
Establish constraints
Establish objective function
Determine optimal product mix

4   *Choose the correct words from those highlighted.*

When dealing with a problem in which there is a requirement to minimise costs, we look for a total cost line touching the feasible area at a tangent **as close to/as far from** the origin as possible.

5   The shadow price of a scarce resource is not the same as its dual price. True or false?

6   In what circumstances does slack arise?

A   At the optimal solution, when the resource used equals the resource available

B   At the optimal solution, when a minimum quantity of a resource must be used, and more than that quantity is used

C   At the optimal solution, when the resource used is less than the resource available

D   At the optimal solution, when a minimum quantity of resource is used

7   Draw the feasibility polygon for the following inequalities.

$2x + 3y \leq 12$
$y \geq 2x$
$x \geq 0, y \geq 0$

8   *Choose the correct words from those highlighted.*

If a **maximum/minimum** quantity of a resource must be used and, at the optimal solution, **more than/less than** that quantity is used, there is a surplus on the **minimum/maximum** requirement.

Answers to Quick Quiz

1   (a)   Non-negativity constraints
    (b)   Inequality
    (c)   Objective function

2   area

    polygon

3   Define variables
    Establish objective function
    Establish constraints
    Draw a graph of the constraints
    Establish the feasible region
    Determine optimal product mix

4   as close to

5   False

6   C. If a resource has a maximum availability and it's not binding at the optimal solution, there will be slack.

7   Start with the inequality $y \geq 2x$. The equation $y = 2x$ is a straight line, and you need to plot two points to draw it, such as (0, 0) and (2, 4).

    Since $y \geq 2x$, feasible combinations of x and y lie above this line (for example if x = 2, y must be 4 or more).

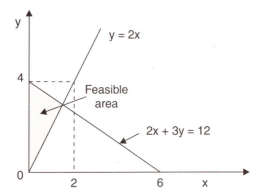

8   minimum
    more than
    minimum

Answers to Questions

3.1 Constraints

These are the constraints that will prevent WX Ltd from producing and selling as much of each product as it chooses.

The constraints are machine hours in each department and sales demand for product B. There is no restriction on the availability of labour hours. Selling price cannot be a constraint.

3.2 Inequalities

The constraint facing the shaping department can be written as follows:

$0.04x + 0.12y \leq 2,400$

The constraint has to be a 'less than equal to' inequality, because the amount of resource used ($0.04x + 0.12y$) has to be 'less than equal to' the amount available of 2,400 hours.

3.3 Formulation of linear programming model

(a)   The objective function is to maximise weekly contribution, given by $C = 124x + 80y$.

(b)   The constraints are:

Department 1	$150x + 90y$	$\leq$	225×60 minutes
Department 2	$100x + 120y$	$\leq$	200×60 minutes
EU quota	y	$\leq$	75
Non-negativity	x, y	$\geq$	0

These constraints can be simplified to:

Department 1	$15x + 9y$	$\leq$	1,350
Department 2	$10x + 12y$	$\leq$	1,200
EU quota	y	$\leq$	75
Non-negativity	x, y	$\geq$	0

3.4 Feasible region

If $0.06x + 0.08y = 2,400$, then if $x = 0$, $y = 30,000$ and if $y = 0$, $x = 40,000$.

If $0.04x + 0.12y = 2,400$, then if $x = 0$, $y = 20,000$ and if $y = 0$, $x = 60,000$.

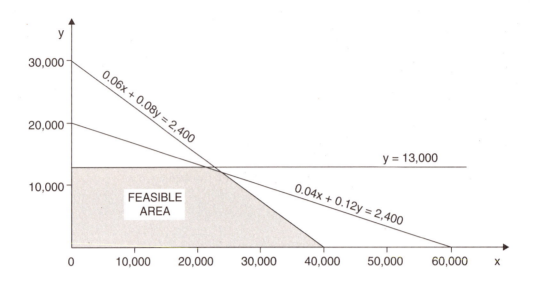

3.5 Determining the optimal solution

Calculate the number of productive hours worked in each department each month

Number of employees x number of productive hours worked each day x number of days each month.

Tanning	=	7 x (7 – 0.5) x 20 = 910 hours
Plunging	=	10 x (6 – 1) x 20 = 1,000 hours
Watering	=	5 x (10 – 0.25) x 20 = 975 hours

 STEP 1 **Define variables**

Let the number of Cretes produced each month = x and the number of Corfus produced each month = y.

 STEP 2 **Establish objective function**

The contribution is \$75 per Crete and \$50 per Corfu. The objective function is therefore maximise C = 75x + 50y subject to the constraints below.

 STEP 3 **Establish constraints**

Tanning	x/6 + y/5 ≤ 910
Plunging	x/4 + y/6 ≤ 1,000
Watering	x/10 + y/4 ≤ 975
Monthly sales units	x ≤ 3,500, y ≤ 4,000
Non negativity	x ≥ 0, y ≥ 0

STEP 4 **Graph the problem**

The problem can be solved using the following graph which includes a sample contribution line 75x + 50y = 150,000.

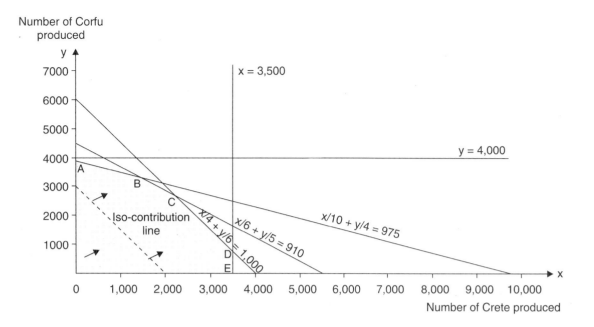

Define the feasible area

The feasible region for a solution is OABCDE.

Determine the optimal solution

Moving the sample contribution line across the feasible region it can be seen that the optimum solution is at any point along the line x/4 + y/6 = 1,000 between C and D (as the sample contribution line has the same gradient as the plunging constraint). The coordinates of point C are (2,175, 2,737.5) while those of point D are (3,500, 750).

The contribution from any of these solutions is $((75 × 3,500) + (50 × 750)) = $300,000 (using the coordinates of D).

3.6 Shadow prices 1

The correct answer is: A shadow price is the **increase** in **contribution** created by the availability of an extra unit of a **limiting resource** at its **original cost**.

3.7 Shadow prices 2

If we assume one **less** hour of machine time in the mixing department is available, the new optimal solution is at the intersection of $0.06x + 0.08y = 2,399$ and $0.04x + 0.12y = 2,400$

Solution by simultaneous equations gives x = 23,970, y = 12,010

Product	Units	Contribution per unit $	Total contribution $
A	23,970	0.20	4,794
B	12,010	0.30	3,603
			8,397
Contribution in original problem			8,400
Reduction in contribution			3

∴ Shadow price of one hour of machine time in the mixing department is $3.

3.8 Ranges for shadow prices

At point Z:	$4x + 3y = 1,200$	.... (1)
	$3x + 5y = 1,725$	.... (2)
Multiply (1) by 3	$12x + 9y = 3,600$	.... (3)
Multiply (2) by 4	$12x + 20y = 6,900$	.... (4)
Subtract (3) from (4)	$11y = 3,300$	
	$y = 300$	
Substituting in (1)	$4x + 900 = 1,200$	
	$4x = 300$	
	$x = 75$	

The shadow price of the minimum demand for X is $2.67 per unit demanded, but only up to a total reduction in the minimum demand of $(100 - 75) = 25$ units per week.

Now try these questions from the Exam Question Bank

Number	Level	Marks	Time
Q7	Examination	25	45 mins
Q8	Examination	10	18 mins

LINEAR PROGRAMMING: THE SIMPLEX METHOD

 The graphical method of linear programming, covered in Chapter 3, can only be used for decision problems with a maximum of **two** decision variables. For more complex problems the **simplex** method is needed as it can deal with **three or more decision variables**.

Section 1 covers the main principles of the method and shows you how to formulate a problem and interpret a solution. Whether the solution is presented in what is known as a tableau (**Section 1**) or as computer output (**Section 3**), sensitivity analysis can be carried out on the results (**Section 2**). Any exam question on simplex is more than likely going to require some form of sensitivity analysis.

Section 4 covers **issues** that you might need to raise to answer a **discursive** question or part question on simplex.

Once you have worked through this chapter you should be able to **formulate** an initial simplex tableau, **interpret** a final simplex tableau and **apply** the information contained in that final tableau.

topic list	learning outcomes	syllabus references	ability required
1 The principles of the simplex method	A2(b), (c)	A2(iii)	analysis
2 Sensitivity analysis	A2(c)	A2(iii)	analysis
3 Using computer packages	A2(c)	A2(iii)	analysis
4 Using linear programming	A2(c)	A2(iii)	analysis

1   The principles of the simplex method   11/10, 3/11, 5/13

Introduction

The simplex method is used to solve problems with two or more decision variables. This section focuses on the main principles of problem-solving using this method. Make sure you understand how to formulate an initial tableau and interpret a final tableau as you could be asked to do this in the exam.

KEY TERM

The SIMPLEX METHOD is a method of solving linear programming problems with two or more decision variables.

KEY POINT

The formulation of the problem using the **simplex method** is similar to that required when the graphical method is used but **slack variables** must be incorporated into the constraints and the objective function.

1.1 General points about the simplex method

KEY POINT

A **slack variable** represents the amount of a constraint that is unused.

In any feasible solution, if a problem involves n constraints and m variables (decision plus slack), n variables will have a positive value and (m–n) variables will have a value of zero.

Feasible solutions to a problem are shown in a **tableau**.

Before introducing an example to explain the technique, we will make a few introductory points. Don't worry if you get confused, working through the example will make things clearer.

(a)   The simplex method involves **testing one feasible solution after another**, in a **succession of tables or tableaux, until the optimal solution is found**. It can be used for problems with **any number of decision variables, from two upwards**.

(b)   In addition to the decision variables, the method introduces additional variables, known as **slack variables** or **surplus variables**. There will be **one slack (or surplus) variable for each constraint in the problem (excluding non-negativity constraints)**.

For example, if a linear programming problem has three decision variables and four constraints, there will be four slack variables. With the three decision variables, there will therefore be a total of seven variables and four constraints in the problem.

(c)   The technique is a **repetitive, step-by-step process**, with each step having the following **purposes**.

(i)   To **establish a feasible solution** (in other words, a feasible combination of decision variable values and slack variable values) and the **value of the objective function** for that solution.

(ii)   To **establish** whether that particular **solution** is one that **optimises** the value of the objective function.

(d)   Each feasible solution is tested by drawing up a **matrix** or **tableau** with the following rows and columns.

(i)   **One row per constraint, plus a solution row**
(ii)   **One column per decision variable and per slack variable, plus a solution column**

(e)   **Every variable**, whether a decision variable, slack variable or surplus variable, **must be ≥ 0 in any feasible solution**.

(f) A feature of the simplex method is that if there are **n constraints**, there will be **n variables with a value greater than 0 in any feasible solution**. Thus, if there are seven variables in a problem, and four constraints, there will be four variables with a positive value in the solution, and three variables with a value equal to 0.

Keep these points in mind as we work through an example.

Exam skills

Note that you do not need to be able to test solutions in the exam. You will be expected to be able to formulate an initial tableau, interpret a final tableau (optimal solution) and apply the information contained in the optimal solution.

Example: The simplex method

An organisation produces and sells two products, X and Y. Relevant information is as follows.

	Materials units	Labour hours	Machine time hours	Contribution per unit $
X, per unit	5	1	3	20
Y, per unit	2	3	2	16
Total available, each week	3,000	1,750	2,100	

Required

Use the simplex method to determine the profit-maximising product mix.

1.2 Formulating the problem

We have just two decision variables in this problem, but we can still use the simplex method to solve it.

Define variables

Let x be the number of units of X that should be produced and sold.

Let y be the number of units of Y that should be produced and sold.

Establish objective function

Maximum contribution (C) = 20x + 16y subject to the constraints below.

Establish constraints

The constraints are as follows.

Materials	$5x + 2y \leq 3,000$	Machine time	$3x + 2y \leq 2,100$
Labour	$x + 3y \leq 1,750$	Non-negativity	$x \geq 0, y \geq 0$

Introduce slack variables

Begin by turning each constraint (ignoring the non-negativity constraints now) into an equation. This is done by introducing slack variables.

Let S_1 be the quantity of unused materials, S_2 be the number of unused labour hours and S_3 be the number of unused machine hours.

Exam alert

An exam question could ask you to analyse the meaning of a number of values within a simplex linear programming model.

KEY TERM

SLACK VARIABLE. 'Amount of each resource which will be unused if a specific linear programming solution is implemented.'
(CIMA *Official Terminology*)

Question 4.1	Slack variables

Learning outcome A2(b)

A problem to be solved using linear programming has three decision variables, six constraints (including two non-negativity constraints) and one objective function.

How many slack variables will be required if the simplex method is used?

We can now express the original constraints as equations.

$$5x + 2y + S_1 = 3,000$$
$$x + 3y + S_2 = 1,750$$
$$3x + 2y + S_3 = 2,100$$

The slack variables S_1, S_2 and S_3 will be equal to 0 in the final solution only if the combined production of X and Y uses up all the available materials, labour hours and machine hours.

Values of variables – non-negative or zero?

In this example, there are **five variables** (x, y, S_1, S_2 and S_3) and **three equations**, and so in any **feasible solution** that is tested, **three variables** will have a **non-negative value** (since there are three equations) which means that **two variables** will have a value of **zero**.

Question 4.2	Values of variables

Learning outcome A2(b)

A problem to be solved using linear programming has seven variables and four equations based on the original constraints.

How many variables will have a value of zero in any feasible solution determined using the simplex method?

Express objective function as an equation

It is usual to express the objective function as an equation with the right hand side equal to zero. In order to keep the problem consistent, the slack (or surplus) variables are inserted into the objective function equation, but as the quantities they represent should have no effect on the objective function they are given zero coefficients. In our example, the objective function will be expressed as follows.

Maximise contribution (C) given by $C - 20x - 16y + 0S_1 + 0S_2 + 0S_3 = 0$.

1.3 Drawing up the initial tableau and testing the initial feasible solution

Exam skills

You will not be required to do this in the exam but seeing how the initial tableau is drawn up will give you additional insight into the technique.

We begin by testing a solution that **all the decision variables have a zero value**, and **all the slack variables have a non-negative value.**

Obviously, this is **not going to be the optimal solution**, but it gives us a starting point from which we can develop other feasible solutions.

Simplex tableaux can be **drawn in several different ways,** and if you are asked to interpret a given tableau in an examination question, you may need to adapt your understanding of the tableau format in this Study Text to the format in the question. The following points apply to all tableaux, however.

(a)   There should be a **column for each variable** and also a **solution column**.

(b)   It helps to add a **further column on the left**, to **indicate the variable which is in the solution to which the corresponding value in the solution column relates**.

(c)   There is a **row for each equation** in the problem, and a **solution row**.

Here is the initial matrix for our problem. Information on how it has been derived is given below.

Variables in solution	x	y	S_1	S_2	S_3	Solution
A (materials)	5	2	1	0	0	3,000
B (labour)	1	3	0	1	0	1,750
C (machine time)	3	2	0	0	1	2,100
Solution	–20	–16	0	0	0	0

(a)   The **figures in each** row correspond with the **coefficients of the variables in each of the initial constraints**. The bottom row or **solution row** holds the **coefficients of the objective function**. For example the materials constraint $5x + 2y + S_1 = 3,000$ gives us the first row, 5 (number of x's), 2 (number of y's), 1 (number of S_1's), then zeros in the S_2 and S_3 columns (since these do not feature in the constraint equation) and finally 3,000 in the solution column.

(b)   The **variables in the solution are S_1, S_2 and S_3** (the unused resources).

   (i)   The **value of each variable is shown in the solution column**. We are testing a solution that all decision variables have a zero value, so there is no production and hence no resources are used. The total resource available is therefore unused.

   (ii)   The **column values** for each variable in the solution are as follows.

      –   1 in the variable's own solution row
      –   0 in every other row, including the solution row.

(c)   The **contribution per unit obtainable from x and y** is given in the **solution row**. These are the **dual prices** or **shadow prices** of the products X and Y. The minus signs are of no particular significance, except that in the solution given here they have the following meanings.

   (i)   A **minus shadow price** indicates that the **value of the objective function can be increased by the amount of the shadow price per unit** of the variable that is introduced into the solution, given no change in the current objective function or existing constraints.

   (ii)   A **positive shadow price** indicates the amount by which the **value of the objective function would be decreased** per unit of the variable introduced into the solution, given no change in the current objective function or the existing constraints.

1.4 Interpreting the tableau and testing for improvement

We can see that the **solution is testing S_1 = 3,000, S_2 = 1,750 and S_3 = 2,100, contribution = 0.** **The coefficients for the variables not in this solution, x and y, are the dual prices or shadow prices** of these variables, given the solution being tested. A **negative value** to a dual price means that the **objective function can be increased**; therefore the **solution in the tableau is not the optimal solution**.

The **shadow prices** in the initial solution (tableau) indicate the following.

(a) The profit would be increased by $20 for every extra unit of x produced (because the shadow price of x is $20 per unit).

(b) Similarly, the profit would be increased by $16 for every extra unit of y produced (because its shadow price is $16 per unit).

Since the **solution is not optimal**, the **contribution may be improved by introducing either x or y into the solution**.

1.5 The next step

The next step is to **test another feasible solution**. We do this by **introducing one variable into the solution, in the place of one variable that is now removed**. In our example, we **introduce x or y in place of S_1, S_2 and S_3.**

The simplex technique continues in this way, producing a feasible solution in each successive tableau, until the optimal solution is reached.

1.6 Interpreting the final tableau

KEY POINT

If the shadow prices on the bottom (solution) row of a tableau are all positive, the tableau shows the optimal solution

- The solution column shows the optimal production levels and the units of unused resource.

- The figure at the bottom of the solution column/right-hand side of the solution row shows the value of the objective function.

- The figures in the solution row indicate the shadow prices of resources.

After a number of iterations, the following tableau is produced.

Variables in solution	x	y	S_1	S_2	S_3	Solution column
X	1	0	0	−0.2857	0.4286	400
S_1	0	0	1	0.5714	−1.8571	100
Y	0	1	0	0.4286	−0.1429	450
Solution row	0	0	0	1.1428	6.2858	15,200

This can be interpreted as follows.

(a) The solution in this tableau is the **optimal** one, because the **shadow prices on the bottom row are all positive.**

(b) The optimal solution is to **make and sell 400 units of X** and **450 units of Y, to earn a contribution of $15,200.**

(c) The solution will leave **100 units of material unused,** but will use up all available labour and machine time.

(d)   The **shadow price of labour time (S_2) is $1.1428 per hour**, which **indicates the amount by which contribution could be increased if more labour time could be made available at its normal variable cost.**

(e)   The **shadow price of machine time (S_3) is $6.2858 per hour**, which **indicates the amount by which contribution could be increased if more machine time could be made available, at its normal variable cost.**

(f)   The **shadow price of materials is nil**, because there are 100 units of **unused** materials in the solution.

Question 4.3	Formulation of problem

Learning outcome A2(b)

TDS manufactures two products, X and Y, which earn a contribution of $8 and $14 per unit respectively. At current selling prices, there is no limit to sales demand for Y, but maximum demand for X would be 1,200 units. The company aims to maximise its annual profits, and fixed costs are $15,000 per annum.

In the year to 30 June 20X2, the company expects to have a limited availability of resources and estimates of availability are as follows.

Skilled labour maximum 9,000 hours

Machine time maximum 4,000 hours

Material M   maximum 1,000 tonnes

The usage of these resources per unit of product are as follows.

	X	Y
Skilled labour time	3 hours	4 hours
Machine time	1 hour	2 hours
Material M	½ tonne	¼ tonne

Required

(a)   Formulate the problem using the simplex method of linear programming.

(b)   Determine how many variables will have a positive value and how many a value of zero in any feasible solution.

Question 4.4	Interpretation of final tableau

Learning outcome A2(c)

The final tableau to the problem in **Question 4.3: formulation of problem** is shown below.

Required

Interpret the tableau.

Variables in the solution	x	y	S_1	S_2	S_3	S_4	Solution column
X	1	0	0	−2	0	0	1,000
Y	0	1	−0.5	1.5	0	0	1,500
S_3	0	0	−0.375	0.625	1	0	125
S_4	0	0	−1	2	0	1	200
Solution row	0	0	1	5	0	0	29,000

Question 4.5

Learning outcome A2(c)

Here is the final tableau of a problem involving the production of products X and Y solved using the simplex method of linear programming.

Variables in solution	x	y	S_1	S_2	S_3	S_4	S_5	Solution column
X	1	0	−2.0	0	3.0	0	0	550
Y	0	1	−0.8	0	0.5	0	0	720
S_2	0	0	1.5	1	1.0	0	0	95
S_4	0	0	0.7	0	−1.1	1	0	50
S_5	0	0	2.0	0	1.8	0	1	104
Solution row	0	0	7.0	0	4.0	0	0	14,110

Required

Draw a ring around the column or row which shows the variables in the solution.

Question 4.6

Learning outcome A2(c)

Refer to the tableau in **Question: identification of variables**.

What is the profit-maximising product mix?

A   Make 95 units of S_2, 50 units of S_4 and 104 units of S_6

B   Make 550 units of X and 720 units of Y

C   Make 4 units of S_3 and 7 units of S_1

D   None of the above

Question 4.7

Learning outcome A2(c)

Refer to the tableau in **Question: identification of variables**. Suppose that variables S_1 to S_5 refer to the unused quantity of resources A to E.

Required

Fill in the blank in the sentence below.

.... units of resource A will be unused.

Question 4.8

Learning outcome A2(c)

Refer to the tableau in **Question: identification of variables**. **The shadow price of resource S_3 is $3**. *True or false?*

Section summary

A **slack variable** represents the amount of a constraint that is unused.

In any feasible solution, if a problem involves n constraints and m variables (decision plus slack), n variables will have a positive value and (m–n) variables will have a value of zero.

Feasible solutions to a problem are shown in a **tableau**.

If the shadow prices on the bottom (solution) row of a tableau are all positive, the tableau shows the optimal solution

- The solution column shows the optimal production levels and the units of unused resource.

- The figure at the bottom of the solution column/right-hand side of the solution row shows the value of the objective function.

- The figures in the solution row indicate the shadow prices of resources.

2   Sensitivity analysis

Introduction

Sensitivity analysis was covered in Chapter 3 in relation to the graphical method of linear programming. This section extends this topic to the simplex method but the aim is still the same. You might be asked to test how the optimal solution would change if the **availability** of a scarce resource **changed**. Alternatively you could be asked to test whether it would be worthwhile to **obtain more** of a scarce resource at a **premium price**.

2.1 The effect of having more or less of a scarce resource

The optimal solution to a linear programming problem is based on the assumption that the constraints are **known with certainty**, and **fixed in quantity**. Sensitivity analysis enables us to test how the solution would alter if the quantity of a scarce resource (the size of a constraint) were to change.

Example: The effect of having more or less of a scarce resource

Return to our previous example, and the optimal solution in Section 1.6, in which both labour hours and machine hours are fully used. How would the solution change if more labour hours (variable S_2) were available?

Solution

The simplex tableau, and in particular the **figures in the S_2 column,** provide the following information for each extra labour hour that is available.

(a)   The **contribution** would **increase** by $1.1428
(b)   The value of **x** would **fall by 0.2857 units**
(c)   The value of S_1 (unused materials) would **increase by 0.5714 units**
(d)   The value of **y** would **increase by 0.4286 units**

In other words, we would be able to make 0.4286 units of Y extra, to earn contribution of ($\times$ $16) $6.8576, but we would make 0.2857 units less of X and so lose contribution of ($\times$ $20) $5.714, leaving a net increase in contribution of $(6.8576 – 5.714) = $1.1436. Allowing for rounding errors of $0.0008, this is the figure already given above for the increase in contribution.

Since x = 400 in the optimal tableau, and extra labour hours would lead to a reduction of 0.2857 units of x, there is a **limit to the number of extra labour hours that would earn an extra $1.1428**. This limit is calculated as 400/0.2857 = 1,400 extra labour hours.

In other words, the **shadow price** of $1.1428 per hour for labour is **only valid for about 1,400 extra labour hours** on top of the given constraint in the initial problem, which was 1,750 hours, (that is up to a **total limit of 3,150 hours**).

If there were **fewer labour hours available**, the same sort of analysis would apply, but in reverse.

(a) The contribution would fall by $1.1428 per hour unavailable
(b) The value of x would increase by 0.2857 units
(c) The value of S_1 would fall by 0.5714 units
(d) The value of y would fall by 0.4286 units

Example: Obtaining extra resources at premium on cost

Suppose we are given the following additional information about our example.

(a) The normal variable cost of labour hours (variable S_2) is $4 per hour, but extra labour hours could be worked in overtime, when the rate of pay would be time-and-a-half.

(b) The normal variable cost of machine time is $1.50 per hour, but some extra machine time could be made available by renting another machine for 40 hours per week, at a rental cost of $160. Variable running costs of this machine would be $1.50 per hour.

Would it be worth obtaining the extra resources?

Solution

We know that the shadow price of labour hours is $1.1428 and of machine hours is $6.2858. We can therefore deduce the following.

(a) **Paying an overtime premium** of $2 per hour for labour **would not be worthwhile**, because the extra contribution of $1.1428 per hour would be more than offset by the cost of the premium, leaving the company worse off by $0.8572 per hour worked in overtime.

(b) **Renting the extra machine would be worthwhile**, but only by $91.43 (which is perhaps too small an amount to bother with).

	$
Extra contribution from 40 hours of machine time (× $6.2858)	251.43
Rental cost	160.00
Net increase in profit	91.43

Note that the variable running costs do not enter into this calculation since they are identical to the normal variable costs of machine time. We are **concerned here only with the additional costs.**

Question 4.9

Formulation

Learning outcome A2(c)

An organisation manufactures three products, tanks, trays and tubs, each of which passes through three processes, X, Y and Z.

Process	Process hours per unit			Total process hours available
	Tanks	Trays	Tubs	
X	5	2	4	12,000
Y	4	5	6	24,000
Z	3	5	4	18,000

The contribution to profit of each product are $2 for each tank, $3 per tray and $4 per tub.

Required

Fill in the blanks in (a) and (b) below, which relate to the formulation of the above data into a simplex linear programming model. Use the following notation.

Let   a be the number of units of tanks produced
        b be the number of units of trays produced
        c be the number of units of tubs produced
        S_1 = quantity of unused process X hours
        S_2 = quantity of unused process Y hours
        S_3 = quantity of unused process Z hours

(a)   Maximise contribution (C) given by .... subject to the following constraints in (b).

(b)   .... (process X hours)

      .... (process Y hours)

      .... (process Z hours)

Question 4.10

Interpretation

Learning outcome A2(c)

The final simplex tableau, based on the data in the question above, looks like this.

Variables in solution	a	b	c	S_1	S_2	S_3	Solution column
C	1.583	0	1	0.417	0	–0.167	2,000
S_2	–2.167	0	0	–0.833	1	–0.667	2,000
B	–0.667	1	0	–0.333	0	0.333	2,000
Solution row	2.333	0	0	0.667	0	0.333	14,000

Required

(a)   Determine how many of each product should be produced and the maximum contribution. Calculate how much slack time, if any, is available in the processes.

(b)   Explain how your solution would vary if an extra 3,000 hours of process X time could be made available.

(c)   Describe what would happen to the production schedule and budgeted contribution if an order were received for 300 units of tanks which the company felt that it had to accept, because of the importance of the customer. **Ignore** the increase of process X time in part (b) above.

Section summary

Sensitivity analysis can be applied to the final tableau to determine the effect of having more or less of a scarce resource (indicated by figures in the column for the resource's slack variable).

Sensitivity analysis can also be applied to test whether or not it would be **worthwhile to obtain more of a scarce resource** by paying a premium for additional supplies (only if the shadow price is greater than the additional cost).

3 Using computer packages

Introduction

Simplex problems are usually solved using one of a variety of computer packages. This section summarises the key outputs of such packages and how to interpret the results.

3.1 General points

Nowadays, modern spreadsheet packages can be used to solve linear programming problems.

Suppose an organisation produces three products, X and Y and Z, subject to four constraints (1, 2, 3, 4).

(a)   **Constraints 1 and 2 are 'less than or equal to' resource constraints**.

(b)   **Constraint 3 provides a limit on the number of X** that can be produced.

(c)   **Constraint 4 is a 'greater than or equal to' constraint** and provides for a **minimum number of Z** to be produced (400).

The organisation wishes to maximise contribution.

Typical output from a spreadsheet package for such a problem is shown below.

Objective function (c)		137,500
Variable	*Value*	*Relative loss*
X	475.000	0.000
Y	0.000	105.000
Z	610.000	0.000
Constraint	*Slack/surplus*	*Worth*
1	17.000	0.000
2	0.000	290.000
3	0.000	1,150.000
4	210.000	0.000

3.2 Interpretation

(a)   Total optimal **contribution (c)** will be $137,500.

(b)   The **variable** and **value columns** mean that x = 475, y = 0 and z = 610.

To maximise contribution, 475 units of X and 610 units of Z should therefore be produced. No units of Y should be produced.

(c)   The **constraint** and **slack/surplus** columns provide information about the slack values of 'less than or equal to' constraints and the surplus values for any 'greater than or equal to' constraints.

(i)   **Constraint 1** is a 'less than or equal to' resource constraint. The slack is 17 and so 17 units of resource 1 will be unused in the optimal solution.

     (ii)   **Constraint 2** is a 'less than or equal to' resource constraint. The slack is zero, indicating that all available resource 2 will be used in the optimal solution.

     (iii)   **Constraint 3** provides a limit on x. The slack is zero, showing that the limit has been met.

     (iv)   **Constraint 4** provides for a minimum z. The surplus is 210, meaning 400 + 210 = 610 units of Z are made.

(d)   **Worth**. This column shows the positive shadow price of resources (the amount that contribution (or, in general terms, c) alters if the availability of the resource is changed by one unit).

     (i)   Contribution would increase by $290 if one extra unit of resource 2 were made available.

     (ii)   Contribution would increase by $1,150 if the limit on the minimum number of Z to be produced altered by 1.

     (iii)   Resource 1 has a worth of 0 because 17 units of the resource are unused in the optimal solution.

KEY POINT

In general, any constraint with a slack of zero has a positive worth figure, while any constraint with a positive slack figure will have a worth of zero.

(e)   **Relative loss.** This indicates that if one unit of Y were produced, total contribution (or generally c) would fall by $105. A relative loss of $105 would therefore be made for every unit of Y made. Units of Y should only be made if unit contribution of Y increases by $105.

     X and Z have relative losses of zero, indicating that they should be made.

KEY POINT

In general, only those decision variables with a relative loss of zero will have a positive value in the optimal solution.

Section summary

Spreadsheet packages can be used to solve linear programming problems.

- The **slack/surplus** columns provide information about the slack values of $\leq$ constraints and the surplus values of any $\geq$ constraints.

- The **worth** column shows the positive shadow price of resources.

- The **relative loss** shows by how much contribution (usually) would fall if extra units of particular decision variables were produced.

4   Using linear programming

Introduction

Although linear programming is a useful technique for solving multi-variable problems, it is still subject to a number of assumptions and practical difficulties. Make sure you are familiar with these as you may be asked to criticise the technique in the exam.

4.1 Assumptions and non-quantifiable factors

The assumptions and non-quantifiable factors highlighted in Chapter 2 in relation to **limiting factor analysis** also apply to **linear programming** so make sure you refresh your memory. Further assumptions that are made in linear programming are:

(a)   The **total amount available of each scarce resource is known with accuracy**.

(b)   There is **no interdependence between the demand** for the different products or services, so that there is a completely free choice in the product or service mix without having to consider the consequences for demand or selling prices per unit.

In spite of these assumptions, linear programming is a useful technique in practice. Some statistical studies have been carried out suggesting that linear cost functions do apply over fairly wide ranges of output, and so the assumptions underlying linear programming may be valid.

4.2 Uses of linear programming

(a)   **Budgeting**. If scarce resources are ignored when a budget is prepared, the budget is unattainable and is of little use for planning and control. When there is more than one scarce resource, linear programming can be used to identify the most profitable use of resources.

(b)   **Calculation of relevant costs**. The calculation of relevant costs is essential for decision making. The **relevant cost** of a **scarce resource** is calculated as **acquisition cost of the resource plus opportunity cost**. When **more than one scarce resource** exists, the **opportunity cost** (or **shadow price**) should be established using linear programming techniques.

(c)   **Selling different products.** Suppose that an organisation faced with resource constraints manufactures products X and Y and linear programming has been used to determine the shadow prices of the scarce resources. If the organisation now wishes to manufacture and sell a modified version of product X (Z), requiring inputs of the scarce resources, the relevant costs of these scarce resources can be determined (see above) to ascertain whether the production of X and Y should be restricted in order to produce Z.

(d)   **Maximum payment for additional scarce resources**. This use of shadow prices has been covered in this chapter.

(e)   **Control.** Opportunity costs are also important for cost control: standard costing can be improved by incorporating opportunity costs into variance calculations. For example, adverse material usage variances can be an indication of material wastage. Such variances should be valued at the standard cost of the material plus the opportunity cost of the loss of one scarce unit of material. Such an approach highlights the true cost of the inefficient use of scarce resources and encourages managers of responsibility centres to pay special attention to the control of scarce factors of production. For organisations using an optimised production technology (OPT) strategy, this approach is particularly useful because variances arising from bottleneck operations will be reported in terms of opportunity cost rather than purchase cost.

(f)   **Capital budgeting**. Linear programming can be used to determine the combination of investment proposals that should be selected if investment funds are restricted in more than one period.

4.3 Practical difficulties with using linear programming

Difficulties with applying the linear programming technique in practice include the following.

(a)   It may be **difficult to identify** which **resources** are likely to be **in short supply** and **what the amount of their availability will be**.

   Estimates of future availability will inevitably be prone to inaccuracy and any such inaccuracies will invalidate the profit-maximising product mix derived from the use of linear programming.

(b)   Management may **not make product mix decisions which are profit-maximising**. They may be more concerned to develop a production/sales plan which has the following features.

   (i)   Realistic
   (ii)   Acceptable to the individual managers throughout the organisation
   (iii)   Acceptable to the rest of the workforce
   (iv)   Promises a 'satisfactory' profit and accounting return

In other words, management might look for a **satisfactory product mix** which achieves a satisfactory return, sales revenue and market share whilst at the same time plans operations and targets of achievement which employees can accept as realistic, not too demanding and unreasonable, and not too threatening to their job security.

(c) The **assumption of linearity may be totally invalid except over smaller ranges**. For example, in a profit maximisation problem, it may well be found that there are substantial changes in unit variable costs arising from increasing or decreasing returns to scale.

(d) The linear programming model is essentially **static** and is therefore not really suitable for analysing in detail the effects of changes in the various parameters, for example over time.

(e) In some circumstances, a practical solution derived from a linear programming model may be of **limited use** as, for example, where the variables may only take on **integer values**. A solution must then be found by a combination of rounding up and trial and error.

(f) The **shadow price** of a scarce resource **only applies up to a certain limit**.

Section summary

Various **assumptions** are made in linear programming, including

- Fixed costs remain the same regardless of the decision taken.
- Unit variable cost is constant regardless of the decision taken.
- Estimates of sales demand and resources required are known with certainty.
- Units of output are divisible.

Chapter Roundup

✓   A **slack variable** represents the amount of a constraint that is unused.

✓   In any feasible solution, if a problem involves n constraints and m variables (decision plus slack), n variables will have a positive value and (m–n) variables will have a value of zero.

✓   Feasible solutions to a problem are shown in a **tableau**.

✓   If the **shadow prices** on the bottom (solution) row of a tableau are all positive, the tableau shows the optimal solution.

  –   The solution column shows the optimal production levels and the units of unused resource.

  –   The figure at the bottom of the solution column/right-hand side of the solution row shows the value of the objective function.

  –   The figures in the solution row indicate the shadow prices of resources.

✓   **Sensitivity analysis** can be applied to the final tableau to determine the effect of having more or less of a scarce resource (indicated by figures in the column for the resource's slack variable).

✓   Sensitivity analysis can also be applied to test whether or not it would be **worthwhile to obtain more of a scarce resource** by paying a premium for additional supplies (only if the shadow price is greater than the additional cost).

✓   **Spreadsheet packages** can be used to solve linear programming problems.

  –   The **slack/surplus** columns provide information about the slack values of ≤ constraints and the surplus values of any ≥ constraints.

  –   The **worth** column shows the positive shadow price of resources.

  –   The **relative loss** shows by how much contribution (usually) would fall if extra units of particular decision variables were produced.

✓   Various **assumptions** are made in linear programming, including

  –   Fixed costs remain the same regardless of the decision taken.
  –   Unit variable cost is constant regardless of the decision taken.
  –   Estimates of sales demand and resources required are known with certainty.
  –   Units of output are divisible.

Quick Quiz

1   *Choose the correct words from those highlighted.*

The simplex method can be used for problems with **one / two / three / more than three / any number of** decision variables.

2   *Fill in the blanks.*

If a linear programming problem has four decision variables and five constraints (excluding non-negativity constraints), there will be .... slack variables and a total of .... variables. Each feasible solution matrix will have .... rows and .... columns. There will be .... variables with a value greater than 0 in any feasible solution.

3   A slack variable represents the amount of constraining resource that is used. True or false?

4   What is the general form of an objective function to maximise contribution (C) for a problem with two decision variables (x and y, with coefficients n and m) and four slack variables (S_1 to S_4)?

A $C + nx + my + S_1 + S_2 + S_3 + S_4 = 0$
B $C - nx - my + OS_1 + OS_2 + OS_3 + OS_4 = 0$
C $C - nx - my + S_1 + S_2 + S_3 + S_4 = 0$
D $C + nx + my - OS_1 - OS_2 - OS_3 - OS_4 = 0$

5   *Choose the correct words from those highlighted.*

If, in a simplex tableau, shadow prices have a negative value, the objective function can be **increased/decreased** and the tableau **shows the optimal solution/does not show the optimal solution.**

6   In an optimal simplex tableau, the figure in the row for decision variable x (product X) and column for slack variable S_1 (resource A) is −1.35. What does this indicate?

A   For each extra unit of X produced, the usage of resource A would fall by 1.35 units
B   For each extra unit of X produced, the usage of resource A would rise by 1.35 units
C   For each extra unit of resource A available, the number of units of X would rise by 1.35 units
D   For each extra unit of resource A available, the number of units of X would fall by 1.35 units

7   If a resource constraint has a worth of 356.92 in a spreadsheet package solution to a linear programming problem, what does this indicate?

A   Contribution will fall by $356.92 if one less unit of the resource is available.
B   Only 356.92 units of the resource are available.
C   356.92 units of the resource are included in the optimal solution.
D   A resource cannot have a worth.

8   It is assumed when using the simplex method of linear programming that there is interdependence between the demand for the different products/services. True or false?

Answers to Quick Quiz

1   any number of

2   five slack variables
   total of nine variables
   six rows
   ten columns
   five variables with a value greater than 0

3   False. It represents the amount unused.

4   B. Slack variables should always have zero coefficients.

5   increased

   does not show the optimal solution

6   D. Here the minus sign indicates a fall for X.

7   A. Remember the worth column shows the shadow price of resources.

8   False. It is assumed there is no interdependence.

Answers to Questions

4.1 Slack variables

A slack variable is required for each constraint (ignoring non-negativity constraints). There are $6 - 2 = 4$ such constraints.

4.2 Values of variables

Four variables will have a non-negative value (since there are four equations), which means that $7 - 4 = 3$ variables will have a value of zero.

4.3 Formulation of problem

(a)   The linear programming problem would be formulated as follows.

Define variables

Let x and y be the number of units made and sold of product X and product Y respectively.

Establish objective function

Maximise contribution (C) = 8x + 14y subject to the constraints below.

Establish constraints

3x + 4y	$\leq$	9,000 (skilled labour)*
x + 2y	$\leq$	4,000 (machine time)
0.5x + 0.25y	$\leq$	1,000 (material M)
x	$\leq$	1,200 (demand for X)
x, y	$\geq$	0

* This constraint is that skilled labour hours cannot exceed 9,000 hours, and since a unit of X needs 3 hours and a unit of Y needs 4 hours, 3x + 4y cannot exceed 9,000. The other constraints are formulated in a similar way.

Introduce slack variables

Introduce a slack variable into each constraint, to turn the inequality into an equation.

Let S_1 = the number of unused skilled labour hours
S_2 = the number of unused machine hours
S_3 = the number of unused tonnes of material M
S_4 = the amount by which demand for X falls short of 1,200 units

Then

3x + 4y + S_1	=	9,000 (labour hours)
x + 2y + S_2	=	4,000 (machine hours)
0.5x + 0.25y + S_3	=	1,000 (tonnes of M)
x + S_4	=	1,200 (demand for X)

and maximise contribution (C) given by $C - 8x - 14y + 0S_1 + 0S_2 + 0S_3 + 0S_4 = 0$

(b)   There are six variables (x, y, S_1, S_2, S_3, S_4) and four equations. In any feasible solution four variables will have a non-negative value (as there are four equations), while two variables will have a value of zero.

4.4 Interpretation of final tableau

There is a column in the tableau for every variable, including the slack variables, but the important parts of the tableau are the 'variables in the solution' column, the solution row, and the solution column. These tell us a number of things.

Identifying the variables in the solution

The variables in the solution are x, y, S_3 and S_4. It follows that S_1 and S_2 have zero values. To be the variable in the solution on a particular row of the table, a value of 1 must appear in the **column** for that variable, with zero values in every other row of that column. For example, x is the variable in the solution for the row which has 1 in the x column. There are zeros in every other row in the x column.

The value of the variables

The solution **column** gives the value of each variable.

x	1,000	(units made of X)
y	1,500	(units made of Y)
S_3	125	(unused material M)
S_4	200	(amount below the 1,200 maximum of demand for X)

This means that contribution will be maximised by making and selling 1,000 units of X and 1,500 units of Y. This will leave 125 unused tonnes of material M, and production and sales of X will be 200 units below the limit of sales demand. Since S_1 and S_2 are both zero, there is no unused labour and machine time; in other words, all the available labour and machine hours will be fully utilised.

The total contribution

The value of the objective function – here, the total contribution – is in both the solution row and the solution column. Here it is $29,000.

Shadow prices

The solution **row** gives the **shadow prices** of each variable. Here, the shadow price of S_1 is $1 per labour hour and that for S_2 is $5 per machine hour.

This means that if more labour hours could be made available **at their normal variable cost per hour**, total contribution could be increased by $1 per extra labour hour. Similarly, if more machine time could be made available, **at its normal variable cost**, total contribution could be increased by $5 per extra machine hour.

4.5 Identification of variables

Variables in solution	x	y	S_1	S_2	S_3	S_4	S_5	Solution column
x	1	0	−2.0	0	3.0	0	0	550
y	0	1	−0.8	0	0.5	0	0	720
S_2	0	0	1.5	1	1.0	0	0	95
S_4	0	0	0.7	0	−1.1	1	0	50
S_5	0	0	2.0	0	1.8	0	1	104
Solution row	0	0	7.0	0	4.0	0	0	14,110

To be a variable in the solution, a value of 1 must appear in the column for the variable, with zero values in every other row.

4.6 Optimal mix

The correct answer is B. The answer can be found in the solution column in the rows for x and y.

4.7 Unused resources

The correct answer is that 0 units of A will be unused. A has a zero value in the solution column and so resource A is fully used.

4.8 Shadow prices

The correct answer is $4, so the statement is false.

The solution row gives the shadow price of each variable.

4.9 Formulation

(a)   C is given by $C - 2a - 3b - 4c + 0S_1 + 0S_2 + 0S_3$

(b)   Constraint for process X hours: $5a + 2b + 4c + S_1 = 12{,}000$
Constraint for process Y hours: $4a + 5b + 6c + S_2 = 24{,}000$
Constraint for process Z hours: $3a + 5b + 4c + S_3 = 18{,}000$

4.10 Interpretation

(a)   **Contribution is maximised at $14,000** by making **2,000 units of tubs** and **2,000 units of trays. No tanks** would be made.

There will be **2,000 slack hours in process Y**. Process X and process Z hours will be fully utilised.

(b)   The shadow price of process X time is $0.667 per hour, and for every extra hour of process X time that can be made available (at its normal variable cost), the production quantities could be altered in such a way that the following would happen.

    (i)   **Contribution would go up by $0.667 per extra process X hour used.**
    (ii)   c (the quantity of tubs) would **go up by 0.417 units**.
    (iii)   b (the quantity of trays) would **go down by 0.333 units**.
    (iv) S_2 (unused process Y time) would **fall by 0.833 hours**.

This is **only true up to the point** where so many extra process X hours have been made available that either b or S_2 reaches 0 in value. This will be at the following points.

    (i)   For S_2, after $\dfrac{2{,}000}{0.833} = 2{,}400$ extra process X hours

    (ii)   For b, after $\dfrac{2{,}000}{0.333} = 6{,}000$ extra process X hours

2,400 is the lowest of these two limits.

The shadow price is therefore valid only for up to 2,400 extra process X hours, so that the full 3,000 available would not be required.

The **new optimal solution** would therefore be to make and sell the following.

    c $2{,}000 + (2{,}400 \times 0.417) = 3{,}000$ units
    b $2{,}000 - (2{,}400 \times 0.333) = 1{,}200$ units

These would require a total of 14,400 hours in process X, 24,000 hours in process Y and 18,000 hours in process Z.

Contribution would be as follows.

		$
Tubs	3,000 × $4	12,000
Trays	1,200 × $3	3,600
		15,600
Contribution in initial solution		14,000
Increase in contribution (2,400 × $0.667)		1,600

(c)   Going back to the original solution, if an order is received for 300 units of tanks, the production schedule would be re-arranged so that **for each unit of tank made the following would happen.**

(i)   **Contribution would fall** by $2.333.

(ii)   1.583 **units less of tubs** (variable c) would be made.

(iii) 0.667 **units more of trays** (variable b) would be made.

(iv)   **Unused process Y time would increase** by 2.167 hours.

The new production and contribution budget would be as follows.

Product		Units	Process X time Hours	Process Y time Hours	Process Z time Hours	Contribution $
Tanks	(a)	300	1,500	1,200	900	600
Trays	(b)	2,200*	4,400	11,000	11,000	6,600
Tubs	(c)	1,525**	6,100	9,150	6,100	6,100
			12,000	21,350	18,000	13,300

*   2,000 + (300 × 0.667)

**   2,000 − (300 × 1.583)

The contribution is $700 lower than in the original optimal solution (which represents 300 tanks × $2.333).

Unused process Y time is 2,650 hours, which is 650 more than in the original solution (which represents 300 × 2.167)

Now try the question from the Exam Question Bank	Number	Level	Marks	Time
	Q9	Examination	25	45 mins

MULTI-PRODUCT
BREAKEVEN ANALYSIS

You will have already encountered breakeven (or CVP) analysis in your earlier studies so you should not be surprised by the terminology or basic techniques that you meet in this chapter. But in case your memory needs refreshing we have included a brief reminder of the material you covered at the beginning of the chapter, and a question on simple breakeven analysis. You could still be asked to carry out straightforward breakeven analysis in the exam so make sure that you are perfectly happy with the basic stuff before moving on to the higher-level material.

You should remember that one of the **major assumptions** underpinning breakeven analysis is that it can **only be applied to one product or to a constant (fixed proportions) mix of products.** So far you will only have studied single product breakeven analysis but as most organisations produce and sell a range of products we are going to look at what is known as multi-product breakeven analysis. We will see how to perform the various calculations you covered at Certificate level but for multiple products, as well as how to draw breakeven and P/V charts.

topic list	learning outcomes	syllabus references	ability required
1 Drawing a basic breakeven chart	A2(b)	A2(ii)	analysis
2 Breakeven analysis in a multi-product environment	A2(b)	A2(ii)	analysis
3 Breakeven point for multiple products	A2(b)	A2(ii)	analysis
4 Contribution to sales (C/S) ratio for multiple products	A2(b)	A2(ii)	analysis
5 Sales/product mix decisions	A2(b)	A2(ii)	analysis
6 Target profits for multiple products	A2(b)	A2(ii)	analysis
7 Margin of safety for multiple products	A2(b)	A2(ii)	analysis
8 Multi-product breakeven charts	A2(b)	A2(ii)	analysis
9 Further aspects of breakeven analysis	A2(b)	A2(ii)	analysis
10 Sensitivity analysis	A2(d)	A2(iv)	analysis

Introduction – knowledge brought forward   9/11

KEY TERM

BREAKEVEN ANALYSIS or COST-VOLUME-PROFIT ANALYSIS (CVP) is 'The study of the effects on future profit of changes in fixed cost, variable cost, sales price, quantity and mix'.

(CIMA *Official Terminology*)

Knowledge brought forward from earlier studies

Breakeven analysis

- Contribution per unit   = unit selling price – unit variable costs

- Profit   = (sales volume × contribution per unit) – fixed costs

- Breakeven point   = activity level at which there is neither profit nor loss

$$= \frac{\text{total fixed costs}}{\text{contribution per unit}} = \frac{\text{contribution required to breakeven}}{\text{contribution per unit}}$$

- Contribution/sales (C/S) ratio   = profit/volume (P/V) ratio = (contribution/sales) × 100%

- Sales revenue at breakeven point   = fixed costs ÷ C/S ratio

- Margin of safety (in units)   = budgeted sales units – breakeven sales units

- Margin of safety (as %) $= \dfrac{\text{budgeted sales} - \text{breakeven sales}}{\text{budgeted sales}} \times 100\%$

- Sales volume to achieve a target profit $= \dfrac{\text{fixed cost} + \text{target profit}}{\text{contribution per unit}}$

- Assumptions

    – Can only apply to one product or constant mix
    – Fixed costs same in total and unit variable costs same at all levels of output
    – Sales prices constant at all levels of activity
    – Production = sales

Breakeven, contribution and P/V charts
- Breakeven chart
- Contribution (contribution breakeven) chart

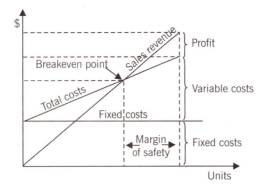

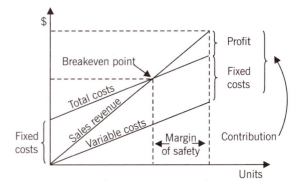

- Profit/volume (P/V) chart

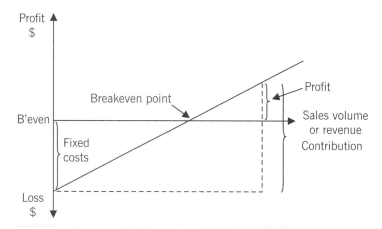

The gradient of the straight line is the contribution per unit (if the horizontal axis is measured in sales units) or the C/S ratio (if the horizontal axis is measured in sales value).

 Section summary

You should have covered the basics of breakeven analysis in your earlier studies. Flick through the relevant chapters of the BPP Study Text or Passcards if your memory needs refreshing.

1 Drawing a basic breakeven chart

 Introduction

You must be able to prepare breakeven charts to scale using data provided. Follow the six steps outlined below.

We will use the following product details to demonstrate how to draw a breakeven chart.

Selling price $60 per unit
Variable cost $40 per unit
Fixed costs $25,000 per month
Forecast sales   1,800 units per month

 Draw the axes and label them. Your graph should fill as much of the page as possible, this will make it clearer and easier to read.

The furthest point on the vertical axis will be the monthly sales revenue.

1,800 units x $60 = $108,000

 Draw the fixed cost line and label it. This will be a straight line parallel to the horizontal axis at the $25,000 level. The $25,000 fixed costs are incurred even with zero activity.

 Draw the total cost line and label it. The best way to do this is to calculate the total costs for the maximum sales level (1,800 units). Mark this point on the graph and join it to the cost incurred at zero activity, that is, $25,000.

	$
Variable costs for 1,800 units (1,800 x $40)	72,000
Fixed costs	25,000
Total cost for 1,800 units	97,000

STEP 4

Draw the revenue line and label it. Once again, start by plotting the revenue at the maximum activity level. 1,800 units x $60 = $108,000. This point can be joined to the origin, since at zero activity there will be no sales revenue.

 STEP 5

Mark any required information on the chart and read off solutions as required. Check that your chart is accurate by reading off the measures that we have already covered in this chapter: the breakeven point, the margin of safety, the profit for sales of 1,800 units.

 STEP 6

Check the accuracy of your readings using arithmetic. If you have time, it is good examination technique to check your answer and make adjustments for any errors in your chart.

The completed graph is shown below.

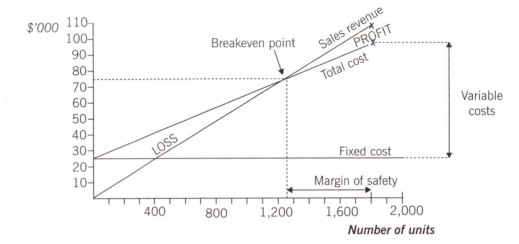

 ### Section summary

You can prepare a **breakeven chart** by plotting sales revenue against total cost. The breakeven point will be where the sales revenue line and total cost line intersect.

2 Breakeven analysis in a multi-product environment

 ### Introduction

This section introduces the important syllabus area of multi-product breakeven analysis. It focuses on one of the major assumptions that is made when calculating multi-product breakeven solutions. Make sure you understand the impact of this assumption.

KEY POINT

To perform breakeven analysis in a multi-product organisation, a **constant product sales mix** must be assumed, or all products must have the **same C/S ratio**.

2.1 A major assumption

Organisations typically produce and sell a variety of products and services. To perform breakeven analysis in a multi-product organisation, however, a constant product sales mix must be assumed. In other words, we have to assume that whenever x units of product A are sold, y units of product B and z units of product C are also sold.

Such an assumption allows us to calculate a weighted average contribution per mix, the weighting being on the basis of the quantities of each product in the constant mix. This means that the unit contribution of the product that makes up the largest proportion of the mix has the greatest impact on the average contribution per mix.

The only situation when the mix of products does not affect the analysis is when all of the products have the same ratio of contribution to sales (C/S ratio).

Section summary

To perform breakeven analysis in a multi-product organisation, a **constant product sales mix** must be **assumed**, or all products must have the **same C/S ratio**.

3 Breakeven point for multiple products   9/12, 11/12

Introduction

This section illustrates the steps involved in calculating the breakeven point for multiple products. Make sure you work through the example and then try the question without looking at the solution. Your understanding of this section is fundamental to your progression through this chapter.

KEY TERM

BREAKEVEN POINT is 'The level of activity at which there is neither profit nor loss.'

(CIMA *Official Terminology*)

This calculation is exactly the same as that for single products but the single product is the standard mix. Let's look at an example.

Example: Breakeven point for multiple products

Suppose that PL produces and sells two products. The M sells for $7 per unit and has a total variable cost of $2.94 per unit, while the N sells for $15 per unit and has a total variable cost of $4.50 per unit. The marketing department has estimated that for every five units of M sold, one unit of N will be sold. The organisation's fixed costs total $36,000.

Solution

We calculate the breakeven point as follows.

STEP 1   Calculate **contribution per unit**

	M	N
	$ per unit	$ per unit
Selling price	7.00	15.00
Variable cost	2.94	4.50
Contribution	4.06	10.50

STEP 2   Calculate **contribution per mix**

= ($4.06 × 5) + ($10.50 × 1) = $30.80

STEP 3 Calculate the **breakeven point** in terms of the number of mixes

= fixed costs/contribution per mix = $36,000/$30.80

= 1,169 mixes (rounded)

 STEP 4 Calculate the **breakeven point** in terms of the **number of units of the products**

= (1,169 × 5) 5,845 units of M and (1,169 × 1) 1,169 units of N (rounded)

 STEP 5 Calculate the **breakeven point** in terms of **revenue**

= (5,845 × $7) + (1,169 × $15)

= $40,915 of M and $17,535 of N = $58,450 in total

It is important to note that the breakeven point is not $58,450 of revenue, whatever the mix of products. The breakeven point is $58,450 provided that the sales mix remains 5:1. Likewise the breakeven point is not at a production/sales level of (5,845 + 1,169) 7,014 units. Rather, it is when 5,845 units of M and 1,169 units of N are sold, assuming a sales mix of 5:1.

 | **Question 5.1** | Breakeven point for multiple products |

Learning outcome A2(b)

Alpha manufactures and sells three products, the beta, the gamma and the delta. Relevant information is as follows.

	Beta $ per unit	Gamma $ per unit	Delta $ per unit
Selling price	135.00	165.00	220.00
Variable cost	73.50	58.90	146.20

Total fixed costs are $950,000.

An analysis of past trading patterns indicates that the products are sold in the ratio 3:4:5.

Required

Fill in the blanks in the sentence below.

Alpha's breakeven point in terms of revenue of the three products is .... of Beta, ... of Gamma and .... of Delta, making .... in total.

 Section summary

The **breakeven point (in number of mixes)** for a standard mix of products is calculated as fixed costs/contribution per mix.

4 Contribution to sales (C/S) ratio for multiple products

Introduction

This section illustrates how to calculate the C/S ratio for multiple products. Remember from your previous studies that the C/S ratio can be used to calculate the breakeven point in terms of sales revenue. This is still the case for multiple products.

LEARN

The **breakeven point in terms of sales revenue** can be calculated as fixed costs/average C/S ratio.

4.1 Calculating the ratio

An alternative way of **calculating the breakeven point** is to use the **average contribution to sales (C/S) ratio** for the standard mix.

As you should already know, the C/S ratio is sometimes called the **profit/volume ratio** or **P/V ratio**.

We can calculate the breakeven point of PL (see Section 3.1) as follows.

Calculate **revenue per mix**

Calculate **contribution per mix**

= $30.80 (see Section 3.1)

Calculate **average C/S ratio**

= ($30.80/$50.00) × 100% = 61.6%

Calculate **breakeven point** (total)

= fixed costs ÷ C/S ratio

= $36,000/0.616 = $58,442 (rounded)

Calculate **revenue ratio of mix**

= 35:15, or 7:3

Calculate **breakeven sales**

M = $58,442 × 7/10 = $40,909 rounded

Question 5.2	C/S ratio for multiple products

Learning outcome A2(b)

Calculate the breakeven sales revenue of product Beta, Gamma and Delta (see Question 5.1 above) using the approach shown in Section 3.1.

Alternatively you might be provided with the individual C/S ratios of a number of products. For example if an organisation sells two products (A and B) in the **ratio 2:5** and if the C/S ratio of A is **10%** whereas that of B is 50%, the average C/S ratio is calculated as follows.

$$\text{Average C/S ratio} = \frac{(2 \times 10\%) + (5 \times 50\%)}{2 + 5} = 38.6\%$$

| Question 5.3 | Average C/S ratio |

Learning outcome A2(b)

TIM produces and sells two products, the MK and the KL. The organisation expects to sell 1 MK for every 2 KLs and have monthly sales revenue of $150,000. The MK has a C/S ratio of 20% whereas the KL has a C/S ratio of 40%. Budgeted monthly fixed costs are $30,000.

What is the budgeted breakeven sales revenue?

The C/S ratio is a measure of how much contribution is earned from each $1 of sales of the standard mix. The **C/S ratio of 33$^1/_3$%** in the question above means that for every $1 of sales of the standard mix of products, a contribution of 33.33c is earned. To **earn a total contribution of, say, $20,000, sales revenue from the standard mix** must therefore be

$$\frac{\$1}{33.33c} \times \$20,000 = \$60,006$$

| Question 5.4 | Using the C/S ratio |

Learning outcome A2(b)

Refer back to the information in the paragraph following Question: C/S ratio for multiple products. Suppose the organisation in question has fixed costs of $100,000, and wishes to earn total contribution of $200,000.

What level of revenue must be achieved?

4.2 Points to bear in mind

KEY POINT

Any change in the proportions of products in the mix will change the contribution per mix and the average C/S ratio and hence the breakeven point.

(a) If the mix shifts towards products with lower contribution margins, the breakeven point (in units) will increase and profits will fall unless there is a corresponding increase in total revenue.

(b) A shift towards products with higher contribution margins without a corresponding decrease in revenues will cause an increase in profits and a lower breakeven point.

(c) If sales are at the specified level but not in the specified mix, there will be either a profit or a loss depending on whether the mix shifts towards products with higher or lower contribution margins.

Section summary

The **breakeven point in terms of sales revenue** can be calculated as fixed costs/average C/S ratio.

Any change in the **proportions of products** in the mix will change the **contribution per mix** and the **average C/S ratio** and hence the breakeven point.

5 Sales/product mix decisions

Introduction

In this section we focus on how to use the methodology above for making sales or product mix decisions. This is an important section so make sure you work through the examples carefully before trying any questions on your own.

KEY POINT

If an organisation sells a number of products, the total C/S ratio is the sum of the individual weighted (by market share) C/S ratios.

Example: Sales mix decisions

JM makes and sells two products, the J and the M. The budgeted selling price of the J is $60 and that of the M, $72. Variable costs associated with producing and selling the J are $30 and, with the M, $60. Annual fixed production and selling costs of JM are $3,369,600.

JM has two production/sales options. The J and the M can be sold either in the ratio two Js to three Ms or in the ratio one J to two Ms.

Required

Determine the optimal mix of products J and M.

Solution

We can decide on the optimal mix by looking at breakeven points. We need to begin by determining contribution per unit.

	J $ per unit	*M* $ per unit
Selling price	60	72
Variable cost	30	60
Contribution	30	12

Mix 1

Contribution per 5 units sold = ($30 × 2) + ($12 × 3) = $96

$$\text{Breakeven point} = \frac{\$3,369,600}{£96} = 35,100 \text{ sets of five units}$$

	J		*M*	
Breakeven point:				
in units	(35,100 × 2)	70,200	(35,100 × 3)	105,300
in $	(70,200 × $60)	$4,212,000	(105,300× $72)	$7,581,600

'Total' breakeven point = $11,793,600

Mix 2

Contribution per 3 units sold = ($30 × 1) + ($12 × 2) = $54

$$\text{Breakeven point} = \frac{\$3,369,600}{\$54} = 62,400 \text{ sets of three units.}$$

Breakeven point:	J		M	
in units	(62,400 × 1)	62,400	(62,400 × 2)	124,800
in $	(62,400 × $60)	$3,744,000	(124,800× $72)	$8,985,600

'Total' breakeven point = $12,729,600

Ignoring commercial considerations, mix 1 is preferable to mix 2. This is because it results in a lower level of sales to break even (because of the higher average contribution per unit sold). The average contribution for mix 1 is $19.20 ($96 ÷ 5). In mix 2 it is $18 ($54 ÷ 3). Mix 1 contains a higher proportion (40% as opposed to $33^1/3$%) of the more profitable product.

The following question looks at the **effect on the overall C/S ratio of changing a product/sales mix.**

Example: Changing the product mix

AL sells three products - Exe, Why and Zed - in equal quantities and at the same selling price per unit. The C/S ratio for the Exe is 50%, that of the Why is 60% and the total C/S ratio is 55%. Suppose the product mix is changed to Exe 20%, Why 50% and Zed 30%.

Required

Calculate the revised C/S ratio.

Solution

Original proportions

	Exe	Why	Zed	Total
C/S ratio	0.5	0.6	0.549(W2)	
Market share	× 1/3	× 1/3	× 1/3	
	0.167	0.200	0.183(W1)	0.55

Workings

1   The total C/S ratio is the sum of the weighted C/S ratios and so this figure is calculated as 0.55 – 0.167 – 0.2 = 0.183

2   This figure is then calculated as 0.183 ÷ $^1/_3$ = 0.549

Revised proportions

	Exe	Why	Zed	Total
C/S ratio (as above)	0.5	0.6	0.549	
Market share	× 0.2	× 0.5	× 0.3	
	0.1	0.3	0.1647	0.5647

The total C/S ratio will increase because of the inclusion in the mix of proportionately more of Why, which has the highest C/S ratio.

Question 5.5   Sales mix decision

Learning outcome A2(b)

LL currently sells three products U, C and Y at the same selling price per unit.

Current product mix	U – 25%	C – 35%	Y – 40%
Current P/V ratio	Total – 43.5%	C – 45%	Y – 35%
LL decides to change the product mix to	U – 30%	C – 40%	Y – 30%

What is the revised total contribution/total sales ratio?

Section summary

If an organisation sells a number of products, the **total C/S ratio is the sum of the individual weighted** (by market share) **C/S ratios**.

---

6 Target profits for multiple products   **9/11**

Introduction

You should already be familiar with the problem of target profits for single products in a CVP context in Certificate Paper C1. This section expands the concept to multiple products, illustrating the calculations in several examples.

6.1 A reminder of the formula for target profits

At **breakeven point** there is no profit – that is:

Contribution = Fixed costs

Suppose an organisation wishes to achieve a certain level of profit during a period. To achieve this profit, contribution must cover fixed costs and leave the required profit:

So **total contribution required = fixed costs + required profit**

Once we know the total contribution required we can calculate the sales revenue of each product needed to achieve a target profit. The method is similar to the method used to calculate the breakeven point.

LEARN

> The number of mixes of products required to be sold to achieve a **target profit** is calculated as (fixed costs + required profit)/contribution per mix.

Example: Target profits for multiple products

An organisation makes and sells three products, F, G and H. The products are sold in the proportions F:G:H = 2:1:3. The organisation's fixed costs are $80,000 per month and details of the products are as follows.

Product	Selling price $ per unit	Variable cost $ per unit
F	22	16
G	15	12
H	19	13

The organisation wishes to earn a profit of $52,000 next month. Calculate the required sales value of each product in order to achieve this target profit.

Solution

 STEP 1 · Calculate **contribution per unit**

	F $ per unit	G $ per unit	H $ per unit
Selling price	22	15	19
Variable cost	16	12	13
Contribution	6	3	6

 STEP 2 · Calculate **contribution per mix**

= ($6 × 2) + ($3 × 1) + ($6 × 3) = $33

 STEP 3 · Calculate the **required number of mixes**

= (Fixed costs + required profit)/contribution per mix

= ($80,000 + $52,000)/$33

= 4,000 mixes

 STEP 4 · Calculate the required sales in terms of the number of units of the products and sales revenue of each product

Product		Units	Selling price $ per unit	Sales revenue required $
F	4,000 × 2	8,000	22	176,000
G	4,000 × 1	4,000	15	60,000
H	4,000 × 3	12,000	19	228,000
Total				464,000

The sales revenue of $464,000 will generate a profit of $52,000 if the products are sold in the mix 2:1:3.

Alternatively the C/S ratio could be used to determine the required sales revenue for a profit of $52,000. The method is again similar to that demonstrated earlier when calculating the breakeven point.

Example: Using the C/S ratio to determine the required sales

We'll use the data from the example above.

Calculate revenue per mix

= (2 × $22) + (1 × $15) + (3 × $19)

= $116

Calculate contribution per mix

= $33 (from Solution in Section 5.1)

Calculate average C/S ratio

= ($33/$116) × 100%

= 28.45%

Calculate required total revenue

= required contribution ÷ C/S ratio

= ($80,000 + $52,000) ÷ 0.2845

= $463,972

Calculate revenue ratio of mix

= (2 × $22) : (1 × $15) : (3 × $19)

= 44:15:57

Calculate required sales

Required sales of F = 44/116 × $463,972 = $175,989

Required sales of G = 15/116 × $463,972 = $59,996

Required sales of H = 57/116 × $463,972 = $227,986

Which, allowing for roundings, is the same answer as calculated in the first example.

Section summary

The number of mixes of products required to be sold to achieve a **target profit** is calculated as (fixed costs + required profit)/contribution per mix.

7 Margin of safety for multiple products

Introduction

It should not surprise you to learn that the calculation of the margin of safety for multiple products is exactly the same as for single products, but the single product is the standard mix. The easiest way to see how it's done is to look at an example which we do in this section.

KEY POINT

The **margin of safety** for a multi-product organisation is equal to the budgeted sales in the standard mix less the breakeven sales in the standard mix. It may be expressed as a percentage of the budgeted sales.

Example: Margin of safety for multiple products

BA produces and sells two products. The W sells for $8 per unit and has a total variable cost of $3.80 per unit, while the R sells for $14 per unit and has a total variable cost of $4.20. For every five units of W sold, six units of R are sold. BA's fixed costs are $43,890 per period.

Budgeted sales revenue for next period is $74,400, in the standard mix.

Required

Calculate the margin of safety in terms of sales revenue and also as a percentage of budgeted sales revenue.

Solution

To calculate the margin of safety we must first determine the **breakeven point.**

 STEP 1 Calculate **contribution per unit**

	W	R
	$ per unit	$ per unit
Selling price	8.00	14.00
Variable cost	3.80	4.20
Contribution	4.20	9.80

 STEP 2 Calculate **contribution per mix**

= ($4.20 × 5) + ($9.80 × 6) = $79.80

 STEP 3 Calculate the **breakeven point** in terms of the **number of mixes**

= fixed costs/contribution per mix = $43,890/$79.80
= 550 mixes

 STEP 4 Calculate the **breakeven point** in terms of the **number of units of the products**

= (550 × 5) 2,750 units of W and (550 × 6) 3,300 units of R

 STEP 5 Calculate the **breakeven point** in terms of **revenue**

= (2,750 × $8) + (3,300 × $14)
= $22,000 of W and $46,200 of R = $68,200 in total

STEP 6 Calculate the **margin of safety**

= budgeted sales – breakeven sales
= $74,400 – $68,200
= $6,200 sales in total, in the standard mix

Or, as a percentage

= ($74,400 – $68,200)/$74,400 × 100%
= 8.3% of budgeted sales

Section summary

The **margin of safety** for a multi-product organisation is equal to the budgeted sales in the standard mix less the breakeven sales in the standard mix. It may be expressed as a percentage of the budgeted sales.

8 Multi-product breakeven charts   9/10

Introduction

As well as being able to carry out CVP calculations you may be asked to produce a breakeven chart in a multiple product situation. This section focuses on the procedure involved in producing multi-product breakeven charts and profit/volume (P/V) charts.

8.1 Breakeven charts

KEY TERM

A BREAKEVEN CHART is 'A chart which indicates approximate profit or loss at different levels of sales volume within a limited range'.   (CIMA *Official Terminology*)

A very serious limitation of breakeven charts is that they can show the costs, revenues, profits and margins of safety for a single product only, or at best for a **single 'sales mix' of products.**

KEY POINT

Breakeven charts for multiple products can be drawn if a constant product sales mix is assumed.

For example suppose that FA sells three products, X, Y and Z which have variable unit costs of $3, $4 and $5 respectively. The sales price of X is $8, the price of Y is $6 and the price of Z is $6. Fixed costs per annum are $10,000.

A breakeven chart cannot be drawn, because we do not know the proportions of X, Y and Z in the sales mix.

Exam alert

If you are not sure about this point, you should try to draw a breakeven chart with the information given. It should not be possible.

There are a number of ways in which we can overcome this problem, however.

8.1.1 Approach 1: output in $ sales and a constant product mix

Assume that budgeted sales are 2,000 units of X, 4,000 units of Y and 3,000 units of Z. A breakeven chart would make the assumption that output and sales of X, Y and Z are in the proportions 2,000: 4,000: 3,000 at all levels of activity, in other words that the sales mix is 'fixed' in these proportions.

We begin by carrying out some calculations.

Budgeted costs		*Costs* $		*Revenue* $
Variable costs of X	(2,000 × $3)	6,000	X (2,000 × $8)	16,000
Variable costs of Y	(4,000 × $4)	16,000	Y (4,000 × $6)	24,000
Variable costs of Z	(3,000 × $5)	15,000	Z (3,000 × $6)	18,000
Total variable costs		37,000	Budgeted revenue	58,000
Fixed costs		10,000		
Total budgeted costs		47,000		

The **breakeven chart** can now be drawn.

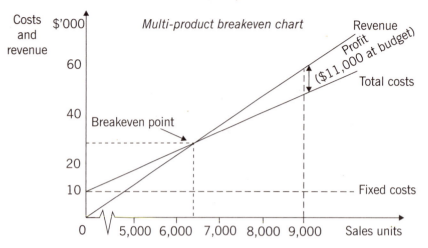

The **breakeven point** is approximately $27,500 of sales revenue. This may either be **read from the chart or computed mathematically**.

(a)   The budgeted C/S ratio for all three products together is contribution/sales = $(58,000 – 37,000)/$58,000 = 36.21%.

(b)   The required contribution to break even is $10,000, the amount of fixed costs. The breakeven point is $10,000/36.21% = $27,500 (approx) in sales revenue.

The margin of safety is approximately $(58,000 – 27,500) = $30,500.

8.1.2 Approach 2: products in sequence

The products could be plotted in a particular sequence (say X first, then Y, then Z).

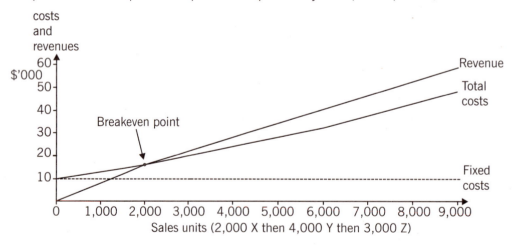

In this case the breakeven point occurs at 2,000 units of sales (2,000 units of product X). The margin of safety is roughly 4,000 units of Y and 3,000 units of Z.

At 2,000 units of X, revenue is $16,000 and variable costs are $6,000, fixed costs $10,000. This is the breakeven point so all further planned production is the margin of safety.

8.1.3 Approach 3: output in terms of % of forecast sales and a constant product mix

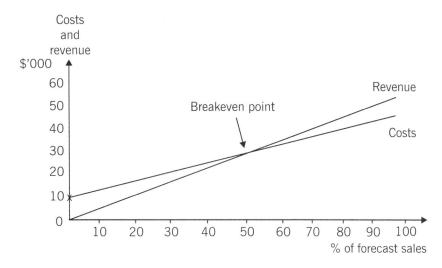

The breakeven point can be read from the graph as approximately 48% of forecast sales ($30,000 of revenue).

Alternatively, with contribution of $(58,000 – 37,000) = $21,000, one percent of forecast sales is associated with $21,000/100 = $210 contribution.

Breakeven point (%) = fixed costs/contribution per 1%

$$= \$10,000/\$210 = 47.62\%$$

∴ Margin of safety = (100 – 47.62) = 52.38%

Exam alert

The general point of setting out these three approaches is to demonstrate that output can be viewed in several different ways.

8.2 Multi-product P/V charts

The same information could be shown on a **P/V chart**, as follows.

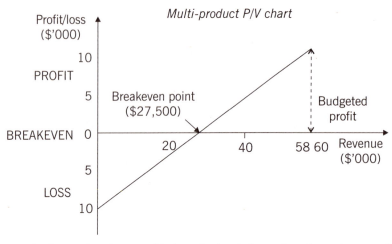

Multi-product P/V chart

An **addition** to the chart would **show further information about the contribution earned by each product individually**, so that their performance and profitability can be compared.

	Contribution $	Sales $	C/S ratio %
Product X	10,000	16,000	62.50
Product Y	8,000	24,000	33.33
Product Z	3,000	18,000	16.67
Total	21,000	58,000	36.21

By convention, the **products are shown individually** on a P/V chart from **left to right**, in **order of the size of their C/S ratio**. In this example, product X will be plotted first, then product Y and finally product Z. A **dotted line** is used to show the **cumulative profit/loss and the cumulative sales** as each product's sales and contribution in turn are added to the sales mix.

Product	Cumulative sales $		Cumulative profit $
X	16,000	($10,000 – $10,000)	–
X and Y	40,000		8,000
X, Y and Z	58,000		11,000

You will see on the graph which follows that these three pairs of data are used to plot the dotted line, to indicate the contribution from each product. The **solid line** which joins the two ends of this dotted line **indicates the average profit** which will be earned from sales of the three products in this mix.

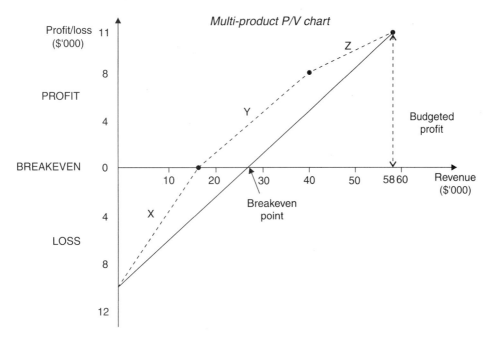

The diagram **highlights** the following points.

(a)   Since X is the most profitable in terms of C/S ratio, it might be worth considering an increase in the sales of X, even if there is a consequent fall in the sales of Z.

(b)   Alternatively, the pricing structure of the products should be reviewed and a decision made as to whether the price of product Z should be raised so as to increase its C/S ratio (although an increase is likely to result in some fall in sales volume).

The **multi-product P/V chart** therefore helps to **identify** the following.

(a)   The overall company breakeven point.

(b)   Which products should be expanded in output and which, if any, should be discontinued.

(c)   What effect changes in selling price and sales volume will have on the company's breakeven point and profit.

 Question 5.6   Multi-product P/V chart

Learning outcome A2(b)

A company sells three products, X, Y and Z. Cost and sales data for one period are as follows.

	X	Y	Z
Sales volume	2,000 units	2,000 units	5,000 units
Sales price per unit	$3	$4	$2
Variable cost per unit	$2.25	$3.50	$1.25
Total fixed costs	$3,250		

Required

Construct a multi-product P/V chart based on the above information on the axes below.

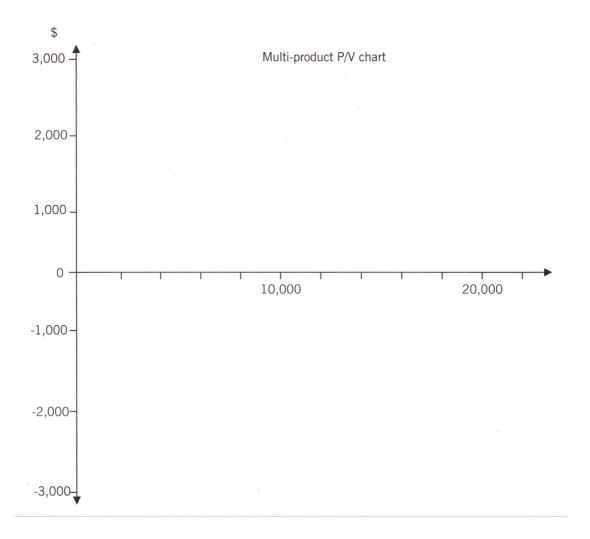

Multi-product P/V chart

Question 5.7

Breakeven point and sales value constraints

Learning outcome A2(b)

Sutton produces four products. Relevant data is shown below for period 2.

	Product M	Product A	Product R	Product P
C/S ratio	5%	10%	15%	20%
Maximum sales value	$200,000	$120,000	$200,000	$180,000
Minimum sales value	$50,000	$50,000	$20,000	$10,000

The fixed costs for period 2 are budgeted at $60,000.

Required

Fill in the blank in the sentence below.

The lowest breakeven sales value, subject to meeting the minimum sales value constraints, is $.............

Section summary

Breakeven charts for multiple products can be drawn if a constant product sales mix is assumed.

The **P/V chart** can show information about each product individually.

9 Further aspects of breakeven analysis

Introduction

As well as being able to carry out CVP calculations, you may be asked to criticise the CVP approach to short-term decision-making. This does not only mean giving the limitations of CVP but also being aware of the advantages as well.

9.1 Limitations and advantages

9.1.1 Limitations

(a)   It is **assumed** that **fixed costs** are the **same in total** and **variable costs** are the **same per unit at all levels of output**. This assumption is a great **simplification**.

     (i)   Fixed costs will change if output falls or increases substantially (most fixed costs are step costs).

     (ii)   The variable cost per unit will decrease where economies of scale are made at higher output volumes, but the variable cost per unit will also eventually rise when diseconomies of scale begin to appear at even higher volumes of output (for example the extra cost of labour in overtime working).

     The **assumption** is only **correct within** a normal range or **relevant range of output**. It is generally assumed that both the budgeted output and the breakeven point lie within this relevant range.

(b)   It is **assumed** that **sales prices** will be **constant** at **all levels of activity**. This may not be true, especially at higher volumes of output, where the price may have to be reduced to win the extra sales.

(c)   **Production** and **sales** are **assumed** to be the **same**, so that the consequences of any increase in inventory levels or of 'de-stocking' are ignored.

(d)   **Uncertainty** in the estimates of fixed costs and unit variable costs is often **ignored**.

9.1.2 Advantages

(a)   **Graphical representation** of cost and revenue data (breakeven charts) can be **more easily understood by non-financial managers**.

(b)   A breakeven model enables **profit or loss at any level of activity** within the range for which the model is valid to be **determined**, and the C/S ratio can indicate the **relative profitability of different products**.

(c)   Highlighting the breakeven point and the margin of safety gives managers some **indication** of the level of **risk** involved.

9.2 Accountant's and economist's models of breakeven analysis and the relevant range

The economist's model of breakeven analysis differs from the accountant's model we have been using for the following reasons:

(a)   The economist's model assumes that **variable** (marginal) **cost per unit changes with the level of output**. It will decrease initially but will start to rise when the factory starts operating at a level beyond its efficient capacity.

(b)   **Selling price per unit is not assumed to be constant** in the economist's model. The economist's philosophy is that in order to sell more a business will have to reduce its price.

The economist's model will therefore look like this:

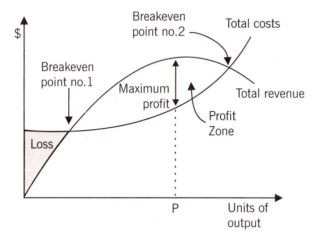

The shape of the total costs and total revenue lines means that there are **two breakeven points**. At the second, decreasing total revenue equals increasing total costs. The first is similar to the single breakeven point shown on an accountant's breakeven chart.

The accountant's breakeven chart is not intended to provide an accurate representation of total costs and total revenue behaviour in all ranges of output but rather to represent behaviour over the **relevant range**.

KEY TERM

RELEVANT RANGE. 'Activity levels within which assumptions about cost behaviour in breakeven analysis remain valid.'
(CIMA Official Terminology)

Within the relevant range the **economist's and accountant's charts are not too different**. The two types of chart are superimposed below.

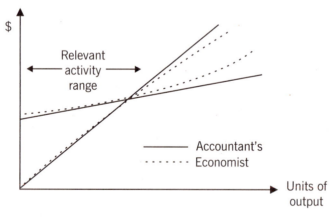

Fixed costs are also **assumed** to be **constant at all levels of output,** so that if there is no output at all, there will be a loss equal to the amount of fixed costs. It might be tempting to assume that this is true, but it could be a seriously **misleading assumption** because many 'fixed cost' items are step costs in nature over a wide range of activity. **Fixed cost** estimates should therefore only **apply within the relevant range** of activity.

Section summary

The usefulness of CVP analysis is restricted by its **unrealistic assumptions**, such as constant sales price at all levels of activity. However CVP has the advantage of being more **easily understood** by non-financial managers due to its graphical depiction of cost and revenue data.

The economist's model of breakeven analysis differs from the accountant's model due to its assumption that **selling price** and **variable cost per unit do not remain constant** as sales and production volumes increase.

However the accountant's model and economist's model tend to be similar in the short-run over the **relevant range**.

10 Sensitivity analysis

Introduction

One issue that is often of interest to companies is how their profit situations are likely to be affected if any of the variables change. In the case of CVP analysis, the variables will be sales mix, variable cost per unit, selling price per unit and total fixed costs. This process – known as sensitivity analysis – is the focus of this section.

10.1 Sensitivity analysis and breakeven analysis

The output from a breakeven model is only as good as the data used as input. Breakeven analysis is based on assumptions about sales mix, total fixed costs, variable costs and unit selling prices. Obviously estimates of the values of these **variables** will be **subject to varying degrees of uncertainty**.

But one way of **analysing the effects of changes in the values of these variables** is **sensitivity analysis**. Sensitivity analysis focuses on how a result will alter if estimates of values of variables or underlying assumptions change. It therefore provides answers to the following types of question.

- By how much will profit change if the sales mix changes from that originally predicted?
- By how much will profit change if fixed costs fall by 5% and variable costs increase by 10%?

It can **highlight the risks that an existing cost structure poses** for an organisation, and hence may lead managers to consider alternative cost structures.

| **Question 5.8** | Sensitivity analysis |

Learning outcome A2(d)

The directors of a family-owned retail department store were shocked to receive the following profit statement for the year ended 31 January 20X0.

	$'000	$'000	$'000
Sales		5,000	
Less cost of sales		3,398	
			1,602
Wages: departments	357		
office	70		
restaurant	26		
		453	
Delivery costs		200	
Departmental expenses		116	
Salaries: directors and management		100	
Directors' fees		20	
Sales promotion and advertising		120	
Store capacity costs (rent, rates and energy)		488	
Interest on bank overdraft		20	
Discounts allowed		25	
Bad debts		15	
Miscellaneous expenses		75	
			1,632
Net loss			(30)

Management accounting techniques have not been employed but the following breakdown has been extracted from the financial records.

	Departments				
	Ladies' wear $'000	Men's wear $'000	General $'000	Toys $'000	Restaurant $'000
Sales	800	400	2,200	1,400	200
Purchases	506	220	1,290	1,276	167
Opening inventory	90	70	200	100	5
Closing inventory	100	50	170	200	6
Wages	96	47	155	59	26
Departmental expenses	38	13	35	20	10
Sales promotion and advertising	10	5	30	75	-
Floor space occupied	20%	15%	20%	35%	10%

The directors are considering reducing selling prices on ladies' wear and men's wear by 5% in the hope of boosting sales.

Required

(a) Present the information for the year to 31 January 20X0 in a more meaningful way to aid decision making. Include any statistics or indicators of performance which you consider to be useful.

(b) Show for the ladies wear and menswear departments, if selling prices are reduced by 5% and unit costs remain the same:

    (i)   the increase in sales value (to the nearest thousand pounds) that would be required for a full year to maintain the gross profits, in $s, earned by each of these departments;

    (ii)   the increase in (i) above expressed as a percentage of the sales for each department to 31 January 20X0.

(c) State your views on the proposal being considered by the directors and recommend any alternative action you think appropriate.

10.2 Sensitivity analysis and breakeven charts

Breakeven charts can be used in a form of sensitivity analysis to show variations in the possible sales price, variable costs or fixed costs and the resulting effects on the breakeven point and the margin of safety.

Example: Sensitivity analysis and breakeven charts

Suppose that an organisation sells a product which has a variable cost of $2 per unit. Fixed costs are $15,000. It has been estimated that if the sales price is set at $4.40 per unit, the expected sales volume would be 7,500 units; whereas if the sales price is lower, at $4 per unit, the expected sales volume would be 10,000 units.

Required

Draw a breakeven chart to show the budgeted profit, the breakeven point and the margin of safety at each of the possible sales prices.

Solution

Workings

	Selling price $4.40/unit $		Selling price $4 per unit $
Fixed costs	15,000		15,000
Variable costs (7,500 × $2.00)	15,000	(10,000 × $2.00)	20,000
Total costs	30,000		35,000
Budgeted revenue (7,500 × $4.40)	33,000	(10,000 × $4.00)	40,000

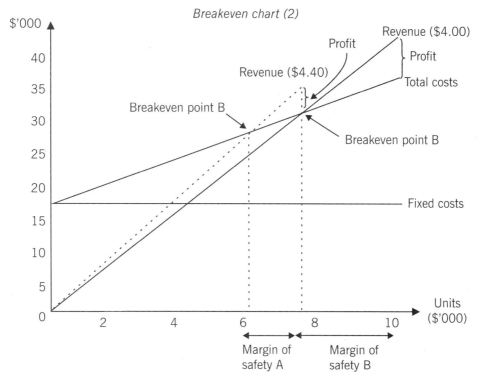

Breakeven chart (2)

(a)   **Breakeven point A** is the breakeven point at a sales price of $4.40 per unit, which is 6,250 units or $27,500 in costs and revenues.

$$(\text{check:} \quad \frac{\text{required contribution to break even}}{\text{contribution per unit}} = \frac{\$15,000}{\$2.40 \text{ per unit}} = 6,250 \text{ units})$$

The **margin of safety (A)** is 7,500 units – 6,250 units = 1,250 units or 16.7% of expected sales.

(b)   **Breakeven point B** is the breakeven point at a sales price of $4 per unit which is 7,500 units or $30,000 in costs and revenues.

(check: $\dfrac{\text{required contribution to break even}}{\text{contribution per unit}} = \dfrac{\$15,000}{\$2 \text{ per unit}} = 7,500 \text{ units})$

The **margin of safety (B)** = 10,000 units – 7,500 units = 2,500 units or 25% of expected sales.

Since a **price of $4** per unit gives a higher expected profit and a wider margin of safety, this price will probably be **preferred** even though the breakeven point is higher than at a sales price of $4.40 per unit.

10.3 Sensitivity analysis and the P/V chart

Just as breakeven charts can be used to show how variations in sales price, variable costs and fixed costs affect the breakeven point and the margin of safety, so too can P/V charts. Two circumstances can be considered.

(a)   **Fixed cost changes** do not alter the slope of the P/V line but change the point of intersection and therefore the breakeven point.

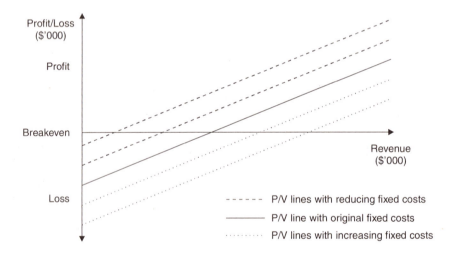

Such a diagram shows how the breakeven point and the level of profit or loss at different levels of revenue will change depending on the level of fixed costs.sss

(b)   **Variable cost and sales price changes** alter the slope of the line and hence the breakeven point and the profit or loss.

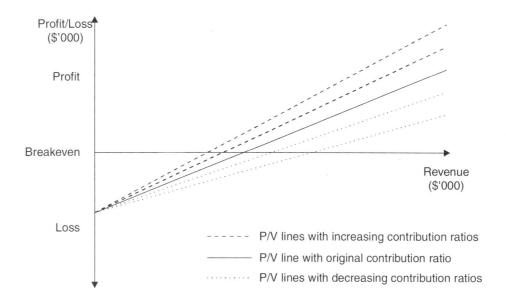

Such a diagram shows how the breakeven point and the level of profit or loss at different levels of revenue will change depending on the contribution ratio.

Example: Sensitivity analysis and P/V chart

The budgeted annual output of a factory is 120,000 units. The budgeted fixed overheads amount to $40,000 and the budgeted variable costs are 50p per unit. The budgeted sales price is $1 per unit.

Contribution will be $120,000 \times \$(1.00 - 0.50) = \$60,000$ and total profit will be $20,000 (fixed costs being $40,000). The breakeven point is shown on the diagram below (breakeven point 1).

Suppose the budgeted selling price is increased to $1.20, with the result that demand drops to 105,000 units despite additional fixed costs of $10,000 being spent on advertising.

At a sales level of 105,000 units, contribution will be $105,000 \times \$(1.20 - 0.50) = \$73,500$ and total profit will be $23,500 (fixed costs being $50,000). The breakeven point is shown on the diagram below (breakeven point 2).

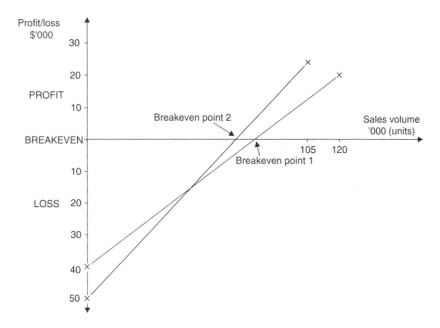

The diagram shows that if the selling price is increased, the breakeven point occurs at a lower level of sales revenue (71,429 units instead of 80,000 units), although this is not a particularly large increase

when viewed in the context of the projected sales volume. It is also possible to see that for sales above 50,000 units, the profit achieved will be higher (and the loss achieved lower) if the price is $1.20. For sales volumes below 50,000 units the first option will yield lower losses.

Changes in the variable cost per unit or in fixed costs at certain activity levels can also be easily incorporated into a P/V chart. The profit or loss at each point where the cost structure changes should be calculated and plotted on the graph so that the profit/volume line becomes a series of straight lines.

Suppose that at sales levels in excess of 120,000 units (when the selling price is $1) the variable cost per unit increases to $0.60, perhaps because of overtime premiums that are incurred when production exceeds a certain level. The resulting P/V chart is shown below.

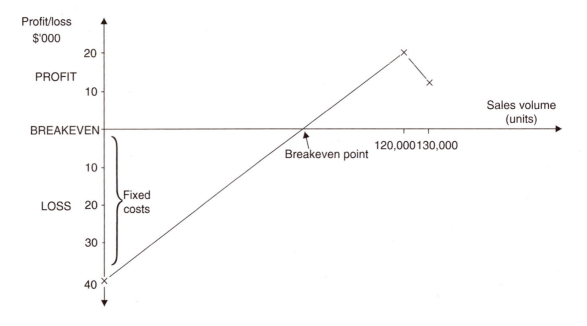

Section summary

Sensitivity analysis is a useful tool for estimating how a company's profit position might be affected by changes in such variables as selling price per unit and total fixed costs. If the profit position is particularly sensitive to a certain variable, the company may wish to consider changing its cost structure.

Chapter Roundup

✓ You should have covered the basics of breakeven analysis in your earlier studies. Flick through the relevant chapters of the BPP Study Text or Passcards if your memory needs refreshing.

✓ You can prepare a **breakeven chart** by plotting sales revenue against total cost. The breakeven point will be where the sales revenue line and total cost line intersect.

✓ To perform breakeven analysis in a multi-product organisation, a **constant product sales mix** must be **assumed**, or all products must have the **same C/S ratio.**

✓ The **breakeven point (in number of mixes)** for a standard mix of products is calculated as fixed costs/contribution per mix.

✓ The **breakeven point in terms of sales revenue** can be calculated as fixed costs/average C/S ratio.

✓ Any change in the **proportions of products** in the mix will change the **contribution per mix** and the **average C/S ratio** and hence the breakeven point.

✓ If an organisation sells a number of products, the **total C/S ratio is the sum of the individual weighted** (by market share) **C/S ratios**.

✓ The number of mixes of products required to be sold to achieve a **target profit** is calculated as (fixed costs + required profit)/contribution per mix.

✓ The **margin of safety** for a multi-product organisation is equal to the budgeted sales in the standard mix less the breakeven sales in the standard mix. It may be expressed as a percentage of the budgeted sales.

✓ **Breakeven charts** for multiple products can be drawn if a constant product sales mix is assumed.

✓ The **P/V chart** can show information about each product individually.

✓ The usefulness of CVP analysis is restricted by its **unrealistic assumptions**, such as constant sales price at all levels of activity. However CVP has the advantage of being more **easily understood** by non-financial managers due to its graphical depiction of cost and revenue data.

✓ The economist's model of breakeven analysis differs from the accountant's model due to its assumption that **selling price and variable cost per unit do not remain constant** as sales and production volumes increase.

✓ However the accountant's model and economist's model tend to be similar in the short-run over the **relevant range**.

✓ Sensitivity analysis is a useful tool for estimating how a company's profit position might be affected by changes in such variables as selling price per unit and total fixed costs. If the profit position is particularly sensitive to a certain variable, the company may wish to consider changing its cost structure.

Quick Quiz

1   Fill in the blanks.

$$\text{Breakeven point} = \frac{\text{\dotfill}}{\text{Contribution per mix}} = \frac{\text{\dotfill}}{\text{Contribution per mix}}$$

2   C/S ratio = P/V ratio × 100. True or false?

3   Fill in the blanks.

$$\text{Margin of safety (as \%)} = \left(\frac{\text{\dotfill sales} - \text{\dotfill sales}}{\text{\dotfill sales}} \right) \times 100\%$$

4   Mark the following on the breakeven chart below.

   • Profit   • Variable costs
   • Sales revenue   • Fixed costs
   • Total costs   • Breakeven point
   • Margin of safety

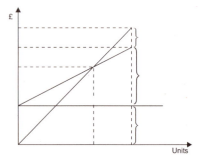

5   Mark the following on the P/V chart below.

   • Breakeven point   • Contribution
   • Fixed costs   • Profit

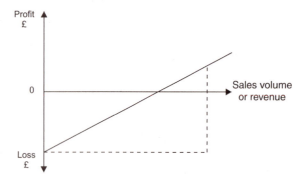

6   Which of the following is not a major assumption of breakeven analysis?

   A   It can only apply to one product or a constant mix.
   B   Fixed costs are the same in total and unit variable costs are the same at all levels of output.
   C   Sales prices vary in line with levels of activity.
   D   Production level is equal to sales level.

7   Choose the appropriate words from those highlighted and fill in the blanks.

When showing multiple products individually on a P/V chart, the products are shown from **left to right/right to left**, in order of **increasing/decreasing** size of C/S ratio. The line joining the two ends of the dotted line (which shows ....) indicates ....

8   Choose the appropriate word from those highlighted.

When choosing between two possible sales mix options, the mix with the **higher/lower** level of sales to break even should be selected.

9   An organisation which sells a number of products in fixed proportions wishes to earn a profit of $P. Its fixed costs are $F. The revenue per mix of products is $R, the contribution per mix $C. What revenue must it achieve to earn profit of $P?

A $R
B   ($F + $P) ÷ ($C/$R)
C $F + $P
D   ($F + $P) ÷ $R/$C

10   Choose the appropriate words from those highlighted.

The assumption in breakeven analysis that variable cost is the same per unit at all levels of output is a great simplification. The variable cost per unit will decrease where (1) **economies/diseconomies** of scale are made at higher volumes of output, but will also eventually rise where (2) **economies/diseconomies** of scale begin to appear at even (3) **higher/lower** volumes of output.

Answers to Quick Quiz

1   Breakeven point $= \dfrac{\text{Total fixed costs}}{\text{Contribution per unit}} = \dfrac{\text{Contribution required to breakeven}}{\text{Contribution per unit}}$

2   False. The C/S ratio is another name for the P/V ratio.

3   Margin of safety (as %) $= \left(\dfrac{\text{Budgeted sales - breakeven sales}}{\text{Budgeted sales}} \right) \times 100\%$

4

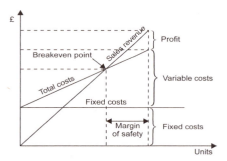

5

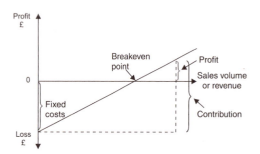

6   C. Sales prices *are constant* at all levels of activity.

7   When showing multiple products individually on a P/V chart, the products are shown from left to right, in order of decreasing size of C/S ratio. The line joining the two ends of the dotted line (which shows the cumulative profit/loss and the cumulative sales) indicates the average profit which will be earned from sales of the products in the mix.

8   Lower

9   B. This is required contribution ÷ C/S ratio

10   (1)   economies
     (2)   diseconomies
     (3)   higher

Answers to Questions

5.1 Breakeven point for multiple products

The correct answer is $393,660 of Beta, $641,520 of Gamma and $1,069,200 of Delta, making $2,104,380 in total.

Calculate **contribution per unit**

	Beta	Gamma	Delta
	$ per unit	$ per unit	$ per unit
Selling price	135.00	165.00	220.00
Variable cost	73.50	58.90	146.20

Calculate **contribution per mix**

= ($61.50 × 3) + ($106.10 × 4) + ($73.80 × 5)

= $977.90

Calculate the **breakeven point** in terms of the **number of mixes**

= fixed costs/contribution per mix

= $950,000/$977.90 = 972 mixes (rounded up)

Calculate the **breakeven point** in terms of the **number of units of the products**

= (972 × 3) 2,916 units of Beta, (972 × 4) 3,888 units of Gamma and (972 × 5) 4,860 units of Delta (rounded)

Calculate the **breakeven point** in terms of **revenue**

= (2,916 × $135) + (3,888 × $165) + (4,860 × $220)

= $393,660 of Beta, $641,520 of Gamma and $1,069,200 of Delta = $2,104,380 in total

---

5.2 C/S ratio for multiple products

Calculate revenue per mix
= (3 × $135) + (4 × $165) + (5 × $220)
= $2,165

Calculate contribution per mix
= $977.90 (from Question: breakeven point for multiple products)

Calculate average C/S ratio
= ($977.90/$2,165) × 100%
= 45.17%

Calculate breakeven point (total)
= fixed costs ÷ C/S ratio
= $950,000/0.4517
= $2,103,166 (rounded)

Calculate revenue ratio of mix
= 405:660:1,100, or 81:132:220

Calculate breakeven sales

Breakeven sales of Beta   = 81/433 × \$2,103,166 = \$393,433
Breakeven sales of Gamma = 132/433 × \$2,103,166 = \$641,150
Breakeven sales of Delta = 220/433 × \$2,103,166 = \$1,068,583

5.3 Average C/S ratio

$$\text{Average C/S ratio} = \frac{(20\% \times 1) + (40\% \times 2)}{3} = 33\tfrac{1}{3}\%$$

$$\text{Sales revenue at the breakeven point} = \frac{\text{fixed costs}}{\text{C / S ratio}} = \frac{\$30,000}{0.333} = \$90,000$$

5.4 Using the C/S ratio

$$\text{Sales revenue must be } \frac{\$1}{38.6c} \times \$200,000 = \$518,135$$

5.5 Sales mix decision

The revised C/S ratio is 45%.

	U	C	Y	Total
P/V ratio	0.55*	0.45	0.35	
Market share	× 0.25	× 0.35	× 0.40	
	0.1375	0.1575	0.140	0.435

* 0.1375/0.25

With revised proportions:

	U	C	Y	Total
P/V ratio	0.55	0.45	0.35	
Market share	× 0.30	× 0.40	× 0.30	
	0.165	0.18	0.105	0.45

5.6 Multi-product P/V chart

	X	Y	Z	Total
				$
Contribution per unit	$0.75	$0.50	$0.75	
Budgeted contribution (total)	$1,500	$1,000	$3,750	6,250
Fixed costs				3,250
Budgeted profit				3,000

Product	Cumulative sales $		Cumulative profit $
Z	10,000	($3,750 – $3,250)	500
Z and X	16,000		2,000
Z, X and Y	24,000		3,000

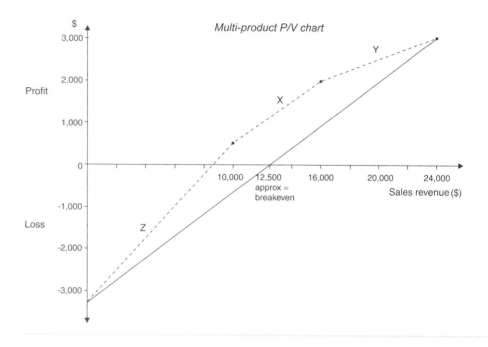

5.7 Breakeven point and sales value constraints

The correct answer is $390,000

Breakeven point occurs when contribution = fixed costs

∴ Minimum breakeven point occurs when contribution is $60,000.

Contribution achieved from minimum sales value

		$
M	5% × $50,000	2,500
A	10% × $50,000	5,000
R	15% × $20,000	3,000
P	20% × $10,000	2,000
		12,500

Product P has the highest C/S ratio and so should be produced first (as it earns more contribution per $ of revenue than the others).

Contribution from sales of P between minimum and maximum points = $170,000 × 20% = $34,000

∴ Required contribution from Product R (which has the next highest C/S ratio)

    = $(60,000 – 12,500 – 34,000)

= $13,500

Revenue from Product R of $13,500/0.15 = $90,000 will produce $13,500 of contribution.

∴ Lowest breakeven sales

= $130,000 (minimum sales) + $170,000 (from P) + $90,000 (from R)
= $390,000

5.8 Sensitivity analysis

(a) **Results for the year ended 31 January 20X0**

	Ladies' wear $'000	%	Men's wear $'000	%	General $'000	%	Toys $'000	%	Restaurant $'000	%	Total $'000	%
Sales	800	100	400	100	2,200	100	1,400	100	200	100	5,000	100
Cost of sales (W1)	496	62	240	60	1,320	60	1,176	84	166	83	3,398	68
Contribution	304	38	160	40	880	40	224	16	34	17	1,602	32
Wages	96		47		155		59		26		383	
Expenses	38		13		35		20		10		116	
Sales promotion and advertising	10		5		30		75		-		120	
	144	18	65	16	220	10	154	11	36	18	619	12
Gross profit/(loss)	160	20	95	24	660	30	70	5	(2)	(1)	983	20

	Total $'000	$'000
Gross profit		983
Indirect costs		
Office wages	70	
Delivery costs	200	
Salaries: directors and management	100	
Directors' fees	20	
Store capacity costs	488	
Interest on bank overdraft	20	
Discounts allowed	25	
Bad debts	15	
Miscellaneous expenses	75	
		1,013
Net loss		(30)

	Ladies' wear	Men's wear	General	Toys	Restaurant
Contribution per 1% of floor space	$15,200	$10,667	$44,000	$6,400	$3,400
Gross profit per 1% of floor space	$8,000	$6,333	$33,000	$2,000	($200)
No of days inventory (W2)	74	76	47	62	13

Workings

1

	Ladies' wear $'000	Men's wear $'000	General $'000	Toys $'000	Restaurant $'000
Opening inventory	90	70	200	100	5
Purchases	506	220	1,290	1,276	167
	596	290	1,490	1,376	172
Closing inventory	100	50	170	200	6
Cost of sales	496	240	1,320	1,176	166

2	(i)	Cost of sales					
		per day (÷ 365)	1.36	0.66	3.62	3.22	0.45
	(ii)	Closing inventory	100	50	170	200	6
		∴ (ii) ÷ (i)	74	76	47	62	13

(b)   *Assumption.* Wages, departmental expenses and sales promotion and advertising expenses are fixed costs which would not be affected by any changes in sales.

	Ladies' wear			*Men's wear*	
	$'000	%		$'000	%
Revised sales value (95%)	760			380	
Cost of sales	496			240	
Revised contribution	264	34.74		140	36.84
Contribution required	304			160	
∴ Sales required (÷ 0.3474)	875		(÷ 0.3684)	434	

(i)   **Sales increase required compared to current sales**   75   34

(ii)   Percentage increase   9.4   8.5

(c)   The calculations in part (b) show that **sales of ladies' wear and men's wear would have to increase** by 9.4% and 8.5% respectively to maintain profits if prices were reduced by 5%. The directors' decision will depend on their assessment of the likelihood of sales increasing by more than these amounts so that profits would increase. The lower prices could attract more people into the store so that the sales of other departments might also increase.

The only area showing a **negative gross profit** is the **restaurant**. However, before taking a decision to close the restaurant the directors should consider whether this will reduce the number of people entering the store and therefore reduce sales in the store as a whole. A review of restaurant prices should be carried out to attempt to improve profitability.

Inventory levels in the **ladies' wear and men's wear departments** are **high compared to the level of sales**. This can be costly in terms of interest charges on the bank overdraft and may lead to large inventory write-offs if fashions change rapidly. A review of the policy over inventory held may help to reduce costs.

Now try the question from the Exam Question Bank	Number	Level	Marks	Time
	Q10	Examination	25	45 mins

PRICING DECISIONS AND PRICING STRATEGIES

Although pricing is no longer viewed as being the most important decision made by the sales and marketing teams, it is still important for **profit-making purposes** and hence the company's survival. It is a **highly competitive tool**, particularly in markets where **product differentiation** is dominant.

This chapter focuses not only on **pricing decisions** but also on **pricing strategies**. The pricing strategy adopted will depend heavily on the **type of market** in which the product is being sold and the product's position in its **life cycle**.

The chapter begins with a look at factors that influence the pricing decision and moves onto pricing to **maximise profits**. As we move through the chapter we will consider **cost-based approaches** to pricing, followed by pricing strategies that are appropriate in particular circumstances.

This is quite a long chapter with a lot of material in it. Read through it slowly, making sure you understand each concept before moving on.

topic list	learning outcomes	syllabus references	ability required
1 Demand	A3(a)	A3(i)	application
2 Other issues that influence pricing decisions	A3(a)	A3(i)	application
3 Deriving the demand curve	A3(a)	A3(i)	application
4 The profit-maximising price/output level	A3(a), (b)	A3(i)	application
5 Full cost-plus pricing	A1(c)	A1(iv)	analysis
6 Marginal cost-plus (mark-up) pricing	A1(c)	A1(iv)	analysis
7 Pricing based on mark-up per unit of limiting factor	A1(c)	A1(iv)	analysis
8 Pricing strategies for new products	A3(b)	A3(ii)	analysis
9 Other pricing strategies	A3(b)	A3(ii)	analysis

1 Demand

Introduction

In the first sections of this chapter you will be learning about the many issues that need to be considered in decisions about the price which can be charged for a product or service. The first issues relate to demand.

1.1 Issue 1: the relationship between price and demand

There are two extremes in the relationship between price and demand. A supplier can either **sell a certain quantity, Q, at any price** (as in graph (a)). Demand is totally unresponsive to changes in price and is said to be **completely inelastic**. Alternatively, **demand might be limitless at a certain price** P (as in graph (b)), but there would be no demand above price P and there would be little point in dropping the price below P. In such circumstances demand is said to be **completely elastic**.

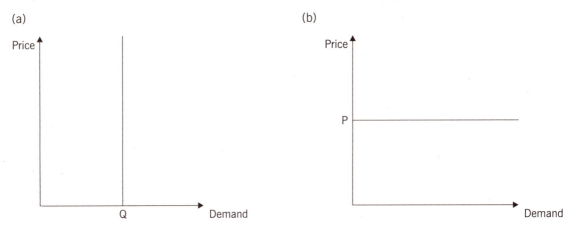

A more **normal situation** is shown below. The **downward-sloping** demand curve shows the inverse relationship between unit selling price and sales volume. As one rises, the other falls. Demand is **elastic** because demand will increase as prices are lowered.

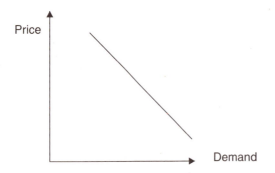

1.1.1 Price elasticity of demand (η)

KEY TERM

PRICE ELASTICITY OF DEMAND (η), which is a measure of the extent of change in market demand for a good in response to a change in its price, is measured as:

$$\frac{\text{The change in quantity demanded, as a \% of demand}}{\text{The change in price, as a \% of the price}}$$

Since the demand goes up when the price falls, and goes down when the price rises, the elasticity has a negative value, but it is usual to ignore the minus sign.

Example: Price elasticity of demand

The price of a good is $1.20 per unit and annual demand is 800,000 units. Market research indicates that an increase in price of 10 pence per unit will result in a fall in annual demand of 75,000 units. What is the price elasticity of demand?

Solution

Annual demand at $1.20 per unit is 800,000 units.

Annual demand at $1.30 per unit is 725,000 units.

% change in demand $\quad = (75,000/800,000) \times 100\% = 9.375\%$
% change in price $\quad\quad = (10p/120p) \times 100\% = 8.333\%$
Price elasticity of demand $\quad = (-9.375/8.333) = -1.125$

Ignoring the minus sign, price elasticity is 1.125.

The demand for this good, at a price of $1.20 per unit, would be referred to as **elastic** because the **price elasticity of demand is greater than 1**.

1.1.2 Elastic and inelastic demand

The value of demand elasticity may be anything from zero to infinity.

Demand is referred to as INELASTIC if the absolute value is less than 1 and **elastic** if the absolute value is greater than 1.

KEY TERM

Exam skills

Think about what this means.

(a)   Where demand is inelastic, the quantity demanded falls by a smaller percentage than the percentage increase in price.

(b)   Where demand is elastic, demand falls by a larger percentage than the percentage rise in price.

1.1.3 Price elasticity and the slope of the demand curve

Generally, **demand curves slope downwards**. Consumers are willing to buy more at lower prices than at higher prices. In general, **elasticity** will **vary** in value **along the length of a demand curve**.

(a)   If a downward sloping demand curve becomes **steeper** over a particular range of quantity, then demand is becoming **more inelastic**.

(b)   A **shallower** demand curve over a particular range indicates **more elastic** demand.

The ranges of price elasticity at different points on a downward sloping straight line demand curve are illustrated in the diagram below.

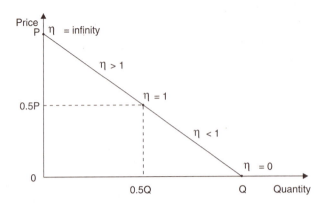

(a)   At **higher prices** on a straight line demand curve (the **top** of the demand curve), **small percentage price reductions** can bring **large percentage increases in quantity** demanded. This means that **demand is elastic** over these ranges, and **price reductions** bring **increases in total expenditure** by consumers on the commodity in question.

(b)   At **lower prices** on a straight line demand curve (the **bottom** of the demand curve), **large percentage price reductions** can bring **small percentage increases in quantity**. This means that **demand is inelastic** over these price ranges, and **price increases** result in **increases in total expenditure**.

1.1.4 Two special values of price elasticity

(a)   **Demand is perfectly inelastic ($\eta = 0$). There is **no change in quantity** demanded, **regardless of the change in price**. The demand curve is **a vertical straight line** (as in graph (a) in Section 1.1).

(b)   **Perfectly elastic demand ($\eta = \infty$)**. Consumers will want to **buy an infinite amount**, but **only up to a particular price level**. Any price increase above this level will reduce demand to zero. The demand curve is a **horizontal straight line** (as in graph (b) in Section 1.1).

1.1.5 Elasticity and the pricing decision

In practice, organisations will have only a rough idea of the shape of their demand curve: there will only be a limited amount of data about quantities sold at certain prices over a period of time *and,* of course, factors other than price might affect demand. Because any conclusions drawn from such data can only give an indication of likely future behaviour, management skill and expertise are also needed. Despite this limitation, an **awareness of the concept of elasticity can assist management with pricing decisions**.

(a)   (i)   With **inelastic demand, increase prices** because revenues will increase and total costs will reduce (because quantities sold will reduce).

(ii)   With **elastic demand**, increases in prices will bring decreases in revenue and decreases in price will bring increases in revenue. Management therefore have to **decide** whether the **increase/decrease in costs will be less than/greater than the increases/decreases in revenue**.

(b)   In situations of **very elastic demand**, overpricing can lead to massive drops in quantity sold and hence profits, whereas underpricing can lead to costly inventory outs and, again, a significant drop in profits. **Elasticity must therefore be reduced by creating a customer preference which is unrelated to price** (through advertising and promotion).

(c)   In situations of **very inelastic demand**, customers are **not sensitive to price. Quality, service, product mix and location** are therefore **more important** to a firm's pricing strategy.

(d)   In practice, the **prices** of many products, such as consumer durables, need to **fall** over time if demand is to rise. **Costs** must therefore **fall by the same percentage to maintain margins**.

1.1.6 Determining factors

Factors that determine the degree of elasticity	Detail
The price of the good	
The price of other goods	For two types of good the market demand is interconnected.
	(a) **Substitutes,** so that an increase in demand for one version of a good is likely to cause a decrease in demand for others. Examples include rival brands of the same commodity (like *Coca-Cola* and *Pepsi-Cola*).
	(b) **Complements,** so that an increase in demand for one is likely to cause an increase in demand for the other (eg cups and saucers).
Income	A rise in income gives households more to spend and they will want to buy more goods. However this phenomenon does not affect all goods in the same way.
	(a) Normal goods are those for which a rise in income increases the demand.
	(b) Inferior goods are those for which demand falls as income rises, such as cheap clothes.
	(c) For some goods demand rises up to a certain point and then remains unchanged, because there is a limit to which consumers can or want to consume. Examples are basic foodstuffs such as salt and bread.
Tastes and fashions	A change in fashion will alter the demand for a good, or a particular variety of a good. Changes in taste may stem from psychological, social or economic causes. There is an argument that tastes and fashions are created by the producers of products and services. There is undeniably some truth in this, but the modern focus on responding to customers' needs and wants suggests otherwise.
Expectations	Where consumers believe that prices will rise or that shortages will occur they will attempt to inventory up on the product, thereby creating excess demand in the short term.
Obsolescence	Many products and services have to be replaced periodically.
	(a) Physical goods are literally 'consumed'. Carpets become threadbare, glasses get broken, foodstuffs get eaten, children grow out of clothes.
	(b) Technological developments render some goods obsolete. Manual office equipment has been largely replaced by electronic equipment, because it does a better job, more quickly, quietly, efficiently and effectively.
Size of the market	The larger the market, the more inelastic the demand for the product in broad terms. For example, the demand for bread is relatively inelastic, whereas that for speciality bread such as olive ciabatta may be more elastic.
Necessities	Demand for basic items such as milk, toilet rolls and bread is, on the whole, price inelastic.

1.2 Issue 2: demand and the market

Economic theory suggests that the volume of **demand** for a good in **the market as a whole** is influenced by a variety of variables.

- The price of the good
- The price of other goods
- Expectations
- Obsolescence

- Tastes and fashion
- The perceived quality of the product
- The size and distribution of household income

1.3 Issue 3: demand and the individual firm

1.3.1 Product life cycle   5/10, 5/11

KEY TERM

PRODUCT LIFE CYCLE is 'The period which begins with the initial product specification, and ends with the withdrawal from the market of both the product and its support. It is characterised by defined stages including research, development, introduction, maturity, decline and abandonment.'

(CIMA *Official Terminology*)

The typical product life cycle can be represented in graphical form:

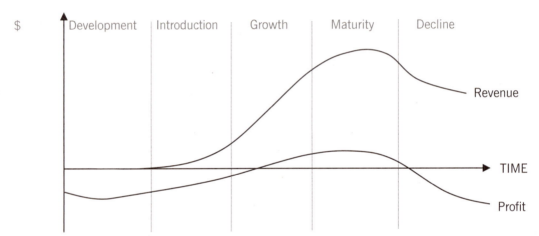

The four phases are described in more detail below:

Phase	Description
Introduction	The product is introduced to the market. Heavy capital expenditure will be incurred on product development and perhaps on the purchase of new non-current assets and building up inventory. On its launch, the product will earn some revenue, but initial demand is likely to be small. Potential customers will be unaware of the product or service, and more advertising spend may be needed to bring it to the attention of the market.
Growth	The product gains a bigger market as demand builds up. Sales revenues increase and the product begins to make a profit. The initial costs of the investment in the new product are gradually recovered.
Maturity	Eventually, growth in demand for the product will slow down and it will enter a period of relative maturity. It will continue to be profitable. The product may be modified or improved, as a means of sustaining demand.
Saturation and decline	At some stage, the market will have bought enough of the product and it will therefore reach 'saturation point'. Demand will fall. For a while, the product will still be profitable despite falling sales, but eventually it will become a loss-maker and this is the time when the organisation should stop selling the product, and so then its life cycle should reach its end.

CASE STUDY

During 2009, Universal Music lowered CD prices in an attempt to 'bring new life' to the flagging format.

The life expectancy of a product will influence the pricing decision. **Short-life products** must be quite **highly priced** so as to give the manufacturer a chance to **recover his investment** and **make a worthwhile** return. This is why fashion goods and new high technology goods, for example, tend to have high prices.

The current tendency is towards shorter product life cycles. Notwithstanding this observation, the **life cycles** of different products may **vary in terms of length of phases, overall length and shape**.

(a)   Fashion products have a very short life and so do high technology products because they become rapidly out-dated by new technological developments.

(b)   **Different versions of the same product may have different life cycles**, and consumers are often aware of this. For example, the prospective buyer of a new car is more likely to purchase a recently introduced Ford than a Vauxhall that has been on the market for several years, even if there is nothing to choose in terms of quality and price.

1.3.2 Quality

One firm's product may be perceived to be better quality than another's, and may in some cases actually be so, if it uses sturdier materials, goes faster or does whatever it is meant to do in a 'better' way. Other things being equal, **the better quality good will be more in demand** than other versions.

1.3.3 Marketing

You may be familiar with the 'four Ps' of the marketing mix, all of which influence demand for a firm's goods.

Ps	Details
Price	This refers to the price at which the product is being sold.
Product	This refers to the particular product being analysed.
Place	This refers to the place where a good can be, or is likely to be, purchased.
	• If a good is difficult to obtain, potential buyers will turn to substitutes.
	• Some goods only have a local appeal.
Promotion	This refers to the various means by which firms draw attention to their products and services.
	• A good brand name is a strong influence on demand.
	• Demand can be stimulated by a variety of promotional tools, such as free gifts, money off, shop displays, direct mail and media advertising.

In recent years, **emphasis** has been placed, especially in marketing, on the importance of **non-price factors in demand**. Thus the roles of product quality, promotion, personal selling and distribution and, in overall terms, brands, have grown. While it can be relatively easy for a competitor to copy a price cut, at least in the short term, it is much **more difficult to copy a successful brand image**.

Some larger organisations go to considerable effort to estimate the demand for their products or services at differing price levels; in other words, they produce estimated demand curves. A **knowledge of demand curves can be very useful**.

For example, a large transport company such as *Stagecoach* might be considering an increase in bus fares. The effect on total revenues and profit of the fares increase could be estimated from a **knowledge of the demand for transport services at different price levels**. If an increase in the price per ticket caused a large fall in demand (that is, if demand were price-elastic) total revenues and profits would fall;

whereas a fares increase when demand is price-inelastic would boost total revenue and since a transport authority's costs are largely fixed, would probably boost total profits too.

Section summary

Demand is normally **elastic** because demand will increase as prices are lowered.

Price elasticity of demand is a measure of the extent of change in market demand for a good in response to a change in its price.

If **demand** is **elastic**, a reduction in price would lead to a rise in total sales revenue. If **demand** is **inelastic**, a reduction in price would lead to a fall in total sales revenue.

The **volume of demand for one organisation's goods rather than another's** is influenced by three principal factors: product life cycle, quality and marketing.

2 Other issues that influence pricing decisions

Introduction

This section follows on from Section 1 by covering additional issues that influence pricing decisions, including competition, quality, price sensitivity and the market in which an organisation operates.

2.1 Issue 4: markets

The price that an organisation can charge for its products will be determined to a greater or lesser degree by the market in which it operates. Here are some familiar terms that might feature as background for a question or that you might want to use in a written answer.

KEY TERMS

(a) PERFECT COMPETITION: many buyers and many sellers all dealing in an identical product. Neither producer nor user has any market power and both must accept the prevailing market price.

(b) MONOPOLY: one seller who dominates many buyers. The monopolist can use his market power to set a profit-maximising price.

(c) MONOPOLISTIC COMPETITION: a large number of suppliers offer similar, but not identical, products. The similarities ensure elastic demand whereas the slight differences give some monopolistic power to the supplier.

(d) OLIGOPOLY: where relatively few competitive companies dominate the market. Whilst each large firm has the ability to influence market prices the unpredictable reaction from the other giants makes the final industry price indeterminate. CARTELS are often formed.

Question 6.1   Markets

Learning outcome A3(a)

A cartel is often formed in which type of market?

2.2 Issue 5: competition

In established industries dominated by a few major firms, it is generally accepted that a price initiative by one firm will be countered by a price reaction by competitors. In these circumstances, prices tend to be fairly **stable**, unless pushed upwards by inflation or strong growth in demand.

If a rival cuts its prices in the expectation of increasing its market share, a firm has several options.

(a)   It will **maintain its existing prices** if the expectation is that only a small market share would be lost, so that it is more profitable to keep prices at their existing level. Eventually, the rival firm may drop out of the market or be forced to raise its prices.

(b)   It may **maintain its prices but respond with a non-price counter-attack**. This is a more positive response, because the firm will be securing or justifying its current prices with a product change, advertising, or better back-up services.

(c)   It may **reduce its prices**. This should protect the firm's market share so that the main beneficiary from the price reduction will be the consumer.

(d)   It may **raise its prices and respond with a non-price counter-attack**. The extra revenue from the higher prices might be used to finance an advertising campaign or product design changes. A price increase would be based on a campaign to emphasise the quality difference between the firm's own product and the rival's product.

2.2.1 Fighting a price war

Peter Bartram (*Financial Management,* March 2001) suggested a number of ways to fight a price war.

(a)   **Sell on value, not price**, where value is made up of service, response, variety, knowledge, quality, guarantee and price.

(b)   **Target service, not product market niches**, to build in the six non-price factors in (a) above.

CASE STUDY

The Marriott hotel chain has chosen to compete in the premium market on service. When guests arrive, instead of queuing at a busy reception, they are met at the front door by a host who gives them their room key.

(c)   **Use 'package pricing' to attract customers**

CASE STUDY

Computer retailers such as PC World have beaten discounters by offering peripherals, discounted software and extended warranties as part of their more expensive packages.

(d)   **Make price comparisons difficult**. Terrestrial and mobile phone companies offer a bewildering variety of rates and discount offers which disguise the core price and make comparisons almost impossible.

(e)   **Build up key accounts**, as it is cheaper to get more business from an existing customer than to find a new one. Customer profitability analysis, covered in Chapter 8, is important here.

(f)   **Explore new pricing models**. E-business provides opportunities to use new pricing models.

   (i)   On-line auctions for a wide range of products are carried out on certain websites.

   (ii)   Other websites use a 'community shopping' pricing model, where the price of an item falls as more people buy it.

   (iii)   Marginal cost pricing is used on certain websites to get rid of inventory such as unsold theatre tickets and holidays.

CASE STUDY

Budget airlines such as EasyJet vary the price of a ticket depending on how early the traveller books.

2.3 Other issues

Issue	Explanation/example
Price sensitivity	This will vary amongst purchasers. Those that can pass on the cost of purchases will be the least sensitive and will therefore respond more to other elements of perceived value. For example, the business traveller will be more concerned about the level of service and quality of food in looking for an hotel than price, provided that it fits the corporate budget. In contrast, the family on holiday are likely to be very price sensitive when choosing an overnight stay.
Price perception	This is the way customers react to prices. For example, customers may react to a price increase by buying more. This could be because they expect further price increases to follow (they are 'stocking up').
Compatibility with other products	A typical example is operating systems on computers, for which a user would like to have a wide range of compatible software available. For these types of product there is usually a **cumulative effect on demand**. The more people who buy one of the formats, the more choice there is likely to be of software for that format. This in turn is likely to influence future purchasers. The owner of the rights to the preferred format will eventually find little competition and will be able to charge a premium price for the product.
Competitors	An organisation, in setting prices, sends out signals. Competitors are likely to react to these signals in some way. In some industries (such as petrol retailing) pricing moves in unison; in others, price changes by one supplier may initiate a price war, with each supplier undercutting the others. Competition is discussed in more detail below.
Competition from substitute products	These are products which could be transformed for the same use or which might become desirable to customers at particular price levels. For example, train travel comes under competition as the quality, speed and comfort of coach travel rises. Similarly, if the price of train travel rises it comes under competition from cheaper coach travel and more expensive air travel.
Suppliers	If an organisation's suppliers notice a price rise for the organisation's products, they may seek a rise in the price for their supplies to the organisation on the grounds that it is now able to pay a higher price.
Inflation	In periods of inflation the organisation may need to change prices to reflect increases in the prices of supplies and so on. Such changes may be needed to keep relative (real) prices unchanged.
Quality	In the absence of other information, customers tend to judge quality by price. Thus a price change may send signals to customers concerning the quality of the product. A price rise may indicate improvements in quality, a price reduction may signal reduced quality, for example through the use of inferior components.
Incomes	In times of rising incomes, price may become a less important marketing variable compared with product quality and convenience of access (distribution). When income levels are falling and/or unemployment levels rising, price will become a much more important marketing variable.

Section summary

As well as demand, a **range of other issues influence pricing decisions** including the market in which an organisation operates, competition, quality and price sensitivity.

3 Deriving the demand curve   9/10, 5/11

Introduction

The demand curve shows the relationship between the price charged for a product and the subsequent demand for that product. This section shows how a demand curve is derived. Don't be put off by the equations – work through the examples slowly and make sure you are comfortable with working with the equations before moving on.

3.1 Demand curve equations

LEARN

Formula text style = icon anchored here. Formula to learn

When demand is linear the **equation for the demand curve is P = a – bx**

Where P = the selling price
    x = the quantity demanded at that price
    a = theoretical maximum price. If price is set at "a" or above, demand will be zero
    b = the change in price required to change demand by one unit.
    a and b are constants and are calculated as follows:

$$a = \$ \text{ (current price)} + \left(\frac{\text{Current quantity at current price}}{\text{Change in quantity when price changed by \$b}} \times \$b \right)$$

$$b = \frac{\text{Change in price}}{\text{Change in quantity}} \quad \text{(it is the gradient of line)}$$

You need to learn these formulae.

Example: Deriving the demand curve

The current price of a product is $12. At this price the company sells 12,000 items a month. One month the company decides to raise the price to $13, but only 9,500 items are sold at this price. Determine the demand equation.

Solution

Find the gradient of the line (b)

Using the formula above, this can be shown as:

$$b = \frac{\$1}{2,500} = 0.0004$$

Extract figures from the question

The **demand equation** can now be determined as P = a – bx

b = 0.0004

x = 12,000 (number of units sold at current selling price)

P = a – (0.0004 x 12,000)

12 = a – 4.80

a = 16.80

∴P = 16.80 – 0.0004x

Check your equation

We can check this by substituting $12 and $13 for P.

12 = 16.80 – 0.0004x = 16.80 – (0.0004 x 12,000)
13 = 16.80 – 0.0004x = 16.80 – (0.0004 x 9,500)

Example: Profit maximisation and the demand curve

Maximum demand for JL's product is 110,000 units per annum. Demand will reduce by 50 units for every $1 increase in the selling price. JL has calculated that the profit-maximising level of sales for the coming year will be 42,000 units.

Required

Calculate the profit maximising selling price for the product.

Solution

Using the demand equation P = a-bx

P = selling price

x = the quantity demanded at that price

a,b = constants

Maximum demand is achieved when the product is free (when P = 0).

When price = 0, demand (x) = 110,000   0 = a – 110,000b (i)

When price = 1, demand (x) = 109,950   1 = a – 109,950b (ii)

Subtract (i) from (ii)   1 = 50b

                                      b = 0.02

Substitute in (i)   a = 110,000 x 0.02

                                        = 2,200

The demand equation for the product is therefore P = 2,200 – 0.02x

When x = 42,000 units   P = 2,200 – (0.02 x 42,000)

                                           = 1,360

Therefore, the profit-maximising selling price is $1,360 per unit

Question 6.2	Profit maximisation

Learning outcomes A3(a)

Maximum demand for AL's product is 8,000 units per annum. Demand will reduce by 50 units for every $1 increase in the selling price.

AL has calculated that the profit-maximising selling price for the coming year will be $10.

What is the profit-maximising sales level in units?

Section summary

When demand is linear the **equation for the demand curve** is **P = a − bx**

Where P = the selling price
     x = the quantity demanded at that price
     a = theoretical maximum price. If price is set at "a" or above, demand will be zero
     b = the change in price required to change demand by one unit.

a and b are constants and are calculated as follows:

$$a = \$ \text{ (current price)} + \left(\frac{\text{Current quantity at current price}}{\text{Change in quantity when price changed by \$b}} \times \$b \right)$$

$$b = \frac{\text{Change in price}}{\text{Change in quantity}} \quad \text{(it is the gradient of line)}$$

You need to learn these formulae.

---

4 The profit-maximising price/output level   9/11, 5/12

Introduction

The overall objective of an organisation should be **profit maximisation**. In this section we look at how the profit-maximising price and output levels can be derived. Remember that, in microeconomic theory, profits are maximised when marginal revenue = marginal cost.

4.1 Microeconomic theory and profit maximisation

Microeconomic theory suggests that as output increases, the marginal cost per unit might rise (due to the law of diminishing returns) and whenever the firm is faced with a downward sloping demand curve, the **marginal revenue per unit will decline**.

Eventually, a level of output will be reached where the **extra cost** of making one extra unit of output is greater than the **extra revenue** obtained from its sale. It would then be unprofitable to make and sell that extra unit.

Profits will continue to be maximised only up to the output level where marginal cost has risen to be exactly equal to the marginal revenue.

Profits are maximised using marginalist theory when **marginal cost (MC) = marginal revenue (MR)**.

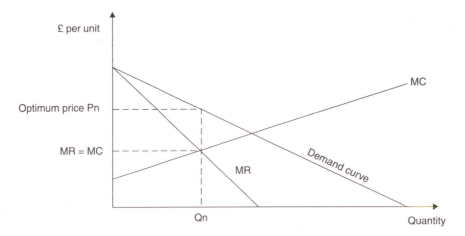

Profits are **maximised** at the point where **MC = MR**, ie at a volume of Qn units. If we add a demand curve to the graph, we can see that at an output level of Qn, the sales price per unit would be Pn.

It is important to make a clear distinction in your mind between the **sales price** and **marginal revenue**. In this example, the optimum price is Pn, but the marginal revenue is much less. This is because the 'additional' sales unit to reach output Qn has only been achieved by reducing the unit sales **price** from an amount higher than Pn for all the units to be sold, not just the marginal extra one. The increase in sales volume is therefore partly offset by a reduction in unit price; hence MR is lower than Pn.

4.2 Determining the profit-maximising selling price: using equations

The **optimal selling price** can be determined using equations (ie when MC = MR).

You could be **provided with equations for marginal cost and marginal revenue** and/or have to **devise them from information** in the question. By **equating the two equations** you can determine the optimal price. Remember, **marginal cost** is the **extra cost of producing one extra unit, marginal revenue** is the **extra revenue from producing one extra unit. Marginal revenue may not be the same as** the **price** charged for all units up to that demand level, as to increase volumes the price may have to be reduced. The following example provides an illustration.

Example: MC = MR

MOC makes and sells a copyrighted, executive game for two distinct markets, in which it has a monopoly. The fixed costs of production per month are $20,000 and variable costs per unit produced, and sold, are $40. (The monthly sales can be thought of as X, where $X = X_1 + X_2$, with X_1 and X_2 denoting monthly sales in their respective markets.) Detailed market research has revealed the demand functions in the markets to be as follows, with prices shown as P_1, P_2.

Market 1: $\qquad\qquad\qquad\qquad$ $P_1 = 55 - 0.05X_1$
Market 2: $\qquad\qquad\qquad\qquad$ $P_2 = 200 - 0.2X_2$

(Note. These formulae are simply **linear equations**. They show how the price (P) can be determined for a given level of demand (X). So in market 1, at a level of demand of 100, the price (P) will be $55 - (0.05 \times 100) = 50$.)

From these, the management accountant has derived that the marginal revenue functions in the two markets are as follows.

Market 1: $MR_1 = 55 - 0.1X_1$
Market 2: $MR_2 = 200 - 0.4X_2$

(Note. In market 1, the marginal revenue if 100 units are sold is $55 - (0.1 \times 100) = 45$.)

The management accountant believes there should be price discrimination; the price is currently $50 per game in either market.

Required

Analyse the information for the executive game and, given the management accountant's belief, do the following.

(a)   Calculate the price to charge in each market, and the quantity to produce (and sell) each month, to maximise profit.

(b)   Determine the revenue function for each market and the maximum monthly profit in total.

(c)   Calculate and comment on the change in total profitability and prices.

Solution

(a)   In both markets, **marginal cost = variable cost per unit = $40**

        Profit is maximised when **marginal revenue = marginal cost**.

        Market 1

        $55 - 0.1X_1 = 40$
        $0.1X_1 = 15$
        $X_1 = 15/0.1 = 150$

        and price $P_1 = 55 - (0.05 \times 150) = \$47.5$.

        Hence the price in market 1 should be $47.50 per unit and 150 units should be produced.

        Market 2

        $200 - 0.4X_2 = 40$

        $0.4X_2 = 160$
        $X_2 = 160/0.4 = 400$

        and price $P_2 = 200 - (0.2 \times 400) = \$120$.

        Hence the price in market 2 should be $120 per unit and 400 units should be produced.

        Total number of items to be produced per month is 550.

(b)   **Revenue = unit price × number of units sold**

        Market 1

        Revenue $= P_1X_1 = 55X_1 - 0.05X_1^2$

        Market 2

        Revenue $= P_2X_2 = 200X_2 - 0.2X_2^2$

        From (a), profit is maximised when

        $X_1 = 150$ and $X_2 = 400$
        $P_1 = 47.5$ and $P_2 = 120$

At maximum profit:

Total revenue = (47.5 × 150) + (120 × 400) = $55,125

Total costs = 20,000 + (40 × 550) = $42,000

Total maximum monthly profit = $13,125

(c)   Currently the price is $50 in both markets.

Market 1	$50 = 55 - 0.05X_1$
	$0.05X_1 = 55 - 50 = 5$
	$X_1 = 5/0.05 = 100$
Market 2	$50 = 200 - 0.2X_2$
	$0.2X_2 = 200 - 50 = 150$
	$X_2 = 150/0.2 = 750$

Therefore the **total number of units** = 100 + 750 = 850.

Total revenue = $50 × 850 = $42,500.
Total cost = 20,000 + (40 × 850) = $54,000.

So the game **currently makes a loss** of $11,500.

Hence, if the prices are changed to $47.50 in market 1 and $120 in market 2, the company can expect to turn a monthly loss of $11,500 into a profit of $13,125.

You will be provided with equations representing MC and MR if they are needed. Note, however, that if a question states that the extra cost of producing one extra item is $20, say, you will be expected to realise that the MC is $20. Likewise, if you are told that **100 units are sold for $10 each**, but **101 can only be sold for $9.99**, the **MR of the 101st item is (101 × $9.99) – (100 × $10) = $8.99**.

 Question 6.3   Deriving a MR equation from the demand curve

Learning outcomes A3(a), (b)

AB has used market research to determine that if a price of $250 is charged for product G, demand will be 12,000 units. It has also been established that demand will rise or fall by 5 units for every $1 fall/rise in the selling price. The marginal cost of product G is $80.

Required

If marginal revenue = a –2bx when the selling price (P) = a – bx, calculate the profit-maximising selling price for product G.

4.3 Determining the profit-maximising selling price: visual inspection of a tabulation of data

 The **optimum selling price** can also be determined using tabulation, graphs and gradients.

KEY POINT

To determine the profit-maximising selling price:

(a)   Work out the **demand curve** and hence the **price** and the **total revenue** (PQ) at various levels of demand.

(b)   Calculate **total cost** and hence **marginal cost** at each level of demand.

(c)   Finally calculate **profit** at each level of demand, thereby determining the price and level of demand at which profits are maximised.

Question 6.4   Tabulation approach to find profit-maximising price

Learning outcomes A3(a), (b)

An organisation operates in a market where there is imperfect competition, so that to sell more units of output, it must reduce the sales price of all the units it sells. The following data is available for prices and costs.

Total output Units	Sales price per unit (AR) $	Average cost of output (AC) $ per unit
0	–	–
1	504	720
2	471	402
3	439	288
4	407	231
5	377	201
6	346	189
7	317	182
8	288	180
9	259	186
10	232	198

The total cost of zero output is $600.

Required

Complete the table below to determine the output level and price at which the organisation would maximise its profits, assuming that fractions of units cannot be made.

Units	Price $	Total revenue $	Marginal revenue $	Total cost $	Marginal cost $	Profit $
0						
1						
2						
3						
4						
5						
6						
7						
8						
9						
10						
10						

4.4 Determining the profit-maximising selling price: graphical approach

The diagrams below show that **profits are maximised** at the point where the **vertical distance** between the total revenue curve and the total costs curve is at a **maximum** (which is fairly obvious if you think about it since profits are maximised when the difference between cost and revenue is maximised). This profit-maximising demand level also **corresponds** to the point at which the **MC and MR curves intersect**, as we would expect. Notice how the profit-maximising price can be read off from the demand curve.

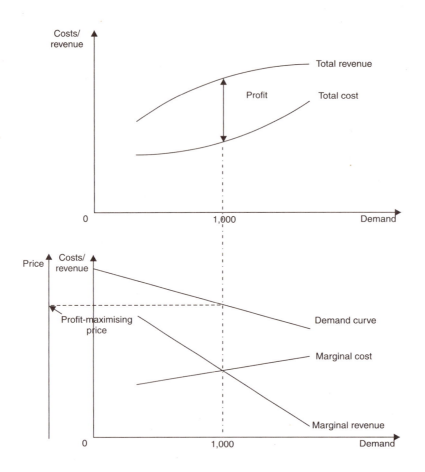

4.5 Determining the profit-maximising selling price: using gradients

Suppose we were to draw **tangents** to the total revenue and total cost curves at the **points at which profit is maximised**. As you can see, the gradients of these tangents **are the same**.

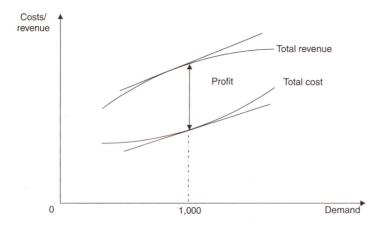

The **gradient of the total cost curve** is the **rate at which total cost changes with changes in volume**, which is simply **marginal cost**. Likewise, the **gradient of the total revenue curve** is the **rate at which total revenue changes with changes in volume**, which is the **marginal revenue**. At the **point of profit maximisation**, the two gradients are **equal** and hence, once again, **MC = MR**.

4.6 Optimum pricing in practice

There are problems with applying the approach described above in practice for the following reasons.

(a)   It assumes that the demand curve and total costs can be **identified with certainty**. This is unlikely to be so.

(b)   It ignores the **market research costs of** acquiring knowledge of demand.

(c)   It assumes the firm has **no production constraint** which could mean that the equilibrium point between supply and demand cannot be reached.

(d)   It assumes the objective is **to maximise profits**. There may be other objectives.

CASE STUDY

Microsoft dominates the market for many types of computer software, but this domination was not achieved by setting short-term profit-maximising selling prices for the MS-DOS and Windows operating systems. By offering cheap licences to PC manufacturers for use of these operating systems, Microsoft word processing, spreadsheet, graphics and database packages have become almost industry-standard.

(e)   It assumes that **price is the only influence** on quantity demanded. We saw in Sections 1 and 2 that this is far from the case.

(f)   It is **complicated by** the issue of **price discrimination** (the practice of charging different unit selling prices for the same product). We look at price discrimination in the next chapter.

(g)   Although there are arguments for the **applicability** of the concept of the profit-maximising unit selling price in **traditional markets** where **homogenous, mass-produced** products are in **continuous supply** (such as public transport), the **modern trend** is towards **short product life cycles** and a **high degree of product differentiation**.

Section summary

Profits are maximised using marginalist theory when **marginal cost (MC) = marginal revenue (MR)**.

The **optimal selling price** can be determined using equations (ie when MC = MR).

The **optimum selling price** can also be determined using tabulation, graphs and gradients.

---

5   Full cost-plus pricing

Introduction

In the next two sections we focus on cost-based approaches to pricing. In this section we concentrate on full cost-plus pricing which adds a percentage onto the full cost of the product to arrive at the selling price.

5.1 Reasons for its popularity

In practice cost is one of the most important influences on price. Many firms base price on simple **cost-plus rules** (costs are estimated and then a mark-up is added in order to set the price). A study by *Lanzilotti* gave a number of **reasons** for the **predominance of this method**.

(a)   Planning and use of scarce capital resources are easier.

(b)   Assessment of divisional performance is easier.

(c)   It emulates the practice of successful large companies.

(d)   Organisations fear government action against 'excessive' profits.

(e)   There is a tradition of production rather than of marketing in many organisations.

(f)   There is sometimes tacit collusion in industry to avoid competition.

(g)   Adequate profits for shareholders are already made, giving no incentive to maximise profits by seeking an 'optimum' selling price.

(h)   Cost-based pricing strategies based on internal data are easier to administer.

(i)   Over time, cost-based pricing produces stability of pricing, production and employment.

KEY TERM

FULL COST-PLUS PRICING is a method of determining the sales price by calculating the full cost of the product and adding a percentage mark-up for profit.

5.2 Setting full cost-plus prices

The 'full cost' may be a fully absorbed production cost only, or it may include some absorbed administration, selling and distribution overhead.

A business might have an idea of the percentage profit margin it would like to earn, and so might **decide on an average profit mark-up** as a general guideline for pricing decisions. This would be particularly **useful for** businesses that carry out a large amount of **contract work or jobbing work**, for which individual job or contract prices must be quoted regularly to prospective customers. However, the percentage profit **mark-up does not have to be rigid and fixed**, but can be varied to suit the circumstances. In particular, the percentage mark-up can be varied to suit demand conditions in the market.

Question 6.5	Cost-plus pricing

Learning outcome A1(c)

A product's full cost is $4.75 and it is sold at full cost plus 70%. A competitor has just launched a similar product selling for $7.99.

Required

Fill in the gap in the sentence below.

The cost-plus percentage will need to be reduced by...... %.

Example: Full cost-plus pricing

Markup has begun to produce a new product, Product X, for which the following cost estimates have been made.

	$
Direct materials	27
Direct labour: 4 hrs at $5 per hour	20
Variable production overheads: machining, ½ hr at $6 per hour	3
	50

Production fixed overheads are budgeted at $300,000 per month and, because of the shortage of available machining capacity, the company will be restricted to 10,000 hours of machine time per month. The absorption rate will be a direct labour rate, however, and budgeted direct labour hours are 25,000 per month. It is estimated that the company could obtain a minimum contribution of $10 per machine hour on producing items other than product X.

The direct cost estimates are not certain as to material usage rates and direct labour productivity, and it is recognised that the estimates of direct materials and direct labour costs may be subject to an error of ± 15%. Machine time estimates are similarly subject to an error of ± 10%.

The company wishes to make a profit of 20% on full production cost from product X.

Required

Ascertain the full cost-plus based price.

Solution

Even for a relatively 'simple' cost-plus pricing estimate, some problems can arise, and certain assumptions must be made and stated. In this example, we can identify two problems.

(a) Should the opportunity cost of machine time be included in cost or not?
(b) What allowance, if any, should be made for the possible errors in cost estimates?

Different assumptions could be made.

(a) **Exclude machine time opportunity costs: ignore possible costing errors**

	$
Direct materials	27.00
Direct labour (4 hours)	20.00
Variable production overheads	3.00
	48.00
Fixed production overheads (at $\dfrac{£300,000}{25,000}$ = $12 per direct labour hour)	
Full production cost	98.00
Profit mark-up (20%)	19.60
Selling price per unit of product X	117.60

(b) **Include machine time opportunity costs: ignore possible costing errors**

	$
Full production cost as in (a)	98.00
Opportunity cost of machine time: contribution forgone (½ hr × $10)	5.00
Adjusted full cost	103.00
Profit mark-up (20%)	20.60
Selling price per unit of product X	123.60

(c) **Exclude machine time opportunity costs but make full allowance for possible under-estimates of cost**

	$	$
Direct materials	27.00	
Direct labour	20.00	
	47.00	
Possible error (15%)	7.05	
		54.05
Variable production overheads	3.00	
Possible error (10%)	0.30	
		3.30
Fixed production overheads (4 hrs × $12)	48.00	
Possible error (labour time) (15%)	7.20	
		55.20
Potential full production cost		112.55
Profit mark-up (20%)		22.51
Selling price per unit of product X		135.06

(d) **Include machine time opportunity costs and make a full allowance for possible under-estimates of cost**

	$
Potential full production cost as in (c)	112.55
Opportunity cost of machine time:	
potential contribution forgone (½ hr × $10 × 110%)	5.50
Adjusted potential full cost	118.05
Profit mark-up (20%)	23.61
Selling price per unit of product X	141.66

Using different assumptions, we could arrive at any of four different unit prices in the range $117.60 to $141.66.

5.3 Problems with and advantages of full cost-plus pricing

There are several serious **problems** with relying on a full cost approach to pricing.

(a) It **fails to recognise** that since demand may be determining price, **there will be a profit-maximising combination of price and demand**.

(b) There may be a need to **adjust prices to market and demand conditions**.

(c) **Budgeted output volume** needs to be established. Output volume is a key factor in the overhead absorption rate.

(d) A **suitable basis for overhead absorption** must be selected, especially where a business produces more than one product.

However, it is a **quick, simple and cheap** method of pricing which can be delegated to junior managers (which is particularly important with jobbing work where many prices must be decided and quoted each day) and, since the size of the profit margin can be varied, a decision based on a price in excess of full cost should ensure that a company working at normal capacity will **cover all of its fixed costs and make a profit**.

Example: Full cost-plus versus profit-maximising prices

Tiger has budgeted to make 50,000 units of its product, timm. The variable cost of a timm is $5 and annual fixed costs are expected to be $150,000.

The financial director of Tiger has suggested that a mark-up of 25% on full cost should be charged for every product sold. The marketing director has challenged the wisdom of this suggestion, and has produced the following estimates of sales demand for timms.

Price per unit ($)	9	10	11	12	13
Demand (units)	*42,000*	*38,000*	*35,000*	*32,000*	*27,000*

Required

(a)   Calculate the profit for the year if a full cost-plus price is charged.
(b)   Calculate the profit for the year if a profit-maximising price is charged.

Assume in both (a) and (b) that 50,000 units of timm are produced regardless of sales volume.

Solution

The full cost per unit comprises $5 of variable costs plus $3 of fixed costs ($8 in total). A 25% mark-up on this cost gives a selling price of $10 per unit so that sales demand would be 38,000 units. (Production is given as 50,000 units.) **Profit using absorption costing** would be as follows.

	$	$
Sales		380,000
Costs of production (50,000 units)		
Variable (50,000 × $5)	250,000	
Fixed (50,000 × $3)	150,000	
	400,000	
Less increase in inventory (12,000 units × 8)	(96,000)	
Cost of sales		304,000
Profit		76,000

Profit using marginal costing instead of absorption costing, so that fixed overhead costs are written off in the period they occur, would be as follows. (The 38,000 unit demand level is chosen for comparison.)

	$
Contribution (38,000 × $(10 − 5))	190,000
Fixed costs	150,000
Profit	40,000

Since the company cannot go on indefinitely producing an output volume in excess of sales volume, this profit figure is more indicative of the profitability of timms in the longer term.

A **profit-maximising price** is one which gives the greatest net (relevant) cash flow, which in this case is the **contribution-maximising price**.

Price $	Unit contribution $	Demand Units	Total contribution $
9	4	42,000	168,000
10	5	38,000	190,000
11	6	35,000	210,000
12	7	32,000	224,000
13	8	27,000	216,000

The profit maximising price is $12, with annual sales demand of 32,000 units.

This example shows that a **cost-plus based price is unlikely to be the profit-maximising price**, and that a **marginal costing approach**, calculating the total contribution at a variety of different selling prices, will be **more helpful** for establishing what the profit-maximising price ought to be.

Section summary

In **full cost-plus pricing** the sales price is determined by calculating the full cost of the product and then adding a percentage mark-up for profit. The most important criticism of full cost-plus pricing is that it fails to recognise that since sales demand may be determined by the sales price, there will be a profit-maximising combination of price and demand.

6 Marginal cost-plus (mark-up) pricing

Introduction

This section follows on from Section 5 by looking at marginal cost-plus pricing. Whereas a full cost-plus approach to pricing draws attention to net profit and the net profit margin, a marginal (variable) cost-plus approach to pricing **draws attention to gross profit** and the **gross profit margin**, or **contribution**.

KEY TERM

MARGINAL COST-PLUS PRICING/MARK –UP PRICING is a method of determining the sales price by adding a profit margin on to either marginal cost of production or marginal cost of sales.

Question 6.6	Marginal cost pricing

Learning outcome A1(c)

A product has the following costs.

	$
Direct materials	5
Direct labour	3
Variable overheads	7

Fixed overheads are $10,000 per month. Budgeted sales per month are 400 units to allow the product to break even.

Required

Fill in the blank in the sentence below.

The mark-up which needs to be added to *marginal* cost to allow the product to break even is ...... %.

6.1 The advantages and disadvantages of a marginal cost-plus approach to pricing

The main advantages are as follows.

(a)   It is a **simple and easy** method to use.

(b)   The **mark-up percentage can be varied**, and so mark-up pricing can be adjusted to reflect demand conditions.

(c)   It **draws management attention to contribution**, and the effects of higher or lower sales volumes on profit. In this way, it helps to create a better awareness of the concepts and implications of marginal costing and cost-volume-profit analysis. For example, if a product costs $10 per unit and a mark-up of 150% is added to reach a price of $25 per unit, management should be clearly aware that every additional $1 of sales revenue would add 60 pence to contribution and profit.

(d)   In practice, mark-up pricing is used in businesses **where there is a readily-identifiable basic variable cost**. Retail industries are the most obvious example, and it is quite common for the prices of goods in shops to be fixed by adding a mark-up (20% or 33.3%, say) to the purchase cost.

There are, of course, drawbacks to marginal cost-plus pricing.

(a)   Although the **size** of the mark-up can be varied in accordance with demand conditions, it **does not ensure that sufficient attention is paid to demand conditions, competitors' prices and profit maximisation**.

(b)   It **ignores fixed overheads** in the pricing decision, but the sales price must be sufficiently high to ensure that a profit is made after covering fixed costs.

Exam alert

In our study of decision-making to date we have adopted a marginal cost approach in that we have considered the effects on contribution and have classed (most) fixed overheads as irrelevant. In pricing decisions, however, there is a conflict with such an approach because of the need for full recovery of all costs incurred.

Section summary

Marginal cost-plus pricing involves adding a profit margin to the marginal cost of production/sales. A marginal costing approach is more likely to help with identifying a profit-maximising price.

7   Pricing based on mark-up per unit of limiting factor

Introduction

This short section demonstrates how to calculate a price based on mark-up per unit of a limiting factor.

Example: Mark-up per unit of limiting factor

Suppose that a company provides a window cleaning service to offices and factories. Business is brisk, but the company is restricted from expanding its activities further by a shortage of window cleaners. The workforce consists of 12 window cleaners, each of whom works a 35 hour week. They are paid $4 per hour. Variable expenses are $0.50 per hour. Fixed costs are $5,000 per week. The company wishes to make a contribution of at least $15 per hour.

The minimum charge per hour for window cleaning would then be as follows.

	$ per hour
Direct wages	4.00
Variable expenses	0.50
Contribution	15.00
Charge per hour	19.50

The company has a total workforce capacity of (12 × 35) 420 hours per week, and so total revenue would be $8,190 per week, contribution would be (420 × $15) $6,300, leaving a profit after fixed costs of $1,300 per week.

Section summary

Another approach to pricing might be taken when a **business is working at full capacity, and is restricted by a shortage of resources** from expanding its output further. By deciding what target profit it would like to earn, it could **establish a mark-up per unit of limiting factor**.

8 Pricing strategies for new products

Introduction

When a new product is launched, it is essential that the company gets the pricing strategy correct, otherwise the wrong message may be given to the market (if priced too cheaply) or the product will not sell (if the price is too high). This section looks at how to approach pricing for new products to ensure a smooth launch.

KEY POINT

Two pricing strategies for **new** products are **market penetration pricing** and **market skimming pricing**.

8.1 Tabulation

Suppose that Novo is about to launch a new product with a variable cost of $10 per unit. The company has carried out market research (at a cost of $15,000) to determine the potential demand for the product at various selling prices.

Selling price $	Demand Units
30	20,000
25	30,000
20	40,000

Its current capacity is for 20,000 units but additional capacity can be made available by using the resources of another product line. If this is done the lost contribution from the other product will be $35,000 for each additional 10,000 units of capacity.

How could we **analyse this information** for senior management in a way that helps them to **decide on the product's launch price**?

Tabulation is the approach to use with a problem of this type.

Selling price $	Demand Units ('000)	Variable costs $'000	Opportunity costs $'000	Total costs $'000	Sales revenue $'000	Contribution $'000
30	20	200	–	200	600	400
25	30	300	35	335	750	415
20	40	400	70	470	800	330

The **optimum price to maximise short-term profits is $25**. However, it is quite possible that the aim will **not** be to maximise short-term profits, and a number of other strategies may be adopted, as discussed below.

The main **objections** to the approach described above are that it only **considers a limited range of prices** (what about charging $27.50?) and it **takes no account of the uncertainty of forecast demand**. However, allowance could be made for both situations by collecting more information.

Question 6.7	Pricing new products

Learning outcome A3(b)

JPM is just about to launch a new product.

Production capacity means that a maximum of 120 units can be manufactured each week and manufacture must be in batches of ten. The marketing department estimates that at a price of $120 no units will be sold but, for each $3 reduction in prices, ten additional units per week will be sold.

Fixed costs associated with manufacturing the product are expected to be $6,000 per week. Variable costs are expected to be $40 per unit for the first eight batches, but after that the unit variable cost of the products in the batch will be $2 more than those in the preceding batch.

Which is the most profitable level of output per week?

A   80 units
B   90 units
C   100 units
D   110 units

8.2 First on the market?

A new product pricing strategy will depend largely on whether a company's product or service is the first of its kind on the market.

(a)   If the **product is the first of its kind**, there will be **no competition** yet, and the company, for a time at least, will be a **monopolist**. Monopolists have more influence over price and are able to set a price at which they think they can maximise their profits. A monopolist's price is likely to be higher, and its profits bigger, than those of a company operating in a competitive market.

(b)   If the new product being launched by a company is **following a competitor's product** onto the market, the pricing strategy will be **constrained by what the competitor** is already doing. The new product could be given a higher price if its quality is better, or it could be given a price which matches the competition. Undercutting the competitor's price might result in a price war and a fall of the general price level in the market.

8.2.1 Market penetration pricing

KEY TERM

MARKET PENETRATION PRICING is a policy of low prices when the product is first launched in order to obtain sufficient penetration into the market.

Circumstances in which a penetration policy may be appropriate

(a)   If the firm wishes to **discourage new entrants** into the market

(b)   If the firm wishes to **shorten the initial period of the product's life cycle** in order to enter the growth and maturity stages as quickly as possible

(c)   If there are **significant economies of scale** to be achieved **from a high volume of output**, so that quick penetration into the market is desirable in order to gain unit cost reductions

(d)   If **demand is highly elastic** and so would respond well to low prices.

Penetration prices are prices which aim to **secure a substantial share in a substantial total market**. A firm might therefore **deliberately build excess production capacity** and set its prices very low. As demand builds up the spare capacity will be used up gradually and unit costs will fall; the firm might even reduce prices further as unit costs fall. In this way, early losses will enable the firm to dominate the market and have the lowest costs.

8.2.2 Market skimming pricing

KEY TERM

MARKET SKIMMING PRICING involves charging high prices when a product is first launched and spending heavily on advertising and sales promotion to obtain sales.

As the product moves into the later stages of its life cycle, **progressively lower prices will be charged** and so the profitable 'cream' is skimmed off in stages until sales can only be sustained at lower prices.

The aim of market skimming is to **gain high unit profits early in the product's life**. High unit prices make it **more likely that competitors will enter the market** than if lower prices were to be charged.

Circumstances in which such a policy may be appropriate

(a)   Where the product is **new and different**, so that customers are prepared to pay high prices so as to be one up on other people who do not own it.

(b)   Where the **strength** of demand and the **sensitivity of demand** to price are **unknown**. It is better from the point of view of marketing to start by charging high prices and then reduce them if the demand for the product turns out to be price elastic than to start by charging low prices and then attempt to raise them substantially if demand appears to be insensitive to higher prices.

(c)   Where **high prices** in the early stages of a product's life might **generate high initial cash flows**. A firm with liquidity problems may prefer market-skimming for this reason.

(d)   Where the firm **can identify different market segments** for the product, each prepared to pay progressively lower prices. If **product differentiation** can be introduced, it may be possible to continue to sell at higher prices to some market segments when lower prices are charged in others. This is discussed further below.

(e)   Where products may have a **short life cycle**, and so need to recover their development costs and make a profit relatively quickly.

Section summary

Two pricing strategies for **new** products are **market penetration pricing** and **market skimming pricing**.

Market penetration pricing is a policy of low prices when the product is first launched in order to obtain sufficient penetration into the market.

Market skimming pricing involves charging high prices when a product is first launched and spending heavily on advertising and sales promotion to attract customers.

9   Other pricing strategies

Introduction

This section looks at other pricing strategies that might be employed by organisations. There are quite a few strategies covered here so make sure you understand the key points of each.

9.1 Product differentiation and price discrimination

KEY TERM

PRICE DISCRIMINATION is the practice of charging different prices for the same product to different groups of buyers when these prices are not reflective of cost differences.

In certain circumstances the **same product** can be sold at different prices to **different customers**. There are a number of bases on which such discriminating prices can be set.

Basis	Detail
By market segment	A cross-channel ferry company would market its services at different prices in England and France, for example. Services such as cinemas and hairdressers are often available at lower prices to old age pensioners and/or juveniles.
By product version	Many car models have **optional extras** which enable one brand to appeal to a wider cross-section of customers. The final price need not reflect the cost price of the optional extras directly: usually the top of the range model would carry a price much in excess of the cost of provision of the extras, as a prestige appeal.
By place	Theatre seats are usually sold according to their location so that patrons pay different prices for the same performance according to the seat type they occupy.
By time	This is perhaps the most popular type of price discrimination. Off-peak travel bargains, hotel prices and telephone charges are all attempts to increase sales revenue by covering variable but not necessarily average cost of provision. Railway companies are successful price discriminators, charging more to rush hour rail commuters whose demand is inelastic at certain times of the day.

Price discrimination can only be effective if a number of **conditions** hold.

(a) The market must be **segmentable** in price terms, and different sectors must show different intensities of demand. Each of the sectors must be identifiable, distinct and separate from the others, and be accessible to the firm's marketing communications.

(b) There must be little or **no** chance of a **black market** developing (this would allow those in the lower priced segment to resell to those in the higher priced segment).

(c) There must be little or **no** chance that **competitors** can and will undercut the firm's prices in the higher priced (and/or most profitable) market segments.

(d) The cost of segmenting and **administering** the arrangements should not exceed the extra revenue derived from the price discrimination strategy.

9.1.1 'Own label' pricing: a form of price discrimination

Many supermarkets and multiple retail stores sell their 'own label' products, often at a lower price than established branded products. The supermarkets or multiple retailers do this by entering into arrangements with manufacturers, to supply their goods under the 'own brand' label.

9.2 Premium pricing

This involves making a product **appear 'different'** through **product differentiation** so as **to justify a premium price**. The product may be different in terms of, for example, quality, reliability, durability, after sales service or extended warranties. Heavy advertising can establish brand loyalty which can help to sustain a premium and premium prices will always be paid by those customers who blindly equate high price with high quality.

9.3 Product bundling

Product bundling is a variation on price discrimination which involves **selling a number of products or services as a package at a price lower than the aggregate of their individual prices**. For example a hotel might offer a package that includes the room, meals, use of leisure facilities and entertainment at a combined price that is lower than the total price of the individual components. This might encourage customers to buy services that they might otherwise not have purchased.

The **success** of a bundling strategy depends on the expected **increase in sales volume** and **changes in margin.** Other cost changes, such as in product handling, packaging and invoicing costs, are possible. **Longer-term issues** such as competitors' reactions must also be considered.

9.4 Pricing with optional extras

The decision here is very similar to that for product bundling. It rests on whether the **increase in sales revenue from the increased price that can be charged** is **greater** than the **increase in costs** required to incorporate extra features. Not all customers will be willing to pay a higher price for additional features if they do not want or need those features.

9.5 Loss leader pricing

A **loss leader** is when a company sets a very low price for one product intending to make customers buy other products in the range which carry higher profit margins. An example is selling inkjet printers at a relatively low price whilst selling the print cartridges at a higher profit margin. People will buy many of the high profit items but only one of the low profit items, yet they are "locked in" to the former by the latter.

9.6 Using discounts

Reasons for using discounts to adjust prices

- To get rid of perishable goods that have reached the end of their shelf life
- To sell off seconds
- Normal practice (eg antique trade)
- To increase sales volumes during a poor sales period without dropping prices permanently
- To differentiate between types of customer (wholesale, retail and so on)
- To get cash in quickly

9.7 Controlled prices

Many **previously nationalised industries** now operate within the private sector and are **overseen by an industry regulator** (such as OFCOM for telecommunications).

Regulators tend to concentrate on **price** so that these near monopolies cannot exploit their position (although the regulators are also concerned with quality of service/product).

If a **price is regulated**, the **elasticity of demand is zero**: 'small' customers pay less than they otherwise would, whereas 'large' customers pay more than in a competitive environment.

Prices have become **more flexible in recent years**, however.

(a)   Introduction of discounted price for very large customers
(b)   Entry of other companies into the market

Question 6.8

Learning outcome A3(b)

As management accountant to a group of companies manufacturing footwear, you have been asked to consider the following two subjects that are to be discussed at the next group pricing committee meeting.

(a) The possibility of differential pricing for different sizes of shoes

(b) The levels of prices at which contracts with a large multiple retailer for 'own label' shoes might be negotiated

Required

Describe briefly the major topics under each of the above headings that you would include in the agenda for discussion.

Exam skills

If asked to **compare** two **pricing strategies** and to determine which is the **better**, you basically need to consider which produces the **higher cash inflows**.

When asked to assess the **financial viability** of the better strategy, however, you need to perform a **DCF appraisal** on the resulting cash flows.

Section summary

Product differentiation may be used to make products appear to be different. **Price discrimination** is then possible.

Price discrimination is the practice of charging different prices for the same product to different groups of buyers when these prices are not reflective of cost differences.

Chapter Roundup

- ✓ **Demand** is normally **elastic** because demand will increase as prices are lowered.

- ✓ **Price elasticity of demand** is a measure of the extent of change in market demand for a good in response to a change in its price.

- ✓ If **demand** is **elastic** a reduction in price would lead to a rise in total sales revenue. If **demand** is **inelastic**, a reduction in price would lead to a fall in total sales revenue.

- ✓ The **volume of demand for one organisation's goods rather than another's** is influenced by three principal factors: product life cycle, quality and marketing.

- ✓ As well as demand, a **range of other issues influence pricing decisions** including the market in which an organisation operates, competition, quality and price sensitivity.

- ✓ When demand is linear the **equation for the demand curve is P = a – bx**

  Where P   = the selling price

        x   = the quantity demanded at that price

        a   = the price at which demand would be nil (theoretical maximum price)

$$a = \$(\text{current price}) + \left(\frac{\text{Current quantity at current price}}{\text{Change in quantity when price changed by \$b}} \times \$b \right)$$

$$b = \frac{\text{change in price}}{\text{change in quantity}}$$

  Gradient of line. Represents the change in price required to change demand by 1 unit.

  You need to learn these formulae.

- ✓ **Profits are maximised** using marginalist theory when **marginal cost (MC) = marginal revenue (MR)**.

- ✓ The **optimal selling price** can be determined using equations (ie when MC = MR).

- ✓ The **optimum selling price** can also be determined using tabulation, graphs and gradients.

- ✓ In **full cost-plus pricing** the sales price is determined by calculating the full cost of the product and then adding a percentage mark-up for profit. The most important criticism of full cost-plus pricing is that it fails to recognise that since sales demand may be determined by the sales price, there will be a profit-maximising combination of price and demand.

- ✓ **Marginal cost-plus pricing** involves adding a profit margin to the marginal cost of production/sales. A marginal costing approach is more likely to help with identifying a profit-maximising price.

- ✓ Another approach to pricing might be taken when a **business is working at full capacity, and is restricted by a shortage of resources** from expanding its output further. By deciding what target profit it would like to earn, it could **establish a mark-up per unit of limiting factor.**

- ✓ Two pricing strategies for **new** products are **market penetration pricing** and **market skimming pricing.**

- ✓ **Market penetration pricing** is a policy of low prices when the product is first launched in order to obtain sufficient penetration into the market.

- ✓ **Market skimming pricing** involves charging high prices when a product is first launched and spending heavily on advertising and sales promotion to attract customers.

- ✓ **Product differentiation** may be used to make products appear to be different. **Price discrimination** is then possible.

- ✓ **Price discrimination** is the practice of charging different prices for the same product to different groups of buyers when these prices are not reflective of cost differences.

Quick Quiz

1   *Choose the correct words from those highlighted.*

The price elasticity of demand for a particular good at the current price is 1.2. Demand for this good at this price is (1) **elastic/inelastic**. If the price of the good is reduced, total sales revenue will (2) **rise/fall/stay the same.**

2   What are the four stages of the product life cycle?

    A   Appearance, growth, maturity, saturation
    B   Birth, growth, adolescence, old age
    C   Introduction, expansion, maturity, death
    D   Introduction, growth, maturity, saturation and decline

3   A company knows that demand for its new product will be highly elastic. The most appropriate pricing strategy for the new product will be market skimming pricing. True or false?

4   *Label the graph with the terms provided.*

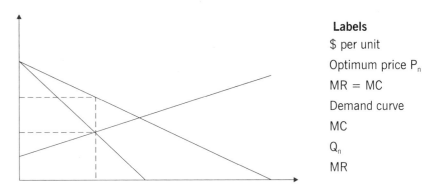

Labels
$ per unit
Optimum price P_n
MR = MC
Demand curve
MC
Q_n
MR

5   *Fill in the blanks.*

When demand is linear, the equation for the demand curve is $P = a - bx$

where

P = ...

x = ...

a = ...

b = ...

The constant a is calculated as $ (....................) + ($\dfrac{\text{...........................}}{\text{.............................}}$ × \$b)

6   At the point of profit maximisation, the gradients of the total cost curve and total revenue curve are the same in absolute terms, but one is positive, one is negative. True or false?

7   *Fill in the blanks.*

    (a)   One of the problems with relying on a full cost-plus approach to pricing is that it fails to recognise that since price may be determining demand, there will be a .... combination of .... and ....

    (b)   An advantage of the full cost-plus approach is that, because the size of the profit margin can be varied, a decision based on a price in excess of full cost should ensure that a company working at .... capacity will cover .... and make a ....

8   A theatre offers a special deal whereby two show tickets and pre-theatre dinner can be purchased as a package for a reduced price. This pricing strategy is usually referred to as

   A   Loss leader pricing
   B   Optional extras
   C   Product bundling
   D   Price discrimination

9   Pricing based on mark-up per unit of limiting factor is particularly useful if an organisation is not working to full capacity. *True or false?*

10   *Fill in the blank.*

   The .... price is the price at which an organisation will break even if it undertakes particular work.

11   Choose the correct word from those highlighted.

   Market **skimming/penetration** pricing should be used if an organisation wishes to discourage new entrants into a market.

12   'Own label' pricing is a form of psychological pricing. True or false?

13   If a price is regulated, the elasticity of demand is:

   A   −1
   B   0
   C   1
   D   Infinity

Answers to Quick Quiz

1   (1) elastic, (2) rise

2   D. Learn them!

3   False. Market penetration pricing would be more appropriate.

4

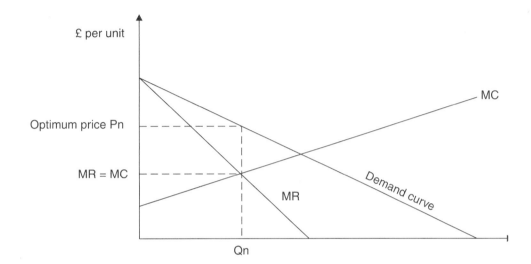

5   P   = selling price

    x   = quantity demanded at that price

    a   = price at which demand will be nil (theoretical maximum price)

    $b = \dfrac{\text{change in price}}{\text{change in quantity}}$ Gradient of line. Represents the change in price required to change demand by 1 unit.

    The constant a is calculated as $ (current price) + $\left(\dfrac{\text{Current quantity at current price}}{\text{Change in quantity when price changed by \$b}} \times \$b\right)$

6   False. The gradients are exactly the same.

7   (a)   profit-maximising combination of price and demand

    (b)   working at normal capacity will cover all of its fixed costs and make a profit

8   C   Product bundling involves selling a number of products or services as a package at a price lower than the aggregate of their individual prices.

9   False. It is useful if the organisation is working at full capacity.

10   Minimum

11   Market penetration

12   False. It is a form of price discrimination.

13   B. The elasticity of demand is zero.

Answers to Questions

6.1 Markets

The correct answer is **an oligopoly**.

6.2 Profit maximisation

Using the demand equation $P = a - bx$

Maximum demand is achieved when the product is free (when $P=0$)

When price = 0, demand (x) = 8,000	$0 = a - 8{,}000b$ (i)
When price = 1, demand (x) = 7,950	$1 = a - 7{,}950b$ (ii)
Subtract (i) from (ii)	$1 = 50b$
	$b = 0.02$
Substitute in (i)	$a = 8{,}000 \times 0.02$
	$= 160$

The demand equation for the product is therefore $P = 160 - 0.02x$

When price = $10	$\$10 = 160 - (0.02x)$
	$x = 7{,}500$

The profit-maximising sales level is 7,500 units.

6.3 Deriving a MR equation from the demand curve

$b = \dfrac{1}{5} = 0.2$

$a = \$250 + (12{,}000 \times 0.2) = \$2{,}650$

Profits are maximised when MC = MR, ie when $80 = a - 2bx$

$80 = 2{,}650 - 0.4x$, $\therefore 0.4x = 2{,}650 - 80$, $\therefore x = (2{,}650 - 80)\,/\,0.4$, $\therefore x = 6{,}425$

Profit-maximising demand $= 6{,}425$

$\therefore$ Profit-maximising price $= \$(2{,}650 - 0.2 \times 1{,}285)$

                                                  $= \$1{,}365$

6.4 Tabulation approach to find profit-maximising price

Profit is maximised at seven units of output and a price of $317, when MR is most nearly equal to MC.

Units	Price $	Total revenue $	Marginal revenue $	Total cost $	Marginal cost $	Profit $
0	0	0	0	600	-	(600)
1	504	504	504	720	120	(216)
2	471	942	438	804	84	138
3	439	1,317	375	864	60	453
4	407	1,628	311	924	60	704
5	377	1,885	257	1,005	81	880
6	346	2,076	191	1,134	129	942
7	317	2,219	143	1,274	140	945
8	288	2,304	85	1,440	166	864
9	259	2,331	27	1,674	234	657
10	232	2,320	(11)	1,980	306	340

6.5 Cost-plus pricing

The correct answer is that the cost-plus percentage will need to be reduced by 2%.

Profits = $(7.99 − 4.75) = $3.24

Mark-up = ($3.24/$4.75) × 100% = 68%

∴ % needs to be reduced by (70 − 68)% = 2%

6.6 Marginal cost pricing

The correct answer is $166^2/_3$%.

Breakeven point is when total contribution equals fixed costs.

At breakeven point, $10,000 = 400 (price − $15)

∴ $25 = price − $15
∴ $40 = price
∴ Mark-up = ((40 − 15) /15) × 100% = $166^2/_3$%

6.7 Pricing new products

The correct answer is C.

Note that we cannot use the profit maximisation model because of the non-linear relationships involved.

Units		Total variable costs $	Selling price per unit $	Total sales revenue $	Total contribution $
80	(× $40)	3,200	96*	7,680	4,480
90	(× $42)	3,780	93	8,370	4,590
100	(× $44)	4,400	90	9,000	4,600
110	(× $46)	5,060	87	9,570	4,510
120	(× $48)	5,760	84	10,080	4,320

*$120 − (8 × $3)

6.8 Pricing strategies

(a)   **Differential pricing for different sizes of shoes**

   (i)   **Cost differences**
      If the differential pricing is to allow for differences in cost, are these cost differences sufficient to justify significant price differentials?

   (ii)   **Administration costs**
      Consideration should be given to the increased cost of administering a differential price structure.

   (iii)   **Custom and practice**
      If it is accepted practice to charge differential prices for shoes, the company may be missing an opportunity to increase profits.

   (iv)   **Reaction of retailers**
      Retailers may not react favourably because their own pricing policy will become more complicated and time consuming.

   (v)   **Effect on demand**
      If higher prices are to be charged for larger shoes, what effect will this have on demand and profits?

(vi) **Competitors' actions**

If competitors are not already practising differential pricing, will they follow our lead? If not, what will be the effect on demand and profits?

(vii) **Differential pricing for marketing purposes**

If, instead of pricing according to cost, the company wishes to offer lower prices for the more popular sizes, will the extra demand justify the reduction in price?

(b) **Prices for own-label shoes**

(i) **Capacity available**

The available capacity will dictate whether or not marginal pricing can be used. It would not be advisable to use marginal pricing if this displaces full-price work.

(ii) **The effect on other business**

Will the sales of own-label shoes affect the demand for our other ranges? If lower prices are offered to the multiple retailer, will other customers start to demand similar reductions?

(iii) **The terms of the negotiated contract**

The company must ensure that they will have the flexibility to change prices if costs fluctuate.

(iv) **The cost of increased working capital**

An expansion in output will result in increased working capital. Will the retailers expect us to hold inventories for them and how much credit will they require? These facts must be evaluated and taken into account in the pricing policy.

(v) **Exclusive designs**

Will the retailer require exclusive designs, or can cost savings be achieved by using the same designs for our own range of footwear?

Now try these questions from the Exam Question Bank

Number	Level	Marks	Time
Q11	Examination	10	18 mins
Q12	Examination	10	18 mins
Q13	Examination	10	18 mins
Q14	Examination	10	18 mins
Q15	Introductory	4	8 mins

COST PLANNING AND ANALYSIS FOR COMPETITIVE ADVANTAGE

Part B

COST PLANNING

This chapter looks at both recently-developed and more established techniques for planning the timing and costs of new products and services. It is the first stage in the three part process of cost planning, analysis (Chapter 8) and management (Chapters 9A and 9B).

Learning curve theory (Section 1) is concerned with the reduction in unit labour times (and hence cost) with the repetition of complex, labour intensive activities. Clearly this has an impact on forecasting future costs of products and services.

Life cycle costing (Section 2) is a technique for reviewing and hence managing the costs of a product (or service or customer) for its entire life, not just during the production stage.

Target costing (Section 3) aims to control and manage costs of production at the product design stage, rather than when production starts.

Value analysis (Section 4) looks at how a product can be produced (or a service delivered) more economically without reducing its value to the customer or user.

Functional analysis (Section 5) uses the functions of a product as the basis for cost management purposes.

topic list	learning outcomes	syllabus references	ability required
1 The learning curve	B1(e)	B1(iv)	application
2 Life cycle costing	B1(i)	B1(vii)	analysis
3 Target costing	B1(h)	B1(vi)	comprehension
4 Value analysis	B1(a)	B1(i)	analysis
5 Functional analysis	B1(a)	B1(i)	analysis

1   The learning curve   5/10, 11/11, 3/12, 5/12, 9/12, 11/12, 3/13, 5/13

Introduction

In this section we look at learning curve theory, when it is used and how to calculate rates of learning. By having an idea how quickly labour efficiency improves, management are better placed to plan how much a product is likely to cost and how long it will take to produce.

KEY TERM

LEARNING CURVE THEORY is used to measure how, in some industries and some situations, the incremental cost per unit of output continues to fall for each extra unit produced.

1.1 When does learning curve theory: apply?

Labour time should be expected to get shorter, with experience, in the production of items which exhibit any or all of the following features.

(a)   **Made largely by labour effort** rather than by a highly mechanised process
(b)   **Brand new** or relatively **short-lived** product (the learning process does not continue indefinitely)
(c)   **Complex** and **made in small quantities for special orders**

1.2 The learning curve theory   11/10

KEY TERM

The LEARNING CURVE is 'The mathematical expression of the commonly observed effect that, as complex and labour-intensive procedures are repeated, unit labour times tend to decrease.' The learning curve models mathematically this reduction in unit production time.'   (CIMA *Official Terminology*)

More specifically, the learning curve theory states that the **cumulative average time per unit** produced is assumed to **decrease by a constant percentage every time total output of the product doubles**.

For instance, where an **80% learning effect or rate** occurs, the **cumulative average time required per unit of output is reduced to 80% of the previous cumulative average time when output is doubled**.

KEY POINT

By cumulative average time, we mean the average time per unit for all units produced so far, back to and including the first unit made.

The **doubling of output** is an **important feature** of the learning curve measurement. With a 70% learning curve, the cumulative average time per unit of output will fall to 70% of what it was before, every time output is doubled.

1.2.1 Example: an 80% learning curve

If the first unit of output requires 100 hours and an 80% learning curve applies, the production times would be as follows.

Cumulative number of units produced		average time per unit		Cumulative Total time required	Incremental time taken		
		Hours		Hours	Total hours		Hours per unit
1		100.0	(× 1)	100.0			
2*	(80%)	80.0	(× 2)	160.0	60.0	÷ 1	60.0
4*	(80%)	64.0	(× 4)	256.0	96.0	÷ 2	48.0
8*	(80%)	51.2	(× 8)	409.6	153.6	÷ 4	38.4

* Output is being doubled each time.

Notice that the incremental time per unit at each output level is much lower than the average time per unit.

1.3 Graph of the learning curve

This learning effect can be shown on a **graph** as a learning curve, either for **unit times (graph (a))** or for **cumulative total times or costs (graph (b))**.

(a)   (b)

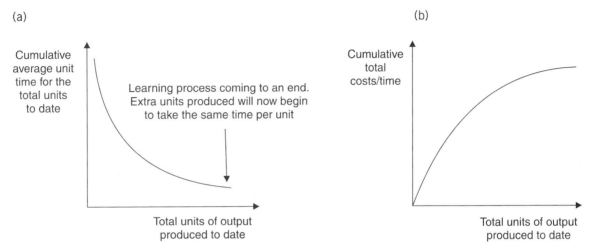

The curve on graph (a) becomes horizontal once a sufficient number of units have been produced. At this point the learning effect is lost and production time should become a constant standard, to which a standard efficiency rate may be applied.

Example: The learning curve effect

Captain Kitts has designed a new type of sailing boat, for which the cost and sales price of the first boat to be produced has been estimated as follows.

	$
Materials	5,000
Labour (800 hrs × $5 per hr)	4,000
Overhead (150% of labour cost)	6,000
	15,000
Profit mark-up (20%)	3,000
Sales price	18,000

It is planned to sell all the yachts at full cost plus 20%. An 80% learning curve is expected to apply to the production work. Only one customer has expressed interest in buying the yacht so far, but he thinks $18,000 is too high a price to pay. He might want to buy two, or even four of the yachts during the next six months.

He has asked the following questions.

(a) If he paid $18,000 for the first yacht, what price would he have to pay later for a second yacht?

(b) Could Captain Kitts quote the same unit price for two yachts, if the customer ordered two at the same time?

(c) If the customer bought two yachts now at one price, what would be the price per unit for a third and fourth yacht, if he ordered them both together later on?

(d) Could Captain Kitts quote a single unit price for the following numbers of yachts if they were all ordered now?

    (i) Four yachts

    (ii) Eight yachts

Assuming there are no other prospective customers for the yacht, how would the questions be answered?

Solution

Number of yachts		Cumulative average time per yacht		Total time for all yachts to date		Incremental time for additional yachts
		Hours		Hours		Hours
1		800.0		800.0		
2	(× 80%)	640.0	(× 2)	1,280.0	(1,280 – 800)	480.0
4	(× 80%)	512.0	(× 4)	2,048.0	(2,048 – 1,280)	768.0
8	(× 80%)	409.6	(× 8)	3,276.8	(3,276.8 – 2,048)	1,228.8

(a)　*Separate price for a second yacht*

	$
Materials	5,000
Labour (480 hrs × $5)	2,400
Overhead (150% of labour cost)	3,600
Total cost	11,000
Profit (20%)	2,200
Sales price	13,200

(b)　*A single price for the first two yachts*

	$
Materials cost for two yachts	10,000
Labour (1,280 hrs × $5)	6,400
Overhead (150% of labour cost)	9,600
Total cost for two yachts	26,000
Profit (20%)	5,200
Total sales price for two yachts	31,200
Price per yacht (÷ 2)	15,600

(c)　*A price for the third and fourth yachts*

	$
Materials cost for two yachts	10,000
Labour (768 hours × $5)	3,840
Overhead (150% of labour cost)	5,760
Total cost	19,600
Profit (20%)	3,920
Total sales price for two yachts	23,520
Price per yacht (÷ 2)	11,760

(d)　*A price for the first four yachts together and for the first eight yachts together*

		First four yachts		First eight yachts
		$		$
Materials		20,000		40,000
Labour	(2,048 hrs)	10,240	(3,276.8 hrs)	16,384
Overhead	(150% of labour cost)	15,360	(150% of labour cost)	24,576
Total cost		45,600		80,960
Profit (20%)		9,120		16,192
Total sales price		54,720		97,152
Price per yacht	(÷ 4)	13,680	(÷ 8)	12,144

Learning outcomes B1(e)

A 90 per cent learning curve applies to the manufacture of product X. If the time taken for the first unit is three hours, what will be the average time per unit for units 5 to 8?

1.4 A formula for the learning curve   3/11

EXAM

The formula for the learning curve shown in Section 1.3(a) is $Y_x = aX^b$

Where Y =	cumulative average time per unit to produce X units	a =	the time required to produce the first unit of output
X =	the cumulative number of units	b =	the learning coefficient or the index of learning/learning index

By calculating the value of b, using logarithms or a calculator, you can calculate expected labour times for certain work.

1.4.1 Logarithms

We need to take a look at logarithms because they appear in the definition of b, the learning coefficient.

KEY TERM

The LOGARITHM of a number is the power to which ten has to be raised to produce that number.

If you have never learnt how to use logarithms, here is a brief explanation.

The **logarithm of a number, x, is the value of x expressed in terms of '10 to the power of'.**

$10 = 10^1$	The logarithm of 10 is 1.0
$100 = 10^2$	The logarithm of 100 is 2.0
$1,000 = 10^3$	The logarithm of 1,000 is 3.0

Your **calculator** will provide you with the logarithm of any number, probably using the **button marked log 10^x**. For example, to find log of 566 using a calculator you will probably press the log button then type in 566 and the close brackets and '=', to get 2.7528, which means that $10^{2.7528} = 566$.

Logarithms are useful to us for two main reasons.

(a)   The logarithm of the product of two numbers is the sum of their logarithms: **log (c × d) = log c + log d**.

(b)   The logarithm of one number (say, f) to the power of another number (say, g), is the second number multiplied by the logarithm of the first: **log (f^g) = g log f.**

Logarithms can therefore be used to derive non-linear functions of the form $y = ax^n$.

If $y = ax^n$, the logarithm of y and the logarithm of ax^n must be the same and so **log y = log a + nlog x.** **This gives us a linear function similar to y = a + nx**, the only difference being that in place of y we have to use the logarithm of y and in place of x we must use the logarithm of x. **Using simultaneous equations, we can get a value for n and a value for log a**, which we can convert back into a 'normal' figure using antilogarithms (the button probably marked 10^x on your calculator).

For example, suppose the relationship between x and y can be described by the function $y = ax^n$, and suppose we know that if x = 1,000, y = 80,000 and if x = 750, y = 63,750.

Substitute these value into log y = log a + n log x.

$\log 80{,}000 = \log a + n \log 1{,}000$
$4.9031 = \log a + 3n$
$\therefore 4.9031 - 3n = \log a$ (1)

$\log 63{,}750 = \log a + n \log 750$
$4.8045 = \log a + 2.8751n$ (2)

Sub (1) into (2).

$4.8045 = 4.9031 - 3n + 2.8751n$
$\therefore 0.1249n = 0.0986$
$\therefore n = 0.7894$

Sub value of n into (1)

$4.9031 - (3 \times 0.7894) = \log a$
$2.5349 = \log a$
$\therefore 342.69 = a$
$\therefore$ Our function is **$y = 342.69x^{0.7894}$**

This technique will be useful when we come to look at the derivation of the learning rate in Section 1.5.4.

1.4.2 Logarithms and the value of b

When $Y_x = aX^b$ in learning curve theory, the value of **b = log of the learning rate/log of 2**. The learning rate is expressed as a proportion, so that for an 80% learning curve, the learning rate is 0.8, and for a 90% learning curve it is 0.9, and so on.

For an 80% learning curve, b = log 0.8/log 2.

Using the button on your calculator marked log 10^x

$$b = \frac{-0.0969}{0.3010} = -0.322$$

Question 7.2	Learning curve formula

Learning outcomes B1(e)

The value of b when a 90% learning curve applies is –0.0458. *True or false?*

Exam alert

You may be asked to prepare a flexed budget or to calculate planning and operational variances using learning curve data.

Example: Using the formula

Suppose, for example, that an 80% learning curve applies to production of item ABC. To date (the end of June) 230 units of ABC have been produced. Budgeted production for July is 55 units.

The time taken to produce the very first unit of ABC, in January, was 120 hours.

Required

Calculate the budgeted total labour time for July.

Solution

To solve this problem, we need to calculate three things.

(a)   The cumulative total labour time needed so far to produce 230 units of ABC

(b)   The cumulative total labour time needed to produce 285 units of ABC, that is adding on the extra 55 units for July

(c)   The extra time needed to produce 55 units of ABC in July, as the difference between (b) and (a)

Calculation (a)

$Y_x = aX^b$ and we know that for 230 cumulative units, a = 120 hours (time for first unit), X = 230 (cumulative units) and b = –0.322 (80% learning curve) and so Y = (120) × ($230^{-0.322}$) = 20.83.

So when X = 230 units, the cumulative average time per unit is 20.83 hours.

Calculation (b)

Now we do the same sort of calculation for X = 285.

If X = 285, Y = 120 × ($285^{-0.322}$) = 19.44

So when X = 285 units, the cumulative average time per unit is 19.44 hours.

Calculation (c)

Cumulative units	Average time per unit Hours	Total time Hours
230	20.83	4,791
285	19.44	5,540
Incremental time for 55 units		749

Average time per unit, between 230 and 285 units = 749/55 = 13.6 hours per unit approx

Instead of the formula you can use the **graphical methodology** (Section 1.3) to determine cumulative average time per unit but you will need considerable drawing skill to obtain an accurate result.

1.4.3 Derivation of the learning rate

The approach to derive the learning rate very much depends on the information given in the question. If you are provided with **details about cumulative production levels of 1, 2, 4, 8 or 16 (etc) units** you can use the **first approach** shown below. If details are given about other levels, however, you need to use the second approach, which involves the use of logarithms.

Question 7.3   Calculation of the percentage learning effect

BL is planning to produce product A. Development tests suggest that 60% of the variable manufacturing cost of product A will be affected by a learning and experience curve. This learning effect will apply to each unit produced and continue at a constant rate of learning until cumulative production reaches 4,000 units, when learning will stop. The unit variable manufacturing cost of the first unit is estimated to be $1,200 (of which 60% will be subject to the effect of learning), while the average unit variable manufacturing cost of four units will be $405.

Required

Calculate the rate of learning that is expected to apply.

Question 7.4   Calculation of percentage learning effect using logs

Learning outcomes B1(e)

XX is aware that there is a learning effect for the production of one of its new products, but is unsure about the degree of learning. The following data relate to this product.

Time taken to produce the first unit	28 direct labour hours
Production to date	15 units
Cumulative time taken to date	104 direct labour hours

What is the percentage learning effect?

Question 7.5   Using the learning curve formula

Learning outcomes B1(e)

Sciento Products manufactures complex electronic measuring instruments for which highly skilled labour is required.

Analysis of production times has shown that there is a learning curve effect on the labour time required to manufacture each unit and it has been decided to allow for this in establishing future forecast times and costs. Records have been kept of the production times for one particular instrument, the V8, an extract of which follows.

Cumulative production Units	Cumulative time Hours	Average time per unit Hours
1	200	200.0
2	360	180.0
4	648	162.0
8	1,166	145.8

The labour time analyses have shown that the learning curve follows the general form $Y = aX^b$

Where Y = average labour hours per unit   X = cumulative number of units
     a = number of labour hours for first unit   b = the learning index

Sciento Products is planning to produce a new version of the V8, the V8II, and believes that the same learning effect will apply to its production.

The company wishes to forecast the cost per V8II in a future period, to which the following data applies.

Estimated cumulative production at start of period	528 units
Estimated production in period	86 units
Estimated overheads	$150,903
Estimated labour cost	$10 per hour
Estimated material cost per unit	$250

Required

(a)   Calculate an estimated cost for the V8II in the period in question.

(b)   Discuss the usefulness of allowing for the learning effect in forecasting future labour costs and times.

1.5 Incremental time model

The model described so far is the cumulative average time model and is the one most commonly encountered. An alternative is the incremental (**or marginal or direct**) model. This model uses the same formula as the cumulative average time model but Y represents the time required to produce the final unit.

Exam alert

When learning curve theory is incorporated in an examination question, you can assume that the cumulative average time model is applicable unless explicit instructions are given to the contrary.

1.6 The practical application of learning curve theory

What costs are affected by the learning curve?

(a) Direct labour time and costs

(b) Variable overhead costs, if they vary with direct labour hours worked

(c) **Materials costs** are usually **unaffected** by learning among the workforce, although it is conceivable that materials handling might improve, and so wastage costs be reduced.

(d) **Fixed overhead expenditure** should be **unaffected** by the learning curve (although in an organisation that uses absorption costing, if fewer hours are worked in producing a unit of output, and the factory operates at full capacity, the **fixed overheads recovered or absorbed per unit** in the cost of the output will decline as more and more units are made).

1.7 The relevance of learning curve effects in management accounting

1.7.1 Situations in which learning curve theory can be used

(a) To **calculate the marginal (incremental)** cost of making extra units of a product.

(b) To **quote selling prices for products/services**, where prices are calculated at cost plus a percentage mark-up for profit.

(c) To **prepare realistic production budgets**.

(d) To design more **efficient production schedules**.

(e) To **prepare realistic standard costs** for cost control purposes.

1.7.2 Experience curves

The learning curve effect can be applied more broadly than just to labour. There are also efficiency gains in other areas;

(a) As methods are standardised **material wastage and spoilage** will decrease

(b) Machine costs may decrease as **better use is made of the equipment**

(c) **Process redesign may take place.** As understanding of the process increases, improvements and short-cuts may be developed.

(d) Learning curve labour efficiency will have a knock-on effect on the **fixed cost per unit**.

1.7.3 Further considerations

Further considerations that should be borne in mind	Detail
Sales projections, advertising expenditure and delivery date commitments	Identifying a learning curve effect should allow an organisation to plan its advertising and delivery schedules to coincide with expected production schedules. Production capacity obviously affects sales capacity and sales projections.
Budgeting with standard costs	Companies that use standard costing for much of their production output cannot apply standard times to output where a learning effect is taking place. This problem can be overcome in practice by establishing standard times for output once the learning effect has worn off or become insignificant and introducing a 'launch cost' budget for the product for the duration of the learning period. Alternatively, a standard average time per unit can be estimated for a budgeted volume of output, which makes allowance for the expected learning rate.
Cash budgets	Since the learning effect reduces unit variable costs as more units are produced, it should be allowed for in cash flow projections.
Work scheduling and overtime decisions	To take full advantage of the learning effect, idle production time should be avoided and work scheduling/overtime decisions should take account of the expected learning effect.
Pay	Where the workforce is paid a productivity bonus, the time needed to learn a new production process should be allowed for in calculating the bonus for a period.
Recruiting new labour	When a company plans to take on new labour to help with increasing production, the learning curve assumption will have to be reviewed.
Market share	The significance of the learning curve is that by increasing its share of the market, a company can benefit from shop-floor, managerial and technological 'learning' to achieve economies of scale.

1.8 Cessation of the learning effect

Improvements in the learning effect will not continue indefinitely. There will come a time when no further improvements can be made (known as a **steady state**). There are practical reasons for this cessation.

1.8.1 Machine efficiency

Machinery only has a **certain capacity of production** it can cope with. Once that capacity has been reached there can be **no further improvements** in efficiency (and thus no further improvements in time taken to produce each unit). If attempts are made to exceed capacity, efficiency could actually **decline**.

1.8.2 Workforce capacity

In a similar manner to machinery, the workforce **can only physically produce a certain amount**. Once they have reached their limit, there can be no further improvements in the time they take to produce each unit. Again, any attempts to push them beyond their capacity could have an **adverse effect** on efficiency.

1.8.3 'Go slow' agreements

Workers might agree to work no faster than a certain rate. Regardless of production conditions and potential for improvements, learning rates will **not increase** if this is the case.

1.9 Problems with applying learning curve theory

(a)   The learning curve phenomenon is **not always present**.

(b)   It **assumes stable conditions at work** which will enable learning to take place. This is not always practicable (for example because of labour turnover).

(c)   It must also **assume a certain degree of motivation** amongst employees.

(d)   **Breaks** between repeating production of an item must not be too long, or **workers will 'forget'** and the learning process would have to begin all over again.

(e)   It might be difficult to **obtain enough accurate data** to determine the learning rate.

(f)   **Workers might not agree** to a gradual reduction in production times per unit.

(g)   **Production techniques might change**, or product design alterations might be made, so that it **takes a long time for a 'standard' production method to emerge**, to which a learning effect will apply.

Section summary

Learning curve theory is used to measure how, in some industries and some situations, the incremental cost per unit of output continues to fall for each extra unit produced.

The theory is that the **cumulative average time per unit produced is assumed to fall by a constant percentage every time total output of the product doubles**. Cumulative average time is the average time per unit for all units produced so far, back to and including the first unit made.

The formula for the learning curve is $Y_x = aX^b$, where b, the learning coefficient or learning index, is defined as (log of the learning rate/log of 2).

2 Life cycle costing   9/10, 9/11, 9/12

Introduction

Life cycle costing is another technique used in cost planning. This section focuses on the concept of life cycle costing and how life cycle costs are linked with marketing strategies are various stages of the product life cycle.

2.1 What are life cycle costs?

Product life cycle costs are incurred **from the design stage through development to market launch, production and sales, and their eventual withdrawal from the market**.

Component elements of a product's cost over its life cycle

(a)   **Research & development costs**. Design, testing, production process and equipment.

(b)   **Technical data cost**. Cost of purchasing any technical data required.

(c)   **Training costs** including initial operator training and skills updating.

(d)   **Production costs**

(e)   **Distribution costs**. Transportation and handling costs.

(f)   **Marketing costs**. Customer service, field maintenance, brand promotion.

(g)   **Inventory costs**. Holding spare parts, warehousing and so on.

(h)   **Retirement and disposal costs**. Costs occurring at the end of the product's life.

Life cycle costs can **apply** to **services** as well as to physical **products**, and to **customers** and **projects**.

Traditional management accounting systems are based on the financial accounting year and tend to dissect the product's life cycle into a series of annual sections. This means that management accounting systems do not accumulate costs over the entire life cycle. They **do not**, therefore, **assess a product's profitability over its entire life** but rather on a periodic basis.

Life cycle costing, on the other hand, **tracks and accumulates actual costs and revenues** attributable to each product **over the entire product life cycle**. Hence the total profitability of any given product can be determined.

KEY TERM

LIFE CYCLE COSTING is 'the profiling of cost over a product's life, including the pre-production stage'.

Lifecycle costs of a product or service

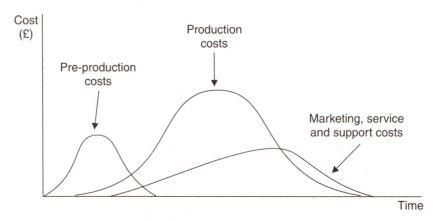

(CIMA Official Terminology)

2.2 The product life cycle

Every product goes through a life cycle, the curve of which resembles the generic curve in the following diagram.

This diagram was introduced in Chapter 6 in relation to pricing strategy.

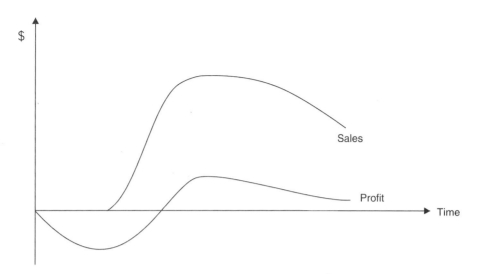

The product represented in the diagram above had a research and development stage prior to production.

The horizontal axis measures the duration of the **life cycle**, which **can last** from, say, **18 months to several hundred years**. Fad products have very short lives while some products, such as binoculars (invented in the eighteenth century) can last a very long time.

2.2.1 Characteristics of the product life cycle

It is important to know where a product is in its life cycle as this will affect **expectations** regarding sales volume and types of costs incurred.

Stage	Sales Volume	Costs
Development	None	Research & development
Introduction	Very low levels	Very high fixed costs (eg Fixed (non-current) assets, advertising)
Growth	Rapid increase	Increase in variable costs Some fixed costs increase (eg. Increase number of fixed (non-current) assets)
Maturity	Stable High volume	Primarily variable costs Variable cost per unit stabilises as economies of scale are achieved and the learning curve may cease to apply
Decline	Falling demand	Primarily variable costs (now decreasing) Some fixed costs (eg decommissioning costs)

Where the product is in its life cycle will also **affect the returns** that are expected.

Performance measure	Stage in the life cycle			
	Introduction	**Growth**	**Maturity**	**Decline**
Cash	Net user	Net user	Generator	Generator
Return on capital	Not important	Not important	Important	Important
Growth	Vital	Vital	Grow with new uses	Negative growth
Profit	Not expected	Important	Important	Very important

If a product is in the **introductory or growth stages** it **cannot be expected to be a net generator of cash** as all the cash it generates will be used in expansion through increased sales and so on. As the product moves from **maturity towards decline**, it is of **prime importance** that the product still **generates a profit and cash** and that its **return on capital** is **acceptable**.

2.3 Problems with traditional accounting systems

Traditional accounting systems **do not tend to relate research and development costs to the products that caused them**. Instead they **write off** these costs on an **annual basis against the revenue generated by existing products**. This makes the **existing products seem less profitable** than they really are and there is a danger that they might be **scrapped** too quickly. If research and development costs are not related to the causal product the true profitability of that product cannot be assessed.

Traditional management accounting systems usually **total all non-production costs** and record them as a **period expense**. With **life cycle costing** these costs are **traced to individual products** over complete life cycles.

2.4 Maximising the return over the product life cycle

2.4.1 Design costs out of products

Between 70% to 90% of a product's life cycle costs are determined by decisions made early in the life cycle, at the design or development stage. Careful design of the product and manufacturing and other processes will keep cost to a minimum over the life cycle.

2.4.2 Minimise the time to market

This is the time from the **conception** of the product to its **launch**. If an organisation is launching a new product it is **vital** to get it to the market place as soon as possible. This will give the product as long a period as possible without a rival in the market place and should mean **increased market share** in the long run. Furthermore, the life span may not proportionally lengthen if the product's launch is delayed and so sales may be permanently lost. It is not unusual for the product's overall profitability to fall by 25% if the launch is delayed by six months. This means that it is usually worthwhile incurring extra costs to keep the launch on schedule or to speed up the launch.

CASE STUDY

When Motorola announced a delay in the launch of its new smartphone in 2011, the share price dropped by 4%. The postponement also meant that Motorola's phone was eventually launched just weeks before the new Apple iphone.

2.4.3 Minimise breakeven time (BET)

A **short** BET is very important in keeping an organisation **liquid**. The sooner the product is launched the quicker the research and development costs will be repaid, providing the organisation with funds to develop further products.

2.4.4 Maximise the length of the life span

Product life cycles are **not predetermined**; they are set by the actions of **management** and **competitors**. Once developed, some products lend themselves to a number of different uses; this is especially true of materials, such as plastic, PVC, nylon and other synthetic materials. The life cycle of the material is then a series of individual product curves nesting on top of each other as shown below.

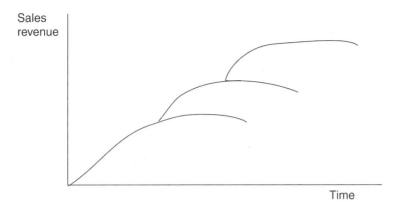

By entering different national or regional markets one after another an organisation may be able to **maximise revenue**. This allows resources to be better applied. On the other hand, in today's fast moving world, an organisation could lose out to a competitor if it failed to establish an early presence in a particular market.

2.4.5 Minimise product proliferation

If products are updated or superseded too quickly, the life cycle is cut short and the product may just cover its R and D costs before its successor is launched.

2.4.6 Manage the product's cashflows

Hewlett-Packard developed a return map to manage the lifecycle of their products. Here is an example.

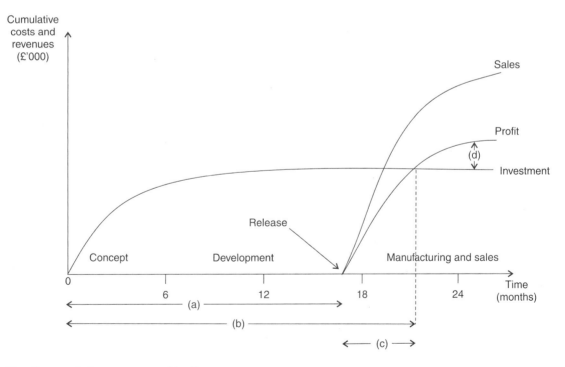

Key time periods are measured by the map:

(a) Time to market
(b) Breakeven time
(c) Breakeven time after product launch
(d) Return factor (the excess of profit over the investment)

Changes to planned time periods can be incorporated into the map (for example, if the development plan takes longer than expected) and the resulting changes to the return factor at set points after release highlighted.

2.5 Service and project life cycles

A service organisation will have services that have life cycles. The only difference is that the **R & D stages will not exist in the same way and will not have the same impact on subsequent costs**. The **different processes that go to form the complete service** are important, however, and **consideration should be given in advance as to how to carry them out and arrange them so as to minimise cost**.

Products that **take years to produce** or **come to fruition** are usually called **projects**, and **discounted cash flow calculations** are invariably used to **cost them over their life cycle in advance**. The projects need to be **monitored** very carefully **over their life** to make sure that they **remain on schedule and that cost overruns are not being incurred**.

2.6 Customer life cycles

Customers also have life cycles, and an organisation will wish to **maximise the return from a customer over their life cycle**. The aim is to **extend the life cycle of a particular customer** or decrease the 'churn' rate, as the Americans say. This means **encouraging customer loyalty**. For example, some supermarkets and other retail outlets issue **loyalty cards** that offer discounts to loyal customers who return to the shop and spend a certain amount with the organisation. As existing customers tend to be more profitable than new ones they should be retained wherever possible.

Customers become more profitable over their life cycle. The profit can go on increasing for a period of between approximately four and 20 years. For example, if you open a bank account, take out insurance or invest in a pension, the company involved has to set up the account, run checks and so on. The initial cost is high and the company will be keen to retain your business so that it can recoup this cost. Once customers get used to their supplier they tend to use them more frequently, and so there is a double benefit in holding on to customers. For example, you may use the bank to purchase shares on your behalf, or you may take out a second insurance policy with the same company.

The projected cash flows over the full lives of customers or customer segments can be analysed to highlight the worth of customers and the importance of customer retention. It may take a year or more to **recoup the initial costs of winning a customer**, and this could be referred to as the **payback period** of the investment in the customer. The investment in the customer and the consequent returns can be analysed in the same way as an investment in a capital project, a topic that we looked at in Part B.

2.7 Life cycle costs and marketing strategies

As a product progresses through its life cycle, it faces different challenges and opportunities which require changes in the marketing mix (covered in Chapter 6) and alternative marketing strategies.

2.7.1 Introduction stage

(a)   The principal aim during this stage is to establish a market and build demand.

(b)   Some organisations may market a product before it is actually introduced, but this will alert competitors and remove any element of surprise.

(c)   Advertising costs are usually high so as to increase customer awareness of the product and to target early adopters.

(d)   Costs associated with the initial distribution of the product are likely to be incurred.

(e)   **Implications for the marketing mix**

    (i)   **Product**. There are one or two, relatively undifferentiated products.

    (ii)   **Price**. Prices are generally high, on the assumption that a market skimming strategy is adopted in order to earn a high profit margin from early adopters and recoup development costs quickly. If a penetration pricing policy is adopted, introductory prices will be low to gain market share.

(iii)   **Distribution**. This will be selective and scattered.

(iv)   **Promotion**. This is aimed at building brand awareness. Early adopters may be offered samples or trial incentives.

2.7.2 Growth stage

(a)   The aim during this stage is to gain consumer preference and increase sales.

(b)   Revenue grows rapidly.

(c)   More customers become aware of the product and additional market segments are targeted.

(d)   As customers begin asking for the product, more retailers will want to carry it.

(e)   Expansion of distribution channels may be required at this point.

(f)   As competitors enter the market, promotional costs may increase (to convince consumers of the superiority of the organisation's version of the product) or price competition may occur.

(g)   **Implications for the marketing mix**

(i)   **Product**. There will be improvements in the quality of the product, new product features may be introduced and alternative packaging options may be considered.

(ii)   **Price**. Prices will be high if demand is high, but will be reduced if demand needs stimulating.

(iii)   **Distribution**. This becomes more intensive.

(iv)   **Promotion**. In order to build a preference for the brand, there may be increased advertising.

2.7.3 Maturity stage

(a)   The aim during this, the most profitable stage, is to maintain market share and extend the product's life cycle.

(b)   The rate of increase in sales slows down.

(c)   Advertising expenditure is reduced as brand awareness should be strong.

(d)   Market share and/or prices may fall as competition increases.

(e)   Product differentiation will become increasingly difficult given the similarity of competitors' offerings.

(f)   Marketing efforts are focused on finding new customers, encouraging customers to switch from competitors and increasing volumes of purchases per customer.

(g)   Sales promotions may be used to encourage retailers to give the product more shelf space than competitors' products.

(h)   **Implications for the marketing mix**

(i)   **Product**. To differentiate the product from those of competitors, modifications are made and features are added.

(ii)   **Price**. In the face of competition and to avoid a price war, prices may be cut.

(iii)   **Distribution**. New distribution channels may be sought. Incentives may be given to maintain shelf space.

(iv)   **Promotion**. The product will need to be differentiated from those of competitors. Brand loyalty should be built. Incentives can be given to entice competitors' customers to switch.

2.7.4 Decline stage

An organisation usually has three options.

(a) Keep the product on the market in the hope that competitors will remove theirs. Reduce costs and find new uses for the product.

(b) Reduce marketing support and let the product continue until profits dry up.

(c) Discontinue the product when profits dry up or a replacement product is available.

Implications for the marketing mix

(a) **Product**. The number of products in a product line may need to be reduced. Remaining products could be rejuvenated.

(b) **Price**. Prices of products to be discontinued may need to be reduced to get rid of remaining inventory.

(c) **Distribution**. Unprofitable channels are no longer used.

(d) **Promotion**. Expenditure is reduced and focuses on reinforcing the brand image of remaining products.

2.7.5 Advantages and disadvantages of the product life cycle concept for marketing strategies

The life cycle curves of different products vary immensely and so the concept is **not always an accurate tool** for sales forecasting purposes.

It has been suggested that the product life cycle may become **self fulfilling**: if it is thought that a product is in the decline stage and the advertising budget is cut, the product will decline further.

The product life cycle does offer a framework within which alternative marketing strategies can be planned, however, which will address the various challenges products are likely to face.

It also offers a means for comparing performance with products with similar life cycles.

Section summary

Life cycle costing involves a number of techniques that assist in the planning and control of a product's life cycle costs by monitoring spending and commitment to spend during a product's life cycle. Its aim is to minimise cost and maximise sales revenue over the life of the product.

3 Target costing   5/11, 5/12

Introduction

Another cost planning technique – target costing – is the focus of this section. You should remember that target costing works in the opposite way to normal methods of pricing, by setting a selling price and then working backwards to find the target cost.

3.1 The importance of product design

In order to compete effectively in today's competitive market, organisations need to **redesign continually their products** with the result that **product life cycles** have become much **shorter**. The **planning, design and development stages of a product's cycle** are therefore **critical to an organisation's cost management process**. Cost reduction at this stage of a product's life cycle, rather than during the production process, is one of the most important ways of reducing product cost.

CASE STUDY

General Motors estimate that 70% of the cost of manufacturing truck transmissions is determined in the design stage. Estimates for other companies and products often exceed 80%.

3.1.1 Factors that build in costs at the design stage

(a)   **The number of different components.** Production time increases as the number increases.

(b)   **Whether the components are standard or not.** Standard components are reliable and reduce inventory and handling costs.

(c)   **The number of extra features** (included as a standard or paid for separately)

(d)   **Type of packaging.** The aim is to protect the product and minimise handling costs by not breaking pallets or cases during distribution.

3.2 What is target costing?

Japanese companies developed **target costing** as a response to the problem of managing **costs over the product life cycle**.

KEY TERM

'TARGET COSTING is an activity which is aimed at reducing the life-cycle costs of new products, while ensuring quality, reliability, and other consumer requirements, by examining all possible ideas for cost reduction at the product planning, research and development, and the prototyping phases of production. But it is not just a cost reduction technique; it is part of a comprehensive strategic profit management system.'   (Kato, 1993)

CASE STUDY

When Toyota developed the Lexus to compete with BMW, Mercedes and Jaguar, it employed two basic concepts: reverse engineering and target costing. In essence, it sought to produce a car with BMW 7-series attributes at a BMW 5-series price. Cost was the dominant design parameter that shaped the development of the Lexus, as it was later with Nissan's Infiniti.

The response from Mercedes Benz, one of the competitors who lost market share through this strategy, was to acknowledge that its cars were over-engineered and too expensive and to change its product-development process to determine target product costs from competitive market prices.

Target costing requires managers to think differently about the relationship between cost, price and profit.

(a)   The **traditional approach** is to **develop a product, determine the expected standard production cost** of that product and **then set a selling price** (probably based on cost) with a resulting profit or loss. Costs are controlled through monthly variance analysis.

(b)   The **target costing approach** is to develop a **product concept** and the primary specifications for performance and design and then to **determine the price customers would be willing to pay** for that concept. The **desired profit margin is deducted from the price leaving a figure that represents total cost**. This is the target cost and the product must be capable of being produced for this amount otherwise the product will not be manufactured. **During the product's life the target cost will constantly be reduced** so that the **price can fall. Continuous cost reduction techniques** must therefore be employed.

KEY TERM

TARGET COST is 'A product cost estimate derived by subtracting a desired profit margin from a competitive market price.'   (CIMA *Official Terminology*)

Because it **encourages cost consciousness** and **focuses on profit margins**, target costing is a **useful tool for strengthening an organisation's competitive position**.

3.3 Setting the target price

Products that are **varieties of existing products** or **new brands of existing products** enter an already established market and therefore a competitive **price should be fairly easy to set**. There is no existing market price for **new products**, however and so **market research** will probably be used to assist in price setting. Many Japanese companies use **functional analysis** and **pricing by function** in such circumstances. We cover functional analysis in Section 5 of this chapter.

Selling price will also be **affected by factors such as the stage in the product life cycle, expected sales volume and the price charged by rivals** in the market.

3.4 Setting the target profit requirement

This should **not be simply a standard mark-up** but instead should be **based on strategic profit plans**. Procedures used to derive the target profit must be agreed by all staff responsible for achieving it and it must be seen as something more than just an expectation. In this way **staff will both accept responsibility for achieving it** and **be committed to achieving it**.

3.5 The target costing process

 Analyse the external environment to ascertain what customers require and what competitors are producing. Determine the **product concept**, the **price** customers will be willing to pay and thus the **target cost**.

 Split the total target cost into broad cost categories such as development, marketing, manufacturing and so on. **Then split up the manufacturing target cost per unit across the different functional areas of the product. Design the product so that each functional product area can be made within the target cost.** If a functional product area cannot be made within the target cost, the targets for the other areas must be reduced, or the product redesigned or scrapped. The product should be developed in an atmosphere of **continuous improvement** using **value engineering techniques** and **close collaboration with suppliers**, to enhance the product (in terms of service, quality, durability and so on) and reduce costs. We cover value engineering in Section 4 of this chapter.

 Once it is decided that it is feasible to meet the total target cost, **detailed cost sheets** will be prepared and **processes formalised**.

It is possible that management may decide to go ahead and manufacture a product whose target cost is well below the currently attainable cost, determined by current technology and processes. If this is the case management will **set benchmarks for improvement** towards the target costs, by specified dates.

Options available to reduce costs

(a)   **Training** staff in more efficient techniques
(b)   Using **cheaper staff**
(c)   Acquiring new, more **efficient technology**
(d)   Cutting out **non-value-added activities**

Even if the product can be produced within the target cost the story does not end there. **Once the product goes into production target costs will gradually be reduced.** These reductions will be incorporated into the budgeting process. This means that cost savings must be actively sought and made continuously. Value analysis will be used to reduce costs if and when targets are missed. Value analysis is covered in Section 4 of this chapter.

3.5.1 Cost tables

Cost tables are useful value engineering tools. They are **high volume, computerised databases of detailed cost information based on various manufacturing variables**. They are a source of information about the effect on product costs of using different resources, production methods, designs and so on.

CASE STUDY

Swedish retailer IKEA continues to dominate the home furniture market with more than 330 stores across 43 countries at the end of 2012. The "IKEA concept" as defined on the company website www.ikea.com is "based on offering a wide range of well designed functional home furnishing products at prices so low as many people as possible will be able to afford them."

IKEA is widely known for pricing products at 30-50% below the price charged by competitors. Extracts from the website outline how the company has successfully employed a strategy of target pricing:

"While most retailers use design to justify a higher price, IKEA designers work in exactly the opposite way. Instead they use design to secure the lowest possible price. IKEA designers design every IKEA product starting with a functional need and a price. Then they use their vast knowledge of innovative, low-cost manufacturing processes to create functional products, often co-ordinated in style. Then large volumes are purchased to push prices down even further.

Most IKEA products are also designed to be transported in flat packs and assembled at the customer's home. This lowers the price by minimising transportation and storage costs. In this way, the IKEA Concept uses design to ensure that IKEA products can be purchased and enjoyed by as many people as possible."

3.6 Target costing support systems

Target costing cannot operate in isolation. **Information** to enable it to operate successfully is needed from a wide range of support systems.

(a) **Sales pricing support systems**, which can, for example, break down product functions into sub-functions and provide information on that basis, and can convert the value placed on each function into a price

(b) **Target profit computation support systems**, which can, for example, calculate the optimal product mix in the future (product portfolio planning system)

(c) **Research and development support systems**, which include computer-aided design and computer-aided engineering

(d) Support systems for **infusing target costs** into products, which include **value engineering** and **variety reduction**

(e) **Human resource management systems**, which are particularly important when an organisation uses target costing for the first time

3.7 Target costing versus standard costing　　　　　9/10

	Standard costing	Target costing
How costs are controlled	Costs must be kept within predetermined standard costs. Variances are calculated to check that this has happened.	There is no cost slashing but continual pressure to ensure costs are kept to a minimum.
Relationship between product concept, cost and price	Predetermined product design ↓ Cost ↓ Price	Product design concept ↓ Selling price ↓ Target cost ↑ Profit margin
Link with strategic plans	None. The approach is short-term cost control through variance analysis.	The product concept and target profit margin take into account medium-term strategic plans.

	Standard costing	Target costing
Time frame for cost control	Standards are usually revised annually.	Continual cost reduction. Target costs are revised monthly.

3.8 Possible adverse effects of target costing

(a) Longer product development times because of numerous changes to designs and costings

(b) Employee demotivation because of pressure to meet targets

(c) Organisational conflict between designers who try to reduce costs and marketing staff who give away promotional items costing even more

Question 7.6	Standard costing v target costing

Learning outcomes B1(h)

Fill in the blank spaces ((a) to (d)) in the table below to show how standard costing and target costing differ.

Stage in product life cycle	Standard costing approach	Target costing approach
Product concept stage	No action	(a)
Design stage	(b)	Keep costs to a minimum
Production stage	Costs are controlled using variance analysis	(c)
Remainder of life	(d)	Target cost reduced, perhaps monthly

Section summary

Target costing is a pro-active cost control system. The target cost is calculated by deducting the target profit from a predetermined selling price based on customers' views. Functional analysis, value engineering and value analysis are used to change production methods and/or reduce expected costs so that the target cost is met.

4 Value analysis

9/11, 11/11, 5/13

Introduction

Value analysis embraces many of the techniques already mentioned. It looks at trying to reduce costs without reducing the value to the customer.

4.1 What is value analysis?

KEY TERMS

VALUE ANALYSIS is 'A systematic inter-disciplinary examination of factors affecting the cost of a product or service, in order to devise means of achieving the specified purpose most economically at the required standard of quality and reliability'.

(CIMA *Official Terminology*)

The **value of the product must therefore be kept the same or else improved, at a reduced cost.**

VALUE ENGINEERING is 'Redesign of an activity, product or service so that value to the customer is enhanced while costs are reduced (or at least increase by less than the resulting price increase).

(CIMA *Official Terminology*)

The distinction between value engineering and value analysis is not clear cut but, in general, **value engineering is cost avoidance or cost prevention before production** whereas **value analysis is cost reduction during production**.

4.2 What is different about value analysis?

There are two features of value analysis that distinguish it from other approaches to cost reduction.

(a)   It **encourages innovation** and a more radical outlook for ways of reducing costs because ideas for cost reduction are **not constrained by the existing product design**.

(b)   It **recognises the various types of value** which a product or service provides, **analyses** this value, and then **seeks ways of improving** or maintaining aspects of this value but at a lower cost.

Conventional cost reduction techniques try to achieve the lowest production costs for a specific product design whereas value analysis tries to find the least-cost method of making a product that achieves its desired function, not the least-cost method of accomplishing a product design to a mandatory and detailed specification.

4.3 Value

KEY TERMS

- COST VALUE is the cost of producing and selling an item.
- EXCHANGE VALUE is the market value of the product or service.
- USE VALUE is what the article does, the purposes it fulfils.
- ESTEEM VALUE is the prestige the customer attaches to the product.

(a)   Value analysis seeks to **reduce** unit costs, and so cost value is the one aspect of value to be reduced.

(b)   Value analysis attempts to provide the same (or a better) use value at the lowest cost. **Use value** therefore involves considerations of the **performance and reliability** of the product or service.

(c)   Value analysis attempts to maintain or enhance the **esteem value** of a product at the lowest cost.

Question 7.7	Value

Learning outcomes B1(a)

Below are three features of a product.

(a)   The product can be sold for £27.50.
(b)   The product is available in six colours to suit customers' tastes.
(c)   The product will last for at least ten years.

What are the correct classifications of the features using the types of value in the key terms box above?

4.4 The scope of value analysis

Any commercial organisation should be continually seeking lower costs, better products and higher profits. These can be achieved in any of the following ways.

(a) Cost elimination or cost prevention
(b) Cost reduction
(c) Improving product quality and so selling greater quantities at the same price as before
(d) Improving product quality and so being able to increase the sales price

Value analysis can achieve all four of these objectives.

| Question 7.8 | Benefits of a VA programme |

Learning outcomes B1(a)

In addition to the above, what other benefits of a VA programme can you think of?

Three areas of special importance are as follows.

Area	Method
Product design	At the design stage value analysis is called value engineering. The designer should be cost conscious and avoid unnecessary complications. Simple product design can avoid production and quality control problems, thereby resulting in lower costs.
Components and material costs	The purchasing department should beware of lapsing into habit with routine buying decisions. It has a crucial role to play in reducing costs and improving value by procuring the desired quality materials at the lowest possible price.
Production methods	These ought to be reviewed continually, on a product-by-product basis, especially with changing technology.

4.5 Carrying out a value analysis

4.5.1 Typical considerations in value analysis

(a) **Can a cheaper substitute material be found** which is as good, if not better, than the material currently used?

(b) **Can unnecessary weight or embellishments be removed** without reducing the product's attractions or desirability?

(c) **Is it possible to use standardised components** (or to make components to a particular standard) thereby reducing the variety of units used and produced? Variety reduction through standardisation facilitates longer production runs at lower unit costs.

(d) **Is it possible to reduce the number of components,** for example could a product be assembled safely with a smaller number of screws?

The origins of value analysis were in the engineering industry, but it **can be applied to services, or aspects of office work, or to management information systems** (for example the value of information, reports and so on).

4.5.2 The steps in value analysis

A value analysis study should be carried out by a team of experts, preferably with varying backgrounds, which blends experience, skill and imagination.

 Selecting a product or service for study. The product selected should be one which accounts for a high proportion of the organisation's costs, since the greatest cost savings should be obtainable from high cost areas. The choice should also take into account the stage of its 'life cycle' that it has reached. A product reaching the end of its marketable life is unlikely to offer scope for substantial savings.

 Obtaining and recording information. The questions to be asked include: what is the product or service supposed to do? Does it succeed? Are there alternative ways of making or providing it? What do these alternatives cost?

 Analysing the information and evaluating the product. Each aspect of the product or service should now be analysed. Any cost reductions must be achieved without the loss of use or esteem value. (Or at least, cost savings must exceed any loss in value suffered, and customers would then have to be compensated for the loss in use or esteem value in the form of a lower selling price.) The types of questions asked in a value analysis include:

(a) Are all the parts necessary?
(b) Can the parts be obtained or made at a lower cost?
(c) Can standardised parts be used?
(d) Does the value provided by each feature justify its cost?

 Considering alternatives. From the analysis, a variety of options can be devised. This is the 'new ideas' stage of the study, and alternative options would mix ideas for eliminating unnecessary parts or features or standardising certain components or features.

 Selection of the least cost alternative. The costs (and other aspects of value) of each alternative should be compared.

 Recommendation. The preferred alternative should then be recommended to the decision makers for approval.

 Implementation and follow-up. Once a value analysis proposal is approved and accepted, its implementation must be properly planned and co-ordinated. The VA team should review the implementation and, where appropriate, improve the new product or method in the light of practical experience.

To be successful, **value analysis programmes must have the full backing of senior management**.

 Section summary

Value analysis is a planned, scientific approach to cost reduction which reviews the material composition of a product and production design so that modifications and improvements can be made which do not reduce the value of the product to the customer or to the user.

Value engineering is the application of value analysis techniques to new products.

Four aspects of value should be considered in value analysis (**cost value, exchange value, use value, esteem value**).

5 Functional analysis   11/11

Introduction

Functional analysis is a cost management technique which has similarities with value analysis. This section looks at the basic steps involved in this technique and compares and contrasts the technique with value analysis.

5.1 Basic steps

KEY TERM

FUNCTIONAL ANALYSIS is 'An analysis of the relationships between product functions, their perceived value to the customer and their cost of provision'.

(CIMA *Official Terminology*)

The technique involves the following nine steps, some of which are similar to those required in value analysis.

Choose the object of analysis (such as product, service or overhead area). If it is not a new product, **a high volume** product with a complex design and relatively large production costs is often an ideal candidate.

Select members for the functional analysis team. The team will usually consist of six to eight members from a number of different departments (such as accounting, production, purchasing, engineering, design and marketing).

Gather information. This will include information both from inside the organisation (detailed design, manufacturing and marketing information, for example) and from outside the organisation (such as information about new technologies).

Define the functions of the object. The various functions of the product should be defined in terms of a verb and a noun. Functions should be classified as basic or secondary in terms of the importance of that particular function for the product.

Draw a functional family tree. The functions identified in step 4 should be arranged in a logical order in a family-tree diagram. A table illustrating the relationship between the functions and the parts of the product, as well as relevant existing costs, should also be drawn up. An extract for a propelling ball point pen is shown below.

Part number	Name of part	Verb	Noun	Cost
			*Function*	
5	ink	put	colour	$0.03
9	clip	prevent	loss	$0.02

Evaluate the functions. The relative value of each function to a total target cost from the customers' point of view has to be estimated (either using market research or by each member of the team placing values and a consensus being reached for each function). This relative value provides a target cost for each function.

Suggest alternatives and compare these with the target cost. Alternatives might include the use of new materials or parts or a different method of manufacturing the product.

Choose the alternatives for manufacturing. The alternatives must be assessed and a final choice made of those to implement.

Review the actual results. An audit or review of the changes implemented should be conducted promptly and the findings reported to senior management. This will prevent over-optimistic assessments of the functional analysis exercise and provide feedback so that future functional analysis can be improved.

5.2 Advantages

(a) Competitive advantage resulting from improved, cost-effective design or redesign of products

(b) Probably of most benefit during the planning and design stages of new products (because up to 90% of the costs of many products are committed by the end of the design stage)

(c) Flexible application (has been applied to services, particular overhead areas, organisational restructuring and corporate strategy) because it views objects in abstract (service potential) terms rather than in physical (parts and people) terms

(d) Information about product functions and about the views of customers is integrated into the formal reporting system

5.3 Comparison of value and functional analysis

The differences between the two techniques can be summarised as follows:

	Value Analysis	Functional Analysis
When used	During production	Prior to production
Focus on	Process to reduce cost	Customer value
Involves	Reducing cost without reducing value	Adding features to improve profits

Value analysis focuses on **cost reduction** through a **review of the processes** required to produce a product or service. **Functional analysis** focuses on the **value to the customer of each function** of the product or service and then makes a decision as to whether cost reduction is necessary.

5.4 Functional analysis and ABC

An activity based costing (ABC) system will provide useful information about what drives specific overheads in the organisation. These **cost drivers** can then be used to **link overhead costs to individual functions or groups of functions** so that when a **function is changed**, a basis for ascertaining the **effect (if any) on the overheads** is available. ABC is explained in detail in the next chapter.

Section summary

Functional analysis is concerned with improving profits by attempting to reduce costs and/or by improving products by adding new features in a cost-effective way that are so attractive to customers that profits actually increase.

Chapter Roundup

✓   **Learning curve theory** is used to measure how, in some industries and some situations, the incremental cost per unit of output continues to fall for each extra unit produced.

✓   The theory is that the **cumulative average time per unit produced is assumed to fall by a constant percentage every time total output of the product doubles**. Cumulative average time is the average time per unit for all units produced so far, back to and including the first unit made.

✓   The formula for the learning curve is $Y_x = aX^b$, where b, the learning coefficient or learning index, is defined as (log of the learning rate/log of 2).

✓   **Life cycle costing** involves a number of techniques that assist in the planning and control of a product's life cycle costs by monitoring spending and commitment to spend during a product's life cycle. Its aim is to minimise cost and maximise sales revenue over the life of the product.

✓   **Target costing** is a pro-active cost control system. The target cost is calculated by deducting the target profit from a predetermined selling price based on customers' views. Functional analysis, value engineering and value analysis are used to change production methods and/or reduce expected costs so that the target cost is met.

✓   **Value analysis** is a planned, scientific approach to cost reduction which reviews the material composition of a product and production design so that modifications and improvements can be made which do not reduce the value of the product to the customer or to the user.

✓   **Value engineering** is the application of value analysis techniques to new products.

✓   Four aspects of value should be considered in value analysis (**cost value, exchange value, use value, esteem value**).

✓   **Functional analysis** is concerned with improving profits by attempting to reduce costs and/or by improving products by adding new features in a cost-effective way that are so attractive to customers that profits actually increase.

Quick Quiz

1   In the formula for the learning curve, $Y_x = aX^b$, how is the value of b calculated?

    A   Log of the learning rate/log of 2
    B   Log of 2/learning rate
    C   Learning rate $\times$ log of 2
    D   Log of learning rate/2

2   Life cycle costing is the profiling of cost over a product's production life. *True or false?*

3   *Put the three terms below in the correct order to represent (a) the target costing process and (b) traditional costing process.*

- Selling price
- Cost
- Profit

4   *Choose the correct words from those highlighted.*

Value **engineering/analysis** is cost avoidance or cost prevention before production whereas value **engineering/analysis** is cost reduction during production.

5   *Match the terms to the correct definitions.*

Terms
Cost value
Exchange value
Use value
Esteem value

Definitions

    (a)   The prestige the customer attaches to the product
    (b)   The market value of the product
    (c)   What the product does
    (d)   The cost of producing and selling the product

6   *Fill in the action to take at each step in a value analysis.*

STEP ① ....

STEP ② ....

STEP ③ ....

STEP ④ ....

STEP ⑤ ....

STEP 6 ....

STEP 7 ....

7   *Fill in the blanks.*

     Functional analysis is an analysis of the relationships between ...., their .... and their ....

8   Draw a curve of a typical product life cycle.

Answers to Quick Quiz

1   A. Make sure you can use the log function on your calculator.

2   False. It includes development costs and so on prior to production and any costs such as dismantling costs when production has ceased.

3   (a)   Selling price, profit, cost
     (b)   Cost, selling price, profit

4   First term should be value engineering, the second term value analysis.

5   Cost value   (d)
     Exchange value   (b)
     Use value   (c)
     Esteem value   (a)

6

    Select a product or service for study

    Obtain and record information

    Analyse the information and evaluate the product

    Consider alternatives

    Select the least cost alternative

    Make a recommendation

    Implement and follow up

7   Functional analysis is an analysis of the relationships between product functions, their perceived value to the customer and their cost of provision.

8

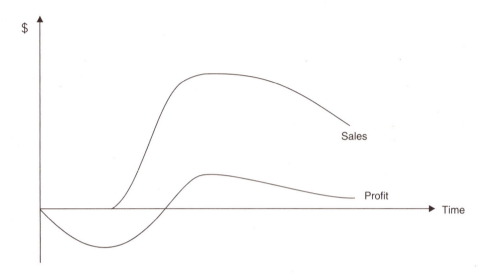

Answers to Questions

7.1 Learning curves

Cumulative number of units produced		Cumulative average time per unit Hours	Total time Hours
1		3	
2	(90%)	2.7	
4	(90%)	2.43	9.720
8	(90%)	2.187	17.496
Time taken for units 5 to 8			7.776
Average time per unit (÷ 4)			1.944 hours

7.2 Learning curve formula

The correct answer is –0.152 and so the statement is false.

$b = \log 0.9/\log 2 = -0.0458/0.3010 = -0.152$

7.3 Calculation of the percentage learning effect

Let the rate of learning be r.

Cumulative production	Cumulative average cost $
1	720*
2	$720 \times r$
4	$720 \times r^2$

$\therefore \quad \$720r^2 \quad = \quad £405$

$r^2 \quad = \quad £405/£720 = 0.5625$

$r \quad = \quad 0.75$

∴ The rate of learning is 75%.

* $\$1,200 \times 60\%$

7.4 Calculation of percentage learning effect using logs

Average time taken per unit to date $= (104 \div 15) = 6.933$ hours

Since	$Y_x =$	aX^b
	$6.933 =$	$28(15)^b$
	$15^b =$	$6.933 \div 28 = 0.2476$
Taking logs	$b \log15 =$	$\log 0.2476$
Since	$\log15 =$	1.1761 (using log 10^x on your calculator)
And	$\log 0.2476 =$	-0.6062

$$b = \frac{\log 0.2476}{\log15} = \frac{-0.6062}{1.1761} = -0.515$$

$$b = \frac{\text{log of learning rate}}{\text{log 2}}$$

$$-0.515 = \frac{\text{log of learning rate}}{0.3010}$$

Log of learning rate $= -0.515 \times 0.3010 = -0.155$

Using the button on your calculator probably marked 10^x, -0.155 converts back to a 'normal' figure of 0.70. Thus the learning rate is 70%.

7.5 Using the learning curve formula

You need to start with a working that provides you with an **average time per unit for the units actually produced within the period**. This means that you need to determine **the number of hours worked in the period**. By calculating the average time per unit for the units produced up to the beginning of the period, you can work out the number of hours worked in total before the beginning of the period by multiplying the average time by the total output. The same calculations can then be performed but for the output produced by the end of the period. The difference between the two total times is the number of hours worked in the period, from which the period average can be calculated.

It might be tempting to take the **average time as an average of the two averages you calculate** $((77.124 + 75.375)/2 = 76.25$ hours per unit). This would be **wrong**, however, since this average would include the time taken for the first unit (200 hours) and the second, third, fourth and so on, whereas we should really be wanting a 'standard' time for the units currently being produced. Our average of 65 hours per unit is the average time needed for the 529th to the 614th units, which is much less than 76.25 hours per unit.

Workings for solution

A 90% learning curve applies because the cumulative average time per unit is 90% of what it was previously each time that cumulative total output doubles.

$Y = aX^b$, where $b = $ log of the learning rate (as a proportion)/log of 2

With a 90% learning curve, $b = $ log 0.9/log 2 $= -0.152$

(1) $X = 528$,

The average labour hours per unit $= aX^{-0.152} = (200)(528)^{-0.152} = 77.124$

(2) $X = (528 + 86) = 614$

The average labour hours per unit $= aX^{-0.152} = (200)(614)^{-0.152} = 75.375$

Total output	Average time	Total time per unit
Units	Hours	Hours
614	75.375	46,280
528	77.124	40,721
86		5,559

The average time per unit for the 86 units produced in the period should be 5,559/86 = 64.64 hours, say 65 hours per unit.

Suggested solution

(a)   The standard overhead rate per hour $= \$150,903/(86 \times 65$ hrs$) = \$27$

	Estimated cost per V8II $
Material cost	250
Labour cost (65 hours × $10 per hour)	650
Overheads (65 hours × $27 per hour)	1,755
Estimated cost per unit	2,655

(b)   **Usefulness**

   (i)   Where there is a learning effect, it would be inaccurate and unrealistic to estimate labour times and labour costs without taking this effect into account.

   (ii)   It is particularly important where the learning effect applies to labour which makes up a large proportion of total costs of production and sales.

   (iii) Accurate estimates of labour times are needed for efficient capacity scheduling and competitive pricing, if prices are set on a cost plus basis.

Limitations

   (i)   An accurate estimate of labour times depends on reliable estimates of:

      (1)   the learning rate; and
      (2)   estimated output in the period.

      There will almost certainly be some margin of error in the estimated times.

   (ii)   The learning effect does not apply in all situations. When a product is long-established, the learning effect will have worn off, and standard times per unit will be constant. The learning effect will not be significant in capital intensive operations.

7.6 Standard costing v target costing

(a)   Set the selling price and required profit and determine the resulting target cost
(b)   Set standard cost and a resulting standard price
(c)   Constant cost reduction
(d)   Standards usually revised annually

7.7 Value

(a)   Exchange value
(b)   Esteem value
(c)   Use value

7.8 Benefits of a VA programme

(a)   Improved product performance and product reliability

(b)   Improved product quality

(c)   An increased product life, in terms of both the marketable life of the product (for the company) and the usable life of each product unit (for the customer)

(d)   Possibly, shorter delivery 'lead times' to customers because of a shorter production cycle

(e)   The increased use of standard parts and components which contribute to lower costs for the customer

(f)   A more economic use of scarce resources

(g)   Encouraging employees to show innovation and creative ideas

Now try these questions from the Exam Question Bank	Number	Level	Marks	Time
	Q16	Examination	10	18 mins
	Q17	Examination	25	45 mins
	Q18	Examination	10	18 mins

COST ANALYSIS

This chapter considers activity based management (ABM) and related topics.

Section 1 sets the scene, while **Section 2** looks at **activity based costing (ABC)**, a topic you may have encountered in your earlier studies.

Activity based management (covered in **Section 3**) is basically the cost management application of ABC.

Sections 4 -6 look at how ABC can be used to determine the **profitability** of products, customers and distribution channels. **Section 7** focuses on activity-based profitability analysis whilst **Section 8** covers **Pareto analysis**, which can be used to present the results of some of the analyses covered in the chapter.

topic list	learning outcomes	syllabus references	ability required
1 The nature of costs	B1(f), (g)	B1(v)	application
2 Activity based costing (ABC)	B1(f)	B1(v)	application
3 Activity based management (ABM)	B1(f)	B1(v)	application
4 Direct product profitability (DPP)	B1(l)	B1(x)	analysis
5 Customer profitability analysis (CPA)	B1(l)	B1(x)	analysis
6 Distribution channel profitability	B1(l)	B1(x)	analysis
7 Activity-based profitability analysis	B1(l)	B1(x)	analysis
8 Pareto analysis	B1(m)	B1(xi)	application

1 The nature of costs

Introduction

In Chapters 1A and 1B we discussed relevant costs in the context of short-term decision-making. This section focuses on the nature of costs in the modern business environment and the problems of accounting for these costs.

KEY POINT

In the **modern business environment**, most costs can be analysed into **short-term variable costs** (that vary with the volume of production) and **long-term variable costs** (that are fixed in the short term and vary not with volume of production but with a different measure of activity).

1.1 The problem of accounting for overheads in the modern business environment

1.1.1 Problem 1

Traditionally, **virtually all costs** with the **exception of material and labour** were classified as **indirect** expenses, meaning that they were not caused by cost objects such as products.

In the **modern business environment**, however, their absorption into products on the **basis of direct labour hours does not recognise the causal factors** of overheads.

1.1.2 Problem 2

Overheads or indirect costs accounted for a **very small proportion of total cost** in the **past.** Their **absorption** into products using **misleading bases** such as in line with direct labour hours **did not therefore produce errors** in product costs that were **too significant**.

Such costs have become a **greater proportion of total production costs**, however, and the **direct labour cost proportion has declined**, in some cases to less than ten per cent of the total cost. This has resulted in a large volume of costs being spread on the basis of the behaviour of a small volume of costs, thereby producing **misleading** and **even inaccurate cost information**.

1.1.3 Problem 3

Nowadays **most costs are fixed in the short term** rather than variable, and so **marginal costing is not a particularly appropriate** costing convention to use. Some method of absorption costing is preferred by the majority of companies – hence the development of ABC and the other systems described in this chapter.

1.2 Cost analysis in the modern business environment

Most costs can be analysed between the following.

(a) **Short-term variable costs**, that vary with the volume of production

(b) **Long-term variable costs**, that are fixed in the short-term and do *not* vary with the volume of production, but that do **vary with a different measure of activity**

It has been suggested that **long-term variable costs** are **related** to the **complexity** and **diversity of production** rather than to simple volume of output. For example, costs for support services such as set-ups, handling of inventory, expediting (progress chasing) and scheduling do not increase with the volume of output. They are fixed in the shorter term but they vary in the longer term according to the range and complexity of product items manufactured. If **another product** or product variation is added to the range,

the **support activities** will become more **complex.** If a **single product** is made **some support activities,** such as production scheduling, will **not exist.**

The problem of producing a **small number of products in volume** against producing a **large variety of products in small runs** is known as **volume versus variety** and can be expressed graphically.

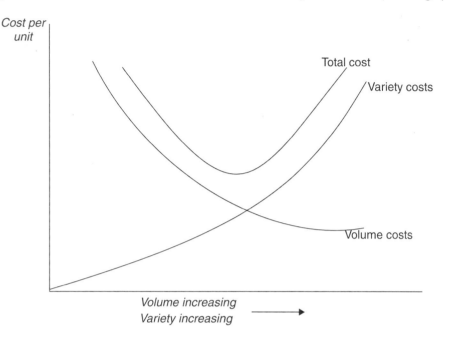

Long production runs (volume) reduce some costs, short production runs (variety) increase some costs. Research has shown that when volume doubles, the average cost per unit decreases by 15% to 25% (the experience curve effect). Stalk & Hout (1990) found that when the variety of products manufactured doubles the average unit costs rise by 20% to 35%.

When a company adopts the **modern philosophy** and **manufactures in variety, costs of support activities** therefore **increase** and **emphasis is inevitably put on controlling these costs,** such as minimising production scheduling and set-up costs. **In order to control costs some attempt must be made to relate these costs to products via their causal factors in as accurate a way as possible.**

Section summary

In the **modern business environment,** most costs can be analysed into **short-term variable costs** (that vary with the volume of production) and **long-term variable costs** (that are fixed in the short term and vary not with volume of production but with a different measure of activity).

2 Activity based costing (ABC) 5/10, 11/10

Introduction

Activity based costing (ABC) has been developed as an **alternative costing system** to traditional overhead absorption costing (which was included in the revision chapter at the beginning of this Study Text). This section focuses on the **features** of this system, the **calculations** involved in cost allocation and **wider applications** of ABC.

KEY TERM

ACTIVITY BASED COSTING (ABC) is 'An approach to the costing and monitoring of activities which involves tracing resource consumption and costing final outputs. Resources are assigned to activities and activities to cost objects based on consumption estimates. The latter use **cost drivers** to attach activity costs to outputs.'

(CIMA *Official Terminology*)

ABC was developed to improve the cost allocation process as traditional techniques assumed that costs were only driven by volume (for example, costs may have been absorbed on a rate per machine hour basis).

Production overheads are **not necessarily driven by volume** therefore allocation using traditional methods is not necessarily meaningful. With ABC, **multiple overhead absorption rates** are calculated based on the different activities that **cause** the costs to **change**.

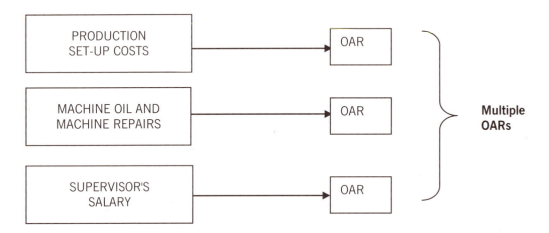

2.1 Cost drivers and cost pools

KEY TERM

A COST DRIVER is 'factor influencing the level of cost. Often used in the context of ABC to denote the factor which links activity resource consumption to product outputs, for example, the number of purchase orders would be a cost driver for procurement cost.'

(CIMA *Official Terminology*)

2.1.1 Examples of cost drivers

Support department costs	Possible cost driver
Set-up costs	Number of production runs
Production scheduling	Number of production runs
Material handling	Number of production runs
Inspection costs	Number of inspections or inspection hours
Raw materials inventory handling etc	Number of purchase orders delivered
Despatch costs	Number of customer orders delivered

All of the costs associated with a particular cost driver (for example production runs) would be grouped into **cost pools**.

In order to understand how ABC operates in detail we need to look at two types of cost driver.

KEY TERMS

A RESOURCE COST DRIVER is a measure of the quantity of resources consumed by an activity. It is used to assign the cost of a resource to an activity or cost pool.

An ACTIVITY COST DRIVER is a measure of the frequency and intensity of demand placed on activities by cost objects. It is used to assign activity costs to cost objects.

An **example** of a **resource cost driver** is **area**, which can be used to assign office occupancy costs to purchasing, the accounts department and so on.

An **example** of an **activity cost driver** is **number of customer orders,** the number of orders measuring the consumption of order entry activities by each customer.

In **traditional absorption costing** overheads are first related to **cost centres** and then to **cost objects** (products). In **ABC** overheads are first related to **activities** or grouped into **cost pools** (depending on the terminology preferred) and then related to the **cost objects**. (Unlike traditional absorption costing, ABC has other cost objects such as customers. This will be discussed later). **The two processes** are therefore **very similar**, but the first stage is different as ABC uses activities instead of cost centres (functional departments).

Proponents of **ABC** therefore claim that it gives a **more realistic picture of cost behaviour.**

(a)   Costs collected into cost pools tend to behave in the same way (they have the same cost driver).

(b)   Costs related to cost centres might behave in different ways.

Like traditional absorption costing rates, **ABC rates** are **calculated in advance**, usually for **a year ahead**.

2.2 Stages in ABC calculations

 Group overheads into cost pools, according to how they are driven. This involves gathering overheads that are caused by the **same activity** into one group and is done by means of **resource cost drivers** (see definition above).

 Identify the cost drivers for each activity (that is, what causes the activity to be incurred). Examples of cost drivers are given in Section 2.1.1 above.

 Calculate a cost per unit of cost driver. This is done in a similar way to the calculation of traditional overhead absorption rates:

Cost driver rate $=$ $\dfrac{\text{Total cost of activity}}{\text{Cost driver}}$

 Absorb activity costs into production based on the usage of cost drivers - for example, rate per production set-up multiplied by number of production set-ups. The **cost driver rate** can be used to **cost products**, as in traditional absorption costing, but it can also cost **other cost objects** such as **customers** or groups of customers.

Example: ABC

The following example illustrates how traditional cost accounting techniques could result in a misleading and inequitable division of costs between low-volume and high-volume products, and demonstrates that ABC may provide a more meaningful allocation of costs.

Suppose that Cooplan manufactures four products, W, X, Y and Z. The direct labour cost per hour is $5. Other output and cost data for the period just ended are as follows.

	Output units	Number of production runs in the period	Material cost per unit $	Direct labour hours per unit	Machine hours per unit
W	10	2	20	1	1
X	10	2	80	3	3
Y	100	5	20	1	1
Z	100	5	80	3	3
		$\overline{14}$			

Overhead costs

Short run variable costs	$3,080	Expediting and scheduling costs	$9,100
Set-up costs	$10,920	Materials handling costs	$7,700

Required

Prepare unit costs for each product using traditional costing and ABC.

Solution

Using a **conventional absorption costing approach** and an absorption rate for overheads based on either direct labour hours or machine hours, the product costs would be as follows.

	W	X	Y	Z	Total
	$	$	$	$	$
Direct material	200	800	2,000	8,000	
Direct labour	50	150	500	1,500	
Overheads *	700	2,100	7,000	21,000	
	950	3,050	9,500	30,500	44,000
Units produced	10	10	100	100	
Cost per unit	$95	$305	$95	$305	

* $30,800 ÷ 440 hours = $70 per direct labour or machine hour.

Using **activity based costing** and assuming that the number of production runs is the cost driver for set-up costs, expediting and scheduling costs and materials handling costs and that machine hours are the cost driver for short-run variable costs, unit costs would be as follows.

	W	X	Y	Z	Total
	$	$	$	$	$
Direct material	200	800	2,000	8,000	
Direct labour	50	150	500	1,500	
Short-run variable overheads (W1)	70	210	700	2,100	
Set-up costs (W2)	1,560	1,560	3,900	3,900	
Expediting, scheduling costs (W3)	1,300	1,300	3,250	3,250	
Materials handling costs (W4)	1,100	1,100	2,750	2,750	
	4,280	5,120	13,100	21,500	44,000
Units produced	10	10	100	100	
Cost per unit	$428	$512	$131	$215	

Workings

1	$3,080 ÷ 440 machine hours =	$7 per machine hour
2	$10,920 ÷ 14 production runs =	$780 per run
3	$9,100 ÷ 14 production runs =	$650 per run
4	$7,700 ÷ 14 production runs =	$550 per run

Summary

Product	Traditional costing Unit cost	ABC Unit cost	Difference per unit	Difference in total
	$	$	$	$
W	95	428	+ 333	+3,330
X	305	512	+ 207	+2,070
Y	95	131	+ 36	+3,600
Z	305	215	− 90	−9,000

The figures suggest that the traditional volume-based absorption costing system is flawed.

(a)   It **under-allocates overhead costs to low-volume products** (here, W and X) and **over-allocates overheads to higher-volume products** (here Z in particular).

(b)   It **under-allocates overhead costs to smaller-sized products** (here W and Y with just one hour of work needed per unit) and **over-allocates overheads to larger products** (here X and particularly Z).

ABC traces the appropriate amount of input to each product. However, it is **important** to realise that although **ABC should be** a **more accurate** way of relating overheads to products **it is not a perfect system** and **product costs** could still be **inaccurate** as ABC is based on a number of assumptions.

2.3 The merits and criticisms of activity based costing

2.3.1 Merits

As the above example illustrates, there is nothing difficult about ABC. Once the necessary information has been obtained it is similar to traditional absorption costing. This **simplicity** is part of its appeal. Further merits of ABC are as follows.

(a)   ABC **recognises the increased complexity** of modern businesses with its **multiple cost drivers**, many of which are transaction-based rather than volume-based.

(b)   ABC is **concerned with all overhead costs**, including such 'non factory-floor' costs as quality control and customer service, and so it takes cost accounting beyond its 'traditional' factory floor boundaries.

(c)   ABC gives a meaningful analysis of costs which should provide a suitable basis for decisions about pricing, product mix, design and production.

(d)   ABC helps with **cost reduction** because it provides an insight into causal activities and allows organisations to consider the possibility of **outsourcing particular activities**, or even of **moving to different areas in the industry value chain**. This is discussed later in the chapter under activity based management.

(e)   ABC can be **used in conjunction with customer profitability analysis (CPA)**, discussed later in this chapter, to determine more accurately the profit earned by serving particular customers.

(f)   ABC can be used by **service and retail organisations**. This will be discussed later in the chapter. Many service and retail businesses have characteristics very similar to those required for the successful application of ABC in modern manufacturing industry.

  (i)   A highly **competitive** market

  (ii)   **Diversity** of products, processes and customers

  (iii) **Significant overhead costs** which are not easily assigned to individual products

  (iv)   **Demands placed on overhead resources** by individual products and customers, which are **not proportional to volume**.

If ABC were to be used in a hotel, for example, attempts could be made to identify the activities required to support each guest by category and the cost drivers of those activities. The cost of a one-night stay midweek by a businessman could then be distinguished from the cost of a one-night stay by a teenager at the weekend. Such information may prove invaluable for customer profitability analysis.

Exam alert

An exam question could ask you to prepare calculations to show the effect on fees charged by a business using activity based costing.

2.3.2 Criticisms

Activity based costing has some serious flaws and concern is now growing that ABC is seen by many as a panacea for management accounting ills, despite the fact that its suitability for all environments remains unproven.

(a) The **cost** of obtaining and interpreting the new information may be considerable. **ABC should not be introduced unless it can provide additional information** for management to use in planning or control decisions.

(b) Some arbitrary **cost apportionment** may still be required at the cost pooling stage for items like rent, rates and building depreciation. If an ABC system has many cost pools the amount of apportionment needed may be greater than ever.

(c) Many **overheads relate neither to volume nor to complexity**. The ability of a **single cost driver** to fully explain the cost behaviour of all items in its associated pool is **questionable**.

(d) There will have to be a **trade off between accuracy, the number of cost drivers and complexity**.

(e) ABC tends to **burden low-volume (new) products** with a punitive level of overhead costs and hence threatens opportunities for successful innovation if it is used without due care.

(f) Some people have questioned the fundamental assumption that activities cause cost, they suggest **that decisions cause cost or the passage of time causes cost** – or that there may be **no clear cause of cost.**

2.4 Wider uses of ABC

2.4.1 Planning

Before an ABC system can be implemented, management must **analyse** the **organisation's activities**, determine the **extent of their occurrence**, and establish the **relationship between activities, products/services and their cost**. This can be used as a basis for **forward planning and budgeting**.

2.4.2 Control

Knowledge of activities also provides an **insight into the way in which costs are structured and incurred in service and support departments**. Traditionally it has been difficult to control the costs of such departments because of the lack of relationship between departmental output levels and departmental cost. With ABC, however, it is possible to **control or manage the costs by managing the activities which underlie them** using a number of key performance measures which must be monitored if costs and the business generally are to be controlled.

2.4.3 Decision-making

Many of **ABC's supporters** claim that it can **assist with decision-making** because it provides accurate and reliable cost information. This is a **contentious issue** among accountants. Many 'purists' consider that **marginal costing** alone provides the correct information on which to **make short-term decisions such as the following.**

(a) Pricing
(b) Make or buy decisions
(c) Promoting or discontinuing products or parts of the business
(d) Developing and designing changed products

ABC establishes a long-run product cost and because it provides data which can be used to evaluate different business possibilities and opportunities it is particularly suited for the types of decision listed above. Those decisions have long-term strategic implications and **average cost** is probably **more important** than **marginal cost** in many circumstances. **An ABC cost is an average cost**, but it is **not always a true cost** because some costs such as depreciation are usually arbitrarily allocated to products. An ABC cost is therefore **not a relevant cost for all decisions**.

2.4.4 ABC and long-term decisions

ABC is **particularly suited for long-term and strategic decisions** (such as long-run pricing, capacity management and product mix decisions) for a number of reasons.

(a)   It assumes all costs are **variable** in relation to product choice or production level decisions.

(b)   It has strategic relevance because it allows for a **full understanding of activities** and their resource consumption.

(c)   **Short-run changes in consumption do not translate into changes in spending** (as real cash savings or expenditure are not made/incurred in the short run).

Question 8.1	Using ABC

Learning outcome B1(f)

(a)   List the features of organisations that would find ABC particularly useful for product costing.

(b)   Briefly explain the reasons why ABC is particularly suitable in a modern business environment and describe any situations where it is not appropriate.

2.5 Pricing and ABC

Example: Activity based costing and pricing

ABP makes two products, X and Y, with the following cost patterns.

	Product X $	Product Y $
Direct materials	27	24
Direct labour at $5 per hour	20	25
Variable production overheads at $6 per hour	3	6
	50	55

Production fixed overheads total $300,000 per month and these are absorbed on the basis of direct labour hours. Budgeted direct labour hours are 25,000 per month. However, the company has carried out an analysis of its production support activities and found that its 'fixed costs' actually vary in accordance with non volume-related factors.

Activity	Cost driver	Product X	Product Y	Total cost $
Set-ups	Production runs	30	20	40,000
Materials handling	Production runs	30	20	150,000
Inspection	Inspections	880	3,520	110,000
				300,000

Budgeted production is 1,250 units of product X and 4,000 units of product Y.

Required

Given that the company wishes to make a profit of 20% on full production costs calculate the prices that should be charged for products X and Y using the following.

(a)   Full cost pricing
(b)   Activity based cost pricing

Solution

(a) The **full cost and mark-up** will be calculated as follows.

	Product X	Product Y
	$	$
Variable costs	50.00	55.00
Fixed prod o/hds ($300,000/25,000 = $12 per direct labour	48.00	60.00
	98.00	115.00
Profit mark-up (20%)	19.60	23.00
Selling price	117.60	138.00

(b) Using **activity based costing**, overheads will be allocated on the basis of cost drivers.

	X	Y	Total
	$	$	$
Set ups (30:20)	24,000	16,000	40,000
Materials handling (30:20)	90,000	60,000	150,000
Inspections (880:3,520)	22,000	88,000	110,000
	136,000	164,000	300,000
Budgeted units	1,250	4,000	
Overheads per unit	$108.80	$41.00	

The price is then calculated as before.

	Product X	Product Y
	$	$
Variable costs	50.00	55.00
Production overheads	108.80	41.00
	158.80	96.00
Profit mark-up (20%)	31.76	19.20
	190.56	115.20

(c) Commentary

The results in (b) are radically different from those in (a). On this basis it appears that the company has **previously been making a huge loss** on every unit of product X sold for $117.60. If the market will not accept a price increase, it may be worth considering ceasing production of product X entirely. It also appears that there is scope for a reduction in the price of product Y, and this would certainly be worthwhile if demand for the product is elastic.

2.5.1 The pricing implications of activity based costing

Many modern companies produce and sell **large volumes** of a **standard product** and a number of variants of the basic product that sell in low volumes at a higher price. Such companies absorb fixed overheads on a conventional basis such as direct labour hours, and price their products by adding a **mark-up** to full cost.

This means that the **majority of the overheads** would be allocated to the **standard** range, and only a small percentage to the up-market products. The result would be that the **profit margin** achieved on the standard range would be much lower than that on the up-market range.

Although the traditional costing system might suggest that the company should concentrate on the lower-volume, higher profit margin products, it should be borne in mind that a large quantity of the overhead costs are likely to be related to the up-market products – for example, production scheduling and marketing and distribution costs. Such costs should therefore be **absorbed by the products that cause them** rather than the standard product.

The problem arises with **marginal cost-plus** approaches as well as with absorption cost based approaches, particularly in a modern manufacturing environment, where a relatively small proportion of the total cost is variable. The implication in both cases is that conventional costing should be abandoned in favour of ABC.

2.6 Using ABC in service and retail organisations

ABC was **first introduced in manufacturing organisations** but it can equally well be used in **other types of organisation**. For example, the management of the Post Office in the USA recently introduced ABC. They analysed the activities associated with cash processing as follows.

Activities	Examples	Possible cost driver
Unit level	Accept cash	Number of transactions
	Processing of cash by bank	Number of transactions
Batch level	'Close out' and supervisor review of clerk	Number of 'close outs'
	Deposits	Number of deposits
	Review and transfer of funds	Number of accounts
Product level	Maintenance charges for bank accounts	Number of accounts
	Reconciling bank accounts	Number of accounts

Retail organisations are considered in more detail in the context of direct product profitability later in this text, but they too **can use ABC**.

Question 8.2	ABC and retail organisations

Learning outcome B1(f)

What activities and drivers might be used in a retail organisation?

Section summary

The ABC approach is to relate costs to the factors that cause or 'drive' them to be incurred in the first place and to change subsequently. These factors are called '**cost drivers**'.

ABC relates overhead/resource costs to the activities that cause or drive them. This is done using **resource cost drivers**. The costs of activities are related to cost units using **activity cost drivers**.

The **information** provided by **analysing activities** can support the management functions of **planning, control and decision-making**, provided it is used carefully and with full appreciation of its implications.

---

3   Activity based management (ABM)

Introduction

Recently the emphasis has switched away from using activity based approaches for product costing to using it to improve cost management. This section covers the cost management version of ABC – that is activity based management (ABM). Make sure you know the differences between the two systems and how ABM can be used by companies to gain competitive advantage.

3.1 What is ABM?

There are a great many different **definitions** of activity based management. We focus on the CIMA official definitions below.

KEY TERMS

ACTIVITY-BASED MANAGEMENT (ABM) is: OPERATIONAL ABM. Actions based on activity driver analysis, that increase efficiency, lower costs and improve asset utilisation.

STRATEGIC ABM Actions based on activity-based cost analysis, that aim to change the demand for activities so as to improve profitability.
(CIMA Official Terminology)

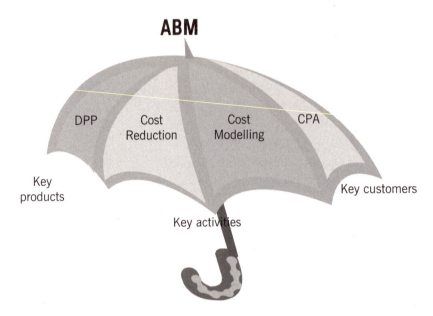

ABM acts as an 'umbrella' for a number of techniques – such as **Direct Product Profitability** (DPP) and **Customer Profitability Analysis** (CPA), both of which will be covered later in this chapter – thus focusing the company's attention on key products, activities and customers. It uses the information generated by ABC to **control or reduce cost drivers** and also to **reduce overheads**. By doing so, the company can gain competitive advantage.

3.2 Cost reduction and process improvement

ABM analyses costs on the basis of cross-departmental activities and thus provides management information on why costs are incurred and on the output of the activity in terms of cost drivers. **By controlling or reducing the incidence of the cost driver, the associated cost can also be controlled or reduced.**

This difference is illustrated in the example below of a customer order processing activity.

Traditional analysis

	$
Salaries	5,700
Stationery	350
Travel	1,290
Telephone	980
Equipment depreciation	680
	9,000

ABC analysis

	$
Preparation of quotations	4,200
Receipt of customer orders	900
Assessment of customer creditworthiness	1,100
Expedition of orders	1,300
Resolution of customer problems	1,500
	9,000

Suppose that the analysis above showed that it cost $250 to process a customer's order. This would indicate to sales staff that it may not be worthwhile chasing orders with a low sales value. By eliminating lots of small orders and focusing on those with a larger value, demand for the activities associated with customer order processing should fall, with spending decreasing as a consequence.

3.2.1 Problems associated with cost reduction and ABM

(a) The extent to which activity based approaches can be applied is very dependent on an organisation's ability to **identify** its main activities and their associated cost drivers.

(b) If a system of 'conventional' responsibility centres has been carefully designed, this may already be a reflection of the key organisational activities.

(c) In some circumstances, the 'pooling' of activity based costs and the identification of a single cost driver for every cost pool may even hamper effective control if the cost driver is not completely applicable to every cost within that cost pool.

3.3 Activity analysis

The activity based analysis above provides information not available from a traditional cost analysis – for example, why was $1,500 spent on resolving customer orders? An **activity analysis** usually **surprises managers** who had not realised the amount being spent on certain activities. This leads to **questions** about the **necessity for particular activities** and, if an activity is required, whether it can be carried out more effectively and efficiently.

Such questions can be answered by classifying activities as value added or non-value added (or as core/primary, support or diversionary/discretionary).

3.3.1 Value-added and non-value-added activities

KEY TERM

An activity may increase the worth of a product or service to the customer; in this case the customer is willing to pay for that activity and it is considered VALUE-ADDED. Some activities, though, simply increase the time spent on a product or service but do not increase its worth to the customer; these activities are NON-VALUE-ADDED.   (Rayborn, Barfield and Kinney, *Managerial Accounting*)

As an example, **getting luggage on the proper flight is a value-added activity** for airlines, **dealing with the complaints from customers whose luggage gets lost is not**.

The **time** spent on **non-value-added activities** creates additional costs that are unnecessary. If such activities were **eliminated**, **costs** would **decrease without affecting the market value or quality of the product or service**.

KEY POINT

Two questions can be used to **assess whether an activity adds value**.

- Would an external customer encourage the organisation to do more of the activity?
- Would the organisation be more likely to achieve its goals by performing the activity?

If both answers are yes, the activity adds value.

The processing **time** of an organisation is made up of four types.

(a)   **Production** or **performance time** is the actual time that it takes to perform the functions necessary to manufacture the product or perform the service.

(b)   Performing quality control results in **inspection time.**

(c)   Moving products or components from one place to another is **transfer time.**

(d)   Storage time and time spent waiting at the production operation for processing are **idle time**.

Production time is value added. The other three are not. The time from receipt of an order to completion of a product or performance of a service equals production time plus non-value-added time.

Sometimes **non-value added activities** arise because of inadequacies in existing processes and so they **cannot be eliminated unless these inadequacies are addressed**.

One of the **costliest** things an organisation can do is to **invest in equipment and people to make non-value-added activities more efficient**. The objective is to **eliminate them altogether** or subject them to a major overhaul, not make them more efficient!

3.4 Cost management of activities

Costs are assigned using cost driver rates (calculated on the basis of available resource) to cost objects on the basis of the objects' demand for an activity or consumption of a resource.

But the amount of resource available in a period is not necessarily the same as the amount of resource consumed by cost objects.

If the staff of a purchasing department are **fully occupied**, **all costs** of the department will be **assigned**, via a cost driver rate based on, say, number of orders, to cost objects. Unlike inventories of material, however, **unused capacity** in the purchasing department **cannot be stored** for the future. Management must therefore **control the provision of activities and the associated resources if costs are to be kept to a minimum**.

A **change in the level of demand for an activity does not necessarily lead to a change in the level of provision of that activity**, however.

(a)   If the demand for orders increases, the existing purchasing department staff may be able to meet this extra demand with overtime working, but in the medium to long term additional staff would be required. It is not usually possible to take on and get rid of staff at short notice, however, and so there is usually a delay between changes in demand for activity and change in the availability of resource for that activity.

(b)   If the demand for orders decreases, the purchasing department staff are not likely to bring to management's attention the fact that they now have slack in their working hours. A traditional absorption costing system would not highlight this situation for management attention, either. If ABC is used, however, the drop in demand for the resource/activity will be obvious as the cost driver rate will be applied to fewer orders/units of output.

The application of **ABC** therefore offers the possibility of **turning costs that were deemed to be fixed into variable costs**: variability is a function of managers' decisions about levels of expenditure and the speed at which the supply of resources should be changed as requirements change.

Whereas **absorption costing aims to recover costs, ABC aims to highlight inefficiencies**, and so cost drivers should be based on the possible level of activity rather than the expected level of activity. If the cost driver rate is $100 per order and 50 orders are handled in a month, the cost assigned is $5,000. If budgeted expenditure is $6,000, the cost of unused capacity is $1,000.

ABC therefore enables management to **identify resources that are not being fully utilised.**

3.5 Design decisions

In many organisations today, roughly 80% of a product's costs are committed at the product design stage, well before production begins. By **providing product designers with cost driver information** they can be encouraged to **design low cost products that still meet customer requirements.**

The identification of appropriate cost drivers and tracing costs to products on the basis of these cost drivers has the potential to **influence behaviour to support the cost management strategies of the organisation.**

A product which is designed so that it uses fewer components will be cheaper to produce. A product using standard components will also be cheaper to produce. Management can **influence the action of designers** through overhead absorption rates if overheads are related to products on the basis of the number of component parts they contain. Hitachi's refrigeration plant uses this method to influence the behaviour of their product designers and ultimately the **cost of manufacture**.

3.6 Cost driver analysis

Exam alert

It is important that you learn the four classification levels as well as understand applications to specific organisations.

KEY TERM

The MANUFACTURING COST HIERARCHY categorises costs and activities as **unit** level, **batch** level, **product** level and **facility sustaining** level.

To reflect today's more **complex business environment**, recognition must be given to the fact that **costs are created and incurred because their cost drivers occur at different levels. Cost driver analysis investigates, quantifies and explains the relationships between cost drivers and their related costs.**

Activities and their related costs fall into four different categories, known as the **manufacturing cost hierarchy**. The **categories determine the type of activity cost driver required**.

Classification level	Cause of cost	Types of cost	Cost driver
Unit level	Production/acquisition of a single unit of product or delivery of single unit of service	Direct materials Direct labour	Units produced
Batch level	A group of things being made, handled or processed	Purchase orders Set-ups Inspection	Batches produced
Product level	Development, production or acquisition of different items	Equipment maintenance Product development	Product lines produced
Facility sustaining level	Some costs cannot be related to a particular product line, instead they are related to maintaining the buildings and facilities. These costs cannot be related to cost objects with any degree of accuracy and are often excluded from ABC calculations for this reason.	Building depreciation Organisational advertising	None - supports the overall production or service process

Traditionally it has been assumed that if costs did not vary with changes in production at the unit level, they were fixed rather than variable. The analysis above shows this assumption to be false, and that costs vary for reasons other than production volume. To determine an accurate estimate of product or service cost, **costs should be accumulated at each successively higher level of costs.**

Unit level costs are allocated over number of units produced, batch level costs over the number of units in the batch, product level costs over the number of units produced by the product line. These costs are all related to units of product (merely at different levels) and so can be gathered together at the product level to match with revenue. Organisational level costs are not product related, however, and so should simply be deducted from net revenue.

Such an approach gives a far greater insight into product profitability.

Question 8.3	Classification of activities

Learning outcome B1(f)

A food processing company operates an ABC system. Which of the following would be classified as a facility-sustaining activity?

(i)   General staff administration
(ii)   Plant management
(iii)   Technical support for individual products and services
(iv)   Updating of product specification database
(v)   Property management

3.7 Continuous improvement

As we will see in the next chapter, continuous improvement **recognises the concept of eliminating non-value-added activities** to reduce lead time, make products or perform services with zero defects, reduce product costs on an ongoing basis and simplify products and processes. It focuses on including employees in the process as they are often the best source of ideas.

3.8 Performance evaluation

ABM **encourages and rewards employees** for developing new skills, accepting greater responsibilities, and making suggestions for improvements in plant layout, product design, and staff utilisation. Each of these improvements reduces non-value-added time and cost. In addition, by focusing on activities and costs, ABM is better able to provide more appropriate measures of performance than are found in more traditional systems.

KEY POINT

To monitor the effectiveness and efficiency of activities using ABM, performance measures relating to volume, time, quality and costs are needed.

(a)   Activity **volume** measures provide an indication of the throughput and capacity utilisation of activities. For example reporting the number of times an activity such as setting-up is undertaken focuses attention on the need to investigate ways of reducing the volume of the activity and hence future costs.

(b)   To increase customer satisfaction, organisations must provide a speedy response to customer requests and reduce the time taken to develop and bring a new product to the market. Organisations must therefore focus on the **time** taken to complete an activity or sequence of activities. This time can be reduced by eliminating (as far as is possible) the time spent on non-value-added activities.

(c)   A focus on value chain analysis is a means of enhancing customer satisfaction. The value chain is the linked set of activities from basic raw material acquisition all the way through to the end-use product or service delivered to the customer. By viewing each of the activities in the value chain as a supplier-customer relationship, the opinions of the customers can be used to provide useful feedback on the **quality** of the service provided by the supplying activity. For example the quality of the service provided by the processing of purchase orders activity can be evaluated by users of the activity in terms of the speed of processing orders and the quality of the service provided by the supplier chosen by the purchasing activity. Such qualitative evaluations can be supported by quantitative measures such as percentage of deliveries that are late.

(d)   **Cost** driver rates (such as cost per set-up) can be communicated in a format that is easily understood by all staff and can be used to motivate managers to reduce the cost of performing activities (given that cost driver rate × activity level = cost of activity). Their use as a measure of performance can induce dysfunctional behaviour, however. By splitting production runs and therefore having more set-ups, the cost per set-up can be reduced. Workload will be increased, however, and so in the long run costs could increase.

3.9 Implementing ABM

In an article in *Financial Management* in 2001 ('Tool of the trade'), Stephanie Gourdie provided the following 'Tips for ABM'.

(a)   Get the support of senior management

(b)   Recognise that ABM requires a major investment in time and resources

(c)   Know what ABM can achieve and what information you want from the system

(d)   Decide which model to use

(e)   Choose the model approach that emphasises the operational understanding of all activities in the business

(f)   Involve people in the field

(g)   Transfer ownership of cost management from the accounts department to the departments and processes where costs are incurred

(h)   Don't underestimate the need to manage the change process

(i)   Link ABM to corporate objectives in the form of increased product profitability and added value for customers'

In 'Voyage of discovery' (*Financial Manager*, May 2002), Selvan Naidoo describes the key decisions to be made and the major pitfalls to be avoided when implementing ABM.

(a)   Decide on whether results are to be used at a strategic level or for cost management, as this will affect the level of analysis of activities required.

(b)   Establish if implementation will be in certain areas only, such as head office, or across the organisation.

(c)   Agree the acceptable level of accuracy.

(d)   Decide on the products and services to be costed. [*BPP note.* Pareto analysis could be applied. See Section 8]

(e)   Involve operational staff from the start of the project.

(f)   Gain full support from senior management.

(g)   Manage expectations. ABC will not solve all of an organisation's problems.

(h)   Implement effective project management.

(i)   Provide regular progress reports for management.

(j)   Do not underestimate the effort needed to obtain the information required in the correct format.

(k)   Consider using a pilot implementation if ABC is being implemented across a number of sites.

(l)   Be wary of running ABC and another project with similar deadlines and demands on resources in a business unit.

3.10 Problems with ABM

ABM is not a 'cure for all ills', however.

(a)   The **amount of work** in setting up the system and in data collection must be considered.

(b)   Organisational and behavioural consequences. Selected activity cost pools may not correspond to the formal structure of cost responsibilities within the organisation (the purchasing activity may spread across purchasing, production, stores, administrative and finance departments) and so determining 'ownership' of the activity and its costs may be problematic. We have already mentioned the behavioural impact of some performance measures.

Section summary

Activity-based management (ABM) is **operational ABM**. Actions based on activity driver analysis that increase efficiency, lower costs and improve asset utilisation.

Strategic ABM: actions based on activity-based cost analysis that aim to change the demand for activities so as to improve profitability.

Two questions can be used to **assess whether an activity adds value**.

- Would an external customer encourage the organisation to do more of the activity?
- Would the organisation be more likely to achieve its goals by performing the activity?

If both answers are yes, the activity adds value.

The **manufacturing cost hierarchy** categorises costs and activities as **unit** level, **batch** level, **product** level and **facility sustaining** level.

To monitor the effectiveness and efficiency of activities using **ABM, performance measures** relating to **volume, time, quality** and **costs** are needed.

---

4   Direct product profitability (DPP)

Introduction

We have been mainly focusing on manufacturing organisations so far in this chapter. Direct product profitability is a costing system used by retail businesses and focuses on the resource consumption of individual products.

KEY TERMS

DIRECT PRODUCT PROFITABILITY (DPP) is 'Used primarily within the retail sector, [and] involves the attribution of both the purchase price and other indirect costs (eg distribution, warehousing, retailing) to each product line. Thus a net profit, as opposed to a gross profit, can be identified for each product. The cost attribution process utilises a variety of measures (eg warehousing space, transport time) to reflect the resource consumption of individual products.'   (CIMA *Official Terminology*)

DIRECT PRODUCT PROFIT is the contribution a product category makes to fixed costs and profits. It is calculated by deducting direct product costs (such as warehousing and transport) from the product's gross margin.

4.1 Calculation of direct product profit

Direct product profit is calculated as follows:

	$	$
Sales price		X
Less: purchase cost		(X)
Gross margin		X
Less: direct product costs		
warehouse direct costs	(X)	
transport direct costs	(X)	
store direct costs	(X)	(X)
Direct product profit		(X)

KEY POINT

Any costs that are **general** to the organisation (but not specific to any particular product) should be **ignored** when calculating direct product profit.

4.1.1 What are direct product costs?

These can be **directly attributed** to the handling and storing of individual products.

Direct product cost	Examples
Warehouse direct costs	Offloading, unpacking, picking and sorting, space costs, inventory financing costs
Transport direct costs	Fuel, depreciation of vehicle, driver's salary, vehicle servicing
Store/supermarket direct costs	Receiving and inspecting, moving, shelf filling, space costs, inventory financing costs

Direct product costs may include other product specific costs such as retailer brand development costs.

In general, warehouse, transport and store costs will tend to be spread across the different goods sold in relation to volume or area occupied, as most costs increase in proportion to the volume of the good or the space it occupies.

Rather confusingly, direct product cost also contains **part of the indirect cost** that can be **apportioned** to the product, **based on one or more product characteristics**. For example, the **cost of shelf space** is apportioned by means of the **physical volume** of the product. All other costs, for example Head Office costs, are not included.

In practice each product would be charged with a number of different costs but the following example deals only with the space costs in a store.

Example: DPP

A supermarket group has estimated that its store space cost is $0.50 per cubic metre per day.

Its product range includes the following products.

(a) Six-packs of lager – volume: 0.01 cubic metres, days in store: 5
(b) Detergent – volume: 0.005 cubic metres, days in store: 4
(c) Double roll of kitchen paper – volume: 0.185 cubic metres, days in store: 3.

Solution

The space costs would be allocated as follows.

Lager $0.50 × 0.01 × 5   = $0.025 per pack
Detergent $0.50 × 0.005 × 4   = $0.01 per pack
Kitchen paper $0.50 × 0.185 × 3 = $0.278 per pack

The results show the need to achieve a high turnover with bulky low price goods. Refrigerated items would carry a higher space cost due to the cost of refrigeration.

4.2 Benefits of using DPP

(a)   Detailed information is provided on the **performance** of an **individual product**.

(b)   Products can be **ranked** according to product profitability.

(c)   **Diagnostic capabilities**. Why did a product under perform? Was the inventory turn acceptable?

(d)   Profitable product lines can be identified and given more **prominent shelf space**.

(e)   Leads to a **mutual understanding** of **product and supply chain** costs and **improves supplier/retailer relationships**

(f)   **Better pricing decisions**

(g)   **Improved management of store** and **warehouse space**

4.3 DPP software systems

These allow 'what if?' analysis to be carried out. A number of key variables can be changed to analyse different scenarios.

(a)   **Prices at which products are bought and sold**. The higher the selling price relative to other retailers, the slower the likely inventory movement.

(b)   **Rate of selling.** This is a key variable and needs to be as high as possible to minimise warehouse and store space costs, and to ensure that interest on money tied up in inventory is not lost.

(c)   **Size of stockholding.** In line with JIT principles, inventory should be kept to a minimum but stock-outs avoided.

(d)   **Size of the product.** This variable requires consideration as it is one of the drivers of space cost per item.

(e)   **Configuration of pallets.** The handling cost per unit falls as the number of cases on a pallet increases.

(f)   **Ordering cost.** A balance has to be found because ordering only occasionally will mean ordering costs are minimised but inventory levels are higher.

(g)   **Distribution routes.** The software can model whether direct delivery to the store or the use of a central warehouse offers the cheaper option. It is likely to be the latter.

Section summary

DPP is a **costing system used by retail businesses**.

Any costs that are **general** to the organisation (but not specific to any particular product) should be **ignored** when calculating direct product profit.

5 Customer profitability analysis (CPA)   9/10, 5/13

> **Introduction**
>
> **Customer profitability analysis** uses ABC principles to identify the most profitable customers or groups of customers to allow marketing efforts to be directed at attracting and retaining these customers.

KEY TERM

CUSTOMER PROFITABILITY ANALYSIS (**CPA**) is 'the analysis of the revenue streams and service costs associated with specific customers or customer groups'.   (CIMA *Official Terminology*)

5.1 Analysing customers

Profitability can vary widely between different customers because various **overhead costs** are, to some extent, **variable and customer driven**.

- Discounts
- Sales force
- Quality control
- Merchandising

- Distribution
- Promotions
- Financing costs
- Enquiries

Suppose a hotel offers a number of services such as a swimming pool, a gym and a nightly dinner dance.

(a) Older guests may attend the dinner dance.
(b) Families may use the swimming pool.
(c) People without children may appreciate the gym.

By charging services to the guests using them, a cost per bed night can be calculated for each guest group. **Strategies for attracting the most profitable guest group** can then be adopted.

Whether individual customers or groups of customers are costed largely depends on the number of customers.

(a) A manufacturing company supplying six companies would cost each customer separately.

(b) A supermarket or bank would cost groups of similar customers. UK banks divide their customers into categories such as single and 30ish, married with young children, older couples with spending money and so on.

Marketing departments should be aiming to **attract and retain profitable customers** but in order to do this they need to **know which customers are profitable** and **how much can be spent on retaining them**. The **costing system** should **provide the necessary answers**.

Customer profitability analysis (CPA) provides important information which allows an organisation to determine both **which classes of customers it should concentrate on** and the **prices it should charge for customer services**. Its use ensures that those customers **contributing sizeably to the profitability** of the organisation receive a **comparable amount of attention** from the organisation.

5.2 Customer revenues

Customer revenues are cash flows from customers. They are influenced by different factors, mainly **allowances and discounts**.

(a) Some types of customer **store and distribute goods** (eg wholesalers) or **promote** the goods in return for an **allowance**.

(b) By giving a **discount** a company may **encourage bulk orders**, which may be cheaper to provide and may result in higher sales volume. However, studies on customer profitability have found large price discounting to be a key explanation for a group of customers being below expected profitability. Sales representatives may have given customers large price discounts unrelated to their current or potential value to the company, perhaps to meet bonuses dependent on sales

volumes. Two customers may be purchasing the same volumes but the price discount given to one may make it unprofitable, while the other is profitable.

CASE STUDY

The USA company *General Electric*, which manufactures and sells refrigerators and so on, used to give substantial discounts to customers who placed large orders. This did not result in customers buying more products. Instead GE's sales orders bunched in particular weeks of the year. In turn this led to an uneven production and distribution flow, which increased costs. The company found that, by removing the discounts while at the same time guaranteeing swift delivery, order size decreased and profits increased.

5.3 Customer costs and ABC

The creation of cost pools for activities in **ABC** systems allows organisations to arrange costs in a variety of different ways. Because different customers use different amounts of activities, it is possible to **build up costs for individual customers or groups of customers** on an activity basis so that their **relative profitability** can be assessed.

Examples of the build up of customer costs using an activity based system

Activity	Cost driver
Order taking	Number of orders taken
Sales visits	Number of sales visits
Emergency orders	Number of rushed orders
Delivery	Miles travelled

CASE STUDY

Drury cites the case of Kanthal, a Swedish company that sells electric heating elements. Customer-related selling costs represented 34% of total costs. In the past Kanthal had allocated these costs on the basis of sales value when customer profitability studies were carried out. The company then introduced an ABC system in order to determine the resources consumed by different customers.

An investigation identified two cost drivers for the resources used to service different customers.

(a) **Number of orders placed.** Each order had a large fixed cost, which did not vary with the number of items ordered. A customer ordering 10 items 100 times cost more to service than a customer placing a single order for 1,000 items.

(b) **Non-standard production items.** These cost more to manufacture than standard items.

A cost per order and the cost of handling standard and non-standard items were calculated and a CPA carried out on the basis of the previous year's sales. The analysis showed that only 40% of customers were profitable, and a further 10% lost 120% of the profits. In other words, 10% of customers incurred losses equal to 120% of Kanthal's total profits. Two of the most unprofitable customers were actually in the top three in terms of total sales volume but made many small orders of non-standard items.

Unprofitable customers identified by CPA should be persuaded to **alter their buying behaviour** so they become profitable customers. In the Kanthal example above, unprofitable customers should be discouraged from placing lots of small orders and/or from buying non-standard products.

The **activity based approach** also **highlights where cost reduction efforts should be focused**. Kanthal should concentrate on reducing ordering cost and the cost of handling non-standard items.

Activity-based CPA allows an organisation to adopt a more **market-orientated approach** to management accounting.

Question 8.4

CPA

Learning outcome B1(i)

BB manufactures components for the heavy goods vehicle industry. The following annual information regarding three of its key customers is available.

	P	Q	R
Gross margin	$897,000	$1,070,000	$1,056,000
General administration costs	$35,000	$67,000	$56,000
Units sold	4,600	5,800	3,800
Orders placed	300	320	480
Sales visits	80	50	100
Invoices raised	310	390	1,050

The company uses an activity based costing system and the analysis of customer-related costs is as follows.

Sales visits	$420 per visit
Order processing	$190 per order placed
Despatch costs	$350 per order placed
Billing and collections	$97 per invoice raised

Using customer profitability analysis, in which order would the customers be ranked?

5.4 Customer profitability statement

There is no set format, but it would normally be similar to the one below. Note that financing costs have been included.

	$'000	$'000
Revenue at list prices		100
Less: discounts given		8
Net revenue		92
Less: cost of goods sold		50
Gross margin		42
Less: customer specific costs (such as those listed above)	28	
financing costs:		
credit period	3	
customer specific inventory	2	
		33
Net margin from customer		9

Question 8.5

Profitable customers

Learning outcome B1(i)

Seth supplies shoes to Narayan and Kipling. Each pair of shoes has a list price of $50 and costs Seth $25. As Kipling buys in bulk it receives a 10% trade discount for every order for 100 pairs of shoes or more. Narayan receives a 15% discount irrespective of order size, because that company collects the shoes, thereby saving Seth any distribution costs. The cost of administering each order is $50 and the distribution cost is $1,000 per order. Narayan makes 10 orders in the year, totalling 420 pairs of shoes, and Kipling places 5 orders for 100 pairs.

Required

The most profitable customer for Seth is ....

5.5 Costing customers

Not all customers cost the same to serve even if they require the same products. A customer will cost more to serve if based a long way from the factory (delivery costs increase), or places rush orders (production scheduling is interrupted, special transport is required), or requires a high level of after-sales service and technical assistance.

In order to analyse different customers it may therefore be useful to review **non-financial data**.

	Customer		
	X	Y	Z
Number of purchase orders	10	20	30
Number of sales visits	5	5	5
Number of deliveries	15	20	55
Distance per delivery	50	20	70
Number of emergency orders	1	0	4

Customer Y may be the cheapest to serve because of the number of deliveries per order, the lower distance travelled and the lack of emergency orders.

5.6 Customers and life cycle costing

Customers can also be **costed over their expected 'life cycle'** and expected future cash flows relating to the customer may be discounted. It is rarely possible to predict accurately the life cycle of a particular customer unless contracts are awarded for a specific time period. Nevertheless the information is valuable as **the longer the customer remains with the organisation** the **more profitable** the customer becomes. This is valuable information and may show the **importance of creating and retaining loyal customers**.

Question 8.6	CPA and competitive advantage

Learning outcome B1(i)

Explain how customer profitability analysis can enhance an organisation's competitive advantage.

Section summary

Customer profitability analysis uses an activity based approach to relate revenues and costs to groups of customers in order to assess their relative profitability.

6 Distribution channel profitability

Introduction

As well as focusing on individual customers or groups of customers (in terms of revenue, number of transactions and so on), a similar analysis can be carried out on different distribution channels. This section looks at distribution channel profitability and why it is so important to manage these channels. It is linked to ABC and ABM which were covered earlier in this chapter.

6.1 Traditional approach to determining distribution channel profitability

Product costs are **allocated** to distribution channels **based on standard costs and the product mix** sold through the channel.

Sales, general and administrative costs are typically **allocated** to distribution channels on the **basis of sales volume or net revenue** for each channel.

This approach is shown diagrammatically below.

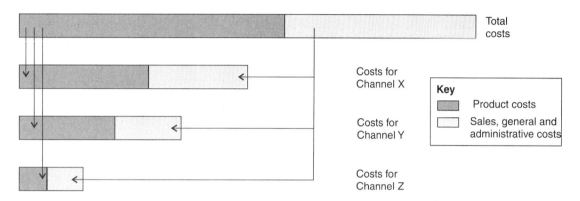

Such an approach may provide **useful information if the organisation is structured on the basis of distribution channels**, but structures tend to be based around regions, product lines or manufacturing locations, making allocation of costs to channels difficult. The approach also obviously has all the **disadvantages associated with the traditional approach to product costing**.

6.2 The ABC approach to determining distribution channel profitability

Material costs and activity costs are allocated direct to products to produce product-related costs, which are **then allocated** to distribution channels on the **basis of the mix of products sold** in each channel.

This approach, which carries with it all the **advantages of ABC**, should result in **more accurate** information.

The main **disadvantage** to this approach is that the allocation is based on the **assumption** that **all costs are driven by the production of particular products** and hence must be allocated to products. For most organisations, however, the **products** they produce is just **one of a range of cost drivers**.

6.3 A refined ABC approach to determining distribution channel profitability

This approach is based on the **assumption** that **costs are driven** not only by **products produced**, but by the **customers served** and the **channels through which the products are offered**. This allows managers to see the effect on the costs of channels of all three categories.

6.3.1 Developing accurate costs for distribution channels

 Separate the organisation's costs into activity-related costs and costs not related to activities

 Identify all costs within the two classifications as product related, customer related or channel related

(a)   Activity costs for a manufacturing organisation might include production scheduling (product related), collection of bad debts (customer related) and advertising brand X (channel related).

(b)   Costs not related to activities might include material costs (product related), customer rebates (customer related) and trade discounts (channel related).

 Trace these costs to individual products, customers and channels
Cost drivers can be used to trace activity-related costs. Direct allocation to the product, customer or channel that caused them should be possible for other costs.

 Link the product-related and customer-related costs to channels
Split total product costs across customers by analysing customer purchases on a product-by-product basis. Then split total customer costs across channels by analysing this customer data on a channel-by-channel basis.

Obviously revenue information for the same products, customers and distribution channels also needs to be captured.

6.4 Comparison of the two ABC approaches

The traditional product-related ABC approach fits in with the way in which most organisations are formed around product lines and product groups.

Nowadays customers are being served through a variety of distribution channels, however (distributors, catalogues, mega-stores, direct mail and so on). Understanding the cost and profitability of using different distribution channels will therefore become increasingly important for good business decision making.

Section summary

Just as **ABC** can be used in conjunction with CPA, it can also be used to determine the relative **profitability of different distribution channels**.

7   Activity-based profitability analysis

Introduction

Activity-based profitability analysis can be linked to ABC techniques that were covered earlier in this chapter.

7.1 Extending activity based techniques to profitability analysis

The hierarchical classification of activities can be extended by applying it to profitability analysis. This is illustrated in the following diagram which is based on one in Drury adapted from an approach advocated by Kaplan ('Contribution margin analysis: no longer relevant', *Journal of Management Accounting Research (USA),* Fall, 1990).

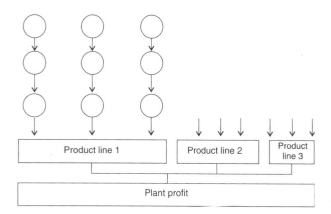

At the point at which **product-level contribution margins for each individual product in the product line** have been calculated, there has been **no cost allocation**. **Some costs incurred at the product-line level**, such as research and development, advertising and distribution, are common to all products in the product line, however, and within this analysis they are **traced to product lines** rather than individual products within the line.

The resulting product-line contribution margin is the sum of the individual product-level contributions sold within the line and shows whether the products sold within the line earn enough contribution to cover the costs of activities required to sustain the line.

Plant profit is arrived at by deducting facility-sustaining costs from the sum of the product-line contributions.

7.2 Using this approach for customers and distribution channels

This approach should not be limited to analysing the profitability of products and product lines. Customers and distribution channels should also be considered, by **summing the product-level contribution margins of the products sold to each customer or through each distribution channel**, and then **deducting costs incurred for individual customers or distribution channels**.

7.3 Dealing with marketing and distribution costs

These costs should be **included** within such an analysis and dealt with in a similar way to production costs. The activity-based analysis therefore assigns the costs to the appropriate level in the hierarchy (depending on whether a cost is incurred in relation to an activity that supports a product, product line/customer/distribution channel) and then aggregates the costs down the hierarchy to determine contribution margins by product, product line, customer and distribution channel.

Section summary

By comparing the costs of products, customers and distribution channels with revenues, a **tier of contribution levels** can be established by applying the concept of the activity based cost hierarchy.

8 Pareto analysis

Introduction

In the final section in this chapter, we look at the concept of Pareto analysis which is based on the general principle that 80% of wealth is owned by 20% of the population. This links to ABM and CPA in that 20% of customers could be viewed as providing 80% of the profit.

KEY TERM

PARETO ANALYSIS is based on the observations of the economist Vilfredo Pareto, who suggested that 80% of a nation's wealth is held by 20% of its population (and so the remaining 80% of the population holds only 20% of the nation's wealth).

8.1 What is Pareto analysis?

Pareto analysis is the **80/20 rule** and it has been applied to many other situations.

(a)   In inventory control, where 20% of inventory items might represent 80% of the value
(b)   In product analysis, where 80% of company profit is earned by 20% of the products

Example: Pareto analysis and products

(a)   A company produces ten products which it sells in various markets. The revenue from each product is as follows.

Product	Revenue $'000
A	231
B	593
C	150
D	32
E	74
F	17
G	1,440
H	12
I	2
J	19
	2,570

(b)   Rearranging revenue in descending order and calculating cumulative figures and percentages gives us the following analysis.

Product	Revenue $'000	Cumulative revenue (W1) $'000	% (W2)
G	1,440	1,440	56.0
B	593	2,033	79.1
A	231	2,264	88.1
C	150	2,414	93.9
E	74	2,488	96.8
D	32	2,520	98.1
J	19	2,539	98.8
F	17	2,556	99.5
H	12	2,568	99.9
I	2	2,570	100.0
	2,570		

Workings

1   This is calculated as follows:

1,440 + 593 = 2,033
2,033 + 231 = 2,264   and so on.

2   (1/2,570 × 1,440 × 100)% = 56.0%
(1/2,570 × 2,033 × 100)% = 79.1%   and so on.

(Enter 1/2,570 into your calculator as a constant – do the calculation and then tap the multiplication button twice until 'k' appears on the screen – and then simply enter each cumulative revenue figure and press the 'equals' button to get the percentage as a decimal.)

(c)   In this case the Pareto rule applies – almost 80% of revenue is brought in by just two products, G and B. The point of Pareto analysis is to highlight the fact that the effort that is put into a company's products is often barely worth the trouble in terms of the sales revenue generated.

KEY POINT

You should not expect that the 80/20 rule will always apply as precisely as in the above example. It may be, that, say, 25% of products will account for 90% of revenue. **The basic principle is that a small number of products often yields a high proportion of income.**

It does not necessarily follow that the products generating the highest income are the most profitable. The costs of producing the products needs to be taken into account. It may be, for example, that products G and B both cost more to produce than the income they bring in, whereas products A, C and E cost virtually nothing. In other words **Pareto analysis can be carried out for costs and contribution as well as for sales**.

Poor performers could also be new products which are establishing themselves in the market and which have more profitable futures.

8.2 Further analysis

Suppose the figures you are given provide some additional information, and you are asked to analyse them and comment on them in a way that will be useful to management.

Product	Revenue	Profit
	$'000	$'000
A	231	46
B	593	108
C	150	52
D	32	7
E	74	16
F	17	4
G	1,440	202
H	12	8
I	2	1
J	19	8
	2,570	452

An analysis might take the following form.

(a)   The revenue figures can be **ranked** and **expressed as percentages** and in **cumulative terms** (as before), and profit can be ranked and analysed in the same way.

The figures are pretty self-explanatory, but make sure that you understand how all of them are calculated, because you may well have to do this yourself in an exam.

Product	Revenue	Rev.	Cum. revenue	Cum.	Product	Profit	Profit	Cum. profit	Cum.
	$'000	%	$'000	%		$'000	%	$'000	%
G	1,440	56.0	1,440	56.0	G	202	44.7	202	44.7
B	593	23.1	2,033	79.1	B	108	23.9	310	68.6
A	231	9.0	2,264	88.1	C	52	11.5	362	80.1
C	150	5.8	2,414	93.9	A	46	10.2	408	90.3
E	74	2.9	2,488	96.8	E	16	3.5	424	93.8
D	32	1.2	2,520	98.1	H	8	1.8	432	95.6
J	19	0.7	2,539	98.8	J	8	1.8	440	97.4
F	17	0.7	2,556	99.5	D	7	1.5	447	98.9
H	12	0.5	2,568	99.9	F	4	0.9	451	99.8
I	2	0.1	2,570	100.0	I	1	0.2	452	100.0
	2,570					452			

This shows us that, whereas the top ranking products are G, B and A in revenue terms, G, B and C are the top three in terms of profit. In **revenue terms** product C produces under 6% of the overall total but in **profit terms** it produces over 10%. Four products each produce 10% or more of the overall **profit**, but only three products individually produce more than 9% of **revenue**.

(b) We can also calculate the **profit margin** (the profit divided by the revenue expressed as a percentage) for individual products and overall. The figures shown below indicate that while most of the products vary slightly around the overall profit margin of 17.6%, some have much higher margins, notably products H, I and J, although these are relatively insignificant in overall revenue terms. The product that provides the greatest amount of revenue and profit, product G, actually has the lowest profit margin of all.

Product	Revenue	Profit	Profit margin
	$'000	$'000	%
A	231	46	19.9
B	593	108	18.2
C	150	52	34.7
D	32	7	21.9
E	74	16	21.6
F	17	4	23.5
G	1,440	202	14.0
H	12	8	66.7
I	2	1	50.0
J	19	8	42.1
	2,570	452	17.6

Your overall recommendations to management might be to make efforts to **save costs** to **improve the profit margin** of product G, and to put **extra marketing effort** into products C, H, I and J where the potential returns are greatest. Obviously what can be done depends on the nature of the products themselves: the smaller revenue items may be specialist add-ons that are only ever likely to be purchased by a few people.

8.3 Analysing customers

Instead of analysing products, customers can be analysed to determine their relative profitability.

When a **customer profitability analysis** is first carried out it is often found that something close to **Pareto's rule** applies. This is illustrated in the following diagram where **20 of the 100** customers generate

approximately **80%** of the company's total margin. As 50 of the 100 customers generate 100% of the total margin, resources appear to be wasted serving the remaining 50 customers.

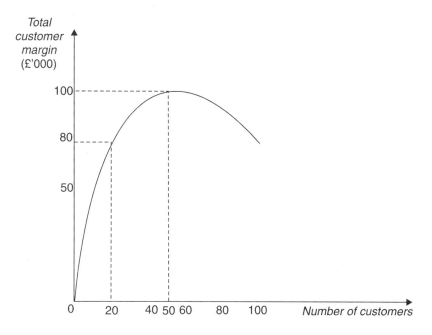

In order to produce a chart such as that above customers need to be **ranked** according to their **relative profitability** to the company. A bar chart, such as that below, produces an alternative view and may prove more useful for the marketing department.

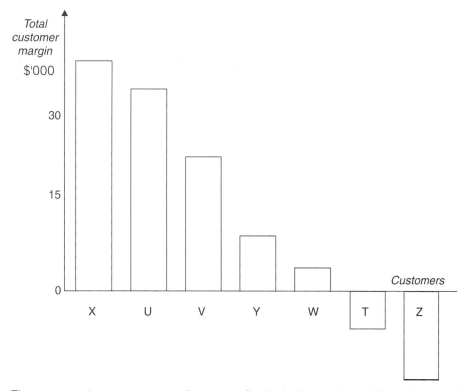

The more evenly customers contribute to profit, the better, as the position of the organisation is stabilised. If customers do not contribute evenly, the loss of two key customers could be disastrous for an organisation.

8.4 Analysing inventory

Pareto analysis can be used to improve inventory control.

(a)   15% of inventory volume might represent 80% of inventory value and so control should be concentrated on that 15%.

(b)   10% of inventory might require 75% of storage space (so that storage costs are particularly high). A just-in-time system could therefore be used for this 10%, saving money and space.

8.5 Analysing overheads

If an organisation uses activity based costing, a Pareto analysis of cost drivers or activities might show that, say, 15% of cost drivers or activities are responsible for 80% of total cost. Analysing, monitoring and controlling these cost drivers or activities will provide improved cost control and increased understanding of the way in which costs behave.

8.6 Pareto diagrams and quality

The term 'Pareto diagram' usually refers to a **histogram or frequency chart on product quality**, following research in the 1950s which showed that a **few causes of poor quality usually accounted for most of the quality problems** – hence the name Pareto. Such diagrams highlight the area or areas to which attention should be given to produce the best returns.

Section summary

Pareto analysis is used to highlight the general principle that 80% of value (inventory value, wealth, profit and so on) is concentrated in 20% of the items in a particular population.

Chapter Roundup

✓ In the **modern business environment**, most costs can be analysed into **short-term variable costs** (that vary with the volume of production) and **long-term variable costs** (that are fixed in the short term and vary not with volume of production but with a different measure of activity).

✓ The ABC approach is to relate costs to the factors that cause or 'drive' them to be incurred in the first place and to change subsequently. These factors are called '**cost drivers**'.

✓ ABC relates overhead/resource costs to the activities that cause or drive them. This is done using **resource cost drivers**. The costs of activities are related to cost units using **activity cost drivers**.

✓ The **information** provided by **analysing activities** can support the management functions of **planning, control and decision making**, provided it is used carefully and with full appreciation of its implications.

✓ **Activity-based management (ABM)** is **operational ABM** – actions based on activity driver analysis that increase efficiency, lower costs and improve asset utilisation.

✓ **Strategic ABM** – actions based on activity-based cost analysis that aim to change the demand for activities so as to improve profitability.

✓ Two questions can be used to **assess whether an activity adds value**.

  – Would an external customer encourage the organisation to do more of the activity?
  – Would the organisation be more likely to achieve its goals by performing the activity?

  If both answers are yes, the activity adds value.

✓ The **manufacturing cost hierarchy** categorises costs and activities as unit level, batch level, product/ process level and organisational/facility level.

✓ To monitor the effectiveness and efficiency of activities using **ABM**, **performance measures** relating to **volume**, **time**, **quality** and **costs** are needed.

✓ DPP is a **costing system used by retail businesses**.

✓ Any costs that are **general** to the organisation (but not specific to any particular product) should be **ignored** when calculating direct product profit.

✓ **Customer profitability analysis** uses an activity-based approach to relate revenues and costs to groups of customers in order to assess their relative profitability.

✓ Just as **ABC** can be used in conjunction with CPA, it can also be used to determine the relative **profitability of different distribution channels**.

✓ By comparing the costs of products, customers and distribution channels with revenues, a **tier of contribution levels** can be established by applying the concept of the activity-based hierarchy.

✓ **Pareto analysis** is used to highlight the general principle that 80% of value (inventory value, wealth, profit and so on) is concentrated in 20% of the items in a particular population.

Quick Quiz

1   The cost driver for quality inspection is likely to be batch size. *True or false?*

2   ABC is not a system that is suitable for use by service organisations. *True or false?*

3   Which of the following is incorrect as a description of part of the ABC process?

    A   Transactions undertaken by support department personnel are appropriate cost drivers for long-term variable overheads.

    B   Longer-term production overhead costs are partly driven by volume of output.

    C   Longer-term production overhead costs are partly driven by the complexity and diversity of production work.

    D   Short-term variable overhead costs should normally be traced to products using volume-related cost drivers.

4   As volume increases, variety costs increase. *True or false?*

5   The processing time of an organisation is made up of four types. Classify the types as either value-added or non-value-added.

6   *Choose the correct word from those highlighted.*

The aim of ABM is to try to eliminate as far as possible the **core/primary/secondary/diversionary/discretionary** activities.

7   BPR can be likened to continuous budgeting. *True or false?*

8   On the axes below, sketch and label correctly a Pareto curve to demonstrate a situation where 75% of an organisation's profit is derived from 25% of its retail outlets.

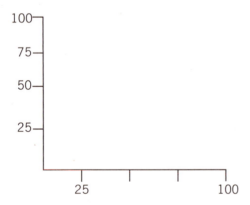

9   A wholesaler has estimated that its store space cost is $1.00 per cubic metre per day.

Its product range includes the following products.

(a)   Six-packs of lager – volume: 0.02 cubic metres, days in store: 5

(b)   Bleach – volume: 0.01 cubic metres, days in store: 4

(c)   Packs of toilet rolls – volume: 0.37 cubic metres, days in store: 3.

State how space costs would be allocated to the products using direct product profitability.

Answers to Quick Quiz

1   True, assuming that the first item in each batch is inspected.

2   False. It is highly suitable.

3   B. Short-term variable overhead costs are driven by volume of output but longer-term costs, such as set-up costs, design and so on, are driven by the number of different products (diversity).

4   False

5   **Value-added**   **Non-value-added**
     Production/performance time   Inspection time
                                        Transfer time
                                        Idle time

6   diversionary or discretionary activities

7   False. It is somewhat akin to ZBB.

8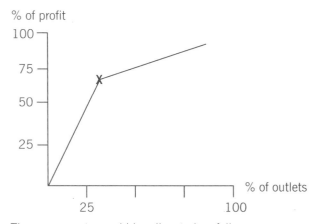

9   The space costs would be allocated as follows.

Lager $1.00 × 0.02 × 5 = $0.1 per pack

Bleach $1.00 × 0.01 × 4 = $0.04 per pack

Packs of toilet rolls $1.00 × 0.37 × 3 = $1.11 per pack

The results show the need to achieve a high turnover with bulky low price goods such as toilet paper. Refrigerated items would carry a higher space cost due to the cost of refrigeration.

Answers to Questions

8.1 Using ABC

(a) Here are our suggestions.

   (i)   Production overheads are a high proportion of total production costs.

   (ii)   The product range is wide and diverse.

   (iii)   The amounts of overhead resources used by products varies.

   (iv)   Volume is not the primary driver of overhead resource consumption.

(b)   **Reasons for suitability**

   (i)   Most modern organisations tend to have a **high level of overhead costs**, especially relating to **support services** such as maintenance and data processing. ABC, by the use of carefully chosen cost drivers, traces these overheads to product lines in a more logical and less arbitrary manner than traditional absorption costing.

   (ii)   The determination and use of cost drivers helps to measure and improve the **efficiency and effectiveness of support departments**.

   (iii)   Many costs included in general overheads can actually be traced to specific product lines using ABC. This **improves product costing** and **cost management** because the costs are made the responsibility of the line manager.

   (iv)   ABC forces the organisation to ask such searching questions as 'What causes the demand for the activity?', 'What does the department achieve?', 'Does it add value?' and so on.

   (v)   ABC systems may **encourage reductions** in throughput time and inventory and improvements in quality.

Unsuitable situations

   (i)   A number of businesses have recently been split into several **small autonomous sections**. In this situation there may be no need for a sophisticated costing system such as ABC because staff should be aware of cost behaviour.

   (ii)   ABC can **work against modern manufacturing methods** such as just-in-time (JIT). JIT seeks to reduce set-up time so that very small batches can be made economically.

   (iii)   The aim of set-up time reduction is to allow more set-ups, not just to reduce set-up costs. The use of a cost driver based on the number of set-ups will therefore **work against JIT principles** as it will tend to encourage larger batches.

8.2 ABC and retail organisations

Activities	Possible cost driver
Procure goods	Number of orders
Receive goods	Number of orders or pallets
Store goods	Volume of goods
Pick goods	Number of packs
Handle returnables/recyclables	Volume of goods

8.3 Classification of activities

The correct answer is options (i), (ii) and (v). Options (iii) and (iv) would be **product level** activities. The level of **internal** support cost would be driven by the degree of **variety** between different products, not by production volume. If item (iii) refers to **external** technical support, this cost would most probably be driven by the fact that the product is too complicated for its market or the instructions provided (product packaging) are inadequate.

8.4 CPA

	P $'000	Q $'000	R $'000
Gross margin	897.00	1,070.00	1,056.00
Less: Customer specific costs			
Sales visits (80/50/100 × $420)	(33.60)	(21.00)	(42.00)
Order processing (300/320/480 × $190)	(57.00)	(60.80)	(91.20)
Despatch costs (300/320/480 × $350)	(105.00)	(112.00)	(168.00)
Billing and collections (310/390/1,050 × $97)	(30.07)	(37.83)	(101.85)
	671.33	838.37	652.95
Ranking	2	1	3

8.5 Profitable customers

The correct answer is Narayan.

It can be shown that Seth earns more from supplying Narayan, despite the larger discount percentage.

	Kipling $	Narayan $
Revenue	25,000	21,000
Less: discount	2,500	3,150
Net revenue	22,500	17,850
Less: cost of shoes	(12,500)	(10,500)
customer transport cost	(5,000)	–
customer administration cost	(250)	(500)
Net gain	4,750	6,850

The difference on a unit basis is considerable.

	Kipling	Narayan
Number of pair of shoes sold	500	420
Net gain per pair of shoes sold	$9.50	$16.31
Net gain per $1 of sales revenue	$0.19	$0.33

8.6 CPA and competitive advantage

By **focusing on the way in which costs are allocated to customers** rather than to the products and services sold, CPA attempts to provide answers to the following types of question.

(a)   What profit or contribution is the organisation making on sales to the customer, after taking account of all costs which can be specifically identified with the customer?

(b)   What would be the financial consequences of losing the customer?

(c)   Is the customer buying in order sizes that are unprofitable to supply?

(d)   What is the return on investment on any plant that is used specifically for this customer?

(e)   Is any inventory held specifically for this customer and what period of credit do they require?

(f)   Are there any other specific costs involved in supplying this customer, such as technical and test facilities, R&D facilities, dedicated sales or administrative staff?

(g)   What is the ratio of the customer's net contribution to the investment made on the customer's behalf?

The technique **enhances an organisation's competitive advantage** because it considers the profits generated by customers and **allows the organisation to focus its efforts on those customers who promise the highest profit**. The organisation is also in a better position to **rationalise its approach** to customers who demonstrate a low potential for generating profit.

Now try these questions from the Exam Question Bank

Number	Level	Marks	Time
Q19	Examination	10	18 mins
Q20	Examination	10	18 mins
Q21	Examination	30	54 mins
Q22	Examination	10	18 mins

COST MANAGEMENT TECHNIQUES 1

'Traditional' methods of inventory control, purchasing, production planning and scheduling, product mix decision making, quality control and management are simply not suitable for the **new manufacturing environment** (which we cover in **Section 1**).

Contemporary techniques such as **total quality management (Section 2), just-in-time (Section 7),** and **theory of constraints (Section 9)** are more relevant to modern manufacturing and can have a major impact on efficiency, inventory and cost.

Throughput accounting (Section 10) is a system of cost and management accounting which can be used with just-in-time, while **continuous improvement (Section 4)** and **Kaizen costing (Section 5)** are central to total quality management.

topic list	learning outcomes	syllabus references	ability required
1 Traditional v modern manufacturing philosophy	B1	B1(ii)	evaluation
2 Total quality management (TQM)	B1(b)	B1(ii)	evaluation
3 Costs of quality and cost of quality reports	B1(d)	B1(iii)	application
4 Continuous improvement	B1(c)	B1(iii)	comprehension
5 Kaizen costing	B1(c)	B1(iii)	comprehension
6 Business process re-engineering (BPR)	B1(g)	B1(iii)	comprehension
7 Just-in-time (JIT)	B1(b)	B1(ii)	evaluation
8 Accounting for pull systems – backflush accounting	B1(b)	B1(ii)	evaluation
9 Theory of constraints (TOC)	B1(b)	B1(ii)	evaluation
10 Throughput accounting (TA)	B1(b)	B1(ii)	evaluation

1 Traditional v modern manufacturing philosophy

Introduction

This section sets the scene for this chapter by looking at traditional and modern manufacturing philosophies.

1.1 Traditional manufacturing philosophy

Traditional manufacturing philosophy focuses on the need to continue to **use valuable resources** (such as manufacturing equipment) to their **full capacity** and to **maximise** the length of production runs. The main features of the traditional approach to manufacturing are as follows.

(a) **Labour** and **manufacturing equipment** are so valuable they should **not be left idle**.

(b) Resulting **inventory** not needed should be **stored** (thus **hiding** inefficient and uneven production methods).

(c) To increase efficiency and reduce production cost per unit, **batch sizes** and **production runs** should be **as large as possible**.

(d) Concerned with **balancing** production run costs and inventory holding costs.

Question 9A.1	Long production run costs

Learning outcome B1

The production manager of AB has advocated long production runs in an attempt to reduce manufacturing costs per unit. The accountant has hit back with the fact that stockholding costs per unit will increase.

Required

List five manufacturing costs per unit that will reduce if production runs are longer, and four stockholding costs per unit that will increase.

Question 9A.2	Interruptions to a stage in production 1

Learning outcome B1

A manufacturing process consists of four stages. There are inventories of raw material, work in progress and finished goods between each stage. At the start of the first stage there are inventories of raw materials and at the end of the final stage there are inventories of finished goods.

What would happen to the entire production process if production was disrupted during the second stage?

1.2 Modern manufacturing philosophy

(a) **Smooth, steady** production flow (**throughput**)

(b) **Flexibility**, providing the customer with exactly what is wanted, exactly when it is wanted (making the organisation a more complex affair to manage), so as to achieve **competitive advantage**.

(c) **Volume versus variety** – greater variety in volumes required by customers

(d) **Just-in-time** – that is, little or no inventory

Section summary

Costing systems have evolved to reflect a **manufacturing philosophy** that is based on the need to achieve **competitive advantage**.

- Flexibility and the ability to respond quickly to customer demands are vital.
- Product life cycles are shorter and products must be brought to the market quickly.
- New technology has been introduced.

2 Total quality management (TQM)   3/11

Introduction

The modern business environment has been progressively switching emphasis from quantity to quality as competition intensifies for customers. This section looks at how total quality management is employed within modern businesses to achieve the best possible quality. The technique is linked with continuous improvement which is the focus of Section 4 below.

2.1 Management of quality

Quality means 'the **degree of excellence of a thing**' – how well made it is, or how well performed if it is a service, how well it serves its purpose, and how it measures up against its rivals. These criteria imply two things.

(a)   That quality is something that **requires care on the part of the provider**.

(b)   That quality is largely **subjective** – it is in the eye of the beholder, the **customer**.

The **management** of quality is the process of:

(a)   Establishing **standards of quality** for a product or service

(b)   Establishing **procedures or production methods** which ought to ensure that these required standards of quality are met in a suitably high proportion of cases

(c)   **Monitoring** actual quality

(d)   Taking **control action** when actual quality falls below standard

Take the postal service as an example. The postal service might establish a standard that 90% of first class letters will be delivered on the day after they are posted, and 99% will be delivered within two days of posting.

(a)   Procedures would have to be established for ensuring that these standards could be met (attending to such matters as frequency of collections, automated letter sorting, frequency of deliveries and number of staff employed).

(b)   Actual performance could be monitored, perhaps by taking samples from time to time of letters that are posted and delivered.

(c)   If the quality standard is not being achieved, management should take control action (employ more postmen or advertise the use of postcodes again).

2.2 Total quality management

Quality management becomes **total (Total Quality Management (TQM)) when it is applied to everything a business does.**

KEY TERM

TOTAL QUALITY MANAGEMENT (TQM) is 'an integrated and comprehensive system of planning and controlling all business functions so that products or services are produced which meet or exceed customer expectations. TQM is a philosophy of business behaviour, embracing principles such as employee involvement, continuous improvement at all levels and customer focus, as well as being a collection of related techniques aimed at improving quality such as full documentation of activities, clear goal setting and performance measurement from the customer perspective.'   (CIMA *Official Terminology)*

2.2.1 Get it right, first time

One of the basic principles of TQM is that the **cost of preventing mistakes is less than the cost of correcting them** once they occur. The aim should therefore be **to get things right first time**. Every mistake, delay and misunderstanding, directly costs an organisation money through **wasted time and effort**, including time taken in pacifying customers. The **lost potential for future sales because of poor customer service must also be taken into account.**

2.2.2 Continuous improvement

A second basic principle of TQM is dissatisfaction with the *status quo*: the belief that it is **always possible to improve** and so the aim should be to **'get it more right next time'**. TQM should foster a consistent, systematic approach to continuous improvement that involves every aspect of the organisation.

2.3 Key elements of TQM

There are nine key elements of TQM.

(a)   Acceptance that the only thing that matters is the **customer**.

(b)   Recognition of the all-pervasive nature of the **customer-supplier relationship**, including internal customers: passing sub-standard material to another division is not satisfactory or acceptable.

(c)   A move from relying on inspecting to a predefined level of quality to **preventing the cause** of the defect in the first place.

(d)   Personal responsibility for each operative or group of operatives for defect-free production or service in their domain. TQM requires an awareness by **all personnel** of the quality requirements compatible with supplying the customer with products of the agreed design specification.

(e)   A move away from 'acceptable' quality levels. **Any** level of defects is **unacceptable.** TQM aims towards an environment of **zero defects** at minimum cost.

(f)   An aim to **eliminate waste**, where waste is defined as anything other than the minimum essential amount of equipment, materials, space and workers' time.

(g)   Obsessive attempts by **all departments** to get things right first time: this applies to misdirected telephone calls and typing errors as much as to production.

(h)   Introduction of **quality certification** programmes.

(i)   Emphasis on the **cost of poor quality**: good quality generates savings.

Exam alert

An exam question could ask you to discuss the importance of a TQM system within a just-in-time environment.

2.4 Quality assurance procedures

Because TQM embraces every activity of a business, quality assurance procedures **cannot be confined to the production process** but must also cover the work of sales, distribution and administration departments, the efforts of external suppliers, and the reaction of external customers.

2.4.1 Quality assurance of goods inwards

The quality of output depends on the quality of input materials, and so quality control should include **procedures for acceptance and inspection of goods inwards and measurement of rejects**. Each supplier can be given a 'rating' for the quality of the goods they tend to supply, and preference with purchase orders can be given to well-rated suppliers. This method is referred to as 'vendor rating'.

Where a **quality assurance scheme** is in place the supplier guarantees the quality of goods supplied and allows the customers' inspectors access while the items are being manufactured. The **onus is on the supplier to carry out the necessary quality checks**, or face cancellation of the contract.

Suppliers' quality assurance schemes are being used increasingly, particularly where extensive sub-contracting work is carried out, for example in the motor industries. One such scheme is **BS EN ISO 9000** certification. A company that gains registration has a certificate testifying that it is operating to a structure of written policies and procedures which are designed to ensure that it can consistently deliver a product or service to meet customer requirements.

2.4.2 Inspection of output

This will take place at various key stages in the production process and will provide a continual check that the production process is under control. The aim of inspection is *not* really to sort out the bad products from the good ones after the work has been done. The **aim is to satisfy management that quality control in production is being maintained.**

The **inspection of samples** rather than 100% testing of all items will keep inspection costs down, and smaller samples will be less costly to inspect than larger samples. The greater the confidence in the reliability of production methods and process control, the smaller the samples will be.

2.5 Monitoring customer reaction

Some sub-standard items will inevitably be produced. Checks during production will identify some bad output, but other items will reach the customer, who is the ultimate judge of quality. **Complaints should be monitored** whether they arrive in the form of complaint letters, returned goods, claims under guarantee, or requests for visits by service engineers. Some companies survey customers on a regular basis.

2.6 Internal customers and internal suppliers

The work done by an internal supplier for an internal customer will eventually affect the quality of the product or service to the external customer. In order to satisfy the expectations of the external customer, it is therefore also necessary to satisfy the expectations of the internal customer at each stage of the overall operation. Internal customers are therefore linked in **quality chains**. Internal customer A can satisfy internal customer B who can satisfy internal customer C who in turn can satisfy the external customer.

The management of each 'micro operation' within an overall operation has the responsibility for managing its internal supplier and internal customer relationships. They should do this by specifying the requirements of their internal customers, for example in terms of quality, speed, dependability and flexibility, and the requirements for the operation itself (for example, in terms of cost).

The **concept of internal supplier-customer relationships in a series of micro-operations** helps to **focus attention on the 'up-stream' activities in an operation**, several stages removed from the external customer. Failure at an early stage of the operation, for example in new product design, has an adverse impact on all the supplier-customer relationships down the line to the external customer. The **cost of rectifying an error** becomes **more expensive the further it goes down the 'supply chain'** without rectification.

Some organisations **formalise the internal supplier-internal customer concept** by requiring each internal supplier to make a **service level agreement** with its internal customer. A service level agreement is a statement of the standard of service and supply that will be provided to the internal customer and will cover issues such as the range of services supplied, response times, dependability and so on. Boundaries of responsibility and performance standards might also be included in the agreement.

Service level agreements have been criticised, however, for over-formalising the relationship between the internal supplier and internal customer, and so creating barriers to the development of a constructive relationship and genuine co-operation between them.

2.7 Employees and quality   11/10

Employees often have a poor attitude towards quality, as a system imposed 'from outside' by non-operational staff and as an implication of lack of trust in workers to maintain quality standards or to apply a control system with objectivity themselves.

Attitudes to quality control and the management of it have, however, been **undergoing changes**.

(a)   As the pace of change in the environment has increased so attention to quality and a commitment to quality standards has become a **vital factor for organisational adaptation and survival**.

(b)   It is being recognised that **workers can be motivated by a positive approach to quality**: producing quality work is a tangible and worthwhile objective. Where responsibility for quality checking has been given to the worker himself (encouraging self-supervision), **job satisfaction may be increased**: it is a kind of job enrichment, and also a sign of trust and respect, because imposed controls have been removed.

(c)   **Non-aversive ways of implementing quality control** have been devised. **Cultural orientation** (the deep 'belief' in quality, filtered down to all operatives) can be enlisted. **Inter-group competition** to meet and beat quality standards, for example, might be encouraged. **Quality circles** may be set up, perhaps with responsibility for implementing improvements which they identify.

Problems can therefore be overcome by **changing people's attitudes** rather than teaching them new tricks. The key issue is to instil **understanding of, and commitment to, working practices that lead to quality**.

Empowerment has two key aspects.

(a)   Allowing workers to have the **freedom to decide how to do** the necessary work, using the skills they possess and acquiring new skills as necessary to be an effective team member.

(b)   Making workers **responsible** for achieving production targets and for quality control.

It is important to **question the value of these developments**, however.

'Do employees and management really find 'empowerment' to be liberating? Empirical studies suggest that 'empowerment' often amounts to the delegation of additional duties to employees. Limits have to be placed on what employees can do, so empowerment is often associated with rules, bureaucracy and form-filling. That apart, many employees find most satisfaction from outside work activities and are quite happy to confine themselves to doing what they are told while at work. The proponents of TQM are often very work-centred people themselves and tend to judge others by their own standards.

Do teams contribute to organisational effectiveness? Just calling a group of people who work in the same office 'a team' does not make it a team. A team requires a high level of co-operation and consensus. Many competitive and motivated people find working in a team environment to be uncongenial. It means that

every time you want to do anything you have to communicate with and seek approval from fellow team members. In practice, this is likely to involve bureaucracy and form-filling.

... it can be argued that TQM merely moves empowerment from management to employees. It has been argued that the latter cannot be expected to succeed where the former have failed.'

'Quality Streak', Bob Scarlett, *CIMA Insider*

2.8 Design for quality

A TQM environment aims to get it right first time, and this means that **quality, not faults, must be designed into the organisation's products and operations from the outset**.

Quality control happens at various stages in the process of designing a product or service.

(a)   At the **product design stage**, quality control means trying to design a product or service so that its specifications provide a suitable balance between price and quality (of sales and delivery, as well as manufacture) which will make the product or service competitive. Modern manufacturing businesses use **Computer Aided Design (CAD)** to identify or rectify design features. This might involve:

(i)   Reducing the **number of parts** in a product overall. The fewer the number of parts, the less parts there are to go wrong.

(ii)   Using parts or materials that are **already used** (or could be used) by other products. The more common parts overall, the less chance there is of a product failing to meet quality standards due to a rogue supplier of just one of many components. For example if a car with electric windows can be designed to use the same glass as a cheaper model with manually-wound windows, there will only be one glass supplier to keep a check on.

(iii)   Improving **physical characteristics** such as shape, size or positioning of controls and so on to make the product more user-friendly.

(b)   **Production engineering** is the **process of designing the methods for making a product** (or service) **to the design specification**. It sets out to make production methods as efficient as possible, and to avoid the manufacture of sub-standard items.

(c)   **Information systems** should be designed to get the required information to the right person at the right time; **distribution systems** should be designed to get the right item to the right person at the right time; and so on.

2.9 Quality control and inspection

A distinction should be made between **quality control** and **inspection**.

(a)   **Quality control** involves setting controls for the process of manufacture or service delivery. It is aimed at **preventing the manufacture of defective items** or the provision of defective services.

(b)   **Inspection** is a technique of **identifying when defective items are being produced at an unacceptable level.** Inspection is usually carried out at three main points.

(i)   Receiving inspection – for raw materials and purchased components
(ii)   Floor or process inspection for WIP
(iii)   Final inspection or testing for finished goods

Question 9A.3 | Quality

Learning outcome B1(b)

Read the following extract from an article in the *Financial Times*, then list the features and methods of a quality information system that *Lloyds Bank* might have devised to collect information on the impact of the 'service challenge' described here.

'If you phone a branch of *Lloyds Bank* and it rings five times before there is a reply; if the person who answers does not introduce him or herself by name during the conversation; if you are standing in a queue with more people in it than the number of tills, then something is wrong.'

'If any of these things happen then the branch is breaching standards of customer service set by the bank... the "service challenge" was launched in the bank's 1,888 branches after being tested in 55 branches ...*Lloyds* already has evidence of the impact. Customers were more satisfied with pilot branches than with others.'

2.10 Benefits of TQM

(a)   Elimination of waste
(b)   Elimination of non-value-adding activities and processes
(c)   Reduced costs
(d)   Increased profitability
(e)   Greater competitive advantage
(f)   Reduction in the variability in processes and outputs to ensure customer satisfaction
(g)   Increased staff morale, leading to greater productivity and efficiency
(h)   Increased customer loyalty and hence more repeat purchases

2.11 Is TQM too expensive?

In the **current economic climate**, companies are trying to eliminate **unnecessary costs** as much as possible. Some people have argued that strategies to improve quality are **too expensive** to implement and run. Training employees is expensive and any changes to quality procedures means additional costs. All quality programmes must be managed which is another costly requirement.

As shareholders are often looking for a **quick return** – and will also be focusing on ways in which management could **reduce costs** – any long-term investment in TQM might be unpopular. Also, if the company is operating in a market with **little competition** it can be tempting to ignore quality issues.

Question 9A.4 | Ignoring quality issues

Learning outcome B1(b)

Why do you think it would be wrong for companies to cut spending on quality in an economic downturn?

Section summary

In the context of **total quality management**, 'quality' means getting it right first time, and improving continuously.

The **main focus** of TQM is **100% satisfaction** of both internal and external customers through the **continuous improvement** of all activities and processes.

Key elements of TQM include preventing the cause of defects in the first place (rather than relying on inspecting to a predefined level of quality) and aiming towards an environment of zero defects at minimum cost.

TQM promotes the concept of the **internal customer** and **internal supplier**.

Workers themselves are frequently the best source of information about how (or how not) to improve **quality**.

3 Costs of quality and cost of quality reports 11/11, 9/12, 3/13

Introduction

Linked with TQM are the costs of quality and cost of quality reports. Make sure you understand the concept that good quality saves money and poor quality costs money.

KEY POINT

When we talk about quality-related costs you should remember that a concern for **good quality saves money**; it is **poor quality that costs money.**

3.1 Costs of quality

Cost of quality reports highlight the total cost to an organisation of producing products or services that do not conform with quality requirements. Four categories of cost should be reported: prevention costs, appraisal costs, internal failure costs and external failure costs.

KEY TERMS

The COST OF QUALITY is 'The difference between the actual cost of producing, selling and supporting products or services and the equivalent costs if there were no failures during production or usage'. The cost of quality can be analysed into the following.

- COST OF PREVENTION – 'the costs incurred prior to or during production in order to prevent substandard or defective products or services from being produced'

- COST OF APPRAISAL – 'costs incurred in order to ensure that outputs produced meet required quality standards'

- COST OF INTERNAL FAILURE – 'the costs arising from inadequate quality which are identified before the transfer of ownership from supplier to purchaser'

- COST OF EXTERAL FAILURE – 'the cost arising from inadequate quality discovered after the transfer of ownership from supplier to purchaser'

(CIMA *Official Terminology*)

External failure costs are the costs of failing to deliver a quality product externally. The sum of internal failure costs, prevention and appraisal costs is the cost of failing to deliver a quality product internally.

Quality-related cost	Example
Prevention costs	Quality engineering Training in quality control
Appraisal costs	Acceptance testing Inspection of goods inwards
Internal failure costs	Failure analysis Losses from failure of purchased items
External failure costs	Administration of customer complaints section Cost of repairing products returned from customers

3.2 Views on quality costs   9/10, 11/10, 11/12

3.2.1 View 1

KEY TERMS

COST OF CONFORMANCE is 'The cost of achieving specified quality standards'.

COST OF NON-CONFORMANCE is 'The cost of failure to deliver the required standard of quality'.

(CIMA *Official Terminology*)

Exam alert

Ensure you are able to explain quality conformance costs and quality non-conformance costs and the relationship between them.

The **cost of conformance** is a **discretionary** cost which is incurred with the intention of **eliminating the costs of internal and external failure**. The **cost of non-conformance**, on the other hand, can **only be reduced by increasing the cost of conformance**. The **optimal investment in conformance costs** is when **total costs of quality reach a minimum** (which may be below 100% quality conformance). This is illustrated in the following diagram.

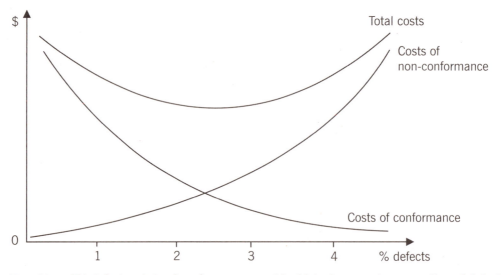

To achieve **0% defects, costs of conformance must be high**. As a **greater proportion of defects are accepted**, however, these costs can be **reduced**. At a level of **0% defects, costs of non-conformance** should be **nil** but these will **increase** as the **accepted level of defects rises**. There should therefore be an **acceptable level of defects** at which the **total costs of quality are at a minimum**.

3.2.2 View 2

A 'traditional' approach to quality management (view one) is that there is an **optimal level of quality effort, that minimises total quality costs**, and there is a point beyond which spending more on quality yields a benefit that is less than the additional cost incurred. Diminishing returns set in beyond the optimal quality level.

The **TQM philosophy** is different.

(a)   Failure and poor quality are unacceptable. It is **inappropriate to think of an optimal level of quality** at which some failures will occur, and the **inevitability of errors is not something that an organisation should accept**. The target should be zero defects.

(b)   Quality costs are difficult to measure, and failure costs in particular are often seriously under estimated. The **real costs of failure include** not just the cost of scrapped items and re-working faulty items, but also the **management time spent sorting out problems** and the **loss of confidence** between different parts of the organisation whenever faults occur.

(c)   A TQM approach does not accept that the prevention costs of achieving zero defects becomes unacceptably high as the quality standard improves and goes above a certain level. In other words, **diminishing returns do not necessarily set in**. If everyone in the organisation is involved in improving quality, the cost of continuous improvement need not be high.

(d)   If an organisation **accepts an optimal quality level** that it believes will minimise total quality costs, there will be **no further challenge** to management to improve quality further.

The **TQM quality cost model** is based on the view that:

(a)   **Prevention costs and appraisal costs** are **subject to management influence** or control. It is **better to spend money on prevention**, before failures occur, than on inspection to detect failures after they have happened.

(b)   **Internal failure costs and external failure costs** are the **consequences of the efforts spent on prevention and appraisal**. Extra effort on prevention will reduce internal failure costs and this in turn will have a knock-on effect, reducing external failure costs as well.

In other words, **higher spending on prevention will eventually lead to lower total quality costs**, because appraisal costs, internal failure costs and external failure costs will all be reduced. The emphasis should be on 'getting things right first time' and 'designing in quality' to the product or service.

Question 9A.5	Quality costs

Learning outcome B1(d)

LL designs and makes a single product, the X4, used in the telecommunications industry. The organisation has a goods received store which employs staff who carry out random checks to ensure materials are of the correct specification. In addition to the random checks, a standard allowance is made for failures due to faulty materials at the completion stage and the normal practice is to charge the cost of any remedial work required to the cost of production for the month. Once delivered to the customer, any faults discovered in the X4 during its warranty period become an expense of the customer support department.

At the end of each month, management reports are prepared for the Board of Directors. These identify the cost of running the stores and the number of issues, the cost of production and the number of units manufactured, and the cost of customer support.

Required

(a)   Briefly discuss why the current accounting system fails to highlight the cost of quality.

(b)   Identify four general categories (or classifications) of LL's activities where expenditure making up the explicit cost of quality will be found and provide an example of a cost found within each category.

(c)   Give one example of a cost of quality not normally identified by the accounting system.

Section summary

Quality costs can be analysed into **prevention**, **appraisal**, **internal failure** and **external failure** costs and should be detailed in a **cost of quality report**.

4 Continuous improvement

Introduction

As the name suggests, continuous improvement aims to constantly improve all aspects of customer value, whilst lowering costs at the same time. This section focuses on the essential factors for continuous improvement and the benefits it brings to an organisation.

4.1 The concept of continuous improvement

In today's highly competitive environment, performance against static historical standards is no longer appropriate and successful organisations must be **open to change** if they are to **maintain their business advantage**. Being **forward looking** and **receptive to new ideas** are **essential elements of continuous improvement**. The concept was popularised in Japan, where it is known as kaizen, and many of Japan's economic advances over the past 20 years have been attributed to it.

KEY TERM

CONTINUOUS IMPROVEMENT is an 'ongoing process that involves a continuous search to reduce costs, eliminate waste, and improve the quality and performance of activities that increase customer value or satisfaction'.   (Drury, *Management and Cost Accounting*)

The implementation of continuous improvement does not necessarily call for significant investment, but it does require a great deal of **commitment and continuous effort**.

Continuous improvement is often associated with **incremental changes** in the day-to-day process of work **suggested by employees** themselves. This is not to say that continuous improvement organisations do not engage in radical change. **Quantum leaps in performance** can occur when cumulative improvements synergise, the sum of a number of small improvements causing a profound net effect greater than the sum of all the small improvements.

The process must be ongoing, and sustained success is more likely in organisations which regularly review their business methods and processes in the drive for improvement.

CASE STUDY

Tata Steel is one of the world's top ten steel producers and the second largest steel producer in The group has a crude steel capacity of more than 28 million tonnes and 80,000 employees..

Tata introduced a continuous improvement culture in their Scunthorpe operations in a five year change process.

They developed a 'current state value stream map' which showed the existing systems and processes, and a 'future state map'.

Cornerstones of Continuous Improvement

Quality – – the creation of Key Performance Indicators (KPIs) with a focus on meeting customer needs was an important step in improving these processes. Previous measures had focussed on output.

Process Improvements. A process of benchmarking its KPIs means that Tata is always reviewing its activities, and by sharing relevant information within Tata, it maintains the drive necessary to keep the system

Teamwork – CI requires everyone to work differently. Every employee needs to feel that they can and should spot areas of weakness and make suggestions about how to make improvements. To help employees make this shift in attitude a phased approach was used whereby initially CI coaches were responsible for CI, then CI champions, managers, team leaders and finally the team.

Tata saw benefits through:

- Reduced wastage
- Improved quality, including less time spent on reworking products
- Faster response times to customer requests

In addition to achieving its production targets Tata also had a more committed and engaged workforce, who were more flexible and enable Tata to be responsive to fluctuations in production demand.

4.2 Essential factors for continuous improvement

(a)   Total **commitment from senior management**

(b)   The **opportunity for all employees to contribute** to the continuous improvement process. Tactical and operational level staff, rather than senior management, usually have the information required. The most successful continuous improvement programs are the ones that have the highest staff involvement.

(c)   Good, objective **information about the organisation's environment** so that its outcomes (what it does) and its processes (how it does it) can be evaluated

(d)   **Employees' awareness of their role** in the achievement of the organisation's strategy

(e)   **Management of the performance and contribution of employees**

(f)   **Good communications** throughout the organisation

(g)   Implementation of **recognised quality management systems and standards**

(h)   **Measurement and evaluation of progress against key performance indicators and benchmarks**. Some organisations have found that simply displaying productivity and quality data every day or week raises production and quality because staff can tell when they are doing things right, and so find themselves in a personal continuous improvement cycle.

It is claimed that if these areas are **regularly reviewed**, change can be managed effectively and **continuous improvement becomes a natural part of the organisational processes**. It should create steady growth and development by keeping the organisation focused on its aims, priorities and performance.

4.2.1 Quality circles

A quality circle consists of a **group of employees**, often from different areas of the organisation, who meet regularly to **discuss problems of quality and quality control** in their area of work, and perhaps to suggest **ways of improving quality**. It is also a way to **encourage innovation**. The aim of quality circles is to **improve employee development and morale** so as to create a **sense of ownership of the quality** of products and services.

Teamwork, in the form of quality circles and **group problem-solving activities**, is the cornerstone of continuous improvement.

4.3 Benefits of continuous improvement

(a)   Better performance, which produces increased profits

(b)   Improvements in customer satisfaction

(c)   Increases in staff morale

(d)   Improvement on a continual, step-by-step basis is more prudent than changing things all at once

(e)   Better communication within the organisation

(f)   Improvements in relations with suppliers

(g)   Better use of resources

(h)   More efficient planning

CASE STUDY

The continuous improvement process has been shown to bring significant benefits to all types of organisation in a variety of sectors, as illustrated by the following case studies. The emphasis is BPP's.

(a)   The Customer Service Excellence standard is a well-established government award scheme promoting and recognising public sector excellence in customer service. **Continuous improvement is a key principle** of the **Customer Service Excellence standard**. The principle requires that organisations continually look for ways to improve their services and the facilities they offer. They do this by:

(i)   Promoting innovation, creativity and striving for excellence.

(ii)   Recognising that, no matter how good, service can always improve.

(iii)   Adopting the latest technologies to change the way business is done.

(b)   One of the aims of North Somerset Council is 'ensuring continuous improvement.....

(i)   ensure that the customer is at the heart of the Council's thinking through a One Council approach to service delivery

(ii)   implement the Human Resources strategy and work towards achieving Investors in People award

(iii)   improve communications

(iv)   improve business and resource planning, financial and performance monitoring.'

Section summary

The essence of **continuous improvement** is the use of an organisation's human resources to produce a constant stream of improvements in all aspects of customer value, including quality, functional design, and timely delivery, while lowering cost at the same time.

5   Kaizen costing   9/10, 5/11, 9/11, 11/11, 3/12

Introduction

Kaizen costing aims to reduce current costs by using such tools as value analysis and functional analysis. These concepts were covered in Chapter 8.

5.1 The Kaizen costing process

KEY TERM

KAIZEN COSTING focuses on obtaining small incremental cost reductions during the production stage of the product life cycle.

Kaizen costing has been used by some Japanese firms for over twenty years and is now widely used in the electronics and automobile industries, for example. 'Kaizen' translates as **continuous improvement**. It is based on the idea of an ongoing process of reviewing how the business operates in order to identify and implement cost savings. Each individual action may result in a small cost saving, but these are incremental and can add up to a material saving.

Kaizen costing has become more important in the modern business environment following a shift from cost-plus pricing to target costing. Traditionally, companies set the price using cost-plus pricing techniques, however, in today's market companies have less control over the price and have to accept the market price. As a result target costing has become increasingly used.

Functional analysis is applied at the design stage of a new product, and a **target cost for each function** is set. The functional target costs are added together and the total becomes the **product target cost**.

Once the product has been in production for a year, the **actual cost of the first year becomes the starting point for further cost reduction**.

It is this **process of continuous improvement, encouraging constant reductions by tightening the 'standards'**, during the production phase that is known as Kaizen costing. The cultural requirements of Kaizen costing are that the whole workforce should be involved, as suggestions for improvements can come from anyone.

The following Kaizen costing chart is based on one used at Daihatsu, the Japanese car manufacturer owned in part by Toyota, and reported in Monden and Lee's 'How a Japanese Auto Maker Reduced Costs' *(Management Accounting* (US Version), 2002).

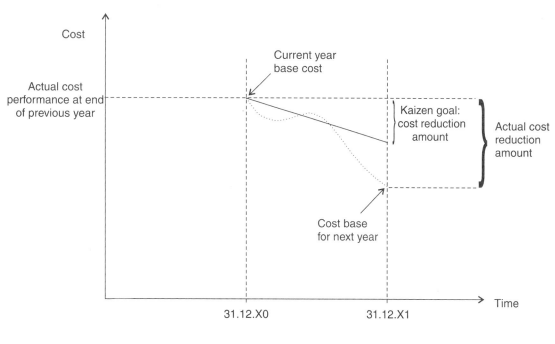

The previous year's actual production cost serves as the cost base for the current year's production cost. A reduction rate and reduction amount are set (**Kaizen cost goals**). **Actual performance** is **compared** to the **Kaizen goals** throughout the year and **variances are monitored**. At the end of the current year, the current actual cost becomes the cost base for the next year. New (lower) Kaizen goals are set and the whole process starts again.

5.2 Kaizen costing v standard costing

Standard costing is used in conjunction with management by exception (management's attention is directed towards situations where actual results differ from expected results). The expected results are based on standards which have been derived from the capability of current organisational processes. **Standard costing** therefore **reflects current levels of performance** and **fails to provide any motivation to improve**.

The following table sets out the **principal differences between Kaizen costing and standard costing techniques**.

	Standard costing	Kaizen costing
Concepts	It is used for cost control.	It is used for cost reduction.
	It assumes that current manufacturing conditions will stay the same.	It assumes continuous improvement.
	The cost focus is on standard costs based on static conditions.	The cost focus is on actual costs assuming dynamic conditions.
	The aim is to meet cost performance standards.	The aim is to achieve cost reduction targets.
Techniques	Standards are set every six or twelve months.	Cost reduction targets are set and applied monthly.
	Costs are controlled using variance analysis based on standard and actual costs.	Costs are reduced by implementing continuous improvement (kaizen) to attain the target profit or to reduce the gap between target and estimated profit.
	Management should investigate and respond when standards are not met.	Management should investigate and respond when target kaizen amounts are not attained.
Employees	They are often viewed as the cause of problems.	They are viewed as the source of, and are empowered to find, the solutions.

(Adapted from Monden and Lee)

5.3 How are Kaizen goals met?

(a) Reduction of non-value added activities and costs
(b) Elimination of waste
(c) Improvements in production cycle time

Section summary

The aim of **Kaizen costing** is to reduce current costs by using various tools such as value analysis and functional analysis..

6 Business process re-engineering (BPR)   **3/12**

Introduction

Business process re-engineering looks at how processes can be redesigned to improve efficiency. Note the link between all these techniques – they are all focused on **improvements**.

6.1 An overview of BPR

BPR *can* lead to fundamental changes in the way an organisation functions. In particular, it has been realised that processes which were developed in a paper-intensive processing environment may not be suitable for an environment that is underpinned by IT.

KEY TERM

BUSINESS PROCESS RE-ENGINEERING (BPR) is the fundamental rethinking and radical redesign of business processes to achieve dramatic improvements in critical contemporary measures of performance, such as cost, quality, service and speed.   (Hammer and Champy: *Reengineering the Corporation*, (1993))

The key words here are **fundamental, radical, dramatic** and **process**.

(a)   **Fundamental** and **radical** indicate that BPR is somewhat akin to zero base budgeting: it starts by asking basic questions such as 'why do we do what we do', without making any assumptions or looking back to what has always been done in the past.

(b)   **Dramatic** means that BPR should achieve 'quantum leaps in performance', not just marginal, incremental improvements.

(c)   **Process**. BPR recognises that there is a need to change functional hierarchies.

KEY TERM

A PROCESS is a collection of activities that takes one or more kinds of input and creates an output.

For example, order fulfilment is a process that takes an order as its input and results in the delivery of the ordered goods. Part of this process is the manufacture of the goods, but under **BPR** the **aim** of **manufacturing** is **not merely to make** the goods. Manufacturing should aim to **deliver the goods that were ordered,** and any aspect of the manufacturing process that hinders this aim should be re-engineered. The first question to ask might be 'Do they need to be manufactured at all?'

A **re-engineered process** has certain **characteristics**.

(a)   Often several jobs are **combined** into one.
(b)   Workers often **make decisions.**
(c)   The **steps** in the process are performed in **a logical order.**
(d)   **Work** is performed where it **makes most sense.**
(e)   Checks and controls may be reduced, and **quality 'built-in'.**
(f)   One manager provides a **single point of contact.**
(g)   The advantages of **centralised and decentralised** operations are combined.

Based on a problem at a *major car manufacturer*.

CASE STUDY

A company employs 25 staff to perform the standard accounting task of matching goods received notes with orders and then with invoices. About 80% of their time is spent trying to find out why 20% of the set of three documents do not agree.

One way of improving the situation would have been to computerise the existing process to facilitate matching. This would have helped, but BPR went further: why accept any incorrect orders at all? What if all the orders are entered onto a computerised database? When goods arrive at the goods inwards department they either agree to goods that have been ordered or they don't. It's as simple as that. Goods that agree to an order are accepted and paid for. Goods that are not agreed are sent back to the supplier. There are no files of unmatched items and time is not wasted trying to sort out these files.

The re-engineering of the process resulted in gains for the company: less staff time wasted, quicker payment for suppliers, lower inventory and lower investment in working capital.

6.2 Principles of BPR

Seven principles of BPR (Hammer)

(a)   Processes should be designed to achieve a desired **outcome rather than** focusing on existing **tasks.**

(b)   **Personnel who use** the **output** from a process should **perform the process**. For example, a company could set up a database of approved suppliers; this would allow personnel who actually require supplies to order them themselves, perhaps using on-line technology, thereby eliminating the need for a separate purchasing function.

(c)   **Information processing** should be **included in the work which produces the information**. This eliminates the differentiation between information gathering and information processing.

(d)   **Geographically dispersed resources** should be **treated** as if they are **centralised.** This allows the benefits of centralisation to be obtained, for example, economies of scale through central negotiation of supply contracts, without losing the benefits of decentralisation, such as flexibility and responsiveness.

(e)   **Parallel activities** should be **linked rather than integrated.** This would involve, for example, co-ordination between teams working on different aspects of a single process.

(f)   **'Doers'** should be allowed to be **self-managing.** The traditional **distinction** between **workers** and **managers** can be **abolished**: decision aids such as expert systems can be provided where they are required.

(g)   **Information** should be **captured once** at **source.** Electronic distribution of information makes this possible.

6.2.1 Examples of business process re-engineering

(a)   A move from a traditional functional plant layout to a JIT cellular product layout is a simple example.

(b)   **Elimination of non-value-added activities.** Consider a materials handling process which incorporates scheduling production, storing materials, processing purchase orders, inspecting materials and paying suppliers.

This process could be re-engineered by sending the production schedule direct to nominated suppliers with whom contracts are set up to ensure that materials are delivered in accordance with the production schedule and that their quality is guaranteed (by supplier inspection before delivery). Such re-engineering should result in the elimination or permanent reduction of the non-value-added activities of storing, purchasing and inspection.

Section summary

Business process re-engineering involves focusing attention inwards to consider how business processes can be redesigned or re-engineered to improve efficiency.

7   Just-in-time (JIT)   5/10, 11/10, 3/11, 5/12, 11/12

Introduction

This section covers a technique that should be familiar to you from your Paper P1 studies. Make sure you are familiar with the JIT philosophy and techniques and how this technique can eliminate non-value added costs.

7.1 Overview of JIT

In **traditional** manufacturing, where there is a production process with several stages, management seek to **insulate each stage** in the process from disruption by another stage, by means of **producing for**, and **holding, inventory**.

Question 9A.6	Interruptions to a stage in production 2

Learning outcome B1(b)

Look again at Question 9A.2.

How would the disruption to stage 2 affect production in a JIT system?

With JIT, a **disruption at any point in the system becomes a problem for the whole operation to resolve**. Supporters of JIT management argue that this will improve the likelihood of the problem being resolved, because it is in the interests of everyone to resolve it. They also argue that **inventories** help to **hide problems** within the system, so that problems go unnoticed for too long.

KEY TERMS

JUST-IN-TIME (JIT) is a system whose objective is to produce or to procure products or components as they are required (by a customer or for use) rather than for inventory. A just-in-time system is a 'pull' system, which responds to demand, in contrast to a 'push' system, in which inventories act as buffers between the different elements of the system, such as purchasing, production and sales.

JUST-IN-TIME PRODUCTION is a production system which is driven by demand for finished products whereby each component on a production line is produced only when needed for the next stage.

JUST-IN-TIME PURCHSING is a purchasing system in which material purchases are contracted so that the receipt and usage of material, to the maximum extent possible, coincide.

(CIMA *Official Terminology*)

7.2 Operational requirements of JIT

High quality	Disruption in production due to errors in quality will reduce throughput and also the dependability of internal supply
Speed	Throughput in the operation must be fast so that customer orders can be met by production rather than from inventory
Reliability	Production must be reliable and not subject to hold-ups
Flexibility	Production must be flexible, and in small batch sizes, to respond immediately to customer orders
Lower cost	High quality production, faster throughput and elimination of errors will result in reduced costs

A consequence of JIT is that if there is **no immediate demand for output**, the operation **should not produce goods for inventory**. Average capacity utilisation could therefore be low (lower than in a traditional manufacturing operation). With a traditional manufacturing system, however, a higher capacity utilisation would only be achieved by producing for inventory at different stages of the production process. Supporters of JIT argue that there is no value in producing for inventory, and, as suggested above, it could damage the overall efficiency of an operation. So whereas **traditional manufacturing systems** are 'push' systems (a delivery from a supplier pushes products through production), **JIT systems** are 'pull' systems (demand from a customer pulls products through production).

'Push' systems	'Pull' systems
Supplier → Production → Customer	Supplier ← Production ← Customer

7.3 The JIT philosophy

JIT can be regarded as an approach to management that encompasses a **commitment to continuous improvement** and the **search for excellence** in the **design and operation of the production management system**. Its aim is to streamline the flow of products through the production process and into the hands of customers.

The JIT philosophy originated in Japan in the 1970s, with companies such as the car manufacturer Toyota. At its most basic, the philosophy is:

(a) To do things well, and gradually do them better (**continuous improvement**)
(b) To **squeeze waste out** of the system

A criticism of JIT, in its extreme form, is that having no inventory between any stages in the production process ignores the fact that some stages, by their very nature, could be less reliable than others, and more prone to disruption. It could therefore be argued that some inventory should be held at these stages to provide a degree of extra protection to the rest of the operation.

7.3.1 Three key elements in the JIT philosophy

Elimination of waste	**Waste** is defined as **any activity that does not add value**. Examples of waste identified by Toyota were: • **Waiting time**. Waiting time can be measured by labour efficiency and machine efficiency. • **Transport**. Moving items around a plant does not add value. Waste can be reduced by **changing the layout of the factory floor so as to minimise the movement of materials**. • **Inventory**. The target should be to eliminate all inventory by tackling the things that cause it to build up.
The involvement of all staff in the operation	JIT is a cultural issue, and its philosophy has to be embraced by everyone involved in the operation if it is to be applied successfully. Critics of JIT argue that management efforts to involve all staff can be patronising.
Continuous improvement	The ideal target is to meet demand immediately with perfect quality and no waste. In practice, this ideal is never achieved. The JIT philosophy is that an organisation should **work towards the ideal**, however.

7.4 JIT techniques

7.4.1 Management techniques

JIT is not just a philosophy, it is also a **collection of management techniques**. Some of these techniques relate to basic working practices.

(a) **Work standards**. Work standards should be established and followed by everyone at all times.

(b) **Flexibility in responsibilities**. The organisation should provide for the possibility of expanding the responsibilities of any individual to the extent of his or her capabilities, regardless of the individual's position in the organisation. Grading structures and restrictive working practices should be abolished.

(c) **Equality of all people working in the organisation**. Equality should exist and be visible. For example, there should be a single staff canteen for everyone, without a special executive dining area; and all staff including managers might be required to wear the same uniform. An example of where such practices occur is the car manufacturer Honda.

(d) **Autonomy**. Authority should be delegated to the individuals directly responsible for the activities of the operation. Management should support people on the shop floor, not direct them. For example, if a quality problem arises, an operative on the production line should have the authority to bring the line to a halt. Gathering data about performance should be delegated to the shop floor and the individuals who use it. Shop floor staff should also be given the first opportunity to solve problems affecting their work, and expert help should only be sought if it is needed.

(e) **Development of personnel**. Individual workers should be developed and trained.

(f) **Quality of working life**. The quality of working life should be improved, through better work area facilities, job security, involvement of everyone in job-related decision making, and so on.

(g) **Creativity**. Employees should be encouraged to be creative in devising improvements to the way their work is done.

7.4.2 Other JIT techniques and methodologies

(a) **Design for manufacture**. In many industries, the way that a product is designed determines a large proportion of its eventual production costs. Production costs can therefore be significantly reduced at the design stage, for example by reducing the number of different components and sub-assemblies required in the product.

(b) **Use several small, simple machines**, rather than a single large and more complex machine. Small machines can be moved around more easily, and so offer greater flexibility in shop floor layout. The risk of making a bad and costly investment decision is reduced, because relatively simple small machines usually cost much less than sophisticated large machines.

(c) **Work floor layout and work flow**. Work can be laid out to promote the smooth flow of operations. Work flow is an important element in JIT, because the work needs to flow without interruption in order to avoid a build-up of inventory or unnecessary down-times. Machines or workers should be grouped by product or component instead of by type of work performed. The non-value-added activity of materials movement between operations is therefore minimised by eliminating space between work stations. Products can flow from machine to machine without having to wait for the next stage of processing or return to stores. Lead times and work in progress are thus reduced.

(d) **Total productive maintenance (TPM).** Total productive maintenance seeks to eliminate unplanned breakdowns and the damage they cause to production and work flow. Staff working on the production line are brought into the search for improvements in maintenance, and are encouraged to take ownership of their machines and carry out simple repairs on them. This frees up maintenance specialists to use their expertise to look for higher-level ways to improve maintenance systems, instead of spending their time on fire fighting repairs and maintenance jobs.

(e) **Set-up reductions**. Set-up is the collection of activities carried out between completing work on one job or batch of production and preparing the process or machine to take the next batch. Set-up time is non-productive time. An aim in JIT is to reduce set-up times, for example by pre-preparing set-up tasks that can be done in advance. Alternatively, set-up time can be reduced by undertaking some tasks previously not done until the machines had stopped whilst the machines are running.

(f) **Total people involvement**. Staff are encouraged to take on more responsibility for using their abilities for the benefit of the organisation. They are trusted and given authority for tasks such as:

    (i) Monitoring and measuring their own performance

    (ii) Reviewing the work they have done each day

    (iii) Dealing directly with suppliers about quality issues and to find out about materials delivery times

    (iv) Dealing with customer problems and queries

    (v) Selecting new staff to work with them

(g) **Visibility**. The work place and the operations taking place in it are made more visible, through open plan work space, visual control systems (such as kanbans, described later), information displays showing performance achievements, and signal lights to show where a stoppage has occurred.

(h) **JIT purchasing**. With JIT purchasing, an organisation establishes a close, long-term relationship with trusted suppliers, and develops an arrangement with the supplier for being able to purchase materials only when they are needed for production. The supplier is required to have a flexible production system capable of responding immediately to purchase orders from the organisation. Responsibility for the quality of goods lies with the supplier. If an organisation has confidence that suppliers will deliver material of 100% quality, on time, so that there will be no rejects, returns and hence no production delays, usage of materials can be matched exactly with delivery of materials and inventories can be kept at near zero levels.

7.5 Elimination of non-value added costs

As you know from the previous chapter, value is only added while a product is actually being processed. Whilst it is being inspected for quality, moving from one part of the factory to another, waiting for further processing and held in store, value is not being added. **Non-value added activities** (or diversionary activities) **should therefore be eliminated**.

Question 9A.7	Non-value-added activities

Learning outcome B1(b)

Solo produces one product, the P. Parts for the product are quality inspected on arrival and stored in a warehouse until needed. They are then moved from the warehouse to the machine room where they are machined to the product specification. This work is then inspected and, if satisfactory, the machined parts are moved to the assembly area. Once this processing is complete, the finished product is inspected and tested. This is then passed to the despatch department, where employees pack it in an attractive box with a printed instruction sheet. Finished goods are stored back in the warehouse until despatched to customers.

Required

Eliminate the non-value-added activities from Solo's current activities listed below to produce the set of activities that would take place under a JIT approach. Comment upon your answer.

Parts received	Machined parts assembled
Parts quality inspected	Finished product inspected and tested
Parts stored in warehouse	Finished goods passed to despatch department
Parts moved to machine room	Finished goods packaged
Parts machined	Packed goods moved back to warehouse
Machined parts inspected	Packed goods stored
Machined parts moved to assembly area	Packed goods despatched to customer

Question 9A.8	Value-added activity

Learning outcome B1(b)

Which of the following is a value-added activity?

A   Setting up a machine so that it drills holes of a certain size
B   Repairing faulty production work
C   Painting a car, if the organisation manufactures cars
D   Storing materials

CASE STUDY

The following extract from an article in the *Financial Times* illustrates how 'just-in-time' some manufacturing processes can be. The emphasis is BPP's.

'Just-in-time manufacturing is down to a fine art at *Nissan Motor Manufacturing (UK)*. **Stockholding of some components is just ten minutes** – and the holding of all parts bought in Europe is less than a day.

Nissan has moved beyond just-in-time to **synchronous supply** for some components, which means manufacturers deliver these components directly to the production line minutes before they are needed.

These manufacturers do not even receive an order to make a component until the car for which it is intended has started along the final assembly line. Seat manufacturer *Ikeda Hoover*, for example, has about 45 minutes to build seats to specification and deliver them to the assembly line a mile away. It delivers 12 sets of seats every 20 minutes and they are mounted in the right order on an overhead conveyor ready for fitting to the right car.

Nissan has **close relationships with this dozen or so suppliers** and deals exclusively with them in their component areas. It involves them and even their own suppliers in discussions about future needs and other issues. These companies have generally established their own manufacturing units close to the Nissan plant.

Other parts from further afield are collected from manufacturers by *Nissan* several times a month at fixed times. This is more efficient than having each supplier making individual haulage arrangements.'

7.6 JIT planning and control with Kanban

Holding inventories is one source of waste in production. Not having materials or parts when they are needed is another. In other words, both having inventory when it is not needed and not having it when it is needed is wasteful practice.

Kanban is the Japanese word for card or signal. A **kanban control system** is a system for **controlling the flow of materials between one stage in a process and the next**. In its simple form, a card is used by an 'internal customer' as a signal to an 'internal supplier' that the customer now requires more parts or materials. The card will contain details of the parts or materials required.

Kanbans are the only means of authorising a flow of materials or parts. The receipt of a card from an internal customer sets in motion the movement or production or supply of one unit of an item, or one standard container of the item. The receipt of two cards will trigger the movement, production or supply of two units or two standard containers, and so on.

There are variants on the basic kanban system. For example, a production system might use **kanban squares**. A space is marked out on the work shop floor. When the space is empty, it acts as a signal for production to start at the previous stage. When it is full, it acts as a signal that production at the previous stage should be halted.

7.7 JIT in service operations

The JIT philosophy can be applied to service operations as well as to manufacturing operations. Whereas JIT in manufacturing seeks to eliminate inventories, JIT in service operations **seeks to remove queues of customers**.

Queues of customers are wasteful because:

(a) They **waste customers' time**.
(b) Queues require **space for customers to wait in**, and this **space is not adding value**.
(c) **Queuing lowers the customer's perception of the quality of the service**.

The application of JIT to a service operation calls for the **removal of specialisation of tasks**, so that the work force can be **used more flexibly and moved from one type of work to another**, in response to demand and work flow requirements.

CASE STUDY

Queue management systems in supermarkets seek to allocate staff according to the customer need. There may be times during the day when there is an influx of shoppers and times when there are few people in the store. Since the timing of these peaks and troughs can be difficult to predict, the 'on duty' checkout staff may be overwhelmed at sometimes and underutilised at others.

To avoid both lengthy queues and idle staff, minimal levels of checkout staff are in place and shop floor staff are reallocated to the tills as needed.

Teamwork and flexibility are difficult to introduce into an organisation because people might be more comfortable with clearly delineated boundaries in terms of their responsibilities. The customer is usually not interested in the company organisation structure, however, because he or she is more interested in receiving a timely service.

In practice, service organisations are likely to use a **buffer operation** to minimise customer queuing times. For example, a hairdresser will get an assistant to give the client a shampoo to reduce the impact of waiting for the stylist.

Question 9A.9   JIT

Learning outcome B1(b)

At the end of the Second World War, Toyota was making losses and was prevented from increasing prices by the weak Japanese car market. It also suffered from major strike action in 1950.

The individual credited with devising JIT in Toyota from the 1940s was Taiichi Ohno, and JIT techniques were developed gradually over time. The kanban system for example, was devised by Toyota in the early 1950s, but was only finally fully implemented throughout the Japanese manufacturing operation in 1962.

Ohno identified seven wastes.

(a) Overproduction
(b) Waste caused by transportation
(c) Waiting
(d) Waste caused by physical movement of items
(e) Over processing
(f) Waste caused by inventory
(g) Defects/corrections

He worked to eliminate them from operations in Toyota. Measures that were taken by the company included the following.

(a) The aim of reducing costs was of paramount importance in the late 1940s.

(b) The company aimed to level the flow of production and eliminate unevenness in the work flow.

(c)   The factory layout was changed. Previously all machines, such as presses, were located in the same area of the factory. Under the new system, different types of machines were clustered together in production cells.

(d)   Machine operators were re-trained.

(e)   Employee involvement in the changes was seen as being particularly important. Team work was promoted.

(f)   The kanban system was eventually introduced, but a major problem with its introduction was the elimination of defects in production.

Required

Explain how each of the changes described above came to be regarded as essential by Toyota's management.

7.8 Problems associated with JIT

JIT should not be seen as a fix for all the underlying problems associated with Western manufacturing. It might not even be appropriate in all circumstances.

(a)   It is **not always easy to predict patterns of demand**.

(b)   JIT makes the organisation **far more vulnerable to disruptions in the supply chain**.

(c)   JIT was designed at a time when all of Toyota's manufacturing was done within a 50 km radius of its headquarters. Wide geographical spread, however, makes this difficult.

Question 9A.10	JIT manufacturing environment

Learning outcome B1(b)

Batch sizes within a JIT manufacturing environment may well be smaller than those associated with traditional manufacturing systems.

What costs might be associated with this feature of JIT?

1   Increased set-up costs

2   Opportunity cost of lost production capacity as machinery and the workforce reorganise for a different product

3   Additional materials handling costs

4   Increased administrative costs

7.9 Modern versus traditional inventory control systems

There is no reason for the newer approaches to supersede the old entirely. A restaurant, for example, might find it preferable to use the traditional economic order quantity approach for staple non-perishable food, but adopt JIT for perishable and 'exotic' items. In a hospital, a lack of inventory could, quite literally, be fatal, and JIT would be quite unsuitable.

7.10 Manufacturing cycle efficiency

7.10.1 Customer response time (CRT)

As product life cycles shorten and customers demand quick response to orders, organisations are seeking to improve **CRT** (the length of time between an order being placed and delivery of goods/services to the customer) and **on-time delivery rate**.

CRT is a measure of an organisation's ability to respond to a customer's request and is in general determined by internal factors (delay between order and work starting, length of time the order spends in the production process), both of which are linked to the length of the manufacturing cycle.

7.10.2 Manufacturing cycle time (MCT)

MCT is the length of time between starting and finishing the production of an order and is typically made up of:

(a)   Processing time
(b)   Waiting time
(c)   Moving time
(d)   Inspection time

Manufacturing cycle efficiency (MCE) shows (in ratio form) the proportion of time during which value is being added during the production process, and is calculated as:

Processing time/(processing time + waiting time + moving time + inspection time)

The closer the ratio is to 1, the **more efficient the production operation**. As the **ratio increases**:

(a)   **WIP investment will fall** (with all the associated benefits). For example, if an organisation has an annual cost of goods sold of $5,000,000 and the MCT reduces from 20 days to 15 days, the average value of WIP will fall by $((20 - 15)/365) \times \$5,000,000 = \$68,493$.

(b)   An organisation's ability to act **flexibly** and **respond to rush orders** or sudden market changes is improved.

(c)   **Production throughput** can be **increased** without increasing plant capacity. The need for overtime may fall or additional production may be possible without increasing fixed production costs.

Reducing MCT links well with Total Quality Management (see Section 2) because of the need to reduce reworking and inspection.

Improving MCE will increase costs, however. A reduction in cycle times may require the manufacturing process to be redesigned or investment in new machinery. The net benefits will very much depend on the circumstances under consideration. Will the investment required be justified by the increase in volumes or reduction in costs? Relevant costing can be used: the proportion of, say, stockholding costs which would be avoidable can be determined, perhaps by using activity based costing. If the reduction in cycle time produces X extra additional saleable units, the opportunity cost of a cycle hour can be calculated and used to assist in the decision of whether or not to invest in reducing cycle time.

7.10.3 MCT and JIT

(a)   The reduction in MCT is a key phase in the introduction of JIT.

(b)   JIT has advantages in certain manufacturing environments, but the benefits of increasing MCE apply to all organisations, irrespective of whether they also use JIT.

(c)   Just as JIT can be applied to the supply chain, so too can the concept of MCE. For example, by requiring a guaranteed level of quality from suppliers, inspection time can be reduced.

Section summary

Just-in-time is an approach to operations planning and control based on the idea that **goods and services should be produced only when they are needed,** and neither too early (so that inventories build up) nor too late (so that the customer has to wait).

Just-in-time systems **challenge** 'traditional' views of manufacturing.

JIT consists of **JIT purchasing** and **JIT production.**

Elimination of waste, involvement of all staff and **continuous improvement** are the three key elements in the JIT philosophy.

JIT aims to **eliminate all non-value-added costs.**

8   Accounting for pull systems – backflush accounting

Introduction

Backflush accounting is a method of accounting that can be used with JIT production systems. It saves a considerable amount of time as it avoids having to make a number of accounting entries that are required by a traditional system.

Backflush accounting is the name given to the method of keeping cost accounts employed if **backflush costing** is used. The two terms are almost interchangeable.

Traditional costing systems use **sequential tracking** (also known as **synchronous tracking**) to track costs sequentially as products pass from raw materials to work in progress, to finished goods and finally to sales. In other words, material costs are charged to WIP when materials are issued to production and direct labour and overhead costs are charged in a similar way as the cost is incurred or very soon after.

If a production system such as **JIT** is used, sequentially tracking means that **all entries are made at almost the same moment** and so a different accounting system can be used. In **backflush costing/accounting, costs are calculated and charged when the product is sold, or when it is transferred to the finished goods store.**

KEY TERM

BACKFLUSH COSTING is 'A method of costing, associated with a JIT production system, which applies cost to the output of a process. Costs do not mirror the flow of products through the production process, but are attached to the output produced (finished goods inventory and cost of sales), on the assumption that such backflushed costs are a realistic measure of the actual costs incurred.'

(CIMA *Official Terminology*)

The CIMA definition above omits the fact that **budgeted or standard costs are used to work backwards to 'flush' out manufacturing costs** for the units produced. (Hence the rather unattractive name for the system!). The application of **standard costs** to finished goods units, or to units sold, is used in order to **calculate cost of goods sold,** thereby **simplifying** the costing system and creating **savings in administrative effort. In a true backflush accounting system, records of materials used and work in progress** are **not required** as material cost can be calculated from either finished goods or goods sold.

Backflush costing runs **counter to the principle enshrined in IAS 2**, and the staple of cost accounting for decades, that inventory and WIP should be accounted for by calculating cost and net realisable value of 'specific individual items of inventory'. The substantial **reduction in inventories that is a feature of JIT** means that **inventory valuation is less relevant,** however, and therefore the **costing system** can be **simplified** to a considerable extent. In the 1980s, Johnson & Kaplan in fact wrote that **management rarely requires a value to be placed on inventory for internal management purposes,** the **value only being required for external reporting.**

Backflush costing is therefore **appropriate** for organisations trying to keep **inventories to the very minimum**. In such circumstances, the **recording** of every little increase in inventory value, as each nut and bolt is added, is simply an expensive and **non-value-added activity** that should be **eliminated**.

Example: working backwards from output

To take a **very simplified example**, if backflush costing is used, the management accountant might extract the following information from the monthly accounting transaction records and production records.

Orders completed and despatched in July	196 units
Orders prepared in advance 1 July	3 units
Orders prepared in advance 31 July	2 units
Scrapped items	5 units
Conversion costs in the month	$250,000
Material costs in the month	$475,000

This is enough to place a value on inventories and production as follows.

	Units		$
B/f	(3)	Conversion costs	250,000
Despatched	196	Material costs	475,000
Scrapped	5	Total costs	725,000
C/f	2		
Units produced	200		

Cost per unit is $725,000 divided by 200 units = $3,625

In this case a single process account could be drawn up as follows.

	Dr ($)	Cr ($)
Inventory b/fwd (3 × $3,625)	10,875	
Materials	475,000	
Conversion costs	250,000	
To finished goods (196 × $3,625)		710,500
Losses etc written off to income statement (5 × $3,625)		18,125
Inventory c/fwd (2 × $3,625)		7,250
	735,875	735,875

8.1 Arguments of traditional management accountants

(a) The figure for **losses** here is **inaccurate**. They would say that in reality the faulty goods would have been scrapped when only partially complete and it is wrong to value them at the same cost as a fully finished good unit.

(b) Using this approach, the figure for inventories b/fwd and c/fwd will not tie up with the accounts for last month and next month, because the material and conversion costs may be different.

8.2 Reply of modern management accountants

(a) **Losses** represent only about 2% of total cost and are **not material**. In any case putting a value to them is less **important** than **improving the quality of production procedures** (on the basis of **TQM** practices and non-financial production information) to ensure that they do not occur again.

(b) **Finished good inventories represent between 1% and 2% of total cost and are immaterial**. Slight discrepancies in valuation methods of b/fwds and c/fwds will amount to a **fraction** of a percentage, and can be written off in the month as a small **variance**.

(c)   Even with computers the **cost of tracing units** every step of the way through production – with 'normal' and 'abnormal' losses, equivalent units and numerous process accounts – **is simply not worth it, in terms of the benefit derived** from the information it provides.

8.3 Variants of backflush costing

(a)   **Trigger points determine when the entries are made in the accounting system.** There will be either one or two trigger points that trigger entries in the accounts.

    (i)   When materials are purchased/received

    (ii)   When goods are completed or when they are sold

In a **true JIT system** where no inventories are held the **first trigger**, when raw materials are purchased, is **unnecessary**.

(b)   Actual conversion costs are recorded as incurred, just as in conventional recording systems. Conversion costs are applied to products at the second trigger point based on a standard cost. It is assumed that any conversion costs not applied to products are carried forward and disposed of at the period end.

(c)   **Direct labour** is included as an **indirect cost in conversion cost with overheads**. (Production is only required when there is demand for it in a JIT system, and so production labour will be paid regardless of the level of activity.)

(d)   All indirect costs are treated as a fixed period expense.

Example: accounting entries at different trigger points

The transactions for period 8 20X1 for Clive are as follows.

Purchase of raw materials	$24,990
Conversion costs incurred	$20,220
Finished goods produced (used in methods 2 & 3 only)	4,900 units
Sales	4,850 units

There are no opening inventories of raw materials, WIP or finished goods. The standard cost per unit is made up of $5.10 for materials and $4.20 for conversion costs.

Required

Show the accounting entries you would expect to see in each of the following scenarios:

(i)   For 1 trigger point – when goods are sold

(ii)   For 1 trigger point – when goods are completed

(iii)   For 2 trigger points.

Solution

For 1 trigger point – when goods are sold (method 1)

This is the simplest method of backflush costing. There is only one **trigger point** and that is **when the entry to the cost of goods sold account is required** when the goods are sold. (This method assumes that units are sold as soon as they are produced.)

			$	$
(a)	DEBIT	Conversion costs control	20,220	
	CREDIT	Expense payables		20,220
	Being the actual conversion costs incurred			
(b)	DEBIT	Cost of goods sold (4,850 × $9.30)	45,105	
	CREDIT	Payables (4,850 × $5.10)		24,735
	CREDIT	Conversion costs allocated (4,850 × $4.20)		20,370
	Being the standard cost of goods sold			

			$	$
(c)	DEBIT	Conversion costs allocated	20,370	
	CREDIT	Cost of goods sold		150
	CREDIT	Conversion costs control		20,220

Being the under or over allocation of conversion costs

Solution

For 1 trigger point – when goods are completed (method 2)

This is very similar to the solution above but in this instance the **trigger** is the completion of a unit and its **movement into finished goods store**. The accounting entries are as follows.

			$	$
(a)	DEBIT	Conversion costs control	20,220	
	CREDIT	Expense payables		20,220

Being the actual conversion costs incurred

(b)	DEBIT	Finished goods inventory (4,900 × $9.30)	45,570	
	CREDIT	Payables (4,900 × $5.10)		24,990
	CREDIT	Conversion costs allocated (4,900 × $4.20)		20,580

Being the standard cost of goods produced

(c)	DEBIT	Cost of goods sold (4,850 × $9.30)	45,105	
	CREDIT	Finished goods inventory		45,105

Being the standard cost of goods sold

(d)	DEBIT	Conversion costs allocated	20,580	
	CREDIT	Cost of goods sold		360
	CREDIT	Conversion costs control		20,220

Being the under or over allocation of conversion costs

The end of period finished goods inventory balance is $465 (50 × $9.30).

Solution

For 2 trigger points – (method 3)

There are two **trigger points**, the **first** when **materials and components are received** and the **other** at the **point of transfer to finished goods**.

			$	$
(a)	DEBIT	Raw materials	24,990	
	CREDIT	Payables		24,990

Being the purchase of raw materials on credit

(b)	DEBIT	Conversion costs control	20,220	
	CREDIT	Expense payables		20,220

Being the actual conversion costs incurred

(c)	DEBIT	Finished goods inventory (4,900 × $9.30)	45,570	
	CREDIT	Raw materials		24,990
	CREDIT	Conversion costs allocated		20,580

Being the standard cost of goods produced

(d)	DEBIT	Cost of goods sold (4,850 × $9.30)	45,105	
	CREDIT	Finished goods inventory		45,105

Being the standard cost of goods sold

(e)	DEBIT	Conversion costs allocated	20,580	
	CREDIT	Cost of goods sold		360
	CREDIT	Conversion costs control		20,220

Being the under or over allocation of conversion costs

Note that the **WIP account is eliminated** using all methods. In a JIT system the vast majority of manufacturing costs will form part of the cost of sales and will not be deferred in closing inventory values. In such a situation the amount of work involved in tracking costs through WIP, cost of sales and finished goods is unlikely to be justified. This considerably **reduces the volume of transactions recorded** in the internal accounting system.

The successful operation of backflush costing rests upon **predictable levels of efficiency** and **stable material prices and usage**. In other words there should be **insignificant cost variances**.

8.4 Possible problems with backflush costing

(a) **It is only appropriate for JIT operations** where production and sales volumes are approximately equal.

(b) Some people claim that it **should not be used for external reporting** purposes. If, however, **inventories are low** or are practically **unchanged** from one accounting period to the next, operating income and inventory valuations derived from backflush accounting will **not be materially different from the results using conventional systems**. Hence, in such circumstances, backflush accounting is acceptable for external financial reporting.

(c) It is vital that adequate production controls exist so that cost control during the production process is maintained.

8.5 Advantages of backflush costing

(a) It is much **simpler**, as there is no separate accounting for WIP.

(b) Even the **finished goods** account is **unnecessary**, as we demonstrated in the first example above.

(c) The number of **accounting entries should be greatly reduced**, as are the supporting vouchers, documents and so on.

(d) The system should **discourage** managers from **producing simply for inventory** since working on material does not add value until the final product is completed or sold.

Section summary

Backflush accounting is a method of accounting that can be used with JIT production systems. It saves a considerable amount of time as it avoids having to make a number of accounting entries that are required by a traditional system.

9 Theory of constraints (TOC)

Introduction

Another cost management technique is theory of constraints whose aim is to ensure the production flows evenly and works as effectively as possible. This section links closely with Section 10 on throughput accounting.

9.1 The concept of the theory of constraints

The use of a JIT operating system, whether in a manufacturing or service organisation, requires a particular type of costing system. **Throughput accounting** is a technique that has been developed to deal

with this. The name was first coined in the late 1980s when *Galloway and Waldron* developed the system in the UK. Throughput accounting is based on the concept of the **theory of constraints** (**TOC**) which was formulated by Goldratt and Cox in the U.S.A. in 1986. Its key financial concept is to **turn materials into sales as quickly as possible**, thereby maximising throughput and the net cash generated from sales. This is to be achieved by striving for **balance in production processes**, and so **evenness of production flow** is an important aim.

KEY TERMS

THEORY OF CONSTRAINTS (TOC) is 'Procedure based on identifying bottleneck (constraints), maximising their use, subordinating other facilities to the demands of the bottleneck facilities, alleviating bottlenecks and re-evaluating the whole system.'

BOTTLENECK is 'facility that has lower capacity than preceding or subsequent activities, and restricts output based on current capacity'.   (CIMA *Official Terminology*)

One process will inevitably act as a bottleneck (or limiting factor) and constrain throughput – this is known as the **binding constraint** in TOC terminology. The important concept behind TOC is that the production rate of the entire factory is set at the pace of the bottleneck. (Goldratt advocates a **drum – buffer – rope system**, with the bottleneck as the drum.) Steps should therefore be taken to remove this bottleneck.

(a)   Buy more equipment
(b)   Provide additional training for slow workers
(c)   Change a product design to reduce the processing time on a bottleneck activity
(d)   Eliminate idle time at the bottleneck (eg machine set-up time)

But ultimately there will always be a binding constraint, unless capacity is far greater than sales demand or all processes are totally in balance, which is unlikely even if it is a goal to be aimed for.

Output through the binding constraint should never be delayed or held up otherwise sales will be lost. To avoid this happening **a buffer inventory should be built up immediately prior to the bottleneck** or binding constraint. **This is the only inventory that the business should hold,** with the exception of possibly a very small amount of finished goods inventory and raw materials that are consistent with the JIT approach. (This is Goldratt's **buffer** in the drum – buffer – rope system.)

Operations prior to the binding constraint should operate at the same speed as the binding constraint, otherwise work in progress (other than the buffer inventory) will be built up. (Here the **rope** links all upstream operations to the pace of the bottleneck.) According to TOC, **inventory costs money** in terms of storage space and interest costs and so inventory is **not desirable**. In a **traditional** production system an **organisation will often pay staff a bonus to produce as many units as possible. TOC** views this as **inefficient** since the organisation is paying extra to build up inventory which then costs money to store until it is required.

Example: An illustration of the theory of constraints

Machine X can process 1,000 kg of raw material per hour, machine Y 800 kg. Of an input of 900 kg, 100 kg of processed material must wait on the bottleneck machine (machine Y) at the end of an hour of processing.

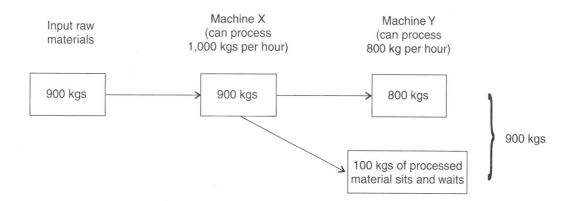

The **traditional view** is that **machines should be working, not sitting idle**. So if the desired output from the above process were 8,100 kgs, **machine X would be kept in continual use** and all 8,100 kgs would be processed through the machine in nine hours. There would be a **backlog** of 900 kgs [8,100 – (9 hrs × 800)] of processed material in front of machine Y, however. All this material **would require handling** and **storage space** and **create the additional costs related to these non-value added activities**. Its **processing would not increase throughput contribution**.

9.2 Key measures

To apply TOC ideas, Goldratt and Cox recommend the use of three key measures.

KEY TERMS

THROUGHPUT CONTRIBUTION (THE RATE OF WHICH PROFIT IS GENERATED THROUGH SALES) = SALES REVENUE – DIRECT MATERIAL COST

CONVERSION COSTS (OTHER OPERATIONAL EXPENSES) = ALL OPERATING COSTS EXCEPT DIRECT MATERIAL COST

INVESTMENTS (INVENTORY) = INVENTORIES + RESEARCH AND DEVELOPMENT COSTS + COSTS FO EQUIPMENT AND BUILDINGS

The aim is to maximise throughput contribution while keeping inventory and operational expenses to a minimum. If a strategy for increasing throughput contribution is being considered it will therefore only be accepted if operational expenses and inventory increase by a lower amount than contribution. TOC considers the short term and assumes operating expenses to be fixed costs.

9.3 Bottlenecks and quality control

Quality control points should be placed before bottlenecks: 'Make sure the bottleneck works only on good parts by weeding out the ones that are defective. If you scrap a part before it reaches the bottleneck, all you have lost is a scrapped part. But if you scrap the part after it's passed through the bottleneck, you have lost time that cannot be recovered.'

(Goldratt and Cox, *The Goal*)

KEY POINT

It is important to realise that TOC is not an accounting system but a **production** system.

CASE STUDY

TOC is not just applicable in manufacturing organisations, but can be applied successfully in the service sector too. The binding constraint in the service sector is often skilled labour.

'Using the "Theory of Constraints" methodology to improve response rates to emergency services in the UK.

Why was the initiative launched?

The UK Police Force was seeking innovative ways to tackle a long standing problem: how to improve the response rate to emergency calls in an affordable way.

Problems

In 2004 10 million emergency calls were made to the 999 number, of which 7 million were not emergencies. These calls block the lines and take up valuable phone operator time which delays the response to genuine emergency calls **Using the TOC approach non-emergency calls need to be weeded out before they get to the operator.** Within the system these calls were 'defective parts' that place excess demand on the bottleneck and need to be eliminated.

Solutions

Diverting the non-emergency numbers to other operators frees up the 999 operators. For the new number, a short, easily memorable number that everyone could use, was chosen, 101. There was concern about whether there would be public acceptance and the demands that it would place on the 101 operators is demand exceeded the existing resources

Tips for success

(a)   Remember TOC is a thinking process and not a list of possible solutions.

(b)   Success is more likely if the methodology is embraced by a core group of senior people in the organisation.

(c)   Involve all staff levels in finding solutions.

(d)   Watch the use of language because the jargon of TOC is not necessary for everyone.

(e)   Don't think of TOC as yet another expensive management tool. It is a relatively simple set of basic principles that are accessible to all.

(f)   Don't allow historical tradition, "we've always done it this way" , to inhibit innovation.

Section summary

Theory of constraints (TOC) is a set of concepts which aim to identify the binding constraints in a production system and which strive for evenness of production flow so that the organisation works as effectively as possible. No inventory should be held, except prior to the binding constraint.

10   Throughput accounting (TA)

Introduction

This section is closely linked with Section 9 on the theory of constraints. Make sure you understand what is meant by 'throughput' and how this technique differs from other management accounting systems.

10.1 A definition

KEY TERM

'THROUGHPUT ACCOUNTING (TA) is an approach to accounting which is largely in sympathy with the JIT philosophy. In essence, TA assumes that a manager has a given set of resources available. These comprise existing buildings, capital equipment and labour force. Using these resources, purchased

materials and parts must be processed to generate sales revenue. Given this scenario the most appropriate financial objective to set for doing this is the maximisation of throughput (Goldratt and Cox, 1984) which is defined as: sales revenue *less* direct material cost.'

(Tanaka, Yoshikawa, Innes and Mitchell, Contemporary Cost Management)

TA is different from all other management accounting systems because of what it **emphasises**.

(a)   Firstly **throughput**

(b)   Secondly minimisation of inventory

(c)   Thirdly **cost control**

10.2 TA concepts

KEY POINT

> **TA is based on three concepts.**
>
> - In the short run, most costs in the factory (with the exception of materials costs) are fixed.
> - The ideal inventory level is zero.
> - Profitability is determined by the rate at which sales are made.

10.2.1 Concept 1

Because TA differentiates between fixed and variable costs it is often compared with marginal costing and **some people argue that there is no difference between marginal costing and throughput accounting.** In marginal costing direct labour costs are usually assumed to be variable costs. Years ago this assumption was true, but employees are not usually paid piece rate today and they are not laid off for part of the year when there is no work, and so labour cost is not truly variable. If this is accepted the two techniques are identical in some respects, but **marginal costing is generally thought of as being purely a short-term decision-making technique** while **TA, or at least TOC, was conceived with the aim of changing manufacturing strategy to achieve evenness of flow. It is therefore much more than a short-term decision technique.**

Because **TA combines all conversion costs** together and does not attempt to examine them in detail it is particularly **suited to use with ABC**, which examines the behaviour of these costs and assumes them to be variable in the long-run.

10.2.2 Concept 2

In a JIT environment, all inventory is a 'bad thing' and the **ideal inventory level is zero**. Products should not be made unless there is a customer waiting for them. This means **unavoidable idle capacity must be accepted in some operations,** but not for the operation that is the bottleneck of the moment. There is one exception to the zero inventory policy, being that a buffer inventory should be held prior to the bottleneck process.

10.2.3 Concept 3

Profitability is determined by the rate at which 'money comes in at the door' (that is, sales are made) and, in a JIT environment, this depends on how quickly goods can be produced to satisfy customer orders. Since the goal of a profit-orientated organisation is to make money, inventory must be sold for that goal to be achieved.

The buffer inventory and any other work in progress or finished goods inventory should be **valued at material cost only** until the output is eventually sold, so that **no value will be added and no profit earned until the sale takes place.** Producing output just to add to work in progress or finished goods inventory creates no profit, and so should not be encouraged.

Learning outcome B1(b)

How are these concepts a direct contrast to the fundamental principles of conventional cost accounting?

10.3 Bottleneck resources

The aim of **modern manufacturing** approaches is to match production resources with the demand for them. This implies that there are **no constraints, termed bottleneck resources** in TA, within an organisation. The throughput philosophy entails the **identification** and **elimination** of these bottleneck resources. Where they **cannot be eliminated production must be limited to the capacity of the bottleneck resource in order to avoid the build-up of work in progress.** If a rearrangement of existing resources (such as moving a machine) or buying-in resources does not alleviate the bottleneck, investment in new equipment may be necessary. The **elimination of one bottleneck is likely to lead to the creation of another** at a previously satisfactory location, however. The **management of bottlenecks** therefore becomes a **primary concern** of the manager seeking to increase throughput.

(a)   There is nothing to be gained by measuring and encouraging the efficiency of machines that do not govern the overall flow of work.

(b)   Likewise, there is little point in measuring the efficiency of production staff working on non-bottleneck processes.

(c)   Bonuses paid to encourage faster working on non-bottleneck processes are wasted and could lead to increased storage costs and more faulty goods.

Other factors that might limit throughput other than a lack of production resources (bottlenecks)

(a)   The existence of a non-competitive selling price

(b)   The need to deliver on time to particular customers, which may disrupt normal production flow

(c)   The lack of product quality and reliability, which may cause large amounts of rework or an unnecessary increase in production volume

(d)   Unreliable material suppliers, which will lead to poor quality products that require rework

10.4 Throughput measures

10.4.1 Return per time period

In a throughput accounting environment, the overall **focus of attention** is the **rate at which the organisation can generate profits**. To monitor this, the return on the throughput **through the bottleneck resource** is monitored using:

$$\text{Return per time period} = \frac{\text{sales revenue - material costs}}{\text{time period}}$$

This measure shows the **value added** by an organisation during a particular time period. Time plays a crucial role in the measure, so **managers** are strongly **encouraged to remove bottlenecks that might cause production delays**.

10.4.2 Return per time period on bottleneck resource

In throughput accounting, the limiting factor is the bottleneck. The return per time period measure can be adapted and used for **ranking products to optimise production** in the **short term**.

$$\text{Product return per minute} = \frac{\text{sales price - material costs}}{\text{minutes on key / bottleneck resource}}$$

Ranking products on the basis of throughput contribution per minute (or hour) on the bottleneck resource is **similar in concept to maximising contribution per unit of limiting factor**. Such product rankings are for **short-term production scheduling only**. In throughput accounting, bottlenecks should be eliminated and so rankings may change quickly. Customer demand can, of course, cause the bottleneck to change at short notice too.

Rankings by TA product return and by contribution per unit of limiting factor may be different. Which one leads to profit maximisation? The correct approach depends on the variability or otherwise of labour and variable overheads, which in turn depends on the time horizon of the decision. Both are short-term profit maximisation techniques and given that labour is nowadays likely to be fixed in the short term, it could be argued that TA provides the more correct solution. An analysis of variable overheads would be needed to determine their variability.

KEY POINT

Bear in mind that the huge majority of organisations cannot produce and market products based on short-term profit considerations alone. Strategic-level issues such as market developments, product developments and stage reached in the product life cycle must also be taken into account.

10.4.3 TA ratio

Products can also be ranked according to the **throughput accounting ratio (TA ratio).**

LEARN

$$\text{TA ratio} = \frac{\text{throughput contribution or value added per time period}}{\text{conversion cost per time period}}$$

$$= \frac{\text{(sales - material costs) per time period}}{\text{(labour + overhead) per time period}}$$

This measure has the **advantage** of **including the costs involved in running the factory**. **The higher the ratio, the more profitable the company**.

Here's an example.

	Product A $ per hour	Product B $ per hour
Sales price	100	150
Material cost	(40)	(50)
Conversion cost	(50)	(50)
Profit	10	50
TA ratio	$\frac{60}{50} = 1.2$	$\frac{100}{50} = 2.0$

Profit will be maximised by manufacturing as much of product B as possible.

Exam skills

If conversion cost cannot be directly allocated to products (because it is not a unit-level manufacturing cost), the TA ratio cannot be calculated and products have to be ranked in terms of throughput contribution per hour or minute of bottleneck resource.

10.4.4 Effectiveness measures and cost control

Traditional efficiency measures such as standard costing variances and labour ratios are **unsuitable** in a TA environment because traditional efficiency should not be encouraged (as the **labour force should not produce just for inventory**).

Effectiveness is a **more important** issue. The **current effectiveness ratio** compares current levels of effectiveness with the standard and is calculated as:

$$\frac{\text{standard minutes of throughput achieved}}{\text{minutes available}}$$

Generally adverse variances are not considered to be a good thing. In a TA environment, however, if overtime is worked at the bottleneck to increase throughput, an adverse labour rate variance would arise. Provided the increase in value added was greater than the extra labour cost, this would be a good thing, however.

10.5 TA and non-value-added activities

Like JIT, TA aims to minimise production time. In order that **process time approaches lead time, all non-value-added activities need to be minimised or eliminated**. Set-up time, waiting time, inspection time and so on should therefore be minimised or eliminated.

10.6 Is it good or bad?

TA is seen by some as **too short term**, as all costs other than direct material are regarded as fixed. This is not true. But TA does **concentrate on direct material costs** and does nothing for the control of other costs. These characteristics make throughput accounting a **good complement for ABC**, as ABC focuses on labour and overhead costs.

TA attempts to maximise throughput whereas traditional systems attempt to maximise profit. By trying to maximise throughput an organisation could be producing more than the profit-maximising output.

Where TA helps direct attention

(a) Bottlenecks
(b) Key elements in making profits
(c) Inventory reduction
(d) Reducing the response time to customer demand
(e) Evenness of production flow
(f) Overall effectiveness and efficiency

A **global measure of throughput** at factory level can produce an insight into the effectiveness of factory management, especially in a multi-product, multi-process organisation in which product demand is unpredictable and prices are set by negotiation between supplier and buyer. With a given level of resources (employees, machines, buildings and so on), an increase period by period in the level of throughput would indicate an improvement in the flow of products through the factory to the customer. If bottleneck resources are highlighted, management can focus their attention on removing factors limiting the profitability of the factory as a whole (as opposed to subunits or product lines).

CASE STUDY

The extract below taken from www.goldratt.co.uk shows that businesses can drastically improve performance by switching focus and committing to measuring elements of throughput.

At the 2005 World Conference of the TOC International Certification Organisation – the certifying body for TOC Professionals - the following was presented. Client names were withheld to maintain confidentiality.

Company 1

Situation: A capital goods manufacturer had been losing money for two and a half years. The owner had given the plant six months to improve significantly otherwise he would close the doors.

Actions: Stopped measuring efficiencies – stopped local performance measures which were causing bad multi-tasking. Started to measure Throughput (T), Investment (I), Operating Expense (OE), OTIF (On Time In Full) and treating Throughput as generated only when CASH was received.

Results: Business turned around in 100 days; OTIF from 5% to 90%+; Sales up by 3000% in five years.

Company 2

Situation: An automotive gears manufacturer. They had been losing money for five years and actions were started to liquidate some assets and parts of the business.

Actions: Stopped measuring quantity and weight of product sales; abolished all the KRAs (Key Result Area measures) of function heads. Started focusing on Throughput instead of sales value; focused on measuring OTIF and cash generation.

Results: OTIF from 4% to 85%+; Receivables reduced from 116 days to 50 days; Throughput increased by 70% over the next two years.

Company 3

Situation: A cement manufacturer with an inconsistent profitability record.

Actions: Stopped measuring Tons per shift, per day, per month. Started measuring T, I OE, Throughput Loss and OTIF; focusing on Throughput instead of sales value for customer orders.

Results: Throughput increased by 25% in first 3 months; OTIF from 75% to 98%.

Example: Throughput accounting

Corrie produces three products, X, Y and Z. The capacity of Corrie's plant is restricted by process alpha. Process alpha is expected to be operational for eight hours per day and can produce 1,200 units of X per hour, 1,500 units of Y per hour, and 600 units of Z per hour.

Selling prices and material costs for each product are as follows.

Product	Selling price $ per unit	Material cost $ per unit	Throughput contribution $ per unit
X	150	70	80
Y	120	40	80
Z	300	100	200

Conversion costs are $720,000 per day.

Requirements

(a)   Calculate the profit per day if daily output achieved is 6,000 units of X, 4,500 units of Y and 1,200 units of Z.

(b)   Calculate the TA ratio for each product.

(c)   In the absence of demand restrictions for the three products, advise Corrie's management on the optimal production plan.

Solution

(a)   Profit per day = throughput contribution – conversion cost

= [($80 × 6,000) + ($80 × 4,500) + ($200 × 1,200)] – $720,000
= $360,000

(b)   TA ratio = throughput contribution per factory hour/conversion cost per factory hour

Conversion cost per factory hour = $720,000/8 = $90,000

Product	Throughput contribution per factory hour	Cost per factory hour	TA ratio
X	$80 × (60 ÷ 0.05 mins) = $96,000	$90,000	1.07
Y	$80 × (60 ÷ 0.04 mins) = $120,000	$90,000	1.33
Z	$200 × (60 ÷ 0.10 mins) = $120,000	$90,000	1.33

(c) An attempt should be made to remove the restriction on output caused by process alpha's capacity. This will probably result in another bottleneck emerging elsewhere. The extra capacity required to remove the restriction could be obtained by working overtime, making process improvements or product specification changes. Until the volume of throughput can be increased, output should be concentrated upon products Y and Z (greatest TA ratios), unless there are good marketing reasons for continuing the current production mix.

Now try a question for yourself.

Question 9A.12	Performance measurement in throughput accounting

Learning outcome B1(b)

Growler manufactures computer components. Health and safety regulations mean that one of its processes can only be operated 8 hours a day. The hourly capacity of this process is 500 units per hour. The selling price of each component is $100 and the unit material cost is $40. The daily total of all factory costs (conversion costs) is $144,000, excluding materials. Expected production is 3,600 units per day.

Required

Calculate

(a) Total profit per day
(b) Return per factory hours
(c) Throughput accounting ratio

10.7 Throughput accounting in service and retail industries

Sales staff have always preferred to use a marginal costing approach so that they can use their discretion on discounts, and **retail organisations** have traditionally thought in terms of sales revenue less the bought in price of goods. The throughput accounting approach is therefore **nothing new** to them.

Throughput accounting can be used very effectively in **support departments and service industries** to **highlight and remove bottlenecks**. For example, if there is a delay in processing a potential customer's application, business can be lost or the potential customer may decide not to proceed. Sometimes credit rating checks are too detailed, slowing the whole procedure unnecessarily and delaying acceptance from say 24 hours to eight days.

A similar problem could occur in hospitals where work that could be done by nurses has to be carried out by doctors. Not only does this increase the cost of the work but it may well cause a bottleneck by tying up a doctor's time unnecessarily.

Question 9A.13	Product costing v TA

Learning outcome B1(b)

Here are some statements about traditional product costing. Provide the equivalent statements about throughput accounting.

Statement 1: Inventory is valued in the financial statements at full production cost.
Statement 2: Labour, material and variable overheads are treated as variable costs.

Statement 3:   A process is deemed efficient if labour and machine time are fully utilised.

Statement 4:   Value is added when a unit of product is produced.

10.8 Differences between throughput accounting and traditional product cost systems

Traditional product costing	Throughput accounting
Labour costs and 'traditional' variable overheads are treated as variable costs.	They are not normally treated as variable costs.
Inventory is valued in the income statement and balance sheet at total production cost.	Inventory is valued at material cost only.
Variance analysis is employed to determine whether standards were achieved.	Variance analysis is used to determine why the planned product mix was not produced.
Efficiency is based on labour and machines working to full capacity.	Efficiency requires schedule adherence and meeting delivery dates.
Value is added when an item is produced.	Value is added when an item is sold.

Section summary

The concept of **throughput accounting (TA)** has been developed from TOC as an alternative system of cost and management accounting in a JIT environment.

TA is based on three concepts.

- In the short run, most costs in the factory (with the exception of materials costs) are fixed.
- The ideal inventory level is zero.
- Profitability is determined by the rate at which sales are made.

The TA philosophy entails the identification and elimination of **bottleneck resources**.

Throughput measures include **return per time period, return per time period on the bottleneck resource** and the **TA ratio**.

Chapter Roundup

- ✓ **Costing systems** have evolved to reflect a **manufacturing philosophy** that is based on the need to achieve **competitive advantage**.

  - Flexibility and the ability to respond quickly to customer demands are vital.
  - Product life cycles are shorter and products must be brought to the market quickly.
  - New technology has been introduced.

- ✓ In the context of **total quality management**, 'quality' means getting it right first time, and improving continuously.

- ✓ The **main focus** of TQM is **100% satisfaction** of both internal and external customers through the **continuous improvement** of all activities and processes.

- ✓ **Key elements of TQM** include preventing the cause of defects in the first place (rather than relying on inspecting to a predefined level of quality) and aiming towards an environment of zero defects at minimum cost.

- ✓ TQM promotes the concept of the **internal customer** and **internal supplier**.

- ✓ **Workers** themselves are frequently the best source of information about how (or how not) to improve **quality**.

- ✓ **Quality costs** can be analysed into **prevention, appraisal, internal failure** and **external failure** costs and should be detailed in a **cost of quality report.**

- ✓ The essence of **continuous improvement** is the use of an organisation's human resources to produce a constant stream of improvements in all aspects of customer value, including quality, functional design, and timely delivery, while lowering cost at the same time.

- ✓ The aim of **Kaizen costing** is to reduce current costs by using various tools such as value analysis and functional analysis.

- ✓ **Business process re-engineering** involves focusing attention inwards to consider how business processes can be redesigned or re-engineered to improve efficiency.

- ✓ **Just-in-time** is an approach to operations planning and control based on the idea that **goods and services should be produced only when they are needed**, and neither too early (so that inventories build up) nor too late (so that the customer has to wait).

- ✓ **Just-in-time** systems **challenge** 'traditional' views of manufacturing.

- ✓ JIT consists of **JIT purchasing** and **JIT production.**

- ✓ **Elimination of waste, involvement of all staff** and **continuous improvement** are the three key elements in the JIT philosophy.

- ✓ JIT aims to **eliminate all non-value-added costs**.

- ✓ **Backflush accounting** is a method of accounting that can be used with JIT production systems. It saves a considerable amount of time as it avoids having to make a number of accounting entries that are required by the traditional system.

- ✓ **Theory of constraints (TOC)** is a set of concepts which aim to identify the binding constraints in a production system and which strive for evenness of production flow so that the organisation works as effectively as possible. No inventory should be held, except prior to the binding constraint.

- ✓ The concept of **throughput accounting (TA)** has been developed from TOC as an alternative system of cost and management accounting in a JIT environment.

✓ **TA is based on three concepts**.

  – In the short run, most costs in the factory (with the exception of materials costs) are fixed.
  – The ideal inventory level is zero.
  – Profitability is determined by the rate at which sales are made.

✓ The TA philosophy entails the identification and elimination of **bottleneck resources**.

✓ Throughput measures include **return per time period, return per time period on the bottleneck resource** and the **TA ratio**.

Quick Quiz

1   What four key words/phrases describe modern manufacturing philosophy?

2   The cost of inspecting a product for quality is a value-added cost. *True or false?*

3   Which of the following is/are correct?

(a)   Cost of conformance = cost of prevention + cost of internal failure
(b)   Cost of conformance = cost of internal failure + cost of external failure
(c)   Cost of non-conformance = cost of internal failure + cost of external failure
(d)   Cost of conformance = cost of appraisal + cost of prevention
(e)   Cost of non-conformance = cost of prevention + cost of appraisal
(f)   Cost of non-conformance = cost of appraisal + cost of external failure

4   *Match the cost to the correct cost category.*

Costs

(a)   Administration of quality control
(b)   Product liability costs
(c)   Acceptance testing
(d)   Losses due to lower selling prices for sub-quality goods

Cost categories

●   Prevention costs
●   Appraisal costs
●   Internal failure costs
●   External failure costs

5   *Choose the appropriate words from those highlighted.*

JIT purchasing requires **small, frequent/large, infrequent** deliveries **well in advance of/as near as possible to** the time the raw materials and parts are needed.

In a JIT environment, the responsibility for the quality of goods lies with the **supplier/purchaser.**

6   Choose the correct words from those highlighted.

(a)   Backflush accounting is a cost accounting system which focuses on the (1) **input/output** of an organisation and then works (2) **forwards/backwards** to allocate costs between cost of goods sold and inventory.

(b)   The point at which a physical activity causes an entry in the accounts which flushes out cost in a backflush system is known as the (3) **trigger point/bottleneck**.

7   *Fill in the blanks in the statements below, using the words in the box. Some words may be used twice.*

    (a)   The theory of constraints is an approach to production management which aims to maximise (1)............. less (2)......... . It focuses on factors such as (3)............... which act as (4)....................

    (b)   Throughput contribution = (5)............. minus (6) ....

    (c)   TA ratio = (7) .... per factory hour ÷ (8) ....per factory hour

- bottlenecks
- material costs
- sales revenue
- throughput contribution
- constraints
- conversion cost

8   Put a tick in the boxes of those statements that relate to Kaizen costing, and a cross for statements about standard costing.

☐   Employees are often viewed as the cause of problems.

☐   Costs are reduced by implementing continuous improvement.

☐   The aim is to meet cost performance targets.

☐   The aim is to achieve cost reduction targets.

☐   It is assumed that current manufacturing conditions remain unchanged.

9   Continuous improvement organisations never engage in radical change. *True or false?*

10   *Fill in the right hand side of the table below, which looks at the differences between throughput accounting and traditional product costing.*

Traditional product costing	Throughput accounting
Labour costs and 'traditional' variable overheads are treated as variable costs.	
Inventory is valued in the income statement and balance sheet at total production cost.	
Variance analysis is employed to determine whether standards were achieved.	
Efficiency is based on labour and machines working to full capacity.	
Value is added when an item is produced.	

11   BPR can be likened to continuous budgeting. *True or false?*

Answers to Quick Quiz

1. (a) Smooth, steady production flow (throughput)
   (b) Flexibility
   (c) Volume versus variety
   (d) JIT

2. False

3. (c) and (d) are correct.

4. (a) Prevention costs
   (b) External failure costs
   (c) Appraisal costs
   (d) Internal failure costs

5. small, frequent
   as near as possible to
   supplier

6. 1 output
   2 backwards
   3 trigger point

7. 1 sales revenue
   2 material costs
   3 bottlenecks
   4 constraints
   5 sales revenue
   6 material costs
   7 throughput contribution
   8 conversion cost

8. ✗ Employees are often viewed as the cause of problems.

   ✓ Costs are reduced by implementing continuous improvement.

   ✗ The aim is to meet cost performance targets.

   ✓ The aim is to achieve cost reduction targets.

   ✗ It is assumed that current manufacturing conditions remain unchanged.

9. False. Quantum leaps in performance can occur.

10.

Traditional product costing	Throughput accounting
Labour costs and 'traditional' variable overheads are treated as variable costs.	They are not normally treated as variable costs.
Inventory is valued in the income statement and balance sheet at total production cost.	It is valued at material cost only.
Variance analysis is employed to determine whether standards were achieved.	It is used to determine why the planned product mix was not produced.
Efficiency is based on labour and machines working to full capacity.	Efficiency requires schedule adherence and meeting delivery dates.
Value is added when an item is produced.	It is added when an item is sold.

11. False. It is somewhat akin to ZBB.

Answers to Questions

9A.1 Long production run costs

If production runs become longer:

Manufacturing costs per unit that will fall:	Stockholding costs per unit that will rise:
Production scheduling costs	Space costs
Set-up costs	Labour costs
Waiting time/costs	Insurance costs
Purchasing costs	Interest charges
Labour costs	

9A.2 Interruptions to a stage in production 1

As inventory is held between each stage, the other stages in the production process would not be immediately affected. Stages 3 and 4 would use the inventories of WIP from stages 2 and 3 and stage 1 would continue to produce inventory for stage 2. There is no immediate urgency to rectify the problem – the responsibility for doing so lies with the manager of stage 2.

9A.3 Quality

A wide variety of answers is possible. The article goes on to explain how the bank is actually going about monitoring the impact of the initiative.

(a)   It has devised a 100 point scale showing average satisfaction with branch service.

(b)   It conducts a 'first impressions' survey of all new customers.

(c)   There is also a general survey carried out every six months which seeks the views of a weighted sample of 350 customers per branch.

(d)   A survey company telephones each branch anonymously twice a month to test how staff respond to enquiries about products.

(e)   A quarter of each branch's staff answer a monthly questionnaire about the bank's products to test their knowledge.

(f)   Groups of employees working in teams in branches are allowed to set their own additional standards. This is to encourage participation.

(g)   Branches that underperform are more closely watched by 24 managers who monitor the initiative.

9A.4 Ignoring quality issues

In an economic downturn companies are **anxious to hold onto existing business** and perhaps secure new business from competitors. **Quality** becomes even **more important** as it is very much a **customer's market** – if customers are not happy with any aspect of the product or service they can go elsewhere.

Although maintaining and improving quality is expensive, it should be seen as an **investment** in the company's long-term future. If companies lose contracts due to reductions in quality their reputation will be damaged (particularly if they were previously known for excellent quality). Ultimately they could go out of business altogether.

9A.5 Quality costs

(a) **Failure of the current accounting system to highlight the cost of quality**

Traditionally, **the costs of scrapped units, wasted materials and reworking** have been **subsumed within the costs of production** by assigning the costs of an expected level of loss (a normal loss) to the costs of good production, while accounting for **other costs of poor quality** within **production or marketing overheads**. Such costs are therefore not only considered as **inevitable** but are not **highlighted** for management attention. Moreover, traditional accounting reports tend to **ignore the hidden but real costs of excessive inventory levels** (held to enable faulty material to be replaced without hindering production) and the facilities necessary for storing that **inventory**.

(b) **Explicit costs of quality**

There are four recognised categories of cost identifiable within an accounting system which make up the cost of quality.

(1) **Prevention costs** are the costs of any action taken to investigate, prevent or reduce the production of faulty output. Included within this category are the costs of training in quality control and the cost of the design/development and maintenance of quality control and inspection equipment.

(2) **Appraisal costs** are the costs of assessing the actual quality achieved. Examples include the cost of the inspection of goods delivered and the cost of inspecting production during the manufacturing process.

(3) **Internal failure costs** are the costs incurred by the organisation when production fails to meet the level of quality required. Such costs include losses due to lower selling prices for sub-quality goods, the costs of reviewing product specifications after failures and losses arising from the failure of purchased items.

(4) **External failure costs** are the costs which arise outside the organisation (after the customer has received the product) due to failure to achieve the required level of quality. Included within this category are the costs of repairing products returned from customers, the cost of providing replacement items due to sub-standard products or marketing errors and the costs of a customer service department.

(c) **Quality costs not identified by the accounting system**

Quality costs which are not identified by the accounting system tend to be of two forms.

(1) Opportunity costs such as the loss of future sales to a customer dissatisfied with faulty goods.

(2) Costs which tend to be subsumed within other account headings such as those costs which result from the disruption caused by stockouts due to faulty purchases.

9A.6 Interruptions to a stage in production 2

As a JIT system holds little or no inventories, the disruption would have an immediate effect. Stages 3 and 4 would have to be suspended as there is no input from stage 2. Stage 1 would have to stop producing as stage 2 will not be able to use its output. There is much greater urgency to rectify the problem at stage 2 as it has brought production to a standstill.

9A.7 Non-value-added activities

The correct answer is:

Parts received	Machined parts assembled
~~Parts quality inspected~~	~~Finished product inspected and tested~~
~~Parts stored in warehouse~~	~~Finished goods passed to despatch department~~
~~Parts moved to machine room~~	Finished goods packaged

Parts machined	~~Packed goods moved back to warehouse~~
~~Machined parts inspected~~	~~Packed goods stored~~
~~Machined parts moved to assembly area~~	Packed goods despatched to customer

Comment

The JIT approach has five value-added activities, compared with 14 activities under the traditional approach – nine non-value-added activities have been eliminated.

Receipt of parts, their machining, assembly, packaging and despatch to the customer are essential activities that increase the saleability of the product.

Solo needs to negotiate with its suppliers to guarantee the delivery of high quality parts to eliminate the need for quality inspection on arrival.

Storage and movement of parts, work in progress and finished goods do not add value; rather they introduce unnecessary delays. The machining, assembly and packaging areas should be in close proximity to avoid excessive movement, and ordering and processing should be scheduled so that there is no need to store parts before they go into production. Similarly, production should be scheduled to finish goods just as they are needed for despatch to avoid storage of finished goods.

Proper maintenance of machinery and good staff training in quality production procedures should ensure finished goods of a consistently high quality, removing the need for inspection and testing.

Thus the JIT approach eliminates all wastage of time in the storage of goods, unnecessary movement of goods and all quality checks, resulting in one continuous string of value-added activities.

9A.8 Value-added activity

The correct answer is C. The other activities are non-value-adding activities.

9A.9 JIT

(a) **Cost reduction**. Toyota was losing money, and market demand was weak, preventing price rises. The only way to move from losses into profits was to cut costs, and cost reduction was probably essential for the survival of the company.

(b) **Production levelling**. Production levelling should help to minimise idle time whilst at the same time allowing the company to achieve its objective of minimum inventories.

(c) The **change in factory layout** was to improve the work flow and eliminate the waste of moving items around the work floor from one set of machines to another. Each cell contained all the machines required to complete production, thus eliminating unnecessary materials movements.

(d) With having **cells of different machines**, workers in each work cell would have to be trained to use each different machine, whereas previously they would have specialised in just one type of machine.

(e) A **change of culture** was needed to overcome the industrial problems of the company. Employee involvement would have been an element in this change. Teamwork would have helped with the elimination of waste: mistakes or delays by one member of a team would be corrected or dealt with by others in the team. The work force moved from a sense of individual responsibility/blame to collective responsibility.

(f) The **kanban system** is a 'pull' system of production scheduling. Items are only produced when they are needed. If a part is faulty when it is produced, the production line will be held up until the fault is corrected. For a kanban system to work properly, defects must therefore be eliminated.

9A.10 JIT manufacturing environment

The correct answer is: 1, 2, 3 and 4.

9A.11 TA v conventional cost accounting

Conventional cost accounting	Throughput accounting
Inventory is an asset.	Inventory is *not* an asset. It is a result of unsynchronised manufacturing and is a barrier to making profit.
Costs can be classified either as direct or indirect.	Such classifications are no longer useful.
Product profitability can be determined by deducting a product cost from selling price.	Profitability is determined by the rate at which money is earned.
Profit is a function of costs.	Profit is a function of throughput as well as costs.

9A.12 Performance measurement in throughput accounting

(a)   Total profit per day

$$= \text{Throughput contribution} - \text{Conversion costs}$$
$$= (3{,}600 \times (100 - 40) - 144{,}000)$$
$$= \$72{,}000$$

(b)   Return per factory hour

$$= \frac{\text{Sales} - \text{direct material costs}}{\text{Usage of bottleneck resource in hours (factory hours)}}$$

$$= \frac{100 - 40}{1/500}$$

$$= \$30{,}000$$

(c)   Throughput accounting ratio

$$= \frac{\text{Return per factory hour}}{\text{Total conversion cost per factory hour}}$$

$$= \frac{30{,}000}{144{,}000/8}$$

$$= 1.67$$

9A.13 Product costing v TA

1   Inventory is valued at material cost only (ie variable cost).
2   Only direct material is treated as a variable cost.
3   Effectiveness is measured in terms of schedule adherence and meeting delivery dates.
4   Value is added when an item is sold.

Now try the question from the Exam Question Bank

Number	Level	Marks	Time
Q23	Examination	25	45 mins

COST MANAGEMENT TECHNIQUES 2

In the final chapter of this part of the syllabus we look at some **externally-orientated** management accounting techniques and how they can be **used to derive competitive advantage**.

The techniques in this chapter consider how the organisation interacts with suppliers and customers.

9B

topic list	learning outcomes	syllabus references	ability required
1 The value chain	B1(j)	B1(viii)	analysis
2 Supply chain management	B1(j)	B1(viii)	analysis
3 Outsourcing	B1(j)	B1(viii)	analysis
4 Partnering, incentives and gain-sharing arrangements	B1(k)	B1(ix)	analysis

1 The value chain

Introduction

This section focuses on the value chain which is a model of the activities of an organisation.

1.1 Basic concepts

According to Porter, the **activities of any organisation** can be divided into nine types and **analysed into a value chain**. This is a model of the activities (which procure inputs, process them and add value to them in some way, to generate outputs for customers) and the relationships between them.

KEY TERM

The VALUE CHAIN is 'The sequence of business activities by which, from the perspective of the end user, value is added to the products and services produced by an entry.'   (CIMA *Official Terminology*)

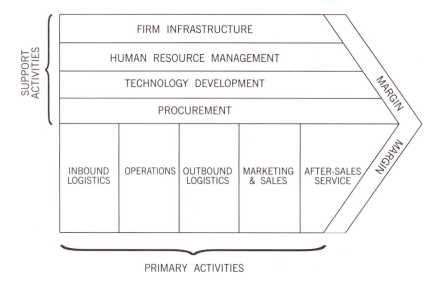

1.2 Activities

KEY TERM

ACTIVITIES are the means by which an organisation creates value in its products.

It is important to realise that **business activities are not the same as business functions**.

(a) Functions are the familiar departments of an organisation (production, finance and so on). They reflect the formal organisation structure and the distribution of labour.

(b) Activities are what actually goes on, and the work that is done. A single activity can be performed by a number of functions in sequence. Activities are the means by which an organisation creates value in its products. (They are sometimes referred to as value activities). Activities incur costs and, in combination with other activities, provide a product or service that earns revenue.

For example, most organisations need to secure resources from the environment. This activity can be called procurement. Procurement will involve more departments than purchasing, however; the accounts department will certainly be involved and possibly production and quality assurance.

1.2.1 Primary activities

Primary activities are directly related to production, sales, marketing, delivery and service.

	Comment
Inbound logistics	Receiving, handling and storing inputs to the production system (warehousing, transport, inventory control and so on)
Operations	Converting resource inputs into a final product. Resource inputs are not only materials. 'People' are a 'resource' especially in service industries.
Outbound logistics	Storing the product and its distribution to customers (packaging, warehousing, testing and so on)
Marketing and sales	Informing customers about the product, persuading them to buy it, and enabling them to do so (advertising, promotion and so on)
After sales service	Installing products, repairing them, upgrading them, providing spare parts and so on

1.2.2 Support activities

Support activities provide purchased inputs, human resources, technology and infrastructural functions to support the primary activities.

	Comment
Procurement	Acquiring the resource inputs to the primary activities (such as purchase of materials, subcomponents equipment)
Technology development	Designing products, improving processes and/or resource utilisation
Human resource management	Recruiting, training, developing and rewarding people
Firm infrastructure	Planning, finance, quality control (Porter believes they are crucially important to an organisation's strategic capability in all primary activities.)

1.3 The value chain in non-manufacturing environments

The diagram below shows an alternative value chain in non-manufacturing environments.

The value chain asserts that whilst excellence in manufacturing is essential for success it is not sufficient to guarantee success.

All business factors should still add value and can run consecutively and concurrently. Value can also be added by the way in which these activities are **linked**.

(a)   R&D – new ideas for products, services or processes
(b)   Design – planning and engineering
(c)   Production – coordination and assembly of resources to produce a product
(d)   Marketing – teaching customers about products and persuading them to purchase
(e)   Distribution – delivery to customers
(f)   Customer service – support to customers

1.4 Creating value

An organisation is profitable if the realised value to customers exceeds the collective cost of performing the activities.

(a) **Customers 'purchase' value**, which they measure by comparing an organisation's products and services with similar offerings by competitors.

(b) **An organisation 'creates' value** by carrying out its activities either more efficiently than other organisations, or by combining them in such a way as to provide a unique product or service. We return to this point below.

Question 9B.1	Creating value

Learning outcome B1(j)

Outline different ways in which a restaurant can 'create' value.

1.5 The focus of the value chain

This contrasts with **traditional management accounting**, which takes a value-added perspective, which has a focus largely **internal** to the organisation, each organisation being viewed in relation to its purchases, its processes, its functions, its products, its customers.

1.6 Value system

Activities that add value do not stop at the organisation's boundaries. For example, when a restaurant serves a meal, the quality of the ingredients – although they are chosen by the cook – is determined by the grower. The grower has added value, and the grower's success in growing produce of good quality is as important to the customer's ultimate satisfaction as the skills of the chef. An **organisation's value chain** is **connected** to what Porter calls a **value system**.

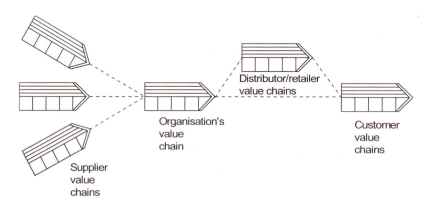

1.7 Linkages

Linkages **connect the activities of the value chain**. Linkages might be with suppliers or with customers, or within the organisation itself.

(a)   Activities in the value chain affect one another.

   (i)   More costly product design or better quality production might reduce the need for after-sales service and post-purchase costs for customers. Designing a product to reduce post-purchase costs can be a major weapon in **capturing competitive advantage**.

   (ii)   JIT requires close partnerships with suppliers. Its introduction might save an organisation storage costs, say, but production schedule instability for suppliers might cause them to raise their prices.

(b)   Linkages require **co-ordination**. Unlike the value-added concept, value chain analysis explicitly recognises the fact that various activities within an organisation are **interdependent**. There is little point in a fast-food chain running a promotional campaign (one value activity) if there is insufficient capacity within 'production' (another value activity) to cope with the increased demand. These linked activities must be coordinated if the full effect of the promotion is to be realised.

Beneficial linkages are linkages with customers or suppliers that are managed in such a way that all parties benefit.

1.8 The value chain and competitive advantage

According to Porter, an organisation can develop sustainable competitive advantage by following one of two strategies.

(a)   **Low-cost strategy.** Essentially this is a strategy of cost leadership, which involves achieving a lower cost than competitors via, for example, economies of scale and tight cost control. Hyundai (in cars) and Timex (wrist watches) are examples of organisations that have followed such a strategy.

(b)   **Differentiation strategy.** This involves creating something that customers perceive as being unique via brand loyalty, superior customer service, product design and features, technology and so on. Mercedes Benz (in cars) and Rolex (wrist watches) are examples of organisations that have followed such a strategy.

As **competitive advantage** is gained either from providing **better customer value for equivalent cost** or **equivalent customer value for lower cost**, value chain analysis is essential to determine **where in an organisation's value chain costs can be lowered or value enhanced**.

1.8.1 Strategic cost management and the value chain

Shank and Govindarajan explained how an organisation's value chain can be used with a view to lowering costs and enhancing value: '.. the value chain framework is a method for breaking down the chain – from basic raw materials to end-use customers – into strategically relevant activities to understand the behaviour of costs and the sources of differentiation'.

They suggest a three-step approach.

 Build up the industry's value chain to determine the various activities in the value chain and to allocate operating costs, revenues and assets to individual value activities. (It is vital to understand the entire value chain, not just the portion of the chain in which the organisation participates. Suppliers and distribution channels have profit margins that impact on an organisation's cost or differentiation positioning, because the final customer has to pay for all the profit margins throughout the value chain.)

 Establish the cost drivers of the costs of each value activity, which are one of two types.

(a) **Structural cost drivers.** These are derived from an organisation's decisions about its underlying economic structure and include:

    (i) Scale of operations (giving rise to economies or diseconomies of scale)
    (ii) Scope (degree of vertical integration)
    (iii) Experience (has the organisation climbed the learning curve?)
    (iv) Technology used in the value chain
    (v) Complexity (number of products/services being sold)

(b) **Executional cost drivers.** These relate to an organisation's ability to deliver the product/service successfully to the customer. According to Shank and Govindarajan, the 'more' of these cost drivers there is, the better. Basic examples include:

    (i) Employee participation
    (ii) TQM
    (iii) Capacity utilisation
    (iv) Plant layout efficiency
    (v) Product configuration
    (vi) Linkages with suppliers or customers

 Develop sustainable competitive advantage, by controlling these drivers better than competitors or by configuring the value chain. For each value activity, **sustainable competitive advantage can be developed by reducing costs whilst maintaining value (sales) and/or increasing value (sales) whilst maintaining costs**.

(a) **Cost reduction.** Compare the value chain of the organisation with the value chain of one or two major competitors, then identify the action required to manage the organisation's value chain better than competitors manage theirs.

(b) **Increasing value.** Identify where in the value chain payoffs could be significant.

1.8.2 Example: using the value chain in competitive strategy

The examples below are based on two supermarket chains, **one concentrating on low prices**, the **other differentiated on quality and service**. See if you can tell which is which.

(a)

Firm infrastructure	Minimum corporate HQ				
Human resource management		De-skilled store operatives	Dismissal for checkout error		
Technology development	Computerised warehousing		Checkouts simple		
Procurement	Branded only purchases Big discounts	Low cost sites			Use of concessions
	Bulk warehousing	1,000 lines only Price points Basic store design		Low price promotion Local focus	Nil
	INBOUND LOGISTICS	OPERATIONS	OUTBOUND LOGISTICS	MARKETING & SALES	SERVICE

(b)

Firm infrastructure	Central control of operations and credit control				
Human resource management	Recruitment of mature staff	Client care training	Flexible staff to help with packing		
Technology development		Recipe research	Electronic point of sale	Consumer research and tests	Itemised bills
Procurement	Own label products	Prime retail positions		Adverts in quality magazines	
	Dedicated refrigerated transport	In store food halls Modern store design Open front refrigerators Tight control of sell-by dates	Collect by car service	No price discounts on food past sell-by dates	No quibble refunds
	INBOUND LOGISTICS	OPERATIONS	OUTBOUND LOGISTICS	MARKETING & SALES	SERVICE

The two supermarkets represented are based on the following.

(a)   The value chain in (a) is similar to that of Lidl, a 'discount' supermarket chain which sells on price. This can be seen in the limited product range and its low-cost sites.

(b)   The value chain in (b) is based on Marks and Spencer, which seeks to differentiate on quality and service. Hence the 'no quibble' refunds, the use of prime retail sites, and customer care training.

CASE STUDY

'By comparing two organisations from the computer retail sector we can observe the strategic choices that organisations make. Dell chooses to use the Internet and telesales as the main channels for its marketing and sales activity, and uses distributors to fulfil its outbound logistics. PC World uses shops as well as the Internet. Both firms employ sales staff, but PC World, consistent with its decision to use retail outlets, has identified that its target customers value the personal touch, so it has chosen to employ trained staff (HR management activity) who can deal with them face to face. Its TV advertising (marketing and sales activity) emphasises this expert personal service as a benefit (differentiating factor) of shopping at PC World.

Compare this approach with that of a retailer such as Ikea, which believes that its target customers do not place a high value on personal customer service and has therefore decided against employing large numbers of sales staff. This allows it to keep employment costs down, supporting its low-cost strategy and its position in the market. Note that competitive advantage and what the customer values are the factors that have driven the decision.'

(Graham Pitcher, 'The Missing Link', CIMA *Insider*)

| **Question 9B.2** | Value chain analysis v conventional management accounting |

Learning outcome B1(j)

Compare and contrast value chain analysis with conventional management accounting by completing the table below.

	Traditional management accounting	Value chain analysis
Focus		
Perspective		
Cost driver concept		
Cost containment philosophy		
Insights for strategic decisions		

Section summary

The **value chain model**, developed by Michael Porter, offers a bird's eye view of an organisation, of what it does and the way in which its business activities are organised.

Activities or **value activities** can be categorised as **primary** or **support**.

The ultimate **value** an organisation creates is measured by the amount customers are willing to pay for its products and services above the cost of carrying out value activities.

The **focus of the value chain** is **external to the organisation**, each organisation being viewed in the context of the overall chain of value-creating activities of which it is only a part, from basic raw materials to end-use consumers.

An organisation's ability to develop and sustain **cost leadership** or **product differentiation**, and hence **gain competitive advantage**, depends on how well it manages its own value chain relative to competitors.

2 Supply chain management

Introduction

This section focuses on how and where a business operates in the supply chain and the ways in which the supply chain can be managed.

2.1 The supply chain

KEY TERM

A SUPPLY CHAIN is a network of facilities and distribution options that performs the functions of procurement of materials, transformation of these materials into intermediate and finished products and the distribution of these finished products to customers.

(Ganeshan and Harrison, *Supply Chain Management*).

Within a supply chain, many processes might take place between the origination of raw materials to the eventual delivery of the finished product or service to the end customer. For each organisation inside a supply chain, some of the processes are carried out by the organisation itself, and others are carried out by suppliers or by other organisations further down the supply chain.

CASE STUDY

For example, a company manufacturing motor vehicles might have a plant where the vehicles are assembled and finished. It might manufacture some parts itself and produce the car body work, but most sub-assemblies and the tyres will be purchased from outside suppliers. The suppliers of sub-assemblies might make some components themselves, but will also purchase many of their components from other suppliers. The manufacturer, suppliers and sub-suppliers might all purchase raw materials, such as steel, from other suppliers. The manufacturer will also purchase capital equipment from equipment suppliers, who are another part of the supply chain. The finished cars will not be sold directly to the end customer, but to distributors, and the distributors will sell to the end customer.

2.2 The concept of supply chain management

If there is a **given amount of profit** in a particular market for a finished product, this profit will be **shared out between all the organisations involved in the supply chain**. In this sense, suppliers and their customers **compete** with each other for **a bigger share of the available profit**. This 'traditional' **adversarial arms' length** attitude is evident in negotiations between an organisation and its suppliers, and efforts by the organisation to get the best terms possible and the lowest prices in their purchasing negotiations.

This view of the supply chain is **challenged by** the concept of **supply chain management**.

KEY TERM

SUPPLY CHAIN MANAGEMENT looks at the supply chain as a whole, and starts with the view that all organisations in the supply chain collaborate to produce something of value for the end customer.

This has two advantages.

(a)   By **adding value** within the supply chain, **customer satisfaction** will be **improved** and **customers** will **pay more** for what they buy.

(b)   **Organisations can also benefit collectively by reducing waste and inefficiency**. A lot of **wasteful activity** (activity that does not add any value to the final product) **occurs at the interface between organisations within the supply chain**. For example, a supplier might spend money on checking outwards supplies for quality, and the same goods will be checked by the organisation buying them when they are delivered. Inspection costs could be reduced by closer collaboration between the organisations, both to improve quality and to reduce inspection activities.

By looking at the supply chain as a collaborative effort, managers can look for ways of enhancing the profitability of the supply chain as a whole, so that everyone, including the end customer, benefits.

2.2.1 Developing relationships

Developing strong relationships is not an easy task, however. The arms' length supplier-purchaser relationship has been based on both sides winning as much short-term gain as possible, and so sharing sensitive information and developing long-term ties is often difficult.

There are a number of practices which can be used to foster improved relationships with key suppliers.

(a)   **Power balancing** occurs if the proportion of a supplier's total output that is sold to a customer roughly equals the proportion of total purchases acquired by the customer from that supplier. Maintaining relative dependence between suppliers and buyers increases the likelihood that both parties will have a vested interest in the success of the other.

(b)   **Codependency.** When a supplier commits substantial specialised resources to meeting the demands of a purchaser and the purchaser chooses to single-source from that supplier, both parties have a vested interest in the success of the purchaser.

(c)   **Target costing.** Suppliers can be rewarded when targets are reached.

(d)   **Personal ties.** The establishment of teams of employees from both supplier and purchaser helps foster good working relationships and develop trust.

CASE STUDY

'To design vehicle and production systems [for the M-class], Mercedes Benz US International used *function groups* that included representatives from every area of the company.... The role of these function groups was to develop specifications and cost projections.

Mercedes included suppliers early in the design stage of the vehicle. By including suppliers as members of the function groups, Mercedes was able to take advantage of their expertise and advice on matters such as supplier capability, cost and quality. The synergy generated by these cross-function groups also allowed the groups to solve larger design issues, such as how to more efficiently and economically switch from manufacturing left-side-drive vehicles to right-side-vehicles. Significant time savings were recognised because of the design improvements implemented by the function groups. Because supplier personnel were at the Mercedes plant on a full-time basis during the launch, other issues (such as quality problems or slight modifications to the product) could be addressed in a more timely fashion.'

(Albright and Davis, 'The Elements of Supply Chain Management', *International Journal of Strategic Cost Management*)

KEY TERM

SUPPLY CHAIN MANAGEMENT (or PIPELINE MANAGEMENT or VALUE STREAM MANAGEMENT) views all the buyers and sellers in this chain as part of a continuum, and the aim should be to look at the supply chain as a whole and seek to optimise the functioning of the entire chain. In other words, a company should look beyond its immediate suppliers and its immediate customers to add value, for example by improving efficiency and eliminating waste.

2.2.2 Adding value

The overall supply chain can be thought of as a **sequence of operations, each of which should add value**. An activity has value if it gives the customer something that the customer considers worth having (ie values), but an activity only adds value if the amount of value added exceeds the cost of creating it. Value is therefore added by making something worth more (in terms of the price the customer will pay, or the quality the customer perceives) or by reducing the cost of the operation (without sacrificing quality).

2.3 Elements of supply chain management

To apply the concept of supply chain management fully, there has to be **close collaboration** between organisations within the supply chain. A company must be able to work constructively with its suppliers. At the same time, it should continually **look for ways of improving the supply chain structure**, and this could involve switching to **different suppliers**, or selling **output through new channels**. The **Internet** has opened up new possibilities for identifying new suppliers worldwide and for **selling direct to customers** instead of through distributors.

There is no single model for the ideal supply chain, and supply chain management can involve:

(a)   Decisions about improving collaboration with suppliers by sharing information and through the joint development of new products

(b)   Switching to new suppliers by purchasing on-line

(c)   Outsourcing some activities that were previously performed in-house

2.4 Issues facing supply chain managers

2.4.1 Production

The customer often wants suppliers to respond to their particular requirements, and to customise orders to their specific needs. A supply chain that can **respond quickly to individual customer requirements** is known as an **'agile' supply chain**.

Issues for management include deciding **what** products or components to make, and **where** to make them. Should the production of components, sub-assemblies or even the final product be done in-house or by external suppliers?

Management **focus** is on **capacity**, **quality** and **order volume**. Production has to be scheduled so as to provide a sufficient workload for the production resources, and to achieve work load balance (so as to avoid both production bottlenecks and under-utilisation of resources). Quality control is an issue, because producing poor-quality output has implications for both cost and customer dissatisfaction.

The **challenge** is to **meet customer orders immediately**, **without** having to invest heavily in **inventories** of finished goods, which are wasteful and expensive.

2.4.2 Supply

Most manufacturing companies cannot make everything themselves and still keep the quality of their output high. Decisions have to be made about how much should be purchased from 'outside'. Some companies have chosen to **close in-house production facilities** and **switch to external suppliers**, so that they can **concentrate on their 'core competences' where they add most value**.

In choosing external suppliers, management need to consider the capabilities of the supplier, and the extent to which a close collaboration will be necessary. (Collaboration is much more important for key supplies, and much less important for low-cost general supplies that can be purchased from numerous sources.) **Distinctive competences** of supplier and the organisation should be **similar**. An organisation selling 'cheap and cheerful goods' will want suppliers who are able to supply 'cheap and cheerful' subcomponents. The management focus should be on the **speed, quality and flexibility of supply**, as well as on cost.

2.4.3 Inventory

If a firm holds large amounts of inventory, it should be able to meet many customer orders immediately out of inventory and should not suffer hold-ups due to inventory shortages. Holding inventory is expensive, however, and there is no certainty that finished goods inventories will ever find a customer, unless they have been made to satisfy specific customer orders. **Ideally, inventory levels should be minimised, but without damaging the ability of the firm to meet customer orders quickly or holding up work flow due to a stock-out of key supplies**.

In managing inventory levels, organisations need to know, with as much certainty as possible, the **lead time** for delivery of supplies and for the production of goods. Unknown lead times increase the chance of too little or too much inventory, both of which are costly for organisations.

2.4.4 Location

Decisions need to be made about where to locate production facilities and warehousing facilities. Cost and tax issues might result in production facilities being constructed in **emerging market economies**.

2.4.5 Transportation

Logistics management is another aspect of supply chain management. Supplies need to be delivered to a firm's premises and finished goods delivered to customers **efficiently, reliably** and at a **low cost**.

2.4.6 Information

Information resources throughout the supply chain need to be **linked together**, for speed of information exchange and to reduce wasteful paper work. Some firms link their computer networks, or share information through the Internet.

2.4.7 Overall management

Managing the supply chain therefore calls for an **understanding of** and **knowledge about**:

(a)   **Customer demand patterns**
(b)   **Service level requirements** (speed of delivery expectations, quality expectations, and so on)
(c)   **Distance considerations** (logistics)
(d)   **Cost**

2.5 Using information and technology

A firm can **share** its **information** about expected customer demand and orders in the pipeline, so that the **suppliers can get ready** themselves for orders that might come to them from the firm. 'Modern' supply chain management uses the **Internet** to share information as soon as it is available. A firm might have an integrated **enterprise resource planning (ERP)** system sitting on a web site or on a server running on the internet. The ERP runs the supply chain database, holding information about a wide range of items, such as customer orders, inventory levels, pricing structures and so on.

The use of EDI, Internet technology and software applications means that **suppliers know what a customer needs before the customer asks**. A supplier that 'knows' what his customers want does not have to guess or wait until the customer places an order. It will be able to **better plan its own delivery systems**. Technology has made the concept of the **'seamless' supply chain** a reality. The development of creative links with suppliers and customers provides organisations with the chance of **competitive advantage over competitors unwilling or unable to invest the time and resources in improving their supply chains**.

A critical issue for successful supply chain management is the **speed** with which activities can be carried out and customer demands met. If a firm, helped by its suppliers and sub-suppliers in the chain, can **respond quickly and flexibly** to customer requirements, the benefits will come from **lower inventories, lower operating costs, better product availability and greater customer satisfaction**.

CASE STUDY

Supply chain management and customisation of orders

Personal computer production provides an interesting example of how supply chain management can be used to provide fast delivery of customised products, thereby creating a 'flexible' or 'agile' supply chain.

When customers expect fast delivery of their orders for personal computers, and at the same time want PCs produced to their individual specifications, the parts needed to deliver the item to the customer must exist somewhere within the supply chain. A PC manufacturer operating in a build-to-order market relies on suppliers keeping inventory available, so that the manufacturer can minimise its own inventories without compromising the time needed to deliver the order to the customer. In the case of Dell Computers (reported in a *Financial Times* supplement on supply chain management), Dell itself held about five days' supply and other firms in the supply chain held about ten days' inventory of supplier-owned items. Replenishment of inventories took between 12 hours and two days.

'Build-to-order involves balancing what is available with what the customers want and Dell has become expert in gently massaging both these factors. Any shortage in a particular component is immediately countered by offering other available products on promotion.... By monitoring component inventory availability in real time, Dell and its suppliers can quickly see problems with any particular part. A first step is to increase lead time, informing customers that their preferred configuration will take eight to 10 days to deliver rather than the usual five. If that does not slow up demand, then would-be customers are offered a more expensive upgrade for the same price. "Everyone wins," [says Dell's vice president in the US]. "Our customers get a better deal, the suppliers get business and we can satisfy demand."'

The efficiency of the Dell build-to-order system depends on data sharing between Dell and its suppliers, and the integrity of the information databases. All systems throughout the supply chain are integrated, with common parts numbers and automated order processing and parts management.

Section summary

A **supply chain** is the network of suppliers, manufacturers and distributors that is involved in the process of moving goods for a customer order from the raw materials stage through the production and distribution stages to the customer. Every organisation operates somewhere within a supply chain.

A **commonly-held view** by management is that **to improve profitability** it is necessary to **get the lowest prices from suppliers** and to **obtain the best prices from the customers** next in line down the supply chain.

Supply chain management looks at the supply chain as a whole, and starts with the view that all organisations in the supply chain collaborate to produce something of value for the end customer.

Supply chain managers need to consider **production, supply, inventory, location, transportation and information.**

The **Internet** and **software applications** have had a huge impact on supply chain management.

---

3 Outsourcing

Introduction

A significant trend in recent years has been for organisations and government bodies to **concentrate on their core competences** – what they are really good at (or set up to achieve) – and **turn other activities over to specialist contractors**. This section looks at reasons for this trend and how outsourcing is likely to move forward in the future.

KEY TERM

OUTSOURCING is 'The use of external suppliers as a source of finished products, components or services. This is also known as **contract manufacturing** or **sub-contracting.**   (CIMA *Official Terminology*)

3.1 Reasons for this trend

(a)   Frequently the decision is made on the grounds that **specialist contractors** can offer **superior quality** and **efficiency**. If a contractor's main business is making a specific component it can invest in the specialist machinery and labour and knowledge skills needed to make that component. However, this component may be only one of many needed by the contractor's customer, and the complexity of components is now such that attempting to keep internal facilities up to the standard of specialists detracts from the main business of the customer. For example, Dell Computers buys the Pentium chip for its personal computers from Intel because it does not have the know-how and technology to make the chip itself.

(b)   Contracting out manufacturing **frees capital** that can then be invested in core activities such as market research, product definition, product planning, marketing and sales.

(c)   **Contractors** have the **capacity** and **flexibility** to start production very quickly to meet sudden **variations in demand**. In-house facilities may not be able to respond as quickly, because of the need to redirect resources from elsewhere.

'... chocolate confectionery companies in the UK will sell Easter eggs promoting their brands and products every spring. Mars, for instance, will provide chocolate eggs containing mini Mars products, or in packaging highlighting Mars products around the egg. The reason that you might be tempted to buy one of these eggs is because it has Mars products associated with it. Mars therefore doesn't have to produce the egg itself – that activity can be outsourced. After all, it would be expensive to maintain production facilities for chocolate eggs for only a couple of months a year.

However, you might buy a Cadbury's Easter egg because it is made of Cadbury's chocolate. Therefore Cadbury's needs the operational capability to produce Easter eggs. The company has focused on marketing and sales activities to develop the Cadbury's Creme Egg into a product that is sold all year round, thereby making the operation viable. The decision whether or not to outsource can often be bound strongly to an organisation's competitive strategy and focuses on how strategic the activity is to the organisation.'

(G Pitcher, 'The Missing Link', *CIMA Student*)

3.2 Internal and external services

In administrative and support functions, too, organisations are increasingly likely to use specialist companies. **Decisions** such as the following are now common.

(a)   Whether the **design and development of a new computer system** should be entrusted to in-house data processing staff or whether an external software house should be hired to do the work

(b)   Whether **maintenance and repairs** of certain items of equipment should be dealt with by in-house engineers, or whether a maintenance contract should be made with a specialist organisation

Even if you are not aware of specialist 'facilities management' companies such as Securicor, you will be familiar with the idea of office cleaning being done by contractors.

3.3 Choosing the activities to outsource

Within the value chain, both primary activities and support activities are candidates for outsourcing, although many can be **eliminated** from the list immediately either **because the activity cannot be contracted out or because the organisation must control it to maintain its competitive position**. Coca Cola does not outsource the manufacture of its concentrate to safeguard its formula and retain control of the product.

Of the remaining activities, an organisation **should carry out only those that it can deliver on a level comparable with the best organisations in the world**. If the organisation cannot achieve benchmarked levels of performance, the activity should be outsourced so that the organisation is **only concentrating on those core activities that enhance its competitive advantage**.

A differential cost analysis should then be carried out on outsourcing possibilities. Some argue that this analysis should be over the long term, using discounted cash flow analysis.

3.4 Advantages and disadvantages

The **advantages** of outsourcing are as follows.

(a)   It **frees up time** taken by existing staff on the contracted-out activities.

(b)   It allows the company to **take advantage of specialist expertise and equipment** rather than investing in these facilities itself and underutilising them.

(c)   It **frees up time spent supporting the contracted-out services** by staff not directly involved, for example supervisory staff, personnel staff.

(d)   It may be **cheaper**, once time savings and opportunity costs are taken into account

(e)   It is particularly **appropriate** when an organisation is **attempting to expand in a time of uncertainty**, because it allows the use of facilities on a short-term (readily-cancelled) basis which

would only otherwise be available via the relatively long-term investments of a permanent employee and the training he or she requires. In other words it is a way of gaining all the benefits of extra capacity without having to find the full cost.

However there are also a number of **disadvantages**.

(a)   Without monitoring there is **no guarantee** that the service will be **performed to the organisation's satisfaction**.

(b)   There is a good chance that contracting out will be **more expensive** than providing the service in-house.

(c)   By performing services itself the organisation retains or develops **skills** that may be needed in the future and will otherwise be **lost**.

(d)   Contracting out any aspect of information-handling carries with it the possibility that **commercially sensitive data will get into the wrong hands.**

(e)   There may be some **ethical reservations**, such as exploitation of staff and inadequate pay and conditions.

(f)   There will almost certainly be **opposition from employees** and their representatives if contracting out involves redundancies.

CASE STUDY

Albright and Davis ('The Elements of Supply Chain Management') describe the extreme outsourcing approach adopted by Mercedes.

Instead of contracting with suppliers for parts, Mercedes outsourced the modules making up a completed M-class to suppliers who purchase the subcomponents and assemble the modules for Mercedes.

This has led to a reduction in plant and warehouse space needed, and a dramatic reduction in the number of suppliers used (from 35 to one for the cockpit, for example).

At the beginning of the production process Mercedes maintained strict control in terms of quality and cost on both the first tier suppliers (who provide finished modules) and the second tier suppliers (from whom the first tier suppliers purchase parts). As the level of trust grew between Mercedes and the first tier suppliers, Mercedes allowed them to make their own arrangements with second tier suppliers.

Benefits of this approach for Mercedes

(i)   Reduction in purchasing overhead

(ii)   Reduction in labour and employee-related costs

(iii)   Higher level of service from suppliers

(iv)   Supplier expertise in seeking ways to improve current operations

(v)   Suppliers working together to continuously improve both their own module and the integrated product

3.5 Current trends in outsourcing

Improvements in technology and telecommunications and more willingness for managers to manage people they can't see have fuelled this trend.

Before taking the decision to outsource overseas, a number of points should be **considered**.

(a)   **Environmental** (location, infrastructure, risk, cultural compatibility, time differences)
(b)   **Labour** (experience in relevant fields, language barriers, size of labour market)
(c)   **Management** (remote management)
(d)   **Bad press** associated with the perception of jobs leaving the home country

Call centres

The inside of a call centre will look virtually the same wherever it is in the world, similar headsets, hardware and software being used, for example. With pressure to provide adequate customer service at low cost, many organisations have closed call centres in parts of Western Europe and relocated to low-cost countries and regions, such as India and South Africa.

It is claimed that savings on call centre costs range from 35% to 55% for near shore outsourcing and 50% to 75% for offshore outsourcing.

3.5.1 Outsourcing to Eastern Europe

The newly-enlarged EU is providing organisations in Western Europe with a range of outsourcing opportunities. The vast **manufacturing facilities that were used to produce for the massive Soviet market,** many of which have been re-equipped, provide the opportunity for manufacturing to be outsourced.

At the moment, **labour is relatively cheap in Eastern Europe**, and it is **closer than the Far East** – an important consideration in today's rapidly-moving environment. The fact that **English is widely taught** and the existence of a **Western culture** are added attractions.

There are problems associated with outsourcing to Eastern Europe, however. Operations in many countries are bound by an **excess of red tape**, for example, and **current political and market uncertainty in Russia** could constrain growth there for some time.

In April 2007, General Motors, the car manufacturer, announced plans to outsource production of elements of its Astra and Vectra models to plants in Russia and other former Soviet-bloc countries.

3.5.2 Outsourcing to India

Moving **back-office functions 'offshore'** began in earnest in the early 1990s when organisations such as American Express, British Airways, General Electric and Swissair set up their own 'captive' outsourcing operations in India.

The **low labour cost** in India has always made the outsourcing option attractive. But not only is it cheap, it is **highly skilled**. India has one of the most developed education systems in the world. One third of college graduates speak more than two languages fluently and of the two million graduates per annum, 80% speak English. These language skills, along with **improved telecomms capabilities**, make it an ideal choice for **call centres**. GE, Accenture and IBM have all set up call centres in India.

The vast majority of service jobs being outsourced offshore are **paper-based back office ones** that can be **digitalised and telecommunicated anywhere around the world**, and **routine telephone enquiries** that can be bundled together into call centres.

3.5.3 Reasons for the popularity of India for outsourcing

(a)   Infrastructure improvements

(b)   Rapid access to the high-quality, numerous and readily-available IT professionals

(c)   Lower costs, not just labour costs (such as falling telecommunications costs)

(d)   The Internet

(e)   Time differences can be used to extend the working day, which is particularly useful if the off-shore organisation provides support or maintenance

(f)   Tax incentives

(g)   Quality certifications (Six Sigma, ISO 9000 and so on)

CASE STUDY

(a)   In October 2009, RBS announced that it expected to save $4 billion in operational costs by outsourcing non-core IT activities to India.

(b)   In June 2009, Rio Tinto announced plans to outsource legal admin work (such as contract review and drafting) to India.

Cost advantages of outsourcing are **being eroded**, however. Salaries in the IT sector in India have been rising in line with demand for skilled workers as firms like Infosys invest heavily in training and facilities.

3.5.4 The future

In **2002**, a study by research group Forrester predicted that 3.3 million white-collar American jobs (500,000 in IT) would shift offshore to countries like India by 2015. At the time of the study, **offshoring** accounted for just 3 – 4% of US organisations' outsourcing and 60% of the US Fortune 1,000 companies had done nothing to investigate the potential for offshoring.

By **2007** the situation had radically changed. Almost 80% of the world's largest companies had outsourced work to India, with about 60% of the contracts coming from the US.

But what about the **future**? The **global financial crisis** has meant that companies are trying to continue operations as **cheaply** as possible. Ironically, when companies need the benefits of outsourcing most, these benefits are drying up. Companies attracted to countries such as India due to the availability **of cheaper skilled labour** – up to 60% cheaper than the going rates in the UK – are now finding that **demand** has started to **drive salaries upwards**.

CASE STUDY

Outsourcing has had its share of disasters as well. There are indications that legal disputes are on the increase, with a landmark case between BSkyB and its IT outsourcer, EDS, in 2010 resulting in a £300m damages payout over a failed £48m system implementation.

In 'Tuning into offshore value,' (*Sunday Business Post On-line*), Fran Gleeson explained why traditional offshore locations (such as Ireland) are losing out to India and Eastern Europe.

(a)   Dell, which was considered to be Ireland's biggest exporter by the Irish Export Association, has quite a sizeable presence in India. For example, in 2001, the company set up Dell International Services in Bangalore, India, to provide technical support by phone and e-mail to its customers in the US, Europe, and the Asia-Pacific region. In less than a year and a half its staff had grown from 180 to 800.

(b)   In the last ten years, Ireland's automotive jobs have moved largely to Eastern Europe and textile facilities were largely relocated to the Far East, giving way to more high tech industries.

(c)   Education is an area where Ireland is having difficulty competing, falling thousands short of India's annual number of PhD graduates, with Eastern European countries and parts of Latin America closing the gap in the education sector as a whole.

(d)   The uncompetitive cost of doing business in Ireland was highlighted in a recent study conducted by AT Kearney and reviewed by the World Bank, Unesco and other research houses, in which 11 countries were assessed to determine their attractiveness for outsourcing.

Ireland was the second least favourable destination in terms of cost, after Canada. The cost factor in the study was broken into the cost of labour, management and infrastructure, and tax or treasury impact. Ireland had the second highest labour costs and management and infrastructure costs after Canada and the impact of taxation here was the greatest of all 11 countries, which included India, China, Russia and the Czech Republic.

India was the most cost competitive. Labour costs in Ireland are three times those in India, according to the report. At that rate, a business moving to India would save over €40,000 on an experienced software programmer, when compared to the IDA (Watson) rate of €61,518.

The same fate that befell Ireland (see case study above) is looking likely to affect India. In 2007 an article in www.theregister.co.uk entitled 'Outsourcing won't save you money' highlighted that, when the first round of skilled workers have been hired, **pay rates** will inevitably **rise**. Skilled workers may **leave the country** in search of high salaries in such areas as the US or Western Europe. Although the population of India is significantly larger than that of Ireland (one billion as opposed to four million), not all of the population will be suitable for outsourcing work. The market is rapidly reaching **saturation point**.

Globalisation has meant that **wage inflation** is happening **more quickly** than in the 1990s when Ireland was the major destination for outsourcing activities. Whilst it took Ireland about 10 years to go from an emerging low-cost outsourcing destination to a level playing field, India is likely to do it in half that time.

However this does not mean the end of outsourcing to such countries as India. As long as companies **outsource for the right reasons** – that is, to take advantage of skills that are not available locally to carry out certain tasks and/or to make use of the specialist skills of companies who are better placed to take responsibility for the provisions of some functions – then **it should not really matter where the tasks or functions are carried out**. **Cost** must be a **secondary** consideration.

Section summary

Some observers predict that in ten to 20 years, most organisations will have **outsourced** every part of the value chain except for the few key components that are unique and sources of **competitive advantage**.

Any activity is a candidate for outsourcing unless the organisation **must control it to maintain its competitive position** or if the organisation can **deliver it on a level comparable with the best organisations in the world**.

To minimise the risks associated with outsourcing, organisations generally enter into **long-run contracts** with their suppliers that specify costs, quality and delivery schedules. They build **close partnerships** or **alliances** with a few key suppliers, collaborating with suppliers on design and manufacturing decisions, and building a culture and commitment for quality and timely delivery.

In an effort to cut costs, many organisations are now outsourcing activities both **near shore (such as Eastern Europe)** and **offshore (such as the Far East and India)**.

4 Partnering, incentives and gain-sharing arrangements

Introduction

Other techniques that focus on external relationships are partnering, incentives and gain-sharing arrangements. Each of these techniques are considered in this section.

4.1 Partnering

KEY TERM

'The term 'PARTNERING' is used about a type of collaboration in a construction project based on DIALOGUE, TRUST, OPENNESS and with EARLY PARTICIPATION from all actors. The project is carried out under a MUTUAL AGREEMENT expressed by MUTUAL ACTIVITIES and based on MUTUAL ECONOMIC INTERESTS.'

Guidelines for partnering, National Agency for Enterprise and Construction, Copenhagen (2004)

Partnering is therefore a **structured management approach** to **facilitate team working across the boundaries of contracts**. It is widely used in the construction industry and within Government departments such as the Ministry of Defence.

4.1.1 Fundamental components of partnering

(a)   Mutual interdependence and trust (as opposed to a blame culture)
(b)   Identification of common goals for success
(c)   Agreed decision-making and problem-solving procedures
(d)   Commitment to continuous improvement
(e)   Team working down the entire product and supply chain
(f)   Gain share and pain share arrangements (incentives)
(g)   Open book accounting
(h)   Targets that provide continuous measurable improvements in performance

4.1.2 Claimed benefits of partnering

(a)	Cost savings	(d)	More predictability of costs and quality
(b)	Improved profit margins	(e)	Increased customer satisfaction
(c)	Reduction in project times	(f)	Improved quality and safety

4.1.3 When to use partnering

For partnering arrangements to be successful, they need the full and visible **support from very senior management** of each organisation. Partnering is not just a bolt on extra that delivers results through one partnering workshop. It is a **continuous process** that needs **sustained effort** by all of the parties to deliver measurable benefits. Partnering arrangements are likely to fail if efforts to contribute to their success are not sustained.

Partnering is **particularly suitable in the following circumstances**.

(a)   If significant input is required from specialist contractors or subcontractors (such as in the construction of a new airport terminal)

(b)   If there is a rapid expansion of a programme of construction (say, if a supermarket chain opens lots of new branches)

(c)   If time is a critical factor

(d)   If projects are repetitive and based upon a set of standard designs (such as the construction of McDonalds restaurants)

(e)   If there is a particular construction problem which is best solved by a team of experts (such as the construction of oil rigs)

Partnering is **less suitable in the following circumstances**.

(a)   If it is important that costs can be predicted with certainty
(b)   If the project is a one-off, commissioned by a one-off customer
(c)   If the customer has little knowledge of the construction process

The table below gives examples of where partnering has been used and the motives for and concerns about the partnering arrangements

Context	Example	Motives	Concerns
Industry and channel partnering	Star Alliance - international passenger air travel	• Customer demands a global service but governments and regulators prevent consolidation • Economies of scale	• Delivering a similar service using different carriers • Firm rivalry • Cultural differences
Project partnering	Civil engineering projects in the UK water sector	• Poor industry profitability • Threat of external competition	• Managing hard contract relationship at the same time as partnering • Internal cultures
Channel and customer partnering	Linking social services and mental health services to provide care in the community through Health Partnerships	• Better health outcomes • Cost savings	• Difficult to work in practice due to poor systems and the lack of investment • Political and professional rivalry
Supply Chain	Internal partnering North Sea Fields	• Cost savings • Limited asset base	• Changing industry mindsets
Integrated Strategic Partnering Strategy (TIPS)	Automotive General Motors	• Cost reduction • Customer value	• Mindsets

4.1.4 Types of partnering

Two key types of partnering arrangement exist.

(a)   **Strategic partnering** (longer-term partnering for agreements involving more than one project)

(b)   **Project specific partnering**.

The Reading Construction Forum report "The Seven Pillars of Partnering" notes that Strategic Partnering has been known to deliver cost savings of 40% and time savings of more than 50%. In comparison, the cost savings for project specific partnering lie in the range 2% to 10%.

The **greater benefits from strategic partnering** arrangements arise because the lessons learnt from one project can be applied to further similar projects through a process of continuous improvement. Strategic partnering arrangements should be adopted in preference to project specific partnering arrangements wherever possible.

Irrespective of the type of partnering relationship that the customer enters into with a primary supplier (such as the main contractor or main consultant), significant benefits (in achieving overall value for money) can be obtained where a primary supplier has entered into strategic partnering arrangements with secondary suppliers (such as sub-contractors or sub-consultants). Supply chain relationships of this type are essential to obtain the maximum benefits from partnering.

4.1.5 Partnering contracts

A contract is required to ensure that all parties are certain of their risks and responsibilities. This encourages **openness and trust**.

An effective partnering contract must be able to deal with any problems in the project and a team-based solution found.

The **defensive attitude embodied in traditional contracts** is a major **obstacle** to the partnering process, however, and so a new form of contractual arrangement is required.

4.2 Incentivisation

Incentives should be **included** in contracts or in **partnering arrangements**, to encourage designers, constructors and/or other suppliers to **provide benefits** to the client significantly **beyond those contracted for** (by using innovation or different working practices to deliver the same or better service whilst yielding cost savings) and **rewarding them for doing so**.

Incentives should **encourage the parties to work together to eliminate wasteful activities that do not add value to the client** and to **identify and implement process improvements, alternative designs, working methods and other activities that result in added value**.

Incentives should **not be given merely for doing a good job** (in other words, meeting the contractual requirements) nor should they be made for improvements in performance that are of no value to the client (such as completing a building contract three months early when the client is still committed to paying rent, rates and other charges on the existing premises).

Here are some examples of features of project performance that can be considered for incentivisation.

- Cost
- Time
- Quality
- Operational efficiency
- Productivity
- Value for the customer
- Safety

Savings can also be **shared amongst members of the supply chain, based on pre-agreed proportions**, so that profits for contractors and suppliers are increased. Alternatively, cost savings can be used by the customer to commission additional work from the partnering team, which again increases the profitability of the supply chain.

Incentive schemes can **also operate 'negatively'**, with the costs of unforeseen risks and problems being shared.

4.2.1 Examples of incentivisation

(a) **Better fee structure**

This applies if the timing and scope of payments deliver a better or lower priced contract.

CASE STUDY

The Highways Agency sets a target completion date for major road maintenance contracts. If contractors 'beat' this date, a bonus is paid. Failure to meet the target date results in a reduction in baseline fees (subject to a maximum figure).

(b) **Enhanced performance and quality**

This applies if a contractor provides a better or faster service than would be delivered under a traditional contract.

CASE STUDY

In a contract for facilities management at one of its sites, the HM Revenue and Customs benchmarked the service required against similar contracts, studied the performance required, established the degree of risk and extent of the profit and savings that might accrue. Fees and costs were fixed and incentives for sharing savings were established. Open book accounting regimes were agreed. Savings were achieved and at the conclusion of each year these savings became a base line for future years. HM Revenue and Customs makes a 50/50 payment share of increased margin to the contractor.

(c) **Target cost incentive scheme**

This applies where a target cost is set based on a given set of parameters. If this fixed target is exceeded or undercut, the outcome is split between the contractor and the customer. These are also known as gain-sharing arrangements.

4.3 Gain sharing arrangements

In pain/gain sharing arrangements, **all cost overruns and cost savings are shared between the customer and the contractor**. A target cost is negotiated and agreed. If the actual cost is less than the target cost, the customer and contractor (and sometimes the contractor's supply chain) split any savings between them in agreed proportions. Likewise any cost overruns are shared by both parties. Sometimes the contractor's share of any cost overrun is up to a pre-arranged limit, and there may be time limits for the gain to be realised.

This does not mean that contractors or suppliers get extra for doing what they are basically contracted to do, but for exceeding those targets. Cost savings should not be seen as incentives to be shared if the scope or standard of work is simply reduced.

Cost savings might be generated from reducing the cost of raw materials, implementing new technologies or suggesting and implementing improvements in operations. The Ministry of Defence see gain sharing as 'a reward for innovative thinking by the contractor'.

Because the resulting benefits from a gain-sharing arrangement are shared, there is an incentive for both parties to look for cost-cutting opportunities.

Many contracts involving these arrangements have **emphasis on greater openness** and **shared development and improvement**.

The Ministry of Defence, for example, is committed to gain sharing as a method of improving the efficient use of the defence procurement budget.

4.3.1 What are the gains?

The gain, benefit or advantage to be shared is **not necessarily financial**, although financial benefits are likely to occur frequently. The Ministry of Defence, for example, will not necessarily take cost savings in the form of a lower contract value but might require a higher specification.

4.3.2 Where might gain-sharing opportunities exist?

Gain-sharing opportunities can exist in various areas of a contract and the associated supply chain.

(a)   Reduced or increased **technical specifications or levels of performance** required, perhaps through advances in technology

(b)   Revised **delivery** times may lead to reduced costs and/or improved performance

(c)   Opportunities for the generation of an **income stream** from the use of the customer's assets by or for a **third party** could emerge or be developed.

(d)   Opportunities may be found **within the supply chain**.

4.3.3 How are financial gains assessed?

In order to assess any financial benefit, both parties should provide each other with access to relevant cost data to determine the basis for the valuation of the benefit and the calculation and sharing of the benefit (**open book accounting**).

CASE STUDY

(a)   Portsmouth City Council and Clenmay Maintenance Services shared gains from a saving of $71,330 on a target cost of $1.4 million.

(b)   Camden Council expanded a roofing refurbishment programme to include window replacement from savings identified by the contractor.

(c)   The consortium which manages the UK arm of the Eurostar train service between London, Paris and Brussels (EUKL) is incentivised to maximise the performance of EUKL with pain-share/gain-share arrangements based on agreed annual targets for EUKL's operating cashflow.

(d)   **Christchurch Junior School Replacement Project Partnering**

'This is a $2.25 million partnering contract between Dorset County Council, Alfred McAlpine Special Projects and other supply chain partners; the **school** and local community were closely involved during design and construction. The **project** incorporated the principles of a guaranteed maximum price within incentivised arrangements using a 50/50 pain/gain share arrangement. The key outcomes and benefits of this **project** are:

(i)   Savings against the guaranteed maximum price of around $0.25 million and a saving against conventional construction of 9%

(ii)   **Project** duration 7 weeks less than prediction using conventional construction

(iii)   Innovative sustainable construction benefits to reduce running costs, energy and water usage including recycling of rainwater to flush WC's.'

(From the website of the Local Government Association www.lga.gov.uk)

(e)   The Army Base Repair Organisation use target cost incentives in contracts for the maintenance of equipment. Bidders are required to quote a target cost and an additional payment is made if that target is bettered, whilst the payment is reduced if it is exceeded. Both minimum and maximum payments are capped by a predetermined percentage.

(f)   The Office of the Gas and Electricity Markets (Ofgem), which supports the Gas and Electricity Markets Authority, the regulator of the gas and electricity industries in Great Britain has a system operator incentive scheme which sets National Grid Company (NGC) a target cost for running the system efficiently and economically. If NGC outperforms this target it keeps a percentage of the savings, if it overspends it bears a percentage of the costs. In this way the incentive scheme encourages NGC to operate the transmission system efficiently and economically by providing it with an appropriate balance of risk and reward. Ofgem has proposed a target of $415m, compared to the current target of $416m. The proposals sharpen the existing incentives and should see further reductions in the costs of system operation over time to the benefit of customers, who ultimately pay these costs.

Question 9B.3	Gain sharing arrangements

Learning outcome B1(k)

The Prime Contracting Initiative marks an innovation in the approach adopted by the Defence Estates on behalf of the Ministry of Defence (MoD) in the UK for the procurement of its capital and maintenance construction work. The Defence Estates arm of the MoD spends well in excess of $1 billion a year and its portfolio ranges from simple structures to complex airfields, garrisons and naval bases.

Required

Describe briefly what you think could be the main features of Prime Contracting.

Note. You are not required to know the specifics of the initiative. You should simply set out some general principles for supply contracts between contractors and the MoD.

Section summary

In some situations, normal competitive pressures do not apply in relationships between customers and contractors. This might be because of the size of the project (say in the construction or civil engineering industries), because there are a limited number of contractors or because of security issues (as in defence work). In such circumstances, **partnering**, **incentives** and **gain-sharing arrangements** are required.

Chapter Roundup

- ✓   The **value chain model**, developed by Michael Porter, offers a bird's eye view of an organisation, of what it does and the way in which its business activities are organised.

- ✓   **Activities** or **value activities** can be categorised as **primary** or **support.**

- ✓   The ultimate **value** an organisation creates is measured by the amount customers are willing to pay for its products and services above the cost of carrying out value activities.

- ✓   The **focus of the value chain** is **external to the organisation**, each organisation being viewed in the context of the overall chain of value-creating activities of which it is only a part, from basic raw materials to end-use consumers.

- ✓   An organisation's ability to develop and sustain **cost leadership** or **product differentiation**, and hence **gain competitive advantage**, depends on how well it manages its own value chain relative to competitors.

- ✓   A **supply chain** is the network of suppliers, manufacturers and distributors that is involved in the process of moving goods for a customer order from the raw materials stage through the production and distribution stages to the customer. Every organisation operates somewhere within a supply chain.

- ✓   A **commonly-held view** by management is that **to improve profitability** it is necessary to **get the lowest prices from suppliers** and to **obtain the best prices from the customers** next in line down the supply chain.

- ✓   **Supply chain management** looks at the supply chain as a whole, and starts with the view that all organisations in the supply chain collaborate to produce something of value for the end customer.

- ✓   Supply chain managers need to consider **production, supply, inventory, location, transportation** and **information**.

- ✓   The **Internet** and **software applications** have had a huge impact on supply chain management.

- ✓   Some observers predict that in ten to 20 years, most organisations will have **outsourced** every part of the value chain except for the few key components that are unique and sources of **competitive advantage**.

- ✓   Any activity is a candidate for outsourcing unless the organisation must **control it to maintain its competitive position** or if the organisation can **deliver it on a level comparable with the best organisations in the world.**

- ✓   To minimise the risks associated with outsourcing, organisations generally enter into **long-run contracts** with their suppliers that specify costs, quality and delivery schedules. They build **close partnerships** or **alliances** with a few key suppliers, collaborating with suppliers on design and manufacturing decisions, and building a culture and commitment for quality and timely delivery.

- ✓   In an effort to cut costs, many organisations are now outsourcing activities both **near shore (such as Eastern Europe)** and **offshore (such as the Far East and India).**

- ✓   In some situations, normal competitive pressures do not apply in relationships between customers and contractors. This might be because of the size of the project (say in the construction or civil engineering industries), because there are a limited number of contractors or because of security issues (as in defence work). In such circumstances, **partnering, incentives** and **gain-sharing arrangements** are required.

Quick Quiz

1   Complete the following diagram of the value chain.

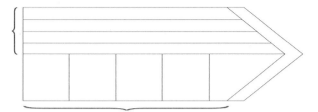

2   *Choose the correct term from those highlighted.*

If the proportion of a supplier's total output that is sold to a customer roughly equals the proportion of total purchases acquired by the customer from that supplier, this is known as **power balancing/ target balancing/codependency/power ties.**

3   Activities that are a source of competitive advantage should be outsourced. *True or false?*

4   List in the spaces below six features of project performance that can be considered for incentivisation.

1 ....   3 ....   5 ....

2 ....   4 ....   6 ....

Answers to Quick Quiz

1

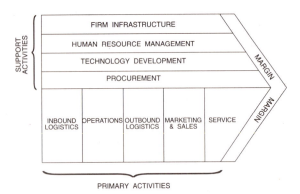

2   The correct answer is power balancing.

3   False. These are the activities an organisation should keep in-house.

4   You could have listed cost, time, quality, operational efficiency, productivity, value for the customer or safety.

Answers to Questions

9B.1 Creating value

Here are some ideas. Each of these options is a way of organising the activities of buying, cooking and serving food in a way that customers will value.

(a)   It can become more efficient, by automating the production of food, as in a fast food chain.

(b)   The chef can develop commercial relationships with growers, so he or she can obtain the best quality fresh produce.

(c)   The chef can specialise in a particular type of cuisine (such as French or Thai).

(d)   The restaurant can be sumptuously decorated for those customers who value 'atmosphere' and a sense of occasion, in addition to a restaurant's purely gastronomic pleasures.

(e)   The restaurant can serve a particular type of customer (such as celebrities).

9B.2 Value chain analysis v conventional management accounting

	Traditional management accounting	Value chain analysis
Focus	Internal	External
Perspective	Value-added	Entire set of linked activities from suppliers to final-use customers
Cost driver concept	Single driver (volume) Applied at organisational level	Multiple cost drivers (structural and executional) Unique cost drivers for each value activity
Cost containment philosophy	'Across the board' cost reductions	By regulating cost drivers Exploit linkages with customers and suppliers Spend to save
Insights for strategic decisions	None readily apparent	Develop cost/differentiation advantage by controlling drivers better than competitors or by reconfiguring the value chain For each value activity, consider make versus buy, forwards/backwards integration and so on Exploit linkages with customers and suppliers

Adapted from Shank and Govindarajan

9B.3 Gain sharing arrangements

Here are some of the actual principles of and details about the Prime Contracting Initiative, taken from 'Prime Contracting – the UK experience and the way forward' by David M Jones, an external adviser to the Defence Estates and a member of the small working party empowered to deliver Prime Contracting. Obviously you are unlikely to have come up with this level of detail but you should have mentioned some of the basic points.

(a)   **Collaborative working**. 'The intention behind the Prime Contracting Initiative in facilitating best value to the customer is to foster a more collaborative and less adversarial relationship between the MoD and the Prime Contractor.....The Core Conditions give opportunities throughout the contract period for collaboration and discussion between the Defence Estates Project Manager (DEPM) for each contract and the Prime Contractor..... There are opportunities for continual adjustment and improvement within the relationship, not least to provide good feedback among the contract members. This will be vital to develop trust, to work on upgrading performance and to add value...... and having a common interest and willingness to co-operate to meet mutual goals'.

(b)   **Gain-sharing arrangement**. 'Of importance, the Core Conditions include a Target Cost pricing mechanism and a pain/gain sharing arrangement between the MoD and the Prime Contractor for both cost under-runs and over-runs up to a Maximum Price Target Cost (MPTC). In the most important area, therefore, there is significant sharing and incentives on both parties......This arrangement is considered to provide the strongest incentive for industry to improve performance and innovate thereby increasing value to the MoD and providing an opportunity for the Prime Contractor's level of profit to increase to reflect his improved performance.... It is expected that Prime Contractors will be entitled to a fair profit margin, bringing tangible benefits from the Prime Contracting approach, which should be passed down through the Supply Chain.'

(c)   **Open book accounting**. 'Throughout the entire contract period the Prime Contractor will be required to operate an "Open Book" accounting regime providing the MoD with access to such relevant financial information as may reasonably be required to, amongst other things:

     (i)   monitor actual incurred costs against Target Cost;
     (ii)   substantiate claims for payment against milestones;
     (iii)   agree changes to the Target Cost to reflect additions/deletions from scope of contract;
     (iv)   assess final out-turn costs and final price payable;
     (v)   consider impact of innovative proposals. '

(d)   **Project teams**. 'One of the critical success factors of Prime Contracting will be the Authority's ability to become a better-informed client. To achieve this, Prime Contracts will be managed by an MoD Integrated Project Team (IPT) consisting of full time members with all the necessary skills and functions required to deliver the project supported, as appropriate, by specialist advice from industry. Any such support provided will be an integral part of the IPT. Throughout the bidding process organisations will be given the opportunity for greater access to the IPT to ensure that a full understanding of the project can be gained. There will in future be a direct MoD/Prime Contractor interface. After contract award the Prime Contractor will become a full member of the IPT along with his supply chain.'

(e)   **Innovative solutions**. 'Throughout the entire Prime Contract process ie, from advertising the requirement through selection and evaluation and ultimately to delivery of the requirement, Prime Contractors will be encouraged to think of innovative ways of delivering the requirements which demonstrate improved value for money and continuous improvement.'

(f)   **Size and length of contract.** 'Prime Contracts because of their size (they will be substantially concerned with geographical areas rather than single sites) and their duration [often five to seven years] will offer better value for money to both the MoD and to the Prime Contractor than traditional procurement contracts. They represent long term commitment and application by both participants and provide an opportunity for shared learning and development.'

Now try the question from the Exam Question Bank	Number	Level	Marks	Time
	Q24	Examination	10	18 mins

BUDGETING AND MANAGEMENT CONTROL

Part C

BUDGETING

This chapter follows on from your Paper P1 studies of budgeting and focuses on how budgets can be used for control purposes.

Budgetary control is the comparison of actual results with budgeted results. **Variances** are calculated to identify the differences between actual and budgeted results and these differences are reported to management so that appropriate **action** can be taken.

Such an approach relies on a system of **flexible** (as opposed to fixed) budgets. We look at the difference between the two types in **Section 1**. **Flexible budgets** are vital for both **planning and control** - **Section 2** shows how they are constructed and **Section 3** looks at their use in the overall **budgetary control process**.

Section 4 introduces the components and characteristics of a budgeting system and **Section 5** examines the use of computer spreadsheets in budget construction. **Section 6** examines how **rolling budgets** encourage management to focus on future performance. **Section 7** looks at two **types of control** which can be used once budgetary control statements have been prepared.

The chapter then considers the **behavioural implications** of operating a budgetary control system. As in all studies of human behaviour, it is difficult to draw concrete conclusions. There is, however, one point which is agreed: **budgeting is more than a mathematical technique**.

The chapter concludes with a review of the criticisms of budgeting and the recommendations of the advocates of 'Beyond Budgeting'.

1 Fixed and flexible budgets

Introduction

This section focuses on the differences between fixed and flexible budgets. Make sure you understand what is meant by each type of budget before moving on.

1.1 Fixed budgets

The master budget prepared before the beginning of the budget period is known as the **fixed** budget. By the term 'fixed', we do not mean that the budget is kept unchanged. Revisions to a fixed master budget will be made if the situation so demands. The term 'fixed' means the following.

(a) The budget is prepared on the basis of an **estimated volume of production** and an **estimated volume of sales**, but no plans are made for the event that actual volumes of production and sales may **differ** from budgeted volumes.

(b) When **actual volumes** of production and sales during a control period (month or four weeks or quarter) are achieved, a fixed budget is **not adjusted** (in retrospect) to represent a new target for the new levels of activity.

The major purpose of a fixed budget lies in its use at the **planning** stage, when it seeks to define the broad objectives of the organisation.

KEY TERM

A FIXED BUDGET is 'A budget set prior to the control period, and not subsequently changed in response to changes in activity or costs or revenues. It may serve as a benchmark in performance evaluation.'

(CIMA *Official Terminology*)

Fixed budgets (in terms of a **pre-set expenditure limit**) are also useful for **controlling any fixed cost**, and **particularly non-production fixed costs** such as advertising, because such costs should be unaffected by changes in activity level (within a certain range).

1.2 Flexible budgets

KEY TERM

A FLEXIBLE BUDGET is a budget which, by recognising different cost behaviour patterns, is designed to change as volume of activity changes.

Two uses of flexible budgets

(a) **At the planning stage**. For example, suppose that a company expects to sell 10,000 units of output during the next year. A master budget (the fixed budget) would be prepared on the basis of these expected volumes. However, if the company thinks that output and sales might be as low as 8,000 units or as high as 12,000 units, it may prepare **contingency** flexible budgets, at volumes of, say 8,000, 9,000, 11,000 and 12,000 units, and then assess the possible outcomes.

(b) **Retrospectively.** At the end of each control period, flexible budgets can be used to compare actual results achieved with what results should have been under the circumstances. Flexible budgets are an essential factor in budgetary control.

   (i) Management needs to know about how good or bad actual performance has been. To provide a measure of performance, there must be a yardstick (budget/ standard) against which actual performance can be measured.

   (ii) Every business is dynamic, and actual volumes of output cannot be expected to conform exactly to the fixed budget. Comparing actual costs directly with the fixed budget costs is meaningless.

(iii)   For useful control information, it is necessary to compare actual results at the actual level of activity achieved against the results that should have been expected at this level of activity, which are shown by the flexible budget.

Section summary

Fixed budgets remain unchanged regardless of the level of activity; **flexible budgets** are designed to flex with the level of activity.

Flexible budgets are prepared using marginal costing and so mixed costs must be split into their fixed and variable components (possibly using the **high/low method**).

Flexible budgets should be used to show what cost and revenues should have been for the actual level of activity. Differences between the flexible budget figures and actual results are **variances**.

2 Preparing flexible budgets   5/10, 5/12, 11/12

Introduction

This section focuses on how to prepare flexible budgets. This is something that should be familiar from your previous studies but make sure you work through the example to reacquaint yourself with the process.

Knowledge brought forward from earlier studies

The preparation of flexible budgets

- The first step in the preparation of a flexible budget is the determination of **cost behaviour patterns**, which means deciding whether costs are fixed, variable or semi-variable.

- Fixed costs will remain constant as activity levels change.

- For non-fixed costs, divide each cost figure by the related activity level. If the cost is a **linear variable cost**, the cost per unit will remain constant. If the cost is a **semi-variable cost**, the unit rate will reduce as activity levels increase.

- Split semi-variable costs into their fixed and variable components using the **high/low method** or the **scattergraph method**.

- Calculate the **budget cost allowance** for each cost item as budget cost allowance = budgeted fixed cost* + (number of units produced/sold x variable cost per unit)**.

    * nil for totally variable cost ** nil for fixed cost

KEY TERM

The BUDGET COST ALLOWANCE/FLEXIBLE BUDGET is the budgeted cost ascribed to the level of activity achieved in a budget centre in a control period. It comprises variable costs in direct proportion to volume achieved and fixed costs as a proportion of the annual budget.

Example: Fixed and flexible budgets

Suppose that Gemma expects production and sales during the next year to be 90% of the company's output capacity, that is, 9,000 units of a single product. Cost estimates will be made using the high-low method and the following historical records of cost.

Units of output/sales	Cost of sales
	Yen
9,800	44,400
7,700	38,100

The company's management is not certain that the estimate of sales is correct, and has asked for flexible budgets to be prepared at output and sales levels of 8,000 and 10,000 units. The sales price per unit has been fixed at Y5 .

Required

Prepare appropriate budgets.

Solution

If we assume that within the range 8,000 to 10,000 units of sales, all costs are fixed, variable or mixed (in other words there are no stepped costs, material discounts, overtime premiums, bonus payments and so on) the fixed and flexible budgets would be based on the estimate of fixed and variable cost.

		Yen
Total cost of 9,800 units	=	44,400
Total cost of 7,700 units	=	38,100
Variable cost of 2,100 units	=	6,300

The variable cost per unit is Yen 3.

		Yen
Total cost of 9,800 units	=	44,400
Variable cost of 9,800 units (9,800 × Yen 3)	=	29,400
Fixed costs (all levels of output and sales)	=	15,000

The fixed budgets and flexible budgets can now be prepared as follows.

	Flexible budget 8,000 units Yen	Fixed budget 9,000 units Yen	Flexible budget 10,000 units Yen
Sales (× Yen 5)	40,000	45,000	50,000
Variable costs (× Yen 3)	24,000	27,000	30,000
Contribution	16,000	18,000	20,000
Fixed costs	15,000	15,000	15,000
Profit	1,000	3,000	5,000

Have a go at the following question. It is more complicated than the last example because it includes inflation. You will need to recall your studies of index numbers from CIMA Certificate C3 *Business Mathematics*.

Question 10.1	High-low method

Learning outcome C2(c)

Rice and Faull Ltd has recorded the following total costs during the last five years.

Year	Output volume Units	Total cost $	Average price level index
0	65,000	145,000	100
1	80,000	179,000	112
2	90,000	209,100	123
3	60,000	201,600	144
4	75,000	248,000	160

What will be the expected costs in year 5 when output is 85,000 units and the average price level index is 180?

2.1 The need for flexible budgets

We have seen that flexible budgets may be prepared in order to plan for variations in the level of activity above or below the level set in the fixed budget. It has been suggested, however, that since many cost items in modern industry are fixed costs, the value of flexible budgets in planning is dwindling.

(a) In many manufacturing industries, plant costs (depreciation, rent and so on) are a very large proportion of total costs, and these tend to be fixed costs.

(b) Wage costs also tend to be fixed, because employees are generally guaranteed a basic wage for a working week of an agreed number of hours.

(c) With the growth of service industries, labour (wages or fixed salaries) and overheads will account for most of the costs of a business, and direct materials will be a relatively small proportion of total costs.

Flexible budgets are nevertheless necessary, and even if they are not used at the planning stage, they must be used for variance analysis.

2.2 The budget committee

The **coordination** and **administration** of budgets is usually the responsibility of a **budget committee** (with the managing director as chairman).

(a) The budget committee is assisted by a **budget officer** who is usually an accountant. Every part of the organisation should be represented on the committee, so there should be a representative from sales, production, marketing and so on.

(b) **Functions of the budget committee**

    (i)   **Coordination** of the preparation of budgets, which includes the issue of the budget manual

    (ii)   **Issuing of timetables** for the preparation of functional budgets

    (iii)   **Allocation of responsibilities** for the preparation of functional budgets

    (iv)   **Provision of information** to assist in the preparation of budgets

    (v)   **Communication of final budgets** to the appropriate managers

    (vi)   **Comparison** of actual results with budget and the investigation of variances

    (vii)   **Continuous assessment** of the budgeting and planning process, in order to improve the planning and control function

Section summary

The **budget cost allowance/flexible budget** is the budgeted cost ascribed to the level of activity achieved in a budget centre in a control period. It comprises variable costs in direct proportion to volume achieved and fixed costs as a proportion of the annual budget.

3 Flexible budgets and budgetary control   9/12

Introduction

Flexible budgets are essential for control purposes. They represent the expected revenues, costs and profits for the actual units produced and sold and are then compared to actual results to determine any differences (or variances). Variances should already be familiar to you from your P1 studies – in this section we show how flexible budgets can be used to identify potential control issues.

KEY TERM

Budgetary control is carried out via a MASTER BUDGET devolved to responsibility centres, allowing continuous monitoring of actual results versus budget, either to secure by individual action the budget objectives or to provide a basis for budget revision.'   (CIMA *Official Terminology*)

In other words, individual managers are held responsible for investigating differences between budgeted and actual results, and are then expected to take corrective action or amend the plan in the light of actual events.

It is therefore vital to ensure that valid comparisons are being made. Consider the following example.

Example: Flexible budgets and budgetary control

Penny manufactures a single product, the Darcy. Budgeted results and actual results for May are as follows.

	Budget	Actual	Variance
Production and sales of the Darcy (units)	7,500	8,200	
	$	$	$
Sales revenue	75,000	81,000	6,000 (F)
Direct materials	22,500	23,500	1,000 (A)
Direct labour	15,000	15,500	500 (A)
Production overhead	22,500	22,800	300 (A)
Administration overhead	10,000	11,000	1,000 (A)
	70,000	72,800	2,800 (A)
Profit	5,000	8,200	3,200 (F)

Note. (F) denotes a favourable variance and (A) an unfavourable or adverse variance.

In this example, the variances are meaningless for the purposes of control. All costs were higher than budgeted but the volume of output was also higher; it is to be expected that actual variable costs would be greater those included in the fixed budget. However, it is not possible to tell how much of the increase is due to **poor cost control** and how much is due to the **increase in activity**.

Similarly it is not possible to tell how much of the increase in sales revenue is due to the increase in activity. Some of the difference may be due to a difference between budgeted and actual selling price but we are unable to tell from the analysis above.

For control purposes we need to know the answers to questions such as the following.

- Were actual costs higher than they should have been to produce and sell 8,200 Darcys?
- Was actual revenue satisfactory from the sale of 8,200 Darcys?

Instead of comparing actual results with a fixed budget which is based on a different level of activity to that actually achieved, the correct approach to budgetary control is to compare actual results with a budget which has been **flexed** to the actual activity level achieved.

Suppose that we have the following estimates of the behaviour of Penny's costs.

(a)   Direct materials and direct labour are variable costs.

(b)   Production overhead is a semi-variable cost, the budgeted cost for an activity level of 10,000 units being $25,000.

(c)   Administration overhead is a fixed cost.

(d)   Selling prices are constant at all levels of sales.

Solution

The **budgetary control analysis** should therefore be as follows.

	Fixed budget	Flexible budget	Actual results	Variance
Production and sales (units)	7,500	8,200	8,200	
	$	$	$	$
Sales revenue	75,000	82,000 (W1)	81,000	1,000 (A)
Direct materials	22,500	24,600 (W2)	23,500	1,100 (F)
Direct labour	15,000	16,400 (W3)	15,500	900 (F)
Production overhead	22,500	23,200 (W4)	22,800	400 (F)
Administration overhead	10,000	10,000 (W5)	11,000	1,000 (A)
	70,000	74,200	72,800	1,400 (F)
Profit	5,000	7,800	8,200	400 (F)

Workings

1   Selling price per unit = $75,000 / 7,500 = $10 per unit
Flexible budget sales revenue = $10 x 8,200 = 482,000

2   Direct materials cost per unit = $22,500/7,500 = $3
Budget cost allowance = $3 x 8,200 = $24,600

3   Direct labour cost per unit = $15,000 / 7,500 = $2
Budget cost allowance = $2 x 8,200 = $16,400

4   Variable production overhead cost per unit = $(25,000 − 22,500)/(10,000 − 7,500)
= $2,500/2,500 = $1 per unit

∴ Fixed production overhead cost = $22,500 − (7,500 x $1) = $15,000

∴ Budget cost allowance = $15,000 + (8,200 x $1) = $23,200

5   Administration overhead is a fixed cost and hence budget cost allowance = $10,000

Comment

(a)   In selling 8,200 units, the expected profit should have been, not the fixed budget profit of $5,000, but the flexible budget profit of $7,800. Instead actual profit was $8,200 ie $400 more than we should have expected.

One of the reasons for this improvement is that, given output and sales of 8,200 units, the cost of resources (material, labour etc) was $1,400 lower than expected. (A comparison of the fixed budget and the actual costs in Example 3.1 appeared to indicate that costs were not being controlled since all of the variances were adverse).

In Paper P1 you saw how these total cost variances can be analysed to reveal how much of the variance is due to lower resource prices and how much is due to efficient resource usage.

(b) The sales revenue was, however, $1,000 less than expected because a lower price was charged than budgeted.

We know this because flexing the budget has eliminated the effect of changes in the volume sold, which is the only other factor that can affect sales revenue. You have probably already realised that this variance of $1,000 (A) is a **selling price variance**.

The lower selling price could have been caused by the increase in the volume sold (to sell the additional 700 units the selling price had to fall below $10 per unit). We do not know if this is the case but without flexing the budget we could not know that a different selling price to that budgeted had been charged. Our initial analysis above had appeared to indicate that sales revenue was ahead of budget.

The difference of $400 between the flexible budget profit of $7,800 at a production level of 8,200 units and the actual profit of $8,200 is due to the net effect of cost savings of $1,400 and lower than expected sales revenue (by $1,000).

The difference between the original budgeted profit of $5,000 and the actual profit of $8,200 is the total of the following.

(a) The savings in resource costs/lower than expected sales revenue (a net total of $400 as indicated by the difference between the flexible budget and the actual results).

(b) The effect of producing and selling 8,200 units instead of 7,500 units (a gain of $2,800 as indicated by the difference between the fixed budget and the flexible budget). This is the **sales volume contribution variance**.

A **full variance analysis statement** would be as follows.

	$	$
Fixed budget profit		5,000
Variances		
Sales volume	2,800 (F)	
Selling price	1,000 (A)	
Direct materials cost	1,100 (F)	
Direct labour cost	900 (F)	
Production overhead cost	400 (F)	
Administration overhead cost	1,000 (A)	
		3,200 (F)
Actual profit		8,200

If management believes that any of the variances are large enough to justify it, they will investigate the reasons for their occurrence to see whether any corrective action is necessary.

Question 10.2

Flexible budget

Learning outcome C2(c)

Flower budgeted to sell 200 units and produced the following budget.

	$	$
Sales		71,400
Variable costs		
Labour	31,600	
Material	12,600	
		44,200
Contribution		27,200
Fixed costs		18,900
Profit		8,300

Actual sales turned out to be 230 units, which were sold for $69,000. Actual expenditure on labour was $27,000 and on material $24,000. Fixed costs totalled $10,000.

Required

Prepare a flexible budget that will be useful for management control purposes.

3.1 Flexible budgets, control and computers

The production of flexible budget control reports is an area in which computers can provide invaluable assistance to the cost accountant, calculating flexed budget figures using fixed budget and actual results data and hence providing detailed variance analysis. For control information to be of any value it must be produced quickly: speed is one of the many advantages of computers.

3.2 Flexible budgets using ABC data

Instead of flexing budgets according to the number of units produced or sold, in an ABC environment it is possible to use **more meaningful bases for flexing the budget**. The budget cost allowance for each activity can be determined according to the number of **cost drivers**.

Suppose the budget for a production department for a given period is as follows.

	$
Wages	220,000
Materials	590,000
Equipment	20,000
Power, heat and light	11,000
	841,000

This budget gives little indication of the link between the level of activity in the department and the costs incurred, however.

Suppose the activities in the department have been identified as sawing, hammering, finishing, reworking and production reporting. The budget might therefore be restated as follows.

Activities	Cost driver	Budgeted cost per unit of cost driver $	Budgeted no of cost drivers	Budget $
Sawing	Number of units sawed	50.00	5,000	250,000
Hammering	Number of units hammered together	10.00	35,000	350,000
Finishing	Number of sq metres finished	0.50	400,000	200,000
Reworking	Number of items reworked	12.40	2,500	31,000
Production reporting	Number of reports	400.00	25	10,000
				841,000

Advantages of this approach

(a) Costs classified as fixed in the first budget can now be seen to be variable and hence can be more readily controlled.

(b) The implications of increases/decreases in levels of activity are immediately apparent. For example, if acceptable quality levels were raised, requiring an additional 200 units per annum to be reworked, budgeted costs would increase by 200 × $12.40 = $2,480.

A **flexible budget** would be prepared as follows.

	Actual no of cost drivers	Budgeted cost per unit of cost driver $	Flexed budget $	Actual cost $	Variance $
Sawing	6,000	50.00	300,000	297,000	3,000 (F)
Hammering	40,000	10.00	400,000	404,000	4,000 (A)
Finishing	264,400	0.50	132,200	113,200	19,000 (F)
Reworking	4,500	12.40	55,800	56,100	300 (A)
Production reporting	30	400.00	12,000	13,700	1,700 (A)
			900,000	884,000	16,000 (F)

3.3 The link between standard costing and budget flexing

The calculation of standard cost variances and the use of a flexed budget to control costs and revenues are **very similar in concept**.

For example, a direct material total variance in a standard costing system is calculated by **comparing the material cost that should have been incurred for the output achieved, with the actual cost that was incurred**.

Exactly the same process is undertaken when a budget is flexed to provide a basis for comparison with the actual cost: **the flexible budget cost allowance for material cost is the same as the cost that should have been incurred for the activity level achieved**. In the same way as for standard costing, this is then compared with the actual cost incurred in order to practice control by comparison.

However, there are differences between the two techniques.

(a) **Standard costing variance analysis is more detailed**. The total material cost variance is analysed further to determine how much of the total variance is caused by a difference in the price paid for materials (the material price variance) and how much is caused by the usage of material being different from the standard (the material usage variance). In flexible budget comparisons only total cost variances are derived.

(b) **For a standard costing system to operate it is necessary to determine a standard unit cost for all items of output**. All that is required to operate a flexible budgeting system is an understanding of the cost behaviour patterns and a measure of activity to use to flex the budget cost allowance for each cost element.

Section summary

Budgetary control is based around a system of **budget centres**. Each centre has its own budget which is the responsibility of the **budget holder**.

4 System design

Introduction

A system is a set of interacting or interdependent parts coordinated to accomplish a set of goals. System management involves the handling or manipulation of resources to produce a set output. Examples of systems include communication systems, budgeting systems and inventory control systems.

4.1 The characteristics and components of a system

There are a number of key characteristics and components of a system.

(a) **Inputs**. The stage at which raw information is entered into the system for processing. Inputs can take the form of materials, money, people or data.

(b) **Process**. The activity of adding value to inputs to produce an output. Processing activities may include manufacturing and recording.

(c) **Outputs**. The stage at which the finished product or service is passed out to the environment. This could involve the transfer of data to a new system or the delivery of goods to a customer.

(d)   **Environment**. External elements that have a direct or indirect influence on the process and the components of a system. Every system operates within and interacts with the environment by receiving inputs from it and delivering outputs to it. Factors that fall within the boundaries of the organisation constitute the internal environment and factors beyond the organisational boundaries form the external environment.

(e)   **Boundary**. System boundaries separate the system and its components from the environment. System boundaries may or may not be physical.

Section summary

There are a number of key characteristics and components of a system. Learn them!

5   Using spreadsheets to build business models

Introduction

Budget construction can be very complicated, particularly if assumptions regarding costs, selling prices or sales volumes are changed several times. Spreadsheets make the process much easier. This section demonstrates how spreadsheet packages can be used to assist in the initial budget-setting process and in the construction of flexible budgets.

KEY TERM

A SPREADSHEET is 'The term commonly used to describe many of the modelling packages available for microcomputers, being loosely derived from the likeness to a 'spreadsheet of paper' divided into rows and columns.'

(CIMA *Computing Terminology*)

It is a type of general purpose software package with **many business applications**, not just accounting ones. It **can be used to build a model**, in which data is presented in **cells** at the intersection of these **rows and columns**. It is up to the model builder to determine what data or information should be presented in the spreadsheet, how it should be presented and how the data should be manipulated by the spreadsheet program. The most widely used spreadsheet packages are Lotus 1-2-3 and Excel.

The idea behind a spreadsheet is that the model builder should **construct a model as follows**.

(a)   Identify what data goes into each row and column and by **inserting text** (for example, column headings and row identifications).

(b)   **Specify how the numerical data in the model should be derived**. Numerical data might be derived using one of the following methods.

    (i)   **Insertion into the model via keyboard input**.

    (ii)   **Calculation from other data in the model** by means of a formula specified within the model itself. The model builder must insert these formulae into the spreadsheet model when it is first constructed.

    (iii)   **Retrieval from data on a disk file** from another computer application program or module.

5.1 The advantages of spreadsheets

The uses of spreadsheets are really only limited by your imagination, and by the number of rows and columns in the spreadsheet, but some of the more **common accounting applications** are listed below.

- Statements of financial position
- Cash flow analysis/forecasting
- General ledger
- Inventory records
- Job cost estimates
- Market share analysis and planning
- Profit projections
- Profit statements
- Project budgeting and control
- Sales projections and records
- Tax estimation

The great value of spreadsheets derives from their **simple format** of rows, columns and worksheets of data, and the ability of the data **users to have direct access themselves** to their spreadsheet model via their own PC. For example, an accountant can construct a cash flow model with a spreadsheet package on the PC on his desk: he can **create** the model, **input** the data, **manipulate** the data and **read or print the output** direct. He will also have fairly **instant access** to the model whenever it is needed, in just the time it takes to load the model into his PC. Spreadsheets therefore bring computer modelling within the everyday reach of data users.

5.2 The disadvantages of spreadsheets

Spreadsheets have disadvantages if they are not properly used.

(a)   A **minor error in the design** of a model at any point can **affect the validity of data** throughout the spreadsheet. Such errors can be very difficult to trace.

(b)   Even if it is properly designed in the first place, it is very **easy to corrupt** a model by accidentally changing a cell or inputting data in the wrong place.

(c)   It is possible to **become over-dependent on them**, so that simple one-off tasks that can be done in seconds with a pen and paper are done on a spreadsheet instead.

(d)   The possibility for experimentation with data is so great that it is possible to **lose sight of the original intention** of the spreadsheet.

(e)   Spreadsheets **cannot take account of qualitative factors** since they are invariably difficult to quantify. Decisions should not be made on the basis of quantitative information alone.

Spreadsheets are a **tool in planning and decision making** with the user making the decision.

In 'Spreadsheets and databases as budgeting tools' (CIMA *Student*), Bob Scarlett expanded on the limitations of spreadsheets for budgeting. (The emphasis is BPP's.)

> 'The process of creating a budget in a large organisation is a **complex** operation. Each area in the organisation needs to prepare a plan and these plans need to be **collated and consolidated**. The system must then accommodate **adjustments** on a **top-down** and **bottom-up** basis. A budgeting operation based on spreadsheets has the following **problems**:
>
> - It is **inflexible** and **error prone**. A large number of spreadsheets can be linked and consolidated but this process presents many difficulties. Calculations are complex and mistakes are easily made. Random 'what if' analyses across centres may become very difficult to carry out.
>
> - It is a **single-user tool in a multi-user environment**. A large number of spreadsheet users are involved using similar templates over periods of weeks. This involves massive duplication of effort and gives rise to risks relating to loss of data integrity and consistency of structure.

- It **lacks 'functionality'**. There are many users in the budget management process ranging from cost centre managers to the chief financial officer. All require ready access to the system in order to input data to it and draw information from it. The budget controller must be able to track revisions. Spreadsheet based systems are notorious for complexity – and they can be anything but easy to use.

Spreadsheet-based budgeting systems may be perfectly adequate for the small and simple operation. However, the limitations of such systems may become increasingly apparent as larger and more complex operations are considered.'

5.3 'What-if?' analysis

KEY TERM

'WHAT-IF?' ANALYSIS involves changing the values of the forecast variables to see the effect on the forecast outcome. The information provided helps managers to understand the sensitivity of the forecast to the value of the variables.

Once a model has been constructed the consequences of changes or amendments to budget/plan assumptions may be tested by asking **'what if?' questions, a form of sensitivity analysis**. For example, a spreadsheet may be used to develop a cash flow model, such as that shown below.

	A	B	C	D
		Month 1	Month 2	Month 3
1				
2	Sales	1,000	1,200	1,440
3	Cost of sales	(650)	(780)	(936)
4	Gross profit	350	420	504
5				
6	Receipts:			
7	Current month	600	720	864
8	Previous month	–	400	480
9		–	–	–
10		600	1,120	1,344
11	Payments	(650)	(780)	(936)
12		(50)	340	408
13	Balance b/f	–	(50)	290
14	Balance c/f	(50)	290	698

Typical 'what if?' questions for sensitivity analysis

(a) What if the cost of sales is 68% of sales revenue, not 65%?

(b) What if payment from receivables is received 40% in the month of sale, 50% one month in arrears and 10% two months in arrears, instead of 60% in the month of sale and 40% one month in arrears?

(c) What if sales growth is only 15% per month, instead of 20% per month?

Using the spreadsheet model, the answers to such questions can be obtained simply and quickly, using the editing facility in the program. The information obtained should **provide management with a better understanding of what the cash flow position in the future might be**, and **what factors are critical to ensuring that the cash position remains reasonable**. For example, it might be found that the cost of sales must remain less than 67% of sales value to achieve a satisfactory cash position.

Question 10.3

Spreadsheets

Learning outcome C2(b)

(a) Write out the formulae that would appear in column C of the spreadsheet shown above.

(b) Comment on the effect on the cash balances if *all* of the 'what if?' conditions listed in Paragraph 4.3 applied. Perform the calculations manually, then if you have access to a spreadsheet package, you could use it to check your answer.

(c) Which cells in column C would have to be changed, and how, if the 'what if?' conditions applied?

(d) How could the design of the spreadsheet model be improved to facilitate sensitivity analysis?

5.4 Analysing relationships

One of the major **assumptions** in **linear regression analysis** is that there is a **linear relationship** between the dependent and independent variables.

The relationship might be **curvilinear**, however. A curvilinear relationship can be expressed in the form $Y = aX^b$ (where Y is the dependent variable, X is the independent variable and a and b are constants).

Before the advent of computers and spreadsheet packages, if we knew that a linear relationship did not exist between, say, cumulative sales (Y) and time (X), we would have needed to use logarithms to find the value of b. ('a' would be sales in the first time period.)

Nowadays, fortunately, a **spreadsheet** package can be used to carry out a series of **repetitive calculations** (substituting the given value of a and the given values of X into $Y = aX^b$ and changing the value of b until the results with a particular value of b are close to the given values of Y).

The resulting equation can then be used for **forecasting** purposes.

5.5 Management reporting

5.5.1 The impact of computer packages

We have looked at the use of spreadsheet packages in budgeting. But what has been the **impact of computer packages in general** on accountants and managers?

(a) **Data** can be provided **more quickly** and in **more detail**.
(b) **Consolidation** of monthly management accounts is **quicker** and **more complete**.
(c) As we have seen, **'what if' analysis** is far easier to carry out.

5.5.2 Monthly reporting

Monthly reports are now **produced more quickly**. The vast majority of organisations prepare management accounts at least once a month, and preparation rarely takes more than ten working days (preparation sometimes taking only five days or less from the period end).

Reports are **more detailed**, often including both **financial and non-financial data**. The majority of **requests** for additional information can be **met**.

Presentation is more **professional**.

Reporting systems are often **broadly standard** across organisations as a result of internal reviews. Such reviews have led to a general **rise in the standards of reporting**, although they have been criticised as offering **standard solutions to unique problems**.

In large organisations reports now contain **lots more figures**. As well as profit for the period just ended, they cover forecast profit, cash flow, working capital and the balance sheet and include reams of non-financial data.

5.5.3 Implications of these developments

Information overload occurs because of the ease with which information can be provided. Reporting by exception is frequently not applied.

There is continuing focus on **information about internal activities** of the organisation, so that monthly reporting remains a system for internal review and control rather than an aid to short-term decision making.

The **level of detail should not be greater than the accuracy of the data**. It is questionable whether period-end cut off procedures and accounting for accruals have improved in line with faster reporting. Systems for recording indirect costs (which in the past did not need to be overly accurate given the small proportion of total costs they represented) may need improvement.

Section summary

Spreadsheet packages can be used to build business models to assist in forecasting and planning.

'What-if?' analysis involves changing the values of the forecast variables to see the effect on the forecast outcome. The information provided helps managers to understand the sensitivity of the forecast to the value of the variables.

6 Rolling budgets   11/10

Introduction

Rolling budgets encourage management to focus on future performance and can be particularly useful when future events cannot be forecast reliably.

KEY TERMS

A ROLLING BUDGET is defined as "A budget continuously updated by adding a further accounting period (month or quarter) when the earliest accounting period has expired. Its use is particularly beneficial where future costs and/or activities cannot be forecast accurately."

(CIMA *Official Terminology*)

For example, a budget may initially be prepared for January to December in year 1. At the end of the first month, that is, at the end of January year 1, the first month's budget is deleted. A further month is then added onto the end of the remaining budget, for January year 2. The remaining portion of the original budget is updated in the light of current conditions.

This contrasts to a PERIODIC BUDGET, which is prepared for a set control period, for example January to December year 1, and a different budget is prepared for the next control period, January to December year 2.

6.1 Advantages and disadvantages of rolling budgets

(a) **Advantages**

(i)   Budgets are reassessed regularly by management and so should be more accurate.

(ii) Uncertainty is reduced. Rolling budgets focus detailed planning and control on short-term prospects where the degree of uncertainty is much smaller, especially in times of change.

(iii) Planning and control is based on a recent updated plan which is likely to be far more realistic than a fixed annual budget prepared months ago.

(iv) The budget is continuous and will always extend a number of months ahead, encouraging managers to think about the future. This is not the case with fixed periodic budgets.

(v)   A realistic budget that takes account of recent performance and market conditions is likely to have a better motivational influence on managers.

(b) **Disadvantages**

(i)   Rolling budgets are time consuming and expensive as a number of budgets must be produced during the accounting period.

(ii) The volume of work required with each reassessment of the budget can be off-putting for managers.

(iii)   Each revised budget may require revision of standards or stock valuations which could put additional pressure on the accounts department each time a rolling budget is prepared.

Section summary

Rolling budgets are continuously updated by adding a further accounting period (month or quarter) when the earliest accounting period has expired.

7   Budgeting as a control system

Introduction

In order to prepare a budget for an organisation as a whole, individual budgets have to be prepared for sub-sections of the organisation, such as individual departments, products or activities. This section looks at the key features of budget control systems and controllable and uncontrollable costs and why it is so important for budgetary control to correctly separate costs into these categories.

7.1 Budget control systems – key features

KEY TERM

A **BUDGET CENTRE** is 'A section of an entity for which control may be exercised through budgets prepared.' (CIMA *Official Terminology*)

Budgetary control is based around a system of budget centres. Each budget centre will have its own budget and a manager will be responsible for managing the budget centre and ensuring that the budget is met.

The **selection of budget centres** in an organisation is therefore a **key first step in setting up a control system**. What should the budget centres be? What income, expenditure and/or capital employment plans should each budget centre prepare? And how will measures of performance for each budget centre be made?

A well-organised system of control should have the following features.

Feature	Explanation
A hierarchy of budget centres	If the organisation is quite large a hierarchy is needed. Subsidiary companies, departments and work sections might be budget centres. Budgets of each section would then be consolidated into a departmental budget, departmental budgets in turn would be consolidated into the subsidiary's budget, and the budgets of each subsidiary would be **combined into a master budget** for the group as a whole.
Clearly identified responsibilities for achieving budget targets	Individual managers should be made responsible for achieving the budget targets of a particular budget centre.
Responsibilities for revenues, costs and capital employed	Budget centres should be organised so that all the revenues earned by an organisation, all the costs it incurs, and all the capital it employs are made the responsibility of someone within the organisation, at an appropriate level of authority in the management hierarchy.

Budgetary control and budget centres are therefore part of the overall system of **responsibility accounting** within an organisation.

RESPONSIBILITY ACCOUNTING is a system of accounting that segregates revenue and costs into areas of personal responsibility in order to monitor and assess the performance of each part of an organisation.

7.2 The controllability principle

Care must be taken to distinguish between controllable costs and uncontrollable costs in variance reporting. The **controllability principle** is that managers of responsibility centres should only be held accountable for costs over which they have **some influence**. From a **motivation** point of view this is important because it can be very demoralising for managers who feel that their performance is being judged on the basis of something over which they have no influence. It is also important from a **control** point of view in that control reports should ensure that information on costs is reported to the manager who is able to take action to control them.

7.3 Controllable and uncontrollable costs

A CONTROLLABLE COST is a 'Cost which can be controlled, typically by a cost, profit or investment centre manager.'

(CIMA *Official Terminology*)

Responsibility accounting attempts to associate costs, revenues, assets and liabilities with the managers most capable of controlling them. As a system of accounting, it therefore distinguishes between **controllable** and **uncontrollable** costs.

Most **variable costs** within a department are thought to be **controllable in the short term** because managers can influence the efficiency with which resources are used, even if they cannot do anything to raise or lower price levels.

A cost which is not controllable by a junior manager might be controllable by a senior manager. For example, there may be high direct labour costs in a department caused by excessive overtime working. The junior manager may feel obliged to continue with the overtime to meet production schedules, but his senior may be able to reduce costs by hiring extra full-time staff, thereby reducing the requirements for overtime.

A cost which is not controllable by a manager in one department may be controllable by a manager in another department. For example, an increase in material costs may be caused by buying at higher prices than expected (controllable by the purchasing department) or by excessive wastage (controllable by the production department) or by a faulty machine producing rejects (controllable by the maintenance department).

Some costs are **non-controllable**, such as increases in expenditure items due to inflation. Other costs are **controllable, but in the long term rather than the short term**. For example, production costs might be reduced by the introduction of new machinery and technology, but in the short term, management must attempt to do the best they can with the resources and machinery at their disposal.

7.3.1 The controllability of fixed costs

It is often assumed that all fixed costs are non-controllable in the short run. This is not so.

(a) **Committed fixed costs** are those costs arising from the possession of plant, equipment, buildings and an administration department to **support the long-term needs of the business**. These costs (depreciation, rent, administration salaries) are largely **non-controllable in the short term** because they have been committed by longer-term decisions affecting longer-term needs. When a company decides to cut production drastically, the long-term committed fixed costs will be reduced, but only after redundancy terms have been settled and assets sold.

(b) A **discretionary cost** is a cost whose amount, within a particular time period, is **determined by**, and can be **altered by**, the **budget holder**. **Discretionary fixed costs**, such as advertising and research and development costs, are incurred as a result of a top management decision, but could

be **raised or lowered at fairly short notice** (irrespective of the actual volume of production and sales).

7.3.2 Controllability and apportioned costs

Managers should only be held accountable for costs over which they have some influence. This may seem quite straightforward in theory, but it is not always so easy in practice to distinguish controllable from uncontrollable costs. **Apportioned overhead costs provide a good example**.

Example: Apportioned costs

Suppose that a manager of a production department in a manufacturing company is made responsible for the costs of his department. These costs include **directly attributable overhead items** such as the costs of indirect labour employed and indirect materials consumed in the department. The department's overhead costs also include an apportionment of costs from other cost centres, such as rent and rates for the building it shares with other departments and a share of the costs of the maintenance department.

Should the production manager be held accountable for any of these apportioned costs?

Solution

(a)   Managers should not be held accountable for costs over which they have no control. In this example, apportioned rent and rates costs would not be controllable by the production department manager.

(b)   Managers should be held accountable for costs over which they have some influence. In this example, it is the responsibility of the maintenance department manager to keep maintenance costs within budget. But their costs will be partly variable and partly fixed, and the variable cost element will depend on the volume of demand for their services. If the production department's staff treat their equipment badly we might expect higher repair costs, and the production department manager should therefore be made accountable for the repair costs that his department makes the maintenance department incur on its behalf.

(c)   Charging the production department with some of the costs of the maintenance department prevents the production department from viewing the maintenance services as 'free services'. Over-use would be discouraged and the production manager is more likely to question the activities of the maintenance department possibly resulting in a reduction in maintenance costs or the provision of more efficient maintenance services.

Question 10.4   Committed and discretionary costs

Try to discover some of your organisation's committed fixed costs and discretionary fixed costs. You will then be able to use them as examples in the exam.

Note: there is no solution to this question at the end of the chapter – this is a research question for you to try.

7.3.3 Controllability and dual responsibility

Quite often a particular cost might be the **responsibility of two or more managers**. For example, raw materials costs might be the responsibility of the purchasing manager (prices) and the production manager (usage). A **reporting system must allocate responsibility appropriately**. The purchasing manager

must be responsible for any increase in raw materials prices whereas the production manager should be responsible for any increase in raw materials usage.

Exam skills

You can see that there are **no clear cut rules** as to which costs are controllable and which are not. Each situation and cost must be reviewed separately and a decision taken according to the control value of the information and its behavioural impact.

7.4 Budgetary control reports

If the **budget holders** (managers of budget centres) are to attempt to meet budgets they must receive regular budgetary control reports so that they can monitor the budget centre's operations and take any necessary control action.

The **amount of detail** included in reports will **vary** according to the needs of management. In general terms, there should be **sufficient detail** within the reports to **motivate the individual manager to take the most appropriate action** in all circumstances. A form of **exception reporting** can be used for **top management,** reports just detailing significant variances.

Section summary

A **budget centre** is defined in CIMA *Official Terminology* as 'A section of an entity for which control may be exercised through budgets prepared.'

Responsibility accounting is a system of accounting that segregates revenue and costs into areas of personal responsibility in order to monitor and assess the performance of each part of an organisation.

Controllable costs are those which can be influenced by the budget holder. **Uncontrollable costs** cannot be so influenced.

8 Feedback and feedforward control mechanisms   11/11, 3/12

Introduction

Following on from the key concepts of budgets as control mechanisms, we move onto how information is relayed to the budget participants.

8.1 Feedback

KEY TERM

The term 'FEEDBACK' is used to describe both the process of reporting back control information to management and the control information itself. In a business organisation, it is information produced from within the organisation **(management control reports)** with the purpose of helping management and other employees with control decisions.

(a) **Single loop feedback**, normally expressed as feedback, is the feedback of relatively small variations between actual and plan in order that corrective action can bring performance in line with planned results. This implies that the existing plans will not change. This type of feedback is associated with budgetary control and standard costing.

(b) **Double loop feedback**, also known as **higher level feedback**, ensures that plans, budgets, organisational structures and the control systems themselves are revised to meet changes in conditions.

(c) Feedback will most often be **negative**: targets were missed and this was **not** what was required. It may, however, be **positive**: targets were missed, but other targets were hit which were better than those we were aiming at. Negative feedback would result in control action to get back onto target. Positive feedback means that the target should be moved.

8.2 The feedback loop in the control cycle

Feedback loop in the control cycle

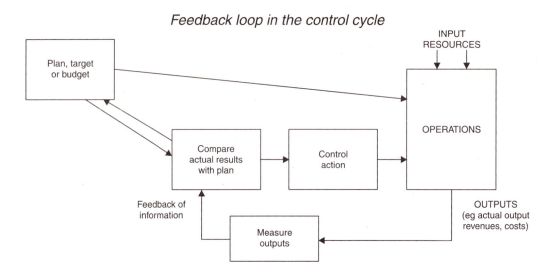

The elements in the control cycle, illustrated in the diagram, are as follows.

 Plans and targets are set for the future. These could be long-, medium- or short-term plans. Examples include budgets, profit targets and standard costs.

 Plans are put into operation. As a consequence, materials and labour are used, and other expenses are incurred.

 Actual results are recorded and analysed.

 Information about actual results is fed back to the management concerned, often in the form of accounting reports. This reported information is **feedback**.

 The feedback is used by management to compare actual results with the plan or targets (what should be or should have been achieved).

 By comparing actual and planned results, management can then do one of three things, depending on how they see the situation.

Management's potential reactions to divergences from planned performance

(a) **They can take controlling action**. By identifying what has gone wrong, and then finding out why, corrective measures can be taken.

(b) **They can decide to do nothing**. This could be the decision when actual results are going better than planned, or when poor results were caused by something which is unlikely to happen again in the future.

(c) **They can alter the plan or target** if actual results are different from the plan or target, and there is nothing that management can do (or nothing, perhaps, that they want to do) to correct the situation.

It may be helpful at this stage to relate the control system to a **practical example, such as monthly sales.**

 A **sales budget** or plan is prepared for the year.

 Management **organises the business's resources** to achieve the budget targets.

 At the end of each month, **actual results** are **reported back to management**.

 Managers **compare actual results against the plan.**

 Where necessary, they **take corrective action to adjust the workings of the system**, probably by amending the inputs to the system- for example, salespeople might be asked to work longer hours or new price discounts might be implemented.

This monthly sales example demonstrates how variance analysis is a form of feedback control. Variances can give negative or positive feedback. An adverse cost variance would be negative feedback and a favourable sales variance may well be seen as positive feedback.

KEY POINT

Variance analysis can be seen as a form of feedback control.

8.3 Feedforward control

KEY TERM

FEEDFORWARD CONTROL is the 'Forecasting of differences between actual and planned outcomes, and the implementation of action, before the event, to avoid such differences.   (CIMA *Official Terminology*)

Most control systems make use of a comparison between results of the current period (historical costs) and the planned results. Past events are therefore used as a means of controlling or adjusting future activity. A major criticism of this approach to control activity is that it is backward looking.

Consider, however, a **cash budget**. This is used to identify likely peaks and troughs in cash balances, and if it seems probable that, say, a higher overdraft facility will be needed later in the year, control action will be taken in advance of the actual need, to make sure that the facility will be available. This is an example of **feedforward control**, that is, control based on comparing original targets or actual results with a **forecast** of future results.

The 'information revolution', which has arisen from computer technology, management information systems theory and the growing use of quantitative techniques has widened the scope for the use of this control technique. Forecasting models can be constructed which enable regular revised forecasts to be prepared about what is now likely to happen in view of changes in key variables (such as sales demand, wage rates and so on).

If regular forecasts are prepared, managers will have both the current forecast and the original plan to guide their action. The original plan may or may not be achievable in view of the changing circumstances. The current forecast indicates what is expected to happen in view of these circumstances.

Examples of control comparisons

 Current forecast versus plan. What action must be taken to get back to the plan, given the differences between the current forecast and the plan? Is any control action worthwhile?

 If **control action** is **planned**, the current forecast will need to be amended to take account of the effects of the control action and a **revised forecast** prepared.

 The next comparison should then be **revised forecast versus plan** to determine whether the plan is now expected to be achieved.

 A comparison between the **original current forecast** and the **revised forecast** will show what the expected effect of the control action will be.

 At the **end of a control period**, actual results will be analysed and two comparisons may be made.

- **Actual results versus the revised forecast.** Why did differences between the two occur?

- **Actual results so far in the year versus the plan.** How close are actual results to the plan?

 At the same time, a **new current forecast** should be prepared, and the cycle of comparisons and control action may begin again.

It is in this way that costs are constantly controlled and monitored.

Another example of a system of feedforward control is target costing. This is when a business sets a target rate of return for its products or services. The results are forecast periodically and if it looks as if the target will not be met, action is taken to bring it back in line with target.

KEY POINT

> **Target costing** can be seen as a form of feedforward control.

 Section summary

The term **'feedback'** is used to describe both the process of reporting back control information to management and the control information itself.

Variance analysis can be seen as a form of feedback control.

Feedforward control is based on comparing original targets or actual results with a **forecast** of future results.

Target costing can be seen as a form of feedforward control.

---

9   Behavioural implications of budgeting   9/10

 Introduction

Although the principal purpose of a budgetary control system is to assist in planning and control, it can also have an effect on the behaviour of those directly affected by the budget. This section looks at how budgets can affect employees' behaviour and motivation.

9.1 Budgets and the provision of control information

The purpose of a budgetary control system is to assist management in **planning and controlling** the resources of their organisation by providing **appropriate control information**. The information will only be valuable, however, if it is **interpreted correctly** and used purposefully by managers *and* employees.

The correct use of control information therefore depends not only on the **content** of the information itself, but also on the **behaviour** of its recipients. This is because control in business is exercised by people. Their attitude to control information will colour their views on what they should do with it and a number of behavioural problems can arise.

(a) The **managers who set the budget** or standards are **often not the managers** who are then made **responsible for achieving budget targets**.

(b) The **goals of the organisation as a whole**, as expressed in a budget, **may not coincide with the personal aspirations of individual managers**.

(c) **Control is applied at different stages by different people**. A supervisor might get weekly control reports, and act on them; his superior might get monthly control reports, and decide to take different control action. Different managers can get in each others' way, and resent the interference from others.

9.2 Motivation

Motivation is what makes people behave in the way that they do. It comes from **individual attitudes**, or group attitudes. Individuals will be motivated by **personal desires and interests**. These may be in line with the objectives of the organisation, and some people 'live for their jobs'. Other individuals see their job as a chore, and their motivations will be unrelated to the objectives of the organisation they work for.

It is therefore vital that the goals of management and the employees harmonise with the goals of the organisation as a whole. This is known as **goal congruence**. Although obtaining goal congruence is essentially a behavioural problem, **it is possible to design and run a budgetary control system which will go some way towards ensuring that goal congruence is achieved**. Managers and employees must therefore be favourably disposed towards the budgetary control system so that it can operate efficiently.

The management accountant should therefore try to ensure that employees have positive attitudes towards **setting budgets, implementing budgets** (that is, putting the organisation's plans into practice) and feedback of results (**control information**).

9.2.1 Poor attitudes when setting budgets

If managers are involved in preparing a budget, poor attitudes or hostile behaviour towards the budgetary control system can begin at the **planning stage.**

(a) Managers may **complain that they are too busy** to spend much time on budgeting.

(b) They may **build 'slack' into their expenditure estimates**.

(c) They may argue that **formalising a budget plan on paper is too restricting** and that managers should be allowed flexibility in the decisions they take.

(d) They may set budgets for their budget centre and **not coordinate** their own plans with those of other budget centres.

(e) They may **base future plans on past results**, instead of using the opportunity for formalised planning to look at alternative options and new ideas.

On the other hand, **managers may not be involved in the budgeting process**. Organisational goals may not be communicated to them and they might have their budget decided for them by senior management or administrative decision. It is **hard for people to be motivated to achieve targets set by someone else**.

9.2.2 Poor attitudes when putting plans into action

Poor attitudes also arise **when a budget is implemented**.

(a)   Managers might **put in only just enough effort** to achieve budget targets, without trying to beat targets.

(b)   A formal budget might **encourage rigidity and discourage flexibility**.

(c)   **Short-term planning** in a budget **can draw attention away from the longer-term consequences** of decisions.

(d)   There might be **minimal cooperation and communication** between managers.

(e)   Managers will often try to make sure that they **spend up to their full budget allowance, and do not overspend**, so that they will not be accused of having asked for too much spending allowance in the first place.

(f)   Particularly in **service departments and public sector organisations,** where performance is assessed by comparing actual and budget spending, managers may consider the **budget** as a **sum of money that has to be spent**. A manager of a local authority department might be given an annual budget of $360,000. The manager knows that he will be punished for spending more than $360,000 but that if he spends less than $300,000 his budget will probably be reduced next year, leading to a loss of status and making his job more difficult next year. To ensure he does not overspend he may spend $26,000 a month for 11 months of the year (by reducing the provision of the department's service), building up a contingency fund of $(11 \times \$4,000)$ $44,000 to be used in case of emergencies. In the final month of the year he would then need to spend ($(\$44,000 + 30,000)$) $74,000 to ensure his whole budget was used (perhaps by using extra labour and/or high quality materials). The manager's **behaviour** has therefore been **distorted by the control system**.

9.2.3 Poor attitudes and the use of control information

The **attitude of managers towards the accounting control information** they receive **might reduce the information's effectiveness**.

(a)   Management accounting control reports could well be seen as having a relatively **low priority** in the list of management tasks. Managers might take the view that they have more pressing jobs on hand than looking at routine control reports.

(b)   Managers might **resent control information**; they may see it as **part of a system of trying to find fault with their work**. This resentment is likely to be particularly strong when budgets or standards are imposed on managers without allowing them to participate in the budget-setting process.

(c)   If budgets are seen as **pressure devices** to push managers into doing better, control reports will be resented.

(d)   Managers **may not understand the information** in the control reports, because they are unfamiliar with accounting terminology or principles.

(e)   Managers might have a **false sense of what their objectives should be**. A production manager might consider it more important to maintain quality standards regardless of cost. He would then dismiss adverse expenditure variances as inevitable and unavoidable.

(f)   **If there are flaws in the system of recording actual costs**, managers will dismiss control information as unreliable.

(g)   **Control information** might be **received weeks after the end of the period to which it relates**, in which case managers might regard it as out-of-date and no longer useful.

(h)   Managers might be **held responsible for variances outside their control**.

It is therefore obvious that accountants and senior management should try to implement systems that are acceptable to budget holders and which produce positive effects.

9.2.4 Pay as a motivator

Many researchers agree that **pay can be an important motivator**, when there is a formal link between higher pay (or other rewards, such as promotion) and achieving budget targets. Individuals are likely to work harder to achieve budget if they know that they will be rewarded for their successful efforts. There are, however, problems with using pay as an incentive.

(a)   A serious problem that can arise is that **formal reward and performance evaluation systems can encourage dysfunctional behaviour**. Many investigations have noted the tendency of managers to pad their budgets either in anticipation of cuts by superiors or to make the subsequent variances more favourable. And there are numerous examples of managers making decisions in response to performance indices, even though the decisions are contrary to the wider purposes of the organisation.

(b)   The targets must be challenging, but fair, otherwise individuals will become dissatisfied. **Pay can be a demotivator as well as a motivator**!

Section summary

Used correctly a budgetary control system can **motivate** but it can also produce undesirable **negative reactions**.

10   Budget participation   3/11, 5/12, 11/12

Introduction

It has been argued that **participation** in the budgeting process **will improve motivation** and so will improve the quality of budget decisions and the efforts of individuals to achieve their budget targets. This section looks at different budget styles and how they affect the participation process.

KEY TERM

There are basically two ways in which a budget can be set: from the TOP DOWN (imposed budget) or from the BOTTOM UP (participatory budget).

10.1 Imposed style of budgeting

KEY TERM

An IMPOSED/TOP-DOWN BUDGET is a 'Budgeting process where budget allowances are set without permitting the ultimate budget holders to have the opportunity to participate in the budgeting process.'

(CIMA *Official Terminology*)

In this approach to budgeting, **top management prepare a budget with little or no input from operating personnel** which is then imposed upon the employees who have to work to the budgeted figures.

The times when imposed budgets are effective

- In newly-formed organisations
- In very small businesses
- During periods of economic hardship
- When operational managers lack budgeting skills
- When the organisation's different units require precise coordination

There are, of course, advantages and disadvantages to this style of setting budgets.

(a) **Advantages**

    (i)   Strategic plans are likely to be incorporated into planned activities.

    (ii)   They enhance the coordination between the plans and objectives of divisions.

    (iii)   They use senior management's awareness of total resource availability.

    (iv)   They decrease the input from inexperienced or uninformed lower-level employees.

    (v)   They decrease the period of time taken to draw up the budgets.

(b) **Disadvantages**

    (i)   Dissatisfaction, defensiveness and low morale amongst employees. It is hard for people to be motivated to achieve targets set by somebody else.

    (ii)   The feeling of team spirit may disappear.

    (iii)   The acceptance of organisational goals and objectives could be limited.

    (iv)   The feeling of the budget as a punitive device could arise.

    (v)   Managers who are performing operations on a day to day basis are likely to have a better understanding of what is achievable.

    (vi)   Unachievable budgets could result if consideration is not given to local operating and political environments. This applies particularly to overseas divisions.

    (vii)   Lower-level management initiative may be stifled.

10.2 Participative style of budgeting

KEY TERM

PARTICIPATIVE/BOTTOM-UP BUDGETING is a 'Budgeting process where all budget holders have the opportunity to participate in setting their own budgets.'

(CIMA *Official Terminology*)

In this approach to budgeting, **budgets are developed by lower-level managers who then submit the budgets to their superiors**. The budgets are based on the lower-level managers' perceptions of what is achievable and the associated necessary resources.

Question 10.5	Participative budgets

Learning outcome C3(a)

In what circumstances might participative budgets *not* be effective?

A   In centralised organisations
B   In well-established organisations
C   In very large businesses
D   During periods of economic affluence

Advantages of participative budgets

- They are based on information from employees most familiar with the department.
- Knowledge spread among several levels of management is pulled together.
- Morale and motivation is improved.
- They increase operational managers' commitment to organisational objectives.
- In general they are more realistic.
- Co-ordination between units is improved.
- Specific resource requirements are included.
- Senior managers' overview is mixed with operational level details.
- Individual managers' aspiration levels are more likely to be taken into account.

Disadvantages of participative budgets

- They consume more time.
- Changes implemented by senior management may cause dissatisfaction.
- Budgets may be unachievable if managers are not qualified to participate.
- They may cause managers to introduce budgetary slack and budget bias.
- They can support 'empire building' by subordinates.
- An earlier start to the budgeting process could be required.
- Managers may set 'easy' budgets to ensure that they are achievable.

10.3 Negotiated style of budgeting

KEY TERM

A NEGOTIATED BUDGET is a 'Budget in which budget allowances are set largely on the basis of negotiations between budget holders and those to whom they report.'   (CIMA *Official Terminology*)

At the two extremes, budgets can be dictated from above or simply emerge from below but, in practice, different levels of management often agree budgets by a process of negotiation. In the imposed budget approach, operational managers will try to negotiate with senior managers the budget targets which they consider to be unreasonable or unrealistic. Likewise senior management usually review and revise budgets presented to them under a participative approach through a process of negotiation with lower level managers. **Final budgets are therefore most likely to lie between what top management would really like and what junior managers believe is feasible.** The budgeting process is hence a **bargaining process** and it is this bargaining which is of vital importance, **determining whether the budget is an effective management tool or simply a clerical device**.

10.4 Budget slack

KEY TERM

BUDGET SLACK is the 'Intentional overestimation of expenses and/or underestimation of revenues during the budget setting.'   (CIMA *Official Terminology*)

In the process of preparing budgets, managers might **deliberately overestimate costs and underestimate sales**, so that they will not be blamed in the future for overspending and poor results.

In controlling actual operations, managers must then **ensure that their spending rises to meet their budget**, otherwise they will be 'blamed' for careless budgeting.

Budget bias can **work in the other direction** too. It has been noted that, after a run of mediocre results, some managers **deliberately overstate revenues and understate cost estimates**, no doubt feeling the need to make an immediate favourable impact by promising better performance in the future. They may merely delay problems, however, as the managers may well be censured when they fail to hit these optimistic targets.

Yet again this is an example of **control systems distorting the processes they are meant to serve**.

Section summary

There are basically two ways in which a budget can be set: from the **top down** (**imposed** budget) or from the **bottom up** (**participatory** budget). Many writers refer to a third style (**negotiated**).

Budget slack occurs when managers deliberately underestimate sales or overestimate costs to avoid being blamed for future poor results.

11   The use of budgets as targets

Introduction

Once decided, budgets become targets. As targets, they can motivate managers to achieve a high level of performance. This section looks at the extent to which managers can be motivated by budget targets and the challenges of ensuring the correct level of difficulty of these targets.

11.1 Setting the target

(a)   There is likely to be a **demotivating** effect where an **ideal standard** of performance is set, because adverse efficiency variances will always be reported.

(b)   A **low standard of efficiency** is also **demotivating**, because there is no sense of achievement in attaining the required standards, and there will be no impetus for employees to try harder to do better than this.

(c)   A **budgeted level of attainment** could be 'normal': that is, the **same as the level that has been achieved in the past**. Arguably, this level will be **too low**. It might **encourage budgetary slack**.

11.2 Aspiration levels

It has been argued that **each individual has a personal 'aspiration level'**. This is a level of performance in a task with which the individual is familiar, which the individual undertakes for himself to reach. This aspiration level might be quite challenging and if individuals in a work group all have similar aspiration levels it should be possible to incorporate these levels within the official operating standards.

Some care should be taken, however, in applying this.

(a)   If a manager's **tendency to achieve success is stronger than the tendency to avoid failure**, budgets with **targets of intermediate levels of difficulty** are the most motivating, and stimulate a manager to better performance levels. Budgets which are either too easy to achieve or too difficult are de-motivating, and managers given such targets achieve relatively low levels of performance.

(b)   A manager's **tendency to avoid failure might be stronger than the tendency to achieve success**. (This is likely in an organisation in which the budget is used as a pressure device on subordinates by senior managers). Managers might then be discouraged from trying to achieve budgets of intermediate difficulty and tend to avoid taking on such tasks, resulting in poor levels of performance, worse than if budget targets were either easy or very difficult to achieve.

11.3 A case for two budgets?

It has been suggested that in a situation where budget targets of an intermediate difficulty *are* motivating, such targets ought to be set if the purpose of budgets is to motivate. However, although budgets which are set for **motivational purposes** need to be stated in terms of **aspirations rather than expectations**, budgets for planning and decision purposes need to be stated in terms of the **best available estimate** of expected actual performance. The **solution** might therefore be to have **two budgets**.

(a)   A **budget for planning and decision-making based on reasonable expectations**.

(b)   A second **budget for motivational purposes**, with **more difficult targets of performance** (that is, targets of an intermediate level of difficulty).

These two budgets might be called an '**expectations budget**' and an '**aspirations budget**' respectively.

Section summary

In certain situations it is useful to prepare an **expectations budget** (for planning and decision-making purposes) and an **aspirations budget** (to act as a motivational tool).

12 Budgets and motivation

5/10

Introduction

We have seen that budgets serve many purposes, but in some instances their purposes can conflict and have an effect on management behaviour. This section examines the need for strategies and methods to deal with the resulting tensions and conflict.

12.1 Is motivation from budgets ever possible?

Can performance measures and the related budgetary control system ever **motivate managers** towards achieving the organisation's goals?

(a)   Accounting measures of performance **can't provide a comprehensive assessment** of what a person has achieved for the organisation.

(b)   It is unfair as it is usually **impossible to segregate controllable and uncontrollable components of performance**.

(c)   Accounting **reports tend to concentrate on short-term achievements**, to the exclusion of the long-term effects.

(d)   Many accounting **reports try to serve several different purposes**, and in trying to satisfy several needs actually satisfy none properly.

12.2 Support from senior management

The management accountant does not have the authority to do much on his or her own to improve hostile or apathetic attitudes to control information. There has to be support, either from senior management or from budget centre managers.

(a)   **How senior management can offer support**

   (i)   Making sure that a **system of responsibility accounting is adopted**.
   (ii)   Allowing **managers to have a say in formulating their budgets**.
   (iii)   Offering **incentives** to managers who meet budget targets.
   (iv)   Not regarding budgetary control information as a way of apportioning blame.

(b)   **Budget centre managers should accept their responsibilities**. In-house training courses could be held to encourage a collective, cooperative and positive attitude among managers.

12.3 Support from the management accountant

The management accountant can offer support in the following ways.

(a)   **Develop a working relationship with operational managers**, going out to meet them and discussing the control reports.

(b)   **Explain the meaning of budgets and control reports**.

(c)   **Keep accounting jargon in these reports to a minimum**.

(d)   Make **reports clear and to the point**, for example using the principle of reporting by exception.

(e)   Provide control information with a **minimum of delay.**

(f)   **Make control information as useful as possible**, by distinguishing between directly attributable and controllable costs over which a manager should have influence and apportioned or fixed costs which are unavoidable or uncontrollable.

(g)   Make sure that **actual costs are recorded accurately**.

(h)   Ensure that **budgets are up-to-date**, either by having a system of rolling budgets, or else by updating budgets or standards as necessary, and ensuring that standards are 'fair' so that control information is realistic.

Question 10.6	Behavioural aspects of budget participation

Learning outcome C3(a)

Discuss the behavioural aspects of participation in the budgeting process and any difficulties you might envisage.

Section summary

There are no ideal solutions to the conflicts caused by the operation of a budgetary control system. Management and the management accountant have to develop their own ways of dealing with them, taking into account their organisation, their business and the personalities involved.

---

13   Beyond Budgeting   5/13

Introduction

This section looks at the arguments put forward by the Beyond Budgeting Round Table that traditional budgeting should be abandoned.

13.1 Criticisms of budgeting

In our discussion of the budgetary planning process we have come across many difficulties with budgets and criticisms of how they are used in organisations. The discussion on behavioural issues in this chapter should help you to appreciate the real danger that budgets can cause unintended dysfunctional behaviour that needs to be guarded against in organisations.

The Beyond Budgeting Round Table (BBRT), an independent research collaborative, propose that budgeting, as most organisations practise it, should be abandoned. Their website at www.bbrt.org lists the following ten criticisms of budgeting as put forward by Hope and Fraser *Beyond Budgeting*, 1st edition, Harvard Business School Press, 2003.

(a)   **Budgets are time consuming and expensive**. Even with the support of computer models it is estimated that the budgeting process uses up to 20 to 30 per cent of senior executives' and financial managers' time.

(b)   **Budgets provide poor value to users**. Although surveys have shown that some managers feel that budgets give them control, a large majority of financial directors wish to reform the budgetary process because they feel that finance staff spend too much time on 'lower value added activities'

(c)   **Budgets fail to focus on shareholder value**. Most budgets are set on an incremental basis as an acceptable target agreed between the manager and the manager's superior. Managers may be rewarded for achieving their short term budgets and will not look to the longer term or take risks, for fear of affecting their own short term results.

(d)   **Budgets are too rigid and prevent fast response**. Although most organisations do update and revise their budgets at regular intervals as the budget period proceeds the process is often too slow compared with the pace at which the external environment is changing.

(e)   **Budgets protect rather than reduce costs**. Once a manager has an authorised budget he can spend that amount of resource without further authorisation. A 'use it or lose it' mentality often develops so that managers will incur cost unnecessarily. This happens especially towards the end of the budget period in the expectation that managers will not be permitted to carry forward any unused resource into the budget for next period.

(f)   **Budgets stifle product and strategy innovation**. The focus on achieving the budget discourages managers from taking risks in case this has adverse effects on their short term performance. Managers do not have the freedom to respond to changing customer needs in a fast changing market because the activity they would need to undertake is not authorised in their budget.

(g)   **Budgets focus on sales targets rather than customer satisfaction**. The achievement of short term sales forecasts becomes the focus of most organisations. However this does not necessarily result in customer satisfaction. The customer may be sold something **inappropriate to their needs**, as in recent years in the UK financial services industry. Alternatively if a manager has already met the sales target for a particular period they might try to **delay sales to the next period**, in order to give themselves a 'head start' towards achieving the target for the next period. Furthermore, there is an incentive towards the end of a period, if a manager feels that the sales target is not going to be achieved for the period, to **delay sales until the next period**, and thus again have a head start towards achieving the target for the next period. All of these actions, focusing on sales targets rather than customer satisfaction, will have a detrimental effect on the organisation in the longer term.

(h)   **Budgets are divorced from strategy**. Most organisations monitor the monthly results against the short term budget for the month. What is needed instead is a system of monitoring the longer term progress against the organisation's strategy.

(i)   **Budgets reinforce a dependency culture**. The process of planning and budgeting within a framework devolved from senior management perpetuates a culture of dependency. Traditional budgeting systems, operated on a centralised basis, do not encourage a culture of **personal responsibility**.

(j)   **Budgets lead to unethical behaviour**. For example we have seen in this chapter a number of opportunities for dysfunctional behaviour such as **building slack into the budget** in order to create an easier target for achievement.

13.2 Beyond Budgeting concepts

Two fundamental concepts underlie the Beyond Budgeting approach.

(a)   **Use adaptive management processes rather than the more rigid annual budget**. Traditional annual plans tie managers to predetermined actions which are not responsive to current situations. Managers should instead be planning on a **more adaptive**, rolling basis but with the focus on cash forecasting rather than purely on cost control. Performance is monitored against world-class benchmarks, competitors and previous periods.

(b)   **Move towards devolved networks rather than centralised hierarchies**. The emphasis is on encouraging a culture of personal responsibility by delegating decision making and performance accountability to line managers.

Beyond Budgeting model

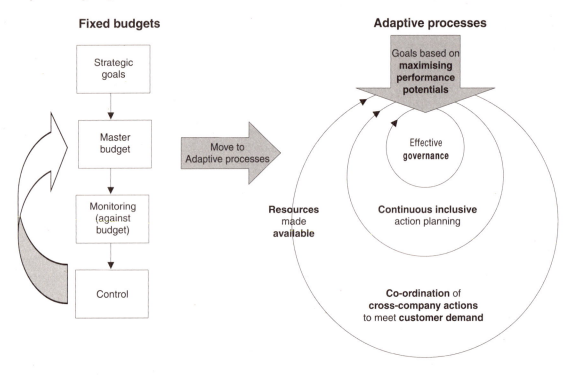

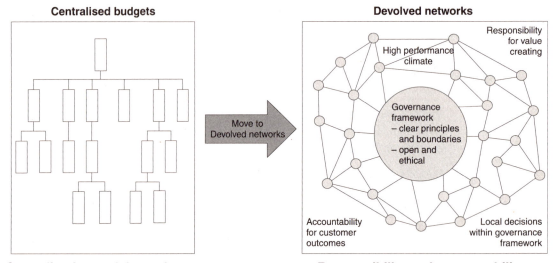

Adapted from www.bbrt.org

13.3 Adaptive management processes

An adaptive management process **does not tie a manager to the achievement of a fixed target** but instead expects managers to deliver **continuous performance improvement in response to changing conditions**. Planning is undertaken on a continuous, participative basis.

Evaluation of a manager's performance is based on **relative improvement** and this evaluation is carried out using a **range of relative performance indicators with hindsight**, ie taking account of the conditions under which the manager was operating.

Managers are **given the resources** they need as they are required and horizontal **cross-company activities are coordinated** to respond to customer demand.

13.4 Devolved organisations

In a devolved organisation managers are enabled and encouraged to make their own local decisions in order to achieve results, **within a governance framework based on clear principles and boundaries**. Managers are not restricted to a specific agreed plan but **can use their own initiative and local knowledge** to achieve the organisation's goals. They are expected to make decisions that create value and are fully **accountable for customer satisfaction** and for **achieving a high level of relative success**.

The emphasis in information systems is on openness and 'one truth' throughout the organisation, thus **encouraging ethical behaviour** that is beneficial to the organisation.

The ability of managers to act immediately, without the restriction of a fixed plan, but **within clear principles, values and strategic boundaries** enables the organisation to respond quickly to identified opportunities and threats.

13.5 Beyond budgeting (BB) implementation

A BB implementation should incorporate the following six main principles.

(a)   The responsibilities of managers within an organisation should be clearly defined.

(b)   Managers should be given goals and targets which are based on key performance indicators and benchmarks. These targets should be linked to shareholder value.

(c)   Managers should be given a degree of freedom to make decisions. A BB organisation chart should be "flat".

(d)   Responsibility for decisions that generate value should be placed with "front line teams" in line with the concept of TQM.

(e)   Front line teams should be made responsible for relationships with customers, associate businesses and suppliers.

(f)   Information support systems should be transparent and align with the activities that managers are responsible for.

| **Question 10.7** | In defence of traditional budgeting |

Learning outcome C3(d)

Identify THREE criticisms that are levelled at the traditional budgeting process by advocates of techniques that are 'beyond budgeting' and explain how the traditional budgeting process can be adapted to address these criticisms.

Section summary

The **Beyond Budgeting Round Table**, an independent research collaborative, have proposed that traditional budgeting should be abandoned. They have published ten main criticisms of the traditional process.

The two fundamental concepts of the **Beyond Budgeting** approach are the use of **adaptive management processes** rather than fixed annual budgets and a move to a more decentralised way of managing the business with a culture of personal responsibility.

Chapter Roundup

- ✓ **Fixed budgets** remain unchanged regardless of the level of activity; **flexible budgets** are designed to flex with the level of activity.

- ✓ **Flexible budgets** are prepared using marginal costing and so mixed costs must be split into their fixed and variable components (possibly using the **high/low method**).

- ✓ Flexible budgets should be used to show what cost and revenues should have been for the actual level of activity. Differences between the flexible budget figures and actual results are **variances**.

- ✓ The **budget cost allowance/flexible budget** is the budgeted cost ascribed to the level of activity achieved in a budget centre in a control period. It comprises variable costs in direct proportion to volume achieved and fixed costs as a proportion of the annual budget.

- ✓ Budgetary control is based around a system of **budget centres**. Each centre has its own budget which is the responsibility of the **budget holder**.

- ✓ There are a number of key characteristics and components of a system. Learn them!

- ✓ **Spreadsheet packages** can be used to build business models to assist the forecasting and planning process.

- ✓ **'What-if?' analysis** involves changing the values of the forecast variables to see the effect on the forecast outcome. The information provided helps managers to understand the sensitivity of the forecast to the value of the variables.

- ✓ **Rolling budgets** are continuously updated by adding a further accounting period (month or quarter) when the earliest accounting period has expired.

- ✓ A **budget centre** is defined in CIMA *Official Terminology* as 'A section of an entity for which control may be exercised through budgets prepared.'

- ✓ **Responsibility accounting** is a system of accounting that segregates revenue and costs into areas of personal responsibility in order to monitor and assess the performance of each part of an organisation.

- ✓ **Controllable costs** are those which can be influenced by the budget holder. **Uncontrollable costs** cannot be so influenced.

- ✓ The term **'feedback'** is used to describe both the process of reporting back control information to management and the control information itself.

- ✓ **Variance analysis** can be seen as a form of feedback control.

- ✓ **Feedforward control** is based on comparing original targets or actual results with a **forecast** of future results.

- ✓ **Target costing** can be seen as a form of feedforward control.

- ✓ Used correctly a budgetary control system can **motivate** but it can also produce undesirable **negative reactions**.

- ✓ There are basically two ways in which a budget can be set: from the **top down** (**imposed** budget) or from the **bottom up** (**participatory** budget). Many writers refer to a third style (**negotiated**).

- ✓ **Budget slack** occurs when managers deliberately underestimate sales or overestimate costs to avoid being blamed for future poor results.

- ✓ In certain situations it is useful to prepare an **expectations budget** (for planning and decision-making purposes) and an **aspirations budget** (to act as a motivational tool).

✓ There are no ideal solutions to the conflicts caused by the operation of a budgetary control system. Management and the management accountant have to develop their own ways of dealing with them, taking into account their organisation, their business and the personalities involved.

✓ The **Beyond Budgeting Round** Table, an independent research collaborative, have proposed that traditional budgeting should be abandoned. They have publicised ten main criticisms of the traditional process.

✓ The two fundamental concepts of the **Beyond Budgeting** approach are the use of **adaptive management processes** rather than fixed annual budgets and a move to a more decentralised way of managing the business with a culture of personal responsibility.

Quick Quiz

1   *Fill in the blanks.*

A flexible budget is a budget which, by recognising ...., is designed to
.... as the level of activity changes.

2   An extract of the costs incurred at two different activity levels is shown. Classify the costs according to
their behaviour patterns and show the budget cost allowance for an activity of 1,500 units.

		1,000 units	2,000 units	Type of cost	Budget cost allowance for 1,500 units
		$	$		$
(a)	Fuel	3,000	6,000	....	....
(b)	Photocopying	9,500	11,000	....	....
(c)	Heating	2,400	2,400	....	....
(d)	Direct wages	6,000	8,000	....	....

3   What is the controllability principle?

4   Feedforward control is based on comparing original targets or actual results with a forecast of future
results. *True or false?*

5   *Match the descriptions to the budgeting style.*

Description

(a)   Budget allowances are set without the involvement of the budget holder

(b)   All budget holders are involved in setting their own budgets

(c)   Budget allowances are set on the basis of discussions between budget holders and those to whom
they report

Budgeting style

Negotiated budgeting
Participative budgeting
Imposed budgeting

6   *Choose the appropriate words from those highlighted.*

An **expectations/aspirations** budget would be most useful for the purposes of planning and decision
making based on reasonable expectations, whereas an **aspirations/expectations** budget is more
appropriate for improving motivation by setting targets of an intermediate level of difficulty.

7   In the context of a balanced scorecard approach to performance measurement, to which of the four
perspectives does each measure relate?

	Performance measure	*Perspective*
(a)	Time taken to develop new products	....
(b)	Percentage of on-time deliveries	....
(c)	Average set-up time	....
(d)	Return on capital employed	....

8   *Choose the appropriate words from those highlighted.*

The correct approach to budgetary control is to compare **actual/budgeted** results with a budget that has
been flexed to the **actual/budgeted** level of activity.

9   Not all fixed costs are non-controllable in the short term. *True or false?*

10   What is goal congruence (in terms of organisational control systems)?

    A   When the goals of management and employees harmonise with the goals of the organisation as a whole

    B   When the goals of management harmonise with the goals of employees

    C   When the work-related goals of management harmonise with their personal goals

    D   When an organisation's goals harmonise with those of its customers

11   For each organisation there is an ideal solution to the conflicts caused by the operation of a budgetary control system and it is the responsibility of the management accountant to find that solution. *True or false?*

12   Which of the following is **not** consistent with the concepts of the Beyond Budgeting approach?

    A   Continuous forecasting
    B   Participative planning
    C   Centralised decision making
    D   Relative performance measures

13   Which of the following definitions is/are correct?

    1   An imposed budget is a budget which, by recognising different cost behaviour patterns, is designed to change as the volume of activity changes

    2   Bottom-up budgeting is a process where all budget holders have the opportunity to participate

    A   Neither are correct
    B   Definition 1 only is correct
    C   Definition 2 only is correct
    D   Both definitions are correct

Answers to Quick Quiz

1   cost behaviour patterns

     flex or change

2   (a)   Variable $4,500
     (b)   Semi-variable $10,250
     (c)   Fixed $2,400
     (d)   Semi-variable $7,000

3   The principle that managers should only be held responsible for costs that they have direct control over.

4   True

5   (a)   Imposed budgeting
     (b)   Participative budgeting
     (c)   Negotiated budgeting

6   expectations
     aspirations

7   (a)   Learning
     (b)   Customer
     (c)   Internal
     (d)   Financial

8   actual
     actual

9   True. Discretionary fixed costs can be raised or lowered at fairly short notice.

10   A

11   False. There are no ideal solutions. Management and the management accountant have to develop their
     own ways of dealing with the conflicts, taking into account the organisation, the business and the
     personalities involved.

12   C

13   C   Definition 1 refers to a flexible budget.

Answers to Questions

10.1 High-low method

The correct answer is $297,000.

Price levels should be adjusted to a common basis, say index level 100.

(a)

	Output	Total cost	Cost at price level index = 100
		$	$
High level	90,000 units	209,100 × (100/123)	= 170,000
Low level	60,000 units	201,600 × (100/144)	= 140,000
Variable cost	30,000 units		= 30,000

The variable cost is therefore $1 per unit.

(b)   Use the variable cost to determine the fixed cost.

	$
Total cost of 90,000 units (Index 100)	170,000
Variable cost of 90,000 units (× $1)	90,000
Fixed costs (Index 100)	80,000

(c)   Costs in year 5 for 85,000 units will be as follows.

	$
Variable costs (Index 100)	85,000
Fixed costs (Index 100)	80,000
Total costs (Index 100)	165,000

At year 5 price levels (Index 180) = $165,000 ×(180/100) = $297,000

10.2 Flexible budget

	Budget 200 units $	Budget per unit $	Flexed budget 230 units $	Actual 230 units $	Variance $
Sales	71,400	357	82,110	69,000	13,110 (A)
Variable costs					
Labour	31,600	158	36,340	27,000	9,340 (F)
Material	12,600	63	14,490	24,000	9,510 (A)
	44,200	221	50,830	51,000	
Contribution	27,200	136	31,280	18,000	13,280 (A)
Fixed costs	18,900		18,900	10,000	8,900 (F)
Profit	8,300		12,380	8,000	4,380 (A)

10.3 Spreadsheets

(a)

C2:	B2*1.2	C10:	@ SUM(C7..C9) or = SUM (C7...C9)
C3:	C2*0.65	C11:	C3
C4:	C2 + C3	C12:	C10 + C11
C7:	C2*0.6	C13:	B14
C8:	B2*0.4	C14:	C12 + C13

Note that the figures are entered into each cell as either positive or negative and so C4, for example, is calculated by *adding* 1,200 and -780.

(b)

A	B		C		D
	Month 1		*Month 2*		*Month 3*
Sales	1,000	(+15%)	1,150	(+15%)	1,323
Cost of sales (68%)	680		782		900
Gross profit	320		368		423
Receipts					
Current month (40%)	400		460		529
Previous month (50%)	–		500		575
Two months in arrears (10%)	–		–		100
	400		960		1,204
Payments	(680)		(782)		(900)
	(280)		178		304
Balance b/f	–		(280)		(102)
Balance c/f	(280)		(102)		202

The cash position would be substantially worse if all of the 'what if?' conditions occurred simultaneously. Although the cash balance would become positive during month 3, the closing balance would be much lower. If these conditions were to apply then management would need to make arrangements to finance a large short-term deficit during months 1 and 2.

(c)

C2:	B2*1.15
C3:	C2*0.68
C7:	C2*0.4
C8:	B2*0.5
C9:	Blank (but D9 would have B2*0.1)

(d) It would be much easier to conduct sensitivity analysis if the items that are variable were allocated specific cells outside the body of the cash flow table. For example rows 15 - 19 could contain the following.

	A	B
15	Cost of sales/Sales	0.68
16	Receipts – current month	0.40
17	– 1 month in arrears	0.50
18	– 2 months in arrears	0.10
19	Sales growth	1.15

The formulae in row C would then read as follows.

C2	B2*B19
C3	C2*B15
C7	C2*B16
C8	B2*B17
C9	A2*B18

(Note that B17, for example, is an absolute cell address whereas C2 is a relative cell address.)

Further sensitivity analysis could be conducted simply by changing the values in cells B15 - B19, rather than having to rewrite each column each time a variable is changed.

At year 5 price levels (Index 180) = $165,000 ×(180/100) = $297,000

10.5 Participative budgets

A participative budget is likely to be least effective in a centralised organisation. An imposed budget will be more effective in such an organisation.

10.6 Behavioural aspects of budget participation

The level of participation in the budgeting process can vary from zero participation to a process of group decision making. There are a number of behavioural aspects of participation to consider.

(a) **Communication**. Managers cannot be expected to achieve targets if they do not know what those targets are. Communication of targets is made easier if managers have participated in the budgetary process from the beginning.

(b) **Motivation**. Managers are likely to be better motivated to achieve a budget if they have been involved in compiling it, rather than having a dictatorial budget imposed on them.

(c) **Realistic targets**. A target must be achievable and accepted as realistic if it is to be a motivating factor. A manager who has been involved in setting targets is more likely to accept them as realistic. In addition, managers who are close to the operation of their departments may be more aware of the costs and potential savings in running it.

(d) **Goal congruence**. One of the best ways of achieving goal congruence is to involve managers in the preparation of their own budgets, so that their personal goals can be taken into account in setting targets.

Although participative budgeting has many advantages, difficulties might also arise.

(e) **Pseudo-participation**. Participation may not be genuine, but merely a pretence at involving managers in the preparation of their budgets. Managers may feel that their contribution is being ignored, or that the participation consists of merely obtaining their agreement to a budget which has already been decided. If this is the case then managers are likely to be more demotivated than if there is no participation at all.

(f) **Coordination**. If participative budgeting is well managed it can improve the coordination of the preparation of the various budgets. There is, however, a danger that too many managers will become involved so that communication becomes difficult and the process complex.

(g) **Training**. Some managers may not possess the necessary skill to make an effective contribution to the preparation of their budgets. Additional training may be necessary, with the consequent investment of money and time. It may also be necessary to train managers to understand the purposes and advantages of participation.

(h) **Slack**. If budgets are used in a punitive fashion for control purposes then managers will be tempted to build in extra expenditure to provide a 'cushion' against overspending. It is easier for them to build in slack in a participative system.

10.7 In defence of traditional budgeting

Three criticisms that could be addressed by adapting the traditional budgeting process are as follows.

(a) Budgets are time consuming and expensive.
(b) Budgets protect rather than reduce costs.
(c) Budgets focus on sales targets rather than customer satisfaction.

The traditional budgeting process can be operated in a fashion that addresses these criticisms as follows.

(a) **Budgets are time consuming and expensive**

A traditional budgeting system need not be more expensive and time consuming than the adaptive management process advocated as a Beyond Budgeting concept. Managers need to appreciate that the cost of obtaining information should not exceed the benefit to be derived from it. A culture of '**sufficiently accurate**' should be encouraged in budget managers and they should understand that their task is to quantify the costs to be incurred in their area **in order to achieve the organisation's strategy**. This does

not necessitate a separate forecast for every paperclip and staple, down to the nearest penny, but budgets can instead be prepared to the nearest thousand or to the nearest million, depending on the size of the organisation.

(b)   Budgets protect rather than reduce costs

The attitude of senior managers needs to change in order to prevent unnecessary expenditure and slack being built into the budget. If a budget manager has not used all of their allocated budget resource during a period they should not expect to lose that resource in the next period. **Each manager should be able to request the resource needed to achieve the organisation's strategy**, regardless of the expenditure incurred in the latest period or the amount that was included in the original budget. Thus a 'use it or lose it' culture can be avoided.

Slack can also be avoided by **using budgetary control reports in a less punitive and rigid manner**. If managers believe they are going to be admonished for exceeding the budget expenditure or they are not going to be allowed more resource than stated in their original budget then they will build in slack at the planning stage in order to provide some leeway.

(c)   Budgets focus on sales targets rather than customer satisfaction

The punitive use of budgetary control reports will again aggravate this situation. Managers must be given the opportunity to justify any sales shortfalls and should not be penalised for any shortfalls that are beyond their control. The use of **non-financial performance measures** combined with the financial budgetary control reports will assist in moving managers' focus away from the sales targets. For example managers' performance could be assessed on a combination of sales targets and the level of customer satisfaction achieved.

Now try these questions from the Exam Question Bank

Number	Level	Marks	Time
Q25	Examination	5	9 mins
Q26	Examination	12	22 mins

BUDGETING: PERFORMANCE EVALUATION

Performance evaluation is important as it allows management to determine how well the company is doing, in comparison with both previous years and with competitors. Variances are an important measure of performance that you have already met in previous studies and in relation to flexible budgeting in Chapter 10.

It is important that the performance of an organisation is monitored, and this is most commonly done by calculating a number of ratios. **Sections 1 and 2** examine the key **financial** and **non-financial** performance indicators.

topic list	learning outcomes	syllabus references	ability required
1 Financial performance indicators (FPIs)	C2(a)	C2(i)	evaluation
2 Non-financial performance indicators (NFPIs)	C3(b)	C3(ii)	analysis
3 The balanced scorecard	C3(c)	C3(iii)	analysis
4 Benchmarking	C3(c)	C3(iii)	analysis
5 Not-for-profit organisations	C3(b)	C3(ii)	analysis

1 Financial performance indicators (FPIs)

Introduction

This section covers the ways in which performance can be measured using financial performance indicators. Make sure you can interpret the ratios as well as calculate them!

1.1 Setting the scene

KEY POINT

Financial performance indicators analyse profitability, liquidity and risk.

Financial indicators (or **monetary** measures) include:

Measure	Example
Profit	Profit is the commonest measure of all. Profit maximisation is usually cited as the main objective of most business organisations: 'ICI increased pre-tax profits to $233m'; 'General Motors... yesterday reported better-than-expected first-quarter net income of $513m.. Earnings improved $680m from the first quarter of last year when GM lost $167m.
Revenue	'The US businesses contributed $113.9m of total group turnover of $409m'.
Costs	'Sterling's fall benefited pre-tax profits by about $50m while savings from the cost-cutting programme instituted in 1991 were running at around $100m a quarter'; 'The group interest charge rose from $48m to $61m'.
Share price	'The group's shares rose 31p to 1,278p despite the market's fall'.
Cash flow	'Cash flow was also continuing to improve, with cash and marketable securities totalling $8.4bn on March 31, up from $8bn at December 31'.

Note that the monetary amounts stated are **only given meaning in relation to something else**. Financial results should be compared against a **yard-stick** such as:

- Budgeted **sales**, **costs** and **profits**

- **Standards** in a standard costing system

- The **trend** over time (last year/this year, say)

- The results of **other parts of the business**

- The results of **other businesses**

- The **economy** in general

- **Future potential** (for example the performance of a new business may be judged in terms of nearness to breaking even).

Exam skills

Knowledge of how to calculate and interpret key ratios is a weak point for many students. Make sure it is one of your strong points.

1.2 Profitability

A company should of course be profitable, and there are obvious checks on **profitability**.

(a)   Whether the company has made a profit or a loss on its ordinary activities.

(b)   By how much this year's profit or loss is bigger or smaller than last year's profit or loss.

It is probably better to consider separately the profits or losses on exceptional items if there are any. Such gains or losses should not be expected to occur again, unlike profits or losses on normal trading.

Question 11.1		Profitability

Learning outcome C2(a)

A company has the following summarised income statements for two consecutive years.

	Year 1	Year 2
	$	$
Turnover	70,000	100,000
Less cost of sales	42,000	55,000
Gross profit	28,000	45,000
Less expenses	21,000	35,000
Net profit	7,000	10,000

Although the net profit margin is the same for both years at 10%, the gross profit margin is not.

Year 1 $\dfrac{28,000}{70,000}$ = 40%   Year 2 $\dfrac{45,000}{100,000}$ = 45%

Is this good or bad for the business?

Profit on ordinary activities before taxation is generally thought to be a **better** figure to use than profit after taxation, because there might be unusual variations in the tax charge from year to year which would not affect the underlying profitability of the company's operations.

Another profit figure that should be calculated is **PBIT: profit before interest and tax**. This is the amount of profit which the company earned **before having to pay interest to the providers of loan capital**. By providers of loan capital, we usually mean longer-term loan capital, such as debentures and medium-term bank loans, which will be shown in the balance sheet as 'Payables: amounts falling due after more than one year.' This figure is of particular importance to bankers and lenders.

PBIT = profit on ordinary activities before taxation + interest charges on long-term loan capital

1.2.1 Sales margin

KEY TERM

SALES MARGIN is turnover less cost of sales.

Look at the following examples.

(a)   **Wyndeham Press, a printer**

	20X5
	$'000
Turnover	89,844
Cost of sales	(60,769)
Gross profit	29,075
Distribution expenses	(1,523)
Administrative expenses	(13,300)
Goodwill amortisation	(212)
Operating profit (15.6%)	14,040
(Interest etc)	

Cost of sales comprises **direct material** cost, such as paper, and **direct labour**. Distribution and administrative expenses include depreciation. **Sales margin = 32%.**

Sales margin at least shows the contribution that is being made, especially when direct variable costs are very significant.

(b) Arriva, a bus company

	20X4
	$m
Turnover	1,534.3
Cost of sales	1,282.6
Gross profit	251.7
Net operating expenses	133.8
Operating profit (7.7%)	117.9

Sales margin = 16%. Clearly a higher percentage of costs are operating costs.

(c) **Lessons to be learnt**

(i) Sales margin as a measure is **not really any use in comparing different industries**.

(ii) Sales margin is **influenced** by the level of **fixed costs**.

(iii) **Trends** in sales margin are of interest. A falling sales margin suggests an organisation has not been able to pass on input price rises to customers.

(iv) **Comparisons** with similar companies are of interest. If an organisation has a lower sales margin than a similar business, this suggests problems in controlling input costs.

In short, the value of sales margin as a measure of performance depends on the **cost structure** of the industry and the **uses** to which it is put.

1.2.2 Earnings per share (EPS)

EPS is a convenient measure as it shows how well the shareholder is doing.

EPS is widely used as a **measure of a company's performance**, especially in **comparing** results over a period **of several years**. A company must be able to sustain its earnings in order to pay dividends and re-invest in the business so as to achieve future growth. Investors also look for **growth in the EPS** from one year to the next.

KEY TERM

EARNINGS PER SHARE (EPS) is defined as the profit attributable to each equity (ordinary) share.

Question 11.2	EPS

Learning outcome C2(a)

Walter Wall Carpets made profits before tax in 20X8 of $9,320,000. Tax amounted to $2,800,000.

The company's share capital is as follows.

	$
Ordinary share (10,000,000 shares of $1)	10,000,000
8% preference shares	2,000,000
	12,000,000

Required

Calculate the EPS for 20X8.

EPS on its own does not really tell us anything. It must be seen **in context**.

(a) EPS is used for comparing the results of a company **over time**. Is its EPS growing? What is the rate of growth? Is the rate of growth increasing or decreasing?

(b) EPS should not be used blindly to compare the earnings of one company with another. For example, if A plc has an EPS of 12c for its 10,000,000 10c shares and B plc has an EPS of 24c for its 50,000,000 25c shares, we must take account of the numbers of shares. When **earnings are used to compare one company's shares with another**, this is done **using** the **P/E ratio or perhaps the earnings yield**.

(c) If EPS is to be a reliable basis for comparing results, it **must be calculated consistently**. The EPS of one company must be directly comparable with the EPS of others, and the EPS of a company in one year must be directly comparable with its published EPS figures for previous years. Changes in the share capital of a company during the course of a year cause problems of comparability.

(d) EPS is a figure based on past data, and it is easily manipulated by changes in accounting policies and by mergers or acquisitions. **The use of the measure in calculating management bonuses makes it particularly liable to manipulation.** The attention given to EPS as a performance measure by City analysts is arguably disproportionate to its true worth. Investors should be more concerned with **future earnings**, but of course estimates of these are more difficult to reach than the readily available figure.

1.2.3 Profitability and return: the return on capital employed (ROCE)

It is impossible to assess profits or profit growth properly without relating them to the amount of funds (the capital) employed in making the profits. An important profitability ratio is therefore **return on capital employed (ROCE)**, which states the profit as a **percentage of the amount of capital employed**.

LEARN

RETURN ON CAPITAL EMPLOYED $= \dfrac{\text{PBIT}}{\text{Capital employed}}$

CAPITAL EMPLOYED = Shareholders' funds *plus* 'payables: amounts falling due after more than one year' *plus* any long-term provisions for liabilities and charges.

= Total assets less current liabilities

What does a company's ROCE tell us? What should we be looking for? There are three **comparisons** that can be made.

(a) The change in ROCE from **one year to the next**

(b) The ROCE being earned by **other companies**, if this information is available

(c) A comparison of the ROCE with **current market borrowing rates**

(i) What would be the cost of extra borrowing to the company if it needed more loans, and is it earning an ROCE that suggests it could make high enough profits to make such borrowing worthwhile?

(ii) Is the company making an ROCE which suggests that it is making profitable use of its current borrowing?

1.2.4 Analysing profitability and return in more detail: the secondary ratios

We may analyse the ROCE, to find out why it is high or low, or better or worse than last year. There are two factors that contribute towards a return on capital employed, both related to turnover.

(a) **Profit margin**. A company might make a high or a low profit margin on its sales. For example, a company that makes a profit of 25c per $1 of sales is making a bigger return on its turnover than another company making a profit of only 10c per $1 of sales.

(b) **Asset turnover**. Asset turnover is a measure of how well the assets of a business are being used to generate sales. For example, if two companies each have capital employed of $100,000, and company A makes sales of $400,000 a year, but company B only makes sales of $200,000 a year, company A is making a higher turnover from the same amount of assets. This means company A will make a higher return on capital employed than company B. Asset turnover is expressed as 'x times' so that assets generate x times their value in annual turnover. Here, company A's asset turnover is 4 times and company B's is 2 times.

Profit margin and asset turnover together explain the ROCE, and if the ROCE is the primary profitability ratio, these other two are the secondary ratios. The relationship between the three ratios is as follows.

Profit margin	×	**asset turnover**	=	**ROCE**
$\dfrac{\text{PBIT}}{\text{Sales}}$	×	$\dfrac{\text{Sales}}{\text{Capital employed}}$	=	$\dfrac{\text{PBIT}}{\text{Capital employed}}$

It is also worth noting the **change in turnover** from one year to the next. Strong sales growth will usually indicate volume growth as well as turnover increases due to price rises, and volume growth is one sign of a prosperous company.

Asset turnover can also be calculated with any category of asset, such as non-current assets, if required.

1.3 Liquidity

Profitability and also debt, or gearing, are important aspects of a company's performance. Neither, however, directly addresses the key issue of liquidity. A company needs liquid assets so that it can meet its debts when they fall due.

LIQUIDITY is the amount of cash a company can obtain quickly to settle its debts (and possibly to meet other unforeseen demands for cash payments too).

KEY TERM

1.3.1 Liquid assets

Liquid funds include:

(a) Cash

(b) Short-term investments for which there is a ready market, such as investments in shares of other companies (NB **not** subsidiaries or associates)

(c) Fixed-term deposits with a bank or building society, for example six month deposits with a bank

(d) Trade receivables

(e) Bills of exchange receivable

Some assets are more liquid than others. Inventories of goods are fairly liquid in some businesses. Inventories of finished production goods might be sold quickly, and a supermarket will hold consumer goods for resale that could well be sold for cash very soon. Raw materials and components in a manufacturing company have to be used to make a finished product before they can be sold to realise cash, and so they are less liquid than finished goods. Just how liquid they are depends on the speed of inventory turnover and the length of the production cycle.

Non-current assets are not liquid assets. A company can sell off non-current assets, but unless they are no longer needed, or are worn out and about to be replaced, they are necessary to continue the company's operations. Selling non-current assets is certainly not a solution to a company's cash needs, and so although there may be an occasional non-current asset item which is about to be sold off, probably

because it is going to be replaced, it is safe to disregard non-current assets when measuring a company's liquidity.

In summary, **liquid assets are current asset items that will or could soon be converted into cash, and cash** itself. Two common definitions of liquid assets are **all current assets** or **all current assets with the exception of inventories.**

The main source of liquid assets for a trading company is sales. A company can obtain cash from sources other than sales, such as the issue of shares for cash, a new loan or the sale of non-current assets. But a company cannot rely on these at all times, and in general, obtaining liquid funds depends on making sales and profits.

1.3.2 The current ratio

The **current ratio** is the standard test of liquidity.

$$\text{CURRENT RATIO} = \frac{\text{Current assets}}{\text{Current liabilities}}$$

A company should have enough current assets that give a promise of 'cash to come' to meet its commitments to pay its current liabilities. Obviously, a ratio in **excess of 1** should be expected. In practice, a ratio comfortably in excess of 1 should be expected, but what is 'comfortable' varies between different types of businesses.

Companies are not able to convert all their current assets into cash very quickly. In particular, some manufacturing companies might hold large quantities of raw material inventories, which must be used in production to create finished goods. Finished goods might be warehoused for a long time, or sold on lengthy credit. In such businesses, where inventory turnover is slow, most inventories are not very liquid assets, because the cash cycle is so long. For these reasons, we calculate an additional liquidity ratio, known as the quick ratio or acid test ratio.

1.3.3 The quick ratio

$$\text{QUICK RATIO or ACID TEST RATIO} = \frac{\text{Current assets less inventories}}{\text{Current liabilities}}$$

This ratio should ideally be **at least 1** for companies with a **slow inventory turnover**. For companies with a **fast inventory turnover**, a quick ratio can be **less than 1** without indicating that the company is in cash flow difficulties.

Do not forget the other side of the coin. The current ratio and the quick ratio can be higher than they should be. A company with large volumes of inventories and receivables might be over-investing in working capital, and so tying up more funds in the business than it needs to. This would suggest poor management of receivables or inventories by the company.

1.3.4 The accounts receivable payment period

ACCOUNTS RECEIVABLE DAYS or ACCOUNTS RECEIVABLE PAYMENT PERIOD

$$= \frac{\text{Trade receivables}}{\text{Credit sales turnover}} \times 365 \text{ days}$$

This is a rough measure of the average length of time it takes for a company's accounts receivable to pay what they owe.

The trade accounts receivable are not the *total* figure for accounts receivable in the statement of financial position, which includes prepayments and non-trade accounts receivable. The trade accounts receivable figure will be itemised in an analysis of the total accounts receivable, in a note to the accounts.

The estimate of accounts receivable days is only approximate.

(a)   The **statement of financial position value** of accounts receivable might be **abnormally high** or low compared with the 'normal' level the company usually has. This may apply especially to smaller companies, where the size of year-end accounts receivable may largely depend on whether a few or even a single large customer pay just before or just after the year-end.

(b)   Turnover in the income statement excludes sales tax, but the accounts receivable figure in the statement of financial position includes sales tax. We are not strictly comparing like with like.

1.3.5 The inventory turnover period

$$\textbf{INVENTORY DAYS} = \frac{\text{Inventory}}{\text{Cost of sales}} \times 365 \text{ days}$$

This indicates the average number of days that items of inventory are held for. As with the average accounts receivable collection period, this is only an approximate figure, but one which should be reliable enough for finding changes over time.

A lengthening inventory turnover period indicates:

(a)   A **slowdown** in **trading**, or

(b)   A **build-up** in **inventory levels**, perhaps suggesting that the investment in inventories is becoming excessive

If we add together the inventory days and the accounts receivable days, this should give us an indication of how soon inventory is convertible into cash, thereby giving a further indication of the **company's liquidity**.

1.3.6 The accounts payable payment period

$$\textbf{ACCOUNTS PAYABLE PAYMENT PERIOD} = \frac{\text{Average trade payables}}{\text{Credit purchases or Cost of sales}} \times 365 \text{ days}$$

The accounts payable payment period often helps to assess a company's liquidity; an increase in accounts payable days is often a sign of lack of long-term finance or poor management of current assets, resulting in the use of extended credit from suppliers, increased bank overdraft and so on.

All the ratios calculated above will **vary by industry**; hence **comparisons** of ratios calculated with other similar companies in the same industry are important.

Question 11.3   Liquidity and working capital ratios

Learning outcome C2(a)

Calculate liquidity and working capital ratios from the accounts of a manufacturer of products for the construction industry, and comment on the ratios.

| | 20X8 | 20X7 |
	$m	$m
Turnover	2,065.0	1,788.7
Cost of sales	1,478.6	1,304.0
Gross profit	586.4	484.7
Current assets		
Inventories	119.0	109.0
Receivables (note 1)	400.9	347.4
Short-term investments	4.2	18.8
Cash at bank and in hand	48.2	48.0
	572.3	523.2
Payables: amounts falling due within one year		
Loans and overdrafts	49.1	35.3
Corporation taxes	62.0	46.7
Dividend	19.2	14.3
Payables (note 2)	370.7	324.0
	501.0	420.3
	$m	$m
Net current assets	71.3	102.9
Notes		
1 Trade receivables	329.8	285.4
2 Trade payables	236.2	210.8

1.4 Reporting a performance evaluation

Once business performance has been analysed using FPIs, the next stage is to report the performance evaluation.

A business may report an evaluation using any of the following approaches.

(a)   **Horizontal analysis**

Horizontal analysis involves a **line-by-line comparison** of one set of data with another. For example, comparing current year financial statements with those of the previous year. Expressing year-on-year movements in percentage terms can help to highlight areas where further analysis is required.

(b)   **Trend analysis**

Trend analysis is horizontal analysis **extended** over a **greater period of time**. For example, comparing financial statements over the past five years may reveal that, on average, company turnover increased at a rate of 5% per annum.

(c)   **Vertical analysis**

Vertical analysis is a method in which data is expressed **as a percentage of a total account balance** within the financial statements. For example, cash, accounts receivable and inventory are likely to be expressed as a percentage of total assets within the statement of financial position. This type of analysis can provide an insight in to the liquidity position and financial condition of a company.

Section summary

Financial performance indicators analyse profitability, liquidity and risk.

A company can be profitable but at the same time get into cash flow problems. Liquidity ratios (**current** and **quick**) and **working capital turnover ratios** give some idea of a company's liquidity.

A business may report an evaluation using **horizontal** analysis, **trend** analysis or **vertical** analysis.

2 Non-financial performance indicators (NFPIs)   5/10, 5/11

Introduction

As well as evaluating performance using financial performance indicators, companies can use non-financial indicators. This section focuses on the different types of non-financial indicators and how they can be used for performance evaluation.

2.1 Increased emphasis on NFPIs

KEY TERM

NON-FINANCIAL PERFORMANCE INDICATORS are 'measures of performance based on non-financial information that may originate in, and be used by, operating departments to monitor and control their activities without any accounting input.'

(CIMA *Official Terminology*)

There has been a growing emphasis on NFPIs for a number of reasons.

(a) **Concentration on too few variables**. If performance measurement systems focus entirely on those items which can be expressed in monetary terms, managers will concentrate on only those variables and ignore other important variables that cannot be expressed in monetary terms.

(b) **Lack of information on quality.** Traditional responsibility accounting systems do not provide information on the quality or relative importance of operations.

(c) **Changes in cost structures.** Modern technology can require massive investment and product life cycles have got shorter. A greater proportion of costs are sunk and a large proportion of costs are designed into a product/service before production/delivery. By the time the product/service is produced/delivered, it is therefore too late to effectively control costs.

(d) **Changes in competitive environment.** Financial measures do not convey the full picture of a company's performance, especially in a modern business environment. They are also open to distortion by the effect of market forces and by the choice of accounting policy.

(e) **Changes in manufacturing environment**. New manufacturing techniques and technologies focus on minimising throughput times, inventory levels and set-up times. But managers can reduce the costs for which they are responsible by increasing inventory levels through maximising output. If a performance measurement system focuses principally on costs, managers may concentrate on cost reduction and ignore other important strategic manufacturing goals.

(f) **NFPIs are a better indicator of future prospects**. Financial indicators tend to focus on the short term and are largely historical. They can give a positive message based on results in the immediate past but problems may be looming. For example, falling quality will ultimately damage profitability.

2.2 The value of NFPIs

Unlike traditional variance reports, NFPIs can be provided **quickly** for managers, per shift, daily or even hourly as required. They are likely to be easy to calculate, and easier for non-financial managers to **understand** and therefore to **use effectively**.

The beauty of non-financial indicators is that **anything can be compared** if it is **meaningful** to do so. The measures should be **tailored** to the circumstances so that, for example, number of coffee breaks per 20 pages of Study Text might indicate to you how hard you are studying!

Many suitable measures combine elements from the chart shown below. The chart is not intended to be prescriptive or exhaustive.

Errors/failure	Time	Quantity	People
Defects	Second	Range of products	Employees
Equipment failures	Minute	Parts/components	Employee skills
Warranty claims	Hour	Units produced	Customers
Complaints	Shift	Units sold	Competitors
Returns	Cycle	Services performed	Suppliers
Stockouts	Day	kg/litres/metres	
Lateness/waiting	Month	m^2/m^3	
Misinformation	Year	Documents	
Miscalculation		Deliveries	
Absenteeism		Enquiries	

Traditional measures derived from these lists like 'kg (of material) per unit produced' or 'units produced per hour' are fairly obvious, but what may at first seem a fairly **unlikely combination** may also be very revealing. 'Absenteeism per customer', for example, may be of no significance at all or it may reveal that a particularly difficult customer is being avoided, and hence that some action is needed.

There is clearly a need for the information provider to work more closely with the managers who will be using the information to make sure that their needs are properly understood. The measures used are likely to be **developed and refined over time**. It may be that some will serve the purpose of drawing attention to areas in need of improvement but will be of no further relevance once remedial action has been taken. A flexible, responsive approach is essential.

Exam alert

Be prepared to explain a number of NFPIs that a business could use.

Question 11.4	NFPIs

Learning outcome C3(b)

Using the above chart develop five non-financial indicators for your organisation or one that you know well, and explain how each might be useful.

2.3 NFPIs in relation to employees

One of the many criticisms of traditional accounting performance measurement systems is that they **do not measure the skills, morale and training of the workforce**, which can be as **valuable to an organisation as its tangible assets**. For example if employees have not been trained in the manufacturing practices required to achieve the objectives of the new manufacturing environment, an organisation is unlikely to be successful.

Employee attitudes and morale can be measured by **surveying** employees. Education and skills levels, promotion and training, absenteeism and labour turnover for the employees for which each manager is responsible can also be monitored.

2.4 Performance measurement in a TQM environment

Total Quality Management is a highly significant trend in modern business thinking which will be considered in detail in Chapter 13. Because **TQM embraces every activity** of a business, performance measures cannot be confined to the production process but must also cover the work of sales, distribution and administration departments, the efforts of external suppliers, and the reaction of external customers.

In many cases the measures used will be non-financial ones. They may be divided into three types.

(a) **Measuring the quality of incoming supplies.** Quality control should include procedures for acceptance and inspection of goods inwards and measurement of rejects.

(b) **Monitoring work done as it proceeds.** 'In-process' controls include statistical process controls and random sampling, and measures such as the amount of scrap and reworking in relation to good production. Measurements can be made by product, by worker or work team, by machine or machine type, by department, or whatever is appropriate.

(c) **Measuring customer satisfaction.'** may be monitored in the form of letters of complaint, returned goods, penalty discounts, claims under guarantee, or requests for visits by service engineers. Some companies adopt a more pro-active approach to monitoring customer satisfaction by surveying their customers on a regular basis. They use the feedback to obtain an index of customer satisfaction which is used to identify quality problems before they affect profits.

2.5 Quality of service

Service quality is measured principally by **qualitative measures**, as you might expect, although some quantitative measures are used by some businesses.

(a) If it were able to obtain the information, a retailer might use number of lost customers in a period as an indicator of service quality.

(b) Lawyers use the proportion of time spent with clients.

2.5.1 Measures of customer satisfaction

You have probably filled in **questionnaires** in restaurants or on planes without realising that you were completing a customer attitude survey for input to the organisation's management information system.

Other possible measures of customer satisfaction include:

(a) Market research on customer preferences and customer satisfaction with specific product features

(b) Number of defective units supplied to customers as a percentage of total units supplied

(c) Number of customer complaints as a percentage of total sales volume

(d) Percentage of products which fail early or excessively

(e) On-time delivery rate

(f)   Average time to deal with customer queries

(g)   New customer accounts opened

(h)   Repeat business from existing customers

Section summary

Changes in cost structures, the competitive environment and the manufacturing environment have lead to an **increased use of non-financial performance indicators** (NFPIs).

NFPIs can usefully be applied to **employees** and product/service **quality**.

3 The balanced scorecard 9/11, 11/11, 3/12, 5/12, 9/12, 3/13

Introduction

So far in our discussion we have focused on performance measurement and control from a financial point of view. Another approach is the use of what is called a 'balanced scorecard' which is the subject of this section.

KEY TERM

The BALANCED SCORECARD APPROACH is an 'Approach to the provision of information to management to assist strategic policy formulation and achievement. It emphasises the need to provide the user with a set of information which addresses all relevant areas of performance in an objective and unbiased fashion. The information provided may include both financial and non-financial elements, and cover areas such as profitability, customer satisfaction, internal efficiency and innovation.'

(CIMA *Official Terminology*)

3.1 The four perspectives

The balanced scorecard focuses on **four different perspectives**, as follows.

Perspective	Question	Explanation
Customer	What do existing and new customers value from us?	Gives rise to targets that matter to customers: cost, quality, delivery, inspection, handling and so on.
Internal	What processes must we excel at to achieve our financial and customer objectives?	Aims to improve internal processes and decision making.
Innovation and learning	Can we continue to improve and create future value?	Considers the business's capacity to maintain its competitive position through the acquisition of new skills and the development of new products.
Financial	How do we create value for our shareholders?	Covers traditional measures such as growth, profitability and shareholder value but set through talking to the shareholder or shareholders direct.

Performance targets are set once the key areas for improvement have been identified, and the balanced scorecard is the **main monthly report**.

The scorecard is '**balanced**' in the sense that managers are required to **think in terms of all four perspectives**, to **prevent improvements being made in one area at the expense of** another.

3.1.1 Types of measures

The types of measure which may be monitored under each of the four perspectives include the following. The list is not exhaustive but it will give you an idea of the possible scope of a balanced scorecard approach. The measures selected, particularly within the internal perspective, will vary considerably with the type of organisation and its objectives.

Perspective	Measures	
Customer	• New customers acquired	• On-time deliveries
	• Customer complaints	• Returns
Internal	• Quality control rejects	• Speed of producing management information
	• Average set-up time	
Innovation and learning	• Labour turnover rate	
	• Percentage of revenue generated by new products and services	
	• Average time taken to develop new products and services	
Financial	• Return on capital employed	• Revenue growth
	• Cash flow	• Earnings per share

Broadbent and Cullen (in Berry, Broadbent and Otley, ed, *Management Control*, 1995) identify the following **important features** of this approach.

•   It looks at both **internal and external matters** concerning the organisation.
•   It is **related to the key elements of a company's strategy**.
•   **Financial and non-financial measures** are linked together.

The balanced scorecard approach may be particularly useful for performance measurement in organisations which are unable to use simple profit as a performance measure. For example the **public sector** has long been forced to use a **wide range of performance indicators**, which can be formalised with a balanced scorecard approach.

3.2 Example

An example of how a balanced scorecard might appear is offered below.

Balanced Scorecard

Financial Perspective

GOALS	MEASURES
Survive	Cash flow
Succeed	Monthly sales growth and operating income by division
Prosper	Increase market share and ROI

Customer Perspective

GOALS	MEASURES
New products	Percentage of sales from new products
Responsive supply	On-time delivery (defined by customer)
Preferred supplier	Share of key accounts' purchases
	Ranking by key accounts
Customer partnership	Number of cooperative engineering efforts

Internal Business Perspective

GOALS	MEASURES
Technology capability	Manufacturing configuration vs competition
Manufacturing excellence	Cycle time
	Unit cost
	Yield
Design productivity	Silicon efficiency
	Engineering efficiency
New product introduction	Actual introduction schedule vs plan

Innovation and Learning Perspective

GOALS	MEASURES
Technology leadership	Time to develop next generation of products
Manufacturing learning	Process time to maturity
Product focus	Percentage of products that equal 80% sales
Time to market	New product introduction vs competition

Question 11.5   Balanced scorecard

Learning outcome C3(c)

Spotlight Productions has in the past produced just one fairly successful product. Recently, however, a new version of this product has been launched. Development work continues to add a related product to the product list. Given below are some details of the activities during the month of November.

Units produced	– existing product	25,000
	– new product	5,000
Cost of units produced	– existing product	$375,000
	– new product	$70,000
Sales revenue	– existing product	$550,000
	– new product	$125,000
Hours worked	– existing product	5,000
	– new product	1,250
Development costs		$47,000

Required

(a)   Suggest and calculate performance indicators that could be calculated for each of the four perspectives on the balanced scorecard.

(b)   Suggest how this information would be interpreted.

Exam alert

Be prepared to discuss the implementation of the balanced scorecard for the specific industry or non-profit-making organisation required by the question.

3.3 Problems

As with all techniques, problems can arise when it is applied.

Problem	Explanation
Conflicting measures	Some measures in the scorecard such as research funding and cost reduction may naturally conflict. It is often difficult to determine the balance which will achieve the best results.
Selecting measures	Not only do appropriate measures have to be devised but the number of measures used must be agreed. Care must be taken that the impact of the results is not lost in a sea of information.
Expertise	Measurement is only useful if it initiates appropriate action. Non-financial managers may have difficulty with the usual profit measures. With more measures to consider this problem will be compounded.
Interpretation	Even a financially-trained manager may have difficulty in putting the figures into an overall perspective.
Too many measures	The ultimate objective for commercial organisations is to maximise profits or shareholder wealth. Other targets should offer a guide to achieving this objective and not become an end in themselves.

Section summary

The **balanced scorecard approach** to the provision of information focuses on four different perspectives: customer, financial, internal, and innovation and learning.

4   Benchmarking

Introduction

Analysing performance by a single comparison of data (eg: current year vs prior year) can be difficult. Benchmarking is another type of comparison exercise through which an organisation attempts to improve performance. The idea is to seek the best available performance against which the organisation can monitor its own performance.

KEY TERM

'BENCHMARKING is the establishment, through data gathering, of targets and comparators, through whose use relative levels of performance (and particularly underperformance) can be identified. By the adoption of identified best practices it is hoped that performance will improve.'

(CIMA *Official Terminology*)

CIMA identified three distinct approaches to benchmarking in *CIMA Insider*.

Type	Description
Metric benchmarking	The practise of **comparing appropriate metrics** to identify possible areas for improvement.
	For example, IT investment as a percentage of total assets may be compared across different departments within the same company to identify areas of the company where additional investment is required.
Process benchmarking	The practise of **comparing processes with a partner** as part of an improvement process. For example, a distributor of personal computers may analyse a competitor's supply chain function in the hope of identifying successful elements of the process that it can use to its advantage.
Diagnostic benchmarking	The practise of **reviewing the processes of a business** to identify those which indicate a problem and offer a potential for improvement.
	For example, a company may critically assess each element of the value chain and conclude that there is potential for improvement within the marketing and sales function.

4.1 Obtaining information

Financial information about competitors is **easier** to acquire than non-financial information. Information about **products** can be obtained from **reverse engineering** (buying a competitor's products and dismantling them in order to understand their content and configuration), **product literature**, **media comment** and **trade associations** in order to undertake **competitive benchmarking** against successful competitors.

Information about **processes** (how an organisation deals with customers or suppliers) is more **difficult to find**.

Such information can be obtained through the following channels.

(a)   In **intra-group benchmarking**, groups of companies in the same industry agree to pool data on their processes. The processes are benchmarked against each other and an 'improvement taskforce' is established to undertake **strategic benchmarking** to **identify** and transfer 'best practice' to all members of the group.

(b)   In **inter-industry benchmarking**, a non-competing business with similar processes is identified and asked to participate in a **functional benchmarking** exercise. The participants in the scheme are able to benefit from the experience of the other and establish 'best practice' in their common business processes.

It is also possible to undertake **internal benchmarking** against other units or departments in the same organisation.

4.2 Why use benchmarking?

4.2.1 For setting standards

Benchmarking allows **attainable standards** to be established following the examination of both **external and internal information**. These standards are most commonly established in the form of key performance indicators. If these standards and indicators are **regularly reviewed** in the light of information gained through benchmarking exercises, they can become part of a programme of **continuous improvement** by becoming increasingly demanding.

4.2.2 Other reasons

(a)   Its **flexibility** means that it can be used in both the public and private sector and by people at different levels of responsibility.

(b)   Cross comparisons (as opposed to comparisons with similar organisations) are more likely to expose radically **different ways of doing things**.

(c)   It is an **effective method** of **implementing change**, people being involved in identifying and seeking out different ways of doing things in their own areas.

(d)   It identifies the **processes** to improve.

(e)   It helps with **cost reduction**.

(f)   It improves the **effectiveness** of **operations**.

(g)   It delivers services to a **defined standard**.

(h)   It provides a **focus** on **planning**.

(i)   It can provide early **warning** of **competitive disadvantage**.

(j)   It should lead to a greater incidence of **team working** and **cross-functional learning**.

Benchmarking works, it is claimed, for the following reasons.

(a)   The **comparisons** are **carried out** by the **managers** who have to live with any changes implemented as a result of the exercise.

(b)   Benchmarking focuses on improvement in key areas and sets targets which are challenging but 'achievable'. What is *really* achievable can be discovered by examining what others have achieved. Managers are therefore able to accept that they are not being asked to perform miracles.

4.3 Benchmarking – the disadvantages

The are a number of potential disadvantages that businesses should consider prior to performing a benchmarking exercise.

(a)   Businesses may experience difficulties in deciding **which activities** to benchmark
(b)   Businesses may find it difficult to **identify the 'best in class'** for each activity
(c)   It is often difficult to **persuade other organisations** to share information
(d)   Successful practices in one organisation **may not transfer** successfully to another
(e)   There is a risk of **drawing incorrect conclusions** from inappropriate comparisons

Exam alert

Be able to discuss the advantages and disadvantages of benchmarking.

Section summary

Benchmarking is an attempt to identify best practices and to achieve improved performance by comparison of operations.

5 Not-for-profit organisations

Introduction

It is not only profit-making organisations whose performance is evaluated. Not-for-profit organisations are expected to account for how their funds are used and are assessed on their efficiency, effectiveness and economy in handling these funds.

Some organisations are set up with a prime objective which is not related to making profits. Charities and government organisations are examples. These organisations exist to pursue non-financial aims, such as providing a service to the community. However there will be financial constraints which limit what any organisation can do.

(a) A not-for-profit organisation needs finance to pay for its operations, and the major financial constraint is the amount of funds that it can obtain from its donors (its customers).

(b) Having obtained funds, a not-for-profit organisation will use the funds to help its 'clients', for example by alleviating suffering. It should seek to use the funds in three ways (sometimes known as 'the three Es'):

- **Economically** – that is, not spending $2 when the same thing can be bought for $1
- **Efficiently** – getting the best use out of what the money is spent on
- **Effectively** – spending funds so as to achieve the organisation's objectives

Section summary

Not-for-profit organisations are assessed on the **effectiveness**, **efficiency** and **economy** with which they use their funds.

Chapter Roundup

- ✓ **Financial performance indicators** analyse profitability, liquidity and risk.

- ✓ A company can be profitable but at the same time get into cash flow problems. Liquidity ratios (**current** and **quick**) and **working capital turnover ratios** give some idea of a company's liquidity.

- ✓ A business may report an evaluation using **horizontal** analysis **trend** analysis or **vertical** analysis.

- ✓ Changes in cost structures, the competitive environment and the manufacturing environment have lead to an **increased use of non-financial performance indicators** (NFPIs).

- ✓ NFPIs can usefully be applied to **employees** and product/service **quality**.

- ✓ The **balanced scorecard approach** to the provision of information focuses on four different perspectives: customer, financial, internal and innovation and learning.

- ✓ **Benchmarking** is an attempt to identify best practices and to achieve improved performance by comparison of operation

- ✓ Not-for-profit organisations are assessed on the **effectiveness**, **efficiency** and **economy** with which they use their funds.

Quick Quiz

1   Give five examples of a financial performance measure.

   - ....   •   ....

   - ....   •   ....

   - ....

2   How do quantitative and qualitative performance measures differ?

3   Choose the correct words from those highlighted.

   In general, a current ratio **in excess of 1/less than 1/approximately zero** should be expected.

4   **Service quality** is measured principally by quantitative measures.

   True ☐   False ☐

5   *Fill in the blanks.*

   NFPIs are less likely to be .... than traditional profit-related measures and they should therefore offer a means of counteracting ....

Answers to Quick Quiz

1.
   - Profit
   - Revenue
   - Costs
   - Share price
   - Cash flow

2. Quantitative measures are expressed in numbers whereas qualitative measures are not.

3. in excess of 1

4. False. Service quality is measured principally by **qualitative** measures.

5. manipulated

   short termism

Answers to Questions

11.1 Profitability

An increased profit margin must be good because this indicates a wider gap between selling price and cost of sales. Given that the net profit ratio has stayed the same in the second year, however, expenses must be rising. In year 1 expenses were 30% of turnover, whereas in year 2 they were 35% of turnover. This indicates that administration, selling and distribution expenses or interest costs require tight control.

Percentage analysis of profit between year 1 and year 2

	Year 1 %	Year 2 %
Cost of sales as a % of sales	60	55
Gross profit as a % of sales	40	45
	100	100
Expenses as a % of sales	30	35
Net profit as a % of sales	10	10
Gross profit as a % of sales	40	45

11.2 EPS

	$
Profits before tax	9,320,000
Less tax	2,800,000
Profits after tax	6,520,000
Less preference dividend (8% of $2,000,000)	160,000
Earnings	6,360,000
Number of ordinary shares	10,000,000
EPS	63.6c

11.3 Liquidity and working capital ratios

	20X8	20X7
Current ratio	572.3/501.0 = 1.14	523.2/420.3 = 1.24
Quick ratio	453.3/501.0 = 0.90	414.2/420.3 = 0.99
Receivables' payment period (days)	329.8/2,065.0 × 365 = 58	285.4/1,788.7 × 365 = 58
Inventory turnover period (days)	119.0/1,478.6 × 365 = 29	109.0/1,304.0 × 365 = 31
Payables' turnover period (days)	236.2/1,478.6 × 365 = 58	210.8/1,304.0 × 365 = 59

As a manufacturing group serving the construction industry, the company would be expected to have a comparatively lengthy receivables' turnover period, because of the relatively poor cash flow in the construction industry. It is clear that the company compensates for this by ensuring that they do not pay for raw materials and other costs before they have sold their inventories of finished goods (hence the similarity of receivables' and payables' turnover periods).

The company's current ratio is a little lower than average but its quick ratio is better than average and very little less than the current ratio. This suggests that inventory levels are strictly controlled, which is reinforced by the low inventory turnover period. It would seem that working capital is tightly managed, to avoid the poor liquidity which could be caused by a high receivables' turnover period and comparatively high payables.

11.4 NFPIs

Here are five indicators, showing you how to use the chart, but there are many other possibilities.

(a)   Services performed late v total services performed
(b)   Total units sold v total units sold by competitors (indicating market share)
(c)   Warranty claims per month
(d)   Documents processed per employee
(e)   Equipment failures per 1,000 units produced

Don't forget to explain how the ones that you chose might be useful.

11.5 Balanced scorecard

(a)   **Customer**

- Percentage of sales represented by new products $= s \times 100$
  $= 18.5\%$

Internal

- Productivity   – existing product $= \dfrac{25,000 \text{ units}}{5,000 \text{ units}}$
  $= 5$ units per hour

  – new product $= \dfrac{5,000 \text{ units}}{1,250 \text{ units}}$
  $= 4$ units per hour

- Unit cost   – existing product $= \dfrac{\$375,000}{25,000 \text{ units}} = \$15$ per unit

  – new product $= \dfrac{\$70,000}{5,000 \text{ units}} = \$14$ per unit

Financial

- Gross profit – existing product

$$= \frac{\$550,000 - 375,000}{\$550,000}$$

$$= 32\%$$

  – new product

$$= \frac{\$125,000 - 70,000}{\$125,000}$$

$$= 44\%$$

Innovation and learning

- Development costs as % of sales

$$= \frac{\$47,000}{\$675,000}$$

$$= 7\%$$

(b) Using a range of performance indicators will allow Spotlight Productions to look at the success of the new product in wider terms than just its profitability. For example, productivity is lower for the new product than the existing product, so managers may wish to examine the processes involved in order to make improvements. Sales of the new product look very promising but some additional measure of customer satisfaction could provide a better view of long-term prospects.

Now try these questions from the Exam Question Bank	Number	Level	Marks	Time
	Q27	Examination	5	9 mins
	Q28	Examination	30	54 mins

CONTROL AND PERFORMANCE MEASUREMENT OF RESPONSIBILITY CENTRES

MEASURING PERFORMANCE IN DIVISIONALISED BUSINESSES

In this chapter we look at a system of **responsibility accounting**. We look at the way that **organisation structure** can be devised to **assist management control** and at the ways in which the **performance** of various parts of the organisation could be assessed.

Section 1 deals with discussion of the various types of responsibility centre that can be used in a system of responsibility accounting. Sections 2 to 5 deal with the calculation and evaluation of return on investment, residual income and economic value added and with discussion of their behavioural implications.

12

topic list	learning outcomes	syllabus references	ability required
1 Responsibility centres	D1(a), 2(b), 3(a), 3(b)	D1(i), 3(i)	analysis
2 Return on investment (ROI)	D2(b), 2(c)	D2(ii)	analysis
3 ROI and decision-making	D2(b), 2(c)	D2(ii)	analysis
4 Residual income (RI)	D2(b), 2(c)	D2(ii)	analysis
5 Economic value added® (EVA)	D2(b), 2(c)	D2(ii)	analysis

1 Responsibility centres   5/10, 11/11, 3/12, 3/13

Introduction

This section focuses on the responsibility centre business model. Make sure you familiarise yourself with the different categories of responsibility centre and what they can control (costs, profit, investment).

1.1 Divisionalisation

In general, a large organisation can be **structured in one of two ways: functionally** (all activities of a similar type within a company, such as production, sales, research, are under the control of the appropriate departmental head) or **divisionally** (split into divisions in accordance with the products or services made or provided).

Divisional managers are therefore responsible for all operations (production, sales and so on) relating to their product, the functional structure being applied to each division. It is possible, of course, that only part of a company is divisionalised and activities such as administration are structured centrally on a functional basis with the responsibility of providing services to *all* divisions.

1.2 Decentralisation

In general, a **divisional structure will lead to decentralisation** of the decision-making process and divisional managers may have the freedom to set selling prices, choose suppliers, make product mix and output decisions and so on. Decentralisation is, however, a matter of degree, depending on how much freedom divisional managers are given.

1.3 Advantages of divisionalisation

(a) Divisionalisation can **improve** the **quality of decisions** made because divisional managers (those taking the decisions) know local conditions and are able to make more informed judgements. Moreover, with the personal incentive to improve the division's performance, they ought to take decisions in the division's best interests.

(b) **Decisions should be taken more quickly** because information does not have to pass along the chain of command to and from top management. Decisions can be made on the spot by those who are familiar with the product lines and production processes and who are able to react to changes in local conditions quickly and efficiently.

(c) The authority to act to improve performance should **motivate divisional managers**.

(d) Divisional organisation **frees top management** from detailed involvement in day-to-day operations and allows them to devote more time to strategic planning.

(e) Divisions provide **valuable training grounds for future members of top management** by giving them experience of managerial skills in a less complex environment than that faced by top management.

(f) In a large business organisation, the central head office will not have the management resources or skills to direct operations closely enough itself. Some authority must be delegated to local operational managers.

1.4 Disadvantages of divisionalisation

(a) A danger with divisional accounting is that the business organisation will divide into a number of self-interested segments, each acting at times against the wishes and interests of other segments. Decisions might be taken by a divisional manager in the best interests of his own part of the business, but against the best interest of other divisions and possibly against the interests of the organisation as a whole.

A task of **head office** is therefore to try to **prevent dysfunctional decision making** by individual divisional managers. To do this, head office must reserve some power and authority for itself so that divisional managers cannot be allowed to make entirely independent decisions. A **balance** ought to be kept **between decentralisation** of authority to provide incentives and motivation, **and retaining centralised authority** to ensure that the organisation's divisions are all working towards the same target, the benefit of the organisation as a whole (in other words, **retaining goal congruence** among the organisation's separate divisions).

KEY TERM

GOAL CONGRUENCE 'In a control system is the state which leads individuals or groups to take actions which are in their self-interest and also in the best interest of the entity.'

(CIMA *Official Terminology*)

(b) It is claimed that the **costs of activities that are common** to all divisions such as running the accounting department **may be greater** for a divisionalised structure than for a centralised structure.

(c) **Top management**, by delegating decision making to divisional managers, may **lose control** since they are not aware of what is going on in the organisation as a whole. (With a good system of performance evaluation and appropriate control information, however, top management should be able to control operations just as effectively.)

1.5 Responsibility accounting

The creation of divisions allows for the operation of a system of responsibility accounting as we saw in Chapter 10. There are a number of types of responsibility accounting unit, or responsibility centre that can be used within a system of responsibility accounting.

In the weakest form of **decentralisation** a system of cost centres might be used. As decentralisation becomes stronger the responsibility accounting framework will be based around profit centres. In its **strongest form investment centres are used**.

Type of responsibility centre	Manager has control over ...	Principal performance measures
Cost centre	Controllable costs	Variance analysis Efficiency measures
Revenue centre	Revenues only	Revenues
Profit centre	Controllable costs Sales prices (including transfer prices)	Profit
Investment centre	Controllable costs Sales prices (including transfer prices) Output volumes Investment in non-current assets and working capital	Return on investment Residual income Other financial ratios

1.6 Cost centres

A cost centre manager is responsible for, and has control over, the costs incurred in the cost centre. The manager has **no responsibility for earning revenues** or for **controlling the assets and liabilities of the centre**.

Cost centre organisations can be relatively easy to establish, because as you will recall from your earlier studies a cost centre is any part of the organisation to which costs can be separately attributed. A cost centre **forms the basis for building up cost records** for cost measurement, budgeting and control.

Functional departments such as product on, personnel and marketing might be treated as cost centres and made responsible for their costs.

A performance report for a cost centre might look like this.

COST CENTRE X

PERFORMANCE REPORT FOR THE PERIOD

Budgeted activity: (units)

Actual activity: (units)

	Budgeted costs (original) $	Budgeted costs (flexed) $	Actual costs $	Variance $
Material costs				
Labour costs				
Variable overhead costs				
Depreciation costs				
etc				

Two important points to note about this report are as follows.

(a)   The report should include **only controllable costs**, although as we saw there is a case for also providing information on certain **uncontrollable costs**. However, there should be a **clear distinction** in the report between controllable costs and uncontrollable costs.

(b)   The actual costs are compared with a budget that has been **flexed to the actual activity level achieved**. We saw in Chapter 10 that this approach provides better information, for the purposes of both control and motivation.

The use of flexible budget information is appropriate for control comparisons in production cost centres but the costs attributed to **discretionary cost centres** are more difficult to control. Examples of discretionary cost centres include advertising, research and development and training cost centres. Management has a **significant amount of discretion** as the amount to be budgeted for the particular activity in question.

Moreover, there is no optimum relationship between the inputs (as measured by the costs incurred) and the outputs achieved. **Fixed budgets** must be used for the control of discretionary costs.

| Question 12.1 | Responsibility accounting |

Learning outcome D2(a)

Explain the meaning and importance of controllable costs, uncontrollable costs and budget cost allowance in the context of a system of responsibility accounting.

1.7 Revenue centres

The manager of a revenue centre is responsible only for raising revenue but has no responsibility for forecasting or controlling costs. An example of a revenue centre might be a sales centre.

Revenue centres are often used for control purposes in not-for-profit organisations such as charities. For example a revenue centre manager may have responsibility for revenue targets **within a overall fund-raising exercise,** but that manager does not control the costs incurred. Such responsibility would pass to a more senior manager to whom the revenue centre manager reports.

1.8 Profit centres

KEY TERM

A PROFIT CENTRE is a part of a business accountable for both costs and revenues.

For a profit centre organisation structure to be established it is necessary to identify units of the organisation to which both revenues and costs can be separately attributed. Revenues might come from sales of goods and services to **external customers**, or from goods and services **provided to other responsibility centres within the organisation**. These internal 'sales' are charged at a notional selling price or **transfer price**. We will return to look at transfer prices in detail in Chapter 13.

A profit centre's performance report, in the same way as that for a cost centre, would identify separately the controllable and non-controllable costs. A profit centre performance report might look like this.

PROFIT CENTRE Y

INCOME STATEMENT FOR THE PERIOD

	Budget	Actual	Variance
	$'000	$'000	$'000
Sales revenue	X	X	
Variable cost of sales	(X)	(X)	
Contribution	X	X	
Directly attributable/controllable fixed costs			
Salaries	X	X	
Stationery costs	X	X	
	etc	etc	
	(X)	(X)	
Gross profit (directly attributable/controllable)	X	X	
Share of uncontrollable costs (eg head office costs)	(X)	(X)	
Net profit	X	X	

Again, the budget for the sales revenue and variable cost of sales will be **flexed according to the activity level achieved**.

The variances could be analysed in further detail for the profit centre manager.

Notice that three different 'profit levels' are highlighted in the report.

(a)   Contribution, which is within the control of the profit centre manager

(b)   Directly attributable gross profit, which is also within the manager's control

(c)   Net profit, which is after charging certain uncontrollable costs and which is therefore not controllable by the profit centre manager.

1.9 Attributable costs and controllable costs

In the example of profit centre Y we have assumed that all attributable costs are controllable costs. Although this is usually the case some care is needed before this assumption is made.

In responsibility accounting, an attributable cost is **a cost that can be specifically identified with a particular responsibility centre**. No arbitrary apportionment is necessary to share the cost over a number of different responsibility centres.

You can see therefore that **most attributable costs will be controllable costs**. An example of an attributable fixed cost is the salary of the supervisor working in a particular responsibility centre.

However, think about the depreciation of the equipment in profit centre Y. This is certainly **attributable to the profit centre**, but is it a controllable cost? The answer is probably 'no'. It is unlikely that the manager has control over the level of investment in equipment in profit centre Y, otherwise the centre would be classified as an investment centre.

Therefore it might be necessary to include a third measure of 'profit' in our performance report, which would be the controllable profit before the deduction of those costs which are attributable to the profit centre, but which are not controllable by the profit centre manager.

Exam alert

If an exam question requires you to prepare a performance report for a responsibility centre, read the information carefully to distinguish controllable attributable and non-controllable costs, and then state clearly any assumptions you need to make in order to distinguish between them.

1.10 Investment centres

KEY TERM

An INVESTMENT CENTRE is a 'Profit centre with additional responsibilities for capital investment and possibly for financing, and whose performance is measured by its return on investment.'

(CIMA *Official Terminology*)

Where a manager of a division or strategic business unit is **allowed some discretion about the amount of investment undertaken** by the division, assessment of results by profit alone (as for a profit centre) is clearly inadequate. The profit earned must be related to the amount of capital invested. Such divisions are sometimes called investment centres for this reason. Performance is measured by **return on capital employed (ROCE)**, often referred to as **return on investment (ROI)** and other subsidiary ratios, or by **residual income (RI)**.

Managers of **subsidiary companies will often be treated as investment centre** managers, accountable for profits and capital employed. Within each subsidiary, the major divisions might be treated as profit centres, with each divisional manager having the authority to decide the prices and output volumes for the products or services of the division. Within each division, there will be departmental managers, section managers and so on, who can all be treated as cost centre managers. All managers should receive regular, periodic performance reports for their own areas of responsibility.

The amount of **capital employed** in an investment centre should consist only of **directly attributable non-current assets and working capital (net current assets)**.

(a) Subsidiary companies are often required to remit spare cash to the central treasury department at group head office, and so directly attributable working capital would normally consist of inventories and receivables less payables, but minimal amounts of cash.

(b) If an investment centre is apportioned a share of head office non-current assets, the amount of capital employed in these assets should be recorded separately because it is not directly attributable to the investment centre or controllable by the manager of the investment centre.

Section summary

There are a number of advantages and disadvantages to **divisionalisation**. The principal disadvantage is that it can lead to dysfunctional decision making and a lack of goal congruence.

Responsibility accounting is the term used to describe decentralisation of authority, with the performance of the decentralised units measured in terms of accounting results.

With a system of responsibility accounting there are three types of **responsibility centre: cost centre, profit centre and investment centre.**

2 Return on investment (ROI)   5/10, 11/11, 3/12

Introduction

Return on investment (ROI) is usually used to monitor the performance of an investment centre. This section looks at how ROI is measured – make sure you understand the concepts before moving on.

2.1 A definition

ROI is generally regarded as the **key performance measure.** The main reason for its **widespread use** is that it **ties in directly with the accounting process**, and is identifiable from the income statement and statement of financial position . However it does have limitations, as we will see later in this chapter.

KEY TERM

RETURN ON INVESTMENT (ROI) (or RETURN ON CAPITAL EMPLOYED (ROCE)) shows how much profit has been made in relation to the amount of capital invested and is calculated as (profit/capital employed) × 100%.

For example, suppose that a company has two investment centres A and B, which show results for the year as follows.

	A $	B $
Profit	60,000	30,000
Capital employed	400,000	120,000
ROI	15%	25%

Investment centre A has made double the profits of investment centre B, and in terms of profits alone has therefore been more 'successful'. However, B has achieved its profits with a much lower capital investment, and so has earned a much higher ROI. This suggests that B has been a more successful investment than A.

2.2 Measuring ROI

ROI can be measured in different ways.

2.2.1 Profit after depreciation as a % of net assets employed

This is probably the **most common method**, but it does present a problem. If an investment centre maintains the same annual profit, and keeps the same assets without a policy of regular replacement of non-current assets, its ROI will increase year by year as the assets get older. This **can give a false impression of improving performance over time**.

For example, the results of investment centre X, with a policy of straight-line depreciation of assets over a 5-year period, might be as follows.

Year	Non-current assets at cost $'000	Depreciation in the year $'000	NBV (mid year) $'000	Working capital $'000	Capital employed $'000	Profit $'000	ROI
0	100			10	110		
1	100	20	90	10	100	10	10.0%
2	100	20	70	10	80	10	12.5%
3	100	20	50	10	60	10	16.7%
4	100	20	30	10	40	10	25.0%
5	100	20	10	10	20	10	50.0%

This table of figures shows that an investment centre can **improve its ROI** year by year, simply **by allowing its non-current assets to depreciate.** There could be a **disincentive to** investment centre managers to **reinvest in new or replacement assets**, because the centre's ROI would initially probably fall.

Question 12.2	ROI calculation (1)

Learning outcome D2(c)

A new company has non-current assets of £460,000 which will be depreciated to nil on a straight line basis over 10 years. Net current assets will consistently be £75,000, and annual profit will consistently be £30,000. ROI is measured as return on net assets.

Required

Calculate the company's ROI in years 2 and 6.

A further disadvantage of measuring ROI as profit divided by net assets is that, for similar reasons, it is not **easy to compare** fairly the **performance of investment centres**.

For example, suppose that we have two investment centres.

	Investment centre P		Investment centre Q	
	$	$	$	$
Working capital		20,000		20,000
Non-current assets at cost	230,000		230,000	
Accumulated depreciation	170,000		10,000	
Net book value		60,000		220,000
Capital employed		80,000		240,000
Profit		$24,000		$24,000
ROI		30%		10%

Investment centres P and Q have the same amount of working capital, the same value of non-current assets at cost, and the same profit. But P's non-current assets have been depreciated by a much bigger amount (presumably P's non-current assets are much older than Q's) and so P's ROI is three times the size of Q's ROI. The conclusion might therefore be that P has performed much better than Q. This comparison, however, would not be 'fair', because the **difference in performance might be entirely attributable to the age of their non-current assets**.

The arguments for using net book values for calculating ROI

(a)   It is the '**normally accepted**' method of calculating ROI.

(b)   Organisations are continually buying new non-current assets to replace old ones that wear out, and so on the whole, the **total net book value** of all non-current assets together **will remain fairly constant** (assuming nil inflation and nil growth).

2.2.2 Profit after depreciation as a % of gross assets employed

Instead of measuring ROI as return on net assets, we could measure it as return on gross assets. This would **remove the problem of ROI increasing over time as non-current assets get older**.

If a company acquired a non-current asset costing $40,000, which it intends to depreciate by $10,000 pa for 4 years, and if the asset earns a profit of $8,000 pa after depreciation, ROI might be calculated on net book values or gross values, as follows.

Year	Profit $	NBV(mid-year value) $	ROI based on NBV	Gross value $	ROI based on gross value
1	8,000	35,000	22.9%	40,000	20%
2	8,000	25,000	32.0%	40,000	20%
3	8,000	15,000	53.3%	40,000	20%
4	8,000	5,000	160.0%	40,000	20%

The ROI based on **net book value** shows an **increasing trend over time**, simply because the asset's value is falling as it is depreciated. The ROI based on gross book value suggests that the asset has **performed consistently** in each of the four years, which is probably a more valid conclusion.

Question 12.3	ROI calculation (2)

Learning outcome D2(c)

Repeat **Question 12.2: ROI calculation (1)**, measuring ROI as return on gross assets.

However, using gross book values to measure ROI has its **disadvantages**. Most important of these is that measuring ROI as return on gross assets ignores the age factor, and **does not distinguish between old and new assets**.

(a)   **Older non-current assets** usually **cost more to repair and maintain**, to keep them running. An investment centre with old assets may therefore have its profitability reduced by repair costs, and its ROI might fall over time as its assets get older and repair costs get bigger.

(b)   **Inflation** and **technological change alter the cost of non-current assets**. If one investment centre has non-current assets bought ten years ago with a gross cost of £1 million, and another investment centre, in the same area of business operations, has non-current assets bought very recently for £1 million, the quantity and technological character of the non-current assets of the two investment centres are likely to be very different.

2.2.3 Constituent elements of the investment base

Although we have looked at how the investment base should be valued, we need to consider its appropriate constituent elements.

(a) If a **manager's performance is being evaluated**, only those **assets** which can be **traced directly to the division** and are **controllable by the manager should be included**. Head office assets or investment centre assets controlled by head office should not be included. So, for example, only those cash balances actually maintained within an investment centre itself should be included.

(b) If it is **the performance of the investment centre that is being appraised, a proportion of the investment in head office assets would need to be included** because an investment centre could not operate without the support of head office assets and administrative backup.

2.2.4 Profits

We have looked at how to define the asset base used in the calculations but what about profit? If the **performance of the investment centre manager is being assessed** it should seem reasonable to **base profit on the revenues and costs controllable by the manager** and exclude service and head office costs except those costs specifically attributable to the investment centre. If it is the **performance of the investment centre that is being assessed, however, the inclusion of general service and head office costs would seem reasonable**.

2.2.5 Tangible and intangible assets

The management accountant is free to capitalise or expense intangible assets. When significant expenditure on an **intangible asset** (such as an advertising campaign) which is expected to provide future benefits is expensed, profits will be reduced and ROI/RI artificially depressed. In the future, the investment should produce significant cash inflows and the ROI/RI will be artificially inflated. **Such expenditure** should therefore be **capitalised so as to smooth out performance measures and to eradicate the risk of drawing false conclusions from them**. The calculation of EVA, which we will learn about later in this chapter, does just this.

A **comparison of the performance of manufacturing divisions and service divisions** should be **treated with caution**. The majority of a **manufacturing division's assets** will be **tangible** and therefore are **automatically capitalised** whereas the treatment of a **service division's** mostly **intangible assets** is **open to interpretation**.

2.2.6 Massaging the ROI

If a manager's large bonus depends on ROI being met, the manager may feel pressure to massage the measure. The **asset base** of the ratio can be **altered** by **increasing/decreasing payables and receivables** (by **speeding up or delaying payments and receipts**).

Section summary

The performance of an investment centre is usually monitored using either or both of **return on investment (ROI)** (also known as return on capital employed (ROCE)) and **residual income (RI)**.

There is no generally agreed method of calculating ROI and it can have **behavioural implications** and lead to dysfunctional decision making when used as a guide to investment decisions. It focuses attention on short-run performance whereas investment decisions should be evaluated over their full life.

3 ROI and decision-making　　　　　　　11/10, 5/11

Introduction

This section is a continuation of Section 2 and looks at how ROI can be used in decision-making.

3.1 New investments

If investment centre performance is judged by ROI, we should expect that the managers of investment centres will probably decide to undertake new capital investments **only if these new investments are likely to increase the ROI of their centre**.

Suppose that an investment centre, A, currently makes a return of 40% on capital employed. The manager of centre A would probably only want to undertake new investments that promise to yield a return of 40% or more, otherwise the investment centre's overall ROI would fall.

For example, if investment centre A currently has assets of $1,000,000 and expects to earn a profit of $400,000, how would the centre's manager view a new capital investment which would cost $250,000 and yield a profit of $75,000 pa?

	Without the new investment	With the new investment
Profit	$400,000	$475,000
Capital employed	$1,000,000	$1,250,000
ROI	40%	38%

The **new investment** would **reduce the investment centre's ROI** from 40% to 38%, and so the investment centre manager would probably decide **not to undertake** the new investment.

If the group of companies of which investment centre A is a part has a target ROI of, say, 25%, the new investment would presumably be seen as **beneficial for the group as a whole**. But even though it promises to yield a return of 75,000/250,000 = 30%, which is above the group's target ROI, it would still make investment centre A's results look worse. The manager of investment centre A would, in these circumstances, be motivated to do not what is best for the organisation as a whole, but what is **best for his division.**

ROI should not be used to guide investment decisions but there is a difficult motivational problem. If management performance is measured in terms of ROI, any decisions which benefit the company in the long term but which reduce the ROI in the immediate short term would reflect badly on the manager's reported performance. In other words, **good investment decisions would make a manager's performance seem worse than if the wrong investment decision were taken instead**.

3.2 Extended example: ROI and decision-making

At the end of 20X3, Division S (part of a group) had a book value of non-current assets of $300,000 and net current assets of $40,000. Net profit before tax was $64,000.

The non-current assets of Division S consist of five separate items each costing $60,000 which are depreciated to zero over 5 years on a straight-line basis. For each of the past years on 31 December it has bought a replacement for the asset that has just been withdrawn and it proposes to continue this policy. Because of technological advances the asset manufacturer has been able to keep his prices constant over time. The group's cost of capital is 15%.

Required

Assuming that, except where otherwise stated, there are no changes in the above data, deal with the following separate situations.

(a) Division S has the opportunity of an investment costing $60,000, and yielding an annual profit of $10,000.

   (i)   Calculate its new ROI if the investment were undertaken.

   (ii) State whether the manager of division S would recommend that the investment be undertaken.

(b) Division S has the opportunity of selling, at a price equal to its written-down book value of $24,000, an asset that currently earns $3,900 p.a.

   (i)   Calculate its new ROI if the asset were sold.

   (ii) State whether the manager of division S would recommend the sale of the asset.

Solution in general

The question does not state whether capital employed should include a valuation of non-current assets at gross historical cost or at net book value. It is assumed that net book value is required. It is also assumed that the non-current asset which has just been bought as a replacement on 31 December 20X3 has not been depreciated at all.

Exam skills

It is worth stating assumptions such as these at the start of a solution to questions of this sort. If the problem has not been properly defined, clarify your own assumptions and definitions for the benefit of the marker of your exam script!

The gross book value of the 5 non-current asset items is 5 × $60,000 = $300,000.

	$
Net book value of asset just bought on 31.12.X3	60,000
NBV of asset bought 1 year earlier	48,000
NBV of asset bought 2 years earlier	36,000
NBV of asset bought 3 years earlier	24,000
NBV of asset bought 4 years earlier	12,000
NBV of all 5 non-current assets at 31.12.X3	180,000
Net current assets	40,000
Total capital employed, Division S	220,000

Solution to part (a)

Part (i)

Begin with a comparison of the existing ROI (which is presumably the typical ROI achieved each year under the current policy of asset replacement) and the ROI with the new investment.

Existing ROI = (64/220) × 100% = 29.1%

For the ROI with the new investment it is assumed that the full asset cost of $60,000 should be included in the capital employed, although the asset will obviously be depreciated over time. It is also assumed that the additional profit of $10,000 is net of depreciation charges.

ROI with new investment = ((64 + 10)/(220 + 60)) × 100% = 26.4%

If the investment centre manager based his investment decisions on whether an investment would increase or reduce his ROI, he would not want to make the additional investment. This investment has a **marginal ROI** of (10/60) × 100% = 16.7%, which is **above the group's cost of capital but below Division S's current ROI** of 29.1%. Making the investment would therefore lower the Division's average ROI.

Part (ii)

This example **illustrates the weakness of ROI as a guide to investment decisions**. An investment centre manager might want an investment to show a good ROI from year 1, when the new investment has a high net book value. In the case of Division S, the average net book value of the asset over its full life will be 50% of $60,000 = $30,000, and so the average ROI on the investment over time will be ($10,000/$30,000) × 100% = 33.3% which is greater than the cost of capital.

Presumably, however, the Division S manager would not want to wait so long to earn a good ROI, and wants to protect his division's performance in the short run as well as the long run. Therefore he would not recommend that the investment be undertaken.

Solution to part (b)

Part (b) of the question deals with a disinvestment proposal, compared to an acquisition in part (a). The same basic principles apply.

The **ROI if the asset is sold** is ((64 − 3.9)/(220 − 24)) × 100% = 30.7%

This compares favourably with the Division's current average ROI of 29.1%, and so if the manager of Division S made his divestment decisions on the basis of ROI, he would **presumably decide to get rid of the asset**.

However, the decision would be misguided, because **decisions should not be based on the short-term effects on ROI**.

The asset which would be sold earns a ROI of (3.9/24) × 100% = 16.3%, which is higher than the group's cost of capital, but lower than the Division S average.

On the assumption that the asset would earn $3,900 after depreciation for the two remaining years of its life, its ROI next year would be (3.9/12) × 100% = 32.5% which again is higher than the cost of capital.

Exam alert

You could be asked to discuss the conflict that may arise between NPV and ROI in an investment decision.

Section summary

If investment centre performance is judged by ROI, we would expect that the managers of these centres would undertake new capital investments only if these new investments increase the centre's ROI.

4   Residual income (RI)   11/10, 3/11

Introduction

Residual income (RI) can also be used to measure the performance of investment centres. However it has a number of weaknesses that make it less preferable to ROI as a performance measure. This section focuses on how to calculate RI and compares it to ROI. Make sure you know the strengths and weaknesses of this measure as well as how to calculate it.

4.1 Calculating RI

An alternative way of measuring the performance of an investment centre, instead of using ROI, is residual income (RI). **Residual income** is a **measure of the centre's profits after deducting a notional or imputed interest cost**.

(a)   The centre's profit is **after deducting depreciation** on capital equipment.

(b)   The imputed cost of capital might be the organisation's cost of borrowing or its weighted average cost of capital.

RESIDUAL INCOME (RI) is 'Profit minus a charge for capital employed in the period.'

(CIMA *Official Terminology*)

Question 12.4   RI

Learning outcome D2(c)

A division with capital employed of $400,000 currently earns an ROI of 22%. It can make an additional investment of $50,000 for a 5 year life with nil residual value. The average net profit from this investment would be $12,000 after depreciation. The division's cost of capital is 14%.

What are the residual incomes before and after the investment?

4.2 The advantages and weaknesses of RI compared with ROI

The advantages of using RI

(a)   Residual income will **increase** when investments earning above the cost of capital are undertaken and investments earning below the cost of capital are eliminated.

(b)   Residual income is **more flexible** since a different cost of capital can be applied to investments with **different risk** characteristics.

The **weakness** of RI is that it **does not facilitate comparisons** between investment centres nor **does it relate the size of a centre's income to the size of the investment**.

4.3 RI versus ROI: marginally profitable investments

Residual income will increase if a new investment is undertaken which earns a profit in excess of the imputed interest charge on the value of the asset acquired. Residual income will go up even if the investment only just exceeds the imputed interest charge, and this means that 'marginally profitable' investments are likely to be undertaken by the investment centre manager.

In contrast, when a manager is judged by ROI, a marginally profitable investment would be less likely to be undertaken because it would reduce the average ROI earned by the centre as a whole.

Example: Residual income and decision-making

In the previous example in section 3.2, **whereas ROI would have worsened with the new investment opportunity (part (a)) and improved with the disinvestment (part (b)), residual income would have done the opposite** – improved with the new investment and worsened with the disinvestment.

The figures would be:

(a)   *Part (a)*

	Without new investment $	*Investment* $	*With new investment* $
Profit before notional interest	64,000	10,000	74,000
Notional interest (15% of $340,000)	51,000	9,000*	60,000
	13,000	1,000	14,000

* 15% of $60,000

If the manager of Division S were **guided by residual income** into making decisions, he would **approve the new investment**.

(b)   *Part (b)*

	Without disinvestment $	Disinvestment $	With disinvestment $
Profit before notional interest	64,000	3,900	60,100
Notional interest	51,000	3,600 *	47,400
Residual income	13,000	300	12,700

*15% of $24,000

If the investment centre manager is guided by residual income, he would decide to **keep the asset** instead of selling it off.

Residual income **does not always point to the right investment decision**. However, residual income is **more likely than ROI to improve when managers make correct investment/divestment decisions**, and so is probably a 'safer' basis than ROI on which to measure performance.

Example: ROI versus residual income

Suppose that Department H has the following profit, assets employed and an imputed interest charge of 12% on operating assets.

	$	$
Operating profit	30,000	
Operating assets		100,000
Imputed interest (12%)	12,000	
Return on investment		30%
Residual income	18,000	

Suppose now that an additional investment of $10,000 is proposed, which will increase operating income in Department H by $1,400. The effect of the investment would be:

	$	$
Total operating income	31,400	
Total operating assets		110,000
Imputed interest (12%)	13,200	
Return on investment		28.5%
Residual income	18,200	

If the Department H manager is made responsible for the department's performance, he would **resist the new investment if he were to be judged on ROI**, but would **welcome the investment if he were judged according to RI**, since there would be a marginal increase of $200 in residual income from the investment, but a fall of 1.5% in ROI.

The marginal investment offers a return of 14% ($1,400 on an investment of $10,000) which is above the 'cut-off rate' of 12%. Since the original return on investment was 30%, the marginal investment will reduce the overall divisional performance. Indeed, any marginal investment offering an accounting rate of return of less than 30% in the year would reduce the overall performance.

Exam skills

Examination questions on residual income may focus on the sort of behavioural aspects of investment centre measurement that we have discussed above, for example why it is considered necessary to use residual income to measure performance rather than ROI, and why residual income might influence an investment centre manager's investment decisions differently.

You should also be able to discuss other methods of assessment alongside ROI and RI. These may include EVA® (see Section 5), balanced scorecard, other non-financial measures, controllable profit and cash generated.

Section summary

RI can sometimes give results that avoid the **behavioural** problem of **dysfunctionality**. Its weakness is that it does not facilitate comparisons between investment centres nor does it relate the size of a centre's income to the size of the investment.

5 Economic value added (EVA®)

Introduction

The final performance measure we are going to look at is economic value added (EVA®). The calculation is similar to that for RI so make sure you don't get them mixed up!

LEARN

EVA® is an alternative absolute performance measure. It is similar to RI and is calculated as follows.

EVA® = net operating profit after tax (NOPAT) less capital charge

where the capital charge = weighted average cost of capital × net assets

5.1 Calculating EVA®

Economic value added (EVA®) is a registered trade mark owned by Stern Stewart & Co. It is a specific type of residual income (RI) calculated as follows.

> EVA® = net operating profit after tax (NOPAT) less capital charge
>
> where the capital charge = weighted average cost of capital × net assets

You can see from the formula that the calculation of EVA® is very similar to the calculation of RI.

The calculation of EVA® is different to RI because the net assets used as the basis of the imputed interest charge are usually valued at their **replacement cost** and are **increased by any costs that have been capitalised** (see below).

There are also differences in the way that NOPAT is calculated compared with the profit figure that is used for RI, as follows.

(a) Costs which would normally be treated as expenses, but which are considered within an EVA® calculation as **investments building for the future**, are added back to NOPAT to derive a figure for 'economic profit'. These costs are included instead as assets in the figure for net assets employed, ie as investments for the future. Costs treated in this way include items such as **goodwill, research and development expenditure and advertising costs**.

(b) Adjustments are sometimes made to the depreciation charge, whereby accounting depreciation is added back to the profit figures, and **economic depreciation** is subtracted instead to arrive at NOPAT. Economic depreciation is a charge for the fall in asset value due to wear and tear or obsolescence.

(c) Any lease charges are excluded from NOPAT and added in as a part of capital employed.

Another point to note about the calculation of NOPAT, which is the same as the calculation of the profit figure for RI, is that **interest** is excluded from NOPAT because interest costs are taken into account in the capital charge.

Example: Calculating EVA®

An investment centre has reported operating profits of $21 million. This was after charging $4 million for the development and launch costs of a new product that is expected to generate profits for four years. Taxation is paid at the rate of 25% of the operating profit.

The company has a risk adjusted weighted average cost of capital of 12% per annum and is paying interest at 9% per annum on a substantial long term loan.

The investment centre's non-current asset value is $50 million and the net current assets have a value of $22 million. The replacement cost of the non-current assets is estimated to be $64 million.

Required

Calculate the investment centre's EVA® for the period.

Solution

Calculation of NOPAT

	$ million
Operating profit	21.00
Taxation @ 25%	(5.25)
	15.75
Add back development costs	4.00
Less one year's amortisation of development costs ($4m/4)	(1.00)
NOPAT	18.75

Calculation of economic value of net assets

	$ million
Replacement cost of net assets ($22 million + $64 million)	86
Add back investment in new product to benefit future	3
Economic value of net assets	89

Calculation of EVA®

The capital charge is based on the **weighted average cost of capital**, which takes account of the cost of share capital as well as the cost of loan capital. Therefore the correct interest rate is 12%.

	$ million
NOPAT	18.75
Capital charge (12% × $89 million)	(10.68)
EVA®	8.07

5.2 Advantages of EVA®

The advantages of EVA® include the following.

(a)   Maximisation of EVA® will create real wealth for the shareholders.

(b)   The adjustments within the calculation of EVA® mean that the measure is based on figures that are closer to cash flows than accounting profits. Hence EVA® may be **less distorted by the accounting policies selected**.

(c)   The EVA® measure is an absolute value which is easily understood by non-financial managers.

(d)   If management are assessed using performance measures based on traditional accounting policies they may be unwilling to invest in areas such as advertising and development for the future because **such costs will immediately reduce the current year's accounting profit**. EVA® recognises such costs as investments for the future and thus they do not immediately reduce the EVA® in the year of expenditure.

5.3 Disadvantages of EVA®

EVA® does have some drawbacks.

(a)   It is still a **relatively short term measure** which can encourage managers to focus on short term performance.

(b)   EVA® is based on historical accounts which may be of **limited use as a guide to the future**. In practice also the influences of accounting policies on the starting profit figure may not be completely negated by the adjustments made to it in the EVA® model.

(c)   Making the necessary adjustments can be problematic as sometimes a **large number of adjustments** are required.

(d)   Investment centres which are larger in size may have larger EVA figures for this reason. **Allowance for relative size** must be made when comparing the relative performance of investment centres.

| Question 12.5 | Calculating EVA® |

Learning outcome D2(c)

Division D operates as an investment centre. The book value of the non-current assets is $83,000 but their replacement value is estimated to be $98,000. Working capital in the division has a value of $19,000.

Latest operating profits for the division were $18,500, after charging historical cost depreciation of $8,100 and the costs of a major advertising campaign which amounted to $6,000. The advertising campaign is expected to boost revenues for two years.

An economic depreciation charge for the period would have been $12,300.

The risk adjusted weighted cost of capital for the company is 11% per annum.

Required

Calculate the EVA® for Division D. Ignore taxation.

Section summary

EVA® is an alternative absolute performance measure. It is similar to RI and is calculated as follows.

EVA® = net operating profit after tax (NOPAT) less capital charge

where the capital charge = weighted average cost of capital × net assets

EVA® and RI are similar because both result in an absolute figure which is calculated by subtracting an imputed interest charge from the profit earned by the investment centre. However there are differences as follows.

(a) The profit figures are calculated differently. EVA® is based on an '**economic profit**' which is derived by making a series of adjustments to the accounting profit.

(b) The notional capital charges use **different bases for net assets**. The replacement cost of net assets is usually used in the calculation of EVA®.

Chapter Roundup

✓ There are a number of advantages and disadvantages to **divisionalisation**. The principal disadvantage is that it can lead to dysfunctional decision making and a lack of goal congruence.

✓ **Responsibility accounting** is the term used to describe decentralisation of authority, with the performance of the decentralised units measured in terms of accounting results.

✓ With a system of responsibility accounting there are three types of **responsibility centre: cost centre, profit centre and investment centre**.

✓ The performance of an investment centre is usually monitored using either or both of **return on investment (ROI)** (also known as return on capital employed (ROCE)) and **residual income (RI).**

✓ There is no generally agreed method of calculating ROI and it can have **behavioural implications** and lead to dysfunctional decision making when used as a guide to investment decisions. It focuses attention on short-run performance whereas investment decisions should be evaluated over their full life.

✓ If investment centre performance is judged by ROI, we would expect the managers of these centres to undertake new capital investments only if these new investments increase the centre's ROI.

✓ RI can sometimes give results that avoid the **behavioural** problem of **dysfunctionality**. Its weakness is that it does not facilitate comparisons between investment centres nor does it relate the size of a centre's income to the size of the investment.

✓ EVA® is an alternative absolute performance measure. It is similar to RI and is calculated as follows.

EVA® = net operating profit after tax (NOPAT) less capital charge

where the capital charge = weighted average cost of capital × net assets

✓ EVA® and RI are similar because both result in an absolute figure which is calculated by subtracting an imputed interest charge from the profit earned by the investment centre. However there are differences as follows.

(a) The profit figures are calculated differently. EVA® is based on an **'economic profit'** which is derived by making a series of adjustments to the accounting profit.

(b) The notional capital charges use **different bases for net assets**. The replacement cost of net assets is usually used in the calculation of EVA®.

Quick Quiz

1   Fill in the table below.

Type of responsibility centre	Manager has control over ...	Principal performance measures

2   Over which of the following can an investment centre manager exercise control?

I   Controllable costs in the division
II   Selling prices of the division's output
III   The division's output volumes
IV   Investment in the division's non-current assets and working capital

A   All of them
B   II and III
C   I only
D   IV only

3   Choose the correct words from those highlighted.

ROI based on profits as a % of net assets employed will (1) **increase/decrease** as an asset gets older and its book value (2) **increases/reduces**. This could therefore create an (3) **incentive/disincentive** to investment centre managers to reinvest in new or replacement assets.

4   An investment centre with capital employed of $570,000 is budgeted to earn a profit of $119,700 next year. A proposed non-current asset investment of $50,000, not included in the budget at present, will earn a profit next year of $8,500 after depreciation. The company's cost of capital is 15%. What is the budgeted ROI and residual income for next year, both with and without the investment?

	ROI	*Residual income*
Without investment	....	....
With investment	....	....

5   'The use of residual income in performance measurement will avoid dysfunctional decision making because it will always lead to the correct decision concerning capital investments.' *True or false?*

6   *Choose the correct words from those highlighted.*

If accounting ROI is used as a guideline for investment decisions, it **should be/should not be** looked at over the full life of the investment. In the short term, the accounting ROI is likely to be **high/low** because the net book value of the asset will be **high/low**.

7   EVA® is calculated as operating profit less a capital charge. *True or false?*

8   Company H has reported annual profits for 20X7 of $83.4m. This is after charging $8.3m for development costs of a new product that is expected to last for the current year and two more years. The cost of capital is 12% per annum. Fixed assets have a historical cost of $110m and the replacement cost of these fixed assets at the beginning of the year is $156m. The assets have been depreciated at 10% per year and the company has working capital of $25.2m. Ignoring the effect of taxation, what is the EVA® of the company?

Answers to Quick Quiz

1

Type of responsibility centre	Manager has control over ...	Principal performance measures
Cost centre	Controllable costs	Variance analysis
		Efficiency measures
Revenue centre	Revenues only	Revenues
Profit centre	Controllable costs	Profit
	Sales prices (including transfer prices)	
Investment centre	Controllable costs	Return on investment
	Sales prices (including transfer prices) Output volumes	Residual income
	Investment in non-current and current assets	Other financial ratios

2   A

3   (a)   increase
       (b)   reduces
       (c)   disincentive

4

	ROI	*Residual income*
Without investment	21.0%	$34,200
With investment	20.7%	$35,200

5   False

6   should be
      low
      high

7   False. EVA® = NOPAT less a capital charge

8

	$m
Profit	83.40
Add	
Current depreciation (110 × 10%)	11.00
Development costs (8.3 × 2/3)	5.53
Less	
Replacement depreciation (156 × 10%)	(15.60)
	84.33
Less cost of capital (W1)	(20.54)
EVA®	63.79

W1   Cost of capital charge

Fixed assets (156 – 15.6)	140.40
Working capital	25.20
Development costs	5.53
	171.13 × 12% = 20.54

Answers to Questions

12.1 Responsibility accounting

In a system of responsibility accounting costs and revenues are **segregated into areas of personal responsibility** in order to monitor and assess the performance of each part of an organisation.

Controllable costs are those costs which are within the control of the manager of a responsibility centre whereas uncontrollable costs are **outside the control** of the centre manager.

A budget cost allowance is the **cost that should be incurred** in a responsibility centre **for the actual activity level that was achieved**. It is the flexible budget cost that is obtained by flexing the variable cost allowance in line with changes in the level of activity.

All three items are important from a point of view of **control** and **motivation**.

Better cost control is achieved if those areas that a manager can control (controllable costs) are **highlighted separately** from those costs that the manger cannot control (uncontrollable costs). Better cost control is also achieved through **more meaningful variances** that are obtained by comparing a realistic flexible budget cost allowance with the actual results that were achieved.

Motivation of managers is improved if uncontrollable items are analysed separately, since otherwise they will feel they are **being held accountable for something over which they have no control**. Similarly the realistic flexible budget of comparison is more likely to have a positive motivational impact because a **more meaningful** comparative measure of actual performance is obtained.

12.2 ROI calculation (1)

Year 2	$	Year 6	$
Non-current assets at net book value	368,000	Non-current assets at net book value	184,000
Current assets	75,000	Current assets	75,000
	443,000		259,000

$$\frac{\$30,000}{\$443,000} \times 100 = 6.8\% \qquad \frac{\$30,000}{\$259,000} \times 100 = 11.6\%$$

Year 2 – 6.8%

Year 6 – 11.6%

12.3 ROI calculation (2)

Year 2 – 5.6%

Year 6 – 5.6%

12.4 RI

	Before investment $	After investment $
Divisional profit ($400,000 x 22%)	88,000	100,000
Imputed interest		
(400,000 × 0.14)	56,000	
(450,000 × 0.14)		63,000
Residual income	32,000	37,000

12.5 Calculating EVA®

	$
Operating profit	18,500
Add back historical cost depreciation	8,100
Less economic depreciation	(12,300)
Add back advertising costs	6,000
Less amortisation of advertising costs ($6,000/2)	(3,000)
NOPAT (ignoring taxation)	17,300
Replacement value of non-current assets	98,000
Working capital	19,000
Add investment in advertising to benefit next year	3,000
Economic value of net assets	120,000
NOPAT	17,300
Capital charge (11% × $120,000)	13,200
EVA®	4,100

Now try these questions from the Exam Question Bank

Number	Level	Marks	Time
Q29	Examination	15	27 mins
Q30	Introductory	30	54 mins
Q31	Examination	30	54 mins

TRANSFER PRICING

In this chapter we look at responsibility accounting and how a transfer pricing system can work in responsibility centres.

Sections 1 and 2 provide you with a **framework** for transfer pricing. **Sections 3 to 7** cover the **various approaches** to transfer pricing required in particular circumstances, while **Section 8** provides a useful summary of these sections.

Section 9 is based on a specific transfer pricing topic mentioned in the syllabus.

This is quite a long chapter but the key points have been highlighted in the section summaries. Make sure you are happy with each point before moving on.

topic list	learning outcomes	syllabus references	ability required
1 The basic principles of transfer pricing	D3(b), 3(c)	D3(ii)	analysis
2 General rules	D3(b), 3(c)	D3(ii)	analysis
3 The use of market price as a basis for transfer prices	D3(b), 3(c)	D3(ii), (iii)	analysis
4 Transfer pricing with an imperfect external market	D3(b), 3(c)	D3(ii)	analysis
5 Transfer pricing when there is no external market for the transferred item	D3(b), 3(c)	D3(ii)	analysis
6 Transfer pricing and changing costs/prices	D3(b), 3(c)	D3(ii), (iii)	analysis
7 Identifying the optimal transfer price	D3(b), 3(c)	D3(ii), (iii)	analysis
8 Negotiated transfer prices	D3(b), 3(c)	D3(iii)	analysis
9 International transfer pricing	D3(d)	D3(iv)	analysis

1 The basic principles of transfer pricing   3/11, 5/13

Introduction

This section introduces the important topic of transfer pricing with a summary of the basic principles. Make sure you understand the main points before moving on as this section forms the basis for the rest of the chapter.

1.1 What is a transfer price?

KEY TERM

A TRANSFER PRICE is the 'Price at which goods or services are transferred between different units of the same company.'   (CIMA *Official Terminology*)

Transfer pricing is used when divisions of an organisation need to charge other divisions of the same organisation for goods and services they provide to them. For example, subsidiary A might make a component that is used as part of a product made by subsidiary B of the same company, but that can also be sold to the external market, including makers of rival products to subsidiary B's product. There will therefore be two sources of revenue for A.

(a)   External sales revenue from sales made to other organisations

(b)   Internal sales revenue from sales made to other responsibility centres within the same organisation, valued at the transfer price

1.2 Main uses of transfer prices

1.2.1 Evaluation of divisional managers' performance

Transfer prices will be a **cost** for the **division receiving the goods** and a **revenue** for the division **supplying the goods**. Just as managers are assessed on their management of costs from external suppliers, they are also assessed on their **ability to control internal costs**. This can lead to disputes between divisional managers as they try to protect their own interests and achieve optimal performance of their own divisions.

1.2.2 To achieve the overall organisational goals

Also known as **goal congruence**, transfer prices in theory should be set to ensure that **organisational goals** (such as profit maximisation) **are achieved**. Although divisional managers are being assessed on their own divisions' performance, their overall objective should be to ensure that their behaviour supports the achievement of organisational goals. Transfer prices should be set at a level that **encourages 'trade'** between divisions rather than driving divisional managers to purchase the goods from external suppliers.

1.2.3 To preserve divisional autonomy

Divisional autonomy refers to the right of a division to govern itself, that is, the **freedom to make decisions without consulting a higher authority first and without interference from a higher body**.

Transfer prices are particularly appropriate for **profit centres** because if one profit centre does work for another the size of the transfer price will affect the costs of one profit centre and the revenues of another.

1.3 Problems with transfer pricing

1.3.1 Maintaining the right level of divisional autonomy

This problem echoes one of the problems of divisionalisation.

A task of **head office** is to try to **prevent dysfunctional decision-making** by individual profit centres. To do this, head office must reserve some power and authority for itself and so **profit centres cannot be allowed to make entirely autonomous decisions**.

Just how much authority head office decides to retain will vary according to the circumstances. **A balance** should be kept **between divisional autonomy** to provide incentives and motivation, and **retaining centralised authority** to ensure that the organisation's profit centres are all working towards the same target, the benefit of the whole organisation (in other words, the divisions should **retain goal congruence**).

1.3.2 Ensuring divisional performance is measured fairly:

Profit centre managers tend to put their own profit performance above everything else. Since profit centre performance is measured according to the profit they earn, no profit centre will want to do work for another and incur costs without being paid for it. Consequently, profit centre managers are likely to dispute the size of transfer prices with each other, or disagree about whether one profit centre should do work for another or not. Transfer prices **affect behaviour and decisions** by profit centre managers.

1.3.3 Ensuring corporate goals are met

These goals could be strategic or financial in nature. Strategic goals could involve market share for a product, where one division is making supplies to the competitor of another division.

Financial goals could be organisation wide, such as minimising the overall tax liability, or divisional such as how much work should be transferred between divisions, and how many sales the division should make to the external market. For this, there is presumably a **profit-maximising level of output and sales for the organisation as a whole**. However, unless each profit centre also maximises its own profit at this same level of output, there will be inter-divisional disagreements about output levels and the profit-maximising output will not be achieved.

The ideal solution

Ideally a transfer price should be set at a level that overcomes these problems.

(a)   The transfer price should provide an 'artificial' selling price that enables the **transferring division to earn a return for its efforts**, and the receiving division to incur a cost for benefits received.

(b)   The transfer price should be set at a level that enables **profit centre performance** to be **measured 'commercially'**. This means that the transfer price should be a fair commercial price.

(c)   The transfer price, if possible, should encourage profit centre managers to agree on the amount of goods and services to be transferred, which will also be at a level that is consistent with the aims of the organisation as a whole such as **maximising company profits**.

In practice it is difficult to achieve all three aims.

| **Question 13.1** | Benefits of transfer pricing |

Learning outcome D3(c)

The transfer pricing system operated by a divisional company has the potential to make a significant contribution towards the achievement of corporate financial objectives.

Required

Explain the potential benefits of operating a transfer pricing system within a divisionalised company.

Section summary

Transfer prices are a way of promoting **divisional autonomy**, ideally without prejudicing the **measurement of divisional performance** or discouraging **overall corporate profit maximisation**.

Transfer prices should be set at a level which ensures that **profits for the organisation as a whole** are **maximised**.

2 General rules   5/10, 9/11, 11/11, 5/12, 11/12

Introduction

This section highlights the boundaries within which transfer prices should fall to make them acceptable to both the supplying and receiving divisions.

2.1 Minimum and maximum prices

KEY POINT

The **limits within which transfer prices should fall** are as follows.

- **The minimum**. The sum of the supplying division's marginal cost and opportunity cost of the item transferred.

- **The maximum**. The lowest market price at which the receiving division could purchase the goods or services externally, less any internal cost savings in packaging and delivery.

The **minimum** results from the fact that the **supplying division will not agree to transfer if the transfer price is less than the marginal cost + opportunity cost of the item transferred** (because if it were the division would incur a loss).

The **maximum** results from the fact that the **receiving division will buy the item at the cheapest price possible**.

Example: General rules

Division X produces product L at a marginal cost per unit of $100. If a unit is transferred internally to division Y, $25 contribution is foregone on an external sale. The item can be purchased externally for $150.

- **The minimum**. Division X will not agree to a transfer price of less than $(100 + 25) = $125 per unit.

- **The maximum**. Division Y will not agree to a transfer price in excess of $150.

The difference between the two results ($25) represents the savings from producing internally as opposed to buying externally.

2.1.1 Opportunity cost

The **opportunity cost** included in determining the lower limit will be one of the following.

(a)   The maximum contribution forgone by the supplying division **in transferring internally rather than selling goods externally**

(b)   The contribution forgone by not using the same facilities in the producing division for their next best alternative use

If there is **no external market** for the item being transferred, and **no alternative uses for** the division's facilities, the **transfer price = standard variable cost of production**.

If there is an **external market** for the item being transferred and **no alternative, more profitable use** for the facilities in that division, the **transfer price = the market price**.

Exam alert

An exam question could ask you to discuss the appropriateness of a company's transfer pricing policy.

Section summary

The **limits within which transfer prices should fall** are as follows.

- **The minimum.** The sum of the supplying division's marginal cost and opportunity cost of the item transferred.

- **The maximum.** The lowest market price at which the receiving division could purchase the goods or services externally, less any internal cost savings in packaging and delivery.

3   The use of market price as a basis for transfer prices

Introduction

This is the first of five sections that explain the various approaches to setting transfer prices. Make sure you follow the example and are aware of the pros and cons of market price as a basis for transfer price.

3.1 When should market price be used as the transfer price?   9/10

If an external market exists for the product being transferred (and there is unsatisfied demand externally) the ideal transfer price will be the market price.

KEY POINT

If **variable costs and market prices are constant**, regardless of the volume of output, a **market-based transfer price** is the ideal transfer price.

If a **perfect external market** exists, **market price** is the **ideal** transfer price.

If an **external market price exists** for transferred goods, profit centre managers will be aware of the price they could obtain or the price they would have to pay for their goods on the external market, and they would inevitably **compare** this price **with the transfer price**.

The external market is also sometimes known as the **intermediate market**.

Example: Transferring goods at market value

A company has two profit centres, A and B. A sells half of its output on the open market and transfers the other half to B. Costs and external revenues in an accounting period are as follows.

	A $	B $	Total $
External sales	8,000	24,000	32,000
Costs of production	12,000	10,000	22,000
Company profit			10,000

Required

What are the consequences of setting a transfer price at market value?

Solution

If the transfer price is at market price, A would be happy to sell the output to B for $8,000.

	A $	A $	B $	B $	Total $
Market sales		8,000		24,000	32,000
Transfer sales		8,000		–	
		16,000		24,000	
Transfer costs	–		8,000		
Own costs	12,000		10,000		22,000
		12,000		18,000	
Profit		4,000		6,000	10,000

The **transfer sales of A are self cancelling with the transfer cost of B**, so that the total profits are unaffected by the transfer items. The transfer price simply spreads the total profit between A and B.

Consequences

(a)   A earns the same profit on transfers as on external sales. B must pay a commercial price for transferred goods, and both divisions will have their profit measured in a fair way.

(b)   A will be indifferent about selling externally or transferring goods to B because the profit is the same on both types of transaction. B can therefore ask for and obtain as many units as it wants from A.

A **market-based** transfer price therefore seems to be the **ideal** transfer price.

3.2 Adjusted market price

Internal transfers are often **cheaper** than external sales, with **savings** in selling and administration costs, bad debt risks and possibly transport/delivery costs. It would therefore seem reasonable for the **buying division to expect a discount** on the external market price. The transfer price might be slightly less than market price, so that **A and B could share the cost savings** from internal transfers compared with external sales. It should be possible to reach agreement on this price and on output levels with a minimum of intervention from head office.

3.3 The merits of market value transfer prices

3.3.1 Divisional autonomy

In a decentralised company, divisional managers should have the **autonomy** to make output, selling and buying **decisions which appear to be in the best interests of the division's performance.** (If every division optimises its performance, the company as a whole must inevitably achieve optimal results.) Thus a **transferor division should be given the freedom to sell output on the open market,** rather than to transfer it within the company.

'Arm's length' transfer prices, which give profit centre managers the freedom to negotiate prices with other profit centres as though they were independent companies, will tend to result in a market-based transfer price.

3.3.2 Corporate profit maximisation

In most cases where the transfer price is at market price, **internal transfers** should be **expected**, because the **buying division** is likely to **benefit** from a better quality of service, greater flexibility, and dependability of supply. **Both divisions** may **benefit** from cheaper costs of administration, selling and transport. A market price as the transfer price would therefore **result in decisions which would be in the best interests of the company or group as a whole**.

3.4 The disadvantages of market value transfer prices

Market value as a transfer price does have certain **disadvantages**.

(a) The **market price may be a temporary one**, induced by adverse economic conditions, or dumping, or the market price might depend on the volume of output supplied to the external market by the profit centre.

(b) A transfer price at market value might, under some circumstances, **act as a disincentive to use up any spare capacity** in the divisions. A price based on incremental cost, in contrast, might provide an incentive to use up the spare resources in order to provide a marginal contribution to profit.

(c) Many products **do not have an equivalent market price** so that the price of a similar, but not identical, product might have to be chosen. In such circumstances, the option to sell or buy on the open market does not really exist.

(d) There might be an **imperfect external market** for the transferred item, so that if the transferring division tried to sell more externally, it would have to reduce its selling price.

Section summary

If **variable costs and market prices are constant**, regardless of the volume of output, a **market-based transfer price** is the ideal transfer price.

If a **perfect external market** exists, **market price** is the **ideal** transfer price.

4 Transfer pricing with an imperfect external market

Introduction

This section focuses on how transfer prices are set when there is an imperfect external market for the product being transferred. The main problem in this situation is that there may be no external market on which a price can be based.

4.1 Problems with having an imperfect external market

Cost-based approaches to transfer pricing are often used in practice, because in practice the following conditions are common.

(a) There is **no external market** for the product that is being transferred (see Section 5).

(b) Alternatively, although there is an external market, it is an **imperfect** one because the market price is affected by such factors as the amount that the company setting the transfer price supplies to it, or because there is only a limited external demand. We cover this situation in this section.

In either case there will **not be a suitable market price** upon which to base the transfer price. Another basis must therefore be used.

4.2 Transfer prices based on full cost

Under this approach, unsurprisingly, the **full cost** (including fixed production overheads absorbed) that has been incurred by the supplying division in making the intermediate product is charged to the receiving division. If a **full cost plus approach** is used a **profit margin is also included** in this transfer price.

Example: Transfer prices based on full cost

Suppose a company has two profit centres, A and B. A can only sell half of its maximum output of 800 units externally because of limited demand. It transfers the other half of its output to B which also faces limited demand. Costs and revenues in an accounting period are as follows.

	A $	B $	Total $
External sales	8,000	24,000	32,000
Costs of production in the division	13,000	10,000	23,000
Profit			9,000

Division A's costs included fixed production overheads of $4,800 and fixed selling and administration costs of $1,000.

There are no opening or closing inventories. It does not matter, for this illustration, whether marginal costing or absorption costing is used. For the moment, we shall ignore the question of whether the current output levels are profit-maximising and congruent with the goals of the company as a whole.

If the transfer price is at full cost, A in our example would have 'sales' to B of $6,000 (($13,000 – 1,000) × 50%). Selling and administration costs are not included as these are not incurred on the internal transfers. This would be a cost to B, as follows.

	A $	A $	B $	B $	Company as a whole $
Open market sales		8,000		24,000	32,000
Transfer sales		6,000		–	
Total sales, inc transfers		14,000		24,000	
Transfer costs			6,000		
Own costs	13,000		10,000		23,000
Total costs, inc transfers		13,000		16,000	
Profit		1,000		8,000	9,000

The **transfer sales of A are self-cancelling with the transfer costs of B** so that total profits are **unaffected by the transfer items**. The transfer price simply spreads the total profit of $9,000 between A and B.

The obvious **drawback** to the transfer price at cost is that **A makes no profit** on its work, and the manager of division A would much prefer to sell output on the open market to earn a profit, rather than transfer to B, regardless of whether or not transfers to B would be in the best interests of the company as a whole.

Division A needs a profit on its transfers in order to be motivated to supply B; therefore transfer pricing at cost is inconsistent with the use of a profit centre accounting system.

4.2.1 Sub-optimal decisions

Note, also, that as the level of transfer price increases, its effect on division B could lead to sub-optimalisation problems for the organisation as a whole.

Example: Sub-optimal decisions

For example, suppose division B could buy the product from an outside supplier for $10 instead of paying $15 ($6,000/(800/2)) to division A. This transfer price would therefore force division B to buy the product externally at $10 per unit, although it could be manufactured internally for a variable cost of $(13,000 − 4,800 − 1,000)/800 = $9 per unit.

Although division B (the buying division) would save $15 − 10) = $5 per unit by buying externally, the organisation as a whole would lose $400 as follows.

	Per unit
	$
Marginal cost of production	9
External purchase cost	10
Loss if buy in	1

The overall loss on transfer/purchase of 400 units is therefore 400 × $1 = $400.

This loss of $1 per unit assumes that any other use for the released capacity would produce a benefit of less than $400. If the 400 units could also be sold externally for $20 per unit, the optimal decision for the organisation as a whole would be to buy in the units for division B at $10 per unit.

	Per unit
	$
Market price	20
Marginal cost	9
Contribution	11
Loss if buy-in	(1)
Incremental profit	10

The overall incremental profit would therefore be 400 × $10 = $4,000.

4.3 Transfer prices based on full cost plus

If the transfers are at cost plus a margin of, say, 10%, A's sales to B would be $6,600 ($13,000 −1,000) × 50% × 1.10).

		A		B	Total
	$	$	$	$	$
Open market sales		8,000		24,000	32,000
Transfer sales		6,600		–	
		14,600		24,000	
Transfer costs			6,600		
Own costs	13,000		10,000		23,000
		13,000		16,600	
Profit		1,600		7,400	9,000

Compared to a transfer price at cost, **A gains some profit** at the expense of B. However, A makes a bigger profit on external sales in this case because the profit mark-up of 10% is less than the profit mark-up on open market sales. The choice of 10% as a profit mark-up was arbitrary and unrelated to external market conditions.

The transfer price **fails on all three criteria** (divisional autonomy, performance measurement and corporate profit measurement) for judgement.

(a) Arguably, the transfer price does not give A fair revenue or charge B a reasonable cost, and so their profit **performance is distorted**. It would certainly be unfair, for example, to compare A's profit with B's profit.

(b) Given this unfairness it is likely that the **autonomy** of each of the divisional managers is **under threat.** If they cannot agree on what is a fair split of the external profit a decision will have to be imposed from above.

(c) It would seem to give A an incentive to sell more goods externally and transfer less to B. This may or **may not be in the best interests of the company as a whole**.

In fact we can demonstrate that the method is **flawed from the point of view of corporate profit maximisation**. Division A's total production costs of $12,000 include an element of fixed costs. Half of division A's total production costs are transferred to division B. However from the point of view of division B the cost is entirely variable.

The cost per unit to A is $15 ($12,000 ÷ 800) and this includes a fixed element of $6 ($4,800 ÷ 800), while division B's own costs are $25 ($10,000 ÷ 400) per unit, including a fixed element of $10 (say). The **total variable cost is really** $9 + $15 = **$24**, but from division **B's point of view** the **variable cost** is $15 + $(25 − 10) = **$30**. This means that division B will be unwilling to sell the final product for less than $30, whereas any price above $24 would make a contribution to overall costs. Thus, if external prices for the final product fall, B might be tempted to cease production.

4.4 Transfer prices based on variable or marginal cost   9/10

A variable or marginal cost approach entails charging the variable cost (which we assume to be the same as the marginal cost) that has been incurred by the supplying division to the receiving division. As above, we shall suppose that A's cost per unit is $15, of which $6 is fixed and $9 variable.

	A $	A $	B $	B $	Company as a whole $	Company as a whole $
Market sales		8,000		24,000		32,000
Transfer sales		3,600		–		
		11,600		24,000		
Transfer costs		–	3,600			
Own variable costs	7,200		6,000		13,200	
Own fixed costs	5,800		4,000		9,800	
Total costs and transfers		13,000		13,600		23,000
(Loss)/Profit		(1,400)		10,400		9,000

4.4.1 Divisional autonomy, divisional performance measurement and corporate profit maximisation

(a) This result is **deeply unsatisfactory for the manager of division** A who could make an additional $4,400 ($(8,000 – 3,600)) profit if no goods were transferred to division B, but all were sold externally.

(b) Given that the manager of division A would prefer to transfer externally, **head office** are likely to have to **insist** that internal transfers are made.

(c)   For the company overall, external transfers only would cause a large fall in profit, because division
        B could make no sales at all.

Point to note. Suppose no more than the current $8,000 could be earned from external sales and the
production capacity used for production for internal transfer would remain idle if not used. Division A
would be indifferent to the transfers at marginal cost as they do not represent any benefit to the division.

If more than the $8,000 of revenue could be earned externally (ie division A could sell more externally
than at present), division A would have a strong disincentive to supply B at marginal cost.

4.5 Dual pricing

One of the problems with a variable cost approach to transfer pricing is that the selling division will not
cover its fixed costs.

Dual pricing, as the name suggests, results in **different prices** being used by the selling and buying
divisions. The selling division will use a price that will allow it to report a **reasonable profit** (usually the
external market price if there is one). The buying division will be charged with the **variable cost**.

The difference between the two prices will be debited to a group account which will then be cancelled out
when divisional results are consolidated to arrive at the group profit.

However, despite its advantages, dual pricing is not widely used in practise for the following reasons.

(a)   Head office will need to be notified of each transaction to ensure that it is accounted for correctly.
        This is likely to take a considerable amount of time and may require a separate accounting
        function to be set up.

(b)   Dual pricing is a complicated system to operate when many goods are being transferred between a
        number of different divisions.

(c)   By continually reporting transactions to head office, managers of divisions may feel that they are
        not being given the freedom to run their division as they see fit.

(d)   If total cost plus pricing is used due to market prices collapsing, it could be argued that managers
        of the supplying division are being "protected" from tough market conditions.

4.6 Two-part tariff system

A two-part tariff system can be used to ensure that the selling division's fixed costs are covered. Transfer
prices are set at variable cost and once a year there is a **transfer of a fixed fee as a lump sum payment to
the supplying division**, representing an allowance for its fixed costs.

This method risks sending the message to the supplying division that it need not control its fixed costs,
however, because the company will subsidise any inefficiencies.

 Section summary

If transfer prices are set at variable cost with an imperfect external market, the supplying division does not
cover its fixed costs. **Dual pricing** or a **two-part tariff system** can be used in an attempt to overcome this
problem.

If **transfers** are made at actual cost instead of **standard cost**, there is no incentive for the supplying
division to control costs as they can all be passed on to the receiving division.

5 Transfer pricing when there is no external market for the transferred item

Introduction

There may be instances when there is no external market for the item being transferred. This section focuses on how to set an appropriate transfer price in such circumstances. Note the argument that profit centre accounting might not even be appropriate in this situation.

5.1 What is the appropriate transfer price?

KEY POINT

When there is **no external market** for the item being transferred, the transfer price should be **greater than or equal to** the variable cost in the **supplying division** but **less than or equal to** the selling price minus variable costs (net marginal revenue) in the **receiving division**.

If there is **no similar item sold on an external market**, and if the **transferred item** is a **major product of the transferring division**, there is a strong argument that **profit centre accounting is a waste of time**. Profit centres cannot be judged on their commercial performance because there is no way of estimating what a fair revenue for their work should be. It would be more appropriate, perhaps, to treat the transferring division as a cost centre, and to judge performance on the basis of cost variances.

If **profit centres are established**, in the **absence of a market price**, the **optimum transfer price is likely to be one based on standard cost plus**, but only provided that the **variable cost per unit and selling price per unit are unchanged at all levels of output**. A standard cost plus price would motivate divisional managers to increase output and to reduce expenditure levels.

Exam alert

In the November 2011 exam students were asked to explain with examples, the performance measurement issues of using actual costs rather than standard costs as the basis of a transfer price.

Example: Standard cost plus as a transfer price in the absence of an external market

Motivate has two profit centres, P and Q. P transfers all its output to Q. The variable cost of output from P is $5 a unit, and fixed costs are $1,200 a month. Additional processing costs in Q are $4 a unit for variable costs, plus fixed costs of $800 a month. Budgeted production is 400 units a month, and the output of Q sells for $15 a unit.

Required

Determine the range of prices from which the transfer price (based on standard full cost plus) should be selected, in order to motivate the managers of both profit centres to both increase output and reduce costs.

Solution

Any transfer price based on standard cost plus will motivate managers to cut costs, because favourable variances between standard costs and actual costs will be credited to the division's profits. Managers of each division will also be willing to increase output (above the budget) provided that it is profitable to do so.

(a)   The **manager of P will increase output if the transfer price exceeds the variable cost** of $5 a unit.

(b)   The **manager of Q** will **increase output if the transfer price is less than the difference between the fixed selling price ($15)** and the **variable costs** in **Q** itself. This amount of $11 ($15 – $4) is sometimes called **net marginal revenue**.

The range of prices is therefore between $5.01 and $10.99.

Check

Suppose the transfer price is $9. With absorption based on the budgeted output of 400 units what would divisional profits be if output and sales are 400 units and 500 units?

Overheads per unit are $1,200/400. The full cost of sales is $(5 + 3) = $8 in division P. In division Q, full cost is $(4 + 2) = $6, plus transfer costs of $9.

(a)   At 400 units:

	P $	Q $	Total $
Sales	–	6,000	6,000
Transfer sales	3,600	–	
Transfer costs	–	(3,600)	
Own full cost of sales	(3,200)	(2,400)	(5,600)
	400	0	400
Under-/over-absorbed overhead	0	0	0
Profit/(loss)	400	0	400

(b)   At 500 units:

	P $	Q $	Total $
Sales	–	7,500	7,500
Transfer sales	4,500	–	–
Transfer costs	–	(4,500)	–
Own full cost of sales	(4,000)	(3,000)	(7,000)
	500	0	500
Over-absorbed overhead	300	200	500
Profit/(loss)	800	200	1,000

Increasing output improves the profit performance of both divisions and the company as a whole, and so decisions on output by the two divisions are likely to be **goal congruent**.

Section summary

When there is **no external market** for the item being transferred, the transfer price should be **greater than or equal to** the variable cost in the **supplying division** but **less than or equal to** the selling price minus variable costs (net marginal revenue) in the **receiving division**.

6 Transfer pricing and changing costs/prices

Introduction

This section is related to Section 5 in that it considers the situation where there is no external market for the transferred item **and** changing costs/prices for the final product. Note the differences in preferred transfer prices between the two sections.

6.1 No external market for the transferred item

KEY POINT

When there is no external market for the transferred item and changing costs/prices for the final output, the transfer price should be greater than or equal to the marginal cost in the supplying division but less than or equal to the net marginal revenue in the receiving division.

If **cost behaviour patterns change** and the **selling price** to the **external market (for the receiving division's product)** is **reduced at higher levels of output**, there will be a **profit-maximising level of output**: to produce more than an 'optimum' amount would cause reductions in profitability.

Under such circumstances, the ideal transfer price is one which would motivate profit centre managers to produce at the optimum level of output, and neither below nor above this level.

Example: The profit-maximising transfer price

MCMR has two divisions, S and T. There is no external intermediate market and so S transfers all its output to T, which finishes the work. Costs and revenues at various levels of capacity are as follows.

Output	S costs	T revenues	T costs	T net revenues	Profit
Units	$	$	$	$	$
600	600	3,190	240	2,950	2,350
700	700	3,530	280	3,250	2,550
800	840	3,866	336	3,530	2,690
900	1,000	4,180	400	3,780	2,780
1,000	1,200	4,480	480	4,000	2,800 *
1,100	1,450	4,780	580	4,200	2,750
1,200	1,800	5,070	720	4,350	2,550

Company profits are maximised at $2,800 with output of 1,000 units. But if we wish to select a transfer price in order to establish S and T as profit centres, what transfer price would motivate the managers of S and T together to produce 1,000 units, no more and no less?

Discussion and Solution

The transfer price will act as revenue to S and as a cost to T.

(a)   **S will continue to produce more output until** the costs of additional production exceed the transfer price revenue, that is where the **marginal cost exceeds the transfer price**.

(b)   **T will continue to want to receive more output from S until** its net revenue from further processing is not sufficient to cover the additional transfer price costs, that is where its **net marginal revenue is less than the transfer price**.

	Division S	Division T
Output	Marginal costs	Net marginal revenues
Units	$	$
600	–	–
700	100	300
800	140	280
900	160	250
1,000	200	220
1,100	250	200
1,200	350	150

Since S will continue to produce more output if the transfer price exceeds the marginal cost of production, a **price of at least $200 per 100 units ($2 per unit) is required to 'persuade' the manager of S to produce as many as 1,000 units**. A price in excess of $250 per 100 units would motivate the manager of S to produce 1,100 units or more.

By a similar argument, T will continue to want more output from S if the net marginal revenues exceed the transfer costs from S. **If T wants 1,000 units, the transfer price must be less than $220 per 100**

units. However, if the transfer price is lower than $200 per 100 units, T will ask for 1,100 units from S in order to improve its divisional profit further.

Summary

(a)   The total company profit is maximised at 1,000 units of output.

(b)   Division S will want to produce 1,000 units, no more and no less, if the transfer price is between $200 to $250 per 100 units, or $2 and $2.50 per unit.

(c)   Division T will want to receive and process 1,000 units, no more and no less, if the transfer price per unit is between $2 and $2.20.

(d)   A transfer price must therefore be selected in the **range $2.00 to $2.20 per unit** (exclusive).

Question 13.2	Transfer pricing and changing costs/prices (no external market)

Learning outcome D3(c)

Explain how the following figures are calculated, or arrived at.

(a)   Example 6.1 – T net revenues
(b)   Example 6.1 Discussion and solution (b) – Division S marginal costs
(c)   Example 6.1 Discussion and solution (b) – Division T net marginal revenue
(d)   Example 6.1 – a transfer price of $2.10 per unit

6.2 With an external market for the transferred item

6.2.1 Imperfect external market

KEY POINT

Where there is an **imperfect external market** for the transferred item and changing costs/prices for the final output, the **transfer price** should again **fall between marginal cost in the supplying division and net marginal revenue in the receiving division**.

The approach is essentially the same as the one shown above, except that the supplying division may also have income, and so its marginal revenue needs to be taken into account.

Example: Profit maximisation with an imperfect external

IMP makes hand-built sports cars. The company has two divisions, M and N. The output of division M can either be sold externally or transferred to division N which turns it into a version for the USA. Due to competition from Japanese car makers the US market is giving poor returns at present. Cost and marginal revenues at various levels of output are as follows.

Cars produced	M Total cost $'000	M Marginal cost $'000	M Marginal revenue $'000	N Net marginal revenue $'000
1	18	18	20 (1)	18 (2)
2	26	8	16 (3)	12 (4)
3	35	9	12 (5)	6
4	45	10	8 (6) will not be built	0
5	56	11	4	(6)
6	68	12	0	(12)
7	81	13	(4)	(18)
8	95	14	(8)	0

You are required to determine the optimal output level.

Solution

(a) In this situation, for any individual car, **marginal revenue will be received by division M *or* net marginal revenue will be received by division N. The same car cannot be sold twice!**

(b) Marginal revenue is the extra amount received for each additional car sold into M's market (or net marginal revenue is the extra amount for additional cars in N's market). Thus the marginal revenue for three cars in M's market is $12,000 only if all three cars have been sold in M's market. If three are produced but one is sold in N's market, the marginal revenue for M for the other two is $16,000.

(c) For each car produced a decision must therefore be made as to which market to sell it in, and this will be done according to which market offers the higher marginal revenue.

(d) As shown by the numbers in brackets, the first car is sold in M's market, the second in N's, the third in M's, and the fourth and fifth in either. By the time six cars have been produced and shared out between the two markets the marginal cost has risen to $12,000. This is greater than the marginal revenue obtainable from either market ($8,000 in M, $6,000 in N).

(e) The sixth car will therefore not be built. Division M will produce five units and sell three cars itself and transfer two to division N. The transfer price must be more than $11,000 to meet M's marginal cost, but less than $12,000 otherwise division N will not buy it.

We now need to consider whether the profit-maximising transfer price should be set using the same approach if **supplies of the transferred item are limited.**

6.3 Maximising profits when the transferred item is in short supply

KEY POINT

Where there is a **capacity constraint** resulting in short supplies of the product, a transfer price based on matching marginal cost and marginal revenue **will not encourage** corporate profit maximisation.

Suppose that one month division M suffered a two-week strike and was only able to produce two cars. If it follows normal policy and transfers the second to division N, its own results for the month will be as follows.

		$'000
Sales	– own	20
	– transfers	11
		31
Total cost		26
		5

However, if division M keeps the second car and sells both in its own market it will earn $36,000 in total ($20,000 + $16,000) increasing its own divisional profit by $5,000.

From the point of view of the company this is a bad decision. If the second car is transferred to division N it can be sold for $18,000. Overall revenue and profit will increase by $2,000 (($18,000 – 16,000)).

The only way to be sure that a profit maximising transfer policy will be implemented is to **dictate the policy from the centre**.

6.3.1 Perfect external market

The approach is the same as that used for an imperfect external market except that marginal revenue for the supplying division is constant at the market price for all volumes of output.

6.4 Profit maximisation with a perfect external market

KEY POINT

When there is a **perfect external market for the transferred item** and **changing costs/prices** for the final output, profits are maximised when **market price** is used on the transfer price.

We will use the example of IMP again but this time the market price achieved by M is $10,000. The costs and marginal revenues at various levels of output are as follows.

Cars produced	M Total cost $'000	M Marginal cost $'000	M Marginal revenue $'000	N Net marginal revenue $'000
1	18	18	10 (3)	18 (1)
2	26	8	10 (4)	12 (2)
3	35	9	10	6
4	45	10	10	0
5	56	11	10	(6)
6	68	12	10	(12)
7	81	13	10	(18)
8	95	14	10	0

Marginal cost is greater than marginal revenue in both markets by car five, so four cars will be built, two sold by M and two transferred to be sold by N. As seen earlier, the market price will be the transfer price.

Question 13.3	Profit-maximising transfer price

Learning outcome D3(c)

Divisions J and A are in M Group. Division J manufactures part N. Three units of part N are used in product Z manufactured by Division A. Division J has no external customers for part N. Division J transfers part N to Division A at variable cost ($35 per part) plus 50%. The variable cost to Division A of manufacturing product Z is $50 per unit. This $50 does not include the cost of part N transferred from Division J.

Division A can sell the following number of units of product Z, earning the associated levels of marginal revenue.

Units sold	1	2	3	4
Marginal revenue	$270	$240	$210	$180

How many units of product Z should management of Division A sell if they wish to maximise divisional profit?

Exam alert

In September 2011 exam students were asked to use NPV to evaluate investment in new equipment. The equipment would increase capacity in a division producing a transferred component. The question asked for the evaluation of both divisional and group impact of the new equipment.

Section summary

When there is **no external market for the transferred item** and changing costs/prices for the final output, the **transfer price** should be **greater than or equal to the marginal cost in the supplying division** but **less than or equal to the net marginal revenue in the receiving division**.

Where there is an **imperfect external market** for the transferred item and changing costs/prices for the final output, the **transfer price** should again **fall between marginal cost in the supplying division and net marginal revenue in the receiving division**.

Where there is a **capacity constraint** resulting in short supplies of the product, a transfer price based on matching marginal cost and marginal revenue **will not encourage** corporate profit maximisation.

Where there is a **perfect external market for the transferred item** and **changing costs/prices** for the final output, profits are maximised when **market price** is used on the transfer price.

7 Identifying the optimal transfer price

Introduction

Throughout the chapter we have been leading up to the following guiding rules for identifying the optimal transfer price. This section focuses on how to determine this price.

7.1 The optimal transfer price

(a) The **ideal transfer price** should **reflect the opportunity cost** of sale to the supply division and the opportunity cost to the buying division. Unfortunately, full information about opportunity costs may not be easily obtainable in practice.

(b) Where a **perfect external market price exists and unit variable costs and unit selling prices are constant**, the **opportunity cost** of transfer will be **external market price** or **external market price less savings in selling costs**.

(c) In the **absence of a perfect external market price for the transferred item, but when unit variable costs are constant**, and the **sales price per unit of the end-product is constant**, the **ideal transfer price** should reflect the opportunity cost of the resources consumed by the supply division to make and supply the item and so should be at standard **variable cost + opportunity cost of making the transfer**.

(d) When **unit variable costs and/or unit selling prices are not constant**, there will be a **profit-maximising level of output** and the **ideal transfer price** will only be found by sensible **negotiation** and careful **analysis**.

(i) Establish the output and sales quantities that will optimise the profits of the company or group as a whole.

(ii) Establish the transfer price at which both profit centres would maximise their profits at this company-optimising output level.

There may be a range of prices within which both profit centres can agree on the output level that would maximise their individual profits and the profits of the company as a whole. Any price within the range would then be 'ideal'.

 Question 13.4   Optimal transfer prices

Learning outcome D3(c)

You should try to learn the above rules, and refer back to the appropriate part of the chapter if you are not sure about any point. Read through the rules again and then answer these questions.

(a) In what situation should the transfer price be the external market price?

(b)   How should the transfer price be established when there are diseconomies of scale and prices have to be lowered to increase sales volume?

(c)   What is the ideal transfer price?

(d)   In what circumstances should the transfer price be standard variable cost + the opportunity cost of making the transfer?

Note: there is no solution at the end of the chapter for this question. The solution can be found in the rules in Section 7.1 above.

Section summary

There are various rules involved in the determination of the optimal transfer price. Make sure you read transfer pricing questions carefully to ensure you recommend the correct price.

8 Negotiated transfer prices   9/10

Introduction

As transfer prices are often difficult to determine, divisional managers may negotiate appropriate prices with each other. This section looks at the implications of negotiated transfer prices.

8.1 Negotiating a transfer price

A transfer price based on opportunity cost is often difficult to identify, for lack of suitable information about costs and revenues in individual divisions.

In this case it is likely that transfer prices will be set by means of negotiation. The agreed price may be finalised from a mixture of accounting arithmetic, politics and compromise.

(a)   A negotiated price might be based on market value, but with some reductions to allow for the internal nature of the transaction, which saves external selling and distribution costs.

(b)   Where one division receives near-finished goods from another, a negotiated price might be based on the market value of the end product, minus an amount for the finishing work in the receiving division.

8.2 Behavioural implications

Even so, inter-departmental **disputes** about transfer prices are likely to arise and these may need the **intervention or mediation of head office** to settle the problem. Head office management may then **impose a price** which maximises the profit of the company as a whole. On the other hand, head office management might restrict their intervention to the **task of keeping negotiations in progress** until a transfer price is eventually settled. The **more head office has to impose** its own decisions on profit centres, the less **decentralisation of authority** there will be and the **less effective the profit centre system** of accounting will be for **motivating** divisional managers.

Section summary

If divisional managers are allowed to **negotiate transfer prices** with each other, the agreed price may be finalised from a mixture of **accounting arithmetic, negotiation and compromise**.

9   International transfer pricing

Introduction

When products are transferred internally between divisions based in different countries, the transfer pricing problem becomes even less clear cut. This section looks at the various problems encountered with international transfer pricing, including currency and taxation issues.

9.1 Factors to be considered

Factor	Explanation
Exchange rate fluctuation	The value of a transfer of goods between profit centres in different countries could·depend on fluctuations in the currency exchange rate.
Taxation in different countries	If tax on profits is 20% in Country A and 50% of profits in Country B, a company will presumably try to 'manipulate' profits (by raising or lowering transfer prices or invoicing the subsidiary in the high-tax country for 'services' provided by the subsidiary in the low-tax country) so that profits are maximised for a subsidiary in Country A, by reducing profits for a subsidiary in Country B.
	Artificial attempts to reduce tax liabilities could, however, upset a country's tax officials if they discover it and may lead to a penalty. Many tax authorities have the power to modify transfer prices in computing tariffs or taxes on profit, although a genuine arms-length market price should be accepted.
	There are three methods the tax authorities can use to determine an arm's length price.
	The **comparable price method (also known as comparable uncontrolled price, or CUs)** involves setting the arm's length price based on the price of similar products (usually the market price). This is the preferred method where possible.
	The **resale price method** involves setting the arm's length price based on the price paid for a final product by an independent party and a suitable mark-up (to allow for the seller's expenses and profit) is deducted. This method is often used for the transfer of goods to distributors where good are sold on with little further processing.
	The **cost-plus method** involves obtaining an arm's-length gross margin and applying it to the seller's manufacturing costs.
	Many countries have double taxation agreements that mean that a company will pay tax on a transaction in only one country. If a tax authority determines that a company has set an unrealistic transfer price and has paid less tax than is due, the company would then pay tax in both countries, plus any applicable penalties.
	A mitigation against this is an Advanced Pricing Agreement, entered into with both of the tax authorities involved.
	We shall work through an example on International transfer pricing and taxation later in this chapter.
Import tariffs/customs duties	Country A imposes an import tariff of 20% on the value of goods imported. A multi-national company has a subsidiary in Country A which imports goods from a subsidiary in Country B. The company would minimise costs by keeping the transfer price to a minimum .

Factor	Explanation
Exchange controls	If a country imposes restrictions on the transfer of profits from domestic subsidiaries to foreign multinationals, the restrictions on the transfer can be overcome if head office provides some goods or services to the subsidiary and charges exorbitantly high prices, disguising the 'profits' as sales revenue, and transferring them from one country to the other. The ethics of such an approach should, of course, be questioned.
Anti-dumping legislation	Governments may take action to protect home industries by preventing companies from transferring goods cheaply into their countries. They may do this, for example, by insisting on the use of a fair market value for the transfer price.
Competitive pressures	Transfer pricing can be used to enable profit centres to match or undercut local competitors.
Repatriation of funds	By inflating transfer prices for goods sold to subsidiaries in countries where inflation is high, the subsidiaries' profits are reduced and funds repatriated, thereby saving their value.
Minority shareholders	Transfer prices can be used to reduce the amount of profit paid to minority shareholders by artificially depressing a subsidiary's profit.

CASE STUDY

Four out of five international disputes involving multinational companies involve transfer pricing – the pricing of cross-border transactions between a company's subsidiaries. Tensions over transfer pricing have been growing as companies have sought to minimise tax bills by shifting profits to low-tax jurisdictions and governments have become increasingly determined to obtain their 'fair share' of multinationals' taxes.

Financial Times, *'Proposal to cut tax disputes across borders'*, 8th February 2007

9.2 The pros and cons of different transfer pricing bases

(a) A transfer price at **market value** is usually encouraged by the tax and customs authorities of both host and home countries as they will receive a **fair share of the profits** made but there are **problems** with its use.

   (i) Prices for the same product may **vary considerably** from one country to another.

   (ii) Changes in exchange rates, local taxes and so on can result in **large variations in selling price**.

   (iii) A division will want to set its prices in relation to the supply and demand conditions present in the country in question to ensure that it can compete in that country.

(b) A transfer price at **cost** is usually acceptable to tax and customs authorities since it provides some indication that the transfer price approximates to the real cost of supplying the item and because it indicates that they will therefore receive a fair share of tax and tariff revenues. Cost-based approaches do not totally remove the suspicion that the figure may have been massaged because the choice of the type of cost (full actual, full standard, actual variable, marginal) can alter the size of the transfer price.

(c) In a multinational organisation, **negotiated** transfer prices may result in overall sub-optimisation because no account is taken of factors such as differences in tax and tariff rates between countries.

Question 13.5   International transfer pricing

Learning outcome D3(d)

RBN is a UK parent company with an overseas subsidiary. The directors of RBN wish to transfer profits from the UK to the overseas company. They are considering changing the level of the transfer prices charged on goods shipped from the overseas subsidiary to UK subsidiaries and the size of the royalty payments paid by UK subsidiaries to the overseas subsidiary.

In order to transfer profit from the UK to the overseas subsidiary should the manager of RBN increase or decrease the transfer prices and the royalty payments?

Question 13.6   More international transfer pricing

Learning outcome D3(d)

LL Multinational transferred 4,000 units of product S from its manufacturing division in the USA to the selling division in the UK in the year to 31 December.

Each unit of S cost $350 to manufacture, the variable cost proportion being 75%, and was sold for £600. The UK division incurred marketing and distribution costs of £8 per unit. The UK tax rate was 30% and the exchange rate £ = $1.5.

If the transfers were at variable cost, what was the UK division's profit after tax?

CASE STUDY

In an article in the Financial Times (14 September 2006), Ernst and Young warned of 'clear signs from the UK that more transfer pricing litigation is heading to the courts'. Tax authorities are stepping up their scrutiny of cross-border transactions, according to the E&Y survey of more than 30 jurisdictions.

Globalisation has increased the importance of transfer pricing rules which determine the allocation of taxable profits between parts of a multinational. According to the Organisation for Economic Co-operation and Development, internal transactions of multinationals account for more than half of world trade.

Officials are becoming increasingly vigilant in their efforts to stop companies manipulating tax rules on internal transactions to minimise their profits. E&Y said its findings showed that tax authorities were under more pressure to deliver revenue 'gains' from anti-avoidance work.

CASE STUDY

In January 2004, GlaxoSmithKline (GSK) was hit with a $5.2 billion bill for additional taxes and interest by the US government, whose Internal Revenue Service (IRS) claimed that the company has used internal pricing procedures to avoid paying full taxes in the US.

The claim centred round the tax treatment of profits and charges for Zantac, the gastro-intestinal drug that was the most important medicine for Glaxo Wellcome, one of the pre-GSK companies.

Whilst the bulk of the revenues from Zantac were generated in the US, the company claimed that most of the research and development and other costs had been incurred in the UK, hence the justification for paying tax outside the US.

The IRS initially launched action against Glaxo Wellcome seeking taxes for the period beginning in 1989. A series of subsequent claims were brought for successive years when the IRS and UK Inland Revenue (which was satisfied with the company's treatment of the expenses and tax) failed to agree on a common position.

This ground-breaking transfer pricing tax dispute was resolved in an out-of-court settlement in September 2006 when GSK agreed to pay the IRS $3.1 billion. When the settlement was made, the partner in charge of transfer pricing at Deloitte said

'There will be a number of pharmaceutical companies keen to find out about the details because it will affect so many of them'.

Example: International transfer pricing and taxation

Division W, which is part of the XYZ group, is based in country A and has the capacity to manufacture 100,000 units of product B each year. The variable cost of producing a unit of B is $15 and the division can sell 85,000 units externally per annum at $25 per unit.

Division D is part of the same group and in based in country L. Division D purchases 40,000 units of product B each year from O (which is not part of XYZ group), which is also based in country L. D pays a dollar equivalent of $20 per unit.

If division D were to purchase product B from division W, division W would set a transfer price of $22. Given that there are no selling costs involved in transferring units to division D, this would give division W the same contribution on internal and external sales.

Division W would give priority to division D and so the orders from some external customers would not be met.

Required

Determine from whom division D should purchase product B in each of the following circumstances if the aim is to maximise group profit.

(a)   The tax rate in country A is 30% and the tax rate in country L is 40%.
(b)   The tax rate in country A is 60% and the tax rate in country L is 15%.

You may assume that changes in contribution can be used as a basis of calculating changes in tax charges and that division D is able to absorb any tax benefits from the profit it generates on other activities.

Solution

We need to consider the relevant costs, which are the changes in contribution and tax paid.

	$'000	(a)	(b)
Current position			
D buys 40,000 units from O @ $20 per unit	(800)		
These purchases reduce D's tax liability by			
$800,000 × 40%		320	
$800,000 × 15%			120
W sells 85,000 units @ $(25 – 15) = $10			
contribution per unit	850		
W's tax on this contribution			
$850,000 × 30%		(255)	
$850,000 × 60%			(510)
If D buys from W			
D buys 40,000 units @ $22 per unit	(880)		
These purchases reduce D's tax liability by			
$880,000 × 40%		352	
$880,000 × 15%			132
W sells 100,000 units @ $10 contribution per unit	1,000,000		
W's tax on this contribution			
$1,000,000 × 30%		(300)	
$1,000,000 × 60%			(600)

Summary

	(a)	(b)
If D switches to W		
Decrease in D's contribution		
$((880) – (800))$	(80)	(80)
Decrease in D's tax liability		
$(352 – 320)$	32	
$(132 – 120)$		12
Increase in W's contribution		
$(1,000,000 – 850,000)$	150	150
Increase in W's tax liability		
$((300) – (255))$	(45)	
$((600) – (510))$		(90)
Net gain to XYZ group	57	(8)

∴ Division D should purchase from Division W to maximise group profit in scenario (a) but from O in scenario (b).

Exam skills

The figures in the summary above are calculated by deducting the cashflow arising in the current position from the cashflows if D buys from W.

9.3 Currency management

When subsidiaries in different countries trade with each other it will be necessary to **decide which currency will be used for the transfer price**.

If the transfer price is set in one of the subsidiaries' home currencies and there is a movement in the exchange rate then one of the subsidiaries will make a **loss on exchange of foreign currencies**.

Example: Transfer prices and exchange rate losses

A subsidiary in the UK sells product P to a US subsidiary. Details are as follows.

	Per unit
Transfer price	$21
Cost incurred in UK subsidiary	£9

At the date that the transfer price was agreed the exchange rate was £1 = $1.50.

The US subsidiary incurs additional costs of $3 per unit to convert product P for sale in the US, at a selling price of $29 per unit.

Due to a weakening of the dollar against the pound, the exchange rate is now £1 = $1.80.

Required

Calculate the effect of the change I exchange rate on the profit per unit earned by each subsidiary, if the agreed transfer price was fixed in terms of:

(a)   Dollars

(b)   Pounds sterling

Solution

When exchange rate is £1 = $1.50

	UK subsidiary £ per unit	US subsidiary $ per unit
Selling price of product ($21 ÷ 1.50)	14	29
Costs incurred in subsidiary – internal	(9)	(3)
– transfer		(21)
Profit per unit	5	5

When exchange rate is £1 = $1.80. Transfer price fixed in dollars ($21)

	UK subsidiary £ per unit	US subsidiary $ per unit
Selling price of product ($21 ÷ 1.80)	11.67	29
Costs incurred in subsidiary – internal	(9.00)	(3)
– transfer		(21)
Profit per unit	2.67	5

When exchange rate is £1 = $1,80. Transfer price fixed in pounds sterling

	UK subsidiary £ per unit		US subsidiary $ per unit
Selling price of product	14		29.00
Costs incurred in subsidiary – internal	(9)		(3.00)
– transfer		(£14 × 1.80)	(25.20)
Profit per unit	5		0.80

Thus the weakening dollar had a detrimental effect on the UK subsidiary when the transfer price was fixed in dollars, but a detrimental effect to the UK subsidiary when the transfer price was fixed in pounds sterling.

As well as having a **behavioural impact** this could also affect the **taxation of the whole group**. If a particular currency weakens, as in this example, then the selection of the correct currency for the transfer price can ensure that currency translation losses occur in the subsidiary which pays the higher rate of taxation.

Exam skills

If you find transfer pricing difficult then try to make sure that you understand the basic principles. Remember that individual managers want to maximise their own profit and this may not be in the best interests of the company as a whole. There must be a system in place which provides an equal distribution of profit between divisions, motivates divisional mangers and promote goal congruence. You can usually use your common sense to calculate this in an exam question.

Section summary

Problems associated with currency exchange rates, taxation, import tariffs, exchange control, anti-dumping legislation and competitive pressures arise **with transfer pricing in multinational companies**.

Chapter Roundup

✓ Transfer prices are a way of promoting **divisional autonomy**, ideally without prejudicing the **measurement of divisional performance** or discouraging **overall corporate profit maximisation**.

✓ Transfer prices should be set at a level which ensures that **profits for the organisation as a whole** are maximised.

✓ The **limits within which transfer prices should fall** are as follows.

   – **The minimum**. The sum of the supplying division's marginal cost and opportunity cost of the item transferred.

   – **The maximum**. The lowest market price at which the receiving division could purchase the goods or services externally, less any internal cost savings in packaging and delivery.

✓ If **variable costs and market prices are constant**, regardless of the volume of output, a **market-based transfer price** is the ideal transfer price.

✓ If a **perfect external market** exists, **market price** is the **ideal** transfer price.

✓ If transfer prices are set at variable cost with an imperfect external market, the supplying division does not cover its fixed costs. **Dual pricing** or a **two-part tariff system** can be used in an attempt to overcome this problem.

✓ If **transfers** are made at actual cost instead of **standard cost**, there is no incentive for the supplying division to control costs as they can all be passed on to the receiving division.

✓ When there is **no external market** for the item being transferred, the transfer price should be **greater than or equal to** the variable cost in the **supplying division** but **less than or equal to** the selling price minus variable costs (net marginal revenue) in the **receiving division**.

✓ Where there is **no external market for the transferred item** and changing costs/prices for the final output, the **transfer price** should be **greater than or equal to the marginal cost in the supplying division** but **less than or equal to the net marginal revenue in the receiving division**.

✓ Where there is an **imperfect external market** for the transferred item and changing costs/prices for the final output, the **transfer price** should again **fall between marginal cost in the supplying division and net marginal revenue in the receiving division**.

✓ Where there is a **capacity constraint** resulting in short supplies of the product, a transfer price based on matching marginal cost and marginal revenue **will not encourage** corporate profit maximisation.

✓ Where there is a **perfect external market for the transferred item** and **changing costs/prices** for the final output, profits are maximised when **market price** is used on the transfer price.

✓ There are various rules involved in the determination of the optimal transfer price. Make sure you read transfer pricing questions carefully to ensure you recommend the correct price.

✓ If divisional managers are allowed to **negotiate transfer prices** with each other, the agreed price may be finalised from a mixture of **accounting arithmetic, negotiation and compromise**.

✓ Problems associated with currency exchange rates, taxation, import tariffs, exchange control, anti-dumping legislation and competitive pressures arise **with transfer pricing in multinational companies**.

Quick Quiz

1   *Put ticks in the appropriate column to highlight whether or not a transfer price should fulfil each of the following criteria.*

	Criteria should be fulfilled	Criteria should not be fulfilled
Should encourage dysfunctional decision making		
Should encourage output at an organisation-wide profit-maximising level		
Should encourage divisions to act in their own self interest		
Should encourage divisions to make entirely autonomous decisions		
Should enable the measurement of profit centre performance		
Should reward the transferring division		
Should be a reasonable cost for receiving division		
Should discourage goal congruence		

2   *Fill in the gaps.*

Market value as a transfer price has certain disadvantages.

(a)   The market price might be ...., induced by adverse economic conditions, say.

(b)   There might be an .... external market, so that if the transferring division tried to sell more externally, it would have to reduce its selling price.

(c)   Many products do not have ....

3   Division P transfers its output to division Q at variable cost. Once a year P charges a fixed fee to Q, representing an allowance for P's fixed costs. This type of transfer pricing system is commonly known as

A   Dual pricing
B   Negotiated transfer pricing
C   Opportunity cost based transfer pricing
D   Two-part tariff transfer pricing

4   Profits are maximised when marginal cost is equal to marginal revenue. *True* or *false*?

5   *Choose the correct words from those highlighted.*

When transfer prices are based on opportunity costs, opportunity costs are either the (1) **contribution/profit** forgone by the (2) **receiving/supplying** division in transferring (3) **internally/externally** rather than (4) **selling externally/transferring internally**, or the (5) **profit/contribution** forgone by not using the relevant facilities for their (6) **next best/cheapest/most profitable** alternative use.

6   Choose the correct words from those highlighted.

Taxation on profits in country C is charged at a higher rate than in country D. When goods are transferred from a subsidiary in country C to a subsidiary in country D it would be beneficial, from the point of view of the whole organisation, to charge a (1) **higher/lower** transfer price so that the total taxation cost for the organisation is (2) **higher/lower**.

7   Transfer prices based on standard cost provide an incentive for the receiving division to control costs. *True or false?*

8   In which of the following circumstances is there a strong argument that profit centre accounting is a waste of time?

A   When the transferred item is also sold on an external market

B   When the supplying division is based in a different country to head office

C   If the transferred item is a major product of the supplying division

D   If there is no similar product sold on an external market and the transferred item is a major product of the supplying division

9   *Choose the correct words from those highlighted.*

The more head office has to impose its own decisions on profit centres, the **more/less** decentralisation of authority there will be and the **more/less** effective the profit centre system of accounting will be for motivating divisional managers.

10   During the year the Dutch manufacturing division of NTN plc transferred 6,000 units of Product C to the UK selling division.

Each unit cost €350 to manufacture and was sold for £650. The variable cost proportion was 75%. The UK division incurred marketing and distribution costs of £20 per unit. The UK tax rate was 30% and the exchange rate was £1 = €1.50. The transfers were at variable cost. What was the UK division's profit after tax on the sale of 6,000 units?

Answers to Quick Quiz

1

	Criteria should be fulfilled	Criteria should not be fulfilled
Should encourage dysfunctional decision making		✓
Should encourage output at an organisation-wide profit-maximising level	✓	
Should encourage divisions to act in their own self interest		✓
Should encourage divisions to make entirely autonomous decisions		✓
Should enable the measurement of profit centre performance	✓	
Should reward the transferring division	✓	
Should be a reasonable cost for receiving division	✓	
Should discourage goal congruence		✓

2   (a)   temporary
     (b)   imperfect
     (c)   an equivalent market price

3   D

4   True

5   (1)   contribution
     (2)   supplying
     (3)   internally
     (4)   selling externally
     (5)   contribution
     (6)   next best

6   (1)   lower
     (2)   lower

7   False. They provide an incentive to the supplying division.

8   D

9   less
     less

10

	£
External sales (6,000 × £650)	3,900,000
Variable cost	
Transfer price of ((€350 × 75%)/€1.50) × 6,000	(1,050,000)
Marketing and distribution (£20 × 6,000)	(120,000)
Profit before tax	2,730,000
Tax at 30%	(819,000)
	1,911,000

Answers to Questions

13.1 Benefits of transfer pricing

Potential benefits of operating a transfer pricing system within a divisionalised company include the following.

(a)   It can lead to **goal congruence** by motivating divisional managers to make decisions, which improve divisional profit and improve profit of the organisation as a whole.

(b)   It can prevent **dysfunctional decision making** so that decisions taken by a divisional manager are in the best interests of his own part of the business, other divisions and the organisation as a whole.

(c)   Transfer prices can be set at a level that enables divisional performance to be measured 'commercially'. A transfer pricing system should therefore report a level of divisional profit that is a **reasonable measure of the managerial performance** of the division.

(d)   It should ensure that **divisional autonomy** is not undermined. A well-run transfer pricing system helps to ensure that a balance is kept between divisional autonomy to provide incentives and motivation, and centralised authority to ensure that the divisions are all working towards the same target, the benefit of the organisation as a whole.

13.2 Transfer pricing and changing costs/prices (no external market)

(a)   T revenues minus T costs
(b)   S costs for 700 units minus S costs for 600 units (and so on)
(c)   T net revenues for 700 units minus T net revenues for 600 units (and so on)
(d)   See Example 7.2 Discussion and solution

This exercise is to make sure that you were following the argument.

13.3 Profit-maximising transfer price

Variable cost of parts for Division A's product Z = $35 \times 3 = $105.

Transfer price = $105 \times 150\% = $157.50

Division A's variable cost per unit of Z = $50

Total variable/marginal cost to division A = $207.50

Division A will sell until marginal cost = marginal revenue.

It will therefore sell 3 units.

13.4 Optimal transfer prices

See Section 7.1 for the answer to this question.

13.5 International transfer pricing

To increase the overseas subsidiary's profit, the **transfer price needs to be higher** (since it is the overseas subsidiary doing the selling) and the **royalty payments** by the UK subsidiaries to the overseas subsidiary company **should also be higher**. Both would add to the overseas subsidiary's revenue without affecting its costs.

13.6 More international transfer pricing

	£
External sales (£600 × 4,000)	2,400,000
Variable cost (transfer price of ($350 × 75%/$1.5) × 4,000)	700,000
Marketing and distribution costs (£8 × 4,000)	32,000
Profit before tax	1,668,000
Tax at 30%	500,400
Profit after tax	1,167,600

	Number	Level	Marks	Time
Now try the question from the Exam Question Bank	Q32	Examination	30	54 mins

APPENDIX:
MATHEMATICAL TABLES AND
EXAM FORMULAE

PRESENT VALUE TABLE

Present value of $1 ie $(1+r)^{-n}$ where r = interest rate, n = number of periods until payment or receipt.

Periods (n)	\multicolumn{10}{c}{Interest rates (r)}
	1%	2%	3%	4%	5%	6%	7%	8%	9%	10%
1	0.990	0.980	0.971	0.962	0.952	0.943	0.935	0.926	0.917	0.909
2	0.980	0.961	0.943	0.925	0.907	0.890	0.873	0.857	0.842	0.826
3	0.971	0.942	0.915	0.889	0.864	0.840	0.816	0.794	0.772	0.751
4	0.961	0.924	0.888	0.855	0.823	0.792	0.763	0.735	0.708	0.683
5	0.951	0.906	0.863	0.822	0.784	0.747	0.713	0.681	0.650	0.621
6	0.942	0.888	0.837	0.790	0.746	0.705	0.666	0.630	0.596	0.564
7	0.933	0.871	0.813	0.760	0.711	0.665	0.623	0.583	0.547	0.513
8	0.923	0.853	0.789	0.731	0.677	0.627	0.582	0.540	0.502	0.467
9	0.914	0.837	0.766	0.703	0.645	0.592	0.544	0.500	0.460	0.424
10	0.905	0.820	0.744	0.676	0.614	0.558	0.508	0.463	0.422	0.386
11	0.896	0.804	0.722	0.650	0.585	0.527	0.475	0.429	0.388	0.350
12	0.887	0.788	0.701	0.625	0.557	0.497	0.444	0.397	0.356	0.319
13	0.879	0.773	0.681	0.601	0.530	0.469	0.415	0.368	0.326	0.290
14	0.870	0.758	0.661	0.577	0.505	0.442	0.388	0.340	0.299	0.263
15	0.861	0.743	0.642	0.555	0.481	0.417	0.362	0.315	0.275	0.239
16	0.853	0.728	0.623	0.534	0.458	0.394	0.339	0.292	0.252	0.218
17	0.844	0.714	0.605	0.513	0.436	0.371	0.317	0.270	0.231	0.198
18	0.836	0.700	0.587	0.494	0.416	0.350	0.296	0.250	0.212	0.180
19	0.828	0.686	0.570	0.475	0.396	0.331	0.277	0.232	0.194	0.164
20	0.820	0.673	0.554	0.456	0.377	0.312	0.258	0.215	0.178	0.149

Periods (n)	\multicolumn{10}{c}{Interest rates (r)}
	11%	12%	13%	14%	15%	16%	17%	18%	19%	20%
1	0.901	0.893	0.885	0.877	0.870	0.862	0.855	0.847	0.840	0.833
2	0.812	0.797	0.783	0.769	0.756	0.743	0.731	0.718	0.706	0.694
3	0.731	0.712	0.693	0.675	0.658	0.641	0.624	0.609	0.593	0.579
4	0.659	0.636	0.613	0.592	0.572	0.552	0.534	0.516	0.499	0.482
5	0.593	0.567	0.543	0.519	0.497	0.476	0.456	0.437	0.419	0.402
6	0.535	0.507	0.480	0.456	0.432	0.410	0.390	0.370	0.352	0.335
7	0.482	0.452	0.425	0.400	0.376	0.354	0.333	0.314	0.296	0.279
8	0.434	0.404	0.376	0.351	0.327	0.305	0.285	0.266	0.249	0.233
9	0.391	0.361	0.333	0.308	0.284	0.263	0.243	0.225	0.209	0.194
10	0.352	0.322	0.295	0.270	0.247	0.227	0.208	0.191	0.176	0.162
11	0.317	0.287	0.261	0.237	0.215	0.195	0.178	0.162	0.148	0.135
12	0.286	0.257	0.231	0.208	0.187	0.168	0.152	0.137	0.124	0.112
13	0.258	0.229	0.204	0.182	0.163	0.145	0.130	0.116	0.104	0.093
14	0.232	0.205	0.181	0.160	0.141	0.125	0.111	0.099	0.088	0.078
15	0.209	0.183	0.160	0.140	0.123	0.108	0.095	0.084	0.074	0.065
16	0.188	0.163	0.141	0.123	0.107	0.093	0.081	0.071	0.062	0.054
17	0.170	0.146	0.125	0.108	0.093	0.080	0.069	0.060	0.052	0.045
18	0.153	0.130	0.111	0.095	0.081	0.069	0.059	0.051	0.044	0.038
19	0.138	0.116	0.098	0.083	0.070	0.060	0.051	0.043	0.037	0.031
20	0.124	0.104	0.087	0.073	0.061	0.051	0.043	0.037	0.031	0.026

CUMULATIVE PRESENT VALUE TABLE

This table shows the present value of $1 per annum, receivable or payable at the end of each year for

n years $\dfrac{1-(1+r)^{-n}}{r}$.

Periods (n)	\multicolumn{10}{c}{Interest rates (r)}
	1%	2%	3%	4%	5%	6%	7%	8%	9%	10%
1	0.990	0.980	0.971	0.962	0.952	0.943	0.935	0.926	0.917	0.909
2	1.970	1.942	1.913	1.886	1.859	1.833	1.808	1.783	1.759	1.736
3	2.941	2.884	2.829	2.775	2.723	2.673	2.624	2.577	2.531	2.487
4	3.902	3.808	3.717	3.630	3.546	3.465	3.387	3.312	3.240	3.170
5	4.853	4.713	4.580	4.452	4.329	4.212	4.100	3.993	3.890	3.791
6	5.795	5.601	5.417	5.242	5.076	4.917	4.767	4.623	4.486	4.355
7	6.728	6.472	6.230	6.002	5.786	5.582	5.389	5.206	5.033	4.868
8	7.652	7.325	7.020	6.733	6.463	6.210	5.971	5.747	5.535	5.335
9	8.566	8.162	7.786	7.435	7.108	6.802	6.515	6.247	5.995	5.759
10	9.471	8.983	8.530	8.111	7.722	7.360	7.024	6.710	6.418	6.145
11	10.368	9.787	9.253	8.760	8.306	7.887	7.499	7.139	6.805	6.495
12	11.255	10.575	9.954	9.385	8.863	8.384	7.943	7.536	7.161	6.814
13	12.134	11.348	10.635	9.986	9.394	8.853	8.358	7.904	7.487	7.103
14	13.004	12.106	11.296	10.563	9.899	9.295	8.745	8.244	7.786	7.367
15	13.865	12.849	11.938	11.118	10.380	9.712	9.108	8.559	8.061	7.606
16	14.718	13.578	12.561	11.652	10.838	10.106	9.447	8.851	8.313	7.824
17	15.562	14.292	13.166	12.166	11.274	10.477	9.763	9.122	8.544	8.022
18	16.398	14.992	13.754	12.659	11.690	10.828	10.059	9.372	8.756	8.201
19	17.226	15.679	14.324	13.134	12.085	11.158	10.336	9.604	8.950	8.365
20	18.046	16.351	14.878	13.590	12.462	11.470	10.594	9.818	9.129	8.514

Periods (n)	\multicolumn{10}{c}{Interest rates (r)}
	11%	12%	13%	14%	15%	16%	17%	18%	19%	20%
1	0.901	0.893	0.885	0.877	0.870	0.862	0.855	0.847	0.840	0.833
2	1.713	1.690	1.668	1.647	1.626	1.605	1.585	1.566	1.547	1.528
3	2.444	2.402	2.361	2.322	2.283	2.246	2.210	2.174	2.140	2.106
4	3.102	3.037	2.974	2.914	2.855	2.798	2.743	2.690	2.639	2.589
5	3.696	3.605	3.517	3.433	3.352	3.274	3.199	3.127	3.058	2.991
6	4.231	4.111	3.998	3.889	3.784	3.685	3.589	3.498	3.410	3.326
7	4.712	4.564	4.423	4.288	4.160	4.039	3.922	3.812	3.706	3.605
8	5.146	4.968	4.799	4.639	4.487	4.344	4.207	4.078	3.954	3.837
9	5.537	5.328	5.132	4.946	4.772	4.607	4.451	4.303	4.163	4.031
10	5.889	5.650	5.426	5.216	5.019	4.833	4.659	4.494	4.339	4.192
11	6.207	5.938	5.687	5.453	5.234	5.029	4.836	4.656	4.486	4.327
12	6.492	6.194	5.918	5.660	5.421	5.197	4.988	4.793	4.611	4.439
13	6.750	6.424	6.122	5.842	5.583	5.342	5.118	4.910	4.715	4.533
14	6.982	6.628	6.302	6.002	5.724	5.468	5.229	5.008	4.802	4.611
15	7.191	6.811	6.462	6.142	5.847	5.575	5.324	5.092	4.876	4.675
16	7.379	6.974	6.604	6.265	5.954	5.668	5.405	5.162	4.938	4.730
17	7.549	7.120	6.729	6.373	6.047	5.749	5.475	5.222	4.990	4.775
18	7.702	7.250	6.840	6.467	6.128	5.818	5.534	5.273	5.033	4.812
19	7.839	7.366	6.938	6.550	6.198	5.877	5.584	5.316	5.070	4.843
20	7.963	7.469	7.025	6.623	6.259	5.929	5.628	5.353	5.101	4.870

Probability

$A \cup B$ = A **or** B. $A \cap B$ = A **and** B (overlap). P(BIA) = probability of B, **given** A.

Rules of addition

If A and B are *mutually exclusive*: $P(A \cup B) = P(A) + P(B)$

If A and B are **not** mutually exclusive: $P(A \cup B) = P(A) + P(B) - P(A \cap B)$

Rules of multiplication

If A and B are *independent*: $P(A \cap B) = P(A) * P(B)$

If A and B are **not** independent: $P(A \cap B) = P(A) * P(BIA)$

$E(X) = \sum (\text{probability} * \text{payoff})$

Descriptive statistics

Arithmetic mean

$$\bar{x} = \frac{\sum x}{n} \text{ or } \bar{x} = \frac{\sum fx}{\sum f} \text{ (frequency distribution)}$$

Standard deviation

$$SD = \sqrt{\frac{\sum (x - \bar{x})^2}{n}}$$

$$SD = \sqrt{\frac{\sum fx^2}{\sum f} - \bar{x}^2} \text{ (frequency distribution)}$$

Index numbers

Price relative = $100 * P_1 / P_0$

Quantity relative = $100 * Q_1 / Q_0$

Price: $\dfrac{\sum W \times P_1 / P_0}{\sum W} \times 100$ where W denotes weights

Quantity: $\dfrac{\sum W \times Q_1 / Q_0}{\sum W} \times 100$ where W denotes weights

Time series

Additive model: Series = Trend + Seasonal + Random
Multiplicative model: Series = Trend * Seasonal * Random

Financial mathematics

Compound Interest (Values and Sums)

Future Value of S, of a sum X, invested for n periods, compounded at r% interest:

$$S = X[1 + r]^n$$

Annuity

Present value of an annuity of £1 per annum receivable or payable, for n years, commencing in one year, discounted at r% per annum:

$$PV = \frac{1}{r}\left[1 - \frac{1}{[1+r]^n}\right]$$

Perpetuity

Present value of £1 per annum, payable or receivable in perpetuity, commencing in one year discounted at r% per annum

$$PV = \frac{1}{r}$$

Learning curve

$$Y_x = aX^b$$

where Y_x = the cumulative average time per unit to produce X units
a = the time required to produce the first unit of output
X = the cumulative number of units
b = the index of learning

The exponent b is defined as the log of the learning curve improvement rate divided by log 2.

Inventory management

Economic Order Quantity

$$EOQ = \sqrt{\frac{2C_oD}{C_h}}$$

Where C_o = cost of placing an order
C_h = cost of holding one unit in inventory for one year
D = annual demand

EXAM QUESTION AND ANSWER BANK

What the examiner means

The very important table below has been prepared by CIMA to help you interpret exam questions.

Learning objectives	Verbs used	Definition
1 Knowledge		
What are you expected to know	• List	• Make a list of
	• State	• Express, fully or clearly, the details of/facts of
	• Define	• Give the exact meaning of
2 Comprehension		
What you are expected to understand	• Describe	• Communicate the key features of
	• Distinguish	• Highlight the differences between
	• Explain	• Make clear or intelligible/state the meaning of
	• Identify	• Recognise, establish or select after consideration
	• Illustrate	• Use an example to describe or explain something
3 Application		
How you are expected to apply your knowledge	• Apply	• Put to practical use
	• Calculate/ compute	• Ascertain or reckon mathematically
	• Demonstrate	• Prove with certainty or to exhibit by practical means
	• Prepare	• Make or get ready for use
	• Reconcile	• Make or prove consistent/compatible
	• Solve	• Find an answer to
	• Tabulate	• Arrange in a table
4 Analysis		
How you are expected to analyse the detail of what you have learned	• Analyse	• Examine in detail the structure of
	• Categorise	• Place into a defined class or division
	• Compare and contrast	• Show the similarities and/or differences between
	• Construct	• Build up or compile
	• Discuss	• Examine in detail by argument
	• Interpret	• Translate into intelligible or familiar terms
	• Prioritise	• Place in order of priority or sequence for action
	• Produce	• Create or bring into existence
5 Evaluation		
How you are expected to use your learning to evaluate, make decisions or recommendations	• Advise	• Counsel, inform or notify
	• Evaluate	• Appraise or assess the value of
	• Recommend	• Propose a course of action

Guidance in our Practice and Revision Kit focuses on how the verbs are used in questions.

1 Restaurant   18 mins

Learning outcome: Revision

W has operated a restaurant for the last two years. Revenue and operating costs over the two years have been as follows.

	Year 1 $'000	Year 2 $'000
Revenue	1,348,312	1,514,224
Operating costs		
Food and beverages	698,341	791,919
Wages	349,170	390,477
Other overheads	202,549	216,930

The number of meals served in year 2 showed an 8% increase on the year 1 level of 151,156. An increase of 10% over the year 2 level is budgeted for year 3.

All staff were given hourly rate increases of 6% last year (in year 2). In year 3 hourly increases of 7% are to be budgeted.

The inflation on 'other overheads' last year was 5%, with an inflationary increase of 6% expected in the year ahead.

Food and beverage costs are budgeted to average $5.14 per meal in year 3. This is expected to represent 53% of sales value.

Required

From the information given above, and using the high-low method of cost estimation, determine the budgeted expenditure on wages and other overheads for year 3.   **(10 marks)**

2 Webber Design   45 mins

Learning outcome: A1(a)

Webber Design had almost completed a specialised piece of equipment when it discovered that the customer who had commissioned the work had gone out of business. Another customer was found to be interested in this piece of equipment but certain extra features would be necessary.

The following data is provided in respect of the additional work.

Direct materials costing $2,500 would be required. Webber Design have these in stock but if not used to manufacture the specialised equipment they would be used on another contract in place of materials which would cost $4,500.

The company has three departments, welding, machining and assembly, within which the extra features would incur the following additional work to be undertaken. In the welding department one worker would be needed for three weeks. The wage rate is $280 per worker per week. The welding department is currently operating at only 50% of normal capacity, but two workers must be kept on the payroll to ensure that the department can respond instantly to any increase in demand.

Two workers would be needed for five weeks in the machining department, which is working normally and the wage rate is $240 per worker, per week.

The assembly department is always extremely busy. Its wage rate is $200 per worker, per week and is currently yielding a contribution of $5 per $1 of direct labour. The additional requirements for this job would be two workers for eight weeks.

Overtime would need to be sanctioned in order to finish the job for the customer. This would cost $1,500. Such costs are normally charged to production overhead.

Variable overhead is 15% of direct wages and a special delivery charge of $3,400 would be incurred. Fixed production overhead is absorbed in each department on the basis of a fixed percentage of direct wages as follows.

Welding at 120%
Machining at 80%
Assembly at 40%

The costs of the equipment as originally estimated and incurred so far are as follows.

	Original quotation $	Work to date $	Work to complete $
Direct materials	13,075	10,745	2,300
Direct wages	7,500	6,700	1,050
Variable overheads	1,125	1,050	150
Fixed production overhead	6,500	5,250	1,200
Fixed administration	1,250	1,050	200

The price to the original customer allowed for a profit margin of 20% on selling price. An advance payment of 15% of the price had been received on confirmation of the order.

If the work of the new customer is not carried out some of the materials in the original equipment would be used for another contract in place of materials that would have cost $4,000 but would need two workers weeks in the machining department to make them suitable. The remaining materials would realise $5,200 as scrap. The design for the equipment, which would normally be included in the selling price could be sold for $1,500.

Required

(a) Calculate the minimum price that Webber Design should quote to the new customer.   **(10 marks)**

(b) State any further considerations you think Webber Design should take into account in setting the price.   **(7 marks)**

(c) Define 'relevant cost', 'opportunity cost' and 'discretionary cost', and state their use to management.   **(8 marks)**

(Total = 25 marks)

3 AB   45 mins

Learning outcomes: A1(a), (c)

AB produces a consumable compound X, used in the preliminary stage of a technical process that it installs in customers' factories worldwide. An overseas competitor, CD, offering an alternative process which uses the same preliminary stage, has developed a new compound, Y, for that stage which is both cheaper in its ingredients and more effective than X.

At present, CD is offering Y only in his own national market, but it is expected that it will not be long before he extends its sales overseas. Both X and Y are also sold separately to users of the technical process as a replacement for the original compound that eventually loses its strength. This replacement demand amounts to 60% of total demand for X and would do so for Y. CD is selling Y at the same price as X ($64.08 per kg).

AB discovers that it would take 20 weeks to set up a production facility to manufacture Y at an incremental capital cost of $3,500 and the comparative manufacturing costs of X and Y would be:

	X	Y
	$ per kg	$ per kg
Direct materials	17.33	4.01
Direct labour	7.36	2.85
	24.69	6.86

AB normally absorbs departmental overhead at 200% of direct labour: 30% of this departmental overhead is variable directly with direct labour cost. Selling and administration overhead is absorbed at one-half of departmental overhead.

The current sales of X average 74 kgs per week and this level (whether of X or of Y if it were produced) is not expected to change over the next year. Because the direct materials for X are highly specialised, AB has always had to keep large inventories in order to obtain supplies. At present, these amount to $44,800 at cost. Its inventory of finished X is $51,900 at full cost. Unfortunately, neither X nor its raw materials have any resale value whatsoever: in fact, it would cost $0.30 per kg to dispose of them.

Over the next three months AB is not normally busy and, in order to avoid laying off staff, has an arrangement with the trade union whereby it pays its factory operators at 65% of their normal rate of pay for the period whilst they do non-production work. AB assesses that it could process all its relevant direct materials into X in that period, if necessary.

There are two main options open to AB:

(a)   to continue to sell X until all its inventories of X (both of direct materials and of finished inventory) are exhausted, and then start sales of Y immediately afterwards;

(b)   to start sales of Y as soon as possible and then to dispose of any remaining inventories of X and/or its raw materials.

Required

(a)   Recommend with supporting calculations, which of the two main courses of action suggested is the more advantageous from a purely cost and financial point of view.   **(13 marks)**

(b)   Identify three major non-financial factors that AB would need to consider in making its eventual decision as to what to do.   **(5 marks)**

(c)   Suggest one other course of action that AB might follow, explaining what you consider to be its merits and demerits when compared with your answer at (a) above.   **(7 marks)**

(Total = 25 marks)

4 X   18 mins

Learning outcome: A1(a)

X manufactures four liquids – A, B, C and D. The selling price and unit cost details for these products are as follows.

	A	B	C	D
	$/litre	$/litre	$/litre	$/litre
Selling price	100	110	120	120
Direct materials	24	30	16	21
Direct labour ($6/hour)	18	15	24	27
Direct expenses	–	–	3	–
Variable overhead	12	10	16	18
Fixed overhead (note 1)	24	20	32	36
Profit	22	35	29	18

Note 1. Fixed overhead is absorbed on the basis of labour hours, based on a budget of 1,600 hours per quarter.

During the next three months the number of direct labour hours is expected to be limited to 1,345. The same labour is used for all products.

The marketing director has identified the maximum demand for each of the four products during the next three months as follows.

A   200 litres   C   100 litres
B   150 litres   D   120 litres

These maximum demand levels include the effects of a contract already made between X and one of its customers, Y Ltd, to supply 20 litres of each of A, B, C and D during the next three months.

Required

Determine the number of litres of products A, B, C and D to be produced/sold in the next three months in order to maximise profits, and calculate the profit that this would yield.

Assume that no inventory is held at the beginning of the three months which may be used to satisfy demand in the period.   **(10 marks)**

5 Research director   **18 mins**

Learning outcome: A1(a)

After completing the production plan in question 4 above, you receive two memos.

The first is from the research director.

'New environmental controls on pollution must be introduced with effect from the start of next month to reduce pollution from the manufacture of product D. These will incur fixed costs of $6,000 per annum.'

The second memo is from the sales director.

'An overseas supplier has developed a capacity to manufacture products C and D on a sub-contract basis, and has quoted the following prices to X.

C $105/litre   D $100/litre

Required

Using the information from *both* of these memos, state and quantify the effect (if any) on X's plans.

(10 marks)

6 Alphabet Ltd   **18 mins**

Learning outcome: A1(a)

Alphabet Ltd have received a proposal to manufacture 12,000 units of T over 12 months at a selling price of $3 per unit.

The following statement has been prepared:

	$	$
Sales revenue		36,000
Costs: Material X at historical cost	5,000	
Material Z at contract price	9,000	
Manufacturing labour	10,000	
Depreciation of machine	4,000	
Variable overheads @ 30c per unit	3,600	
Fixed overheads		
(absorbed @ 80% of manufacturing labour)	8,000	
		(39,600)
		(3,600)

Further information

1   Material X cannot be used or sold for any other product. It would cost $200 to dispose of the existing inventories.

2   Each unit of new production uses two kilos of material Z. The company has entered into a long-term contract to buy 24,000 kilos at an average price of 37.5c per kilo. The current price is 17.5c per kilo. This material is regularly used in the manufacture of the company's other products.

3   The machine which would be used to manufacture T was bought new three years ago for $22,000. It had an estimated life of five years with a scrap value of $2,000.

   If the new product is not manufactured the machine could be sold immediately for $7,000. If it is used for one year it is estimated that it could then be sold for $4,000.

4   The new product requires the use of skilled labour, which is scarce. If product T were not made this labour could be used on other activities, which would yield a contribution of $1,000.

Required

Prepare a statement of relevant costs and revenues and determine whether or not the proposal should be accepted. **(10 marks)**

7 RAB Consulting   45 mins

Learning outcome: A2(c)

RAB Consulting specialises in two types of consultancy project.

•   Each Type A project requires twenty hours of work from qualified researchers and eight hours of work from junior researchers.

•   Each Type B project requires twelve hours of work from qualified researchers and fifteen hours of work from junior researchers.

Researchers are paid on an hourly basis at the following rates:

| Qualified researchers | $30/hour |
| Junior researchers | $14/hour |

Other data relating to the projects:

Project type

	A	B
	$	$
Revenue per project	1,700	1,500
Direct project expenses	408	310
Administration*	280	270

* Administration costs are attributed to projects using a rate per project hour. Total administration costs are $28,000 per four-week period.

During the four-week period ending on 30 June 20X0, owing to holidays and other staffing difficulties the number of working hours available are:

| Qualified researchers | 1,344 |
| Junior researchers | 1,120 |

An agreement has already been made for twenty type A projects with XYZ group. RAB Consulting must start and complete these projects in the four-week period ending 30 June 20X0.

A maximum of 60 type B projects may be undertaken during the four-week period ending 30 June 20X0.

RAB Consulting is preparing its detailed budget for the four-week period ending 30 June 20X0 and needs to identify the most profitable use of the resources it has available.

Required

(a) (i) Calculate the contribution from each type of project. **(4 marks)**

  (ii) Formulate the linear programming model for the four-week period ending 30 June 20X0.
  (4 marks)

  (iii) Calculate, using a graph, the mix of projects that will maximise profit for RAB Consulting for the four-week period ending 30 June 20X0.

  (Note: projects are not divisible.) **(9 marks)**

(b) Calculate the profit that RAB Consulting would earn from the optimal plan. **(3 marks)**

(c) Explain the importance of identifying scarce resources when preparing budgets and the use of linear programming to determine the optimum use of resources. **(5 marks)**

(Total = 25 marks)

8 Zaman   18 mins

Learning outcome: A2(c)

Zaman Ltd manufactures two products, the Qa and the Mar. Details of the two products are as follows:

	Qa	Mar
Selling price per unit	$200	$109
Labour required per unit	20 hours	8 hours
Raw material required per unit	4 kgs	5 kgs
Variable overheads per unit	$20	$15
Maximum annual demand	1,000 units	4,000 units

Both products require the same grade of labour (costing $3 per hour) and the same type of raw material (costing $10 per kg).

In the coming year, Zaman Ltd expects to have available a maximum of 40,000 labour hours and 20,000 kgs of raw material. The company has no stocks of either Qa or Mar, and does not wish to have any stocks of either product at the end of the coming year.

Required

(a) Prepare calculations to show the quantities of Qa and Mar that should be manufactured and sold in the coming year in order to maximise the profit of Zaman Ltd; and **(7 marks)**

(b) Discuss the limitations of your calculations. **(3 marks)**

(Total = 10 marks)

9 XYZ   45 mins

Learning outcomes: A2(b), (c)

(a) The following details are taken from the forecasts for 20X1 of XYZ.

  Thousands of units

	Sales demand per annum, maximum
Super deluxe model (x_1)	500
Deluxe model (x_2)	750
Export model (x_3)	400

  Two production facilities are required, machining and assembly, and these are common to each model.

Capacity in each facility is limited by the number of direct labour hours available.

	Direct labour, total hours available in millions	Direct labour hours per unit		
		x_1	x_2	x_3
Machining	1.4	0.5	0.5	1.0
Assembly	1.2	0.5	0.5	2.0

Contribution is estimated as follows.

Model	Contribution per thousand units $
x_1	1,500
x_2	1,300
x_3	2,500

Required

Prepare formulae for this problem using the Simplex method of linear programming.   **(10 marks)**

(b)   Interpret the following tableau, given that it is the final solution to the above problem. The s variables (s_1, s_2, s_3, s_4, s_5) relate to the constraints in the same sequence as presented in (a) above.

x_1	x_2	x_3	s_1	s_2	s_3	s_4	s_5	
1	0	0	1	0	0	0	0	500
0	0	0	0.25	0.25	1	0	-0.5	112.5
0	0	1	-0.25	-0.25	0	0	0.5	287.5
0	0	0	-0.25	-0.25	0	1	-0.5	487.5
0	1	0	0	1	0	0	0	750
0	0	0	875	675	0	0	1,250	2,443,750

(15 marks)

(Total = 25 marks)

10 BB Company   45 mins

Learning outcomes: A2(b), 2(d)

For some time the BB company has sold its entire output of canned goods to supermarket chains which sell them as 'own label' products. One advantage of this arrangement is that BB incurs no marketing costs, but there is continued pressure from the chains on prices, and margins are tight.

As a consequence, BB is considering selling some of its output under the BB brand. Margins will be better but there will be substantial marketing costs.

The following information is available.

	Current year's results – 20X2 (adjusted to 20X3 cost levels)	Forecast for 20X3 (assuming all 'own label' sales)
Sales (millions of cans)	18	19
	$ million	$ million
Sales	5.94	6.27
Manufacturing costs	4.30	4.45
Administration costs	1.20	1.20
Profit	0.44	0.62

For 20X3 the unit contribution on BB brand sales is expected to be $33^{1}/_{3}$% greater than 'own label' sales, but variable marketing costs of 2c per can and fixed marketing costs of $400,000 will be incurred.

Required

(a) Prepare a contribution breakeven chart for 20X3 assuming that all sales will be 'own label'.

(9 marks)

(b) Prepare a contribution breakeven chart for 20X3 assuming that 50% of sales are 'own label' and 50% are of the BB brand. **(9 marks)**

Note. The breakeven points and margins of safety must be shown clearly on the charts.

(c) Comment on the positions shown by the charts and your calculations and discuss what other factors management should consider before making a decision. **(7 marks)**

Ignore inflation. **(Total = 25 marks)**

11 PN Motor Components

18 mins

Learning outcome: A3(a)

(a) In an attempt to win over key customers in the motor industry and to increase its market share, PN Motor Components plc have decided to charge a price lower than their normal price for component WB47 when selling to the key customers who are being targeted. Details of component WB47's standard costs are as follows.

Standard cost data

	Component WB47 Batch size 200 units			
	Machine group 1	Machine group 7	Machine group 29	Assembly
	$	$	$	$
Materials (per unit)	26.00	17.00	–	3.00
Labour (per unit)	2.00	1.60	0.75	1.20
Variable overheads (per unit)	0.65	0.72	0.80	0.36
Fixed overheads (per unit)	3.00	2.50	1.50	0.84
	31.65	21.82	3.05	5.40
Setting-up costs per batch of 200 units	$10	$6	$4	–

Required

Compute the lowest selling price at which one batch of 200 units could be offered, and describe the other factors to consider when adopting such a pricing policy. **(6 marks)**

(b) The company is also considering the launch of a new product, component WB49A, and have provided you with the following information.

	Standard cost per box
	$
Variable cost	6.20
Fixed cost	1.60
	7.80

Market research – forecast of demand

Selling price ($)	13	12	11	10	9
Demand (boxes)	5,000	6,000	7,200	11,200	13,400

The company only has enough production capacity to make 7,000 boxes. However, it would be possible to purchase product WB49A from a sub-contractor at $7.75 per box for orders up to 5,000 boxes, and $7 per box if the orders exceed 5,000 boxes.

Required

Prepare and present a computation which illustrates which price should be selected in order to maximise profits. **(4 marks)**

(Total = 10 marks)

12 DX

18 mins

Learning outcome: A3(a)

DX manufactures a wide range of components for use in various industries. It has developed a new component, the U. It is the practice of DX to set a 'list' selling price for its components and charge this price to all customers. It sells its components directly to customers all over the UK and abroad.

DX has surplus capacity available to enable it to produce up to 350,000 units per year without any need to acquire new facilities or cut back on the production of other products.

Market research indicates that:

(a)   If demand is 100,000 units or less, marginal revenue is 9 – 0.06x, where x is demand in thousands of units.

(b)   If demand is above 100,000 units, marginal revenue is 10 – 0.08x, where x is demand in thousands of units.

Research into production costs indicates that the marginal costs for a unit of production in any given year are as follows.

(a)   **Labour**. Initially $2.00 per unit but falling by 2.5p per unit for each extra 1,000 units produced, thus up to the first 1,000 units produced incurs a labour cost of $2,000, the second 1,000 incurs a labour cost of $1,975, the third 1,000 incurs a labour cost of $1,950 and so on until output reaches 80,000; output can be increased beyond 80,000 units per year without incurring any additional labour costs.

(b)   **Materials**. 50p per unit constant at all levels of output.

(c)   **Overhead**. Initially $1.00 per unit and remaining constant until output reaches 100,000 units per year; the overhead cost per unit of producing at above that level rises by 0.25p for each extra 1,000 units produced, thus the 101st thousand units produced incur an overhead cost of $1,002.50, the 102nd thousand units produced incur an overhead cost of $1,005 and so on.

Required

Calculate the output level that will maximise DX's profit from U production.   **(10 marks)**

13 Plastic tools

18 mins

Learning outcomes: A1(a), 3(a)

A small company is engaged in the production of plastic tools for the garden.

Subtotals on the spreadsheet of budgeted overheads for a year reveal the following.

	Moulding department	Finishing department	General factory overhead
Variable overhead $'000	1,600	500	1,050
Fixed overhead $'000	2,500	850	1,750
Budgeted activity			
Machine hours (000)	800	600	
Practical capacity			
Machine hours (000)	1,200	800	

For the purposes of reallocation of general factory overhead it is agreed that the variable overheads accrue in line with the machine hours worked in each department. General factory fixed overhead is to be reallocated on the basis of the practical machine hour capacity of the two departments.

It has been a long-standing company practice to establish selling prices by applying a mark-up on full manufacturing cost of between 25% and 35%.

A possible price is sought for one new product which is in a final development stage. The total market for this product is estimated at 200,000 units per annum. Market research indicates that the company could expect to obtain and hold about 10% of the market. It is hoped the product will offer some improvement over competitors' products, which are currently marketed at between $90 and $100 each.

The product development department have determined that the direct material content is $9 per unit. Each unit of the product will take two labour hours (four machine hours) in the moulding department and three labour hours (three machine hours) in finishing. Hourly labour rates are $5.00 and $5.50 respectively.

Management estimate that the annual fixed costs which would be specifically incurred in relation to the product are supervision $20,000, depreciation of a recently acquired machine $120,000 and advertising $27,000. It may be assumed that these costs are included in the budget given above. Given the state of development of this new product, management do not consider it necessary to make revisions to the budgeted activity levels given above for any possible extra machine hours involved in its manufacture.

Required

Prepare full cost and marginal cost information which may help with the pricing decision.   **(10 marks)**

14 Costs and pricing   18 mins

Learning outcomes: A1(c), 3(a)

(a)   Comment on the cost information in question 13 above and suggest a price range which should be considered.   **(5 marks)**

(b)   Briefly explain the role of costs in pricing.   **(5 marks)**

(Total = 10 marks)

15 Hilly plc   8 mins

Learning outcome: A3(a)

Hilly plc is a well-established manufacturer of high-quality goods. The company has recently developed a new product 'The Lauren' to complement its existing products.

Each Lauren requires 2 kilograms of material. Each kilogram costs $60.

The labour cost of manufacturing a 'Lauren' is estimated at $40 per unit.

Variable overheads are estimated to be $20 per unit.

The marketing director has estimated that at a selling price of $500 per Lauren, an annual sales volume of 500,000 would be achieved. He has further estimated that an increase/decrease in price of $20 will cause quantity demanded to decrease/increase by 25,000 units. He has provided you with the following formulae:

Price function: $P = a - bx$

Marginal revenue (MR) function: $= a - 2bx$

Where: a = the price at which demand would be nil

             b = the amount by which the price falls for each stepped change in demand

Required

Calculate the profit-maximising output level for sales of 'The Lauren' and the price that should be charged. **(4 marks)**

16 Dench   18 mins

Learning outcome: B1(e)

Dench Manufacturing has received a special order from Sands Ltd. to produce 225 components to be incorporated into Sands' product. The components have a high cost, due to the expertise required for their manufacture. Dench produces the components in batches of 15, and as the ones required are to be custom-made to Sands' specifications, a "prototype" batch was manufactured with the following costs:

	$
Materials	
4 kg of A, $7.50/kg	30
2 kg of B, $15/kg	30
Labour	
20 hrs skilled, $15/hr	300
5 hrs semi-skilled, $8/hr	40
Variable overhead	
25 labour hours, $4/hr	100
	500

Additional information with respect to the workforce is noted below:

Skilled   virtually a permanent workforce that has been employed by Dench for a long period of time. These workers have a great deal of experience in manufacturing components similar to those required by Sands, and turnover is virtually non-existent.

Semi-Skilled   hired by Dench on an "as needed" basis. These workers would have had some prior experience, but Dench management believe the level to be relatively insignificant. Past experience shows turnover rate to be quite high, even for short employment periods.

Dench's plans are to exclude the prototype batch from Sands' order. Management believes an 80% learning rate effect is experienced in this manufacturing process, and would like a cost estimate for the 225 components prepared on that basis.

Required

(a)   Prepare the cost estimate, assuming an 80% learning rate is experienced.   **(6 marks)**

(b)   briefly discuss some of the factors that can limit the use of learning curve theory in practice.

(4 marks)

(Total = 10 marks)

17 Cost reduction   45 mins

Learning outcome: B1(a)

It has been suggested that much of the training of management accountants is concerned with cost control whereas the major emphasis should be on cost reduction.

Required

(a)   Distinguish between cost control and cost reduction.   **(7 marks)**

(b)   Give *three* examples *each* of the techniques and principles used for (i) cost control and (ii) cost reduction.   **(8 marks)**

(c)   Discuss the proposition contained in the statement.   **(10 marks)**

(Total = 25 marks)

18 Life cycle costing

18 mins

Learning outcome: B1(i)

Explain life cycle costing and state what distinguishes it from more traditional management accounting techniques.

(10 marks)

19 ABC

18 mins

Learning outcome: B1(f)

(a) It is sometimes claimed that activity based costing (ABC) simply provides a **different** picture of product costs to traditional absorption costing, rather than a more accurate picture. **(5 marks)**

Explain the concepts that underlie ABC and discuss the claim above.

(b) Some advocates of ABC claim that it provides information which can be used for decision making. Critically appraise this view. **(5 marks)**

(Total = 10 marks)

20 ABC systems

18 mins

Learning outcome: B1(f)

'ABC systems are *resource-consumption models.* That is, they attempt to measure the cost of *using* resources, not the cost of *supplying* resources.'

Colin Drury, *Management Accounting Business Decisions*

Required

Discuss the statement above using figures, if you wish, to illustrate the points made.

(10 marks)

21 Abkaber plc

54 mins

Learning outcome: B1(f)

Abkaber plc assembles three types of motorcycle at the same factory: the 50cc Sunshine; the 250cc Roadster and the 1000cc Fireball. It sells the motorcycles throughout the world. In response to market pressures Abkaber plc has invested heavily in new manufacturing technology in recent years and, as a result, has significantly reduced the size of its workforce.

Historically, the company has allocated all overhead costs using total direct labour hours, but is now considering introducing Activity Based Costing (ABC). Abkaber plc's accountant has produced the following analysis.

	Annual output (units)	Annual direct labour Hours	Selling price ($ per unit)	Raw material cost ($ per unit)
Sunshine	2,000	200,000	4,000	400
Roadster	1,600	220,000	6,000	600
Fireball	400	80,000	8,000	900

The three cost drivers that generate overheads are:

Deliveries to retailers – the number of deliveries of motorcycles to retail showrooms

Set-ups – the number of times the assembly line process is re-set to accommodate a production run of a different type of motorcycle

Purchase orders – the number of purchase orders.

The annual cost driver volumes relating to each activity and for each type of motorcycle are as follows:

	Number of deliveries to retailers	Number of set-ups	Number of purchase orders
Sunshine	100	35	400
Roadster	80	40	300
Fireball	70	25	100

The annual overhead costs relating to these activities are as follows:

	$
Deliveries to retailers	2,400,000
Set-up costs	6,000,000
Purchase orders	3,600,000

All direct labour is paid at $5 per hour. The company holds no inventories.

At a board meeting there was some concern over the introduction of activity based costing.

The finance director argued: 'I very much doubt whether selling the Fireball is viable but I am not convinced that activity based costing would tell us any more than the use of labour hours in assessing the viability of each product.'

The marketing director argued: 'I am in the process of negotiating a major new contract with a motorcycle rental company for the Sunshine model. For such a big order they will not pay our normal prices but we need to at least cover our incremental costs. I am not convinced that activity based costing would achieve this as it merely averages costs for our entire production'.

The managing director argued: 'I believe that activity based costing would be an improvement but it still has its problems. For instance if we carry out an activity many times surely we get better at it and costs fall rather than remain constant. Similarly, some costs are fixed and do not vary either with labour hours or any other cost driver.'

The chairman argued: 'I cannot see the problem. The overall profit for the company is the same no matter which method of allocating overheads we use. It seems to make no difference to me.'

Required

(a) Calculate the total profit on each of Abkaber plc's three types of product using each of the following methods to attribute overheads:

    (i) The existing method based upon labour hours.

    (ii) Activity based costing. **(12 marks)**

(b) Write a report to the directors of Abkaber plc, as its management accountant. The report should:

    (i) Evaluate the labour hours and the activity based costing methods in the circumstances of Abkaber plc.

    (ii) Examine the implications of activity based costing for Abkaber plc, and in so doing evaluate the issues raised by each of the directors. **(12 marks)**

(c) In a manufacturing environment, activity based costing often classifies activities into unit, batch, product sustaining and facility sustaining. Explain these terms. **(6 marks)**

Refer to your calculations in requirement (a) above where appropriate.

(Total = 30 marks)

22 CPA

18 mins

Learning outcome: B1(I)

As the management accountant of XY Ltd you have undertaken an analysis of the company's profitability in relation to the number of customers served. The results of your analysis are shown in the graph below.

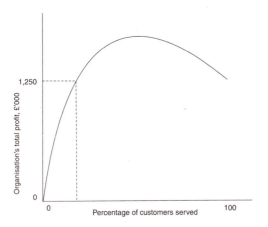

Required

Write a report to management which:

(a) Explains the general concept that is encapsulated by the graph. **(4 marks)**

(b) Advises management on the actions that are open to it to improve the profitability of the organisation. **(6 marks)**

(Total = 10 marks)

23 Just-in-time

45 mins

Learning outcome: B1(b)

Many organisations believe that a key element of just-in-time (JIT) systems is JIT production.

Required

(a) Discuss five main features of a JIT production system. **(20 marks)**
(b) State the financial benefits of JIT. **(5 marks)**

(Total = 25 marks)

24 Outsourced services

18 mins

Learning outcome: B1(j)

Explain how control can be exercised over the cost of outsourced services.

(10 marks)

25 Responsibility accounting

9 mins

Learning outcome: C1(b)

Explain the importance of an established system of responsibility accounting in the construction of functional budgets that support the overall master budget. **(5 marks)**

26 Budgets and people

22 mins

Learning outcome: C3(a)

In his study of *The Impact of Budgets on People* Argyris reported inter alia the following comment by a financial controller on the practice of participation in the setting of budgets in his company.

'We bring in the supervisors of budget areas, we tell them that we want their frank opinion but most of them just sit there and nod their heads. We know they're not coming out with exactly how they feel. I guess budgets scare them.'

Required

Suggest reasons why managers may be reluctant to participate fully in setting budgets, and suggest also unwanted side effects which may arise from the imposition of budgets by senior management. **(12 marks)**

27 Balanced scorecard

9 mins

Learning outcome: C3(c)

For each perspective of the balanced scorecard, suggest ONE key performance indicator that could be monitored by a company that provides training courses to the general public, and explain why each might be a useful indicator. **(5 marks)**

28 MPL

54 mins

Learning outcomes: C2(c), 3(b)

(a) MPL is a company specialising in providing consultancy services to the catering industry. The operating statement for period 5 for the IT division is as follows. The division operates as a profit centre.

	Budget	*Actual*	*Variance*
Chargeable consultancy hours	2,400	2,500	100
	€	€	€
Central administration costs – fixed	15,000	15,750	750 (A)
Consultants' salaries – fixed	80,000	84,000	4,000 (A)
Casual wages – variable	960	600	360 (F)
Motor and travel costs – fixed	4,400	4,400	-
Telephone – fixed	600	800	200 (A)
Telephone – variable	2,000	2,150	150 (A)
Printing, postage & stationery – variable	2,640	2,590	50 (F)
Depreciation of equipment – fixed	3,200	3,580	380 (A)
Total costs	108,800	113,870	5,070 (A)
Fees charged	180,000	200,000	20,000 (F)
Profit	71,200	86,130	14,930 (F)

While the manager of the IT division is pleased that the actual profit exceeded the budget expectation she is interested to know how this has been achieved. After the budget had been issued to her she had queried the meaning of variable costs and had been told that they were variable in direct proportion to chargeable consultancy hours.

Required

As the newly appointed management accountant, prepare a report addressed to the board of directors of MPL which:

(i) Explains the present approach to budgeting adopted in MPL and discusses the advantages and disadvantages of involving consultants in the preparation of future budgets; **(8 marks)**

(ii) Critically discusses the format of the operating statement for period 5; **(5 marks)**

(iii) Prepare an alternative statement for the profit centre which distinguishes clearly between controllable profit and attributable profit and which provides a realistic measure of the variances for the period. State any assumptions you make. **(7 marks)**

(b) Briefly explain the balanced scorecard approach and the problems that can arise when it is applied. **(10 marks)**

(Total = 30 marks)

29 Divisional performance   27 mins

Learning outcomes: D2(b), 2(c)

(a) Compare and contrast the use of residual income and return on investment in divisional performance measurement, stating the advantages and disadvantages of each. **(10 marks)**

(b) Division Y of Chardonnay currently has capital employed of $100,000 and earns an annual profit after depreciation of $18,000. The divisional manager is considering an investment of $10,000 in an asset which will have a ten-year life with no residual value and will earn a constant annual profit after depreciation of $1,600. The cost of capital is 15%.

Calculate the following and comment on the results.

(i) The return on divisional investment, before and after the new investment
(ii) The divisional residual income before and after the new investment **(5 marks)**

(Total = 15 marks)

30 B and C   54 mins

Learning outcomes: D1(a), 2(b), 2(c), 3(a)

(a) The following figures for the years ending 31 December 20X4 and 20X3 relate to the B and C divisions of Cordeline.

The return on capital employed (ROCE) figure is the basis for awarding a 20% bonus to the manager of B division (actual ROCE/target ROCE). The below target ROCE for C division has resulted in a zero bonus award to its manager.

	Division			
	B		C	
	20X4	20X3	20X4	20X3
	$'000	$'000	$'000	$'000
Sales	9,850	7,243	4,543	2,065
Profit before interest and taxes (PBIT)	1,336	1,674	924	363
Included in profit calculation:				
Depreciation for year	960	919	1,300	251
Net book value (NBV) of non-current	5,540	6,000	7,700	2,600
Original cost of non-current assets	12,600	12,100	9,500	3,100
Replacement cost of non-current assets	25,000	24,500	9,750	3,350
New investment in non-current assets	500	750	6,400	2,400
Cost of capital	8%	8%	8%	8%
Return on capital employed**	24%	28%	12%	14%
Target return on capital	20%	20%	20%	20%

* Net book value is original cost less accumulated depreciation to date.

** Cordeline consider ROCE for bonus purposes to be PBIT as a % of NBV.

Required

Cordeline's board are meeting to review the company's management performance appraisal and reward system. Prepare a short paper for the board, drawing on the above information, which contains the following.

BPP
LEARNING MEDIA

(i)   An explanation of possible counter-productive behaviour resulting from using the current ROCE calculation for performance appraisal   **(14 marks)**

(ii)   A revised ROCE measure together with justification for your suggestion   **(6 marks)**

(b)   Briefly explain the advantages and disadvantages of divisionalisation.   **(10 marks)**

(Total = 30 marks)

31 Pasta Division   54 mins

Learning outcomes: D2(b), 2(c), 3(a)

A well-established food manufacturing and distribution company, specialising in Italian food products, currently has an annual turnover in excess of $15 million. At present, the company has three production and distribution divisions, each responsible for specific product groups and a cost of capital of 15%.

The summary information of the pasta division relating to divisional assets and profitability is as follows.

Pasta division

This division produces a wide range of both dried and fresh pasta products which it sells to both the supermarket sector and the restaurant trade.

Last year the divisional figures were as follows.

	$m
Investment in non-current assets	1.5
Investment in working capital	1.0
Operating profit	0.5

The company is keen to ensure that each division operates as an autonomous profit-making unit to ensure efficiency prevails and motivation and competitiveness are maximised. Managers are given as much freedom as possible to manage their divisions. Divisional budgets are set at the beginning of each year and these are then monitored on a month by month basis. Divisional managers are rewarded in terms of divisional return on investment.

The company is currently considering expansion into a new but allied product range. This range consists of sauces and canned foods. Projected figures for the expansion into sauces and canned foods are:

	$m
Additional non-current assets required	0.75
Additional investment in working capital	0.35
Budgeted additional profit	0.198

The manager of the pasta division has produced successful results over the past few years for her division. She and her staff have enjoyed handsome bonuses on the basis of return on investment. The company has traditionally calculated return on investment as operating profit as a percentage of return on all net divisional assets, and bonuses are paid as a percentage on this basis. The board proposes that the pasta division will be responsible for the expansion into sauces and canned foods.

Required

(a)   Calculate the return on investment for the division both before and after the proposed divisional expansion.   **(5 marks)**

(b)   Calculate the residual income for the division both before and after the proposed divisional expansion.   **(5 marks)**

(c)   Using return on investment as a performance measure, determine whether the divisional manager will be happy to accept the proposed expansion. Explain how your answer would differ if residual income was used as a performance measure instead of return on investment.   **(5 marks)**

(d)   Briefly outline the advantages and disadvantages of return on investment and residual income as divisional performance measures. **(8 marks)**

(e)   Briefly explain the main features of Economic Value Added (EVA®) as it would be used to assess the performance of divisions. **(3 marks)**

(f)   Briefly explain how the use of EVA® to assess divisional performance might affect the behaviour of divisional senior executives. **(4 marks)**

(Total = 30 marks)

32 Transfer pricing   54 mins

Learning outcome: D3(c)

(a)   Explain the potential benefits of operating a transfer pricing system within a divisionalised company. **(6 marks)**

(b)   A company operates two divisions, Able and Baker. Able manufactures two products, X and Y. Product X is sold to external customers for $42 per unit. The only outlet for product Y is Baker.

Baker supplies an external market and can obtain its semi-finished supplies (product Y) from either Able or an external source. Baker currently has the opportunity to purchase product Y from an external supplier for $38 per unit. The capacity of division Able is measured in units of output, irrespective of whether product X, Y or combination of both are being manufactured. The associated product costs are as follows.

	X	Y
Variable costs per unit	32	35
Fixed overheads per unit	5	5
Total unit costs	37	40

Required

Using the above information, provide advice on the determination of an appropriate transfer price for the sale of product Y from division Able to division Baker under the following conditions.

(i)   When division Able has spare capacity and limited external demand for product X. **(3 marks)**

(ii)   When division Able is operating at full capacity with unsatisfied external demand for product X. **(4 marks)**

(c)   A group has two companies, K, which is operating at just above 50% capacity and L, which is operating at full capacity (7,000 production hours).

L produces two products, X and Y, using the same labour force for each product. For the next year its budgeted capacity involves a commitment to the sale of 3,000 kg of Y, the remainder of its capacity being used on X. Direct costs of these two products are as follows.

	X		Y	
	$ per kg		$ per kg	
Direct materials	18		14	
Direct wages	15	(1 production hour)	10	(²/₃ production hour)

The company's overhead is $126,000 per annum relating to X and Y in proportion to their direct wages. At full capacity $70,000 of this overhead is variable. L prices its products with a 60% mark-up on its total costs.

For the coming year, K wishes to buy from L 2,000 kg of product X which it proposes to adapt and sell, as product Z, for $100 per kg. The direct costs of adaptation are $15 per kg. K's total fixed costs will not change, but variable overhead of $2 per kg will be incurred.

Required

As group management accountant, make the following recommendations.

(i) The range of transfer prices, if any, at which 2,000 kg of product X should be sold to K.

(ii) The other points that should be borne in mind when making any recommendations about transfer prices in the above circumstances. **(12 marks)**

(d) Discuss briefly whether standard costs or actual costs should be used as the basis for cost-based transfer prices. **(5 marks)**

(Total = 30 marks)

1 Restaurant

Wages

> **Top tip**. You need to work out the variable wages cost using the high-low method. There are only two years, so one is taken as 'high' and one as 'low'.

	Year 1	Year 2	Increase
Number of meals	151,156	(× 8%) 163,248	12,092
	$	$	$
Wages cost	349,170	390,477	41,307

We must account for inflation, however, by adjusting year 1 to year 2 costs. The figure used is the 6% hourly rate increase.

	$	$	$
$349,170 \times 106\%$ =	370,120	390,477	20,357

In year 2, the variable wages cost of a meal is $\dfrac{\$20,357}{12,092} = \$1.68$

	$
Variable wages cost (year 2) ($1.68 × 163,248)	274,257
Fixed wages cost (year 2) (balance)	116,220
Total wages cost (year 2)	390,477

	$
So, in year 3, variable cost = (163,248 × 110%) meals × $1.68 × 107%	322,800
Fixed cost = $116,220 × 107%	124,355
Total wages cost (year 3)	447,155

Overheads

	Year 1	Year 2	Increase
Number of meals	151,156	163,248	12,092
	$	$	$
Overhead costs	202,549	216,930	14,381
Adjusting year 1 costs to year 2 cost (× 105%)	212,676	216,930	4,254

Variable overhead cost in year 2 is $\dfrac{\$4,254}{12,092} = \$0.352$ per meal

	$
∴ In year 2, variable overhead cost ($0.352 × 163,248)	57,463
Fixed overhead cost (balance)	159,467
Total overhead cost (year 2)	216,930
∴ In year 3, variable cost = (163,248 × 110%) meals × $0.352 × 106%	67,002
Fixed cost = $159,467 × 106%	169,035
Total overhead cost (year 3)	236,037

2 Webber Design

> **Top tips.** This is a relevant costing question so don't get led astray by the references to pricing.
>
> Part (c) is a standalone question that can be answered independently of the rest of the question. It also asks for **definitions** so you should be able to answer this using knowledge rather than application.

(a)   Incremental costs and revenues of altering equipment

	Note	Alter $	Scrap $	Difference $
Materials	1	4,500	–	4,500
Welding	2	–	–	–
Machining	2	–	–	–
Assembly	3	3,680	(16,000)	19,680
Overtime	4	1,500	–	1,500
Variable overhead	5	–	–	–
Delivery	6	3,400	–	3,400
Fixed overheads	7	–	–	–
Original costs	8	–	–	–
Advance	9	–	–	–
Original materials	10	–	(4,000)	4,000
Scrap	10	–	(5,200)	5,200
Design	10	–	(1,500)	1,500
				39,780

The minimum price to be charged is $39,780, but this is subject to clarification of a number of matters which could significantly affect the figure given. See the notes for details.

Notes

1   The cost of proceeding is the $4,500 which will have to be spent on materials for the other contract.

2   Although additional work is required in the welding and machining departments there is no indication that workers can be taken on or laid off at will: we assume that all workers involved in the alteration work will be paid their weekly wages whether or not the work proceeds.

3   Assembly department workers appear to be in short supply and they can generate $5 for every $1 of direct labour. By redeploying 2 workers for eight weeks at $200 per worker the company will forgo $2 \times \$5 \times \$200 \times 8 = \$16,000$ contribution. Contribution is earned after having covered labour and variable overhead costs and therefore wages of $(2 \times 8 \times \$200) = \$3,200$ and variable overheads of 15% ($480) are also included in this case. Total reduced cost is $19,680.

4   Overtime is incurred as a direct result of the alteration work and will not be paid otherwise.

5   Variable overhead, like direct wages, will be incurred whatever decision is taken.

6   The special delivery charge is directly relevant to the new customer.

7   Fixed overheads do not change as a result of the decision to proceed and so no extra cost is included.

8   We do not know whether the 'additional work' is in place of or in addition to the work required to complete the equipment to the original specification. We do not know whether the completion costs are 'estimated' or already 'incurred'. We do not know whether direct wages costs are committed or not. Fixed costs are not relevant, since presumably they will not be saved whatever decision is taken.

        None of the completion costs are included in our calculation but further information would have to be obtained before finalising the minimum price.

9   The advance can be calculated as follows.

		$
Original quotation –	cost	29,450.00
	– margin (20/80)	7,362.50
		36,812.50

Advance (15%) = $5,522

However, we do not know whether this is to be returned to the original customer or not – this will depend upon the terms of the contract. If it were returnable only in the event that the equipment were sold to another customer it would be a relevant cost of proceeding; we have assumed that this is not the case.

10   Savings of $4,000 in materials (ignoring machining costs (see note 2)) would be made if the original equipment were scrapped, and disposal proceeds of $5,200 for other materials and $1,500 for the design would be forgone.

(b)   In addition to the queries raised in the notes above, Webber should consider the following matters in setting the price.

(i)   Whether any of the costs incurred to date can be recovered from the original customer under the terms of the contract.

(ii)   If not, whether the price should attempt to recover costs incurred to date as well as future costs.

(iii)   Whether repeat work is likely from the new customer, in which case it might be worthwhile to grant favourable terms on this order.

(c)   Relevant costs are 'costs appropriate to a specific management decision. They are future cash flows arising as a direct consequence of a decision.

Opportunity cost is 'the value of the benefit sacrificed when one course of action is chosen, in preference to an alternative'.

Discretionary cost is 'expenditure whose level is a matter of policy', for example advertising costs or research and development expenditure.

Relevant costs are (or should be) used by management to make decisions, as stated above. Opportunity costs are a type of relevant cost. The concept is particularly useful where resources are scarce. Discretionary costs do not have to be incurred in order to continue in business: it is thus useful to management to know which costs can be so classified where cost reductions are necessary or when budgeting.

3 AB

> **Top tips.** This question has four ingredients of a good and testing problem on decision-making.
>
> - It tests your ability to grasp the **nature of a decision problem**, and think about the assumptions you may have to make. It is assumed that inventory in hand of finished X, valued at $51,900 at full cost, is valued at the full cost of production and not at the full cost of sale.
>
> - It tests your knowledge of **relevant costs**. For example, the $3,500 capital cost of Y will be incurred whatever course of action is taken, although with the alternative recommendation we have made the spending could be deferred by 33 weeks. Selling and administration overhead has been assumed to be a fixed cost and so is irrelevant to the decision.
>
> - It includes a consideration of **non-financial factors**. We looked at the workforce, customers' interests and competition – you may have focused on different areas.
>
> - Part (c) of the question introduced the very practical issue **of searching for alternative opportunities**. For example, the alternative course of action we have suggested seems the most obvious one, but you might think otherwise, and a sensible alternative would be equally acceptable as a solution.

(a) **Full cost of production per kg of X**

	$
Direct materials	17.33
Direct labour	7.36
Production overhead (200% of labour)	14.72
	39.41

The quantity of stock-in-hand is therefore $51,900/$39.41 = 1,317 kg

At a weekly sales volume of 74 kg, this represents 1,317/74 = about 18 weeks of sales

It will take 20 weeks to set up the production facility for Y, and so inventory in hand of finished X can be sold before any Y can be produced. This **finished inventory** is therefore **irrelevant** to the decision under review; it will be sold whatever decision is taken.

The problem therefore centres on the inventory in hand of direct materials. Assuming that there is no loss or wastage in manufacture and so 1 kg of direct material is needed to produce 1 kg of X then inventory in hand is $44,800/$17.33 = 2,585 kg.

This would be converted into 2,585 kg of X, which would represent sales volume for 2,585/74 = 35 weeks.

If AB sells its existing inventories of finished X (in 18 weeks) there are **two options**.

(i) To produce enough X from raw materials for 2 more weeks, until production of Y can start, and then dispose of all other quantities of direct material – ie 33 weeks' supply.

(ii) To produce enough X from raw materials to use up the existing inventory of raw materials, and so delay the introduction of Y by 33 weeks.

The relevant costs of these two options

(i) **Direct materials**. The relevant cost of existing inventories of raw materials is $(0.30). In other words the 'cost' is a benefit. By using the direct materials to make more X, the company would save $0.30 per kg used.

(ii) **Direct labour**. It is assumed that if labour is switched to production work from non-production work in the next three months, they must be paid at the full rate of pay, and not at 65% of normal rate. The *incremental* cost of labour would be 35% of the normal rate (35% of $7.36 = $2.58 per kg produced).

Relevant cost of production of X

	$
Direct materials	(0.30)
Direct labour	2.58
Variable overhead (30% of full overhead cost of $14.72)	4.42
Cost per kg of X	6.70

Relevant cost per kg of Y

	$
Direct materials	4.01
Direct labour	2.85
Variable overhead (30% of 200% of $2.85)	1.71
	8.57

(*Note*. Y cannot be made for 20 weeks, and so the company cannot make use of spare labour capacity to produce any units of Y.)

It is cheaper to use up the direct material inventories and make X ($6.70 per kg) than to introduce Y as soon as possible, because there would be a saving of ($8.57 – $6.70) = $1.87 per kg made.

AB must sell X for at least 20 weeks until Y could be produced anyway, but the introduction of Y could be delayed by a further 33 weeks until all inventories of direct material for X are used up. The saving in total would be about $1.87 per kg × 74 kg per week × 33 weeks = $4,567.

(b) **Non-financial factors that must be considered in reaching the decision**

  (i) **The workforce**. If the recommended course of action is undertaken, the workforce will produce enough units of X in the next 13 weeks to satisfy sales demand over the next year, (with 18 weeks' supply of existing finished goods inventories and a further 35 weeks' supply obtainable from direct materials inventories). When production of Y begins, the direct labour content of production will fall to $2.85 per kg – less than 40% of the current effort per kg produced – but sales demand will not rise. The changeover will therefore mean a big drop in labour requirements in production. Redundancies seem inevitable, and might be costly. By switching to producing Y as soon as possible, the redundancies might be less immediate, and could be justified more easily to employees and their union representatives than a decision to produce enough X in the next 3 months to eliminate further production needs for about 9 months.

  (ii) **Customers' interests**. Product Y is a superior and 'more effective' compound than X. It would be in customers' interests to provide them with this improved product as soon as possible, instead of delaying its introduction until existing inventories of direct materials for X have been used up.

  (iii) **Competition**. CD is expected to start selling Y overseas, and quite possibly in direct competition with AB. CD has the advantage of having developed Y itself, and appears to use it in the preliminary stage of an alternative technical process. The competitive threat to AB is two-fold:

  (1) CD might take away some of the replacement demand for Y from AB so that AB's sales of X or Y would fall.

  (2) CD might compete with AB to install its total technical process into customers' factories, and so the competition would be wider than the market for compound Y.

(c) **Alternative course of action**

  (i) Produce enough units of X in the next 13 weeks to use up existing inventories of direct materials.

  (ii) Start sales of Y as soon as possible, and offer customers the choice between X and Y. Since X is an inferior compound, it would have to be sold at a lower price than Y.

Merits of this course of action

(i)   The workforce would be usefully employed for the next 13 weeks and then production of Y would begin at once. Although redundancies would still seem inevitable, the company would be creating as much work as it could for its employees.

(ii)   AB's customers would be made aware of the superiority of Y over X in terms of price, and of AB's commitment to the new compound. AB's marketing approach would be both 'honest' and would also give customers an attractive choice of buying the superior Y or, for a time, an inferior X but at a lower price. This might well enhance AB's marketing success.

Demerits of this course of action

(i)   It is unlikely to be a profit-maximising option, because selling X at a discount price would reduce profitability.

(ii)   Customers who get a discount on X might demand similar discounts on Y.

(iii) Some customers might query the technical differences between X and Y, and question why AB has been selling X at such a high price in the past – this might lead to some customer relations difficulties.

(iv)   AB must decide when to reduce the price of X, given that Y cannot be made for 20 weeks. The timing of the price reduction might create some difficulties with customers who buy X just before the price is reduced.

4 X

> **Top tips.** The ranking of the products is relatively straightforward, provided you adopt a systematic approach.

	A $/litre	B $/litre	C $/litre	D $/litre
Selling price	100	110	120	120
Variable cost	54	55	59	66
Contribution	46	55	61	54
Labour hours used per litre	3	2.5	4	4.5
Contribution per labour hour	$15.33	$22	$15.25	$12
Ranking	2	1	3	4

The available **labour hours** should be allocated **first** to the **contract already made** with Y Ltd. The **remaining hours** should then be allocated to **products according to this ranking**, and **subject to the maximum demand.**

	Product	Litres		Hours used	Cumulative hours used
Y Ltd	A, B, C, D	20 each	(× 14)	280	280
Ranking	B	130	(× 2.5)	325	605
	A	180	(× 3)	540	1,145
	C	50	(× 4)	200	1,345

Summary of recommended production for next three months

Product	Litres
A	200
B	150
C	70
D	20

Calculation of profit for next three months

Product		Contribution	
	Litres	$ per litre	$
A	200	46	9,200
B	150	55	8,250
C	70	61	4,270
D	20	54	1,080
Total contribution			22,800
Fixed overhead (see working)			12,800
Profit			10,000

Working

Calculation of fixed overhead per quarter

Using product A, fixed overhead per hour = $24/3 = $8 per hour

∴ Budgeted fixed overhead = 1,600 hours × $8 = $12,800

Note. The calculation of the hourly rate of $8 per hour could have been based on any of the four products.

5 Research director

Top tips. The information provided changes the ranking compared with question 4, and so you will need to recalculate the production plan. Don't forget that the minimum quantity of D has to be produced.

Products **C and D** can both be **sold** for a **higher price than that offered by the overseas supplier**. The **unsatisfied demand** should therefore be **met** by using the **overseas supplier** next quarter.

	C	D
	$ per litre	$ per litre
External supplier's price	105	100
Internal variable cost of manufacture	59	66
Saving through internal manufacture	46	34
Labour hours used per litre	4	4.5
Saving per labour hour	$11.50	$7.56

Even when the extra cost of the pollution controls for product D is ignored, **it is therefore preferable to manufacture product C internally and purchase D from the overseas supplier.**

The capacity which would have been used to manufacture 20 litres of product D can now be allocated to product C (20 litres × 4.5 hours = 90 hours).

Summary of revised recommended production for the next three months

Product		Hours	Litres	Litres
A	Internal manufacture	600		200
B	Internal manufacture	375		150
C	Internal manufacture	370	92.5	
C	External purchase		7.5	100
D	External purchase			120
		1,345		570

Calculation of revised profit for next three months

Product	Litres		$ per litre	Contribution $
			Contribution	
A	200.0		46	9,200.00
B	150.0		55	8,250.00
C	92.5		61	5,642.50
	7.5	(120 – 105)	15	112.50
D	120.0	(120 – 100)	20	2,400.00
				25,605.00
Fixed overhead				12,800.00
Revised profit				12,805.00

Reasons that profit will increase by $2,805 per quarter are as follows.

(a) Production of product D is subcontracted and the time saved is used on production of product C.

(b) The additional fixed cost is not incurred because Product D production is subcontracted.

(c) Maximum demand for products C and D can be met.

A number of factors should be considered, however, including the following.

(a) The reliability of the supplier, which is particularly important in the case of an overseas supplier

(b) The quality of supply

(c) Any other sources of sub-contract supply

6 Alphabet Ltd

Sales revenue	(1)		36,000
Costs			
Material X	(2)	(200)	
Material Z	(3)	4,200	
Labour	(4)	11,000	
Variable overhead	(5)	3,600	
Depreciation	(6)	–	
Fixed overheads	(7)	–	
Lost scrap proceeds	(8)	3,000	
			(21,600)
Net Relevant Contribution			14,400

Conclusion: the proposal should be accepted as it makes a positive contribution of $14,400 based on relevant costs.

(1) Revenue earned as a result of producing and selling T.

(2) No other use for X in business, but $200 disposal costs are saved by using X to make Ts.

(3) Z is used in the business and will have to be replaced for $0.175 x 2 x 12,000 = $4,200.

Assuming inventories can be bought at this price.

(4) Opportunity cost of using labour   = contribution foregone + cost of labour
                = $1,000 + $10,000
                = $11,000

(5) Variable overhead is only incurred when units are made.

∴ relevant cost = 12,000 x $0.30

(6) Depreciation is not a cash flow and ∴ not relevant

(7) These fixed overheads will be incurred regardless of whether or not Ts are made, therefore cost is not relevant.

(8) If machine is used, instead of scrapped the business loses $(7,000 – 4,000) of scrap proceeds.

However, the following non-financial factors also need to be considered:

(a) The likelihood of a more profitable proposal being received;
(b) Whether repeat orders would be expected at the same price in future years;
(c) Whether the company's present customers can be differentiated from this special order price.

7 RAB Consulting

Top tips. This is a straightforward linear programming question from a previous pilot paper.

The best way to approach graphical linear programming questions is to work through the **six steps** we recommend in the text.

- Define variables
- Establish objective function
- Establish constraints
- Graph the problem
- Define feasible area
- Determine optimal solution

Notice the approach we have taken to choosing our sample **iso-contribution line**. This is something that students often find difficult, so choose easy **numbers (related to the coefficients of the variables)**, making sure that the line then falls within the feasible area.

Don't forget that there will always be **marks** in the exam for **presentation** of the **graph**, so remember to label your axes, use a ruler and so on.

(a) (i)

		Type A $ per project		Type B $ per project
Revenue		1,700		1,500
Variable costs				
Labour				
– qualified researchers	(20 hrs × $30)	600	(12 hrs × $30)	360
– junior researchers	(8 hrs × $14)	112	(15 hrs × $14)	210
Direct project expenses		408		310
		1,120		880
Contribution		580		620

(ii)

 Define variables

Let a = number of type A projects

Let b = number of type B projects

 Establish objective function

Maximise contribution (C) = 580a + 620b, subject to the constraints below.

 Establish constraints

Qualified researchers time:	$20a + 12b \leq 1,344$
Junior researchers time:	$8a + 15b \leq 1,120$
Agreement for type A:	$a \geq 20$
Maximum for type B:	$b \leq 60$
Non-negativity:	$a \geq 0, b \geq 0$

(iii)

Graphing the problem

Constraints

Qualified researcher time:	if a = 0, b = 112
	if b = 0, a = 67.2
Junior researcher time:	if a = 0, b = 74.67
	if b = 0, a = 140
Agreement for type A:	graph the line a = 20
Maximum for type B:	graph the line b = 60

Define feasible area

Iso-contribution line

580a + 620b = 35,960 (where 35,960 = 58 × 62 × 10) goes through the points (62, 0) and (0, 58)

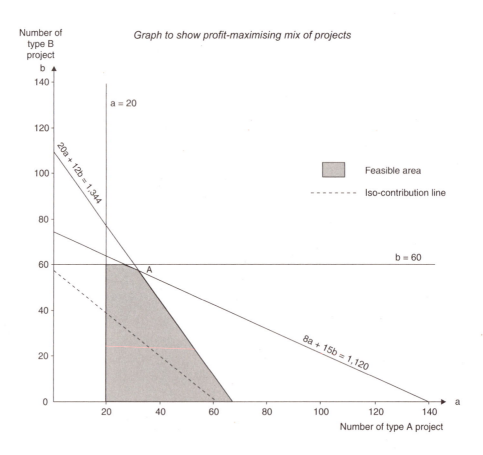

Moving the iso-contribution line away from the origin, we see that it leaves the feasible area at the intersection of the two time constraints (point A).

STEP 6 *Determine optimal solution*

Find the coordinates of A

20a + 12b	= 1,344	(1)
8a + 15b	= 1,120	(2)
20a + 37.5b	= 2,800	(3) (2) × 2.5
25.5b	= 1,456	(3) – (1)
b	= 57.09	
20a + 685.08	= 1,344	substitute into (1)
A	= 32.946	

The profit-maximising mix of projects is 33 of type A and 57 of type B.

(b) **Profit for profit-maximising mix**

	$
Contribution from type A: 33 × $580	19,140
Contribution from type B: 57 × $620	35,340
Total contribution	54,480
Less: fixed costs	(28,000)
	26,480

(c) **The importance of identifying scarce resources when preparing budgets**

Scarce resources restrict the activity level at which an organisation can operate. For example, a sales department might estimate that it could sell 1,000 units of product X, which would require 5,000 hours of grade A labour. If there are no units of product X in inventory, and only 4,000 hours of grade A labour available in the period, the company would be unable to make and sell 1,000 units of X because of the shortage of labour hours. Management must choose one of the following options.

- Reduce budgeted sales by 20%.
- Increase the availability of grade A labour by recruitment or overtime working.
- Sub-contract some production to another manufacturer.

If the fact that grade A labour is a **scarce resource** is **ignored** when the **budget** is prepared, it will be **unattainable** and of **little relevance for planning and control.**

Most organisations are **restricted** from making and selling more of their products because there would be **no sales demand for the increased output** at an acceptable price. The organisation should therefore budget to produce and sell the volume of its product(s) demanded.

The **scarce resource** might be machine capacity, distribution and selling resources, raw materials or cash.

(i) If an organisation **produces just one product**, the **budget for the scarce resources is usually the starting point in the budget preparation process**.

(ii) If an organisation **produces two or more products** and there is only **one scarce resource**, **limiting factor analysis** must be used to determine the most profitable use of the scarce resource.

(iii) When there is **more than one scarce resource**, **linear programming** must be used to identify the most profitable use of resources.

The use of linear programming to determine the optimum use of resources

Linear programming is a technique which **determines the most profitable production mix, taking into account resource constraints and limitations** faced by an organisation. **All costs are assumed to be either fixed or variable in relation to a single measure of activity (usually units of output)**.

The **problem is formulated** in terms of an **objective function** and **constraints** are then **graphed**. This process **highlights all possible output combinations given** the resource constraints and limitations and allows for the **identification of the output combination which would maximise contribution (the optimal solution)**.

If there are **more than two types of output**, the graphical approach is not possible and the **simplex method** must be used instead.

8 Zaman

> **Top tips**. The question does not ask for a graph but we have sketched one here. It helps you to find the optimal production level if you plot your axes correctly and use a rule to find the optimal point in the feasible region.

(a)   Let q = number of Qa units produced next year

and m = number of Mar units produced next year

Contribution per unit:

Qa   =   \$200 – (20 × \$3) – (4 × \$10) – \$20 = \$80
Mar   =   \$109 – (8 × \$3) – (5 × \$10) – \$15 = \$20

Objective function is to maximise contribution \$80q + \$20m.

Constraints:

Labour: $20q + 8m \leq 40{,}000$ (hours)

Material: $4q + 5m \leq 20{,}000$ (kgs)

Sales: $q \leq 1{,}000$ & $m \leq 4{,}000$ (units)

Non-negativity: $q \geq 0$ & $m \geq 0$

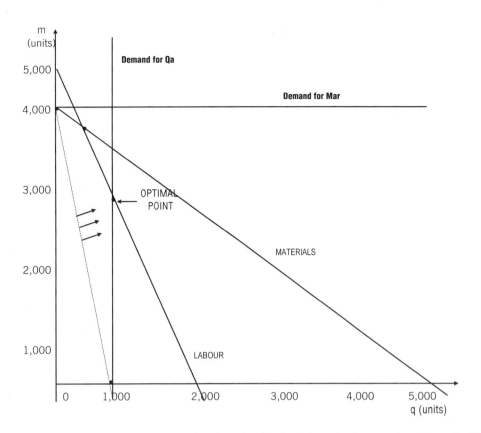

From the graph it will be seen that the optimal production level is at the intersection of q = 1,000 and labour 20q + 8m = 40,000, i.e. where q = 1,000 and m = 2,500.

Optimal production plan is 1,000 units of Qa and 2,500 units of Mar.

(b)   The following limitations are inherent in the calculations:

(i)   the model assumes linear relationships between the variables. This assumption may not always be true. For example, it may be possible to charge a higher price when production is at a restricted level. Similarly at higher levels of production, costs may be reduced either by mass production techniques, the learning effect and faster performance of employees or bulk discounts on materials.

(ii)   All information is taken as certain which is unlikely to be the case in practice. Sensitivity analysis may be applied to deal with this problem.

(iii)   The sale of Qa and Mar may be in markets with different debt collection patterns – this has been ignored in the solution.

(iv)   It is assumed that there is no latitude in the availability of resources. In practice it will almost certainly be possible to obtain extra labour by payment of an overtime premium.

(v)   The products may be complementary or substitutes. This may impose other limitations on the demand.

9 XYZ

Top tips. The formulation of a problem using the simplex method of linear programming (part (a)) involves **five key stages**.

- Define variables
- Establish objective function
- Establish constraints
- **Introduce slack variables**
- **Express constraints as equations**

The method only really differs from the graphical approach in the fourth and fifth stages. A **slack variable** is **needed for each constraint** (other than non-negativity constraints), and so five will be needed in this solution. The **constraints are then turned into equations** by **including the relevant slack variable** (which represents the amount of resource unused, the difference between actual production and maximum possible production and so on) so that the **two sides of the equation are equal.**

Interpretation of a final tableau may appear daunting at first, but once you have done a few questions you will find it becomes far easier. Honestly! Read through our solution and ensure that you really understand the meaning of the figures in the tableau.

The **optimal solution** is determined by looking for **variables** that have a **zero in every row of their column except for one row that has a figure 1**. This is the **solution** for that variable. The figure 1 in the x_2 column is in the same row as the 750 in the solution column, and so 750,000 units of the deluxe model should be produced.

By the way, did you notice that **the figures** were in **thousands**?

(a) **Define variables**

Let x_1 be the number of Super deluxe produced

Let x_2 be the number of Deluxe produced

Let x_3 be the number of Export produced

Establish objective function

Maximise contribution (C) = $1{,}500x_1 + 1{,}300x_2 + 2{,}500x_3$ (subject to the constraints below).

Establish constraints

$$
\begin{aligned}
x_1 &\leq 500 && \text{(super deluxe demand)} \\
x_2 &\leq 750 && \text{(deluxe demand)} \\
x_3 &\leq 400 && \text{(export model demand)} \\
0.5x_1 + 0.5x_2 + x_3 &\leq 1{,}400 && \text{(machining capacity)} \\
0.5x_1 + 0.5x_2 + 2x_3 &\leq 1{,}200 && \text{(assembly capacity)} \\
x_1, x_2, x_3 &\geq 0
\end{aligned}
$$

Introduce slack variables

Slack variables are introduced as follows.

s_1 is the amount by which demand for x_1 falls short of 500

s_2 is the amount by which demand for x_2 falls short of 750

s_3 is the amount by which demand for x_3 falls short of 400

s_4 is the unused machine capacity in thousands of hours

s_5 is the unused assembly capacity in thousands of hours

Then $x_1 + s_1 = 500$

$x_2 + s_2 = 750$

$x_3 + s_3 = 400$

$0.5x_1 + 0.5x_2 + x_3 + s_4 = 1,400$

$0.5x_1 + 0.5x_2 + 2x_3 + s_5 = 1,200$

and $C - 1,500x_1 - 1,300x_2 - 2,500x_3 + 0s_1 + 0s_2 + 0s_3 + 0s_4 + 0s_5 = 0$

(b)   (i)   Produce   500,000 units of the super deluxe model ($x_1 = 500$)

750,000 units of the deluxe model   ($x_2 = 750$)

and   287,500 units of the export model   ($x_3 = 287.5$)

(ii)   This means that demand for the export model will be 112,500 units short of the maximum demand ($s_3 = 112.5$)

(iii)   There will be 487,500 unused direct labour hours in machining ($s_4 = 487.5$)

(iv)   The total contribution will be $2,443,750.

(v)   The shadow price of s_1 is $875 and that of s_2 is $675.

(1)   Contribution would therefore increase (or decrease) by $875 for each one thousand units by which the demand constraint for the super deluxe model increased (or decreased). For example if the maximum demand for the super deluxe fell to 490,000 ($x_1 \leq 490$), maximum contribution would fall by $10 \times \$875 = \$8,750$ to $2,435,000.

(2)   Similarly, contribution would increase (or decrease) by $675 for each one thousand units by which the demand constraint for the deluxe model increased (or decreased).

(vi)   The shadow price of assembly time is $1,250 per thousand hours. This means that for every thousand hours extra (or less) of assembly time available, provided that the cost of this time remains at its normal variable cost per hour, maximum contribution would be $1,250 higher (or lower). This is readily apparent in this particular problem, because the extra time would have to be used to make the export model (since the other two models are already being produced up to maximum demand). One thousand extra hours of assembly time would be sufficient to produce 500 units of the export model, to earn a contribution of 50% of $2,500 = \$1,250$. This shadow price is only valid up to the point where demand for the export model is satisfied (an extra 112,500 units, or 225,000 hours), given that sufficient machining capacity does exist to produce all of these extra units.

10 BB Company

> **Top tips**. The P2 exam could include a full question on the topic so ensure you make a good attempt at this one.
>
> To draw up a **contribution breakeven chart** you need to **know** three things.
>
> - Selling price per can
> - Variable cost per can
> - Fixed costs
>
> These can all be calculated from information in the question with varying degrees of difficulty/ease.
>
> As CVP analysis is based on **marginal costing principles** and given that information in the question is provided for two time periods, you have a rather large hint that you need to split the manufacturing costs into fixed and variable components using the **high-low method**. It is safe to assume that the **administration** costs are **fixed** as they are the **same** in both time periods. Selling price per unit is a straightforward calculation.
>
> You then have enough information to draw up the chart. You can always calculate breakeven point and margin of safety and compare them with your chart to ensure that you have marked them on the chart correctly. (Did you actually see the note in the requirements asking you to show them on the chart?)
>
> Part (b) involves **multi-product** CVP analysis. The data for the chart is not difficult to derive, but the calculation of breakeven point must be based on contribution per mix, **the standard mix being one own label, one BB brand**.
>
> An exam question will invariably ask for some written analysis, and this question is no exception. The points you need to make are not particularly technical, but are simply grounded in common sense. If option 2 shows the higher profit, **lower breakeven point** (so that **not so many sales are required to cover costs**) and **a higher margin of safety** (which means that the **difference between expected sales and breakeven sales is likely to be higher**), it should be the better option. There are, of course, **other factors** that might affect that decision.

Assumption. Manufacturing costs for the BB brand will be the same as for own label brands.

Initial workings

Manufacturing costs

We need to analyse the cost behaviour patterns by separating the manufacturing costs into their fixed and variable elements, using the high-low method.

	Sales Millions	Costs $ million
20X3	19	4.45
20X2	18	4.30
	1	0.15

Variable manufacturing cost per can = $0.15

Fixed manufacturing cost = $4.45 million – (19 million × $0.15)
  = $1.6 million

Selling prices

Selling price per can in 20X3	= 6.27/19	= $0.33
∴ Unit contribution per can	= $0.33 – $0.15	= $0.18
∴ Contribution per can of BB brand	= $0.18 × 133 1/3%	= $0.24
Variable cost per can of BB brand	= $0.15 + $0.02	= $0.17
∴ Selling price per can of BB brand	= $0.17 + $0.24	= $0.41

(a) **Data for chart**

		$ million	$ million
Variable costs	(19 million × $0.15)		2.85
Fixed costs: manufacturing		1.60	
administration		1.20	
			2.80
Total costs			5.65

Breakeven point $= \dfrac{\text{fixed costs}}{\text{contribution}} = \dfrac{\$2.8\text{m}}{\$0.18}$

$= 15.55$ million cans

$= \$5.13$ million sales

Margin of safety $= 19\text{m} - 15.55\text{m} = 3.45$ million cans $= \$1.14$ million sales

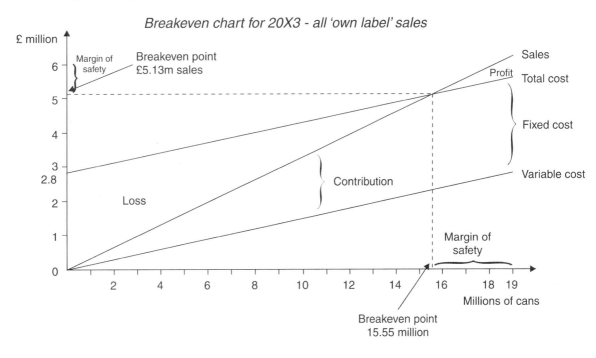

Breakeven chart for 20X3 - all 'own label' sales

(b) **Data for chart**

		$ million	$ million
Variable costs:	own label (9.5m × $0.15)		1.425
	BB brand (9.5m × $0.17)		1.615
			3.040
Fixed costs: manufacturing		1.600	
administration		1.200	
marketing		0.400	
			3.200
Total costs:			6.240
Sales value: own label (9.5m × $0.33)			3.135
BB brand (9.5m × $0.41)			3.895
			7.030

Our standard mix is 1 own label, 1 BB brand.

$$\text{Breakeven point} = \frac{\text{fixed costs}}{\text{contribution per mix}} = \frac{\$3.2m}{\$(0.18 + 0.24)} = \frac{\$3.2m}{\$0.42}$$

$$= 7.62 \text{ million mixes} = 15.24 \text{ million cans}$$

$$= 7.62 \times (\$(0.33 + 0.41)) \text{ million sales} = \$5.64 \text{ million sales}$$

Margin of safety $= 19m - 15.24 \text{ million} = 3.76 \text{ million cans} = 1.88 \text{ million mixes}$

$$= 1.88 \times (\$(0.33 + 0.41)) \text{ million sales}$$

$$= \$1.39 \text{ million sales}$$

Profit $= \$7.03 \text{ million} - \$6.24 \text{ million} = \$790,000$

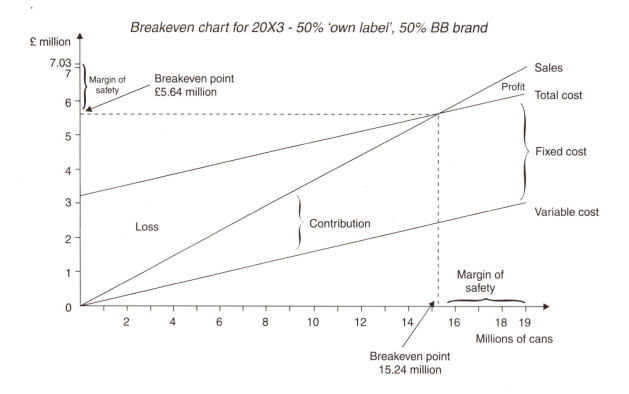

Breakeven chart for 20X3 - 50% 'own label', 50% BB brand

(c) The **first chart** shows a breakeven point of 15.55 million cans ($5.13m sales value) and a margin of safety of 3.45 million cans ($1.14m sales value). Forecast profit for sales of 19 million cans is $620,000.

The **second chart** shows a breakeven point of 15.24 million cans ($5.64m sales value) and a margin of safety of 3.76 million cans ($1.39m sales value). Forecast profit for sales of 19 million cans is $790,000.

Option 2 therefore results in a higher profit figure, as well as a lower breakeven point and increased margin of safety. On this basis it is the better of the two options.

Other factors which management should consider before making a decision

(i) The supermarket chains may put the same pressure on margins and prices of the BB brand as they do on the own label brands.

(ii) Customers may realise that the BB brand is the same product as the own label brand and may not be willing to pay the premium price.

(iii) If the mix of sales can be changed in favour of the BB brand then profits will improve still further.

11 PN Motor Components

> **Top tips.** In part (a) you should have disregarded the information about fixed costs. You should have taken into account the setting-up costs, however, as they do vary with the volume of production and so are marginal costs.
>
> Many candidates find the discussion parts of questions the most difficult and so don't worry if your list of 'factors' in part (a) is far shorter than ours.

(a)   The **lowest selling price** of one batch of 200 units is **one which covers the marginal cost of production**. This comprises the variable costs of materials, labour, overheads and setting up.

Marginal cost per unit calculation

	Machine group 1 $	Machine group 7 $	Machine group 29 $	Assembly $	Total $
Materials	26.00	17.00	–	3.00	46.00
Labour	2.00	1.60	0.75	1.20	5.55
Variable overheads	0.65	0.72	0.80	0.36	2.53
Setting-up costs (÷ 200)	0.05	0.03	0.02	–	0.10
	28.70	19.35	1.57	4.56	54.18

The lowest selling price per batch is therefore $54.18 × 200 = $10,836.

The calculations show that the marginal cost of one batch of 200 units is $10,836 and this is therefore the lowest possible price that can be offered. However, to sell at such a price would mean that the component would make no contribution to fixed costs and such costs must be covered if the company is to make a profit.

Other factors to be considered when adopting such a pricing policy include the following.

(i)   It is inappropriate to set prices with reference only to an organisation's internal cost structure. Of equal **importance** is the **wider market environment** and the **pricing strategy of competitors**.

(ii)   The organisation must **take into account the likely reaction of competitors**. For example, such a policy could trigger off a price war in which the company could lose more than it gains.

(iii)   The organisation **cannot continue to sell at the minimum price indefinitely**. It must therefore decide its future plans for the component. Will it reduce costs or increase prices? It may, however, take longer than the organisation imagines to be able to charge the full price for the component.

(iv)   The organisation should consider the approach to be taken if existing customers for the component discover the 'special price' being offered to other customers. **Will the organisation gain a few new customers at the expense of alienating existing valuable customers?**

(b)   **We begin by calculating the contribution per unit at different sales prices and sales volumes.**

Outputs and sales up to 7,000 units

Total demand	Selling price $	Variable cost $	Contribution $
5,000 boxes	13.00	6.20	6.80
6,000 boxes	12.00	6.20	5.80
7,200 boxes	11.00	6.20	4.80
11,200 boxes	10.00	6.20	3.80
13,400 boxes	9.00	6.20	2.80

BPP
LEARNING MEDIA

Outputs and sales above 7,000 units

Total demand	Supplied by sub-contractor	Selling price $	Variable cost $	Contribution $
7,200 boxes	200 boxes	11.00	7.75	3.25
11,200 boxes	4,200 boxes	10.00	7.75	2.25
13,400 boxes	6,400 boxes	9.00	7.00	2.00

The total contribution at different sales levels can now be found.

Selling Price $	Demand $	Own boxes sold	Unit contrib'n $	Sub contr's boxes	Unit contrib'n $	Total contrib'n $
13.00	5,000	5,000	6.80	0		34,000
12.00	6,000	6,000	5.80	0		34,800
11.00	7,200	7,000	4.80	200	3.25	34,250
10.00	11,200	7,000	3.80	4,200	2.25	36,050
9.00	13,400	7,000	2.80	6,400	2.00	32,400

The calculations show that contribution and therefore profit are maximised at a selling price of $10 with sales of 11,200 boxes.

12 DX

> **Top tips.** The way to tackle this sort of question is to read through the information twice and then to formulate it mathematically, taking care to define your variables as you go. You should then find that you have condensed all the information into a few simple equations.

Profit will be maximised when marginal cost (MC) equals marginal revenue (MR).

Let x = the number of thousands of units sold

For values of x up to 80,

$$MC = 2 - 0.025x + 0.5 + 1$$
$$MC = 3.5 - 0.025x$$

For values of x between 80 and 100,

$$MC = 0.5 + 1 = 1.5$$

For values of x above 100,

$$MC = 0.5 + 1 + 0.0025(x - 100)$$
$$MC = 1.25 + 0.0025x$$

If the profit-maximising output is below 80,000 units, it is at

$$9 - 0.06x = 3.5 - 0.025x$$
$$5.5 = 0.035x$$
$$x = 157.14$$

This is above 80,000 units, so the profit-maximising output is not below 80,000 units.

If the profit-maximising output is between 80,000 and 100,000 units, it is at

$$9 - 0.06x = 1.5$$
$$7.5 = 0.06x$$
$$x = 125$$

This is above 100,000 units, so the profit-maximising output is not between 80,000 and 100,000 units.

The profit-maximising output is therefore at

$$10 - 0.08x = 1.25 + 0.0025x$$
$$8.75 = 0.0825x$$
$$x = 106.061$$

The profit-maximising output is 106,061 units.

13 Plastic tools

> **Top tips.** The techniques required in this question are extremely **straightforward** (calculation of overhead absorption rates for example) so beware of making a silly arithmetical error.

Calculation of overhead absorption rates

	Moulding dept $'000	*Finishing dept* $'000	*General factory overhead* $'000
Variable overhead			
Initial allocation	1,600	500	1,050
Reapportion general overhead (800:600)	600	450	(1,050)
Total variable overhead	2,200	950	–
Budgeted machine hours	800	600	
Variable overhead rate per hour	$2.75	$1.58	
	$'000	$'000	$'000
Fixed overhead			
Initial allocation	2,500	850	1,750
Reapportion general overhead (1,200:800)	1,050	700	(1,750)
Total fixed overhead	3,550	1,550	–
Budgeted machine hours	800	600	
Fixed overhead rate per hour	$4.44	$2.58	

Information to assist with the pricing decision

		$ per unit	$ per unit
Direct material			9.00
Direct labour:	moulding dept (2 × $5)	10.00	
	finishing dept (3 × $5.50)	16.50	
			26.50
Variable overhead:	moulding dept (4 × $2.75)	11.00	
	finishing dept (3 × $1.58)	4.74	
			15.74
Variable manufacturing cost			51.24
Fixed overhead:	moulding dept (4 × $4.44)	17.76	
	finishing dept (3 × $2.58)	7.74	
			25.50
Full manufacturing cost			76.74

A **full-cost plus price** will be **based on this cost** of $76.74 **plus a mark-up** of between 25% and 35%. Taking a high, low and average mark-up, the potential prices are as follows.

	25% mark-up $ per unit	*30% mark-up* $ per unit	*35% mark-up* $ per unit
Full manufacturing cost	76.74	76.74	76.74
Mark-up	19.19	23.02	26.86
Full cost-plus price	95.93	99.76	103.60

Certain incremental or specific fixed costs have been identified, however, and these should be borne in mind for a well-informed pricing decision.

Product cost based on incremental fixed costs

	$'000	$ per unit
Variable manufacturing cost		51.24
Incremental fixed costs: supervision	20	
depreciation	120	
Advertising	27	
	167	
Incremental fixed cost per unit (÷ 20,000 (W))		8.35
Incremental total cost per unit		59.59

Working

Total market = 200,000 units per annum

Ten per cent market share = 20,000 units per annum

14 Costs and pricing

> **Top tips.** In part (a), there is a lot of information in question 13 that you can use when suggesting a suitable price range. Your **higher-level skills** are required, however. Make sensible comments on the various possible prices.
>
> The most important point to make in (b) is that **cost is not the only factor to consider** when setting prices, although of course it must be considered. This part of the question is only worth 5 marks, so you should only spend a maximum of **9 minutes** on it. It would have been very easy to wander from the point and discuss the various pricing approaches in detail.

(a)   The cost information provides a range of bases for a pricing decision.

Variable manufacturing cost

The variable manufacturing cost is $51.24 per unit. At a price below this level there would be no contribution to fixed overheads. Since the prevailing market price is between $90 and $100 each, such a low price might suggest that the product is of inferior quality.

Incremental total cost

The incremental total cost per unit is $59.59. Management must select a price above this level to be sure of covering all costs associated with this product. This unit rate depends on achieving an annual volume of 20,000 units.

Full manufacturing cost

The full manufacturing cost per unit is $76.74. A price based on this cost will ensure that all costs are covered in the long run, if the annual volume of 20,000 units is achieved. Since competitors' prices range between $90 and $100 it seems possible that the company can compete with a price calculated on a full cost-plus basis.

The range of prices suggested, using the company's usual mark-up of between 25 per cent and 35 per cent, is $95.93 to $103.60 per unit.

Given the current price range of the competitors' products and the fact that the product is expected to offer some improvement over competitors' products, a price towards the upper end of the suggested range would be appropriate.

(b)   In general, the **price charged** for a product should **exceed its cost**. There are a number of different cost-based approaches to pricing, however, and each is appropriate in different circumstances.

Full-cost plus pricing involves adding a profit margin to the fully absorbed total cost of a product. In certain situations, for example if an organisation has spare capacity, it may be appropriate to use **marginal cost** as the basis for pricing. Alternatively if the lowest possible price is sought, perhaps for strategic reasons, a **minimum** price based on **relevant costs** may be used as the basis for a pricing decision. Management must not lose sight of the need to cover fixed costs in the long run, however.

Whichever cost basis is used, it is important to appreciate that a cost-based price merely provides a **starting point for informed management decisions and pricing negotiations.**

Cost is **only one of the factors to bear in mind** when making a price-setting decision. Other factors to consider will include the organisation's objectives, the market in which the organisation operates and the effect which price has on the volume of demand for its goods.

15 Hilly plc

Demand function $\quad$ P $= a - bx$

$\qquad\qquad\qquad$ b $= 20/25{,}000 = 0.0008$

$\qquad\qquad\qquad\qquad$ When P = 500, x = 500,000

$\therefore$ 500 $= a - (500{,}000 \times 0.0008)$

$\therefore$ 500 $= a - 400$

$\therefore a = 900$

Demand function is therefore

P $= 900 - 0.0008x$

Maximise profit when MR $=$ MC

Marginal or variable cost per unit

	$ per unit
Material (2kg × $60)	120
Labour	40
Variable overhead	20
Total variable cost per unit (MC)	180

The marginal revenue (MR) function is

$\qquad$ MR $\qquad = a - 2bx$

$\qquad \therefore$ 180 $\qquad = 900 - (2 \times 0.0008)\, x$

$\qquad \therefore$ 720 $\qquad = 0.0016x$

$\qquad \therefore$ x $\qquad = 450{,}000$ units

Substituting x = 450,000 in the demand function

P $= 900 - (0.0008 \times 450{,}000)$
P $= \ 540$

The profit-maximising level of sales is 450,000 units at a price of $540 per unit.

16 Dench

> **Top tips**. Part (a) uses a table to calculate the cumulative average time per batch. This is based on output doubling (cumulative batches) and the time taken reducing by 0.80 for each doubling of batches. You can also use the formula $Y_x = aX^b$ to work out the cumulative average time per batch.

(a)   Cost estimate for 225 components is based upon the following assumptions:

   (1)   the first batch of 15 is excluded from the order (and total cost for first batch is likewise excluded); and

   (2)   the 80% learning rate only applies to the skilled workforce (and related variable overhead), due to their high level of expertise/low turnover rate.

Cumulative batches	Cumulative units	Total time (hrs)	Cum. ave time/batch (hrs)
1	15	20	20
2	30	32	16
4	60	51.2	12.8
8	120	81.92	10.24
16	240	131.072	8.192

Total cost for 16 batches (240 components):

		$
Material A:	$30/batch	480
Material B:	$30/batch	480
Labour:	Skilled 131.072 hr @ $15/hr	1,966
	Semi-skilled $40/batch	640
Variable O.H.:	131.072 hr @ $4/hr	524
	5 hr/batch at $4/hr	320
		4,410
Less: cost for 1st batch (15 components)		(500)
... cost for 225 components		$3,910

(b)   The limited use of learning curve theory is due to several factors:

   (i)   the learning curve phenomenon is not always present;

   (ii)   it assumes stable conditions at work (e.g. of the labour force and labour mix) which will enable learning to take place. This is not always practicable (e.g. because of labour turnover);

   (iii)   it must also assume a certain degree of motivation amongst employees;

   (iv)   extensive breaks between production of items must not be too long, or workers will 'forget' and the learning process would have to begin all over again;

   (v)   it is difficult to obtain enough accurate data to decide what the learning curve rate is;

   (vi)   there will be a cessation to learning eventually, once the job has been repeated often enough.

17 Cost reduction

> **Top tips**. Parts (a) and (b) shouldn't have given you major problems. Or did you find it difficult to think of three **cost control techniques**? As you will see from our answer, however, these include some of the principal **conventional management accounting techniques**, only it is not always usual to explicitly describe them as such!
>
> **Part (c)** required a little more thought. Try to give **reasoned arguments** that look at **both sides** of the proposition. Don't be afraid to be vaguely critical of management accounting training, but be extremely polite about it, as we have been. Always provide some sort of **conclusion** to your discussion.

(a)   **Cost control** is the regulation of the costs of operating a business and is concerned with keeping costs within acceptable limits.

In contrast, **cost reduction** is a planned and positive approach to reducing expenditure. It starts with an assumption that current or planned cost levels are too high and looks for ways of reducing them without reducing effectiveness.

Cost control action ought to lead to a reduction in excessive spending (for example when material wastage is higher than budget levels or productivity levels are below agreed standards). However, a cost reduction programme is directed towards reducing expected cost levels below current budgeted or standard levels.

Cost control tends to be carried out on a routine basis whereas cost reduction programmes are often ad hoc exercises.

(b)   **Three examples of cost control techniques**

   (i)   **Budgetary control**. Cost control is achieved by setting predetermined absolute levels for expenditure. If flexible budgeting is used then the budget cost allowance can be flexed in line with changes in activity. Control action is taken if actual expenditure differs from planned expenditure by an excessive amount.

   (ii)   **Standard costing**. Designed to control unit costs rather than absolute levels of expenditure, the use of standard costing depends on the existence of a measurable output which is produced in standard operations. Control action is taken if the actual unit costs differ from standard unit costs by an excessive amount.

   (iii)   **Limits on authority to incur expenditure**. Many organisations restrict the authority for their managers to incur expenditure. For example a budget manager may have an overall budget for overheads in a period, but even within this budget the manager may be required to seek separate authorisation for individual items of expenditure which are above a certain amount.

Three examples of cost reduction techniques

   (i)   **Value analysis**. CIMA defines value analysis as 'a systematic inter-disciplinary examination of factors affecting the cost of a product or service, in order to devise means of achieving the specified purpose most economically at the required standard of quality and reliability.' The aim in a value analysis exercise is to eliminate unnecessary costs without reducing the use value, the esteem value or the exchange value of the item under consideration.

   (ii)   **Work study**. This is a means of raising the production efficiency of an operating unit by the reorganisation of work. The two main parts to work study are method study and work measurement. Method study is the most significant in the context of cost reduction. It looks at the way in which work is done and attempts to develop easier and more effective methods in order to reduce costs.

      (iii)   **Variety reduction**. This involves standardisation of parts and components which can offer enormous cost reduction potential for some manufacturing industries. Variety reduction can also be used to describe the standardisation or simplification of an organisation's product range.

(c)   The **statement suggests** that the training of management accountants should place the major **emphasis on cost reduction**.

This is true to some extent because of the changes in the competitive environment and the globalisation of markets. In order to remain competitive an organisation must provide goods and services of the right quality at prices which are attractive to the customer.

The **Japanese** in particular view costs as a **target** which must be reached rather than as a limit on expenditure. They employ cost reduction techniques to bring costs down below a target price with the result that prices dictate costs and not vice versa.

If companies are to compete effectively then they must adopt a similar philosophy. The management accountant needs to be trained to provide information which is useful for cost planning and cost reduction. An emphasis on cost control might create a tendency to concentrate effort and resources on the mechanics of recording and reporting historic costs, rather than on the planning and reducing of future costs.

On the other hand it is **still necessary to control costs** and to record and report actual costs so that management can take control action if necessary. An efficient plan will ensure that the organisation is starting out with the most effective cost targets, but only by recording the actual costs and comparing them with the targets will management know whether those targets have been achieved.

Despite the implied criticism of management accounting training, an increasing awareness of the need for a **more strategic approach to management accounting** does exist, both among trainee and qualified management accountants. Active discussion is also taking place on the need to adapt information systems to be more useful in an advanced manufacturing technology environment.

In **conclusion** while there may be a case for a **slight change in emphasis** in the training of management accountants, this should not lead to the total abandonment of cost control principles and techniques.

18 Life cycle costing

> **Top tips**. See how we have set out our answer with two headings addressing the two requirements in the question.

Life cycle costs

Life cycle costs are the **costs incurred on products and services from their design stage, through development to market launch, production and sales, and their eventual withdrawal from the market**. A product's life cycle costs might therefore be classified as follows.

(a)   Acquisition costs (costs of research, design, testing, production and construction)

(b)   Product distribution costs (transportation and handling)

(c)   Maintenance costs (customer service, field maintenance and 'in-factory' maintenance)

(d)   Operation costs (the costs incurred in operations, such as energy costs, and various facility and other utility costs)

(e)   Training costs (operator and maintenance training)

(f)   Inventory costs (the cost of holding spare parts, warehousing and so on)

(g)   Technical data costs (cost of purchasing any technical data)

(h)   Retirement and disposal costs (costs occurring at the end of the product's life)

Life cycle costing versus traditional management accounting systems

(a)   **Traditional management accounting practice**

This is, in general, to report costs at the physical production stage of the life cycle of a product; costs are not accumulated over the entire life cycle. Such practice **does not, therefore, assess a product's profitability over its entire life but rather on a periodic basis**. Costs tend to be accumulated according to function; research, design, development and customer service costs incurred on all products during a period are totalled and recorded as a period expense.

(b)   **Life cycle costing**

(i)   Using **life cycle costing**, on the other hand, such **costs are traced to individual products over complete life cycles**. These accumulated costs are compared with the revenues attributable to each product and hence the **total profitability of any given product can be determined**. Moreover, by gathering costs for each product, the relationship between the choice of design adopted and the resulting marketing and production costs becomes clear.

(ii)   The **control function** of life cycle costing lies in the **comparison of actual and budgeted life cycle costs for a product**. Such comparisons allow for the refinement of future decisions about product design, lead to more effective resource allocation and show whether expected savings from using new production methods or technology have been realised.

Life cycle costing and AMT environments

Research has shown that, for organisations operating within an **advanced manufacturing technology environment**, approximately **90% of a product's life-cycle cost is determined by decisions made early within the life cycle**. In such an environment there is therefore a **need to ensure that the tightest cost controls are at the design stage**, because the majority of costs are committed at this point. This necessitates the need for a management accounting system that assists in the planning and control of a product's life cycle costs, which monitors spending and commitments to spend during the early stages of a product's life cycle and which recognises the reduced life cycle and the subsequent challenge to profitability of products produced in an AMT environment. Life cycle costing is such a system.

Summary

Life cycle costing **increases the visibility of costs such as those associated with research, design, development and customer service**, and also enables **individual product profitability to be more fully understood** by attributing all costs to products. As a consequence, more **accurate feedback** information is available **on the organisation's success or failure in developing new products. In today's competitive environment, where the ability to produce new and updated versions of products is of paramount importance to the survival of the organisation**, this information is vital.

19 ABC

> **Top tips.** Requirements such as these are just the sort of thing you might encounter as parts of questions in the exam. You are expected to be able to critically appraise the management accounting techniques and methods included in the syllabus so don't be afraid to be critical of a view used as the basis for a question.

(a) **ABC** attempts to **relate all costs**, with the possible exception of facility sustaining costs, to **cost objects** such as products, services or customers. It does this by **collecting costs/resources** and **relating them to either primary or support activities via resource cost drivers. Support activity costs are then spread across primary activities**. Finally the **costs of the primary activities** are **related** to **cost units using activity cost drivers**.

It is likely that ABC will **provide a different picture of product costs than that produced using traditional absorption costing**. This is because different assumptions are made because the costs are spread across the activities, etc. As both methods make assumptions about the behaviour and cause of costs, it is impossible to say categorically that ABC results are more accurate than those produced using traditional absorption costing.

Nevertheless there are usually more activities than cost centres and this should make the process **more accurate**. Furthermore it is **easier to justify the selection of cost driver rates** with ABC than the absorption rates used with traditional absorption costing. ABC also allows costs to be accumulated per batch or per number of products made, as well as per unit.

These factors all suggest that in most cases ABC will produce a more accurate answer.

(b) Some commentators argue that only marginal costing provides suitable information for decision making. This is untrue. Marginal costing provides a crude method of differentiating between different types of cost behaviour by splitting costs into their variable and fixed elements. **Marginal costing** can only be used for **short-term decisions** and usually even these have longer-term implications which ought to be considered.

ABC spreads costs across products or other cost units according to a number of different bases. The analysis may show that one activity which is carried out for one or two products is expensive. If costs have been apportioned using the traditional method prior to this the cost of this activity is likely to have been spread across all products, thus hiding the fact that the products using this activity may be loss making. If these costs are not completely variable costs but are, for example, batch costs, marginal costing would not have related them to the products at all. Therefore **ABC** can be used to make **decisions about pricing, discontinuing products**, and so on.

20 ABC systems

> **Top tips.** This old syllabus pilot paper question was not easy, in that you may have had difficulty in finding enough to write about to justify 10 marks. To get close to full marks you should expand your argument to include ABM.

To a certain extent Drury is correct when he states that ABC systems are resource-consumption models.

When ABC systems were first discussed companies were using other systems, usually absorption-based, for the purposes of inventory valuation. ABC analysis and supporting calculations would be carried out using actual data to see what the 'actual' costs of products were as a way of improving decision making and operational control.

In this retrospective context ABC starts with the processes of allocating costs to cost pools and determining an appropriate cost driver. For example $250,000 may have been spent on labour and materials for the packing department which processed 25,000 customer orders. This results in a cost of $10 per order to trace back to products, where 'number of orders' is the identified cost driver.

Clearly, in this context, ABC is looking at the **cost of using resources** within the packing department.

Increasingly, however, companies are using ABC as their main costing system but as part of a broader system of **activity based management** (ABM). Here an **activity based budget** (ABB) will be prepared, using budgeted costs and levels of activity, and compared to the ABC figures over the period for the purposes of exercising control.

It is likely that when the ABB is being prepared it will start with expected sales volumes and from there consider what activities will be required in order to generate the required volume of product. Thus the example above would shift emphasis from 'we spent $250,000 in packing last year' to 'how much resource should we supply the packing department with so as to have them pack the expected volume?' If the ABB is accurate then the ABB figure for packing will be the same as the figures obtained through ABC.

Hopefully companies that are using ABC are using it in the broader context of ABM so as to be able to obtain a broader range of benefits. Although ABC in isolation does focus on resource consumption, **ABM will consider both the consumption and the supply of resources.**

21 Abkaber plc

> **Top tips.** There is a lot of information in this question and in an exam situation it is one you would probably make use of some of the 20 minutes' reading time. Make sure you show your workings clearing (cross-referencing if possible) – there are quite a few easy marks that can be picked up in part (a). In part (b) make sure your answer is in the form of a report, as specified in the question and relate your answer to the company in the scenario.

(a)(i) **Existing method**

	Sunshine	Roadster	Fireball
	$	$	$
Direct labour ($5 per hr) (W1)	1,000,000	1,100,000	400,000
Materials (W2)	800,000	960,000	360,000
Overheads (at $24) (W3)	4,800,000	5,280,000	1,920,000
Total costs	6,660,000	7,340,000	2,680,000
Output (Units)	2,000	1,600	400
	$	$	$
Selling price	4,000	6,000	8,000
Cost per unit (W4)	3,300	4,587.5	6,700
	700	1,412.5	1,300
Total profit	$	$	$
(output in units × profit/unit)	1,400,000	2,260,000	520,000

Total profit = $4,180,000

Workings

1   **Labour cost**

Sunshine 200,000 hrs × $5 per hour =1,000,000

Roadster 220,000 hrs × $5 per hour =1,100,000

Fireball   80,000 hrs × $5 per hour =400,000

2   **Material cost**

Sunshine $2,000 \times 400 =$ 800,000

Roadster $1,600 \times 600 =$ 960,000

Fireball $400 \times 900 =$ 360,000

3   **Overhead per labour hour**

	$
Total overhead cost =	12,000,000
Total labour hours =	500,000 hrs

$$\text{Overhead per labour hour} = \frac{\$12,000,000}{500,000} = \$24$$

4   **Cost per unit**

Sunshine: $\dfrac{\text{Total costs}}{\text{Units produced}} = \dfrac{6,600,000}{2,000} = \$3,300$

Roadster: $\dfrac{\text{Total costs}}{\text{Units produced}} = \dfrac{7,340,000}{1,600} = \$4,587.50$

Fireball: $\dfrac{\text{Total costs}}{\text{Units produced}} = \dfrac{2,680,000}{400} = \$6,700$

(ii)   **Activity based costing**

	Sunshine	Roadster	Fireball
	$	$	$
Direct labour ($5 per hr) (as (W1) above)	1,000,000	1,100,000	400,000
Materials (as (W2) above)	800,000	960,000	360,000
Overheads			
Deliveries (W5(a))	960,000	768,000	672,000
Set up costs (W5(b))	2,100,000	2,400,000	1,500,000
Purchase orders (W5(c))	1,800,000	1,350,000	450,000
	6,600,000	6,578,000	3,382,000
Output units	2,000	1,600	400
	$	$	$
Selling price	4,000	6,000	8,000
Cost per unit (W4)	3,330	4,111.25	8,455
Profit/(loss) per unit	670	1,888.75	(455)
Total profit/(loss)	$1,340,000	$3,022,000	($182,000)

Total profit = $4,180,000

Workings

5   **Overheads**

$$\frac{\text{Overhead cost of deliveries to retailers}}{\text{Total number of deliveries}} = \frac{2,400,000}{250} = \$9,600$$

$$\frac{\text{Overhead cost of set - ups}}{\text{Total number of set - ups}} = \frac{6,000,000}{100} = \$60,000$$

$$\frac{\text{Overhead cost of purchase orders}}{\text{Total number of purchase orders}} = \frac{3,600,000}{800} = \$4,500$$

5(a)   **Deliveries overheads**

Sunshine $9,600 × 100 = $960,000

Roadster $9,600 × 80 = $768,000

Fireball $9,600 × 70 = $672,000

5(b)   **Set-up cost overheads**

Sunshine $60,000 × 35 = $2,100,000

Roadster $60,000 × 40 = $2,400,000

Fireball $60,000 × 25 = $1,500,000

5(c)   **Purchase order overheads**

Sunshine $4,500 × 400 = $1,800,000

Roadster $4,500 × 300 = $1,350,000

Fireball $4,500 × 100 = $450,000

(b)   **REPORT**

To: Directors, Abkaber plc
From: Management accountant
Subject: The implications of activity based costing
Date: 12.12.X2

(i)   **Labour hours and activity based costing allocation**

Labour hours

For the allocation of overheads on the basis of labour hours to be appropriate, there would need to be a direct relationship between overheads and labour hours. From the information available, this does not appear to be the case.

A traditional method of cost allocation, such as the one based on labour hours, was developed when an enterprise produced a narrow range of products which underwent similar operations and consumed similar proportions of overheads. Moreover, when such methods were being widely used, overhead costs were only a very small proportion of total costs, with direct labour and material costs accounting for the largest proportion of total costs.

Abkaber plc has invested in new technology and as a result has significantly reduced the size of its workforce. Direct labour costs now account for a relatively smaller proportion of total costs with overheads making up the highest single cost item. Allocation of overheads on the basis of labour costs would tend to allocate too great a proportion of overheads to the higher volume Sunshine than the lower volume Fireball, ignoring the fact that the lower volume product may require relatively more support services. It therefore seems likely that attributing overheads on the basis of labour hours may lead to inappropriate decisions.

Activity based costing

Activity based costing attempts to overcome this problem by identifying the factors which cause the costs of an organisation's major activities.

The idea behind activity based costing is that activities such as ordering, materials handling, deliveries and set up cause costs. Producing goods creates demand for activities. Costs are assigned to a product on the basis of the product's consumption of activities.

Supporters of ABC argue that it is activities that generate costs, not labour hours.

The accuracy of any ABC system will depend on the appropriateness of the activities as cost drivers. Each cost driver selected should be appropriate to the overheads to which it relates. There should be a direct and proportionate relationship between the relevant overhead costs and the cost driver selected.

The labour hours costing system and ABC result in markedly different profit figures, especially with respect to the Fireball which appears profitable under the first system but loss making under ABC.

The reason for this is that, although the Fireball uses twice as many hours per unit as the Sunshine, its low output volume of only 400 units (compared with 2,000 units of Sunshine) means that a proportionately lower amount of overheads is absorbed.

Under activity based costing, the Fireball shows a loss because ABC recognises the relatively high set-up costs, deliveries and purchase orders.

(ii) **Finance director's comments**

The finance director is questioning the viability of the Fireball, but doubts whether ABC provides more information than the labour hours costing method.

ABC helps to company focus on the fact that the low volumes of Fireball involve a disproportionate amount of set-up costs, deliveries and purchase orders, resulting in a relatively higher allocation of overheads.

It may be the case that a review of current activities relating to Fireball may reduce costs. There are also other, non-financial, considerations for continuing to produce the Fireball. As the more expensive of the three products, it may have brand value and help raise the reputation of the company as well as that of the other models.

Marketing director's comments

The marketing director is questioning the suitability of ABC in helping price a major new contract.

(1) The accuracy of ABC depends on the appropriateness of the cost drivers identified. Although more appropriate than the labour hours allocation basis, for the type of one-off decision the marketing director needs to make, an incremental cost approach may be better.

(2) There may be factors both financial and non-financial that ABC may not be able to capture. For example, there may be costs common to more than one product, interdependencies between costs and revenues, or interdependencies between the sales volumes of the different products.

The relationship between costs and activities is based on historic observations which may not be a reliable guide to the future.

Managing director's comments

The MD is correct to question the fact that ABC assumes that the cost per activity is constant. In practice, the existence of a learning curve may mean that the costs per activity are going down as the activity is repeated.

The MD is correct in questioning the inclusion of fixed costs which do not vary with either labour hours or any cost driver and thus show no cause and effect relationship under ABC.

Chairman's comments

As (i) and (ii) above illustrate, the overall profit under the two methods is the same. However, it would not be appropriate to dismiss the two approaches as irrelevant.

(1) If the company carried inventory, then the method of cost allocation would affect the inventory valuation and consequently profit.

(2)   It is important to understand both the strengths and limitations of ABC as a decision making tool. Although it may appear to be more appropriate than labour hours in the allocation of overheads there are financial and non-financial factors that ABC does not capture. A decision to discontinue production of the Fireball should not be made without the consideration of these factors. These may include:

- Existence of a learning curve
- The inclusion of fixed costs that do not vary with level of activity
- Interdependencies of cost and revenues
- Interdependencies of sales of the three products

Further considerations

Abkaber plc will need to continue evaluating the activities identified and the relationship between cost drivers and overheads.

(c)   Unit level costs are costs that are driven by the number of units produced or delivered.

Batch costs are those costs which increase when a batch of items is made, for example, set up costs.

Product sustainability costs are costs that are incurred by the production/development of a product range. Advertising costs are often driven by the number of product lines.

Facility sustaining costs are not related to particular products but instead relate to maintaining the building and facilities, eg. rent, rates.

22 CPA

Top tips. This is a fairly straightforward question. You can pick up marks straight away by using a report format as requested.

REPORT

To: Management of XY Ltd
From: Management accountant
Date: 20/05/X0

Title: **XY Ltd's profitability in relation to the number of our customers served**

1   **Concept encapsulated by the graph**

1.1   The graph illustrates what is often referred to as the 80:20 rule, that is that 80% of our profits are generated by a core 20% of our customer base.

2   **Application of the principle**

2.1   The same principle (known as Pareto analysis) can be applied in other spheres. For example, in information systems, 20% of systems design effort may provide systems meeting 80% of business requirements, with 80% of the effort being expended to meet the final 20% of requirements.

2.2   In the case of profitability in relation to the customer base, those 20% of customers who buy our standard product, pay invoices in full and on time and in all other respects conform to our procedures will be the ones who generate 80% of our profits. The other 80% of our customers will generate further costs through their non-compliance with our processes.

3   **Improving the profitability of the organisation**

3.1   To build upon the principles of the 80:20 rule there are a number of steps which can be taken.

3.2   **Conduct a survey of Customer Profitability**. It may be possible to identify specific customers who, as a result of particular requirements they have regarding the product they buy or special ordering or payment procedures they demand, are not being fully charged for the costs which they generate.

3.3 If this is the case a new selling price should be established which does cover the additional costs they generate and if they are not willing to pay this higher price it may be necessary to consider discontinuing supply. Although this may reduce sales revenues it will increase profits because dealings with these customers are likely to be generating losses.

3.4 **Review internal processes**. It may be possible to align these more closely to those of our customers, thus increasing our overall profit.

3.5 The 20% most profitable customers need to be recognised and steps taken to ensure that they are retained and, if possible, sales to them are increased. Marketing need to ensure that these customers' needs are continually being identified and met. Investigations should be conducted to see whether it is possible to increase sales to these customers, for example by encouraging them to use XY Ltd as their sole supplier.

Signed: Management accountant

23 Just-in-time

> **Top tips**. In the exam you would probably only need to provide five (relevant) financial benefits in part (b) to gain the full five marks.

(a) JIT production systems will include the following features.

Multiskilled workers

In a JIT production environment, production processes must be shortened and simplified. **Each product family is made in a workcell based on flowline principles**. The variety and complexity of work carried out in these work cells is increased (compared with more traditional processes), necessitating a group of dissimilar machines working within each work cell. **Workers must therefore be more flexible and adaptable, the cellular approach enabling each operative to operate several machines**. Operatives are trained to operate all machines on the line and undertake **routine preventative maintenance**.

Close relationships with suppliers

JIT production systems often go hand in hand with JIT purchasing systems. **JIT purchasing** seeks to **match the usage of materials with the delivery of materials** from external suppliers. This means that **material inventories can be kept at near-zero levels**. For JIT purchasing to be successful this requires the organisation to have confidence that the supplier will deliver on time and that the supplier will deliver materials of 100% quality, that there will be no rejects, returns and hence no consequent production delays. The **reliability of suppliers is of utmost importance** and hence the company must **build up close relationships** with their suppliers. This can be achieved by doing **more business with fewer suppliers** and placing **long-term orders** so that the supplier is assured of sales and can produce to meet the required demand.

Machine cells

With JIT production, factory layouts must change to reduce movement of workers and products. Traditionally machines were grouped by function (drilling, grinding and so on). A part therefore had to travel long distances, moving from one part of the factory to the other, often stopping along the way in a storage area. All these are non-value-added activities that have to be reduced or eliminated. **Material movements between operations are therefore minimised by eliminating space between work stations and grouping machines or workers by product or component** instead of by type of work performed. Products can flow from machine to machine without having to wait for the next stage of processing or returning to stores. **Lead times and work in progress are thus reduced**.

Quality

Production management within a JIT environment seeks to both **eliminate scrap and defective** units **during production and avoid the need for reworking of units**. Defects stop the production line, thus creating rework and possibly resulting in a failure to meet delivery dates. Quality, on the other hand, reduces costs. Quality is assured by **designing products and processes with quality in mind, introducing quality awareness programmes and statistical checks on output quality**, providing **continual worker training** and implementing **vendor quality assurance programmes** to ensure that the correct product is made to the appropriate quality level on the first pass through production.

Set-up time reduction

If an organisation is able to **reduce manufacturing lead time** it is in a better position to **respond quickly to changes in customer demand**. Reducing set-up time is one way in which this can be done. Machinery set-ups are non-value-added activities which should be reduced or even eliminated. **Reducing set-up time** (and hence set-up costs) also makes the manufacture of **smaller batches more economical and worthwhile**; managers do not feel the need to spread the set-up costs over as many units as possible (which then leads to high levels of inventory). Set-up time can be reduced by the **use of one product or one product family machine cells**, by **training workers** or by the use of **computer integrated manufacturing (CIM)**.

(b)   JIT systems have a number of financial **benefits**.

- Increase in labour productivity due to labour being multiskilled and carrying out preventative maintenance

- Reduction of investment in plant space

- Reduction in costs of storing inventory

- Reduction in risk of inventory obsolescence

- Lower investment in inventory

- Reduction in costs of handling inventory

- Reduction in costs associated with scrap, defective units and reworking

- Higher revenue as a result of reduction in lost sales following failure to meet delivery dates (because of improved quality)

- Reduction in the costs of setting up production runs

- Higher revenues as a result of faster response to customer demands

24 Outsourced services

The **most significant controls** will need to be **implemented at the planning stage of the process of outsourcing a service**.

(a)   The organisation should **document details** of the level and quality of the service it requires from the external organisation.

(b)   External organisations should then be invited to **tender** for providing the service. A documented policy as to the tendering process is required and should cover factors such as the number of bids required, whether the bids should be sealed and so on.

(c)   The organisation must confirm a **price** for the service with the successful bidder.

(d)   **On-going control** involves ensuring that the service delivered is actually of the contracted level and quality.

(e) The organisation must also give consideration to drawing up **policies** to deal with problems which could arise in the following areas.

- Judging the quality of service provided

- Approving any costs in excess of those agreed

- Including a get-out clause in the contract (to be used if the contractor becomes complacent following a desire by the organisation to build up a long-term relationship)

- Including a price increase clause in the contract

- Reducing prices if the level of service is lower than anticipated

25 Responsibility accounting

Top tips. A good exam technique with this type of question is to quickly clarify all of the main technical terms at the beginning of your answer. But don't take too long on this; you have only nine minutes at the very most to write out your complete answer.

Responsibility accounting is a system of accounting that identifies **specific areas of responsibility** or budget centres for all costs incurred by or revenues earned by an organisation. **Functional budgets** are budgets prepared for **each department** or process within an organisation. These functional budgets are then summarised to produce the overall summary or master budget for the whole organisation.

The main function of the system of responsibility accounting is **to identify clear responsibilities** for preparing and achieving budget targets. An individual manager is made responsible for each budget centre and for ensuring that their budget coordinates with all others that are affected by or affect their own activities. **The budgeting process cannot begin without such a system of defined responsibilities**. If individual responsibilities are not clarified at the outset then there may be duplication of effort, some areas may be overlooked completely and managers would not know who to consult when they require information about specific areas of the business.

A clearly defined hierarchy of budget centres is necessary in order to **consolidate and coordinate the master budget for the whole organisation**. The hierarchy can consist of a responsibility centre for each section, department or subsidiary company. For example in a large group the budget for each section would be **summarised** into a **budget** for each **function**. The **functional budgets** in turn would be **summarised** or consolidated into the **subsidiary company's budget** and the individual subsidiaries' budgets would then be summarised into an overall master budget for the group.

The hierarchy of individual budget centres should be organised to ensure that all the revenues earned by an organisation, all the costs it incurs, and all the capital it employs are made the responsibility of someone within the organisation, at an appropriate level in the hierarchy.

26 Budgets and people

Top tips. This question covers a wide range of the possible issues that you could encounter. Make sure that you **deal with both parts** of the question (the reasons for reluctance and the side effects of imposed budgets). Beware, however, of writing down everything you can possibly think of which is remotely related to the behavioural aspects of management accounting.

There is one major **reason why managers may be reluctant to participate** fully in setting up budgets and that is a **lack of education in the purposes of the budgeting process**. The budget's major role is to communicate the various motivations that exist among management so that everybody sees, understands and co-ordinates the goals of the organisation.

Specific reasons for the reluctance of managers to participate are as follows.

(a) Managers view budgets as **too rigid a constraint on their decision making.** For example, a manager may be unable to sanction an item of expenditure if it has not been budgeted for. The natural reaction to this supposed restriction of their autonomy is resistance and self defence.

(b) Managers feel that the top management **goals expressed by the budget will interfere with their personal goals** (for example their desire to 'build an empire' with substantial resources under their control, large personal income and so on). A successful budgetary system will harmonise the budget goals with the managers' personal goals, but it is by no means easy to achieve a successful system.

(c) Managers imagine that the purpose of budgets is to provide senior management with a **rod** with which to chastise those who do not stay within budget. They will be unwilling to help in the construction of such a rod.

(d) Managers view the budgeting process as one in which they must **fight for a fair share** of the organisation's **resources** in competition with colleagues with other responsibilities.

(e) Managers misinterpret the **control function** of the budgeting system to be a method whereby **blame** can be **attached**. By not participating in the budget setting process, they are able to blame an 'unattainable' or 'unrealistic' budget for any poor results they may have.

As a reaction to these uneducated notions, the behaviour of managers involved in budget preparation can conflict with the desires of senior management. Such behaviour is often described as **dysfunctional**; it is counter-productive because it is **not goal congruent.**

The **unwanted side effects** which may arise from the **imposition of budgets** by senior management (for example under an authoritative rather than a participative budgetary system) are examples of **dysfunctional behaviour** and include the following.

(a) There may be a **reluctance to reduce costs** for fear that future budget allowances may be reduced as a consequence of successful cost cutting.

(b) Managers may **spend up to their budget** in order to justify levels of expenditure. This is particularly the case in local government circles where there is a tendency to spend any available cash at the end of a financial year.

(c) There may be **padding**, whereby managers request inflated allowances. In turn senior management may cut budgets where they suspect padding exists. Padding is sometimes called slack and represents the difference between the budget allowance requested and the realistic costs necessary to accomplish the objective.

(d) In extreme cases of authoritative budgeting, the **'emotional' responses** of managers can be highly detrimental to the goals of the organisation, for example non-cooperation.

27 Balanced scorecard

> **Top tips**. We have provided more than one measure for each perspective but you must **not** do this in the exam otherwise you will waste time. You may have thought of other measures that are just as useful but the two key points to remember is that your measures must be **measurable** and **useful**. There is no point in thinking up with the most wonderful item to be monitored if it would not be feasible to collect the relevant data. Also, once the performance indicator is reported to management it **must initiate appropriate action**. There is nothing to be gained by reporting information to managers that they will not be able to act upon.
>
> You might find it difficult at times to decide in which perspective a certain measure belongs. Don't worry about this. There will often be overlap between the perspectives. If you think of a measure just try to put it into the most sensible category and try to ensure that your measures are not all too similar.
>
> Don't forget to explain **why** each measure might be a useful indicator.

Performance indicators that might usefully be monitored by a training company include the following.

Customer perspective

- Number of customer complaints; monitors customer satisfaction
- Average time to complete a booking; monitors customer service

Innovation and learning perspective

- Training expenditure per employee; monitors ability to update staff and lecturer skills
- Percentage of revenue generated by new courses; monitors ability to maintain competitiveness by continual development

Internal perspective

- Number of courses cancelled due to lack of demand; monitors ability to publicise available courses adequately and forecast the demand in the training market
- Response time in producing management accounting information; monitors ability to maintain competitiveness by keeping management informed

Financial perspective

- Return on capital employed; monitors ability to create value for the shareholders
- Revenue growth; monitors ability to maintain market share

28 MPL

> **Top tips**. The key point to note in the scenario detail is that budgets are issued to the responsibility centre managers, implying that an **imposed system** of budgeting is in place. Make sure that you do discuss the advantages **and disadvantages** of participation as requested in the question, as all too often students focus on just the advantages, seeing a participative approach as the panacea for all organisational ills.
>
> In part (a)(iii) you will need to distinguish between controllable and uncontrollable costs. Attributable profit is the profit after all attributable costs have been deducted. Controllable profit is profit before deduction of uncontrollable costs.

(a)   (i)

REPORT

To: Board of Directors of MPL
From: Management accountant
Date: 23 April 20X0
Subject: Budgeting

This report considers our present approach to budgeting, including the appropriateness of the format of the opening statement currently prepared.
Present approach to budgeting

Given that the budgets are **'issued to' budget holders**, they clearly have very **little or no input to the budget process**. Budgets are **set centrally by senior management** and are **imposed** on managers without the managers participating in their preparation.

Although there are advantages to such an approach (for example, strategic plans are likely to be incorporated into planned activities, there is little input from inexperienced or uninformed employees and the period of time taken to draw up the budgets is shorter), **dissatisfaction, defensiveness and low morale** amongst employees who must work with the budgets is often apparent. The budget may be seen as a **punitive device** and **initiative may be stifled**. More importantly, however, it is **difficult for people to be motivated to achieve targets that have been set by somebody else.**

- **Targets** that are **too difficult** will have a **demotivating** effect because **adverse efficiency variances** will always be reported.

- **Easy targets** are also **demotivating** because there is **no sense of achievement** in attaining them.

- **Targets set at the same levels as have been achieved in the past** will be too low and might **encourage budgetary slack**.

Academics have argued that each individual has a **personal 'aspiration level'** which the individual undertakes for himself to reach, and so it may be more appropriate to adopt a **participative approach** to budgeting. Budgets would be developed by the budget holders and would be based on their perceptions of what is achievable and the associated necessary resources.

Managers are more likely to be **motivated** to achieve targets that they have set themselves and overall the budgets are likely to be more **realistic** (as senior management's overview of the business is mixed with operational level details and the expectations of both senior management and the budget holders are considered).

Allowing participation in the budget-setting process is **time consuming**, however, and can produce **budget bias.** It is generally assumed that the bias will operate in one direction only, consultants building **slack** into their budgets so targets are easy to achieve. But **bias can work in two directions.** Optimistic forecasts may be made with the intention of pleasing

senior management, despite the risk of displeasing them when optimistic targets are not met.

(ii) **Format of the operating statement**

The current format of the operating statement classifies costs as either fixed or variable in relation to the number of chargeable consultancy hours and compares expected costs for the budgeted number of chargeable consultancy hours with actual costs incurred.

For **control purposes**, however, there is little point in comparing costs and revenues for the budgeted numbers of chargeable hours with actual costs and revenues if budgeted and actual hours differ. Rather, the **costs that should have been incurred given the actual number of chargeable consultancy hours should be compared with the actual costs incurred.** Although fixed costs should be the same regardless of the hours charged, such a comparison requires **variable costs to be flexed** to the actual activity level. More appropriate **variances** could then be calculated and denoted as either **adverse or favourable.**

The report should also **distinguish** between those **costs** which are **controllable** by the profit centre manager and those which are **uncontrollable.** The manager's attention will then be focused on those variances for which they are responsible and which, if significant, require action.

(iii) **Assumptions**

(1) Central administration costs are not directly attributable to the profit centre and they are outside the control of the profit centre manager.

(2) Depreciation of equipment is an attributable cost, since it ca be specifically identified with the profit centre. However, it is not a controllable cost since the profit centre manager has no control over investment decisions.

Revised operating statement for period 5

	Original budget	Flexed budget	Actual	Variance
Chargeable consultancy hours	2,400	2,500	2,500	100
	€	€	€	€
Fees charged	180,000	187,500	200,000	12,500 (F)
Variable costs				
Casual wages	960	1,000	600	400 (F)
Telephone	2,000	2,083	2,150	67 (A)
Printing, postage and stationery	2,640	2,750	2,590	160 (F)
	5,600	5,833	5,340	493 (F)
Contribution	174,400	181.667	194,660	12,993 (F)
Controllable fixed costs				
Consultant's salaries	80,000	80,000	84,000	4,000 (A)
Motor and travel costs	4,400	4,400	4,400	–
Telephone	600	600	800	200 (A)
	85,000	65,000	89,200	4,200 (A)
Controllable profit	89,400	96,667	105,460	8,793 (F)
Attributable uncontrollable fixed cost	3,200	3,200	3,580	380 (A)
Attributable profit	86,200	93,467	101,880	8,413 (F)
Uncontrollable fixed cost	15,000	15,000	15,750	750 (A)
Division net profit	71,200	78,467	86,130	(7,663) (F)

(b) The balanced scorecard approach was originally developed by Kaplan and Norton and consists of a variety of **indicators** both **financial** and **non-financial**. It focuses on **four different perspectives**.

Customer

The balanced scorecard asks what existing and new customers value from us. This gives rise to targets that matter to customers such as cost, quality, delivery and inspection.

Internal

The balanced scorecard asks at what processes we must excel to achieve our financial and customer objectives. This aims to improve internal processes and decision making.

Innovation and learning

The balanced scorecard asks if we can continue to improve and create future value. This considers the business's capacity to maintain its competitive position through the acquisition of new skills and the development of new products.

Financial

The balanced scorecard asks how we can create value for our shareholders. This covers traditional measures such as growth, profitability and shareholder value but set through talking to the shareholder or shareholders direct.

The balanced scorecard approach is not without its problems.

Conflicting measures

Some measures in the scorecard such as research funding and cost reduction may naturally conflict. It is often difficult to determine the balance which will achieve the best results.

Selecting measures

Not only do appropriate measures have to be devised but the number of measures used must be agreed. Care must be taken that the impact of the results is not lost in a sea of information.

Expertise

Measurement is only useful if it initiates appropriate action. Non-financial managers may have difficulty with the usual profit measures. With more measures to consider this problem will be compounded.

Interpretation

Even a financially-trained manager may have difficulty in putting the figures into an overall perspective.

Too many measures

The ultimate objective for commercial organisations is to maximise profits or shareholder wealth. Other targets should offer a guide to achieving this objective and not become an end in themselves.

29 Divisional performance

Top tips. Parts (a) and (b) require you to demonstrate knowledge you should have picked up directly from the text. No application skills are required at all in this instance.

That being said, it is vital that you do not learn the advantages and disadvantages of ROI and RI in a parrot fashion as they underlie the very core of the chapter. You **must understand how and why ROI affects managerial behaviour**, for example. You are just as likely to get a written question on this area as a calculation-based one.

The calculations required in (b) should not have caused you any problems.

(a)   The **residual income (RI)** for a division is calculated by deducting from the divisional profit an imputed interest charge, based on the investment in the division.

The **return on investment (ROI)** is the divisional profit expressed as a percentage of the investment in the division.

Both methods use the **same basic figure for profit and investment**, but **residual income** produces an **absolute** measure whereas the **return on investment** is expressed as a **percentage**.

Both methods suffer from **disadvantages** in measuring the profit and the investment in a division which include the following.

(i)   Assets must be valued consistently at historical cost or at replacement cost. Neither valuation basis is ideal.

(ii)   Divisions might use different bases to value inventory and to calculate depreciation.

(iii) Any charges made for the use of head office services or allocations of head office assets to divisions are likely to be arbitrary.

In addition, **return on investment** suffers from the following **disadvantages**.

(i)   Rigid adherence to the need to maintain ROI in the short term can discourage managers from investing in new assets, since average divisional ROI tends to fall in the early stages of a new investment. Residual income can overcome this problem by highlighting projects which return more than the cost of capital.

(ii)   It can be difficult to compare the percentage ROI results of divisions if their activities are very different: residual income can overcome this problem through the use of different interest rates for different divisions.

(b)   (i)   **Return on divisional investment (ROI)**

	Before investment	After investment
Divisional profit	$18,000	$19,600
Divisional investment	$100,000	$110,000
Divisional ROI	18.0%	17.8%

The ROI will fall in the short term if the new investment is undertaken. This is a problem which often arises with ROI, as noted in part (a) of this solution.

(ii)   **Divisional residual income**

	Before investment	After investment
	$	$
Divisional profit	18,000	19,600
Less imputed interest: $100,000 × 15%	15,000	
$110,000 × 15%		16,500
Residual income	3,000	3,100

The residual income will increase if the new investment is undertaken. The use of residual income has highlighted the fact that the new project returns more than the cost of capital (16% compared with 15%).

30 B and C

> **Top tips**. Part (a)(i) requires both regurgitation of book knowledge and **application of the data provided** in the question to illustrate your answer. The examiner needs evidence that you can apply the techniques and principles you have learnt to particular scenarios.
>
> We suggested use of **ROCE based on gross book value of assets** in part (a)(ii) as this overcomes the counterproductive behaviour caused by the current approach.

Paper for board meeting to review the company's performance appraisal and reward system

(a)   (i)   Possible counter-productive behaviour resulting from using the current ROCE calculation for *performance appraisal*

Under the current method of performance appraisal, managers are judged on the basis of the ROCE that their divisions earn, the ROCE being calculated using the net book value of non-current assets. The use of **ROCE** as a method of appraising performance has **disadvantages**, whilst there are **additional disadvantages** of using ROCE **based** on the **net book value** of **non-current assets**.

(1)   As managers are judged on the basis of the ROCE that their divisions earn each year, they are likely to be **motivated** into taking **decisions** which increase the division's **short-term ROCE** and rejecting projects which reduce the short-term ROCE even if the project is in excess of the company's target ROCE and hence is desirable from the company's point of view.

Suppose that the manager of B division was faced with a proposed project which had a projected return of 21%. He would be likely to reject the project because it would reduce his division's overall ROCE to below 24%. The investment would be desirable from Cordeline's point of view, however, because its ROCE would be in excess of the company's target ROCE of 20%. This is an example of sub-optimality and a **lack of goal congruence** in decision making.

(2)   A similar misguided decision would occur if the manager of C division, say, was worried about the low ROCE of his division and decided to reduce his investment by **scrapping** some **assets** not currently being used. The **reduction** in both **depreciation** charge and **assets** would immediately **improve** the **ROCE**. When the assets were eventually required, however, the manager would then be **obliged** to buy **new equipment**.

(3)   The current method bases the calculation of ROCE on the net book value of assets. If a division maintains the same annual profits and keeps the same asset without a policy of regular replacement of non-current assets, its **ROCE** will **increase** year by year as the **assets get older**. Simply by allowing its assets to depreciate a divisional manager is able to give a false impression of improving performance over time.

The level of new investment in non-current assets by C division was over three times that of B division in 20X3 and nearly 13 times that of B division in 20X4. B division is using old assets that have been depreciated to a much greater extent than those of C division and hence the basis of the ROCE calculation is much lower. Consequently it is able to report a much higher ROCE.

(4)   The method used to calculate ROCE therefore also provides a **disincentive** to divisional mangers to **reinvest** in new or replacement **assets** because the division's ROCE would probably fall. From the figures provided it is obvious that C division has replaced assets on a regular basis, the difference between original and replacement costs of its assets being small. The manager of B division, on the other hand, has not replaced assets, there being a marked difference between original and replacement cost of the division's assets.

(5)   A further disadvantage of measuring ROCE as profit divided by the net book value of assets is that it is **not easy** to **compare** fairly the **performance** of one **division** with another. Two divisions might have the same amount of working capital, the same value of non-current assets at cost and the same profit. But if one division's assets have been depreciated by a much bigger amount, perhaps because they are older, that division's ROCE will be bigger.

In some respects this is the case with B and C divisions. Both the profit and the original asset cost of C division are about the same proportion of B division's profit and original asset cost but the ROCE of B division is twice that of C division.

The use of ROCE per se and ROCE calculated using the net book value of assets therefore produces a number of examples of **counter-productive behaviour**.

(ii) *A revised ROCE measure*

Instead of using the net book value of non-current assets to calculate ROCE, it could be calculated using the **gross book value** of non-current assets. This would **remove** the problem of ROCE increasing over time as assets get older and will enable **comparisons** to be made more **fairly**.

Using the alternative method, the ROCE for the two divisions in the two years would be as follows.

B	20X3	13.8%
	20X4	10.6%
C	20X3	11.7%
	20X4	9.7%

Although B division still has a greater ROCE, the difference between the ROCE of the two divisions is much less.

(b) In general, a large organisation can be structured in one of two ways: functionally (all activities of a similar type within a company) or divisionally (split into divisions in accordance with the products or services made or provided).

Advantages of divisionalisation

(i) Divisionalisation can **improve** the **quality of decisions** made because divisional managers (those taking the decisions) know local conditions and are able to make more informed judgements. Moreover, with the personal incentive to improve the division's performance, they ought to take decisions in the division's best interests.

(ii) **Decisions should be taken more quickly** because information does not have to pass along the chain of command to and from top management. Decisions can be made on the spot by those who are familiar with the product lines and production processes and who are able to react to changes in local conditions quickly and efficiently.

(iii) The authority to act to improve performance should **motivate divisional managers**.

(iv) Divisional organisation **frees top management** from detailed involvement in day-to-day operations and allows them to devote more time to strategic planning.

(v) Divisions provide **valuable training grounds for future members of top management** by giving them experience of managerial skills in a less complex environment than that faced by top management.

(vi) In a large business organisation, the **central head office will not have the management resources or skills to direct operations closely enough itself**. Some authority must be delegated to local operational managers.

Disadvantages of divisionalisation

(i) A danger with divisional accounting is that the business organisation will divide into a number of self-interested segments, each acting at times against the wishes and interests of other segments. Decisions might be taken by a divisional manager in the best interests of his own part of the business, but against the best interest of other divisions and possibly against the interests of the organisation as a whole.

(ii) It is claimed that the **costs of activities that are common** to all divisions such as running the accounting department **may be greater** for a divisionalised structure than for a centralised structure.

(iii)   **Top management**, by delegating decision making to divisional managers, may **lose control** since they are not aware of what is going on in the organisation as a whole. (With a good system of performance evaluation and appropriate control information, however, top management should be able to control operations just as effectively.)

31 Pasta Division

> **Top tips.** Remember to calculate the ROI and RI for both situations in parts (a) and (b). In part (c), you must relate your answer to the scenario and your answers to part (a) – you will get 'own figure' marks in the exam if your calculations are incorrect. Parts (d) – (f) are quite general but pay attention to the word 'briefly' in each case – don't be tempted to write pages and pages!

(a)

	Before expansion	*Additions*	*After proposed expansion*
	$m	$m	$m
Investment in non-current assets	1.5	+0.75	2.25
Investment in working capital	1.0	+0.35	1.35
Net divisional assets	2.5		3.60
Operating profit	0.5	+0.198	0.698
Return on investment	20.0%		19.4%

(b)

		Before expansion		*After proposed expansion*
		$m		$m
Operating profit		0.500		0.698
Imputed interest on				
Net divisional assets	($2.5m × 15%)	0.375	($3.6m × 15%)	0.540
Residual income		0.125		0.158

(c)   Using return on investment (ROI) as a performance measure, the divisional manager would not be happy to accept the proposed expansion. The ROI would reduce if the expansion went ahead, indicating a deterioration in the division's performance, and because bonuses are paid as a percentage on this basis, the manager would receive a lower bonus.

If residual income (RI) was used as a performance measure the manager would be happy to accept the proposed expansion. This is because the RI would increase as a result of the expansion. This indicates an improvement in the division's performance and so the manager would receive a higher bonus.

(d)   ROI has the obvious advantages of being compatible with accounting reports and is easier to understand.

There are a number of disadvantages associated with both ROI and RI, however.

- Both methods suffer from disadvantages in measuring profit (how should inventory be valued, how should arbitrary allocations of head office charges be dealt with) and investment (what basis to use).

- It is questionable whether a single measure is appropriate for measuring the complexity of divisional performance.

- If a division maintains the same annual profit, keeps the same assets without a policy of regular non-current asset replacement and values assets at net book value, ROI and RI will increase year by year as the assets get older, even though profits may be static. This can give a false impression of improving performance over time and acts to discourage managers from undertaking new investments.

In addition, ROI suffers from the following disadvantages.

- The need to maintain ROI in the short term can discourage managers from investing in new assets (since the average ROI of a division tends to fall in the early stages of a new investment) even if the new investment is beneficial to the group as a whole (because the investment's ROI is greater than the group's target rate of return). This focuses attention on short-run performance whereas investment decisions should be evaluated over their full life. RI can help to overcome this problem of sub-optimality and a lack of goal congruence by highlighting projects which return more than the cost of capital.

- It can be difficult to compare percentage ROI results of divisions if their activities are very different. RI can overcome this problem through the use of different interest rates for different divisions.

    There are also a number of disadvantages associated with RI: it does not facilitate comparison between divisions; neither does it relate the size of a division's income to the size of the investment. In these respects ROI is a better measure.

    The disadvantages of the two methods have a number of behavioural implications. Managers tend to favour proposals that produce excellent results in the short term (to ensure their performance appears favourable) but which, because they have little regard for the later life of their division's projects, are possibly unacceptable in the longer term. They will therefore disregard proposals that are in the best interests of the group as a whole. ROI and RI can therefore produce dysfunctional decision making.

(e) The main features of Economic Value Added (EVA®) as it would be used to assess the performance of divisions:

EVA like Residual Income (RI) is a performance measure expressed in absolute terms. It is based on the concept of net economic profit after tax less a deduction for an imputed interest charge.

The relationship between economic and accounting profit is explained below. The imputed interest charge is based on the company's weighted average cost of capital. The assets are at their replacement cost as explained below. The imputed interest charge is based on the company's weighted average cost of capital.

EVA = net operating economic profit after tax less capital charge where the capital charge = weighted average cost of capital × net assets

The weighted average cost of capital is based on the capital asset pricing model.

(f) How the use of EVA to assess divisional performance might affect the behaviour of divisional senior executives:

- It is argued that maximisation of the EVA® target will lead to managers maximising wealth for shareholders.

- The adjustments within the calculation of EVA mean that the measure is based on figures closer to cash flows than accounting profits. Hence, EVA is less likely to be distorted by the accounting policies selected.

- EVA like RI is an absolute measure, as compared to a relative one such as ROCE. As such it will not lead to sub-optimal decisions with respect to new investment as it is the absolute increase in shareholder value which is used as a criterion. The ROCE criterion might lead to sub-optimal decisions if new investment has a lower relative return than existing investment, even though it may result in higher shareholder value.

- EVA is based on **economic profit** which is derived by making a series of adjustments to **accounting profits**. Examples of such adjustments are set out below:

    - Accounting depreciation is added back to the profit figures and **economic depreciation** which seeks to reflect the fall in asset values is subtracted to arrive at economic profit.

    - Goodwill is amortised over its useful life

    - Research and development and advertising expenditure written off are added back to profit and amortised over their useful lives (ie the period over which the benefit from this expenditure will accrue).

- The assets used for the calculation of EVA are valued at their replacement cost and not at their historic accounting cost. They are also increased by any costs that have been capitalised as a result of the above adjustments.

32 Transfer pricing

Top tips. Part (a) is basic book knowledge so you should have been able to score at least four of the six marks. If you can answer **part (b)** successfully then there is every chance that you really understand transfer pricing. The reasoning required is not at all difficult but goes to the very **heart of the topic**. If you couldn't answer part (b) yourself, work through our answer really carefully until you understand what's going on.

The **first thing** to do in part (c)(i) is to **calculate** the **unit costs** and **selling price** of product X. We are told that overheads are apportioned to X and Y in proportion to direct wages. Since hourly rates for labour are the same for both products, the same results will be obtained by **apportioning** the **overheads** according to **labour hours**.

The **next step** is to work out **whether** or not the 2,000 kgs of product **X** should be **sold** to **K**. This depends on whether product Z earns a **positive contribution** based on an appropriate **relevant** cost.

Finally, the range of transfer prices can be established. You will need to use your **common sense** in this part of the question in terms of suggesting an appropriate level of **variable costs** that may be **saved** with **internal** transfers.

As usual we have included a **discursive** requirement. We know that it is tempting just to read our answer and tell yourself that you would be able to reproduce something similar in the exam, but it doesn't work like that. You must **practice** these requirements as conscientiously as the numerical ones.

(a) **Potential benefits of operating a transfer pricing system within a divisionalised company**

  (i) It can lead to **goal congruence** by motivating divisional managers to make decisions, which improve divisional profit and improve profit of the organisation as a whole.

  (ii) It can prevent **dysfunctional decision making** so that decisions taken by a divisional manager are in the best interests of his own part of the business, other divisions and the organisation as a whole.

  (iii) Transfer prices can be set at a level that enables divisional performance to be measured 'commercially'. A transfer pricing system should therefore report a level of divisional profit that is a **reasonable measure of the managerial performance** of the division.

  (iv) It should ensure that **divisional autonomy** is not undermined. A well-run transfer pricing system helps to ensure that a balance is kept between divisional autonomy to provide incentives and motivation, and centralised authority to ensure that the divisions are all working towards the same target, the benefit of the organisation as a whole.

(b) (i) **Division Able has spare capacity and limited external demand for product X**

In this situation, the incremental cost to the company of producing product Y is $35. It costs division Baker $38 to buy product Y from the external market and so it is cheaper by $3 per unit to buy from division Able.

The **transfer price** needs to be fixed at a price **above $35** both to **provide** some **incentive** to division Able to supply division Baker and to provide some **contribution** towards fixed overheads. The transfer price must be **below $38** per unit, however, to **encourage** division Baker to **buy** from division Able rather than from the **external supplier**.

The transfer price should therefore be set in the range above $35 and below $38 and at a level so that both divisions, acting independently and in their own interests, would choose to buy from and sell to each other.

(ii) **Division Able is operating at full capacity with unsatisfied external demand for product X**

If division Able chooses to supply division Baker rather than the external market, the **opportunity cost** of such a decision must be incorporated into the transfer price.

For every unit of product Y produced and sold to division Baker, division Able will lose $10 ($(42-32)) in contribution due to not supplying the external market with product X. The relevant cost of supplying product Y in these circumstances is therefore $45 ($(35 + 10)). It is therefore in the interests of the company as a whole if division Baker sources product Y externally at the cheaper price of $38 per unit. Division Able can therefore continue to supply external demand at $42 per unit.

The company can ensure this happens if the transfer price of product Y is set above $38, thereby encouraging division Baker to buy externally rather than from division Able.

(c) (i) **Product X**

	$ per kg
Direct materials	18.00
Direct wages	15.00
Variable overhead (($70,000/7,000 hours) × 1 hr)	10.00
	43.00
Fixed overhead (($56,000/7,000 hours) × 1 hr)	8.00
	51.00
Profit mark up 60%	30.60
Selling price	81.60

If product X is used by K in manufacturing product Z, the **opportunity cost** to the company is the sales revenue forgone, $81.60 per kg.

Relevant cost per kg of Z = $81.60 + $15 adaptation + $2 variable overhead
= $98.60

Contribution per kg of Z = $100 – $98.60 = $1.40 per kg

Product Z earns a positive contribution and therefore 2,000 kg of product X should be sold to K.

We can now consider the **transfer price**.

$81.60 would be the arm's length price at which a transfer could be made, and this price would make K aware of the full opportunity cost of using X to make product Z.

However, K may argue that certain variable costs may be saved with internal transfers, for instance packaging, credit control and transport costs. If these are, say, $3 per kg, then the transfer price could be reduced by $3 + 60% = $4.80, to say $(81.60 – 4.80) = $76.80.

K is also likely to be unhappy that L is taking a much larger profit mark up, 60% compared with $1.40/$17 × 100% = 8.2% mark up on K's costs.

However, it is unlikely that K can justify a substantial reduction in the transfer price, because of the opportunity costs involved.

The **suggested range of transfer prices** is therefore $76.80 to $81.60 per kg.

(ii) **Other points which should be borne in mind when making any recommendations about transfer prices in these circumstances**

(1) What are the personal goals and aspirations of the individual managers, and the consequent motivational impact of any transfer price?

(2) Are there any other uses for L's and K's facilities?

(3) What will be the short-term and long-term effect on L's sales, if 2,000 kg of product X are withdrawn from the external market?

(4) What is the likely effect of the new product on the morale of K's staff, who must be aware of the current under-utilisation of capacity?

(5) What are the long-term prospects for product Z?

(6) Can the constraint on production hours in L be removed without any significant effect on unit costs?

(7) The forecast profit margin on Product Z is fairly small. It may therefore be risky to rely on this forecast for a new product.

(d) **Actual cost versus standard cost**

When a transfer price is based on cost, **standard cost should be used**, not actual cost. A transfer at **actual cost** would give the **supplying division** no **incentive to control costs** because all of the costs could be passed on to the receiving division. **Actual cost** plus transfer prices might even **encourage** the manager of the supplying division to **overspend**, because this would increase divisional profit, even though the organisation as a whole (and the receiving division) suffers.

Standard cost based transfer prices should **encourage** the supplying division to become **more efficient** as any variances that arise would affect the results of the supplying division (as opposed to being passed on to the receiving division if actual costs were used).

The problem with the approach, however, is that it **penalises** the **supplying division** if the standard cost is **unattainable**, while it **penalises** the **receiving division** if it is **too easily attainable**.

LIST OF VERBS USED IN THE QUESTION REQUIREMENTS

A list of the learning objectives and verbs that appear in the syllabus and in the question requirements for each question in this paper.

It is important that you answer the question according to the definition of the verb.

Learning objective	Verbs Used	Definition
Level 1 - Knowledge		
What you are expected to know	List	Make a list of
	State	Express, fully or clearly, the details of/facts of
	Define	Give the exact meaning of
Level 2 - Comprehension		
What you are expected to understand	Describe	Communicate the key features
	Distinguish	Highlight the differences between
	Explain	Make clear or intelligible/state the meaning or purpose of
	Identify	Recognise, establish or select after consideration
	Illustrate	Use an example to describe or explain something
Level 3 - Application		
How you are expected to apply your knowledge	Apply	Put to practical use
	Calculate	Ascertain or reckon mathematically
	Demonstrate	Prove with certainty or to exhibit by practical means
	Prepare	Make or get ready for use
	Reconcile	Make or prove consistent/compatible
	Solve	Find an answer to
	Tabulate	Tabulate Arrange in a table
Level 4 - Analysis		
How you are expected to analyse the detail of what you have learned.	Analyse	Examine in detail the structure of
	Categorise	Place into a defined class or division
	Compare and contrast	Show the similarities and/or differences between
	Construct	Build up or compile
	Discuss	Examine in detail by argument
	Interpret	Translate into intelligible or familiar terms
	Prioritise	Place in order of priority or sequence for action
	Produce	Create or bring into existence
Level 5 - Application		
How you are expected to use your learning to evaluate, make decisions or recommendations.	Advise	Counsel, inform or notify
	Evaluate	Appraise or assess the value of
	Recommend	Propose a course of action

INDEX

Note: **Key terms** and their references are given in **bold**.

Note: **Key terms** and their references are given in **bold**.

Notes

Notes

Notes

Notes

Notes

Notes

Notes

Notes

Review Form – Paper P2 Performance Management (6/13)

Please help us to ensure that the CIMA learning materials we produce remain as accurate and user-friendly as possible. We cannot promise to answer every submission we receive, but we do promise that it will be read and taken into account when we update this Study Text.

Name: _____   Address: _____

_____

_____

How have you used this Study Text?
(Tick one box only)

☐ Home study (book only)

☐ On a course: college _____

☐ With 'correspondence' package

☐ Other _____

Why did you decide to purchase this Study Text? *(Tick one box only)*

☐ Have used BPP Texts in the past

☐ Recommendation by friend/colleague

☐ Recommendation by a lecturer at college

☐ Saw information on BPP website

☐ Saw advertising

☐ Other _____

During the past six months do you recall seeing/receiving any of the following?
(Tick as many boxes as are relevant)

☐ Our advertisement in *Financial Management*

☐ Our advertisement in *PQ*

☐ Our brochure with a letter through the post

☐ Our website www.bpp.com

Which (if any) aspects of our advertising do you find useful?
(Tick as many boxes as are relevant)

☐ Prices and publication dates of new editions

☐ Information on Text content

☐ Facility to order books off-the-page

☐ None of the above

Which BPP products have you used?

Text	☑	*Success CD*	☐
Kit	☐	*i-Pass*	☐
Passcard	☐	*Interactive Passcard*	☐

Your ratings, comments and suggestions would be appreciated on the following areas.

	Very useful	Useful	Not useful
Introductory section	☐	☐	☐
Chapter introductions	☐	☐	☐
Key terms	☐	☐	☐
Quality of explanations	☐	☐	☐
Case studies and other examples	☐	☐	☐
Exam skills and alerts	☐	☐	☐
Questions and answers in each chapter	☐	☐	☐
Fast forwards and chapter roundups	☐	☐	☐
Quick quizzes	☐	☐	☐
Question Bank	☐	☐	☐
Answer Bank	☐	☐	☐
OT Bank	☐	☐	☐
Index	☐	☐	☐

	Excellent	Good	Adequate	Poor
Overall opinion of this Study Text	☐	☐	☐	☐

Do you intend to continue using BPP products?   Yes ☐   No ☐

On the reverse of this page is space for you to write your comments about our Study Text We welcome your feedback.

The BPP Learning Media author of this edition can be e-mailed at: ianblackmore@bpp.com

Please return this form to: Douglas Haste, CIMA Product Manager, BPP Learning Media Ltd, FREEPOST, London, W12 8BR

TELL US WHAT YOU THINK

Please note any further comments and suggestions/errors below. For example, was the text accurate, readable, concise, user-friendly and comprehensive?